THE BRITISH INVASION OF MARYLAND
1812–1815

D1563869

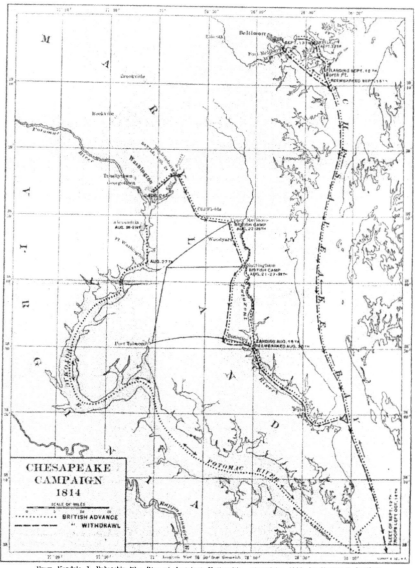

CHESAPEAKE
CAMPAIGN
1814

SCALE OF MILES

········· BRITISH ADVANCE
▬▬▬▬ " WITHDRAWL

From Kendric J. Babcock's *The Rise of American Nationality.* Copyright, 1906, by Harper & Brothers.

ii

THE
BRITISH INVASION OF MARYLAND
1812-1815

BY

WILLIAM M. MARINE

EDITED, WITH AN APPENDIX, CONTAINING ELEVEN THOUSAND NAMES, BY

LOUIS HENRY DIELMAN

CLEARFIELD

Originally published
Baltimore, Maryland, 1913

Reprinted by
Genealogical Publishing Co., Inc.
Baltimore, Maryland 1977

Printed for Clearfield Company by
Genealogical Publishing Company
Baltimore, Maryland
2010

Library of Congress Catalogue Card Number 77-70368
ISBN 978-0-8063-0760-2

Made in the United States of America

PREFACE

This volume is an attempt to present in permanent form the history of the British invasion of Maryland during the War of 1812. The story has not heretofore been fully told; the record is deplorably incomplete, and the following pages are intended to be an adequate chronicle of the events of that period in Maryland, and to that end even trifling circumstances have been interwoven in the narrative.

It was the good fortune of the author to be associated, for a number of years, with the survivors of the battle of North Point and of the defense of Fort McHenry. He has received from them the story of those struggles and has endeavored to imprint the letter and convey the spirit of their language in these annals. Indeed, but for his personal relations with the Defenders, this work, which has been a labor of love, might never have been undertaken. As time passes the preservation of the record becomes not only more desirable and important but also more difficult. The archives of the State afford but slight assistance, the few official papers being scattered and difficult of access. Every known source of information has been examined and the collection of the Maryland Historical Society was found to include various publications from which much valuable material has been obtained. No effort has been made to settle minor disputed points and the reader has been allowed the privilege of reaching his own conclusions from the facts impartially presented.

The historical value of the defense of Baltimore has been dwarfed by the brevity of treatment accorded it and only when taken in connection with the full campaign on the waterways of Maryland and the adjacent territory, can the importance of the defense be realized.

The author acknowledges his indebtedness for valuable facts to Ingersoll's History of the War of 1812, now out of print. Other authorities are noted on the margins.

W. M. M.

BALTIMORE, MD., 1899.

CONTENTS

CHAPTER I

EVENTS LEADING UP TO THE WAR

The causes which led up to the declaration of war against Great Britain on June 18, 1812, were too complex, and extended over too great a period of time, to be set forth here at length.[1] The union of states was so loosely knit as to be little more than a confederation, and the long political struggle of the Federalist and Anti-Federalist parties, accentuated by sectional jealousies, had strained the bonds almost to the breaking-point. When war was declared, the country was discordant, disunited and unprepared. The majority in Congress in favor of war was small, being but thirty-nine in the House and six in the Senate. Of the Maryland delegation in the House six voted for and three against war, while in the Senate they were divided.[2]

In Maryland, as elsewhere throughout the country, party feeling was bitter and violent and found its expression in deeds as well as words. The enemies of President Madison proclaimed in derision that "his administration was like the street in Baltimore, called by his name, which began at the poor-house, went by the jail, then passed the penitentiary, and ended on Gallows Hill."

The drift of the war sentiment is well expressed in the resolutions introduced in the Maryland Legislature during the sessions from 1811 to 1815, the eighth Senate having been elected in the former year and continuing throughout the period, while a new House of Delegates was elected each year. The following resolutions were passed at the November session, 1811:

"Whereas, It is highly important at this eventful crisis in our foreign relations, that the opinions and feelings of every section of the union should be fairly and fully expressed; Therefore, we the legislature of Maryland do *Resolve,* That in the opinion of this

---

[1] For important evidence concerning the declaration of war, see "Joseph Gales on the War Manifesto of 1812," in *American Historical Review,* 13:303.

[2] House, yeas: Stevenson Archer, Joseph Kent, Peter Little, Alexander McKim, Samuel Ringgold, Robert Wright. Nays: Charles Goldsborough, Philip Barton Key, Philip Stuart.

Senate, yea: Samuel Smith. Nay. Philip Reed.

legislature, the measures of the administration with respect to Great Britain have been honorable, impartial and just; that in their negotiations they have evinced every disposition to terminate our differences on terms not incompatible with our national honor, and that they deserve the confidence and support of the nation:

" *Resolved,* That the measures of Great Britain have been, and still are destructive of our best and dearest rights, and being inconsistent with justice, with reason and with law, can be supported only by force; therefore if persisted in, by force should be resisted.

" *Resolved,* That the measures of the administration with respect to France we highly approve, they have been authorised by the law and the fact.

" *Resolved,* That the acts of injustice and violence committed on our neutral rights by France have excited all that indignation which a lawless exercise of power could not fail to do; but having now ceased to violate our neutral rights, we trust that the period is not far distant, when by acts of ample justice, all cause of complaint will be removed.

" *Resolved,* That the President's message, moderate, impartial and decisive, deserves all our praise; it points out the best course to an honorable independence.

" *Resolved,* That the independence established by the aid and valor of our fathers, will not tamely be yielded by their sons; the same spirit which led the Maryland regulars to battle, still exists in the state, and waits only for its country's call."

These resolutions originated in the Senate, where they were unanimously adopted; but they were held up in the House for three weeks and after a number of ballots had been taken on proposed amendments thereto, were finally adopted by a vote of 34 to 23.

In addition to placing on record its views as to the justice of the impending conflict, this legislature passed two acts (chapters 182 and 213, Nov. sess. 1811) for " regulating and governing the militia of the State." The first is a very long document of twenty-eight closely printed octavo pages, covering every contingency that could possibly arise, from the enlistment of men to details concerning courts martial. All white male citizens between the ages of eighteen and forty-five were required to perform military duty;

and provision was made for the enrollment from time to time of all youths who reached the age of eighteen. Civil officers of the United States and the state, professors in schools and colleges, practising physicians, ferrymen, pilots, sailors in the coasting trade and all those who entertained religious scruples concerning war were exempted from the operation of the act, but all exempts were required to pay annually into the treasury the sum of three dollars. Directions were given for the muster and drill of the troops, for the meeting of field officers, for uniforms and for the conduct of the militia while in camp.

The militia was arranged in divisions consisting of brigades, regiments, battalions and companies, all numbered and recorded. A brigade was composed of four regiments; a regiment of two battalions; a battalion of five companies; a company of sixty-four privates, four sergeants, four corporals, one drummer and one fifer or bugler. A brigade, therefore, consisted of about three thousand men.

Chapter 213 established a cavalry organization, the state being divided into eleven cavalry districts, with one extra squadron, as follows:

1st, Washington and Frederick Counties; 2d, Montgomery and Prince George's; 3d, Calvert and Anne Arundel; 4th, Charles and St. Mary's; 5th, Baltimore City; 6th, Baltimore County; 7th, Harford County with Howard troop from Baltimore City; 8th, Cecil and Kent; 9th, Queen Anne's and Talbot; 10th, Caroline and Dorchester; 11th, Somerset and Worcester; extra squadron in Allegany County. Each regiment was composed of two squadrons of two troops each, commanded by a lieutenant colonel; each squadron by a major; each troop consisted of two lieutenants, one cornet, one quarter-master sergeant, four sergeants, four corporals, one farrier, one saddler, one trumpeter and thirty-two privates, commanded by a captain.

In order to meet the changes in population and to secure uniformity of drill and discipline, the commanding officers were required to order a meeting of the field officers prior to May 1, 1812, at which meeting the bounds of the several districts should be fixed; and they were further required to hold at least two meetings annually thereafter in order that the officers might be drilled and instructed in all the necessary duties of a soldier.

Early in 1812 the advocates of war determined on a public expression of their opinions, and on May 16 a called meeting was held at the Fountain Inn in Baltimore City by supporters of President Madison's administration, over which Joseph H. Nicholson presided. In the course of an address he said: "No one can be insensible to the great crisis to which the affairs of our country are rapidly approaching. The two great belligerent powers of Europe, who have embroiled one-half of the civilized world in their quarrels, unwilling that any nation should continue to enjoy its prosperity, have for some years past extended to us that system of rapine and plunder, which in the ordinary course of human events, ought only to have been directed against others. Our citizens have been forcibly impressed and detained in the most odious servitude; our commerce has been impeded in every channel through which it has been accustomed to flow, and injury and insult has been heaped upon us until it has begun to be almost questionable even among ourselves whether we have the spirit to resist. One of these nations has indeed of late held out to us a semblance of justice; but it is much to be feared that even this will prove vain and illusory. The period, however, cannot be very distant when, by the return of our messengers from Europe, we shall learn whether the solemn stipulations in which we have heretofore confided are any longer deserving of confidence. But the other has not even pretended to do us justice. Our government, sincerely desirous of maintaining peace, has remonstrated until their remonstrances are regarded with indifference; our ministers, sent abroad for the purpose, have continued to appeal until their appeals are answered by insult; and negotiations have been carried on until negotiation has become a term of national reproach. Under these circumstances it is for us, my countrymen, in common with the rest of the American people, to decide upon the course which ought to be pursued. The time has at length arrived when we must determine whether by tameness and submission we shall sink ourselves below the rank of an independent nation, or whether by a glorious or manly effort we shall permanently secure that independence which our forefathers handed down to us as the price of their blood and their treasure. The government of our choice—I thank God, of our yet free and unbiased choice—has resolved upon its course, and is preparing for the conflict. We have assembled here to-night for the purpose of determining whether we will give it our support in the mighty struggle into which it is about to enter. This, my countrymen, is the awful subject for deliberation, and on such a subject can there be any difference of opinion? Shall we suffer any matter of local concern to withdraw us from a cause like this? Is there an American heart that does not pant with resentment? Is there an American sword that will not leap from its scabbard to avenge the wrongs and contumely under which we have so long suffered? No, my countrymen! It is impossible! Let us act with one heart, with one hand; let us show to an admiring world that however we may differ among ourselves about some of our internal concerns, yet in the great cause of our country the American people are animated by one soul and by one spirit."

The resolutions subsequently adopted, recited the critical situation of our foreign relations, which were considered of the utmost concern; that it was important that the sentiments of the friends of the Union and of the government as administered should be publicly declared with reference to public measures, upon which depended the future safety and prosperity of the United States. It was recommended by the resolutions, that a meeting of the citizens of Baltimore, of democratic proclivities be held in their respective wards on a Tuesday evening at seven o'clock, at the usual places of ward meetings, and in each ward elect five delegates to meet the general committee at the Fountain Inn, on the following Thursday evening to take into consideration the means most likely to conduce to the support and aid of the government in its effort to maintain, protect and defend national rights, honor and independence. Democratic brethren in the eastern and western precincts were also invited to assemble at Chamberlain's and Gorsuch's taverns, for the purpose of selecting delegates. The call met with a hearty response from the various wards and precincts of the city, into which the municipality was at that time divided.

On the twenty-first of May the delegates, selected from among the most prominent citizens of the town, met at the Fountain Inn. Joseph H. Nicholson occupied the chair, with John Montgomery as secretary. The following resolutions, signed by the members

of the general committee, were adopted and ordered to be trans-
mitted to the President of the United States:

" We, the delegates of the city and precincts of Baltimore, in
general committee assembled, for the purpose of taking into consideration the present situation of public affairs, do resolve unanimously:

1st. That in the conduct of Great Britain towards the United
States for some years past, we can perceive nothing but a determined hostility to our national rights. She forcibly impresses our
seamen, and detains them inhumanly in an odious servitude; she
obstructs our commerce in every channel through which it has
been accustomed to flow; she has murdered our citizens within our
own waters, and has made one attempt at least to dissolve the
union of these States, thereby striking at the foundation of our
government itself.

2d. That the government of the United States has manifested
the strongest desire to maintain peace and harmony with all
nations, not only by observing a course of equal and exact justice
to all, but by proposing to those with whom any differences have
arisen, terms the most honorable and conciliatory.

3d. That inasmuch as Great Britain has rejected those terms,
and still persists in violating every principle heretofore held sacred
among nations, no alternative is left to the United States but to
choose between war and degradation. In the choice of these it
is impossible freemen should hesitate, and in the prosecution of
such a war we pledge ourselves to support our government at
every hazard.

4th. That the conduct of France, and of other powers in alliance
with her and under her immediate influence, towards the United
States, has been scarcely less atrocious than that of England; and
if the pending negotiations should terminate without an honorable
adjustment of existing differences, we have full confidence that our
government will direct the most active hostilities to be commenced
against her for a redress of our grievances and the maintenance
of our rights; at the same time we wish it explicitly understood,
that in our well founded complaints against foreign nations,
Russia and Sweden are not to be included."

Fifty citizens attached their signatures to these resolutions,
and it is interesting to note that those who thus loudly clamored

for war, later on took an active part in the defense of Baltimore, either as soldiers in the ranks or as members of the Committee of Vigilance and Safety.

On the 18th of June, 1812, Congress declared war against Great Britain;[a] and on Saturday, the 20th of June, the *Federal Republican,* edited by Jacob Wagner and Alexander C. Hanson, published the following editorial: "'*Thou hast done a deed whereat valor will weep.*' Without funds, without taxes, without an army, navy, or adequate fortifications—with one hundred and fifty millions of our property in the hands of the declared enemy, without any of his in our power, and with a vast commerce afloat, our rulers have promulgated a war against the clear and decided sentiments of a vast majority of the nation. As the consequences will be soon felt, there is no need of pointing them out to the few who have not sagacity enough to apprehend them. Instead of employing our pen in this dreadful detail, we think it more apposite to delineate the course we are determined to pursue as long as the war shall last. We mean to represent in as strong colors as we are capable, that it is unnecessary, inexpedient, and entered into from partial, personal, and as we believe, motives bearing upon their front marks of undisguised foreign influence, which cannot be mistaken. We mean to use every constitutional argument and every legal means to render as odious and suspicious to the American people, as they deserve to be, the patrons and contrivers of this highly impolitic and destructive war, in the fullest persuasion that we shall be supported and ultimately applauded by nine-tenths of our countrymen, and that our silence would be treason to them. We detest and abhor the endeavors of faction to create civil contest through the pretext of a foreign war it has rashly and premeditatedly commenced, and we shall be ready cheerfully to hazard everything most dear, to frustrate anything leading to the prostration of civil rights, and the establishment of a system of terror and proscription announced in the Government paper at Washington as the inevitable consequence of the measure now proclaimed. We shall cling to the rights of freemen, both in act and opinion, till we sink with the liberties of our country or sink

[a] The declaration was drafted by Attorney-General William Pinkney of Maryland.

alone. We shall hereafter, as heretofore, unravel every intrigue and imposture which has beguiled or may be put forth to circumvent our fellow-citizens into the toils of the great earthly enemy of the human race. We are avowedly hostile to the presidency of James Madison, and we never will breathe under the dominion, direct or derivative, of Bonaparte, let it be acknowledged when it may. Let those who cannot openly adopt this confession, abandon us; and those who can, we shall cherish as friends and patriots worthy of the name."

Wagner, the editor-in-chief, who had served as chief clerk in the State Department for some years, was a Federalist of the black cockade school. As such he had denounced the administration with a bitterness which stirred up the deadly hatred of the Democrats. Long before war was declared this conduct had called forth fierce replies in the newspapers and had led a number of distinguished people to say that, if it were continued after war was declared, the *Federal Republican* should be silenced.

On the evening of Monday the 22d of June, two days after the publication of this ill-advised editorial, a well organized mob wrecked the printing office, destroyed the type, smashed the presses, and razed the building in which the *Federal Rebublican* was printed. One of the mob, while engaged in tearing a window from the building, fell from the second story and was instantly killed. The *Federal Gazette* of June 24, in commenting on this disgraceful affair said: " The Mayor of the city, the Judge of the Court of Oyer and Terminer, and several magistrates and military officers, were present and witnessed this dreadful outrage which their *peaceful efforts* were insufficient to prevent, although it was generally known during the preceding day that the attack was meditated."

Hanson, who lived at Rockville, Montgomery County, not having been in Baltimore on the night the printing office was destroyed, was quickly informed of the fact by John Howard Payne, who urged him not to be downed by the mob, but to go on with his paper, assert the liberty of the press which every Republican from Jefferson down to the lowest demagogue had prated so persistently, and, if need be, defend it with arms.

After many consultations with friends, the editors decided to print the *Federal Republican* at Georgetown, where the plant would be safe, and issue it from the house on Charles street, lately occupied by Wagner, the editor-in-chief. Accordingly, on Sunday the 26th of July, Hanson, accompanied by a number of friends who had volunteered their services " in maintaining the rights of person and property and defending the liberty of the press," took possession of the house which had been supplied with provisions and arms to withstand a siege. On the following day they were joined by more volunteers, making the total number in the party about thirty. Copies of the paper arrived and were distributed without interference, but at night the mob rose in force, stoned the house, beat in the door, brought up a cannon and were about to blow the building to pieces, when a compromise was effected through the mediation of the Mayor and the commander of the militia, General Stricker. In consideration of the promise of a military guard the garrison agreed to surrender to the civil authorities, and the mob agreed to do no further harm to life or property. During the night a number of the defenders had been sent out to notify the authorities, or for other purposes, and were unable to return so that at the time of the surrender the garrison was reduced to twenty-three. The following persons were conducted to jail and committed for further examination: Alexander C. Hanson, Gen. Henry Lee, Gen. James M. Lingan, William Schroeder, John Thompson, William B. Bend, Otho Sprigg, Henry Kennedy, Robert Kilgour, Henry Nelson, John E. Hall, George Winchester, Dr. Peregrine Warfield, George Richards, Edward Gwinn, David Hoffman, Horatio Bigelow, Ephraim Gaither, William Gaither, Jacob Schley, Mark U. Pringle, Daniel Murray and Richard S. Crabb. After the removal of the prisoners, the house was instantly gutted by the mob.

During the following night, the militia having been withdrawn and dismissed, the jail was stormed. Eight of the prisoners mingled with the mob and escaped; nine were taken, dragged to the door where a butcher beat them down with a club and flung their bodies in a pile at the foot of the stairway. The mob fell on the senseless bodies, beat them with clubs, thrust pen-knives into their cheeks, poured candle grease into their eyes and finally gave them to the jail doctor to make skeletons of. General Lingan was killed and General Lee was made a cripple for life. John Thompson, after being terribly beaten and mutilated was tarred and feathered. Some of the others were hidden in hay carts and sent to friends in town, while those remaining, being too badly hurt to be moved, were cared for at the jail hospital.

The affair was investigated by a joint committee of the two branches of the City Council and later by the Committee of Grievances and Courts of Justice in the General Assembly. Presentments were found against many individuals of each party, but all were acquitted and discharged.

The effect of this shameful riot was far-reaching. All over the country decent people of both parties were alarmed, as they realized that something more than a riot had happened. The freedom of the press had been attacked. The Federal newspapers reminded their readers of the days of the Sedition Law and of the violence with which the Republicans then cried out for free speech and a free press. Their columns were filled with all the details of the riot, Baltimore was nicknamed Mobtown and the blame was laid on the administration.[1]

The immediate effect in Maryland was shown at the state election in October, when the Federalists elected a preponderating majority in the General Assembly on joint ballot, enabling them to elect a Governor and Council and a United States Senator. On the crest of this wave Mr. Hanson was elected to Congress; and was later reimbursed for the losses inflicted on him by the mob. Under date of October 10, 1812, *Niles' Register* said: " The political aspect of the State of Maryland has been completely changed by the election held on Monday last. Various causes are assigned as producing this effect; the chief of which, probably was, the existing diversity of sentiment in some of the counties (always nearly balanced) as to the presidency of the United States."

The issue of October 17 of the *Register* contains this startling announcement: " Mr. Alexander Contee Hanson and his associates who defended the house in Charles street in this city, on the night of the 27th July, *indicted for manslaughter,* have had their trial at Annapolis, and are acquitted! "

[1] McMaster, History of the People of the U. S., 3:555. For details of the riot see *Niles Register* 2:373 and 2:405.

CHAPTER II

THE PRIVATEERSMEN

When President Madison delivered his war message to Congress on June 1, 1812, the available naval force of the United States consisted of seven frigates and a few smaller vessels, many of which were unseaworthy. The British navy at this time consisted of more than a thousand vessels and it was believed by the opponents of the war that with this force our coasts might be completely blockaded. Congress lost no time in calling for private vessels of war and the declaration of war itself conferred authority upon the President " to issue to private armed vessels of the United States, commissions or letters of marque and general reprisal in such form as he shall think proper and under the seal of the United States."[1]

A few days later another act was passed regulating in detail the issue of commissions. It contains provisions for a written description of the vessel to be filed with the Secretary of State; for security of five or ten thousand dollars, according to the number of the crew; for the transfer of the whole property in the prizes to the captors, subject to their written agreement for the bringing in of prizes and their adjudication in the district courts of the United States; for the delivery of prisoners to a United States Marshal or other district officer; for a bounty of twenty dollars for each man alive on board hostile ships of equal or superior force at the beginning of the engagement leading to their capture; for journals of cruises to be kept under penalties, and shown on demand to the public vessels of the United States; and for obedience to any instructions issued by the President. As the war was undertaken by the United States in defence of neutral rights, the instructions of the Secretary of State were explicit upon this point: " You are to pay the strictest regard to the rights of neutral powers and the usages of civilized nations. . . . You are particularly to avoid even the appearance of using force or seduction with a view to deprive such vessels of their crews or of their passengers . . . ."

[1] 2 Stat. at Large, ch. 102, p. 755.

In spite of the apparent disparity between the opposing forces, the possibilities of American sea power were appreciated both in England and America as is shown by the following quotations: The *London Statesman*,[2] under date of June 10, said: " It has been stated that in a war with this country, America has nothing to gain. In opposition to this assertion it may be said, with equal truth, that in a war with America, this country has nothing to gain, but much to lose. Let us examine the relative situation of the two countries. America certainly cannot pretend to wage a maritime war with us; she has no navy to do it with. But America has nearly 100,000 as good seamen as any in the world, all of whom would be actively employed against our trade in every part of the ocean in their fast sailing ships of war, many of which will be able to cope with our small cruizers; and they will be found to be sweeping the West India seas, and even carrying desolation into the chops of the channel. Every one must recollect what they did in the latter part of the American war. The books at Lloyd's will recount it; and the rate of assurances at that time will clearly prove what their diminutive strength was able to effect in the face of our navy, and that when nearly one hundred pennants were flying on their coast. Were we then able to prevent their going in and out, or stop them from taking our trade and our storeships even in sight of our garrisons. Besides, were they not in the English and Irish channel picking up our homeward bound trade— sending their prizes into French and Spanish ports, to the great terror and annoyance of our merchants and ship-owners?

" These are facts that can be traced to a period when America was in her infancy; without ships—without seamen—without money—and at a time when our navy was not much less in strength than at present. The Americans will be found to be a different sort of enemy by sea than the French.

" They possess nautical knowledge with equal enterprise to our-selves; they will be found attempting deeds which a Frenchman would never think of ; and they will have all the ports of our enemy open, in which they can make good their retreat with their booty. In a predatory war on commerce, Great Britain would have more to lose than to gain, because the Americans would retire within

[2] Reprinted in *Niles' Register*, Aug. 1, 1812, v. 2: 360.

themselves, having everything they want for supplies, and what foreign commerce they might have, would be carried on in fast sailing armed ships, which as heretofore, would be able to fight or run away as best suited their force or inclination."

A few weeks later, under the head of "Political Remarks," Mr. Niles said: "How far will the revenue [of Great Britain] be touched by the irresistible activity and enterprise of 100,000 American seamen, prepared or preparing themselves to assail the British commerce in every sea—to cut off supplies from abroad, and forbid exportations, with safety. The Americans will prove themselves an enemy more destructive than Great Britain ever had on the ocean—they will do deeds that other sailors would hardly dare to reflect on. Witness their exploits in the revolutionary war, and at Tripoli; in which, perhaps, not a single instance occurred of their being defeated by an equal force, though cases of the contrary are numerous. What part of the enemy's trade will be safe? France, duly estimating the capacity of America to injure a common enemy, will open all the ports of the continent as places of refuge and deposit for our privateers, and all the fleets of England cannot confine them to their harbors, at home or abroad. The British channel itself will be vexed by their enterprises; and 100 sail of armed vessels be inadequate to the protection of the trade passing through it. For the probability of these things, let Lloyd's lists from 1777 to '83 be referred to. Terror will pervade the commercial mind, and mighty bankruptcies follow; to all which will be superadded the great privations of the manufacturers, and the increased distresses of the poor. More money must be raised—for the national expenditure will be greatly augmented—every ship must be put in commission, if possible— and the war being prosecuted chiefly at a distance, will be the more costly."[2] And again in the same issue, under the caption "Privateering," he says ".... In the United States every possible encouragement should be given to privateering in war with a commercial nation. We have tens of thousands of seamen, that, without it, would be destitute of the means of support, and useless to their country. Our national ships are too few to give employment to a twentieth part of them, or retaliate the acts of the enemy.

[2] *Niles' Register*, v. 2: 395.

But by licensing private armed vessels the whole naval force of the nation is truly brought to bear on the foe; and while the contest lasts, that it may have the speedier termination, let every individual contribute his mite, in the best way that he can, to distress and harass the enemy, and compel him to peace."

During the embargo and non-intercourse struggles, particular attention was given to the building of swift sailing "clipper" ships to engage in the carrying trade and the Baltimore shipbuilders were pre-eminently successful in developing this type of vessel which soon became noted the world over for its beauty and fine sailing qualities. The models were borrowed all along the Atlantic seaboard and Baltimore ship carpenters were in great demand everywhere. Carrying an enormous spread of canvas, these vessels sat so lightly upon the water that they appeared "as if about to rise and fly in the air." Niles said of them: "These wonderfully constructed schooners cannot easily be taken. They go where they please; they chase and come up with anything they see, and run away at pleasure."

Conditions in 1812 were especially favorable for privateering. For nineteen years American commerce had run the gauntlet of French decrees and British orders in council, under which visit meant capture and condemnation at the hands of either nation and the safety of the vessels depended more upon their sails than upon their papers. At the outbreak of the war the American ships were the best built and best manned in the world, and as many hundreds of vessels were temporarily out of commission, both shipowners and sailors were eager for a chance to make prize of the enemy's ships. "In the summer of 1812, any craft that could keep the sea in fine weather set out as a privateer to intercept vessels approaching the coast. The typical privateer of the first few months was the pilot boat, armed with one or two long, nine or twelve-pound guns. Of twenty-six privateers sent from New York in the first four months of war, fifteen carried crews of 80 men or less. . . . After the seas had been cleared of such prey as these petty marauders could manage, they were found to be unprofitable—too small to fight and too light to escape. The typical privateer of 1813 was a larger vessel—a brig or schooner of two or three hundred tons, armed with one long pivot-gun, and six or eight lighter guns in broadside; carrying crews which varied in number from one hundred and twenty to one hundred and sixty men; swift enough to escape under most circumstances even a frigate, and strong enough to capture any armed merchantman." [4]

Within a month after the declaration of war a little volunteer navy of sixty-five vessels was at sea and prizes were arriving almost daily. From the beginning of the war until its close *Niles' Register* published a list of American prizes, at the head of which was kept standing this quotation from the *British Naval Register:*

> "The winds and seas are Britain's wide domain,
> And not a sail, but by *permission* spreads!"

The list included "only such enemy vessels as safely arrive in our ports, or are sunk or burnt or otherwise *'satisfactorily'* accounted for." The extent of the loss inflicted on British commerce by American privateers cannot be definitely determined as statistics differ so widely, but it ran up into many millions. Niles says: "The number of vessels captured and 'satisfactorily accounted for' during a war of two years and eight months is 1634. There may be a few duplicates in our lists; but there are certainly many omissions. The vessels captured, which arrived safely in port, were divested or destroyed at sea, including a few ransomed, I estimate at not less than 1750; and the whole amount captured at 2,500, allowing 750 to have been recaptured. I think my opinion on this subject is entitled to some weight; considering that I have read the journal of every vessel that was published, and examined in the course of the war not less than ten and perhaps twelve thousand columns of 'ship news' to make up the list of prizes, and collect the facts that belonged to the war on the ocean . . . ."

Emmons in his Statistical History of the United States Navy puts the number at 1341; Schouler, probably quoting from Niles, gives 1750; Ingersoll places the number at 2425, and Coggeshall, whose work is largely made up of verbatim transcripts from Niles, says the number exceeded 2000. We know, however, that the money loss inflicted was stupendous; that marine insurance rose to unheard of figures and that by the end of 1814 the British merchants were heartily sick of the war and complained bitterly of the state of affairs, for in spite of the heavy convoy duty paid

[4] Henry Adams, History of the U. S. 7: 314.

by them, the Admiralty was unable to afford them adequate protection. More than anything else, the wholesale destruction wrought by the privateers brought about a disposition for peace in the British classes most responsible for the war.

By act of March 3, 1813, Congress offered to pay to any persons who should " burn, sink or destroy " any British *armed vessel of war,* one half the value of such vessel and Niles, in his numerous editorials on the subject strongly advocated the destruction of British vessels and the nationalization of privateers. At the outset of the war it was customary to man privateers with all the seamen they could hold, in order that sufficient prize crews might be detached to man the prizes taken. In consequence, it frequently happened that being heavily laden with the spoils from prizes and weakened by the heavy drafts of prize crews, the privateers came to grief and their successful careers ended in disaster to the shipowners and in imprisonment for the crew.

In a letter to Monroe on the subject of privateers Jefferson wrote: " Encourage them to burn their prizes and let the public pay for them. They will cheat us enormously. No matter; they will make the merchants of England feel and squeal and cry out for peace." Jefferson's idea was to extend the provisions of the above mentioned act to *all* British vessels instead of restricting it to national vessels of war, and there is but little doubt that this policy would have proved very effective and would have prevented the loss of many American privateers, overloaded and undermanned, through zeal for the interests of their owners as well as their own pockets. In spite of these drawbacks, however, that the system of privateering was the most powerful agent for peace is shown by dispatches and comments in the English press, of which the following is a specimen:

"At a meeting of ship-owners, merchants, manufacturers and underwriters of the City of Glasgow, held September 7, 1814, it was unanimously resolved,

" ' That the number of American privateers with which our channels have been infested, the audacity with which they have approached our coasts, and the success with which their enterprise has been attended, have proved injurious to our commerce, humbling to our pride and discreditable to the directors of the naval power of the British nation, whose flag till of late waved over every sea and triumphed over every rival.

" ' That there is reason to believe, in the short space of less than twenty-four months, above eight hundred vessels have been captured by the power, whose maritime strength we have hitherto impolitically held in contempt.

" ' That at a time when we were at peace with all the rest of the world, when the maintenance of our marine costs so large a sum to the country, when the mercantile and shipping interests pay a tax for protection under the form of convoy duty, and when, in the plenitude of our power we have declared the whole American coast under blockade, it is equally distressing and mortifying that our ships cannot with safety traverse our own channels, that insurance cannot be effected but at an excessive premium, and that a horde of American cruisers should be allowed, unheeded, unresisted and unmolested to take, burn or sink our own vessels in our own inlets and almost in sight of our own harbors . . . .' " [5]

While the achievements of some of the Maryland privateers have become famous and have passed into history, the whole story will never be known. Only a few of the log books are known to be in existence and these for single cruises; and as the privateersmen were more facile with the cutlass than the pen, these sources of information leave much to be desired. The original records of commissions issued by the Collector of the Port of Baltimore were all destroyed by fire in 1904, none are on file at Annapolis, and if any remain in the state, they are at the smaller ports of entry. Of the cruisers themselves, many reporting as " at sea " at the close of the war, were never heard of again.

The form of commission issued from 1794 to 1816 (apparently under the Act of 1794, Chap. 50, U. S. Stat. at large), was as follows:

BY THE PRESIDENT OF THE UNITED STATES OF AMERICA.

Suffer the brig *Inca* of Baltimore, Alexander Thompson, master or commander, of the burthen of two hundred and thirty and 3/95 tons or thereabouts, mounted with two guns, navigated with twenty-two men, to pass with her company, passengers, goods

[5] *Niles' Register,* 7: 190.

and Merchandise without any hindrance, seizure or molestation, the said ship appearing by good testimony to belong to one or more of the citizens of the United States and to him or them only.

Given under my hand and the seal of the United States of America the 23rd day of October, in the year of our Lord, one thousand, eight hundred and eleven.

JAMES MADISON,

Number 76.   By the President.

JAMES MONROE,
    Secretary of State.

State of Maryland, District of Baltimore,
    Countersigned by JAMES H. McCULLOUGH, Coll'r.

During the war of 1812 one hundred and twelve letters of marque or privateers were commissioned from Maryland, of which number fifty-eight were fitted out from Baltimore, the largest number from any port in the United States. Many of these were never mentioned in the contemporary newspapers and the careers of some that are mentioned, were brief indeed. The names of Commodore Barney, Captains Boyle, Coggeshall, Dooley, Miller, Moon, Murphy and Stafford are well known as active, successful privateersmen, whose exploits made Baltimore famous and earned for her the venomous dislike of some of the peace-loving New England states. Unflattering items frequently appeared in the papers of that section, as the following specimen reprinted in *Niles' Register* will show:

" From the *New Bedford Mercury*.

" ' Mr. Lindsey is requested by one of his subscribers to insert in his paper, that the doctor of the privateer *Saratoga* (now fitting for a cruise at Fairhaven) applied some days since, to several apothecaries of this place for a *medicine chest;* all of whom peremptorily refused supplying him with that article, or with any drugs or medicines for the use of the privateer.

" ' We think the gentlemen did themselves much credit ; and we hope their example will be followed by the citizens of this place generally. Let it be distinctly understood, that privateers cannot obtain supplies of any kind at this place, and we shall no longer be infested with those nuisances. Let them fit and refit from that sink of corruption, that *Sodom* of our country, called *Baltimore,* and not by seeking refuge here, put in jeopardy our shipping and our town, and necessitate our yeomanry at this busy season to leave their farms uncultivated to defend our harbor, which were it not a place of refuge for what has been emphatically denominated "licensed pirates," would not need a soldier to insure its safety.   A SHIP OWNER.'" [6]

Commodore Barney made but one cruise as a privateersman, sailing from Baltimore in the *Rossie,* July 12, 1812, and returning November 10, during which time he captured four ships, eight brigs, three schooners and three sloops, valued with their cargoes at more than one million, five hundred thousand dollars. Seven of the prizes were burnt at sea and 217 prisoners were sent to Newfoundland in one of the brigs. Shortly after his return from this cruise, Commodore Barney was taken into the service of the United States in the regular navy. Captain Boyle was the most famous as well as the most successful of the Maryland privateersmen. He was born at Marblehead, Mass., June 29, 1776, and had command of a ship when only sixteen years of age; he married and settled in Baltimore October 6, 1794, and died at sea October 12, 1825. First in the *Comet* and later in the *Chasseur* he destroyed thousands of tons of shipping, the value of which ran into millions, sent in hundreds of prisoners, and on more than one occasion attacked the lighter vessels of the British regular navy.

A letter written by Henry Fulford of Baltimore, under date of November 21, 1813, throws an interesting sidelight on the business side of privateering as well as the potential risks and profits.

"The *Transit* and *Patapsco* have sailed; the former got under way Wednesday morning and the latter on Friday. From the winds we have had, I judge they are both somewhere about the Patuxent, where are several other vessels that sailed before them; they are both well fitted out for their voyage and I hope Dame Fortune may protect them. We have directed Captain Richardson to proceed to Porto Rico where we are in hopes he may sell his flour and purchase a cargo of coffee on advantageous terms with which to proceed to New York or some other eastern port. Kelly is bound to Havana for White Sugar suitable to the French market; he will probably on his return proceed to New York. However, the owners of the *Patapsco* have given up the management

---

[6] *Niles' Register,* v. 7: 112.

of the voyage to Holden and Kelly and I feel perfectly satisfied
that the matter is in good hands.

" The *Patapsco* has on board 1075 barrels of superfine flour and
48 barrels of Navy bread on owners account and twenty-five barrels of flour belonging to Kelly being the privileges allowed him
in the vessel. He has besides wages of $60.00 per month, three
hundred dollars to be paid on his safe arrival at Havanna and
three hundred more on his safe arrival at New York or any other
port in the United States. Holden is to get a commission of 5
per cent on the gross sales with liberty of investing it and bringing
it home in the vessel freight free.

" I think them both valuable men and believe that some, not
equal to them, have quite as good terms. The flour I imagine
will average somewhere about seven dollars per barrel on board.
We began to purchase at six dollars and fifty cents and finished
at seven dollars and fifty cents. The seamens' wages in both
vessels are thirty dollars per month. We had however to pay their
expences down from Philadelphia which amounts to something. I
am in great hopes that they will get safe out and safe back. Every
boat has got out that attempted it lately. You recollect the vessel
commanded by Tom Wilson that you and I saw get under way on
Sunday when we were upon Hampstead Hill. She proceeded
directly to sea, and two days afterward captured a British brig
loaded with rum and ordered her to enter a port in North Carolina, where she has safely arrived and will pay well. We intend
loading the *Diamond* immediately for the West Indies, suitable
guns for an armament are not to be had. She must therefore go
if we can get men, with anything we can catch. For a man of my
capacity I shall have a good deal afloat. And if NERVE lasts I
mean to run the risk, for if two of the three arrive safe, I ought to
make money. Mr. Clopper got back shortly after you went away.
He is much pleased with the *Grampus's* voyage, having made
about thirty thousand dollars thereby."

We do not know the result of these ventures, but it was probably most satisfactory to the owners, as both the *Patapsco* and the
Diamond were afloat in 1815, and were credited with having made
prizes. The *Transit* is not mentioned in any of the lists of privateers fitted out or of those taking prizes, so the chances are even that
her cruise was uneventful and successful as a business venture.

CHAPTER III

THE CHESAPEAKE EXPEDITION

During the first six months of the war, Maryland was busily engaged in arming and equipping her quota of troops and in making preparations for the defence of Annapolis and Baltimore. The fortifications of Baltimore were manned by the city militia; and the companies of Captains Collins and Sterrett's Baltimore militia were stationed at Fort Madison, Annapolis, then under the command of Lieut.-Colonel Small of the 39th Regiment, Maryland Militia. The " Homespun Volunteer Company " of Hagerstown, commanded by Captain Thomas Quantrill was sent on the same service.

Within six weeks after the declaration of war Captain Nathan Towson of the 2nd United States Artillery, with a company of volunteer artillery from Baltimore City and County, marched north to take part in the Canadian invasion. A little later the City of Baltimore sent nearly a full regiment of infantry under the command of Colonel William H. Winder, for the Canadian service, fifteen thousand dollars having been subscribed by the citizens for the equipment of the regiment. On October 5, 1812, another company of a hundred men, under the command of Captain Stephen H. Moore, marched from Baltimore to join Colonel Winder's forces.

The British government issued a proclamation on December 26, 1812, declaring a blockade of the Delaware and Chesapeake bays, but it was not until February 4, 1813, that a hostile fleet consisting of four ships of the line, six frigates and several smaller vessels, under the command of Admiral Sir George Cockburn, entered the waters of the Chesapeake and cast anchor in Hampton Roads.[1]

---

[1] The fleet was made up as follows: The *Marlborough,* 74, Captain Charles Bayne Hodgson Ross, Rear-Admiral Cockburn's flagship; *Dragon,* 74, Captain Berry; *Poictiers,* 74, Commodore Beresford; *Victorious,* 74, Captain Talbot; *Acasta,* 44, Kerr; *Junon,* 38, Sanders; *Statira,* 38, Stackpoole; *Maidstone,* 36, Burdett; *Belvidera,* 36, Byron; *Narcissus,* 32, Aylmer; *Lauristinus,* 21, Gordon; and *Tartarus,* 20, Paseo.

In the course of the spring[2] this force was materially increased, and on the 20th of March the entire coast of the United States was declared to be in a state of blockade, with the exception of Rhode Island, Massachusetts, and New Hampshire. This apparently singular exception was in line with the avowed British policy of encouraging the peace party by leaving unmolested those sections of the country in which the war was unpopular.

" Until the overthrow of Napoleon disengaged more of their navy and all of their army, there were few land forces with the ships of war sent to this country early in 1813. Some two or three thousand foreign renegades, called ' Chasseurs Brittaniques,' enlisted in Spain, from among the prisoners and vagabonds taken or found there, if not intended, too well calculated for marauding and despicable incursions, came with Warren's squadron, whose second in command was a notorious freebooter, Admiral George Cockburn."[3]

The conduct of the Chesapeake expedition gained for Admiral Cockburn the undying hatred of the American people and he was probably the best hated British officer engaged in the war. His exploits at Havre de Grace, and the head of the bay, occasioned the production of James Kirke Paulding's " Lay of the Scottish Fiddle," an almost forgotten satire on the commanding officers of the squadron, and the plunder and burning of the towns of Havre de Grace, Fredericktown and Georgetown. The contemporary newspapers are full of accounts of pillage, rapine and burning,

---

[2] Admiral Sir John Borlase Warren, in command of the American station, was not with the fleet when it first entered the Chesapeake. He arrived early in March, 1813, the *San-Domingo, 74,* Captain Charles Gill, bearing his flag.

[3] Ingersoll, 1 : 196. The events of Admiral Cockburn's career are thus set forth in the Dictionary of National Biography, in which his conduct of the Chesapeake expedition is characterized as dashing but desultory : " Born 1772 ; put on the ships' book as captains' servant, 1781, though he did not join his ship until 1786 ; commanded ship in the Mediterranean, 1793-1802 ; rear admiral, 1812 ; sent to harass the American coast, 1812-15 ; took part in capture of Washington ; K. C. B., 1815 ; conveyed Napoleon to St. Helena, 1815 ; governor of St. Helena, 1815-16 ; M. P. and a lord of the admiralty, at intervals, 1820-46 ; admiral of the fleet, 1851 ; succeeded to baronetcy, 1852 ; died 1853."

and *Niles' Register* has many columns headed "Barbarities of the Enemy." The Boston *Gazette* published the following flattering notice in July, 1813: "It is stated as a fact that the notorious barbarian Admiral Cockburn has gone to England in the *Cressy,* British ship of war. We know not for what purpose he has gone home; but this we do know, that there breathes not in any quarter of the globe a more savage monster than this same British Admiral. He is a disgrace to England and to human nature; and we do not hesitate to say that, by his profligate and barbarous conduct to the Americans, he has forfeited all right to be treated as other prisoners of war, should he ever chance to be taken." At a banquet at Annapolis, about the same period, the following toast was drunk with great enthusiasm: "Admirals Warren and Cockburn; may the eternal vengeance of Heaven hurl them to some station that will terminate their inhuman butcheries and savage cruelties—they disgrace human nature."

A recent writer, K. C. Babcock, in volume 13, page 119, "The American Nation," makes the following statement: "The most that could be done by the blockading squadrons was to seize, carry off, or burn everything that floated, and to destroy all that could contribute to national resistance. The harassing of the shores, however, was carried on in a mild and gentlemanly fashion—private property being respected, or if it were levied upon, payment was made, unless the owners offered resistance." A little further on (page 136), this remarkable statement is somewhat qualified:

"In the war of 1812 it was one of the prime objects of the British to bring the Republican government into such disrepute and scorn that it would have to make peace on British terms, or yield to a revolution favorable to British interests. Therefore, by the rules of war and of political strategy, the Chesapeake expedition in itself was wise and proper, though some of its incidents cannot be justified on any grounds."

It is interesting to turn to the account of one of the most distinguished British officers, who took part in this expedition. Sir Charles James Napier, after having served with distinction in the Peninsular campaign, was sent to Bermuda to join the expedition forming "to harass the American coast." One of the regiments under his command had recently returned from

Botany Bay where they had been stationed as a punishment. The "Chasseurs Brittaniques" were Frenchmen enlisted from the war prisons. The following quotations from "The Life and Opinions of Sir Charles James Napier," by Sir William Napier, are very conclusive: "Very anxious also I am to ascertain my own force in command of an awkward brigade; for the marines, being ever on board ship, are necessarily undrilled, and the foreigners under me are *duberous.* Fight these last shall, all men will fight when they begin, but delay enables rogues to evaporate. My self-confidence makes me wish for the chief command; yet am I fearful of estimating my powers too high, and much I dislike sacking and burning of towns, it is bad employment for British troops. This authorized, perhaps needful plundering, though to think so is difficult, is very disgusting, and I will with my own hand kill any perpetrator of brutality under my command . . . .

"I have never said anything publicly, but am inclined to think that more might have been done in the Chesapeake; but whether doing more would be doing good, is a point to dispute. Taking an extended view of the expedition, as a diversion in favour of Canada, it was a complete one; but it ended too soon or too late—too late if the troops were to be afterwards sent to Canada for reinforcing Sir George Prevost; too soon if not to go there . . . . But the faults of this expedition sprung from one simple cause—there were three commanders! It was a council of war, and what council of war ever achieved a great exploit?

"Had either Sir John Warren, Sir Sydney Beckwith, or Admiral Cockburn acted singly and without consultation, we should not have done such foolish things. Sir Sydney wanted neither head, nor heart, nor hand for his business; but he was not free to do what he thought wise, and run sulky when required to do what he deemed silly, which in my opinion made it more silly. He is certainly a very clever fellow, but a very odd fish. I like him, yet do not like to serve under him in his Chesapeake fashion. He ought to have hanged several villains at little Hampton; had he so done, the Americans would not have complained; but every horror was committed with impunity, rape, murder, pillage; and not a man punished! . . . .

"Well! whatever horrible acts were done at Hampton, they were not done by the 102nd, for they were never let to quit their ranks, and they almost mutinied at my preventing them joining in the sack of that unfortunate town. The marine artillery behaved like soldiers; they had it in their power to join in the sack and refused. I said to that noble body of men, I cannot watch your conduct, but trust you will not join those miscreants. They called out, Colonel we are picked men, *we blush for what we see,* depend upon us, not a man of the marine artillery will plunder. We are well paid by his majesty and we will not disgrace him or ourselves *by turning robbers and murderers . . . .*

"We have sent off our Frenchmen, who are the greatest rascals existing. Much I wished to shoot some, but had no opportunity. They really murdered without an object but the pleasure of murdering. One robbed a poor Yankee and pretended all sorts of anxiety for him; it was the custom of war he said to rob a prisoner, but he was sorry for him. When he had thus coaxed the man into confidence he told him to walk on before, as he must go to the general; the poor wretch obeyed, and when his back was turned the musket was fired into his brains. *This is one of many instances* of their killing without any object but murder, and they intend to desert in a body. I would rather see ten of them shot than one American. It is quite shocking to have men who speak our own language brought in wounded; one feels as if they were English peasants and that we are killing our own people.

"Strong is my dislike to what is perhaps a necessary part of our job, viz., plundering and ruining the peasantry. We drive all their cattle and of course ruin them; my hands are clean, but it is hateful to see the poor Yankees robbed, and to be the robber."

His opinion of the system followed in this expedition was evinced in the following note, endorsed on a rejected proposal of his to prevent excesses at Ocracoke:

"Ocracoke, 1813. A proposal to Admiral Cockburn, in the hope of preventing a second edition of the *horrors of Little Hampton, equally disgraceful to the British name and to human nature.*"

In the light of this testimony of a participant and eye-witness, it is probable that the accounts published in the current prints are not unduly colored, and all the evidence tends to show that the outrages perpetrated during the Chesapeake expedition were not only sanctioned by the British government, but that the command-ing officers were deliberately selected as those best qualified to carry out the policy of "harassing the American coast."

Concerning this same occurrence (the attack on Hampton, June 25, 1813), James[4] has this to say:

"A subject next presents itself for relation, upon which it is painful to proceed. As soon as the Americans were defeated, and driven from Hampton, the British troops, or rather, the foreign troops, for they were the principals, forming part of the advanced force, commenced perpetrating upon the defenceless inhabitants acts of rapine and violence, which unpitying custom has, in some degree, rendered inseparable from places that have been carried by storm; but which are revolting to human nature, as they are dis-graceful to the flag that would sanction them. The instant these circumstances of atrocity reached the ears of the British command-ing officer, orders were given to search for, and bring in, all the Canadian chasseurs distributed through the town; and, when they were so brought in, a guard was set over them. The officers could do no more; they could not be at every man's elbow, as he roamed through the country in search of plunder; and plunder the soldier claims as a right, and will have, when the enemy has compelled him to force his way at the point of the bayonet.

"No event of the war was so greeted by the government editors as the affair at Hampton. All the hireling pens in the United States were put in requisition, until tale followed tale, each out-doing the last in horror. The language of the brothel was ex-hausted, and that of Billingsgate surpassed, to invent sufferings for the American women, and terms of reproach for their 'British' ravishers. Instances were not only magnified, but multiplied, ten-fold; until the whole republic rang with peals of execration against the British character and nation. A few of the boldest of the anti-government party stood up to undeceive the public; but the voice of reason was drowned in the general clamour, and it became as dangerous, as it was useless, to attempt to gain a hearing.

[4] William James. The Naval History of Great Britain, London, 1859, vol. 6:94.

The *George-town Federal-Republican* of July 7, a newspaper published just at the verge of Washington City, and whose editor possessed the happy privilege of remaining untainted amidst a corrupted atmosphere, contained the following account: 'The statement of the women of Hampton being violated by the British, turns out to be false. A correspondence upon that subject and the pillage said to have been committed there, has taken place between General Taylor and Admiral Warren. Some plunder appears to have been committed, but it was confined to the French troops employed. Admiral Warren complains on his part, of the Americans having continued to fire upon the struggling crews of the barges after they were sunk.' "

Hitherto the people of Maryland had not felt acutely the stress of war, though business was gradually becoming demoralized and militia service (which was compulsory), entailed considerable hardships on mechanics and others. After the blockade was effectually established, conditions became much worse as the privateers and coast-wise vessels came in and out of the Chesapeake with great difficulty, if at all, and in Baltimore especially the price of food stuffs increased enormously. All business came to a standstill owing to the stoppage of the ordinary supplies of provisions and the general financial stringency. The distress became acute, and many worthy people were obliged to choose between emigration or dependence on charity.

In the spring of 1813 the enemy's squadron left the anchorage at Lynn Haven Bay and moved slowly up the Chesapeake, creating great alarm among the inhabitants of both shores by the system of plunder, rapine and destruction inaugurated by Cockburn and his savage men. The people of the lower counties, being cut off from their executive head, were embodied into companies at the discretion of the militia officers, according to the militia laws of the State.

Early in April, while moving up the bay, Cockburn sent his tenders and barges into most of the navigable inlets, plundering and burning as he went. At each point threatened, the militia was called out, sometimes exchanging shots with the attacking parties, but offering little obstacle to the marauders; they were usually disbanded as soon as the immediate danger was past. So much anxiety was felt for the safety of Annapolis, that the Governor not only called out additional militia but removed the public records to a place of safety, inland.

On the 16th of April the fleet threatened the City of Baltimore, and while it lay off the city, preparations for defence were carried forward with great activity, the Mayor and City Council having appropriated $20,000 for that purpose, and this was supplemented by a loan to the citizens' committee of $500,000. The militia, under the command of General Samuel Smith, erected a water-battery mounted with 42-pounders, and built furnaces for heating shot. Signal boats were established down the Patapsco, while cavalry, infantry and artillery were stationed along the shores of the river and bay with a code of signals. Fort McHenry was strengthened under the direction of Colonel Wadsworth of the United States Engineers, and a number of old hulks were stationed in the river for the purpose of being sunk in the channel if necessary. The works known as the six gun battery were thrown up by brick-makers without charge.

While off the mouth of the Patapsco, Admiral Cockburn sent a flag of truce under pretext of forwarding a letter to the Secretary of State, his real object being to obtain a view of the fort and to sound the river. The flag was not permitted to approach nearer than four miles to the city, where it was met by an aid-de-camp and detained by Captain Chayter, commander of one of the barges. The officer in charge of the flag of truce asked whether our forces had mounted the guns of the French seventy-four, and was told that the heaviest of them were in position. This information, it is supposed, deterred the British from attempting the reduction of the fort at that time.

The frequent landings of small marauding parties in search of fresh water and provisions for the enemy's fleet caused many alarms, and the whole city was in a state of suspense, as thirty hostile vessels lay in sight of Baltimore. The landings were made first on one side of the river and then on the other. *Niles' Register* for April 17 said: "The means of defence of this important place have assumed great activity. The United States Government has promptly supplied all that General Smith requested. Look-out boats are stationed down the river, and the shores near the bay are watched by companies of riflemen and troops of horse. The fortifications are improved and increased, and a number of thirty-two pounders are mounting. Thousands of volunteers and militia are immediately taken into pay. Besides these, we have fifteen hundred or two thousand men well disciplined and completely equipped belonging to the city brigade; and arms have been purchased for the use of other citizens. Money, the sinew of war, is furnished as well by patriotic donations as otherwise. An attack cannot be feared." This sounds very much like whistling to keep up courage, for owing to the frequent marauding expeditions of the enemy, the alarms were almost constant and the invaders appeared to be ubiquitous. On April 23, Spesutie Island was occupied by an armed force, and many cattle and hogs were carried off or wantonly destroyed. The inhabitants fled on the approach of the enemy, but on being assured that they would not be molested, returned to their homes. On the 26th an attack on Annapolis was rumored, and again it was reported that a landing had been made at North Point; the Annapolitans made hurried requisitions for ammunition and more troops, and for the latter alarm the Baltimore militia was called to arms. Concerning this the *American* said:

"The alarm which summoned our citizens to arms has been discovered to have been groundless. From what source it originated is not material, nor was it unfortunate that it was given. It may have a tendency to render us more vigilant, and to accustom those on whom the city relies for defence to promptitude in turning out whenever occasion may demand. We know not at what moment of the day or night we may be assailed. The enemy has given sufficient proof of his disposition to wreak vengeance on us whenever an opportunity of success shall present itself. The best way to insure our safety is never to permit an opportunity to occur, but be always on the alert and prepared to repel him with vigor. The hour of danger can test our energy and firmness. And in this view of the subject the alarms which have been given are useful, because they show us on what numbers we can really calculate for efficient service."

The blockade of the Patapsco was so close that during the week ending April 24, not a single vessel was able to get into or out of the Baltimore harbor.

In a letter addressed to the President of the United States, under date April 26, 1813, Governor Winder said, in part: " We have the honor to transmit herewith a copy of a letter with sundry enclosures, just received by us from Jacob Gibson, esquire, of Talbot county. From these papers, of the correctness of which we entertain no doubt, it appears that the enemy visited Sharpe's Island, of which he is proprietor, last week, kept the possession thereof for several days, and took therefrom such supplies as they were in want of. Mr. Gibson was not in a situation to resist any demands that might be made on him, and, of course, *is not to be censured for the conduct of the enemy.* It is now for the constituted authorities of the country to decide whether, under the circumstances disclosed, and when that protection which is the just claim of every citizen has not been afforded him, this gentleman shall receive the compensation which the enemy authorizes, or it would be better, by refusing such permission in all cases, and indemnifying the injured out of the national resources, taking from individuals the temptation which might some times be offered to an underhand and dangerous traffic with the enemy. The determination of the Government upon this subject, as soon as it can be given, we respectfully ask.

" We cannot close this communication without some observations on the unprotected and defenceless state in which many parts of Maryland are left. Applications from various quarters are constantly pouring in upon us, and so far as the very limited means within our power will enable us, we are endeavoring to afford protection. But besides that, we have not sufficient arms and ammunition to supply the demands of every section of the State; the inevitable expense of calling out the militia for its protection would greatly exceed the ability of the State government. By the Constitution of the United States, the common defence is committed to the National Government, which has to protect each state against invasion, and to defray all the necessary expenses of a National war; and to us it is a most painful reflection that after every effort we have made, or can make, for the security of our citizens and their property, they have little to rely on but the possible forbearance of the enemy. The Capital of the State, notwithstanding the late call of the militia we are informed by the commanding officer, has not a sufficient force for its protection. Indeed, it must be obvious that while there are only from twenty to thirty regulars stationed in its forts, the militia in addition to this force, cannot give to it that protection which it has a right to claim, and without which Maryland may be essentially injured. A communication from the Secretary of War a few days since gave us to understand that a regiment of troops to be raised under the late Act of Congress, would be assigned to Maryland, and that a train of light artillery of fourteen pieces would be stationed north of the Potomac. We beg leave to urge the necessity of some immediate aid being ordered to the seat of government, as well as other parts of this state. Another delay may be of fatal consequence, as from the force which the enemy now has in our bay, we have much to apprehend, unless other means of defence than those which we now have are afforded to us."

CHAPTER IV

FRENCHTOWN AND HAVRE DE GRACE

After having plundered Sharp's, Poole's, Tilghman's and Poplar Islands, in the latter part of April, Admiral Cockburn made several expeditions for the destruction of the towns and villages at the head of the bay. On the 29th of April, Lieutenant Westphal of the *Marlborough,* in command of thirteen barges manned by four hundred armed men, made an attack on Frenchtown, a small hamlet nearly opposite to Elkton. This place was of small importance, being merely a point of relay for the stages between Baltimore and Philadelphia. The fortification consisted of a small redoubt, upon which were mounted four small four-pounders that had seen service during the Revolution, and which had later been used as ballast in a fishing vessel. The garrison consisting of some stage drivers, wagoners and a few militia from Elkton, made a resolute stand, but after twice repulsing the enemy, were forced to retire before overwhelming numbers.[1]

The wharf, fishery, and warehouses, with goods valued at from $20,000 to $30,000 were plundered and burned, but no dwelling was injured. Captain Howell's Susquehanna packet and four other small vessels were also burned.

After completing the work of destruction at Frenchtown, the enemy proceeded to White Hall, and from there marched over to the opposite battery at Elk Landing, where, after the exchange of a few shots, they returned and embarked immediately.

Havre de Grace, then a thriving town of about sixty houses, situated about two miles from the head of the bay, was visited on the morning of May 3. While the greater portion of the inhabitants were still in their beds, nineteen barges suddenly appeared before the place and opened a fire of shot, shells and rockets. A citizen by the name of Webster was struck on the head by a rocket

---

[1] Another account says that the defenders expended all their ammunition, consisting of about fifteen rounds, long before the enemy was within range, and then quietly removed themselves to a place of safety.

and instantly killed. Upon the high bank just below the town stood the so-called " Potato Battery," mounted with one 9-pounder and two 6-pounders, while on the lower, or Concord Point, where the lighthouse now stands, was another small battery. The only actual resistance offered to the landing of the British was made from the " Potato Battery; " and from his own account, John O'Neill was virtually the sole defender of the town.

O'Neill was born in Ireland, November 23, 1768, and came to the United States when eighteen years of age. He was in the military service under General Henry Lee, in quelling the Whiskey Insurrection in 1794, and in 1798 entered the naval service against the French. He became a prosperous merchant at Havre de Grace, and the destruction of the place ruined his business. When the present lighthouse was built on Concord Point, in 1829, he became its keeper and continued as such until his death, the 26th of January, 1838. For his gallantry at the " Potato Battery," the City of Philadelphia presented him with a beautiful sword.

Niles' Register printed the following letter of O'Neill's, dated May 10: " No doubt before this you have heard of my *defeat.* On the third instant we were attacked by fifteen English barges at break of day. We had a small breastwork erected, with two 6- and one 9-pounder in it, and I was stationed at one of the guns. When the alarm was given I ran to the battery and found but one man there, and two or three came afterwards. After firing a few shots they retreated, *and left me alone in the battery.* The grape-shot flew very thick about me. I loaded the gun myself, without any one to serve the vent, which you know is very dangerous, and fired her, when she recoiled and ran over my thigh. I retreated down to town, and joined Mr. Barnes, of the nail manufactory, with a musket, and fired on the barges while we had ammunition, and then retreated to the common, where I kept waving my hat to the militia who had run away, to come to our assistance, but they proved cowardly and would not come back. At the same time an English officer on horseback, followed by the marines, rode up and took me with two muskets in my hand. I was carried on board the *Maidstone* frigate, where I remained until released, three days since."

4

It having been reported that the British intended to hang O'Neill as a traitor taken with arms against his sovereign, Brigadier-General Henry Miller wrote to Admiral Warren, threatening to hang two British subjects in reprisal, but as Admiral Warren's letter shows, O'Neill had already been released on parole at the request of the magistrates of Havre de Grace.

The following letter from General Miller to Admiral Warren was sent with a flag of truce by Major Hanson, with instructions to proceed with all possible dispatch to the Admiral's ship, that the protection of the government of the United States might be extended in defence of a citizen from dangers they believed to menace him.

HEADQUARTERS, Baltimore, May 8, 1813.

SIR:

It becomes my duty to write to your Excellency that a citizen of the United States and an inhabitant of Havre de Grace for the last fifteen years, named O'Neill, has recently been taken in arms in defence of his property and his family in that place by a detachment from his Brittanic Majesty's fleet under your command, and that the said O'Neill has been menaced with immediate capital punishment as a traitor to the country of his Brittanic Majesty, on the ground of his being by birth an Irishman. Nothing in the course of public duty would be more painful to me than the application, or resorting to the law of retaliation on this or any other occasion; but, sir, in the event of the execution of O'Neill, painful as may be the duty, it becomes inevitable and I am authorized and commanded to state to your Excellency that two British subjects shall be selected by lot, or otherwise, and immediately executed. It is for your Excellency to decide whether a character of such barbarism shall or not be given to the war waged under your immediate direction.

I beg, sir, that you will do me the honor to accept the assurances of my very high respect and consideration.

HENRY MILLER,
Brigadier-General.

His Excellency, Sir J. B. WARREN,
H. M. S. *San Domingo.*

To which communication the following reply was received:

CHESAPEAKE, May 10, 1813.

SIR:

I have the honor to acknowledge the receipt of your letter of the 8th instant respecting a man named O'Neill taken by a detachment from the squadron under the orders of Rear-Admiral Cockburn. This man has been released upon the application of the magistrates of Havre de Grace upon parole. I was not informed of this man being an Irishman, or he would certainly have been detained to account to his sovereign for being in arms against British colors.

I have the honor to be, sir, your most obedient and humble servant,

JOHN BORLASE WARREN.

HENRY MILLER, ESQ.,
    Brigadier-General, etc.

The Reverend Jared Sparks, who was an eye-witness of the burning of Havre de Grace, contributed the following account of the affair to the *North American Review*, for July, 1817:

"In two or three histories of the late war, we have noticed erroneous statements respecting the operations of the British at the head of the Chesapeake, and particularly at Havre de Grace. The truth is, no official or correct account of these transactions was given in the papers of the day. No one, we believe, who was at all acquainted with the occurrences from personal observation, made any communication on the subject, and the short notices, which were published, were rather the result of vague report, than of any accurate knowledge of facts. We think it will gratify some of our readers, and serve, perhaps, to guard future historians against errours, if we offer them in this place a more detailed narrative of those events, than has yet appeared, founded on facts, which came under the observation of the writer, and for the correct statement of which we hold ourselves responsible.

"Considerable alarm had been excited as early as the 20th of April, 1813, among the inhabitants residing around the head of the bay, by reports continually circulated, that the British were rapidly advancing, and were resolved, for reasons not very distinctly known, to commit depredations on them particularly, and to make them acquainted, not only with the apprehensions, but with some of the realities of war. The enemy had already burnt several small vessels in the bay north of Baltimore, and landed in a few places, but without doing much injury, except occasionally driving off cattle for provision, where the owners had fled and left them behind. They were always desirous of making a fair purchase, and of paying the full value of what they received. We feel it incumbent on us to remark, however, that instances of so criminal a violation of the laws of their country, as that of voluntarily affording supplies to an enemy, if they occurred at all among the inhabitants, were exceedingly rare; and it is no more than justice to the enemy to state, that in some instances money was left behind, in a conspicuous place, to the full amount of what had been taken away.

"They took, plundered, and burnt the small vessels passing from one shore of the bay to the other, belonging to individuals, and loaded entirely with private property. This was their uniform practice. Even fishermen's boats did not escape; and some individuals, and even families, were reduced to absolute want, by the losses they sustained from this species of depredation.

"On the 28th of April, a brig and two or three schooners came to anchor in the bay, a little below Havre de Grace. This village is beautifully situated on the west side of the Susquehanna, a short distance above the confluence of that river with the Chesapeake. It is a port of entry, and was once a place of considerable trade, and were it not for the obstruction of navigation by a bar at the mouth of the river, and falls a few miles above, it would probably be one of the most important commercial points in that part of the country. These obstacles were found sufficient to counteract some very energetic attempts, which were made several years ago by a few gentlemen of wealth and enterprise, to promote its growth and importance. At the time when it was attacked by the British, it might perhaps be considered rather on the decline. It was principally engaged in the herring fishery, which is carried on to a great extent in the vicinity, and with large profits to the proprietors.

"On the next morning another brig and schooner joined those which came up the day before, and together with them anchored on the precise spot where the fleet was stationed in 1777, which brought up the forces under Lord Howe, before the battle of Brandywine. During the day, they all disappeared, passed round Turkey Point, and proceeded up Elk River as far as the small village of French Town, where the enemy burnt one or two warehouses, but no private dwellings, as has been erroneously stated. They burnt also two vessels in the river. They returned the next day, and resumed their former station. A large number of barges was seen for several hours making various movements in the bay, and it was generally thought that an immediate visit to the town was intended; but after landing a body of marines on a neighbouring island, they returned quietly to the shipping.

" The inhabitants of Havre de Grace had, for three weeks previous to this period, been making preparations for defence, and several companies of militia were called in to their aid. But these were in a very disorderly state, without discipline or arms. They were soon supplied with the latter, however, by the Governour, and, under the command of a colonel were reduced to some degree of order. A battery was thrown up at Point Concord, where the river unites with the bay, behind which were mounted an eighteen-pounder and two nines. These were manned by a company of volunteers, principally exempts from military service. Patrols were stationed every night, for two or three miles along the river and the bay, and everything seemed to indicate a resolution to be prepared for any event.

" This vigilance continued till within three or four days of the time, when they were actually attacked. At this time, the inhabitants, wearied with continual excitement and laborious exercise, began to relax from their exertions, and as the English had continued tranquil for some time, without discovering any hostile intentions, they fancied themselves in less danger than they had apprehended. By some unaccountable want of foresight, all the cavalry and some of the infantry were suffered to return to their homes, and those who remained became uneasy and disorderly. The officers were often absent, and even at the time of the attack, the commanding officer was several miles from town, and did not arrive there, till after the work of destruction was accomplished, and the authors of it had retired.

" Such was the state of things till Saturday afternoon, the first of May, when information was received from a deserter, that an attack would certainly be made on the town the following night— that orders had already been given, and everything was in complete readiness in the squadron. This report was immediately circulated and produced a general agitation. Many of the women and children were sent from the town. No time was lost in making every preparation for defence. The militia, amounting to about two hundred and fifty men, were kept at their arms all night, patrols were stationed in every place where they could possibly be of any service, the volunteers at the battery were at their guns, and a general determination seemed to prevail of giving the enemy a warm reception.

" But the night passed away, and no enemy had been seen. This alarm, however, was not without just ground. The story of the deserter was substantially true; but a timely discovery in the squadron that a man had escaped, and the supposition that he would give the information which he did, caused the expedition to be deferred till the next night. It was the general belief afterwards, that had the attack been made at the time first proposed, it would have been successfully repelled.

" Exhausted with fatigue, and believing themselves to have been deceived, the inhabitants retired quietly to rest the next night, seemingly without any apprehension of danger, or any preparation for meeting it. The militia, except a small number necessarily on duty every night, were dispersed in various parts of the town. But in the midst of this imaginary security, at daybreak, on the 3d of May, the drums beat an alarm, and the discharge of cannon immediately followed. At that moment were seen twenty barges filled with the enemy, advancing rapidly towards the town. The people, who were nearly all in bed, being thus suddenly awakened, were thrown into the greatest consternation. The guns at the battery, however, were soon manned, and began to operate on the barges as they advanced toward Point Concord, around which they were obliged to pass before they could enter the town. The women and children fled in every direction to the neighboring hills and woods. The militia were called to their arms with all possible speed, but in such a state of confusion, that they could not be rallied. Congreve rockets began to be thrown from the barges, the threatening appearance of which produced a still greater agitation, and when one of the militia was killed by a rocket, it was a signal for a general retreat. They left their ground, and escaped with great precipitation and disorder to the nearest woods, even before a man of the enemy had landed.

" In the meantime, the enemy passed round the point under a smart fire from the guns at the battery, and soon effected a landing. They had kept up a tremendous discharge of balls, rockets, and shells, and the town was already in flames. A party immediately advanced to the battery, and took possession of the guns, which had been deserted, but not until it would have been rashness to remain by them longer. These guns were turned upon the town, and did much injury.

" The sun had scarcely risen, when all the enemy's forces were landed, and marched to an open square in the centre of the town. They were here separated into bands of thirty or forty each, and sent to plunder and burn such houses as were not already on fire. A division of fifty men marched nearly a mile into the country in pursuit of the militia, but returned unsuccessful. Those engaged in plundering and burning did more execution. Their manner was, on entering a house, to plunder it of such articles as could be of any service to them, and easily transported, and convey them to their barges. Every man had his hatchet in his girdle, and when wardrobes and bureaus happened to be locked, they were made to yield to the force of this instrument. This was not a work of much time, and as soon as it was accomplished, they set fire to the house and entered another for the same purposes.

" The firing of cannon had ceased, and no other noise was heard, than the roaring of flames, the crash of falling timbers, and the occasional lamentations and entreaties of a few of the inhabitants, who had braved every danger with the hope of preserving from destruction their only means of subsistence. Their entreaties, however, were unavailing. General orders had been given to burn every house, and these were rigorously executed, till they were at length countermanded by the admiral. Immediately after he came on shore, which was not until some time after the landing of the forces, two or three ladies, who had courageously remained in their houses, during the whole commotion, endeavored by all the powers of female eloquence to dissuade him from his rash purposes. He was unmoved at first; but when they represented to him the misery he was causing, and pointed to the smoking ruins under which was buried all that could keep their proprietors from want and wretchedness, he relented and countermanded his original orders.

"This was not done 'till more than half of the town had been consumed. It has been said in a very respectable history of the times, that *one house* only escaped the flames; but this is a mistake. Havre de Grace consisted of about sixty houses, and of these not more than forty were burnt. Many others were plundered and much injured, and scarcely one remained which was not perforated with balls or defaced by the explosion of shells.

"During these operations, two barges ascended the river five miles, to the head of navigation, where their crews burnt a warehouse. They expected to have found there a number of vessels, but these had previously been sunk for protection. They were easily raised afterwards without having received essential injury.

"The enemy did not remain in Havre de Grace more than four hours. They then went on board their barges, passed out of the river and ascended a small creek to a furnace, belonging to Colonel Hughes, about eight miles north of Havre de Grace, where large numbers of public cannon had been made, and were still making. This establishment, comprising very curious machinery for boring cannon, was valued at twenty thousand dollars. It was entirely destroyed, as well as the cannon, which had been finished, and not yet been taken away. At sunset the barges were seen passing down the bay, and before dark they had arrived at the shipping.

"It is not easy to assign any cause, other than the caprice of its projector, for this violent attack on a defenceless and unoffending village. No public property was deposited there, nor were any of its inhabitants engaged in aiding the prosecution of the war.

"The conduct of the sailors while on shore was exceedingly rude and wanton. The officers gave such of the inhabitants, as remained behind liberty to carry out such articles of furniture as they chose, while the sailors were plundering their houses; but the sailors, not content with pillaging and burning, broke and defaced these also, as they were standing in the streets. Elegant looking-glasses were dashed in pieces, and beds were ripped open for the sport of scattering the feathers in the wind. These outrages, to be sure, were not commanded by the officers, but they were not restrained by them.

"Little can be said, indeed, in favor of the officers conduct in this particular. They selected tables and bureaus for their private use, and after writing their names on them, sent them on board the barges. The admiral himself was pleased with an elegant coach, which fell in his way, and commanded it to be put on board a boat, which belonged to the proprietor of the ferry, and taken to his ship. This order was executed, although he was told it belonged to a poor coach maker, whose family must suffer by its loss.

" But the most distressing part of the scene, was at the close of the day, when those, who fled in the morning, returned to witness the desolation of their homes, and the ruin of all their possessions. Most of them had escaped without being able to take anything away, except the clothes which covered them. They returned wretched and disconsolate, and seemed overwhelmed with the thoughts of the misery and want which awaited them. But their immediate necessities were relieved by the benevolence and liberality of a few gentlemen in the neighbourhood, who received them kindly into their houses, and supplied them with provisions.

" A deputation with a flag of truce was soon after sent, by the inhabitants of Havre de Grace, to the admiral's ship. He released the prisoners, but was obstinate in refusing to return any private property, or to make any reparation to individuals for their losses. He expressed disappointment at having met with so feeble a resistance, and said he could not commend the courage of the people of Havre de Grace, who had suffered five hundred men to land and plunder their town.

" Two days afterwards a party of marines went up the river Sassafras in several barges, and burnt the small villages of Frederick and Georgetown, which stood near its banks. All the British vessels immediately after left this part of the Chesapeake, and joined the squadron below.

"We ought not, perhaps, to close this account without saying a word of O'Neill, who has been celebrated in song, and who made some noise in the official correspondence of the day. He was a sturdy, vociferous Irishman, from the west of Ireland, who had been fifteen years in this country, and had during several of them superintended a nail manufactory in Havre de Grace. He seemed, for some reasons connected with his country, to have contracted a fiend-like hatred for the English, and appeared rejoiced at the opportunity he was likely to have of satisfying his vengeance. He was the most active man at the guns, and the last who left them, and was finally taken prisoner with his musket in his hands in the posture of defence, while marching alone from the battery into the town. He was afterward released with the other prisoners."

The account of the Chesapeake expedition is thus set forth by James:[2]

"Unfortunately, the capture of frigate after frigate by the Americans could not persuade the British Government that the United States were in earnest about going to war. Hence, instead of one of the ten or twelve dashing flag-officers, whose names have recently figured in these pages, being sent out to fight the Americans into compliance, a superannuated admiral, whose services, such as they were, bore a very old date, arrived, early in March, 1813, in Chesapeake Bay, to try the effect of diplomacy and procrastination. Had not Sir John Warren's second in command, Rear-Admiral Cockburn, been of a more active turn, the inhabitants of that very exposed part of the American sea-frontier, the coast around the bay in which the two admirals had cast anchor, would scarcely have known, except by hearsay, that war existed. . . . .

"Rear-Admiral Cockburn was now directed, with a squadron of small vessels, to penetrate the rivers at the head of the bay, and endeavour to cut off the enemy's supplies, as well as to destroy his foundries, stores and public works; particularly a depôt of flour, military and other stores, ascertained, by the information

[2] Naval History of Great Britain, 6:82, *et seq.*

of some Americans, to be at a place called Frenchtown, situated a considerable distance up the River Elk. Accordingly, on the evening of the 28th of April, taking with him the brigs *Fantom* and *Mohawk,* and the *Dolphin, Racer,* and *Highflyer* tenders, the rear-admiral moved towards the river. Having anchored the brigs and schooners as far within the entrance as could be effected after dark, the rear-admiral took with him in the boats of his little squadron, commanded by Lieutenant George Augustus West-phal, first of the *Marlborough,* one hundred and fifty marines, under Captains Marmaduke Wybourn and Thomas Carter, and five artillerymen, under Lieutenant Robertson, of that corps, and proceeded to execute his orders.

" Having, owing to ignorance of the way, entered the Bohemia, instead of keeping in the Elk River, the boats did not reach the destined place till late on the following morning. This delay enabled the inhabitants of Frenchtown to make arrangements for the defence of the stores and town, for the security of which a six-gun battery had lately been erected. As soon as the boats approached within gunshot of it, a heavy fire was opened upon them. Disregarding this, however, the marines quickly landed; and the American militia fled from the battery to the adjoining woods. The inhabitants of the town, which was situated at about a mile distant, having, as far as could be ascertained, taken no part in the contest, were not in the slightest degree molested; but a considerable quantity of flour, of army clothing, saddles, bridles, and other equipments for cavalry; also various articles of mer-chandise and the two stores in which they had been contained, together with five vessels lying near the place, were entirely con-sumed. The guns of the battery, being too heavy to be carried away, were disabled; and the boats departed, with no other loss than one seaman wounded in the arm by a grape-shot. The Americans lost one man killed by a rocket, but none wounded.

" The rear-admiral's system, and which he had taken care to impart to all the Americans captured by, or voluntarily coming on board the squadron, was to land without offering molestation to the unopposing inhabitants, either in their persons or properties; to capture or destroy all articles of merchandise and munitions of war; to be allowed to take off, upon paying the full market price, all such cattle and supplies as the British squadron might require, but, should resistance be offered, or menaces held out, to consider the town as a fortified post, and the male inhabitants as soldiers; the one to be destroyed, the other, with their cattle and stock, to be captured.

"As the boats on their way down the Elk were rounding Turkey Point, they came in sight of a large estate, surrounded by cattle. The rear-admiral landed; and, directing the bailiff, or overseer, to pick out as many oxen, sheep, or other stock, as were deemed sufficient for the present use of the squadron, paid for them to the full amount of what the bailiff alleged was the market price. Not the slightest injury was done; or doubtless one of the industrious American historians would have recorded the fact. Having learnt that cattle and provisions, in considerable quantity, were at Specucie Island, the rear-admiral, with the brigs and tenders proceeded to that place. In his way thither, it became necessary to pass in sight of Havre de Grace, a village of about sixty houses, situated on the west side of the Susquehanna, a short distance above the confluence of that river with the Chesapeake. Although the British were a long way out of gun-shot, the Americans at Havre de Grace, as if inspired by the heroism of their townsman, Commodore Rodgers, fired at them from a six-gun battery, and displayed to their view, as a further mark of defiance, a large American ensign. This determined the rear-admiral to make that battery and town the next object of attack. In the meanwhile he anchored off Specucie Island. Here a part of the boats landed, and obtained cattle upon the same terms as before. A complaint having been made that some of the subordinate officers had destroyed a number of turkeys, the rear-admiral paid the value of them out of his own pocket. The Americans, as they were driving the cattle to the boats, jeered the men, saying, 'Why do you come here? Why don't you go to Havre de Grace? There you'll have something to do.' About this time a deserter gave the people at Havre de Grace, who had already been preparing, notice of the intended attack.

"After quitting Specucie Island, the rear-admiral bent his course towards Havre de Grace; but the shallowness of the water admitting the passage of boats only, the one hundred and fifty marines and 'the five artillerymen embarked at midnight on the 2d of May, and proceeded up the river. The *Dolphin* and *Highflyer* tenders attempted to follow in support of the boats, but shoal water compelled them to anchor at the distance of six miles from the point of attack. By daylight the boats succeeded in getting opposite to the battery; which mounted six guns, 12- and 6-pounders, and opened a smart fire upon the British. The marines instantly landed to the left; which was a signal to the Americans to withdraw from their battery. Lieutenant Westphal, having in the meantime stationed his rocket-boat close to the battery, now landed with his boat's crew, turned the guns upon the American militia, and drove them to the extremity of the town. The inhabitants still kept up a fire from behind the houses, walls and trees, Lieutenant Westphal, by the admiral's orders, held out a flag of truce, and called upon them to desist. Instead of so doing, these ' unoffending citizens' fired at the British lieutenant, and actually shot him through the very hand that was bearing the flag of truce. After this, who could wonder if the British seamen and marines turned to the right and left, and demolished everything in their way? The townspeople themselves had constructed the battery; and yet not a house in which an inhabitant remained was injured. Several of the inhabitants, principally women, who had fled at first, came again into the town and got back such articles as had been taken. Some of the women actually proceeded to the boats; and upon identifying their property, obtained its restoration.

" Many of the inhabitants who had remained peaceably in their houses, as a proof that they were well informed of the principle upon which Sir George Cockburn acted, frequently exclaimed to him: 'Ah, sir, I told them what would be the consequence of their conduct. It is a great pity so many should suffer for a headstrong few. Those who were the most determined to fire upon you the other day, saying it was impossible you could take the place, were now the first to run away.' Several of the houses that were not burnt did, in truth, belong to the chief agents in those violent measures which caused such severity on the part of the British; and the very townspeople themselves pointed out the houses. Lieutenant Westphal, with his remaining hand, pursued and took prisoner an American captain of militia; and others of the party brought in an ensign and several privates, including an old Irish-man, named O'Neill. After embarking the six guns from the battery, and taking or destroying about one hundred and thirty stands of small-arms, the British departed from Havre de Grace.

"One division of boats, headed by the rear-admiral, then pro-ceeded to the northward in search of a cannon-foundry, of which some of the inhabitants of Havre de Grace had given information. This was found and quickly destroyed, together with five long 24-pounders, stationed in a battery for its protection; twenty-eight long 32-pounders, ready for sending away; and eight long guns and four carronades in the boring house and foundry. Another division of boats was sent up the Susquehanna, and returned after destroying five vessels and a large store of flour.

"On the night of the 5th of May, the same party of British marines and artillerymen again embarked in the boats, and pro-ceeded up the river Sassafras, separating the counties of Kent and Cecil, towards the villages of Georgetown and Fredericktown, situ-ated on opposite sides of the river, nearly facing each other. Having intercepted a small boat with two of the inhabitants, Rear-Admiral Cockburn halted the detachment about two miles from the town; and then sent forward the two Americans in their boat, to warn their countrymen against acting in the same rash manner as the people of Havre de Grace had done; assuring them that if they did, their towns would inevitably experience a similar fate; but that, on the contrary, if they did not attempt resistance, no injury should be done to them or their towns; that vessels and public property only would be seized; that the strictest discipline would be maintained; and that whatever provision, or other property of individuals, the rear-admiral might require for the use of the squadron, would be instantly paid for in its fullest value. The two Americans agreed in the propriety of this; said there was no battery at either of the towns; that they would willingly deliver the message, and had no doubt the inhabitants would be peaceably disposed.

"After waiting a considerable time, the rear-admiral advanced higher up; and, when within about a mile from the towns, and be-tween two projecting points of land which compelled the boats to proceed in close order, a heavy fire was opened upon them from one field-piece, and as conjectured, three hundred or four hundred militia, divided and entrenched on the opposite sides of the river. The fire was promptly returned, and the rear-admiral pushed on shore with the marines; but the instant the American militia observed them fix their bayonets, they fled to the woods, and were neither seen nor heard of afterwards. All the houses, excepting those whose owners had continued peaceably in them, and taken no part in the attack, were forthwith destroyed; as were four vessels lying in the river, together with some stores of sugar, of lumber, of leather, and other merchandise. On this occasion, five of the British were wounded. One of the Americans who entreated to have his property saved, wore military gaiters; and, had no doubt, assisted at the firing upon the British. Agreeably to his request, however, his property was left untouched.

"On his way down the river the rear-admiral visited a town situated on a branch of it. Here a part of the inhabitants actually pulled off to him; and requesting to shake hands, declared he should experience no opposition whatever. The rear-admiral accordingly landed, with the officers, and, chiefly out of respect to his rank, a small personal guard. Among those that came to greet him on his landing, were observed two inhabitants of Georgetown. These men, as well as an inhabitant of the place who had been to Georgetown to see what was going on, had succeeded in persuading the people to adopt as their best security, a peaceable demeanor. Having ascertained that there were no warlike stores nor public property, and obtained upon payment of the full value such articles as were wanted, the rear-admiral and his party reembarked. Soon afterwards a deputation was sent from Charlestown on the Northeast River, to assure the rear-admiral that the place was considered as at his mercy; and, similar assurances coming from other places in the upper part of the Chesapeake, the rear-admiral and his light squadron retired from that quarter.

"Persons in England may find it difficult to consider as soldiers, men neither embodied nor dressed in regimentals. That circumstance has not escaped the keen discernment of the American government. Hence the British are so often charged in proclamations and other state papers, with attacking the 'inoffensive citizens of the republic.' The fact is, every man in the United States, under 45 years of age, is a militiaman; and during the war attended in his turn, to be drilled or trained. He had always in his possession either a musket or a rifled-barrel piece; knew its use from his infancy; and with it, therefore, could do as much execution in a smock frock or plain coat as if he wore the most splendid uniform. These soldiers in citizens' dresses were the men whom Rear-Admiral Cockburn so frequently attacked and routed; and who, when they really acted up to the character of non-combatants, were invariably spared, both in their persons and properties. The rear-admiral wished them, for their own sakes only, to remain neutral; but General Hull, in his famous proclamation, prepared with so much care at Washington, invited the Canadian people to become open traitors to their country; and visited upon the heads of those that refused, all ' the horrors and calamities of war.' "

The legislature met in extra session, May 17, 1813, having been convened by the proclamation of Governor Winder. In his message the Governor said: " Since the adjournment of the legislature considerable alarms have harassed the state, in consequence of a large naval force within the waters of the Chesapeake, and the wanton destruction of our houses and other property by the squadron of the enemy.

" We have furnished all the means within our power to repel the invasion of the enemy, and as our resources are too limited to afford complete protection, it is for the wisdom of the legislature to make such further provision as the exigencies of the state, in their opinion, may require . . . .

" By letters from the Secretary of War, dated March the 20th and 24th, the Governor was required to call out five hundred militia to be stationed at Annapolis. One of the exigencies mentioned in the Constitution on which the militia may be called forth having occurred, it was considered the duty of the executive to comply with the requisition, and the necessary orders for that purpose were issued. By another letter from the Secretary of War, dated April 16, a further requisition of two thousand men to be stationed at Baltimore was made: Orders have been issued in consequence of this requisition . . . ."

This legislative session was a short one, lasting only from May 17th to the 30th. A large part of the time was taken up in the discussion of resolutions, which could not be passed owing to the difference of opinion between the Senate and House. Of the twenty-three acts passed, three had to do with the matter for which the legislature had been convened: Chapter 15, " An act to provide for the payment of the militia which has been called into actual service, and expenses incurred by reason thereof "; Chapter 19, " An act providing for the calling out and detaching the militia of this State and for other purposes "; and Chapter 22, " An act authorising the several banks in this State to loan money to the State of Maryland."

On May 28 Mr. Lewis Duvall read the following preamble and resolutions in the House, which was largely Federalist:

" WHEREAS, An expression of the sentiments of this legislature is expected by the good people of the State of Maryland, in relation to the conduct of the enemy while in our waters; and viewing the British squadron, under the command of Admiral Warren, as having violated the dignified character of humanity and national honor; Therefore

" *Resolved,* That this legislature view with horror and disgust, the unmanly and perfidious procedure of the enemy recently in the Chesapeake Bay, and well deserving universal execration, more especially among civilized nations, in wantonly destroying, and indiscriminately plundering the private property of individuals at Havre de Grace, Fredericktown and Georgetown, and thereby endangering the lives of innocent and helpless women and children.

" *Resolved,* That Brigadier-General Miller have the thanks of this legislature for his prompt and dignified demand of a fellow-citizen captured by the enemy at Havre de Grace, and that his threat of retaliation was just and honorable.

" *Resolved,* That the reply of Admiral Warren to General Miller, merits and ought to receive the severest animadversion."

On the next day Mr. Duvall's resolutions were brought up for the consideration of the House, when Mr. Dorsey submitted the following amendment: and

" WHEREAS, The national government has perverted the national

5

revenue to foreign conquest, and yielded up the property on our seaboard to the conflagration and vengeance of an incensed foe, under a full knowledge that the enemy against whom they had declared hostilities, had ample means by their naval superiority to deal out destruction to an extent even beyond that which has been experienced; Therefore

" *Resolved,* In the opinion of this general assembly, that the conduct of the national government in diverting our resources to foreign conquest (an event never contemplated by the framers of our constitution) and abandoning our homes to an enemy, brought into operation by their own act, and inflamed by the recollection of the conquest achieved by the American arms, has been guilty of an improvident departure from the genius of our constitution.

" *Resolved,* That those persons who have emigrated to this country and have been naturalized by the laws of the United States, are entitled to complete protection within our territorial jurisdiction; but that a war waged for the only declared object of extending to them an inviolability against the claims of their deserted country when beyond the scope of our national limits, is impolitic and must necessarily be attended with public and individual sacrifices, entitled to more consideration than any good likely to result from the recognition of the contested principle; Therefore

" *Resolved,* That our senators and representatives in the Congress of the United States, be instructed and required to use every constitutional means to bring to an immediate and honorable peace the present harassing and oppressive war, and in the meantime to obtain from the general government that efficient protection which as a confederate State, Maryland is entitled to claim."

The amendment was immediately passed by a vote of 43 to 15, and after some verbal corrections the original resolutions were likewise passed, the word " savage " being inserted in place of " perfidious," in the first resolution.

On Sunday, May 30, the Senate passed and sent to the House the following resolutions:

" WHEREAS, The just and unavoidable war in which we are engaged, waged not for conquest or from motives of ambition, but to secure some of the most sacred rights which appertain to free and independent nations. Yet as our only object is peace as soon as it can be attained upon equal and honorable terms; Therefore

"*Resolved unanimously,* That the evidences of a ready and earnest disposition so promptly manifested on all occasions by the government of the United States, to meet the government of Great Britain upon fair and honorable conditions, command our warmest approbation, and leave us fully persuaded that nothing but the want of a desire equally sincere on the part of the enemy can procrastinate the war or delay a peace, the end and object of all our wishes and efforts."

On being put to a vote, there were ten affirmative votes and thirty-seven negative, so it was returned to the Senate.

"On May 22 Mr. Lusby delivered to the House a petition from sundry inhabitants of Fredericktown, in Cecil County, praying relief in consequence of the destruction of their property by the enemy: which was read and referred to Messrs. Lusby, Dorsey, Bayley, Bowles and Belt.

"On May 25 Mr. John Forwood of Jacob, delivered a petition in behalf of the inhabitants of Havre de Grace, praying relief in consequence of the losses sustained by them by an incursion of the enemy; which was read and referred to the committee on the petition of sundry inhabitants of Fredericktown, in Cecil County, and the committee enlarged by the addition of Messrs. Forwood of Jacob, and Lewis Duvall.

"On the 26th, Mr. Lusby, from the committee, delivered the following report:

"'The committee to whom were referred the memorials of sundry inhabitants of Harford and Cecil Counties, praying for some immediate relief to their wants occasioned by the conflagrations recently perpetrated by the British at Havre de Grace and Fredericktown, beg leave to report, that they find the facts therein stated to be true. While your committee regret that the exhausted state of our revenue, and the pressing calls which are made for defence against the enemy, will not permit the State to indulge in that liberality which the character of the State for humanity and. munificence would require, they cannot but express their belief, that some legislative relief should be granted to the pressing and immediate distresses of the indigent; they therefore submit the following resolutions:

"'*Resolved,* That the Treasurer of the Western Shore pay to the order of Messrs. Samuel Hughes, Elijah Davis and Mark Pringle, or a majority of them, the sum of one thousand dollars, out of any unappropriated money in the treasury, to be by them distributed among the needy and indigent of those who suffered by the burning of Havre de Grace.

"'*Resolved,* That the Treasurer of the Western Shore pay the sum of seven hundred dollars to the order of Messrs. James Scanlan, Lambert Baird, Richard Davis, Peregrine Biddle, and John Mercer, or a majority of them, out of any unappropriated money in the treasury, to be by them distributed among the needy and indigent of those who suffered by the burning of Fredericktown, in Cecil County; which was read the first and second time by special order, and the question put, that the house concur in the said report and assent to the resolution therein contained.'"[3]

Messrs. Samuel Hughes and Mark Pringle had applied to the Mayor and City Council of Baltimore, on the 14th of May, in behalf of the sufferers at Havre de Grace. But, as the city had no charter privileges to enable it to render the aid required, the citizens of Baltimore, in their individual capacity, subscribed liberally and raised a large sum for the relief of the stricken town.

Admiral Warren, who had quitted the Chesapeake for Bermuda, returned to his command on the 1st of June, with a considerable naval reenforcement, having on board a large number of land troops and marines under the command of Sir Sidney Beckwith, consisting of a detachment of battalion-marines, 1800 strong, 300 of the 102d regiment, 250 of the Independent Foreigners or Canadian Chasseurs, and 300 of the Royal Marine Artillery, a total of 2650 men. By the capture of bay craft the British were supplied with numerous tenders well adapted to the navigation of our inland waters. With these and their barges, they made repeated expeditions and kept the country in a constant state of alarm.

During the spring and summer of 1813, the marauding expeditions of the enemy made frequent inroads among the farmers of St. Mary's County in the vicinity of Point Lookout. In July

---

[3] House Journal, May session, 1813, p. 14.

they made an attempt to land in Mattoax Creek, but were driven off with severe loss by Captain Hungerford's company of light infantry. The enemy afterwards took possession of Blackistone's and St. George's Islands, and soon afterwards landed a force of about two thousand men two and a half miles from Point Lookout. Here they organized small parties, which committed all kinds of depredations along the shores of the Potomac and Patuxent rivers, capturing and burning a great number of small vessels, together with houses and other valuable property. "They plundered anything and everything, robbing even the women and children of their clothes, and destroying such articles as it did not suit them to carry away.⁴

In consequence of these depredations, the inhabitants of the eastern half of St. Mary's County were compelled to perform military duty with very little intermission from early in April. Their plantations, therefore, were neglected and pillaged, their slaves ran off to the enemy, and sickness prevailed to a great extent among these poverty stricken people. A large number of the inhabitants, unable to bear the burdens of war, abandoned their homes to the pillagers and moved to the new settlements then opening in the far west.

The enemy evacuated Point Lookout on the 27th of July, and on the 30th the whole fleet stood up the bay. After threatening Baltimore and Annapolis, they took possession of Kent Island which had been almost abandoned by its inhabitants. Here, as there was much sickness in the fleet (seventy-four dead having been left on the banks of the Potomac), they landed about three thousand men, and from the ships which lay at anchor, expeditions of the usual sort were sent out.

On the 8th of August a squadron of about fifteen vessels moved in sight of Baltimore as if designing an attack. The forts were promptly manned and seven hundred men of Colonel Jamison's regiment of the Baltimore County Brigade, were ordered to defend a narrow pass of high land seven or eight miles from the city, toward North Point. On the high grounds east of the city (now Patterson Park), forty pieces of artillery mounted upon carriages were collected; and the Marine Artillery Company, Captain

⁴ *Niles' Register,* 4: 356-375.

George Stiles, manned their marine battery of 42-pounders on the water-front of Fort McHenry. In a few days the enemy moved off and threatened Annapolis, where Captain Morris and his crew of two hundred and twenty seamen and one hundred marines, together with a large body of militia, were prepared to give him a warm reception.

Admiral Cockburn, in conversation with a Maryland gentleman, stated that no vessel would be permitted to leave the bay with a cargo under any circumstances whatsoever. He congratulated the inhabitants of Annapolis upon the prudence which they displayed in not having made an attack on a British brig which grounded near the city. Their forbearance alone, he said, saved the city from destruction, as he had pledged his superior officer, Admiral Warren, that should a gun be fired, he would sack the town in half an hour. The brig to which Cockburn referred was one sent in pursuit of the schooner *Active* from Laguira and the *Patapsco* from Rochelle, bound up the bay for Baltimore. The brig chased them into the Severn River, and while in pursuit, grounded on the " Spit." She was afterwards gotten off by the aid of one of the enemy's frigates. In the conversation at that time Cockburn gave as his reason for destroying Havre de Grace, the killing of four of his men in one of the barges, and the wounding of Lieutenant Westphal of the *Marlborough,* after he had landed with a flag of truce. He said his original intention was simply to destroy the iron works.

While on Kent Island the British officers were actively engaged in electioneering for " England and her friends in Congress and the House of Delegates." They represented to those of our citizens with whom they conversed that the British Government was desirous of peace with America, and to this end they hoped that the American administration would be changed by the election of Federalists to office. Should this not be accomplished by the following spring, it was the intention of the Admiral to destroy Baltimore, and to desolate both shores of the bay.

From Kent Island operations on the Eastern Shore were renewed. On August 7 a large force was embarked in forty-five barges, and fifteen hundred men were marched to attack Queenstown on the Chester River. It was the intention of the enemy to cut off a body of about three hundred militia under the command of Major Nicholson, by marching up a considerable force in front of the town, while another body of men was sent around in the barges to land in the rear. A detachment of eighteen men under Captain Massey was out scouting about two miles from the town in the direction of Kent Island, when they discovered the British advancing. Captain Massey ordered his men to take shelter behind a fence and lie quiet until the enemy came within thirty yards. When within pistol shot, the militia opened fire upon the advancing column and retreated in good order through a corn field. By taking a circuitous route and marching rapidly, they again took position in front of the enemy and having a second time fired into the advancing column, fell back to the town where the main body of the militia was stationed. Upon learning the size of the enemy's force, Major Nicholson immediately ordered a retreat.

In the meantime the detachment in the barges landed by mistake on " Blakeford Shore," which left a creek between them and the town, and owing to this circumstance the militia escaped to Centreville without the loss of a man.

Three days later, on the 10th of August, the town of St. Michaels was assailed and gallantly defended by the militia under Brigadier-General Benson. Being apprehensive that an attack would be made on the town. a force of about five hundred volunteers had assembled from Easton and other sections of the county, including the companies of Captain Henrix, Captain Kerr and Lieutenant Vickers' Eastern Point Artillery. A boom was thrown across the entrance to the harbor, from Parrott's Point to Three Cedar Point and small batteries were erected on each point, as well as one in front of Fairview. The attack was made in the night, and being unable to force the boom, the British effected a landing about a hundred yards above the battery on Parrotts' Point. Here Lieutenant Dodson with two nine-pound guns and fifteen men awaited the coming of the enemy. As it was very dark, and raining, the enemy was not discovered until they leaped from the barges. Hastily forming, they charged upon the battery, and when they were within thirty yards, Lieutenant Dodson, having added a charge of grape to the caliber shot, discharged both guns into the advancing columns with considerable effect. For a moment the enemy was checked, but finding that they were gathering around him in overwhelming numbers, Lieutenant Dodson spiked his guns and ordered a retreat. The enemy took possession of the battery, supposing that St. Michaels was already in their grasp; but immediately afterwards Captain Vickers, with the Easton Artillery opened on them an active and well-directed fire, which was returned from the battery and barges until daylight. The British finding the battery untenable, abandoned it soon after sunrise and made off. It is said that in this engagement the enemy lost two officers and twenty-seven men in killed and wounded, while several of the barges were destroyed. Although grape shot flew like hail in the town and many houses were riddled, not a man was hurt among the defenders. Tradition says that among the British dead was Cockburn's favorite nephew, over whose body he exclaimed: " His life was worth the whole d——d town."

General Benson's report of the affair was as follows: " The enemy with eleven barges made an attack on the little fort at the mouth of the harbor of St. Michaels on Tuesday morning, the 10th instant, and under a dark cloud, and were not seen until they were landing. They were fired on by two guns and the men from the fort retreated, with the loss of three muskets. The guns were spiked and the enemy embarked and commenced a cannonade upon the town. There were fifteen well directed shots from our guns which made the enemy retreat. Ten of the shots were fired by Lieutenant Graham from his battery and five from Lieutenant Vicker's. There was much blood on the grass at the water. One pair of boarding pistols, two boarding cutlasses, two cartridge boxes and a pair of pumps [were] left. The barges fell down to the brig, three or four miles, and remained until nine or ten o'clock. Nine of them went to Kent Island in slow order; two went down to the Admiral's ship. The militia generally behaved well, and I have no doubt the same body would renew the conflict with redoubled ardor. Some of the houses were perforated, but no injury to any human being. This showeth the hand of a protecting Providence." [*]

---

[*] From the papers of Dr. Samuel A. Harrison.

Aside from some trifling marauding expeditions, the attack on St. Michaels closed the active operations in the Chesapeake for the year 1813. The principal objects of Admiral Cockburn seem to have been to gratify his men with plunder, and to so harass the inhabitants of Maryland as to drive them into a union with the eastern states to compel the government to make peace on any terms. In this latter, however, he failed of his purpose, for every act of barbarity caused the war to become more popular, and induced the people to make greater sacrifices for its support.

From the 1st to the 7th of November, 1813, the enemy's vessels in the Potomac captured a number of schooners and sloops laden with flour and other merchandise. On the 2d they landed on St. George's Island and burned the buildings, consisting of four houses and a barn, and on the 7th destroyed two captured vessels. A hundred and seventy negroes were embarked on several of the captured schooners, and in company with a large part of the blockading squadron, sent to Bermuda for the winter; Captain Robert Barrie of the 74-gun ship *Dragon* being left in command of the remainder of the fleet.

CHAPTER V

BARNEY'S FLOTILLA

"After fifteen or sixteen precious months had been wasted in the experiment, the British government discovered that Admiral Sir John Warren was too old and infirm to carry on the war as it ought to be carried on against the Americans. Sir John was therefore recalled, and in the summer of 1814, Vice-Admiral Sir Alexander Cochrane arrived at Bermuda to take command on the coast of North America. During the preceding winter the command of the British forces in the Chesapeake had been intrusted to Captain Robert Barrie, of the 74-gun ship *Dragon*. In the latter end of May, Rear-Admiral Cockburn, in the 74-gun ship *Albion* (into which he had shifted his flag from the *Sceptre*), Captain Charles Bayne Hodgson Ross arrived in the bay and relieved Captain Barrie. The first operation of any importance in the bay of the Chesapeake, after Rear-Admiral Cockburn's arrival, was an attack upon a strong American flotilla fitted out at Baltimore, and intrusted to the command of a brave officer of the revolutionary war, Commodore Joshua Barney.[1]

In the summer of 1813, Commodore Joshua Barney received an offer from the Secretary of the Navy to command a flotilla of gunboats, then fitting out in Baltimore for the defence of the Chesapeake and its tributaries. It was a command without connection with the navy and independent of it, though orders were issued by the National Government. Having accepted the offer, Commodore Barney was occupied throughout the year in fitting out his flotilla, and in April, 1814, was ready to commence active operations, having under his command twenty-six gun-boats and barges, and nine hundred men, officered by shipmasters and mates enrolled in the City of Baltimore. In the latter part of May he moved with sixteen of his vessels down the Chesapeake with the intention of attacking Tangier Island, of which the enemy had taken possession and upon which they had established a negro encampment.

[1] James, 6: 168.

On the first of June, Commodore Barney, with thirteen barges and five hundred men, sailed out of the Patuxent, but falling in with several vessels of the enemy, was compelled to retreat. He was closely pursued by their whole force, and after the exchange of a few solid shot, proceeded three or four miles up the river. Having perceived the arrival of re-enforcements to the blockading squadron, he deemed it prudent to retire, and instead of running up the Patuxent River, took refuge in St. Leonard's Creek. Here the flotilla was attacked by the boats of the enemy's squadron on the 8th, 9th, and 10th of June.

Captain Barrie had under his command the 74s *Albion* and *Dragon,* the schooner *St. Lawrence,* of 13 guns and 55 men, the 38-gun frigate *Loire,* Captain Thomas Brown, and the 18-gun brig-sloop *Jasseur,* Captain George Edward Watts.

The English and American accounts of the action or actions, differ materially. James says: (6:169) " The flotilla retreated about two miles up St. Leonard's creek, where it could be reached by boats only; but the force of the latter was not equal to the attack. Captain Barrie endeavored, however, by a discharge of rockets and carronades from boats, to provoke the American vessels, which were moored in a close line abreast across the channel, to come down within reach of the guns of the ship, brig and schooner, at anchor near the mouth of the creek. At one time the American flotilla got under way, and chased the boats to a short distance and then returned to their moorings. With a view to force the flotilla to quit its station, detachments of seamen and marines were landed on both sides of the river, and the American militia, estimated at 300 or 400, retreated before them to the woods. The marines destroyed two tobacco stores, and several houses converted into military posts; but still the flotilla remained at its moorings.

" On the 15th of June the 32-gun frigate Narcissus, Captain John Richard Lumley, joined the little squadron; and Captain Barrie, taking with him twelve boats, containing 180 marines, and thirty of the black colonial corps, proceeded up the river to Benedict. Here the men disembarked, and drove into the woods, without a struggle, a number of militia, who left behind a part of their muskets and camp equipage, as well as a 6-pounder field-piece. After spiking the latter, and destroying a store containing tobacco, the British again took to their boats, except five or six men, who had probably strayed too far into the woods.

"After quitting Benedict, Captain Barrie ascended the river to Lower Marlborough, a town about 28 miles from the capital of the United States. The party landed and took possession of the place; the militia, as well as the inhabitants, flying into the woods. A schooner, belonging to a Captain David, was captured and loaded with tobacco. After this, having burnt at Lower Marlborough and at Magruders, on the opposite side of the river, tobacco-stores containing 2800 hogsheads, and loaded the boats with stock, the detachment re-embarked. The Americans collected a force, estimated at about 350 regulars, besides militia, on Holland's cliffs; but some marines, being landed, traversed the skirts of the heights, and re-embarked without molestation, the American troops not again showing themselves till the boats were out of gun-shot.

"The blockade of Commodore Barney's flotilla, and the depredations on the coasts of the Patuxent, by Captain Barrie's squadron, caused great inquietude at Washington. At length an order reached the American commodore, directing him to destroy the flotilla, in the hope that the British, having no longer such a temptation in their way, would retire from a position so near to the capital. The order was suspended, owing to a proposal of Colonel Wadsworth, of the engineers; who, with two 18-pounders upon travelling carriages, protected by a detachment of marines and regular troops, engaged to drive away the two British frigates from the mouth of the creek. The colonel established his battery behind an elevated ridge, which sheltered him and his men; and on the morning of the 26th of June a simultaneous attack by the gun-boats and battery was made upon the *Loire* and *Narcissus*. Owing to the effect of the colonel's hot shot, the impracticability of bringing a gun to bear upon his position from either frigate, and the want of a sufficient force to storm and carry the battery, Captain Brown retreated with the *Loire* and *Narcissus* to a station near Point Patience; and, with the exception of two barges, which put back disabled apparently by the shot from the frigates, the American flotilla moved out of the creek and ascended the Patuxent. The frigates sustained no loss on this occasion; but Commodore Barney admits a loss of one midshipman and three men killed and seven men wounded. On the 4th of July the 40-gun frigate *Severn,* Captain Joseph Nourse, joined the *Loire* and *Narcissus;* and Captain Nourse immediately despatched Captain Brown, with the marines of the three ships, 150 in number, up St. Leonard's Creek. Here two of Commodore Barney's barges were found scuttled, owing to the damage they had received in the action with the frigates. The barges and several other vessels were burnt, and a large tobacco-store destroyed. Soon after this, the British quitted the Patuxent.

"On the 19th of July, Rear-Admiral Cockburn, having been joined by a battalion of marines, and a detachment of marine artillery, proceeded up the river Potomac, for the purpose of attacking Leonard's town, the capital of St. Mary's County, where the 36th United States regiment was stationed. The marines of the squadron under Major George Lewis were landed, whilst the boats pulled up in front of the town; but on discovering the marines, the enemy's armed force quitted the place, and suffered the British to take quiet possession. A quantity of stores belonging to the 36th regiment, and a number of arms of different descriptions, were found there and destroyed; and a quantity of tobacco, flour, provisions, and other articles, were brought away in the boats, and in a schooner which was lying off the town. Not a musket being fired, nor an armed enemy seen, the town was spared."

Commodore Barney's version, somewhat condensed, from his memoirs and his official dispatches to the Secretary of War is as follows:

"On the first of June, a little below the mouth of Patuxent, Commodore Barney discovered two of the enemy's schooners and several barges, to which he gave chase; but at the moment when he flattered himself they were within his grasp, the *Dragon,* seventy-four gun ship, came up to their rescue, and he was compelled in his turn to retreat. He was closely pursued by the whole force of the enemy, and before he reached the Patuxent, one of the schooners, mounting eighteen guns, and several of the barges, had approached within gunshot of his flotilla—the *Dragon* being still at a distance, he made the signal for action, and a fire was opened from all the flotilla, which in a few minutes compelled the enemy to seek protection under the battery of the seventy-four; having thus driven them from his heels, he entered the river in safety, and the *Dragon* and her attendants took post at its mouth. On the seventh the blockading squadron was re-inforced by the arrival of a frigate and sloop of war, and he deemed it prudent to move the flotilla up the river as far as St. Leonard's Creek. The wisdom of this measure was very soon apparent, for on the following day, the 8th, the enemy's frigate, brig, and schooners entered the river, and advanced to the mouth of the creek, but being unable to proceed further, they manned a number of barges and sent them to the attack of the flotilla. The barges, however, being armed with rockets, which they were able to throw to a much greater distance than the shot of the flotilla would reach, showed no disposition to come to closer quarters, and the commodore put his force in motion that he might approach the enemy within the power of his guns: but they retired as he advanced, until they gained the cover of their ships. A second attempt with a still larger force, was made in the afternoon of the same day, and with a like result—the enemy's barges were again driven to the protection of their ships. On the 9th they renewed the attack, and were a third time driven to seek refuge under their larger batteries; but all these various demonstrations were but experiments of the enemy, to exercise their men, and prepare them for the " grand attack," which was made on the 10th with a force sufficient, as they no doubt believed, to ensure them an easy victory. Twenty-one barges, one rocket boat, and two schooners, each mounting two thirty-two pounders, with eight hundred men, entered the creek with colors flying, and music sounding its animating strains, and moved on with a proud confidence of superiority. Barney's force consisted of thirteen barges, and five hundred men—his sloop and two gun vessels being left at anchor above him, as unmanageable in the shoal water—but he did not hesitate a moment to accept the challenge offered, and gave the signal to meet the enemy, as soon as they had entered the creek. They commenced the attack with their schooners and rockets, and in a few minutes every boat was engaged; the Commodore in his barge with twenty men, and his son, Major William B. Barney—who, in a small boat, acted as his aide on the occasion—were seen rowing about everywhere in the most exposed situations, giving the necessary orders to the flotilla; the action was kept up for some time with equal vigor and gallantry, but at length the enemy, struck with sudden confusion, began to give way, and turning their prows, exerted all their force to regain the covering ships. They were pursued to the mouth of the creek by the flotilla with all the eagerness of assured victory; but here lay the schooner of eighteen guns beyond which it was impossible to pass without first silencing her battery, and for this purpose the whole fire of the flotilla was directed at her—she made an attempt to get out of the creek, and succeeded so far as to gain the protection of the frigate and sloop of war, but so cut to pieces, that, to prevent her sinking, she was run aground and abandoned. The two larger vessels now opened a tremendous fire upon our gallant little flotilla, during which they threw not less than seven hundred shot, but without doing much injury: the flying barges of the enemy having thus succeeded in recovering their safe position under the heavy batteries of the ships, the flotilla was drawn off, and returned to its former station up the creek.

" That the enemy suffered severely in this engagement, was too manifest to be denied, even if their own subsequent conduct had not clearly proved the fact. Several of their boats were entirely cut to pieces, and both schooners were so damaged as to render them unserviceable during the remainder of the blockade—they had a number of men killed, and we have learned from an eye witness of the fact that the hospital rooms of the flag-ship were long afterwards crowded with the wounded in this engagement. On the part of the flotilla, not a man was lost—one of the barges was sunk by a shot from the enemy, but she was taken up again on the very day of the action, and two days afterwards was as ready as ever for service.

" On the first day of these repeated attacks, an incident occurred which is well worthy of being recorded. One of the enemy's rockets fell on board one of our barges, and, after passing through one of the men, set the barge on fire—a barrel of powder and another of musket cartridges, caught fire and exploded, by which several of the men were blown into the water, and one man very severely burned—his face, hands, and every uncovered part of his body, being perfectly crisped. The magazines were both on fire, and the commander of the boat, with his officers and crew, believing that she must inevitably blow up, abandoned her, and sought safety among the other barges. At this moment Major Barney, who commanded the cutter *Scorpion,* hailed his father and asked permission to take charge of the burning boat. Major Barney immediately put himself on board, and by dint of active labor of bailing water into the boat and rocking her constantly from side to side, he very soon succeeded in putting out the fire and saving the boat, to the very great delight as well as astonishment of the commodore, who acknowledged afterwards that he considered the duty as a forlorn hope.

" After the severe chastisement inflicted upon them for their last attempt, the enemy made no further efforts to disturb the tranquility of the flotilla, but contented themselves with converting the seige into a blockade, by mooring in the mouth of the creek, where they were soon reinforced by another frigate. Having come to this resolution, they turned their attention to the plunder of the surrounding country, in which frequent experience had given them an unenviable expertness. Tobacco, slaves, farm stock of all kinds, and household furniture, became the objects of their daily enterprises, and possession of them in large quantities was the reward of their honorable achievement. What they could not conveniently carry away, they destroyed by burning. Unarmed, unoffending citizens were taken from their very beds—sometimes with beds and all—and carried on board their ships, from which many of them were not released until the close of the war.

" In this state of things, the Secretary of the Navy despatched a hundred marines, under the command of Captain Samuel Miller, with three pieces of cannon, to the assistance of Commodore Barney. The Secretary of War also sent Colonel Wadsworth, with two pieces of heavy artillery, and ordered about six hundred of the regular troops to be marched to St. Leonard's Creek for the same purpose. The militia of Calvert County had been already called out, but like most other troops of that class, they were to be seen everywhere but just where they were wanted—whenever the enemy appeared, *they* disappeared; and their commander was never able to bring them into action. There was one officer among them, Major Johns, who deserved to be better supported—he appeared to be active and gallant, and labored hard to inspirit his men, but without success: they rendered no assistance whatever to the flotilla, nor did they even attempt to defend their own houses and plantations from pillage and conflagration. The conduct of the 36th regiment, under Colonel Carberry,[2] was unfortunately but little more worthy of praise than that of the militia, though several of its officers were well disposed to meet the enemy upon any terms, the men had neither discipline nor subordination, and receiving no check from their commanding officer in their irregularities, gave themselves up to disgraceful inaction, so that the presence of this regiment added nothing to the effective force of the commodore.

" Upon the arrival of Colonel Wadsworth, on the twenty-fourth of June, a consultation was held between him and the commodore to which Captain Miller, of the Marines, was invited; it was decided by these officers, that a battery and furnace should be erected on the commanding height near the mouth of the creek, upon which the colonel's two 18-pounders should be placed, and that, on the 26th before daylight, a simultaneous attack should be made by the flotilla and battery upon the blockading ships. The commodore placed one of his best officers, Mr. Groghegan (a sailing master) and twenty picked men, under the command of Colonel Wadsworth, for the purpose of working his two guns. Everything was now bustle and active preparation in the flotilla; the men were in high spirits, all looking impatiently to the 26th as a day of victory and triumph. On the evening of the 25th after dark, the commodore moved with his flotilla down the creek, that he might be near the enemy at the appointed hour next morning. He divided his boats into three divisions, each under its separate chief, and a distinctive broad flag—his own was the red, that of his first officer, Mr. Rutter, the white—the third, blue, under his second officer, Mr. Frazier: both these officers were old and experienced shipmasters, as indeed were many others in the flotilla. In this order they moved to the scene of action, and at

[2] Col. Henry Carberry. See Appendix.

6

early dawn of the 26th they were gratified and cheered by the sound of the guns from the opening battery on the height—the barges now seemed to fly under the rapid strokes of the oar, and in a few minutes reached the mouth of the creek, where they assumed the line of battle, and opened their fire upon the moored ships. Their position was eminently critical and hazardous, but this in the view of the gallant souls on board only rendered it the more honorable. They were within four hundred yards of the enemy; and the mouth of the creek was so narrow as to admit no more than eight barges abreast, to use their guns—the men were wholly unprotected by any species of bulwarks, and the grape and canister shot of the enemy, which was poured upon them in ceaseless showers, kept the water around them in a continual foam. It was a scene to appall the inexperienced and the faint-hearted; but there were few of these among the daring spirits of the flotilla. In this situation, the firing was kept up on all sides for nearly an hour; the commodore was then surprised and mortified to observe that not a single shot from the battery fell with assisting effect, and that the whole fire of the enemy was directed against his boats: shortly afterwards the battery, from which so much had been expected, became silent altogether, and the barges were hauled off as a matter of consequent necessity, for it would have been an act of madness in such a force, unassisted, to contend against two frigates, a brig, two schooners, and a number of barges, in themselves equal to the force that could be brought into action from the flotilla. Three of our barges, under the respective commands of sailing masters Worthington, Kiddall and Sellars, suffered very much in the action, and ten of their men were killed and wounded. A few minutes after the flotilla had retired. it was perceived that the enemy's frigates were in motion, and in a little time the whole blockading squadron got under way and stood down the river. The way being thus unexpectedly opened to him, the commodore immediately left the creek and moved up the Patuxent River.

" On the night after the engagement the flotilla was anchored opposite the town of Benedict, on the Potomac. As they were moving up the river, Captain Miller, of the marines, went on board the commodore's boat, and gave him the first information he had received from the inefficient battery—except to some of his own men, the guns there had done no mischief, and there was evidently bad management somewhere; but he shortly afterwards had a full report from Mr. Groghegan, who commanded the guns—from this he ascertained to his own satisfaction, that the fault was not in *his* officer or men. It appears that Mr. Groghegan, on the evening of the 25th, waited upon Colonel Wadsworth to receive instructions as to the place where the two guns were to be stationed; the colonel replied to his inquiry in these words: 'As you are to command and fight them, place them where you please.' The officer immediately set to work with his men and began to construct his battery, exactly upon the spot where it unquestionably ought to have been, the summit of the hill which completely commanded the ship—he continued at work all night and had nearly finished his platform, when about one o'clock in the morning Colonel Wadsworth came upon the ground, and after examining the work declared that his guns should not be put there as they would be too much exposed to the enemy. Having given his reason, he ordered a platform to be made in the *rear* of the summit; and in consequence, the guns being placed on a declivity, must either be fired directly into the hill, or be elevated so high in the air as to preclude the possibility of all aim, they were rendered useless. At the very first fire, the guns recoiled half way down the hill and in this situation they continued to be fired in the air at random, until the colonel gave orders to have them spiked and abandoned! The guns were served with hot shot, and in loading one of them rather too carelessly, she was accidently discharged before the servers had got out of the way, and thus two of the men were severely wounded."

Colonel Wadsworth, in his official report to the Secretary of War, dated June 26, 1814, said (in part): "The ground I was obliged to occupy for a battery consisted of a high bluff point having the Patuxent on the right and St. Leonard's Creek on the left, with which the communication was over a flat piece of ground subject to be enfiladed from the Patuxent to the hill on which the guns were placed, and liable to a severe fire from the same quarter; therefore, in case of an attack, the enemy might have rendered our situation very uncomfortable by stationing a small vessel so as to command the low ground I speak of.

" We committed a great many blunders during the action, or our success would probably have been more complete. I forbear to enter into minute particulars lest I should cast an indiscreet censure on some of the officers, perhaps undeserved. But the fact is, the infantry and light artillery decided upon a retreat without my orders before they had lost a single man killed or wounded; and at the time, too, when the enemy was manœuvering to the rear of our position with their barges. The consequence of this movement was very disadvantageous; the men at the guns, perceiving the infantry retreating and the enemy getting into the rear, their numbers began sensibly to diminish, and I was pretty soon left with only men enough to work one gun, which I was necessitated to turn to the rear for the sake of keeping the barges in check. Finally the few men that remained were so exhausted with fatigue, we found it impracticable to fire any more and the limbers and horses, which had been ordered down the hill, having disappeared and gone, I knew not where, I found myself under the painful necessity of spiking the guns to prevent their being used by the enemy, should he get possession of them.

" I might, in justice to the infantry, acknowledge that they did not take to flight, but quitted the ground in perfect order; after a while I was able to halt them and bring them back. In the meantime the enemy were getting under way and retiring down the river—from the precipitancy of his retreat, I infer he must have suffered considerably. From some untoward circumstances I had it not in my power to observe the effect of each shot fired, otherwise I think its (sic) destruction would be complete.

" Commodore Barney furnished me with twenty excellent men from his flotilla to work the guns. By some mismanagement, loading with hot shot, one poor fellow had his arm blown off, which is the only material accident we sustained. One of the enemy's rockets passed through the ammunition box which had been injudiciously placed, and exploded it, which did some damage. The ammunition cart near it was covered with fire, but fortunately did not explode. Some other trivial accidents were sustained.

" We commenced in the height an epaulement to cover our guns; but the work progressed so slowly from the shortness of time, I did not think it best to occupy it. We stationed our guns so as to barely allow the muzzles to peep over the hill. This brought us on descending ground in a ploughed corn-field. The recoil of the guns downward every time they were fired gave us excessive labor to bring them to their positions. In every respect it answered admirably. The enemy found it impossible to hit us; every shot either fell short and struck the bank or flew clear over us. Towards the close of the firing, they adopted the method of using small charges of powder, which just threw the shot over the hill—probably firing from his carronades—but the effect was not more decisive.

"I should mention that the situation in which the infantry and light artillery were placed was a trying one for new raised troops. Most of the shot which missed the battery fell among them. I had anticipated that disadvantage, but it was unavoidable. It was indispensable to have some cover by some rising ground from the waters of the Patuxent, and the position chosen was considered the only one compatible with that view, and the design I had in posting them, to protect the rear of our battery.

"The battalion of the 38th regiment joined us last evening after a hard day's march, and were immediately marched to the ground. Some of their men were completely exhausted and the whole excessively fatigued and half famished.

"I hope on the whole, taking into consideration our not being fully prepared, the excessive fatigue of the men, and that we have attained the object in view, which was the release of Commodore Barney's flotilla, the affair will not reflect dishonor on our troops."

On the 1st of July Commodore Barney received orders requesting his presence in Washington. On his arrival there, the subjects of consultation on which his views were required were the situation of the flotilla, the probable intentions of the enemy, and the measures necessary to be taken by the government for the protection of Washington and Baltimore. The result of the deliberation was that he should keep his thirteen barges and the sloop *Scorpion,* with five hundred men, in the Patuxent, and that his first lieutenant, Mr. Rutter, should be despatched to Baltimore to take command of the fourteen barges and five hundred men remaining there; so that in the event of an attack on either city, they could march respectively to the assistance of each other. Barney returned to his command after two days absence, and immediately despatched Mr. Rutter to Baltimore. After this, to place himself more conveniently within reach of either city in the event of invasion, he moved his flotilla up to Nottingham, about forty miles from Washington. Here he found the inhabitants in a state of alarm, and everything in confusion—the militia, to use his own expressive terms "*were here and there, but never where the enemy was.*" [3]

General Winder, who commanded the army destined for the defence of the two important cities, came to Nottingham soon afterwards and held a short consultation with Commodore Barney upon some unimportant points, but disclosed nothing of his own plans or views. Thus things remained until the 16th of August, when two of the officers who had been stationed at the mouth of the river for the purpose of watching the movements of the enemy, arrived with information that a fleet had entered the Patuxent and was standing up the river. Barney dispatched an express to the Secretary of the Navy, and in return received orders to retire with his flotilla as high up the river as he could get, and, if the enemy landed, to set fire to the boats and join General Winder with his men.

On the 21st of August information reached Commodore Barney that the enemy had landed an army at Benedict, and were then in full march on the road to Washington. He immediately landed with four hundred of his men, leaving the flotilla under the command of his second lieutenant, Mr. Frazier, a little above Pig Point, with positive orders, should the enemy appear near him in force, to set fire to every boat, and after seeing them in full conflagration to join him with the rest of his men. Commodore

---

[3] Commodore Barney's opinion of the Maryland militia was not a high one. At a dinner in his honor, at Frankfort, Kentucky, he said: "I had the good fortune to be in seventeen battles during the revolution, in all of which the star-spangled banner triumphed over the bloody cross, and in the late war I had the honor of being engaged in nine battles with the same glorious result, except in the last, in which I was unfortunate, though not in fault. If there had been with me 2,000 *Kentuckians,* instead of 7,000 *Marylanders,* Washington City would not have been sacked, nor our country disgraced."

Barney marched to Upper Marlborough that evening; and on the following morning, having heard from General Winder that he was with his army at the Woodyard, continued his march to that place, where he was joined by Captain Miller, of the marines, with eighty men and five pieces of artillery, under orders from the Secretary of the Navy.

Having learned that the enemy had turned off to the right, on the road to Upper Marlborough General Winder put his forces on the march in order to keep a position between the British and the City of Washington. He continued to retreat before the enemy until he reached a place called the " Battalion Old Field," where, upon hearing that the British were at Upper Marlborough, he encamped for the night.'

' William Henry Winder was born in Somerset County, Maryland, February 18, 1775. After being graduated at the University of Pennsylvania, he studied law under Judge Gabriel Duval, and in 1789 settled in Baltimore. In March, 1812, he was appointed lieutenant-colonel of the 14th U. S. infantry; on July 6 was placed in command, and on November 28 led a successful expedition from Black Rock, near Buffalo, N. Y., to the Canadian shore below Fort Erie. On March 12, 1813, Winder was promoted brigadier-general. At the battle of Stony Creek, June 1, 1813, he was taken prisoner and held as a hostage until some time in the year 1814. In May, 1814, he was appointed adjutant-general and placed in command of a newly created military district embracing Maryland and Virginia, the actual force consisting of 400 men only. General Winder was court-martialed for the defeat at Bladensburg, but the trial resulted in a report of "commendation" for having heroically done his duty under circumstances beyond his control. The court found that Winder showed great zeal and energy, but in a misdirected manner; that the loss of the battle was not due to lack of energy on the part of the commanding officer, but to his lack of skill and ability to handle troops properly! He was again sent to the Niagara frontier, and at the close of the war returned to Baltimore, broken in health and fortune. On the reduction of the army in June, 1815, he was retired and resumed the practice of law in Baltimore, where he died May 24, 1824.

A recent writer says of him: " The officer in command, General W. H. Winder, appointed for political rather than military reasons, was worse than useless, the very incarnation of incompetency, a fussy, nerveless man, who owed his appointment as brigadier-general in command of the military district to his kinship with the Federalist governor of Maryland."

CHAPTER VI

BLADENSBURG AND WASHINGTON

"On the second of June the British 74-gun ship *Royal Oak*, Rear-Admiral Pulteney Malcolm, Captain Edward Dix, accompanied by three frigates, three sloops, two bomb-vessels, five ships armed *en flûte*, and three transports having on board a body of troops under Major-General Ross, sailed from Verdon road at the mouth of the Gironde. On the twenty-fourth of July the squadron arrived at Bermuda, and there joined Vice-Admiral Cochrane, in the 80-gun ship *Tonnant*. On the second of August, having received on board the *Tonnant* Major-General Ross and his staff, Sir Alexander sailed, in company with the 36-gun frigate *Euryalus*, Captain Charles Napier, for Chesapeake Bay; and on the fourteenth of August arrived, and joined the *Albion*, Rear-Admiral Cockburn, off the mouth of the Potomac. On the next day Major-General Ross, accompanied by Rear-Admiral Cockburn, went on shore to reconnoitre.

"Cockburn's knowledge of the country, as well as the plan adopted to prevent surprise, enabled the two officers to penetrate further than would otherwise have been prudent. In his frequent walks through the country he invariably moved forward between two parties of marines, occupying in open order the woods by the roadside. Each marine carried a bugle, to be used as a signal, in case of casual separation, or the appearance of an enemy. It was during the excursion with General Ross, that Admiral Cockburn suggested the facility of an attack upon the City of Washington;[1] and General Ross determined, as soon as the troops should arrive from Bermuda, to make the attempt.

"On the seventeenth of August, Rear-Admiral Malcolm arrived with the troops, and joined Vice-Admiral Cochrane off the mouth of the Potomac; and the whole proceeded to the Patuxent, situated about twenty miles further up the bay. In the meantime Captain James Alexander Gordon, of the 38-gun frigate *Seahorse*, with some vessels of the squadron, had been detached up the

[1] See "Admiral Cockburn's Plan," *Md. Hist. Mag.*, vol. VI, p. 16.

Potomac, to bombard Fort Washington, situated on the left bank of that river, about fourteen miles below the federal city; and Captain Sir Peter Parker, with the 38-gun frigate *Menelaus,* had been sent up the Chesapeake, above Baltimore, to create a diversion in that quarter. The direct route to Washington, from the mouth of the Potomac, was up that river, about fifty miles to Port Tobacco; thence, overland by the village of Piscataway, thirty-two miles, to the lower bridge across the eastern branch of the Potomac; but, as no doubt could be entertained that this bridge, which was half a mile long, and had a draw at the west end, would be defended as well by a body of troops, as by a heavy sloop-of-war and an armed schooner, known to be in the river, a preference was given to the route up the Patuxent, and by Bladensburg; where the eastern branch, in case of the bridge at that spot being destroyed, could be easily forded.

" Commodore Barney's gun-boats were still lying in the Patuxent. An immediate attempt against this flotilla offered two advantages; one, in its capture or destruction; the other, as a pretext for ascending the Patuxent, with the troops destined for the attack of the federal city. Part of the ships, having advanced as high up the river as the depth of the water would allow, disembarked the troops, about four thousand in number, on the 19th and 20th of August, at Benedict, a small town about fifty miles southeast of Washington. On the 20th, in the evening, Admiral Cockburn, taking with him the armed boats and tenders of the fleet, having on board the marines under Major Robyns, and the marine-artillery under Captain James H. Harrison, proceeded up the river, to attack Commodore Barney's flotilla; and to supply with provisions, and, if necessary, afford protection to the army as it ascended the right bank. The boats and tenders were separated into three divisions. The first division was commanded by Captains Thomas Ball Sullivan and William Stanhope Badcock, the second, by Captains Rowland Money and James Somervell, and the third, by Captain Robert Ramsay; and the whole was under the superintendence and immediate management of Captain John Wainwright, of the *Tonnant.* The frigates *Severn* and *Hebrus,* Captains Joseph Nourse and Edmund Palmer, accompanied by the brig-sloop *Manly,* Captain Vincent Newton, had been also directed to follow the boats up the river as far as might be practicable.

"On opening the reach above Pig Point, Admiral Cockburn, who had just before been joined by Captains Nourse and Palmer with the boats of their two frigates, which they could get no higher than Benedict, discovered Commodore Barney's broad pennant in the headmost vessel, a large sloop, and the remainder of the flotilla extending in a long line astern of her. The British boats now advanced as rapidly as possible, but on nearing the flotilla, the sloop bearing the broad pennant was observed to be on fire, and soon afterwards blew up; as did fifteen out of the sixteen remaining gun-boats.[2]

"The destruction of the flotilla secured the right flank of the army under Major-General Ross; who on the afternoon of the 22d, with the troops, arrived and encamped at the town of Upper Marlborough, situated about four miles up the western branch of the Patuxent. The men, therefore, after having been nearly three months on board ship, had, in less than three days, marched forty miles; and that in the month of August, when the sultriness of the climate could scarcely be tolerated. While General Ross and his men were resting themselves at Upper Marlborough, General Winder and his army, now joined by Commodore Barney and the men of his flotilla, were lying at their encampment at the Long Old Fields, only eight miles distant. On the next morning the American troops were reviewed by President Madison. Soon after the review, a detachment from the American army advanced along the road to Upper Marlborough and after exchanging a few shots with the British skirmishers, fell back to the main body.

"On the 23rd, in the morning, Admiral Cockburn having left at Pig Point, directly opposite to the western branch, the marines of the ships under Captain Robyns, and two divisions of the boats, crossed over with the third division to Mount Calvert, and proceeded by land to the British encampment at Upper Marlborough. The little opposition experienced by the army in its march from

[2] Barney's flotilla blown up in the Patuxent, consisted only of one cutter, one gun-boat and thirteen barges. Barney's memoir, p. 315.

Benedict, and the success that had attended the expedition against Commodore Barney's flotilla, determined General Ross to make an immediate attempt upon the city of Washington, distant from Upper Marlborough not more than sixteen miles. At the desire of Ross, the marine and naval forces at Pig Point were moved over to Mount Calvert; and the marines, marine-artillery, and a proportion of the seamen under Captains Palmer and Money joined the army at Upper Marlborough.

As if by concert, the American army retired from the Long Old Fields about the same time that the British army advanced from Upper Marlborough, and the patrols of the latter actually occupied before midnight the ground which the former had abandoned. The American army did not stop until it reached Washington, where it encamped for the night near the navy yard. On the same evening upwards of two thousand troops arrived at Bladensburg from Baltimore. On the 24th, at daylight, General Ross put his troops in motion for Bladensburgh, twelve miles from his camp, and having halted by the way, arrived at about eleven-thirty a. m. at the heights facing the village."[3]

The British troops which took part in the Battle of Bladensburg, according to Gleig, consisted of three brigades. "The first, or light brigade, consisted of the 85th, the light infantry companies of the 4th, 21st, and 44th regiments, with the party of disciplined negroes, and a company of marines, amounting in all to about eleven hundred men; to the command of which Colonel Thornton, of the 85th regiment, was appointed. The second brigade, composed of the 4th and 44th regiments, which mustered together fourteen hundred and sixty bayonets, was entrusted to the care of Colonel Brooke, of the 44th; and the third, made up of the 21st, and the battalion of marines, and equaling in number the second brigade, was commanded by Colonel Patterson of the 21st. The whole infantry may, therefore be estimated at four thousand and twenty men. Besides these, there were landed about a hundred artillery-men, and an equal number of drivers; but for want of horses to drag them, no more than one 6-pounder and two small 3-pounder guns were brought on shore. Ex-

---

[3] James. Naval History, 6: 174 *et seq.*

cept those belonging to the general and staff-officers, there was not a single horse in the whole army. To have taken on shore a large park of artillery would have been, under such circumstances, absolute folly; indeed, the pieces which were actually landed, proved in the end of very little service, and were drawn by seamen sent from the different ships for the purpose. The sailors thus employed, may be rated at a hundred, and those occupied in carrying stores, ammunition, and other necessaries, at a hundred more; and thus by adding these, together with fifty sappers and miners, to the above amount, the whole number of men landed at St. Benedicts may be computed at four thousand five hundred."

The American force hastily called together to meet the invaders, consisting of about seven thousand men, principally raw militia, poorly armed, undisciplined, and with no great confidence in their commanders, was made up as follows: A brigade under the command of General Walter Smith, of Georgetown, was composed of two regiments of Washington and Georgetown militia, commanded respectively by Major George Peter and Captain Benjamin Burch; and two companies of riflemen, armed with muskets, commanded by Captains Doughty and Stull; in all 1070 men. Another brigade of district militia, organized by General Robert Young, reported to General Winder on August 18, but having been employed to defend the approach to Fort Washington, were not engaged at Bladensburg. This was made up of volunteer companies from Alexandria and vicinity; a company of cavalry under Captain Thornton; and a company of light-artillery with two brass 6-pounders and one 4-pounder commanded by Captain Marsteller; in all about five hundred men.

On the 20th of August General Tobias Stansbury's brigade, composed of two regiments of militia, one of five hundred and fifty men under Lieutenant-Colonel Ragan, and another of eight hundred and three men under Lieutenant-Colonel Schutz, marched from Baltimore to join General Winder. On the evening of the 23rd, Lieutenant-Colonel Sterett's command consisting of the Fifth Baltimore regiment of volunteers, with the rifle battalion of Major William Pinkney and two companies of volunteer artillery under Captains Myers and Magruder, with six

6-pounders, in all about eight hundred men, reached Bladensburg and joined General Stansbury. On the morning of the 24th, seven hundred and fifty men, comprising a part of two regiments, under Colonel William D. Beall and Colonel Hood, arrived on the field; and two hundred and forty men under Colonel Kramer and two battalions, mustering one hundred and fifty men under Majors Waring and Magruder also came in.

Colonel George Minor commanded the Virginia militia, consisting of one regiment of about six hundred men and a cavalry company of about one hundred. The regular United States infantry, three hundred strong, together with a company of eighty men from the 12th regiment, was under the command of Colonel William Scott. Barney's flotilla-men, numbering about four hundred and fifty, and one hundred and fifty marines, with two 18-pounders, joined the army on the 22d. The Maryland cavalry, about three hundred men, were commanded by Lieutenant-Colonel Tilghman, Major Otho H. Williams and Major Charles Sterett. Captain J. C. Herbert commanded the "Bladensburg Troop of Horse." The U. S. cavalry, about one hundred and twenty-five strong, was commanded by Lieutenant-Colonel Laval.

In spite of the fact that the British fleet had been in full command of the Chesapeake for nearly a year and a half, no adequate preparations for defence were made by the federal government, and there was neither fortification of any strength nor army of size or efficiency for the protection of Washington. Late in June, 1814, information was received by the President, from Messrs. Gallatin and Bayard, that an expedition was being fitted out with reinforcements for the British invaders in America. A cabinet meeting was held on the 1st of July, at which it was determined to create a new military district to be known as the tenth, comprising that part of Virginia between the Rappahannock and the Potomac rivers, the District of Columbia and Maryland.

On the 4th of July a requisition for 93,500 men was made by the Secretary of War, to be organized and held in readiness. Under this order Maryland was required to furnish six regiments (six thousand men) to consist of six hundred artillery and four thousand four hundred infantry, which was to be organized and held in readiness for future service, within the state, until the tenth district should be actually invaded, or menaced with invasion, when, and not sooner, General Winder was authorized to call for a part or for the whole of the quota assigned to the State of Maryland.

General Armstrong, the Secretary of War, undertook to comply with the cabinet decision and issued orders to that effect. The result was humiliating, as of the quota of 5000 men from Pennsylvania, none were furnished, owing to a defect in the state militia law; Virginia furnished 2000 men, who were never mustered into service; and of Maryland's quota, only 2000 men, principally from Baltimore, appeared. When General Winder took command of his district, he found it without magazines of provisions or forage, without transport, tools or implements, without a commissariat or efficient quartermaster's department. Neither rifles nor flints were available to arm the prospective forces. Not a cannon was in position and within twelve miles of Washington there was not a fortification or breastwork. Early in July General Winder wrote to the Secretary of War explaining the situation, and stating that the total force at his command, including the men garrisoning the several forts, would not exceed one thousand; that, until the troops to be supplied under the requisition should reach him, the detachments of the 36th and 38th regiments, amounting to about seven hundred men, would be all he would have in the field. No answer was sent to this letter, nor was any attention given to the suggestions contained in it.

In spite of the lack of all the essentials necessary for a successful defence of his district, General Winder immediately proceeded to examine personally, into the condition and possibilities thereof. The numerous letters from Winder published in the first volume of "American State Papers, Military Affairs," show that he was diligent in business and judicious in selecting a spot as the center of operations. His itinerary during the months of July and August was as follows: On July 12th he was at Baltimore; on the 16th, at Marlborough; on the 17th, at Nottingham; on the 22nd, at Marlborough; on the 23d, at the Woodyard; on the 25th, at Fort Washington; on the 26th, at Port Tobacco; on the 27th, at Piscataway; on August 1st, at Washington; on the 4th, at Port Tobacco; on the 6th, at Washington and on the 8th, at Baltimore.

Bladensburg was appointed as the place of rendezvous, where arms and military stores were to be sent, and for strategic purposes no better place could have been selected.

Concerning the inglorious battle of Bladensburg, a wealth of literature is extant, for the most part explanatory or exculpatory; but the account universally conceded to be the fairest and least biased, is that of G. R. Gleig, an English subaltern officer. He says: "Having started on the 24th at an early hour, our march was for some time both cool and agreeable. The road—if road it could be called—wound for the first five miles through the heart of an immense forest, and being, in every sense of the word, a by-path, was completely overshadowed by projecting branches of trees, so closely interwoven, as to prevent a single sunbeam from making its way, even at noon, within the arch. We continued to move on, therefore, long after the sun had risen, without being sensible that there was not a cloud in the sky to screen us from his influence; whilst a heavy moisture continually emitted from the grass and weeds on both sides of us, produced a coolness, which, had it been less confined, would have proved extremely pleasant. So far, then, we proceeded without experiencing any other inconvenience than what was produced by the damp and fetid atmosphere which we breathed; but no sooner had we begun to emerge from the woods and to enter the open country, than an overpowering change was perceived. The sun, from which we had been hitherto defended, now beat upon us in full force; and the dust arising in thick masses from under our feet, without a breath of air to disperse it, flew directly into our faces, occasioning the greatest inconvenience both to the eyes and respiration. I have stated this at length, because I do not recollect a period of my military life during which I suffered more severely from heat and fatigue; and as a journey of a few miles, under such circumstances, tells more than one of thrice the distance in a cool day and along a firm wintry road, it is not surprising that before many hours had elapsed numbers of men began to fall behind from absolute inability to keep up.

" Yet, in spite of all this, there was that in to-day's march which rendered it infinitely more interesting than any we had performed since the landing. We had learnt, from various quarters, that the enemy was concentrating his forces for the purpose of hazarding a battle in defence of his capital. The truth of these rumors we had no cause to doubt, confirmed as they were by what we had our-selves witnessed only the evening before; indeed the aspect of various fields on each side of the high road (which we had now regained), where smoking ashes, bundles of straw, and remnants of broken victuals were scattered about, indicated that considerable bodies of troops had passed the night in this neighborhood. The appearance of the road itself, likewise, imprinted as it was with fresh marks of many feet and hoofs, proved that these troops could be no great way before us; whilst our very proximity to Washington, being now distant from it not more than ten or twelve miles, all tended to assure us that we should at least see an American army before dark. . . .

" We had now proceeded about nine miles, during the last four of which the sun's rays had beat continually upon us, and we had inhaled almost as great a quantity of dust as of air. Numbers of men had already fallen to the rear, and many more could with difficulty keep up; consequently, if we pushed on much farther without resting, the chances were that at least half of the army would be left behind. To prevent this from happening, and to give time for the stragglers to overtake the column, a halt was determined upon, and being led forward to a spot of ground well wooded, and watered by a stream which crossed the road, the troops were ordered to refresh themselves. Perhaps no halt ever arrived more seasonably than this, or bid fair to be productive of more beneficial effects; yet so oppressive was the heat, that we had not resumed our march above an hour, when the banks by the wayside were again covered with stragglers; some of the finest and stoutest men in the army being literally unable to go on.

" The hour of noon was approaching, when a heavy cloud of dust, apparently not more than two or three miles distant, attracted our attention. From whence it originated there was little difficulty in guessing, nor did many minutes expire before surmise was changed into certainty; for on turning a sudden angle in the road, and passing a small plantation, which obstructed the vision toward the left, the British and American armies became visible to one another. The position occupied by the latter was one of great strength and commanding attitude. They were drawn up in three lines upon the brow of a hill, having their front and left flanks covered by a branch of the Potomac, and their right resting upon a thick wood and a deep ravine. This river flowed between the heights occupied by the American forces and the little town of Bladensburg. Across it was thrown a narrow bridge, extending from the chief street in that town to the continuation of the road, which passed through the very center of their position; and its right bank (the bank above which they were drawn up) was covered with a narrow strip of willows and larch trees, whilst the left was altogether bare, low and exposed. Such was the general aspect of their position as at the first glance it presented itself; of which I must endeavor to give a more detailed account, that my description of the battle may be in some degree intelligible.

"I have said that the right bank of the Potomac was covered with a narrow strip of willow and larch trees. Here the Americans had stationed strong bodies of riflemen, who in skirmishing order, covered the whole front of their army. Behind this plantation, again, the fields were open and clear, intersected at certain distances by rows of high and strong palings. About the middle of the ascent, and in the rear of one of these rows, stood the first line, composed entirely of infantry; at a proper interval from this, and in a similar situation, stood the second line; while the third, or reserve, was posted within the skirts of a wood, which crowned the heights. The artillery, again, of which they had twenty pieces in the field, was thus arranged: On the high road and commanding the bridge, stood two heavy guns; and four more, two on each side of the road, swept partly in the same direction, and partly down the whole of the slope into the streets of Bladensburg. The rest were scattered, with no great judgment, along the second line of infantry, occupying different spaces between the right of one regiment and the left of another; whilst the cavalry showed itself in one mass, within a stubble field, near the extreme left of the position. Such was the nature of the ground which they occupied, and the formidable posture in which they waited our approach; amounting by their own account, to nine thousand men, a number exactly doubling that of the force which was to attack them.

7

"In the meantime, our column continued to advance in the same order which it had hitherto preserved. The road, having conducted us for about two miles in a direction parallel with the river, and of consequence with the enemy's line, suddenly turned, and led directly towards the town of Bladensburg. Being of course ignorant whether this town might not be filled with American troops, the main body paused here till the advanced guard should reconnoitre. The result proved that no opposition was intended in that quarter, and while the whole of the enemy's army had been withdrawn to the opposite side of the stream, whereupon the column was again put in motion, and in a short time arrived in the streets of Bladensburg, and within range of the American artillery. Immediately on our reaching this point, several of their guns opened upon us, and kept up a quick and well-directed cannonade, from which, as we were again commanded to halt, the men were directed to shelter themselves as much as possible behind the houses. The object of this halt, it was conjectured, was to give the General an opportunity of examining the American line, and of trying the depth of the river, because at present. there appeared to be but one practicable mode of attack, by crossing the bridge, and taking the enemy directly in front. To do so, however, exposed as the bridge was, must be attended with bloody consequences, nor could the delay of a few minutes produce any mischief which the discovery of a ford would not amply compensate.

"But in this conjecture we were altogether mistaken; for without allowing time to the column to close its ranks, or to be joined by such of the many stragglers as were now hurrying, as fast as weariness would permit, to regain their places, the order to halt was countermanded, and the word given to attack, and we immediately pushed on at a double quick time, towards the head of the bridge. While we were moving along the street, a continued fire was kept up, with some execution, from those guns which stood to the left of the road; but it was not till the bridge was covered with our people that the two-gun battery upon the road itself began to play. Then, indeed, it also opened, and with tremendous effect; for at the first discharge almost an entire company was swept down; but whether it was that the guns had been previously laid with measured exactness, or that the nerves of the gunners became afterwards unsteady, the succeeding discharges were much less fatal. The riflemen likewise began to gall us from the wooded bank with a running fire of musketry; and it was not without trampling upon many of their dead and dying comrades that the light brigade established itself on the opposite side of the stream.

"When once there, however, everything else appeared easy. Wheeling off to the right and left of the road, they dashed into the thicket, and quickly cleared it of the American skirmishers; who, falling back with precipitation upon the first line, threw it into disorder before it had fired a shot. The consequence was, that our troops had scarcely shown themselves when the whole of that line gave way and fled in the greatest confusion, leaving the two guns upon the road in possession of the victors.

"But here it must be confessed that the light brigade was guilty of imprudence. Instead of pausing till the rest of the army came up, the soldiers lightened themselves by throwing away their knapsacks and haversacks; and extending their ranks so as to show an equal front with the enemy, pushed on to the attack of the second line. The Americans, however, saw their weakness, and stood firm, and having the whole of their artillery, with the exception of the pieces captured on the road, and the greater part of their infantry in this line, they first checked the ardour of the assailants by a heavy fire, and then, in their turn, advanced to recover the ground which was lost. Against this charge the extended order of the British troops would not permit them to offer an effectual resistance, and they were accordingly borne back to the very thicket upon the river's brink; where they maintained themselves with determined obstinacy, repelling all attempts to drive them through it; and frequently following, to within a short distance of the cannon's mouth, such parts of the enemy's line as gave way.

"In this state the action continued till the second brigade had likewise crossed, and formed upon the right bank of the river; when the 44th regiment moving to the right, and driving in the skirmishers, debouched upon the left flank of the Americans and completely turned it. In that quarter, therefore, the battle was won; because the raw militia-men, who were stationed there as being the least assailable point, when once broken could not be rallied. But on their right the enemy still kept their ground with much resolution; nor was it until the arrival of the 4th regiment, and the advance of the British forces in firm array to the charge, that they began to waver. Then, indeed, seeing their left in full flight, and the 44th getting in their rear, they lost all order and dispersed, leaving clouds of riflemen to cover their retreat, and hastened to conceal themselves in the woods, where it would have been madness to follow them. The rout was general throughout the line. The reserve, which ought to have supported the main body, fled as soon as those in its front began to give way; and the cavalry, instead of charging the British troops now scattered in pursuit, turned their horses heads and galloped off, leaving them in undisputed possession of the field, and of ten out of the twenty pieces of artillery.

" This battle, by which the fate of the American capital was decided, began about one o'clock in the afternoon, and lasted till four. The loss on the part of the English was severe, since, out of two-thirds of the army, which were engaged, upwards of five hundred men were killed and wounded; and what rendered it doubly severe was, that among these were numbered several officers of rank and distinction. Colonel Thornton, who commanded the light brigade, Lieutenant-Colonel Wood, commanding the 85th regiment, and Major Brown, who led the advanced guard, were all severely wounded; and General Ross himself had a horse shot under him. On the side of the Americans the slaughter was not so great. Being in possession of a strong position they were of course less exposed in defending than the others in storming it; and had they conducted themselves with coolness and resolution, it is not conceivable how the battle could have been won. But the fact is, that, with the exception of a party of sailors from the gun-boats, under the command of Commodore Barney, no troops could behave worse than they did. The skirmishers were driven in as soon as attacked, the first line gave way without offering the slightest resistance, and the left of the main body was broken within half an hour after it was seriously engaged. Of the sailors, however, it would be injustice not to speak in the terms which their conduct merits. They were employed as gunners, and not only did they serve their guns with quickness and precision which astonished their assailants, but they stood till some of them were actually bayoneted with fuses in their hands; nor was it till their leader was wounded and taken, and they saw themselves deserted on all sides by the soldiers, that they quitted the field. With respect to the British army, again, no line of distinction can be drawn. All did their duty, and none more gallantly than the rest; and though the brunt of the affair fell upon the light brigade, this was owing chiefly to the circumstance of its being at the head of the column and perhaps also, in some degree, to its own rash impetuosity. The artillery, indeed, could do little, being unable to show itself in presence of a force so superior; but the 6-pounder was nevertheless brought into action, and a corps of rockets proved of striking utility.

"Our troops being worn down from fatigue, and of course as ignorant of the country as the Americans were the reverse, the pursuit could not be continued to any distance. Neither was it attended with much slaughter. Diving into the recesses of the forests, and covering themselves with riflemen, the enemy were quickly beyond our reach; and having no cavalry to scour even the high road, ten of the lightest of their guns were carried off in the flight. The defeat, however, was absolute, and the army which had been collected for the defence of Washington was scattered beyond the possibility of, at least, an immediate reunion; and as the distance from Bladensburg to that city does not exceed four miles, there appeared to be no further obstacle in the way to prevent its immediate capture."

General Winder's statement[*] gives a detailed account of his movements from the date of his appointment to the military district, until the day after the battle. The essential parts are as follows:

"I will state as nearly as possible the forces which were in the field under these various demands and requisitions, the time of

[*] American State Papers, Military Affairs, vol. 1; also in appendix to J. S. Williams' "History of the Invasion and Capture of Washington."

their assembling, their condition, and subsequent movements. The returns first made, when I came into command, gave me

Fort McHenry, under the command of Major Armistead, non-commissioned officers, musicians and privates for duty.............. 194
At Annapolis, in Forts Severn and Madison, under Lieutenant Fay... 39
At Fort Washington, under Lieutenant Edwards.................... 49
The detachments of the 36th and 38th and a small detachment of
artillery under Lieutenant-Colonel Scott...................... 330

                                                              ___
                                                              612

These corps received no addition, but were gradually diminishing by the ordinary causes which will always operate to this effect.

"The two thousand Maryland militia who were ordered to assemble at Baltimore had been drafted in pursuance of a requisition made by the Secretary of War on General Smith of the 20th of April, and as full time had been allowed to make the draft deliberately, they were, as far as practicable, ready to come without delay; notwithstanding, Brigadier-General Stansbury was unable to bring to Bladensburg more than one thousand four hundred, including officers, and arrived at Bladensburg on the evening of the 22nd of August.

"From General Stricker's brigade in the city of Baltimore, which had been called out *en masse,* I required a regiment of infantry, the battalion of riflemen, and two companies of artillery —not deeming it practicable to reconcile the people of Baltimore to march a greater number, and leave it without any force, and being strongly persuaded that the exigency would have drawn in time a greater force from the adjacent country. The detachment from Stricker's brigade, under Colonel Sterett, arrived at Bladensburg in the night of the 23rd of August, and the total amount was nine hundred and fifty-six.

"The detachment which had been stationed at Annapolis under Colonel Hood, arrived at Bladensburg about fifteen minutes before the enemy appeared and I suppose were from six to seven hundred strong.

"The brigade of General Smith, consisting of the militia of the District of Columbia on this side the Potomac, were called out on Thursday, the 18th of August, on Friday were assembled, and on Saturday the 20th, they crossed the Eastern Branch Bridge, and advanced about five miles toward the Wood Yard. They amounted, I suppose, to about twelve hundred.

"General Young's brigade, from Alexandria, between five and six hundred strong, crossed the Potomac Saturday or Sunday and took post near Piscataway.

"The call for three thousand militia, under the requisition of the 4th of July, had produced only two hundred and fifty men at the moment the enemy landed at Benedict. In addition to the causes hereinbefore mentioned, the inefficacy of this call is to be attributed to the incredulity of the people on the danger of invasion; the perplexed, broken and harassed state of the militia in St. Mary's, Calvert, Charles and Prince George's, and a part of Anne Arundel counties, which had rendered it impossible to make the draft in some of them, or to call them from the exposed situations where they had been on duty two months, under the local calls for Maryland.

"Several other small detachments of Maryland militia, either as volunteers, or under calls on the brigadiers, joined about the day before the action, whose numbers or commanding officers I did not know. They may have amounted to some four or five hundred.

"Lieutenant-Colonel Tilghman of the Maryland cavalry, under an order of the Governor of Maryland, with about eighty dragoons, arrived at Washington on the 16th of August.

"Lieutenant-Colonel Laval of the U. S. Light Dragoons, with a small squadron of about one hundred and twenty, who had been mounted at Carlisle the preceding Monday, arrived at Montgomery Court House on the evening of the 19th of August. He moved on the next morning and crossed the Eastern Branch.

"Captain Morgan, with a company of about eighty of the 12th U. S. Infantry, joined at the Long Old Fields on the evening of the 22d.

"Colonel Minor, from Virginia arrived at the city on the evening of the 23rd with about five hundred men, wholly unarmed, and without equipments. Under the direction of Colonel Carberry, who had been charged with the subject, they received arms, ammunition, etc. next morning, but not until after the action at Bladensburg.

" On Thursday evening Colonel Monroe proposed, if I would detach a troop of cavalry with him, to proceed in the most probable direction to find the enemy and reconnoitre him. Captain Thornton's troop from Alexandria was detailed on this service, and on Friday morning the colonel departed with them. At this time it was supposed the enemy intended coming up the bay, as one of his ships was already in view from Annapolis, and his boats were sounding South River. It was Colonel Monroe's intention to have proceeded direct to Annapolis; but before he had got without the city, he received intelligence that the enemy had proceeded up the Patuxent, and were debarking at Benedict. He therefore bent his course to that place.

" On Saturday, Lieutenant-Colonel Tilghman, with his squadron of dragoons, was despatched by way of the Wood Yard to fall down upon the enemy, to annoy, harass, and impede their march by every possible means, to remove or destroy forage and provisions from before the enemy, and gain intelligence. Captain Caldwell, with his troop of city cavalry, was despatched with the same views toward Benedict by Piscataway, it being wholly uncertain what route the enemy would take if it was his intention to come to Washington. . . . .

" My patrols and vedettes not having yet brought me any intelligence of a movement of the enemy, and being still doubtful whether he might not move upon Annapolis, Fort Warburton, or toward the bridge rather than Bladensburg, I held the position near the bridge as that which, under all circumstances, would enable me to act against the enemy in any alternative. I learned about this time, with considerable mortification, that General Stansbury, from misunderstanding or some other cause, instead of holding a position during the night in advance of Bladensburg, had taken one about a mile in its rear, and that his men, from a causeless alarm, had been under arms the greater part of the night, and moved once or twice, and that he was at that moment on his march into the city. I instantly sent him an order to resume his position at Bladensburg; to post himself to the best advantage; to make the utmost resistance, and to rely upon my supporting him if the enemy should move upon that road. I had, at a very early hour in the morning, detached Captain Graham with his troop of Virginia cavalry, to proceed by Bladensburg down upon the road toward the enemy, and insure, by that means, timely notice to General Stansbury and myself, should the enemy turn that way. With this addition to the cavalry already on those roads, it became impossible for the enemy to take any steps unobserved. Additional cavalry patrols and vedettes were also detached upon all the roads across the bridge, to insure the certainty of intelligence, let the enemy move as he might.

"Colonel Minor had also arrived in the city the evening before, with five or six hundred militia from Virginia, but they were without arms, accoutrements, or ammunition. I urged him to hasten his equipment, which I learned was delayed by some difficulty in finding Colonel Carberry, charged with that business; and he had not received his arms, etc., when, about ten o'clock, I received intelligence that the enemy had turned the head of his column toward Bladensburg. Commodore Barney had, upon my suggestion, posted his artillery to command the bridge early in the morning.

"As soon as I learned the enemy were moving toward Bladensburg, I ordered General Smith, with the whole of the troops, to move immediately to that point.

"The necessary detention arising from orders to issue, interrogations and applications to be answered from all points being past, I proceeded on to Bladensburg, leaving the President and some of the heads of departments at my quarters, where they had been for an hour or more.

"I arrived at the bridge at Bladensburg about twelve o'clock, where I found Lieutenant-Colonel Beall had at that moment passed with his command, having just arrived from Annapolis. I had passed the line of Stansbury's brigade, formed in the field upon the left of the road, at about a quarter of a mile in the rear of the bridge; and on the road, a short distance in the rear of Stansbury's line, I met several gentlemen, and among others, Mr. Francis Key, of Georgetown, who informed me that he had thought that the troops coming from the city could be most advantageously posted on the right and left of the road near that point. I left General Smith to make a disposition of these troops and proceeded to the bridge, where I found Lieutenant-Colonel

Beall, as before stated. I inquired whether he had any directions
as to his position; he replied that he had been shown a high hill
upon the right of the road, ranging with the proposed second
line. It being a commanding position, and necessary to be occupied by some corps, I directed him to proceed agreeably to the
instructions he had received. I then rode up to a battery which
had been thrown up to command the street which entered Bladensburg from the side of the enemy and the bridge, where I found
the Baltimore artillery posted, with the Baltimore riflemen to
support them. Upon inquiry, I learned that General Stansbury
was on a rising ground upon the left of his line. I rode immediately thither, and found him and Colonel Monroe together.
The latter gentleman informed me that he had been aiding General Stansbury to post his command, and wished me to proceed
to examine it with them, to see how far I approved of it. The
column of the enemy at this moment appeared in sight, moving
up the Eastern Branch parallel to our position. From the left,
where I was, I perceived that if the position of the advanced
artillery were forced, two or three pieces upon the left of Stansbury would be necessary to scour an orchard which lay between
his line and his artillery, and for another rifle company to increase
the support of this artillery.

"These were promptly sent forward by General Smith, and
posted as hastily as possible, and it was barely accomplished
before I was obliged to give orders to the advanced artillery to
open upon the enemy, who was descending the street toward
the bridge. All further examination or movement was now impossible, and the position where I then was, immediately in the
rear of the left of Stansbury's line, being the most advanced
position from which I could have any commanding view, I remained there. The fire of our advanced artillery occasioned the
enemy, who were advancing, and who were light troops, to leave
the street, and they crept down under cover of houses and trees,
in loose order, so as not to expose them to risk from the shot;
it was therefore, only occasionally that an object presented at
which the artillery could fire.

" In this sort of suspension, the enemy began to throw rockets,
and his light troops began to accumulate down in the lower parts

of the town and near the bridge, but principally covered from view by the houses. Their light troops, however, soon began to issue out and press across the creek, which was everywhere fordable, and in most places lined with bushes or trees, which were sufficient to conceal the movements of light troops, who act, in the manner of theirs, singly. The advanced riflemen now began to fire, and continued it for half a dozen rounds, when I observed them to run back to the skirts of the orchard on the left, where they became visible, the boughs of the orchard trees concealing their original position, as also that of the artillery, from view. A retreat of twenty or thirty yards from their original position toward the left brought them in view on the edge of the orchard. They halted there, and seemed for a moment returning to their position; but in a few minutes entirely broke, and retired to the left of Stansbury's line. I immediately ordered the 5th Baltimore Regiment, Lieutenant-Colonel Sterett, being the left of Stansbury's line, to advance and sustain the artillery. They promptly commenced this movement; but the rockets, which had for the first three or four passed very high above the heads of the line, now received a more horizontal direction, and passed very close above the heads of Schutz's and Ragan's regiments, composing the centre and left of Stansbury's line. A universal flight of these regiments was the consequence. This leaving the right of the 5th wholly unsupported, I ordered it to halt, rode swiftly across the field toward those who had so shamefully fled, and exerted my voice to the utmost to arrest them. They halted, began to collect, and seemed to be returning to their places. An ill-founded reliance that their officers would succeed in stopping the greatest part of them, induced me immediately to return to the 5th, the situation of which was likely to become critical, and that position gave me the best command of view. To my astonishment and mortification, however, when I had regained my position, I found the whole of these regiments (except thirty or forty of Ragan's, rallied by himself, and as many perhaps of Schutz's, rallied, I learn by Captain Shower and Captain ——, whose name I do not recollect) were flying in the utmost precipitation and disorder.

" The advanced artillery had immediately followed the riflemen, and retired by the left of the 5th. I directed them to take post on a rising ground which I pointed out in the rear. The 5th, and the artillery on its left, still remained, and I hoped that their fire, notwithstanding the obstruction of the boughs of the orchard, which being below, covered the enemy, would have been enabled to scour this approach and prevent his advance. The enemy's light troops, by single men, showed themselves on the lower edge of the left of the orchard, and received the fire of this artillery and the 5th, which made them draw back. The cover to them was, however, so complete, that they were enabled to advance singly, and take positions from which their fire annoyed the 5th considerably, without either that regiment or the artillery being able to return the fire with any probability of effect. In this situation I had actually given an order to the 5th and the artillery to retire up to the hill, toward a wood more to the left and a little in the rear, for the purpose of drawing them farther from the orchard, and out of reach of the enemy's fire while he was sheltered by the orchard. An aversion, however, to retire before the necessity became stronger, and the hope that the enemy would issue in a body from the left of the orchard and enable us to act upon him on terms of equality, and the fear that a movement of retreat might in raw troops produce some confusion and lose us this chance, induced me instantly to countermand this order, and direct the artillery to fire into a wooden barn on the lower edge of the orchard, behind which I supposed the enemy might be sheltered in considerable numbers. The fire of the enemy now began to annoy the 5th still more in wounding several of them, and a strong column of the enemy having passed up the road as high as the right of the 5th, and beginning to deploy into the field to take them in flank, I directed the artillery to retire to the hill to which I had directed the Baltimore artillery to proceed and halt, and ordered the 8th regiment also to retire. This corps, which had heretofore acted so firmly, evinced the usual incapacity of raw troops to make orderly movements in the face of the enemy, and their retreat in a very few moments became a flight of absolute and total disorder.

" The direct line of retreat to the whole of this first line being to the hill on which I had directed the artillery to halt, and immediately in connection with the positions of General Smith's corps, which were not arrayed in line, but posted on advantageous positions in connection with and supporting each other, according as the nature of the ground admitted and required, I had not for a moment, dispersed and disordered as was the whole of Stansbury's command, supposed that their retreat would have taken a different direction. But it soon became apparent that the whole mass were throwing themselves off to the right on the retreat toward Montgomery Court House, and flying wide of this point; the whole of the cavalry, probably from the pressure of the infantry that way, were also thrown wide of the line of retreat toward the right.

" After making every effort to turn the current more toward General Smith's command and the city in vain, and finding that it was impossible to collect any force to support the artillery, which I had directed to halt, and finding also that the enemy's light troops were extending themselves in that direction, and pressing the pursuit, I directed the artillery to continue their retreat on the road they were then on, toward the Capitol, it being impossible for them to get across to the turnpike road or unite with General Smith's brigade.

" The hope of again forming the first line at this point, and there renewing the retreat, or at all events, of being able to rally them between the Capitol and that point and renewing the contest, induced me, at the moment I directed the 5th regiment to retreat, to request Mr. Riggs, of Georgetown, to proceed to the President and inform him that we had been driven back, but that it was my hope and intention to form and renew the contest between that place and the Capitol.

" As soon as I found it vain longer to endeavor to turn the tide of retreat toward the left, I turned toward the positions occupied by Lieutenant-Colonel Beall, Commodore Barney, and General Smith. By this time the enemy had advanced up the road, had driven back Lieutenant-Colonel Kramer's command, posted on the right of the road, and in advance of Commodore Barney, after having well maintained his position and much hurt the enemy, and also continued to fire during his retreat. He had come under the destructive fire of Commodore Barney, which had turned him up the hill toward Lieutenant-Colonel Beall, whose detachment gave one or two ineffective fires and fled. Their position was known to me, was very conspicuous, and the extreme right. The enemy, therefore, had gained this commanding position, and was passing our right flank; his force pursuing on the left had also advanced to a line with our left, and there was nothing there to oppose him. To preserve Smith's command from being pressed in front by fresh troops of the enemy, who were coming on at the same time, while they were under the certainty of being assailed on both flanks and the rear by the enemy, who respectively gained them, in which circumstances their destruction or surrender would have been inevitable, I sent (my horse being unable to move with the rapidity I wished) to General Smith to retreat. I am not acquainted with the relative position of the different corps composing his command, and can not, therefore, determine who of them engaged the enemy, nor could I see how they acted; but when I arrived in succession at his different corps, which I did as soon as practicable, I do not recollect to have found any of them that were not in order, and retreating with as little confusion as could have been expected. When I reached the road I found Commodore Barney's men also retiring on the road, he having been overpowered by those who drove off Beall's regiment about the time I sent the order to retreat.

"I still had no doubt but that Stansbury's command and the cavalry would have fallen down upon the Capitol by the roads which enter that part of the city from the north, and still solaced myself with the persuasion that I should be able to rally them upon the city and Georgetown troops, who were retiring in order, and make another effort in advance of the Capitol to repulse the enemy.

"After accompanying the retreating army within two miles of the Capitol, I rode forward for the purpose of selecting a position, and endeavoring to collect those who I supposed, from the rapidity of their flight, might have reached that point. A half a mile in advance of the Capitol I met Colonel Minor with his detachment, and directed him to form his men, wait until the retreating army passed, and protect them if necessary. When I arrived at the Capitol I found not a man had passed that way, and, notwithstanding the commanding view which is there afforded to the north,

I could see no appearance of the troops. I despatched an order to call in the cavalry to me there. In a few moments the Secretary of State and the Secretary of War joined me. Both these gentlemen concurred that it would subject my force to certain capture or destruction [to attempt to defend Washington]; and in its reduced and exhausted condition, it was wise and proper to retire through Georgetown, and take post in the rear of it, on the heights, to collect my force. I accordingly pursued this course, and halted at Tenleytown, two miles from Georgetown, on the Frederick road. Here was evinced one of the great defects of all undisciplined and unorganized troops; no effort could rouse officers and men to the exertion necessary to place themselves in such a state of comfort and security as is attainable even under very disadvantageous circumstances. Such of them as could be halted, instead of making those efforts, gave themselves up to the uncontrolled feelings which fatigue, exhaustion, and privation produced, and many hundreds, in spite of all precautions and efforts, passed on and pursued their way, either toward home, or in search of refreshments and quarters. After waiting in this position until I supposed I collected all the force that could be gathered, I proceeded about five miles further on the river road, which leads a little wide to the left of Montgomery Court House, and in the morning gave orders for the whole to assemble at Montgomery Court House."

After the rout, and while attempting to gather together the fragments of his shattered army, General Winder tried to secure a muster of the troops remaining. In this he failed entirely; and inasmuch as he had but slight knowledge of his command prior to the battle, and none at all after it, it is not surprising that there should be no measurable account of the losses. General Winder estimated the loss to be about thirty to forty killed, fifty to sixty wounded and one hundred and twenty made prisoners.

The official statement of the British losses was as follows: Killed, one captain, two lieutenants, five sergeants, fifty-six rank and file; total, sixty-four. Wounded, two lieutenant-colonels, one major, one captain, fourteen lieutenants, two ensigns, twenty sergeants, one hundred and fifty-five rank and file; total, one hundred and ninety-five. Total losses, two hundred and fifty-nine.

The American estimate of the British losses was upward of five hundred, but the former statement is probably more nearly accurate.

The one redeeming feature of the disastrous fight at Bladensburg was the part played by Commodore Barney and his men. Ample testimony to the bravery and efficiency of this command is furnished by both American and British chroniclers.

When the British arrived at Bladensburg, General Ross, with a few of his officers ascended a hill to the residence of Colonel Bowie, where, from the second story, they had an unobstructed view of the whole slope of country. The lines of American troops, with their reserves were plainly visible. They made a formidable appearance, apparently fresh and ready for battle and seemingly aware of the exhausted condition of the enemy, who had made a forced march of sixty miles, under the August sun, each man loaded down with the weight of eighty rounds of ammunition, provisions, knapsacks and accoutrements. The column was put in motion, advancing down the street in front of and in full view of the American line. The four or five 6-pounders of the Americans opened fire, the balls at first passing over the heads of the advancing column, until it arrived at the bridge between Bladensburg and the American line, when several balls did execution, but did not interrupt the progress across the bridge, nor prevent the British from fording the shallow stream. After crossing, the column deployed to the right and left of the main road, in the middle of which was a 6-pounder. The British were now within musket range of the American infantry, which opened fire, doing but little execution; while the Congreve rockets of the British proved very much more effective. The gleam of the approaching bayonets caused a precipitate flight of the entire line, with the exception of two Washington companies, which made a momentary stand. The British then marched in solid column on the main road and crossed Turncliff's bridge, over a run passing by the duelling ground, up the gradual ascent of a long, steep hill, where Barney's and Miller's forces were supported by Beall's regiment, the District militia and a regiment of regular infantry composed of parts of the 36th and 38th regiments.

The column advanced to within a few hundred yards of Barney's battery before he opened fire, when it burst forth with most destructive effect, sweeping the road and staggering the column; but so determined were they that they renewed the attempt three several times, till at length the carnage became so great that they were obliged to desist from the direct attack and flank off to the right and left to get under cover from Barney's fire; this was afforded by a ravine parallel to and at the distance of four or five hundred yards from Barney's line, or the second line of defence. It became the duty of Colonel Wood to lead a portion of the left, with orders to turn the American right, and on emerging from the ravine they approached within striking distance of the line, consisting of a regiment of Maryland militia under the command of Colonel Beall, from which they received a shower of musket balls, which Colonel Wood said he had scarcely known to be equaled in all the battles in which he had participated on the Spanish peninsula. By this discharge Colonel Wood was severely wounded, and while being conducted to a place of safety, was knocked down by the concussion from a discharge of Barney's battery.

Colonel Beall, having only raw militia under his command, could not induce them to stand the shock of the bayonet to which the British troops had been ordered to bring the contest, and they retired, leaving the right and rear of Barney's position exposed to a heavy column of British which now approached under cover of a heavy wood. While this movement was going on at Barney's right, the right flank of the British had pushed up the ravine with a view of turning the American left; and at the debouch of the ravine, the head of the British column approached the front of the 36th and 38th, who remained without orders to fire, until the enemy approached within pistol range, when the officers and men retreated. A small battalion of Washington and Georgetown volunteers, under Major Peter, made a spirited resistance, but were soon driven back, leaving Barney's left entirely unprotected. Barney's ammunition wagons having gone off in the general flight, and he being wounded and on the ground, with the British closing in on his rear, ordered his guns spiked. His officers refused to leave him, but he ordered them all to leave him except Mr. Huffington, and they made good their retreat.

8

Shortly afterward Captain Wainwright came up, and on learning Barney's identity, went in search of Admiral Cockburn, who soon afterward made his appearance, accompanied by General Ross. They both accosted the prisoner in the most polite and respectful terms, offering immediate assistance, and the attendance of their surgeon. General Ross, turning to the admiral, remarked, " I told you it was the flotilla men!" Admiral Cockburn replied: "Yes, you were right, though I could not believe you—they have given us the only fighting we have had." After some further conversation between the two commanders in a low tone, General Ross turned again to the prisoner and said: " Commodore Barney, you are paroled, where do you wish to be conveyed?" Barney's wound had in the meantime been dressed by the British surgeon, and he requested to be conveyed to Bladensburg. The general immediately ordered a sergeant's guard to attend with a litter, and Captain Wainwright was directed by the admiral to accompany it, and see that every attention was paid to the commodore. Captain Wainwright, observing that he was very weak and suffering much pain from the motion of the litter, ordered the soldiers to put down the litter, saying they did not know how to handle a man, and directed a young naval officer to bring a gang of sailors to carry the litter. The order was speedily executed, and as Captain Wainwright had predicted, the sailors handled the patient like a child.

With the withdrawal of Barney's command from the field, all resistance was at an end, and the victorious troops marched leisurely into the city of Washington. While the two brigades which had been in action remained upon the field to recover their order, the third, which had formed the reserve, and was consequently unbroken, took the lead and pushed forward to Washington. Concerning the destruction of the city, Gleig says: " As it was not the intention of the British government to attempt permanent conquests in this part of America, and as the general was well aware that, with a handful of men, he could not pretend to establish himself for any length of time in an enemy's capital, he determined to lay it under contribution, and to return quietly to the shipping. Nor was there anything unworthy of the character of a British officer in this determination. By all the customs of war, whatever public property may chance to be in a captured town, becomes confessedly the just spoil of the conqueror; and in thus proposing to accept a certain sum of money in lieu of that property, he was showing mercy rather than severity to the vanquished. It is true that if they chose to reject his terms he and his army would be deprived of their booty, because without some more convenient mode of transporting it than we possessed, even the portable part of the property itself could not be removed. But, on the other hand, there was no difficulty in destroying it; and thus, though we should gain nothing, the American government would lose probably to a much greater amount than if they had agreed to purchase its preservation by the money demanded.

"Such being the intention of General Ross, he did not march the troops immediately into the city, but halted them upon a plain in its immediate vicinity, whilst a flag of truce was sent forward with terms. But whatever his proposal might have been, it was not so much as heard; for scarcely had the party bearing the flag entered the street, when it was fired upon from the window of one of the houses, and the horse of the general himself, who accompanied it, killed. The indignation excited by this act throughout all ranks and classes of men in the army, was such as the nature of the case could not fail to occasion. Every thought of accomodation was instantly laid aside; the troops advanced forthwith into the town, and having first put to the sword all who were found in the house from which the shots were fired, and reduced it to ashes, they proceeded without a moments delay to burn and destroy everything in the most distant degree connected with the government. In this general devastation were included the Senate-house, the President's palace, an extensive dock-yard and arsenal, barracks for two or three thousand men, several large storehouses filled with naval and military stores, some hundreds of cannon of different descriptions, and nearly twenty twousand stand of small arms. There were also two or three public ropewalks which shared the same fate, a fine frigate pierced for sixty guns, and just ready to be launched, several gun brigs and armed schooners, with a variety of gun-boats and small craft. The powder magazines were set on fire and exploded with a tremendous crash, throwing down many houses in their vicinity;

whilst quantities of shot, shell and hand-grenades, which could not otherwise be rendered useless were cast into the river. In destroying the cannon a method was adopted which I had never before winessed, and which, as it was both effectual and expeditious, I cannot avoid relating. One gun of rather a small calibre was pitched upon as the executioner of the rest, and being loaded with ball and turned to the muzzles of the others, it was fired, and thus beat out the breechings.

"All this was as it should be, and had the arm of vengeance been extended no further, there would not have been room given for so much as a whisper of disapprobation. But unfortunately it did not stop there; a noble library, several printing offices, and all the national archives were likewise committed to the flames, which, though no doubt the property of the government, might better have been spared. . . . .

"Whilst the third brigade was thus employed, the rest of the army, having recalled its stragglers, and removed the wounded into Bladensburg, began its march towards Washington. Though the battle came to a close by four o'clock, the sun had set before the different regiments were in a condition to move, consequently this short journey was performed in the dark. The work of destruction in the city had also begun before they quitted their ground; and the blazing of houses, ships and stores, the report of exploding magazines, and the crash of falling roofs, informed them, as they proceeded, of what was going forward. It would be difficult to conceive a finer spectacle than that which presented itself as they approached the town. The sky was brilliantly illuminated by the different conflagrations; and a dark red light was thrown upon the road, sufficient to permit each man to view distinctly his comrade's face. . . . .

"Our troops were this day kept as much together as possible upon the Capitol hill. A powerful army of Americans already began to show themselves upon some heights, at the distance of two or three miles from the city; and as they sent out detachments of horse even to the very suburbs, for the purpose of watching our motions, it would have been unsafe to permit more straggling than was absolutely necessary. The army which we had overthrown the day before, though defeated, was far from annihilated; it had by this time recovered its panic, began to concentrate itself in our front, and presented quite as formidable an appearance as ever. We learnt also, that it was joined by a considerable force from the back settlements, which had arrived too late to take part in the action, and the report was that both combined amounted to nearly twelve thousand men.

"Whether or not it was their intention to attack, I cannot pretend to say, because it was noon before they showed themselves; and soon after, when something like a movement could be discerned in their ranks, the sky grew suddenly dark, and the most tremendous hurricane ever remembered by the oldest inhabitant in the place came on. Of the prodigious force of the wind it is impossible for one who was not an eye-witness to its effects to form a conception. Roofs of houses were torn off by it, and whirled into the air like sheets of paper; whilst the rain which accompanied it resembled the rushing of a mighty cataract rather than the dropping of a shower. The darkness was as great as if the sun had long set, and the last remains of twilight had come on, occasionally relieved by flashes of vivid lightning streaming through it; which together with the noise of the wind and the thunder, the crash of falling buildings, and the tearing of roofs as they were stript from the walls, produced the most apalling effect I ever have, and probably ever shall, witness. The storm lasted for nearly two hours without intermission, during which time many of the houses spared by us were blown down, and thirty of our men, besides several of the inhabitants, buried beneath the ruins. Our column was as completely dispersed as if it had received a total defeat; some of the men flying for shelter behind walls and buildings, and others falling flat upon the ground to prevent themselves from being carried away by the tempest; nay, such was the violence of the wind, that two pieces of light cannon, which stood upon the eminence, were fairly lifted from the ground and borne several yards to the rear.

" When the hurricane had blown over, the camp of the Americans appeared to be in as great a state of confusion as our own; nor could either party recover themselves sufficiently during the rest of the day to try the fortune of a battle. Of this General Ross did not fail to take advantage. He had already attained all that he could hope, and perhaps more than he originally expected to attain; consequently, to risk another action would only be to spill blood for no purpose. Whatever might be the issue of the contest, he could derive from it no advantage. If he were victorious, it would not do away with the necessity which esisted of evacuating Washington; if defeated, his ruin was certain. To avoid fighting was therefore his object, and perhaps he owed its accomplishment to the fortunate occurrence of the storm. Be that, however, as it may, a retreat was resolved upon; and we now only waited for night, to put the resolution into practice.

"There was, however, one difficulty to be surmounted in this proceeding. Of the wounded, many were so ill as to preclude all possibility of their removal, and to leave them in the hands of an enemy whom we had beaten was rather a mortifying anticipation. But for this there was no help; and it now only remained to make the best arrangements for their comfort, and to secure for them, as far as could be done, civil treatment from the Americans.

"It chanced that, among other prisoners taken at Bladensburg, was Commodore Barney, an American officer of much gallantry and high sense of honour. Being himself wounded, he was the more likely to feel for those who were in a similar condition, and having received the kindest treatment from our medical attendants, as long as he continued under their hands, he became, without solicitation, the friend of his fellow sufferers. To him, as well as to the other prisoners, was given his parole, and to his care were our wounded, in a peculiar manner, intrusted—a trust which he received with the utmost willingness, and discharged with the most praiseworthy exactness. Among other stipulations, it was agreed that such of our people as were left behind should be considered as prisoners of war, and should be restored to us as soon as they were able to travel; and that as soon as they reached the ships, the commodore and his countrymen would, in exchange, be released from their engagements.

"As soon as these arrangements were completed, and darkness had come on, the third brigade, which was posted in the rear of our army, began to withdraw. Then followed the guns, and

afterwards the second, and last of all the light brigade, exactly
reversing the order which had been maintained during the advance. Instead of an advance guard, this last now furnished a
party to cover the retreat, and the whole procession was closed
by the mounted drivers.

" It being a matter of great importance to deceive the enemy
and to prevent pursuit, the rear of the column did not quit its
ground upon the Capitol till a late hour. During the day an
order had been issued that none of the inhabitants should be
seen in the streets after eight o'clock, and as fear renders most
men obedient, the order was punctually attended to. All the
horses belonging to different officers were removed to drag the
guns, no one being allowed to ride, lest a neigh or even the trampling of hoofs should excite suspicion. The fires were trimmed,
and made to blaze brightly; fuel enough was left to keep them so
for some hours; and finally about half-past nine o'clock the
troops formed in marching order, and moved off in the most profound silence. Not a word was spoken, nor a single individual
permitted to step one inch out of his place, by which means they
passed along the streets perfectly unnoticed, and cleared the
town without any alarm being given. Our pace, it will be
imagined, was none of the most tardy, consequently it was not
long before we reached the ground which had been occupied by
the other brigades. Here we found a second line of fires blazing
in the same manner as those deserted by ourselves; and the same
precautions in every respect adopted, to induce a belief that our
army was still quiet. Beyond these again, we found two or three
solitary fires, placed in such order as to resemble those of a chain
of piquets. In a word, the deception was so well managed, that
even we ourselves were at first doubtful whether the rest of the
troops had fallen back. . . . .

" In Bladensburg the Brigade halted for an hour, while those
men who had thrown away their knapsacks endeavoured to
recover them. During this interval I strolled up to a house which
had been converted into an hospital, and paid a hasty visit to the
wounded. I found them in great pain, and some of them deeply
affected at the thought of being abandoned by their comrades,

and left to the mercy of their enemies. Yet, in their apprehension of evil treatment from the Americans, the event proved that they had done injustice to that people, who were found to possess at least one generous trait in their character, namely, that of behaving kindly and attentively to their prisoners. . . . .

"We had now proceeded a distance of thirty-five miles, and began to consider ourselves beyond the danger of pursuit. The remainder of the retreat was accordingly conducted with more leisure; our next march carrying us no farther than to Nottingham, where we remained during an entire day, for the purpose of resting the troops. It cannot be said that this resting time was spent in idleness. A gun-brig, with a number of ships' launches and long boats had made their way up the stream, and were at anchor opposite to the town. On board the former were carried such of the wounded as had been able to travel, whilst the latter were loaded with flour and tobacco, the only spoil which we found it practicable to bring off.

" Whilst the infantry were thus employed, the cavalry was sent back as far as Marlborough to discover whether there were any American forces in pursuit; and it was well for the few stragglers who had been left behind that this recognizance was made. Though there appeared to be no disposition on the part of the American general to follow our steps and to harass the retreat, the inhabitants of that village, at the instigation of a medical practitioner called Bean, had risen in arms as soon as we departed, and falling upon such individuals as strayed from the column, put some of them to death, and made others prisoners. A soldier whom they had taken, and who had escaped, gave information of these proceedings to the troopers, just as they were about to return to headquarters; upon which they immediately wheeled about, and galloping into the village, pulled the doctor out of his bed (for it was early in the morning), compelled him by a threat of instant death to liberate the prisoners, and mounting him before one of the party, brought him in triumph to the camp.

" The wounded, the artillery and plunder, being all embarked on the 28th, at daybreak on the 29th we took the direction of St. Benedict's where we arrived without any adventure at a late hour in the evening."

The following graphic account from the autobiography[5] of John Pendleton Kennedy, gives the experiences of a young volunteer, and incidentally sheds some light on the citizen soldier and his fitness to cope with the Peninsular veterans.

"We marched on Sunday, the twenty-first—our regiment, the Fifth—accompanied by a battalion of riflemen, commanded by William Pinkney, then recently returned from England, where he had been our minister for several years, and now, at the date of this campaign, Attorney General of the United States. We had also with us a company of artillery, commanded by Richard Magruder, another member of the bar, and a small corps of cavalry from the Baltimore Light Dragoons—Harry Thompson's company—the detachment being under the command of Lieutenant Jacob Hollingsworth.

"A portion of Sterett Ridgeley's Hussars were also in the detachment. These were all volunteers of the city. My father was a member of Hollingsworth's command, and, with John Brown, an old schoolmate of mine, and three or four privates of the corps, served as videttes to our brigade.

"It was a day of glorious anticipation, that Sunday morning; when, with all the glitter of a dress parade, we set forth on our march. As we moved through the streets, the pavements were crowded with anxious spectators; the windows were filled with women; friends were rushing to the ranks to bid us good-bye—many exhorting us to be of good cheer and do our duty; handkerchiefs were waving from the fair hands at the windows—some few of the softer sex weeping as they waved adieux to husbands and brothers; the populace were cheering and huzzahing at every corner, as we hurried along in brisk step to familiar music, with banners fluttering in the wind and bayonets flashing in the sun. What a scene it was, and what a proud actor I was in it! I was in the ecstacy of a vision of glory, stuffed with any quantity of romance. This was a real army marching to a real war. The enemy, we knew, was in full career, and we had the certainty of meeting him in a few days. Unlike our customary parades, our

[5] In Henry T. Tuckerman's Life of John Pendleton Kennedy, N. Y., 1871, p. 71 *et seq.*

march now had all the equipments of a campaign. Our wagon-train was on the road; our cartridge-boxes were filled; we had our crowd of camp servants and followers. Officers rode backward and forward along the flanks of the column, with a peculiar air of urgent business, as if it required everything to be done in a gallop—the invariable form in which military conceit shows itself in the first movements towards a campaign. The young officers wish to attract attention, and so seem to be always on the most important messages. As for me—not yet nineteen—I was too full of the exultation of the time to think of myself—all my fervor was spent in admiration of this glittering army.

'It were worth ten years of peaceful life
One glance at their array.'

" I thought of these verses, and they spoke of my delight. It was not long before we were outside of the town, in full career on the Washington road. It was afternoon in warm August weather when we started. By sundown we reached Elk Ridge Landing, and there turned in upon the flat meadow ground that lies under the hills upon the further bank of the Patapsco, to pitch our tents for the night. Camp-kettles were served out to us and our rations of pork and hard bread. We formed our messes that evening. and mine, consisting of six members, who were consigned to one tent, was made up of pleasant companions. This was all new to us, and very amusing. The company consisted of gentlemen of good condition and accustomed to luxurious life, and the idea of a supper of fat pork and hard biscuit was a pleasant absurdity which we treated as a matter of laughter. We had our own stores in the wagon to rely upon when we could get at them, and a short, active negro man as a servant for the mess, whom we took into service that evening from the crowd of stragglers who followed the column of march. The first care after getting our tent up was to hold a consultation about our domestic affairs, and it was then resolved that two of us should in turn serve as house-keeper, successively from week to week. The choice to-day fell upon Ned Schroeder and myself. We were to attend at the giving out of the rations and then to cook them. The mess was not likely to grow fat under our administration. Upon repairing to the quartermaster for our supplies, we were given a piece of pork of five or six pounds, a new camp-kettle, and a quantity of hard biscuit. Ned and I had a consultation upon the process of the cooking, the result of which was that we determined to put our pork in the kettle, to fill this with water to the brim, and then set it over a brisk fire for two hours; so we set about it. To make the fire we resolved to signalize our service by that soldierly act which is looked upon as a prescriptive right—the robbing of the nearest fence of as many rails as suited our purpose—which we did like veterans, satisfying our conscience with the reflection that some time or other, perhaps, Congress would pay for the damage. We got up a magnificent flame, and by placing our kettle on a support of stones in its midst, we made sure that the cooking would soon become a happy success. This being done, we sauntered off to look at the evening parade, from which our culinary labors gave us exemption. In less than an hour we lounged back to take a view of the kettle. There it was, buried in a little mound of hot coals, the water all boiled out, and the iron red hot. In the bottom of this lurid pot we discovered a black mess which seemed to be reduced to a stratum of something resembling a compound of black soap in a semi-liquid state, and on drawing the kettle out of the fire, and cooling it as quickly as we could, by setting it in water, we came to the perception that our supper, or at least as much of it as we had cooked, was a compost of charred bones, and a deposit of black fat, the whole plated over with the scales of iron which the heat had brought off in flakes from the kettle. Our comrades of the mess gathered around this ruin with amused interest, and we were voted a diploma for our admirable experiment in the art of dressing pork. We had found our company's wagon by the time this experiment was so finely concluded, and, with the help of Elijah, or Lige—as our servant was called—found a very good resource for supper without the aid of the pork. We had coffee and chocolate, good bread and ham in abundance. The night was chilly, and I had come away without a blanket, trusting to a great coat which I thought would be sufficient for a summer campaign. Luckily, my father came along by our quarters, and perceiving my condition, went out and supplied my need by a contribution from a friend in the neighborhood. At the regulation hour, the members of the mess who were not detailed for guard duty—some four of us—crept into our tent, and arranging our blankets into a soft bed, laid down and fell into a hearty sleep which was only broken by the reveille the next morning. This was my first night of a regular campaign. The next day we marched from the Landing to Vansville, about twenty miles—halting an hour or so at Waterloo, then McCoy's Tavern, where we got our dinner—I mean my comrades and myself, having no need and not very willing to try another experiment in cooking for ourselves. The day was hot and portions of the road in deep sand. It was a great trial. We were in winter cloth uniform, with a most absurd helmet of thick jacked leather and covered with plumes. We carried, besides, a knapsack, in which—in my own case—I had packed a great coat, my newly acquired blanket, two or three shirts, stockings, etc. Among these articles I had also put a pair of pumps, which I had provided with the idea, that, after we had beaten the British army and saved Washington, Mr. Madison would very likely invite us to a ball at the White House, and I wanted to be ready for it. The knapsacks must have weighed at least ten pounds. Then there was a Harper's Ferry musket of fourteen pounds. Take our burden altogether, and we could not have been tramping over those sandy roads, under the broiling sun of August, with less than thirty pounds of weight upon us. But we bore it splendidly, toiling and sweating in a dense cloud of dust, drinking the muddy water of the little brooks which our passage over them disturbed, and taking all the discomforts of this rough experience with a cheerful heart and a stout resolve. We joked with our afflictions, laughed at each other, and sang in the worst of time. The United Volunteers was the finest company in the regiment, about one hundred strong when in full array, but now counting eighty effective men. These were the *elite* of the city—several of them gentlemen of large fortunes. William Gilmor was one of them—a merchant of high standing; Meredith, who had so long been among the most distinguished at the bar, was another. It was what is called the crack company of the city, and composed of a class of men who are not generally supposed to be the best to endure fatigue, and yet there was no body of men in all the troops of Baltimore who were more ready for all service, more persistent in meeting and accomplishing the severest duty. To me personally labor and fatigue were nothing. I was inured to both by self-discipline, and I had come to a philosophic conviction that both were essential to all enjoyments of life, and beside this bit of philosophy, I was lured by the romance of our enterprise into an oblivion of its hardships.

"The second day brought us to Vansville, by the way, a town consisting of one house, on the top of a hill, where stage-passengers stopped for a change of horses on the road to Washington; and at early dawn the next day—Tuesday morning, the 22d of August—we resumed the road, and reached Bladensburg about five in the afternoon, having marched very slowly, with many halts during the day, waiting for orders from the commander-in-chief. Reports were coming to us every moment of the movements of the enemy. They had passed Marlborough, and were marching on Washington, but whether they were on the direct road to the city, or were coming by Bladensburg, was uncertain. Our movements depended somewhat upon them. General Winder, who commanded the army immediately in front of the enemy, and was retiring slowly before him, was advised of our march, and was sending frequent instructions to our commander. Of course we in the ranks knew nothing about these high matters. All that we could hear were the flying rumors of the hour, which were stirring enough. One of Winder's videttes had come to us. He had a great story to tell. He was carrying orders to Stansbury, who was ahead of us, and fell in with a party of British dragoons, from whom he fled at speed for his life. The country in Prince George is full of gates; the highroads often lie through cultivated field, without side fences to guard them, and every field is entered through a gate which is always old and rickety, and swings to after your horse with a rapid sweep and a bang that threatens to take off his tail. One vidette, a Mr. Floyd, known to us in Baltimore, told us he had been pursued several miles by four of these dragoons. He reported that the British army had a corps of cavalry with them, and that being splendidly mounted, as we saw he was, and having General Winder's servant with him also mounted on a fleet horse, to open and *hold open* the gates for him, he had escaped and had got up to us. This was all true as he told it, except that he was mistaken, as we found out the next day when we joined Winder, in one important particular, and that was, that his pursuers were not British dragoons, but four members of the Georgetown cavalry who fell into the same mistake. They supposed him a British dragoon, straggling from his corps, and gave him chase, feeling very sure from the direction they had pressed him to take, that they must soon drive him into our hands. It was only because they could not keep up with him that they failed to witness that happy denouement. This report of cavalry in the enemy's army, of course, furnished us, as green soldiers, with much occasion for remark and reflection. We had a pleasant evening in camp near Bladensburg. Our tents were pitched on the slope of the hill above the town on the eastern side of the river. Stansbury's brigade of drafted militia were there, and Winder, with the rest of the army, which altogether perhaps counted nine thousand men, was not far off. He was falling back before the march of the enemy, who could not have been more than ten or twelve miles off.

" The afternoon towards sunset was mild and pleasant, and we had leisure to refresh ourselves by a bath in the Eastern Branch. Our camp was supplied with every comfort, and we did not depend upon the United States for our supper, for Lige was sent out to forage, with money to purchase what we wanted. He returned about dark with a pair of chickens and a handful of tallow candles, which seemed to be an odd combination ; and upon being interrogated by me what it meant, he said he found them under the flap of a tent in Stansbury's brigade, and being perfectly sure they were stolen, he thought he would restore them to their proper owners. The stealing was probable enough, and we therefore had little scruple in consigning the fowls to Lige's attentions in the kitchen, and finding ourselves with an extra supply of candles, we indulged the luxury of lighting some three or four, which, being fitted into the band of a bayonet with the point stuck in the ground, gave an unusual splendor to the interior of our tent. The keg in which we kept our biscuit—Jamison's best crackers—made the support of our table—a board picked from some neighboring house, and here we enjoyed our ease, and ham, chicken and coffee.

" My feet were swollen and sore from my day's march in boots, such as none but a green soldier would ever have put on; so for my comfort, I had taken them off, and substituted my neat pair of pumps from the pocket of my knapsack, and in this easy enjoyment of rest and good fellowship, we smoked our cigars and talked about the battle of to-morrow until the hour when the order of the camp obliged us to extinguish our lights and 'turn in.'

" I was too much excited by the novelty and attraction of my position and by the talk of my comrades in the tent, to get asleep much before midnight. About an hour after this—one o'clock— we were aroused by the scattered shots of our pickets, some four or five in succession, in the direction of the Marlborough road, and by the rapid beating of the long roll from every drum in the camp. Every one believed that the enemy was upon us, and there was consequently an immense bustle in getting ready to meet him. We struck a light to be able to find our coats, accoutrements, etc., but in a moment it was stolen away by some neighbor who came to borrow it only for a moment to light his own candle, and in the confusion forgot to return it. This gave rise to some ludicrous distresses. Some got the wrong boots, others a coat that didn't fit, some could not find their cross-belts. There was no time allowed to rectify these mistakes. I, luckily was all right, except that I sallied out in my pumps. We were formed in line and marched off towards the front, perhaps a mile, and when we came to a halt, we were soon ordered to march back again to camp.

" What was the cause of this sudden excursion and quick abandonment of it I never learned. But it was evident there was a false alarm. On our return march our attention was called to the sudden reddening of the sky in the direction of the lower bridge of the Eastern Branch, by which the river road from Marlborough crossed to Washington. The sky became more lurid every moment, and at last we could discern the flames. A despatch which reached us when we got back to camp, and had just laid down again to sleep, brought us information that Winder had crossed the bridge and then burnt it to impede the march of the enemy, who, in consequence, was forced to direct his march upon the Bladensburg road. Winder himself was *en route* to join us, and we were ordered forthwith to break up our camp and march towards Washington. Here was new excitement—everything was gathered up in a few moments. All our baggage was tossed into our regimental wagon—knapsacks, provisions, blankets, everything but our arms. Among them went my boots. The tents were struck and packed away with the speed of the shifting of a scene upon the stage, and in half an hour from the time of receiving the order we were in full column of march upon the road. Descending into the village we crossed the bridge and moved toward Washington; but after making about two miles at a very slow pace, we found ourselves brought to a halt, and after this we loitered, as slow as foot could fall, along the road, manifestly expecting some order that should turn us back towards the village we had left. What a march that was! I never was so sleepy in my life. We had been too much exhilarated in the early part of the night to feel the fatigue of our day's march, but now that fatigue returned upon me with double force. It was but an hour or two before day—that hour when the want of sleep presses most heavily upon all animals that go abroad by day. Nothing could keep us awake. I slept as I walked. At every halt of a moment whole platoons laid down in the dusty road and slept till the officers gave the word to move on. How very weary I felt! The burning of the bridge lighted up the whole southern sky, but it had no power to attract our gaze. At length when we had reached a hill some three miles on our route, we were marched into a stubble field and told we might rest until daylight. Here we threw ourselves upon the ground without any covering, exposed to the heavy dew which moistened the earth and hung upon the stubble, and slept. Mine was the sleep of Endymion. When I awoke I was lying on my back with the hot sun of a summer morning beaming upon my face. Our orders then were to march back to Bladensburg. Soon we had the famous 'trial of souls'—the battle of Bladensburg. The drafted militia ran away at the first fire, and the 5th regiment was driven off the field with the bayonet. We made a fine scamper of it. I lost my musket in the melee while bearing off a comrade, James W. McCulloch, afterwards the cashier of the Branch Bank of the United States in Baltimore, whose leg was broken by a bullet. The day was very hot, and the weight of my wounded companion great, and not being able to carry both, I gave my musket to a friend who accompanied me, and he, afterwards being wounded himself, dropped his own weapon as well as mine."

Thus abruptly ends Mr. Kennedy's account of the battle, but among his posthumous papers is one endorsed " Memoranda taken from the company book of the Baltimore United Volunteers in reference to the campaign in 1814." This document is (in part) as follows: " Keener has lent me the company book of the United Volunteers. I entered this corps, I think, in the fall of 1812, just after I graduated. I find my name attached to resolutions volunteering to march to any part of the state, but not to perform guard duty out of Baltimore County. These resolutions are dated March 16th, 1813. By this record, there were at Bladensburg in the action of the 24th August, 1814, including a few who joined as volunteers:

66 members of the company in action,
10 absent on guard duty with the wagons,
3 volunteers—Frank Davidge, Dick Dorsey and Ed. Hollingsworth in the action.

The wounded were:
Lieutenant Cooke, Commanding,
Sergeant W. H. Murray,
Corporal J. W. McCulloch,
Privates George Clarke,
George Golder,
William Williams,
Dennis F. Magruder,
Francis H. Davidge."

Another Baltimore volunteer, a member of the Independent Company, has also left an account of his experiences. He says:

" On Wednesday last at twelve o'clock the British attacked our army in a large field at Bladensburg where we had been drawn up in line for a considerable time to receive them. A stream of water passes through the town where the enemy entered on the opposite side from where we were posted. We had two companies of Baltimore artillery, commanded by Captains Magruder and Myers, placed a long way in front of our line of infantry,

9

so as to rake the enemy as they passed over the bridge. The fire I think, must have been dreadfully galling, but they took no notice of it; their men moved like clock-work; the instant a part of a platoon was cut down it was filled up by the men in the rear without the least noise and confusion whatever, so as to present always a solid column to the mouths of our cannon; they advanced so fast that our artillery had to give way and fall back upon our line, where they commenced again and fired for a short time, when the 5th regiment was ordered to advance on the enemy and fire, which was obeyed and kept up for a considerable time. The British force was greatly superior in numbers to ours. It is my opinion that not one third of their army came into action at all, any further than by amusing themselves by throwing Congreve rockets at us. They were so strong that we had to give way. I think if we had remained ten minutes longer they would have either killed or taken the whole of us.

" When the retreat was ordered, I shaped my course for a woods in the rear, where I intended to lay down and rest, being almost fatigued to death, but the bullets and grape shot flew like hailstones about me and I was compelled to make headway for a swamp where I remained until I had strength sufficient to get to a little farm house where I was hospitably received and got refreshed. I started from this house about nine o'clock at night with a guide through woods and by-paths about five miles to Ross's Tavern, where I spent the remainder of the night. A part of the British force proceeded directly to Washington, which place they took possession of, destroyed everything in the Navy Yard, the Capitol and all other public buildings. They will be here in a few days and we have no force that can face them. I think the only way to save the town and state will be to capitulate." [6]

Chaplain Gleig's conclusions on the tactical mistakes of Bladensburg are so convincing and reasonable that they are here inserted:

" With respect to the Americans, again, criticism necessarily degenerates into unqualified censure. From the beginning to the

---

[6] Unpublished correspondence of Henry Fulford, dated Baltimore, Aug. 26, 1814.

end of the affair, they acted in no one instance like prudent or sagacious men. In the first place, they ought on no account to have risked a general action in an open country, however strong and steep; and, secondly, they deserve to suffer much more severely than they did suffer, for permitting an enemy's army to penetrate beyond Nottingham. In allowing us to land without opposition, they were perhaps guilty of no great mistake; but having done so, instead of concentrating their forces in one place, they ought to have harassed us with continual skirmishing; felled trees on each side, and thrown them across the road; dug deep ditches at certain intervals; in a word, it was their wisdom to adopt the mode of warfare to which their own habits, as well as the nature of the country invited them.

" In America, every man is a marksman from his very boyhood, and every man serves in the militia; but to bring an army of raw militia-men, however excellent they might be as marksmen, into a fair field against regular troops, could end in nothing but defeat. When two lines oppose each other, very little depends upon the accuracy with which individuals take aim. It is then that the habit of acting in concert, the confidence which each man feels in his companions, and the rapidity and good order in which different movements can be executed, are alone of real service. But put these raw militia-men into thick woods, and send your regular troops to drive them out, and you will immediately lose all the advantages of discipline, and reduce your battle to so many single combats.

" Here, therefore, lay their principal error; had they left all clear, and permitted us to advance as far as Nottingham, and then broken up the roads, and covered them with trees, it would have been impossible for us to go a step beyond. As soon as this was effected, they might have skirmished with us in front, and kept our attention alive with part of their troops, till the rest, acquainted as they doubtless were with every inch of the country, had got into our rear, and, by a similar mode of proceeding, cut off our retreat. Thus we should have been taken in a snare, from which it would have been no easy task to extricate ourselves, and might, perhaps, have been obliged in the end to surrender at discretion.

" But so obvious and so natural a plan of defence they chose to reject; and determining to trust all to the fate of a battle, they were guilty of a monstrous error again. Bladensburg ought not to have been left unoccupied. The most open village, if resolutely defended, will cost many men before it falls; whereas Bladensburg, being composed of substantial brick houses, might have been maintained for hours against all our efforts. In the next place, they displayed great want of military knowledge in the disposition of both their infantry and artillery. There was not, in the whole space of their position, a single point where an enemy would be exposed to a cross fire. The troops were drawn up in three straight lines, like so many regiments upon a gala parade; whilst the guns were used as connecting links to a chain, being posted in the same order, by ones and twos, at every interval.

" In maintaining themselves, likewise, when attacked, they exhibited neither skill nor resolution. Of the personal courage of the Americans there can be no doubt; they are, individually taken, as brave a nation as any in the world. But they are not soldiers; they have not the experience nor the habits of soldiers. It was the height of folly, therefore, to bring them into a situation where nothing except that experience and those habits will avail; and it is on this account that I repeat what I have already said, that the capture of Washington was more owing to the blindness of the Americans themselves than to any other cause."

CHAPTER VII

CAULK'S FIELD

When the main body of the British forces moved up the Patuxent and on toward Washington, the frigate *Menelaus* with several smaller vessels, under the command of Sir Peter Parker, was sent to make a demonstration in the Chesapeake in the direction of Baltimore, in order to draw the attention of the people of that section from the movements of the main body.

On August 20, Sir Peter Parker came in sight of Rock Hall and from his flag-ship organized a number of marauding parties on the shore. After bombarding Worten, a detachment landed and burned the dwelling, barn and crops of Mr. Henry Waller. On the 30th they landed at Fairlee and burned the buildings of Mr. Richard Frisby and carried off four of his colored men. About midnight, they landed again with about two hundred and sixty men, under the immediate command of Sir Peter Parker, the first division led by Captain Henry Crease and the second by Lieutenant Pearce. Led by one of Mr. Frisby's slaves, they set out to capture a camp of one hundred and seventy men of the 21st regiment, commanded by Lieutenant-Colonel Philip Reed, which had been located a half a mile from the beach and about nine miles from Chestertown. The official accounts of what transpired are as usual, widely different, especially as to the relative strength of the forces engaged. In his report to Brigadier-General Benjamin Chambers, Colonel Reed said:

"About half past eleven o'clock on the night of the 30th ult., I received information that the barges of the enemy, then lying off Waltham's farm were moving in shore. I concluded their object was to land and burn the houses, &c., at Waltham's and made the necessary arrangement to prevent them and to be prepared for an opportunity which I had sought for several days to strike the enemy. During our advance to the point threatened, it was discovered that the blow was aimed at our camp. Orders were

immediately given to the quartermaster to remove the camp and
baggage, and to the troop to countermarch, pass the road by
the right of our camp, and form on the rising ground about
three hundred paces in the rear—the right towards Caulk's
house and the left retiring on the road, the artillery in the centre,
supported by the infantry on the right and left. I directed Captain Wickes and his Second-Lieutenant Beck, with a part of the
rifle company to be formed, so as to cover the road by which the
enemy marched, and with this section I determined to post myself,
leaving the line to be formed under the direction of Major Wickes
and Captain Chambers.

" The head of the enemy's column soon presented itself and
received the fire of our advance party, at seventy paces distance,
and, being pressed by numbers vastly superior, I repaired to my
post in the line, having ordered the riflemen to return and form
on the right of the line. The fire now became general along the
whole line, and was sustained by our troops with the most determined valor. The enemy pressed our front; foiled in this he
threw himself on our left flank, which was occupied by Captain
Chambers' company. Here, too, his efforts were equally unavailing. His fire had nearly ceased, when I was informed that in
some parts of our line the cartridges were entirely expended, nor
did any of the boxes contain more than a very few rounds,
although each man brought twenty into the field. The artillery
cartridges were entirely expended. Under these circumstances
I ordered the line to fall back to a convenient spot where a part
of the line was fortified, when the few remaining cartridges were
distributed amongst a part of the line, which was again brought
into the field, where it remained for a considerable time, the night
preventing a pursuit. The artillery and infantry for whom there
were no cartridges were ordered to this place. The enemy having
made every effort in his power, although apprized of our having
fallen back, manifested no disposition to follow us up, but retreated
about the time our ammunition was exhausted.

" When it is recollected that very few of our officers or men had
ever heard the whistling of a ball; that the force of the enemy, as
the most accurate information enables us to estimate, was double
ours; that it was commanded by Sir Peter Parker of the *Menelaus*,

one of the most distinguished officers in the British navy, and composed (as their officers admitted in a subsequent conversation) of as fine men as could be selected from the British service, I feel fully justified in the assertion that the gallantry of the officers and men engaged on this occasion, could not be excelled by any troops. The officers and men performed their duty. It is, however, but an act of justice to notice those officers who seemed to display more than a common degree of gallantry. Major Wickes and Captain Chambers were conspicuous—Captain Wickes and his Lieutenant Beck of the rifle corps, Lieutenant Ennick and Ensign Shriven of Captain Chambers' company exerted themselves, as did Captain Hynson and his Lieutenant Grant, Captain Usselton of the brigade artillery and his Lieutenants Reed and Brown. Lieutenant Tilghman, who commanded the guns of the volunteer artillery, in the absence of Captain Hands who is in ill health and from home, was conspicuous for his gallantry, his Ensign Thomas also manifested much firmness.

"I am indebted to Captain Wilson, of the cavalry, who was with me, for his exertions, and also to Adjutant Hynson, who displayed much zeal and firmness throughout. To Dr. Blake, Dr. Gordon and to Isaac Spencer, Esq., who were accidently in camp, I am indebted for their assistance in reconnoitering the enemy on his advance.

"You will be surprised sir, when I inform you that an engagement of so long continuance in an open field, when the moon shone brilliantly on the rising ground occupied by our troops, while the shade of the neighboring woods, under the protection of which the enemy fought, gave us but an indistinct view of anything but the flash of his guns; that under the disparity of numbers against us and the advantage of regular discipline on the side of the enemy, we had not one man killed, and only one sergeant, one corporal and one private wounded, and those slightly. The enemy left one midshipman and eight men dead on the field, and nine wounded; six of whom died in the course of a few hours. Sir Peter Parker was amongst the slain—he was mortally wounded with a buck-shot and died before he reached the barges, to which he was conveyed by his men. The enemy's force, consisting of marines and musqueteers, was in part armed with boarding pikes, swords and pistols, no doubt intended for our tents, as orders had been given by Sir Peter not to fire. Many of these arms, with rockets, muskets, &c., have fallen into our hands, found by the picket guard under Ensign Shriven, which was posted on the battle ground for the remainder of the night. Nothing but the want of ammunition saved the enemy from destruction.

"Attached are the names of the wounded; and as an act of justice to those concerned, I enclose you a list of the names of every officer and soldier engaged in the affair. Certain information from the enemy assures us that his total loss in killed and wounded was forty-two or forty-three, including two wounded lieutenants.

Names of the wounded of Captain Chambers' company:

John Magnor, sergeant, slightly, in the thigh.

Philip Crane, corporal, ball in the thigh, near the knee.

Wounded of Captain Page's company:

John Glanville, private; in the arm."

The British official account is as follows:

"With grief the deepest it becomes my duty to communicate the death of Sir Peter Parker, Bart., late commander of his Majesty's ship *Menelaus*, and the occurrences attending an attack on the enemy's troops, on the night of the 30th ult., encamped at Bel-air. The previous and accompanying letters of Sir Peter Parker, will, I presume, fully point out the respect the enemy on all occasions evinced at the approach of our arms, retreating at every attack, though possessing a superiority of numbers of five to one; an intelligent black man gave us information of two hundred militia being encamped behind a wood, distant half a mile from the beach, and described their situation, so as to give us the strongest hopes of cutting off and securing the largest part as our prisoners, destroying the camp, field pieces, &c., and possessing also certain information that one man out of every five had been levied as a requisition on the eastern shore, for the purpose of being sent over for the protection of Baltimore, who were only prevented crossing the bay by the activity and vigilance of the tender and ship's boats. One hundred and four bayonets, with twenty pikes, were landed at eleven o'clock at night, under the immediate direction of Captain Sir Peter Parker, Bart., the first division headed by myself, and the second division by Lieutenant Pearce. On arriving at the ground we discovered the enemy had shifted his position, as we were then informed, to the distance of a mile farther; having taken the look out picket immediately on our landing, we were in assurance our motions had not been discovered, and with the deepest silence followed on for the camp. After a march of between four and five miles in the country, we found the enemy posted on a plain, surrounded by woods, with the camp in their rear; they were drawn up in a line and perfectly ready to receive us; a single moment was not to be lost; by a smart fire and instant charge, we commenced the attack, forced them from their position, putting them before us in full retreat to the rear of their artillery, where they again made a stand, showing a disposition to outflank us on the right; a movement was instantly made by Lieutenant Pearce's division to force them from that quarter and it was at this time, while animating his men in the most heroic manner that Sir Peter Parker received his mortal wound which forced him to quit the field, and he expired in a few minutes. Lieutenant Pearce, with his division, soon routed the enemy, while that under my command gained and passed the camp. One of the field pieces was momentarily in our possession, but obliged to quit it from superior numbers.

" The marines under Lieutenants Beynon and Post formed our centre, and never was bravery more conspicuous. Finding it impossible to close on the enemy, from the rapidity of their retreat, having pursued them upwards of a mile, I deemed it prudent to retire towards the beach, which was effected in the best possible order, taking with us from the field twenty-five of our wounded— the whole we could find, the enemy not even attempting to regain the ground they had lost; from three prisoners (cavalry) taken by us, we learn their force amounted to five hundred militia, a troop of horse, and five pieces of artillery, and since by flags of truce, I am led to believe their number much greater.

" Repelling a force of such magnitude with so small a body as we opposed to them, will I trust speak for itself; and although our loss has been severe, I hope the lustre acquired to our arms will compensate for it . . . . Herewith I beg leave to enclose you a list of the killed, wounded and missing in this affair.

I have the honor to be &c.,

HENRY CREASE, Acting Commander.

Total, 14 killed, 27 wounded."[1]

The list of the officers and men who were in the action at Caulk's Field on the night of August 30, referred to in the report of Colonel Reed, was published in the *General Advertiser,* at Easton, under date of October 4, 1814, and is as follows:

Of Captain Chambers' company:

Ezekiel F. Chambers, Captain,
Thomas Ennick, Lieutenant,
William Skirven, Ensign.
Aaron Alford,
Benjamin Benton,
Benjamin Lee Chambers,
David Chambers,
Edward Coleby,
Isaiah Coleman,
Lemuel Comegys,
Robert Constable,
Philip Crane,
Samuel Deal,
Thomas Dugan,
Alexander Dunk,
William Elliott,
David Falls,
Samuel Floyd,
James Gooding,
Samuel Griffith,
James Haley,
Zebedie Harbert,

James Hickinbottom,
George Holtzman,
John Jones,
John Kemp (drummer),
Richard Kennard,
Thomas I. Kennard,
William C. Lassell,
William S. Lassell,
John Magnor,
James Mansfield,
James D. Miller,
William Notts,
James Robinson,
Samuel Rumney,
Theoph. Russell,
Andrew Toulson,
John Usselton,
James Vickers,
Jesse Vickers,
George Watts,
Joseph Wickes, 4th,
Thomas Wickes,

[1] Both of the foregoing accounts are published in *Niles' Register,* v. 7, p. 150.

Of Captain Hand's company:

Henry Tilghman, Lieutenant,
Richard S. Thomas, Ensign,
Robert Barnes,
James F. Brown,
Henry Copper,
John B. Eccleston,
John Edwards,
Samuel Elbert,
Joseph Gibbs,
William Hague,
William Hyland,
Thomas J. James,
Robert McGuire,
William Martin,
James Middleton,
Jeremiah Nicols,
Arthur Parsley,
Joseph Redue,
James Ringgold, Jr.,
Richard Seymour,
Wilson Stavely,
Thomas Taylor,
Nath. Tonson,
Thomas Vickers,
James Wilcox,
John R. Wilmer,
Lemuel Wilmer.

Of Captain Wickes' rifle corps:

Simon Wickes, Captain,
Joseph Brown, 1st Lieutenant,
John Beck, 2nd Lieutenant,
John Airy,
John Beck,
Peregrine Beck,
Samuel Coleman,
Eliphan Donlin,
Robert Fellingham,
Richard Freiks,
Thomas Hartley,
John Hyland,
John Jones,
Richard Kennard,
William Lamb,
John Pearce,
Levin Rolinson,
James Smith,
Richard Smith,
Bazilla Sparks,
Horatio Stokes,
Elisha Swift,
James Tharp,
Henry Urie,
Samuel C. Wickes,
James Yeates.

Of Captain Griffith's company:

Samuel Griffith, Captain,
Samuel Baker,
Hyram Brown,
James Crouch,
John Crouch,
Birney DeCourse,
Henry Dunk,
Jonathan Harris,
David Jones,
William Kendall,
George G. Simmonds,
Joseph Thomas.

Of Captain Hynson's company:

Thomas B. Hynson, Captain,   James Shaw,
Richard Grant, Ensign,   John Waram,
William Hague,   Peregrin Whaland.
Robert Love,

Of Captain Page's company:

Samuel Wickes, Lieutenant,   John Dunn,
Merritt Miller, Ensign,   James Eagle,
Gabriel Alloway,   William Frisby,
George Apsley,   John Glanville,
Elishia Beck,   Nathan Gleaves,
Benj. Benton,   James Hudson,
Francis Benton,   John Humphries,
Thomas Benton,   Benj. Hynson,
Stephen Bryan,   William Ivry,
Jesse Clark,   James Legg,
Ezekiel Coleman,   William Miller,
Robert Collin,   William Simmons,
Jesse Covington,   Thomas Spencer,
Thomas Covington,   Abraham Waram,
Thomas Crouch,   William Wickes, Jr.,
James Downey,   John Yearley, Jr.
Nicholas Dudley,

Artillery company:

Aquila M. Usselton, Captain,   James Hatcherson,
John Reed, Lieutenant,   Charles Letherbury,
Morgan Brown, Lieutenant,   Edward Nicholson,
Dulaney Apsley,   Philip Raisin, Jr.,
William Apsley, Jr.,   Sirus Raisin,
Edward Cannon,   Henry H. Stewart,
Philip Carroll,   James Usselton,
John Dugan,   William T. Usselton,
Ezekiel Foreman,   William Weaver,
Joseph Gidley,   Matthew Wickes.

Philip Reed was born in Kent County, Maryland, in 1760. He was commissioned lieutenant in the 3d regiment of the Maryland Line, on October 13, 1778, served throughout the War of the Revolution, and particularly distinguished himself in the attack of Stoney Point, July 16, 1779. In recognition of his services at Caulk's Field (or " Moorsfield ") he was made a brigadier-general of Maryland militia. He was United States Senator from Maryland from 1806 to 1813, and was a representative in Congress from 1817 to 1819 and from 1822 to 1823. He died at Huntingfield, Kent County, November 2, 1829. His grave was unmarked until October, 1902, when a memorial slab was placed over his resting place, with appropriate ceremonies.

On Saturday, December 31, 1814, the following resolutions and preamble were read in the House of Delegates of Maryland, on motion of Mr. Hamilton:

" WHEREAS, It has always been considered, not only a generous, but wise policy in all free governments, to evince in the most pointed manner, their high sense of the gallantry and good conduct of such of their citizens as have devoted their time and talents to the public good; and whereas, Col. Philip Reed, did on the thirtieth day of August last, in a masterly and heroic manner, with an inferior force, composed of militia, defeat and repel a marauding party of the enemy in Kent County, killing their leader, Sir Peter Parker, and fourteen of his men, and wounding a number of others, thereby evincing to the enemy and the world, that the arms of freemen, when used in defense of their liberties, their wives, their children, and their firesides, are invincible: and also thereby evincing to his countrymen, that the same statesmen who, in his legislative capacity, of Senator from Maryland, voted against the declaration of war, was the patriot and hero who was amongst the foremost in his military capacity, to step forward and repel an invading foe, when polluting the sovereignty of our soil by their unhallowed tread; therefore,

Resolved, That the governor of this state be, and he is hereby requested, to address, in the name of the State of Maryland, a letter to Colonel Philip Reed, of Kent County, expressive of the very high sense entertained of the intrepidity, gallantry, and good conduct of him, and his brave associates, in repelling the enemy in his attack on the militia of Kent County, on the 30th day of August last, and driving him with confusion and loss to his shipping."

Sir Peter Parker, baronet, son of Rear-Admiral Christopher Parker, was born in 1786. In consideration of his distinguished gallantry in the West Indies, he was made a post captain at the age of nineteen. The attack on Colonel Reed's camp was to have been the last demonstration prior to rejoining the fleet and Sir Peter said " he must have one more frolic with the Yankees before he left them." His body, preserved in Jamaica Rum, together with that of General Ross, who was killed a few days later, was sent in the *Tonnant* to Halifax, and thence to England, and was finally laid in St. Marguerite's Church in London.

Lord Byron, who was his cousin, wrote a poem on the death of Sir Peter Parker; and two other contemporary effusions, but little known, are herewith reproduced:

SIR PETER PETRIFIED.

On the modern Sir Peter Parker's expedition to Kent Island, in Chesapeake Bay, 1814.

> Sir Peter came, with bold intent,
> To persecute the men of Kent,
>   His flag aloft display'd:
> He came to see their pleasant farms,
> But ventured not without his arms
>   To talk with man or maid.
>
> And then the gallant Colonel Reed
> Said, " We must see the man, indeed;
>   He comes, perhaps, in want—
> Who knows but that his stores are out:
> 'Tis hard to dine on mere sour-krout,
>   His water may be scant."
>
> He spoke—but soon the men of Kent
> Discover'd what the errand meant,
>   And some discouraged, said,
> " Sir Peter comes to petrify,
> He points his guns, his colours fly,
>   His men for war array'd!"

Secure as if they owned the land,
Advanced this daring naval band,
  As if in days of peace;
Along the shore they prowling went,
And often ask'd *some friends in Kent,*
  Where dwelt the fattest geese?

The farmers' geese were doom'd to bleed;
But some there were with Colonel Reed,
  Who would not yield assent;
And said, before the geese they take,
Sir Peter must a bargain make
  With us, the boys of Kent."

The Britons march'd along the shore,
Two hundred men, or somewhat more;
  Next, through the woods they stray'd:
The geese, still watchful, as they went,
To save the capitol of Kent
  Their every step betray'd.

The British march'd with loaded gun,
To seize the geese that gabbling run
  About the isle of Kent;
But, what could hardly be believed,
Sir Peter was of life bereaved
  Before he pitched his tent.

Some Kentish lad, to save the geese,
And make their noisy gabbling cease
  Had took a deadly aim:
By Kentish hands Sir Peter fell,
His men retreated with a yell,
  And lost both geese and game!

Now, what I say, I say with grief,
That such a knight, or such a chief,
  On such an errand died!
When men of worth their lives expose
For little things, where little grows,
They make the very geese their foes;
  The geese his fall deride:

And, sure, they laugh, if laugh they can,
To see a star and garter'd man
For life of goose expose his own,
And bite the dust with many a groan;
  "Alas!" a gander cried,
  "Behold, (said he) a man of fame
Who all the way from England came
No more than just to get the name
  Of *Peter Petrified.*"

PHILIP FRENEAU.

SIR PETER PARKER.

Tune—"Maggy Lauder."

By CHARLES L. S. JONES.

Let others sing, whilst loudly ring
  The valleys to their measures,
Of love, or wine, or sports divine,
  Made vocal by their pleasures;
    Be mine the theme,
    No fancied dream
  Of visionary barker;
    The warlike cheer,
    And welcome here,
  Of brave Sir Peter Parker.

Let not the muse her strains refuse,
  Accordant to my metre,
Whilst I declare the exploits rare
  Of valiant-hearted Peter;
    Nor deem me wrong
    To raise the song—
  Of praise I am no sharker;
    But let my shell
    The wonders tell
  Of brave Sir Peter Parker.

He oft would boast to rule the roast
  Upon the briny ocean;
And scold and jeer with glorious cheer,
  Expecting high promotion:
    Whilst from his fun
    The Yankees run,

As fearful of a jeering;
　Lest like Van Tromp
　Their hides he'd thump,
His broom at mast-head rearing.

Long had he sail'd, and nothing hail'd,
　As worthy of a winner;
So did desire, to ease his ire,
　A Baltimorean dinner;
　　And in he sent
　　With that intent
His compliments, high sounding,
　　Whilst from on board,
　　His thunders roar'd,
Their Yankee souls astounding.

But not to be behind in glee,
　Or hospitable freedom,
They answer sent, he might have twent—
　Y dinners if he'd need them;
　　O glorious feast,
　　For prince, or priest,
'Twould cure the gout or cholic;
　　Sir Peter swore,
　　He ne'er, before,
Saw such a Yankee frolic.

But most his tongue thy praises rung,
　Jamaica's lively liquor;
And swore, 'twas fit to enliven the wit
　Of laymen or of vicar:
　　So not in fun
　　To be outdone,
They sent this gallant sparker,
　　Well seasoned, home,
　　In his favourite rum,
The far-famed Peter Parker.

CHAPTER VIII

NORTH POINT AND BALTIMORE

During the operations of the British squadron in the Chesapeake, in the years 1813-14, a permanent encampment was made on Tangier Island, which became the base of operations for their numerous marauding expeditions. One of the inhabitants of Tangier, at this period, was the Reverend Joshua Thomas, a rather illiterate Methodist preacher, who has left some interesting notes of the British occupation of that place.[1]

On the arrival of the British squadron, in Tangier Harbor, about two hundred men were landed and set to work on the lower beach. While preparing the grounds for the encampment, some trees in what was known as the Camp Meeting Ground were felled, but on the personal application of the " Parson " to Admiral Cockburn, the remainder of the grove was spared.

Two forts were erected a little to the south of the camp ground, about three hundred yards apart. The tents for the army were pitched in a semi-circle, extending about half way round on the north side of the island, and a number of buildings for the accomodation of the officers were erected. Thomas became on very friendly terms with the invaders (all the inhabitants were considered prisoners of war), and he reports that the British treated the island people with " high-toned honor and generosity." What they needed in the way of provisions, they paid for liberally, and small boats or vessels taken from the poor people, were invariably returned on application to the admiral.

Towards the close of the summer of 1814 it became apparent that some important movement was on foot. Preparations began both on shore and through the fleet in the harbor. Some of the officers informed Thomas that they intended to take Baltimore. Before they left Tangier it was arranged that Thomas should

---

[1] Wallace, Adam, The Parson of the Islands: a biography of the Rev. Joshua Thomas. Phila., 1861.

hold a religious service for the army, on the last Sunday of their stay in camp. " Early that morning the flags were hoisted, the drums beat, every preparation was made for a full turnout. Boats were plying from the ships to the shore, and bands of music were playing on board. At the hour appointed the soldiers were all drawn up in solid columns, about twelve thousand men, under the pines of the old camp ground which faced the open space in the center of their tents. I stood on a little platform erected at the end of the camp nearest the shore, all the men facing me with their hats off and held by the right hand under the left arm . . . .

" I warned them of the danger and distress they would bring upon themselves and others by going to Baltimore with the object they had in view. I told them of the great wickedness of war and that God said ' Thou shalt not kill.' If you do, He will judge you at the last day; or before then, He will cause you to 'perish by the sword.' I told them it was given me from the Almighty that they *could not* take Baltimore, and would not succeed in their expedition. I exhorted them to prepare for death, for many of them would in all likelihood die soon, and I should see them no more till we met at the sound of the great trumpet before our final Judge."

After the service many stepped up to the Parson and thanked him for his faithful warnings, and said they hoped it would not go so hard with them as he had foretold. He shook his head and said he felt that many that day had received their last call.

The encampment on Tangier was not abandoned until February, 1815, when the news of peace was received. That part of the island where the camp ground stood has long since been washed away and is now covered by four or more feet of water.

On the 6th of September, a flag of truce having come from Baltimore, all was bustle and alacrity on board the British squadron. The *Royal Oak* and troop ships stood out of the Patuxent, and Admiral Cochrane, quitting his anchorage off Tangier Island, proceeded with the remainder of the fleet up the bay to North Point, at the mouth of the Patapsco River. On the 10th and 11th the fleet anchored; and by noon, on the 12th, the whole of the troops, marines of the fleet, black colonial marines and seamen, numbering altogether 3270[2] rank and file, had disembarked at North Point.

In the meanwhile the citizens of Baltimore had not been idle. Up to this time half a million dollars subscribed by citizens, had been spent for the defense of the city, under the direction of Mayor Edward Johnson, and a committee of safety composed of James Mosher, Luke Tiernan, Henry Payson, Dr. J. C. White, James A. Buchanan, Samuel Sterrett and Thorndike Chase. A chain of fortifications to the east of the city, extended from the Patapsco, west of Harris' Creek to what is now Greenmount Cemetery. The crest of Loudenslager's Hill was fortified, and at numerous points a second line of breastworks was constructed and barricades were placed between the earthworks.

In his official report, made after the battle, Commodore Rogers, who had general command of the batteries, gave the following statement as to the respective batteries and the forces stationed therein:

" In the general distribution of the forces employed in the defence of Baltimore, with the concurrence of the commanding general, I stationed Lieutenant Gamble, first of the *Guerriere,* with about one hundred seamen, in command of a seven-gun battery, on the line between the roads leading from Philadelphia and Sparrows Point.

"Sailing Master De La Zouch, of the *Erie,* and Midshipman Field, of the *Guerriere,* with twenty seamen, in command of a two-gun battery, fronting the road leading from Sparrow's Point.

" Sailing Master Ramage, of the *Guerriere,* with twenty seamen, in command of a five-gun battery, to the right of the Sparrow's Point road.

" And Midshipman Salter, with twelve seamen, in command of a one-gun battery, a little to the right of Mr. Ramage.

" Lieutenant Kuhn, with the detachment of marines belonging to the *Guerriere,* was posted in the entrenchment between the batteries occupied by Lieutenant Gamble and Sailing Master Ramage.

"Lieutenant Newcomb, third of the *Guerriere,* with eighty seamen, occupied Fort Covington, on the Ferry Branch, a little below Spring Gardens.

[2] James, 6: 188

"Sailing Master Webster, of the flotilla, with fifty seamen of that corps, occupied a six-gun battery on the Ferry Branch known by the name of Babcock.

"Lieutenant Frazier, of the flotilla, with forty-five seamen of the same corps, occupied a three-gun battery near the Lazaretto.

"And Lieutenant Rutter, the senior officer of the flotilla, in command of all the barges, which were moored at the entrance of the passage between the Lazaretto and Fort McHenry, in the left wing of the water battery, at which was stationed Sailing Master Rodman, and fifty-four seamen of the flotilla." [3]

On the 23d of August, the day of the Bladensburg fight, the mayor convened a meeting of citizens in the council chamber, when a Committee of Vigilance and Safety was formed. The minutes of this committee, of which the following is (in part) a verbatim transcript, are now in the possession of the Maryland Historical Society,[4] and have never before been published.

BALTIMORE, 24th August, 1814.

In conformity to the recommendation and resolves of a meeting of a number of citizens convened by the Mayor at the Council Chamber on the 23rd instant. Meetings were held in the different wards at 10 o'clock yesterday morning, when the following persons were duly elected, in each ward, to form a general Committee of Vigilance and Safety during the present time of alarm, to wit:

1st Ward.

Henry Stouffer,
Solomon Etting,
Elias Ellicott,
Wm. Jessup.

Elias Ellicott, Chairman, and
Solomon Etting, Sec't. of the
meeting.

2d Ward.

Samuel Hollingsworth,
Benjamin Berry,
Henry Payson.

Henry Payson, Chairman.
A. S. Schwartz, Sec't.

[3] *Niles' Register,* v. 7, supplement, p. 156.
[4] Presented by Mr. William Bowly Wilson.

3d Ward.

William Lorman,
James A. Buchanan,
William Wilson.

James Calhoun, Chairman.
John Hollins, Sec't.

4th Ward.

William Patterson,
Adam Fonerden,
James Wilson.

Jacob Myers, Chairman.
Joshua Jones, Sec't.

5th Ward.

Joseph Jamison,
Cumberland Dugan,
William Camp.

Cumberland Dugan, Chairman.
George Franciscus, Sec't.

6th Ward.

James Armstrong,
James Taylor,
Peter Bond.

James Taylor, Chairman.
James Wilson, Sec't.

7th Ward.

Robert Stewart,
Frederick Schaffer,
Richard Stevens.

Robert Stewart, Chairman.
William B. Barney, Sec't.

8th Ward.

Hezekiah Waters,
David Burke,
George Woelpert.

Hezekiah Waters, Chairman.
John Snyder, Sec't.

Eastern Precincts.

Hermanus Alricks,
John Kelso,
Richard Frisby.

Hermanus Alricks, Chairman.
Richard Frisby, Sect'y.

Western Precincts.

Col. John E. Howard,
George Warner,
Theoderick Bland.

Emanuel Kent, Chairman.
Theoderick Bland, Sec't.

BALTIMORE, 24th August, 1814.

At a meeting of the Committee of Vigilance and Safety elected from the several wards and each of the Precincts of the City of Baltimore held at the Council Chamber at 5 o'clock P. M. this day in pursuance of public notice when Edward Johnson, Esq. the Mayor, being called to the chair, and Theoderick Bland, Esq. appointed Secretary. The Mayor in a short address opened to the Committee the general nature and objects of the business proposed to be submitted to their consideration.

On motion, *Resolved* that Mr. Buchanan, Mr. Bland and Mr. Payson be a committee to prepare an address to the citizens, which shall be submitted to this committee for their approbation at their next meeting.

Resolved, That this committee meet every day at 10 o'clock A. M. in the Council Chamber.

The Committee then adjourned.

BALTIMORE, 25th August, 1814.

The Committee of Vigilance and Safety met pursuant to adjournment—when the proceedings of yesterday were read.

The Committee charged with the drafting of an address to the Citizens made a report which was ordered to lie on the table.

The following resolutions were then moved and adopted:

1. *Resolved,* That all good citizens be and they are hereby requested to give to this committee any information they may have relative to suspected persons or places and that the members of this committee be and they are hereby required to appoint such person or persons as they may think proper in each ward and precinct to search suspected persons and places; and the persons so appointed shall report to this committee any information that may be obtained.

2. *Resolved,* That the owners of vessels now moored and made fast at or near the wharves of the City are hereby directed to remove their vessels to some place below Harris' Creek for the greater security.

3. *Resolved,* That all deserters from the enemy shall during the present time of alarm be confined to the gaol and gaol yard, where their situation shall be made as comfortable as the nature of

things will admit; that any extra expense for that purpose shall be provided for by this committee, and that Mr. Frisby, Mr. Kelso and Mr. Bland be and they are hereby appointed to adjust with the gaoler the amount of such extra expense and to report to this committee.

4. WHEREAS, It has been communicated to this committee by Brig. Genl. Stricker, Com. Perry, Maj. Armstead and Capt. Spence in person that it is their wish that Maj. Genl. Smith be requested to take the command of the forces which may be called into service for the defence of the city, therefore,

Resolved, That Col. John E. Howard, Mr. Frisby and Mr. Stewart be appointed to wait on Maj. Genl. Smith and to communicate to him the information this committee have received, to state that they unanimously concur with the same, and to request that he would at this important crisis take upon himself the command of the forces that may be called out for the defence of our city.

5. *Resolved,* That the gentlemen named in the foregoing resolution wait on Maj. Genl. Smith and report his answer to this committee forthwith.

The gentlemen who were so appointed accordingly retired and after a short time reported that Maj. Genl. Smith was at this time willing and would take upon himself the command of the forces that might be called out for the defence of the city, but that he wished to be sanctioned in so doing by the Executive of this State and that his powers might be extended, whereupon it was,

6. *Resolved,* That Mr. Buchanan, Mr. Bland and Mr. Frisby be and they are hereby appointed to address a letter to the Governor of this State, requesting him to invest Maj. Genl. Smith with powers in every respect commensurate to the present exigency, which shall be forwarded immediately by express; and that they report to this committee at their next meeting.

The committee then adjourned.

BALTIMORE, 26th August, 1814.

The Committee of Vigilance and Safety met according to adjournment. The proceedings of yesterday were read and the first, second, and fourth resolutions and the names of this committee were ordered to be published. Mr. Bland from the committee reported that the gaoler had agreed to receive, hold and maintain in a comfortable manner any deserters that might be committed to him for the sum of twenty-five cents per day.

On motion it was resolved that four seamen who have presented themselves as deserters from the enemy, be placed under the care of a constable and at the expense of this committee conveyed beyond the Susquehanna, where there shall be given to each out of the funds of the committee, the sum of two dollars.

2. *Resolved,* That Mr. Daniel Conner be and he is hereby requested to place himself in the service of the committee for a compensation to be hereafter agreed upon; and that it be his duty, vigilantly to search for all suspected strangers or other persons, and in a discreet exercise of this authority, to report such persons to, or bring them before the mayor.

3. *Resolved,* That the Mayor be and he is hereby authorized and directed to employ an additional watch, to guard the city and precincts, and that the expense be paid out of the funds of the committee of Vigilance and Safety; and that the city commissioner and the companies of the Eastern and Western precincts be requested to aid him in the execution thereof.

4. WHEREAS in the present exigency money will be wanted for various purposes, therefore,

Resolved, That the inhabitants of the city and precincts be and they are hereby invited to contribute thereto by calling at the Mayor's office, who will receive such contributions, and will publish the names of the contributors and the sums by them severally given, to be appropriated to such objects as the committee of Vigilance and Safety may authorize and direct.

Ordered that the third and fourth of the foregoing resolutions be published.

Mr. Buchanan from the committee appointed to address a letter to the Governor reported that they had forwarded a letter by express a copy of which was read and approved. A letter from the Governor in answer to that which was addressed to him from the committee respecting Maj. Gen'l. Smith's command was received and read. The committee then adjourned.

BALTIMORE, 27th August, 1814.

The committee of Vigilance and Safety met pursuant to adjournment. The proceedings of yesterday were read.

On motion the following resolutions were adopted to wit:

WHEREAS, The commanding officer has requested the aid of the citizens, in the erection of works for the defense of the city, and the committee of Vigilance and Safety having full confidence in the patriotism of their fellow citizens, have agreed on the following organization for the purpose of complying with the request of the Major General.

The inhabitants of the city and precincts are called on to deposit at the Court House in the third ward, Centre Market in the fifth ward, Riding school in the seventh ward, Market House Fells' Point, and take with them to the place required all wheelbarrows, pick-axes, spares and shovels that they can procure.

That the city and precincts be divided into four sections, the first section to consist of the Eastern precincts and the eighth ward, the second to comprise the 5th, 6th, and 7th, wards, and the third to comprise the 2d, 3d, and 4th, wards, and the fourth to comprise the 1st ward and the Western precincts.

That the exempts from militia duty and the free people of colour, of the first district, consisting of the 8th ward and the Eastern Precincts, assemble tomorrow, Sunday morning, at 6 o'clock, at Hampstead Hill, with provisions for the day, and that Arthur Mitchell, Daniel Conn, Henry Pennington, John Chalmers, William Starr, Thomas Weary, Henry Harwood, and Philip Cunmiller, be charged with the superintendence during the day.

That the second district, comprising the 5th, 6th, and 7th wards assemble at Myers Garden on Monday morning under the superintendence of William Parks, Capt. Watts, Ludwick Herring, William Ross, William Carman, Daniel Howland, Caleb Ernest and James Hutton.

That those of the third district comprising the 2d, 3d and 4th wards assemble at Washington Square on Tuesday morning, under the superintendence of Frederick Leypold, William McClary, John McKim, Jr., Henry Schroeder, Alexander McDonald, Eli Hewitt, Peter Gold and Alexander Russell.

That those of the fourth district comprising the 1st ward and Western precincts assemble at the intersection of Eutaw and Market streets on Wednesday under the superintendence of William W. Taylor, William Jessup, Edward Harris, George Decker, William Hawkins, Isaac Philips, William Jones and John Hignet.

The owners of slaves are requested to send them to work on the days assigned in the several districts. Such of our patriotic fellow citizens of the country or elsewhere as are disposed to aid in the common defense are invited to partake in the duties now required, on such days as may be most convenient to them. Ordered that the foregoing resolution be published.

Ordered, That John Kelso, George Woelpert, Robert Stewart, Peter Bond, William Camp, Adam Fonerden, William Lorman, Benjamin Berry, Henry Stouffer and George Warner, members of the committee be and they are hereby requested to give notice to the persons appointed to carry into effect the foregoing resolution, in the several districts and to aid them with their advice and assistance.

Ordered, That Adam Fonerden, James Wilson, and James Armstrong be and they are hereby appointed as a standing committee of accounts. The committee then adjourned.

BALTIMORE, 28th August, 1814.

The committee of Vigilance and Safety met pursuant to adjournment. The proceedings of yesterday were read.

The committee were informed by a letter from Elias Ellicott that as his religious principles, (to wit, those of a quaker) would not permit him to interfere in military affairs, he therefore resigned his station as a member of this committee.

On motion *resolved,* That this committee will fill up all vacancies occasioned in its own body by resignation or otherwise.

Resolved, That Mr. William Jessup be and he is hereby appointed a member of this committee to fill the vacancy occasioned by the resignation of Elias Ellicott.

Resolved, That Mr. Etting, Mr. Taylor and Capt. Stevens be and they are hereby appointed to provide a hospital or suitable accommodation for the sick and wounded of the forces that are or may be called out for the defense of the city and to report to this committee at their next meeting. The committee then adjourned.

BALTIMORE, 29th August, 1814.

The committee of Vigilance and Safety met pursuant to adjournment. The proceedings of yesterday were read.

On motion, *Resolved,* That Samuel Hollingsworth, Adam Fonerden, Cumberland Dugan and Joseph Jamison or any three of them with the Mayor, be and they are hereby appointed to examine all deserters from the enemy that may be apprehended and brought before them and to report to this committee.

The members appointed to provide quarters for the sick and wounded made report that they obtained the use of the public hospital from Doctors McKenzie and Smythe in which there were accomodations for about one thousand and that the compensation for the same was to be such as this committee should hereafter deem reasonable.

Mr. Jessups who was appointed to fill the vacancy occasioned by the resignation of Mr. Ellicott appeared and took his seat as a member.

Resolved, That it be and is hereby most earnestly recommended to the good people of the State of Maryland to be extremely circumspect in their communications respecting the movements of the enemy and our preparations and disposition to resist him. In a particular manner they are exhorted to abstain from the expression of any opinions calculated to inspire a belief that the people of Baltimore will be found wanting in what is due to themselves. The committee are urged to this measure by perceiving as they do, with indignation, that letters degrading to our character have appeared in some of the distant papers; the writers and publishers of such must be alike objects of contempt to all who have any attachment for their country.

Ordered, That the foregoing resolution be published immediately.

Resolved, That Mr. Payson, Mr. Lorman and Mr. James Wilson be and they are hereby appointed to wait on Maj. Genl. Smith and inform him that from the zeal manifested by our fellow citizens in the erection of works of defense as directed, they feel great pleasure in assuring him that, if he should deem it necessary to order the extension of those or the erection of other works, that they will be promptly undertaken. And that they be further instructed to inform the Major General that in whatever way the services of the committee of Vigilance and Safety can be useful in providing for the comforts of their patriotic fellow citizens in arms, they will cheerfully undertake the same; and that they report to this committee at their next meeting. The committee then adjourned.

BALTIMORE, 30th August, 1814.

The committee of Vigilance and Safety met pursuant to adjournment. The proceedings of yesterday were read.

On Motion, *Resolved,* That the resolution passed by this committee on the 25th of this month relative to deserters from the enemy be and the same is hereby repealed.

Resolved, That George Warner, Solomon Etting, William Jessup, David Burke and George Woelper be and they are hereby appointed a committee to wait on the Quarter-master General and tender to him their aid and that of this committee in providing suitable accommodations for our fellow citizens in arms, who are assembling for the common defense.

Resolved, That it be the particular and permanent duty of the above named committee diligently to enquire into the wants of the troops on their arrival and that they make known the same from time to time to this committee and to those authorities in the staff department who are competent to supplying the same.

WHEREAS, The committee of Vigilance and safety have received information from a reputable source that certain individuals are in the constant habit of making use of very improper and intemperate expressions, calculated to produce discussion, and to defeat the preparations making for the defense of our city, therefore

Resolved, That Richard Frisby, William Camp and Peter Bond be and they are hereby appointed to investigate cases of this kind and make an immediate report to this board.

On motion the following address and appeal to our fellow citizens of the country was adopted, to wit,

The ardour with which our fellow citizens in arms of this and the neighbouring States are hastening to the defense of our city affords the strongest evidence of the patriotism of our yeomanry and inspires the committee with an earnest desire to make their situation here perfectly comfortable. The committee reposes unlimited confidence in the disposition of the good people in this and the neighboring states who are not employed in a military capacity to aid in this laudable purpose and they therefore confidently call upon them individually and collectively to bring to the city *for sale* such supplies as may contribute to the comfort of those to whom, under Providence, the safety of this city is confided. The committee are authorized by the Major General to assure those who visit our city with the laudable intention of contributing to the comforts of its brave defenders, that they shall be permitted to transact their business free from the danger of impressment to their wagons, carts or horses or of any species of interruption to themselves, and that if there be any cause of complaint the same shall be promptly removed on application to this committee. Editors of newspapers are requested to give this publicity.

Ordered, That the foregoing address be published immediately, printed in handbills and disseminated as widely as possible.

WHEREAS, The commanding officer has requested the *further* aid of the citizens in completing the works already so far advanced; and in erecting others for the defense of the city; and the committee of Vigilance and Safety having full confidence in the patriotism of their fellow citizens, therefore

Resolved, That the city and precincts be divided into four districts, and that the exempts from militia duty and the free people of color of the first district, consisting of the 8th ward and Eastern precincts, be and they are hereby requested to assemble on Thursday next, and that Arthur Mitchell, Daniel Conn, Henry Pennington, John Chalmers, William Starr, Thomas Weary, Henry Harwood, Philip Cunmiller, John Price, Bazil Smith, John Gracy, John Schunck, John Smith, and Calvin Cooper, be charged with the superintendence during the day.

That those of the second district, comprising the 5th, 6th, and 7th wards, assemble on Friday next, under the superintendence of William Parks, Capt. Watts, Ludwick Herring, William Ross, William Carman, Caleb Arnest, Jacob Miller, Robert Fisher, John Gross, James Hutton and George Auckerman.

That those of the third district comprising the 2d, 3rd, and 4th wards assemble on Saturday next under the superintendence of Frederick Leypold, William McClary, John McKim, Jr., Henry Schroeder, Alexander McDonald, Eli Hewitt, Peter Gold and Alexander Russell; and

That those of the fourth district, comprising the first ward and western precincts, assemble on Sunday next, under the superintendence of William W. Taylor, William Jessup, Edward Harris, George Decker, William Hawkins, Isaac Philips, William Jones, John Hignet, Charles Bohn, Alexander Irvine, Ferdinando Gourdon and Jonas Clopham.

That John Kelso, George Woelpert, Robert Stewart, Peter Bond, William Camp, Adam Fonerden,. William Lorman, Benjamin Berry, Henry Stouffer and George Warner, members of this committee be and they are hereby requested to give notice to the persons appointed as superintendents in their several districts, and to aid them with their advice and assistance.

The owners of slaves are requested to send them to work on the days assigned to the several districts, and such of our patriotic fellow citizens of the country, or elsewhere as are disposed to aid in the common defense are invited to partake in the further duties now required on such days as may be most convenient.

The committee then adjourned.

BALTIMORE, August 31, 1814.

The committee of Vigilance and Safety met pursuant to adjournment. The proceedings of yesterday were read.

Mr. Warner from the committee appointed to wait on the Quarter-master General reported that they had done so and acquainted him with the readiness of this committee to cooperate in any way for the common good.

Mr. Hollingsworth from the committee appointed to examine deserters from the enemy reported that they had examined three of whom they entertained no apprehensions but submitted to this committee for their consideration the propriety of sending such persons, at least some distance into the country.

Resolved, That the chairman of this committee be and he is hereby authorized and requested to give to each of the above mentioned deserters five dollars from the funds of this committee, a passport, and order them to go out of the State of Maryland.

Ordered, That the letter from the Major-General to this committee respecting a deposit in the banks on loan be and the same is hereby referred to Mr. William Wilson, Mr. Waters and Mr. Payson, with power, and a request to communicate with the other Presidents and directors of banks and to report to this committee at its next meeting.

This committee were informed by their chairman that Mr. Robert C. Long with thirty carpenters in his employ had tendered their services to this committee whenever called on and in whatever manner they might be required.

WHEREAS, The duties imposed on this committee, engrossing much of their attention, and it being necessary that immediate steps be taken to raise a *Committee of Relief* whose duty it shall be, to solicit subscriptions in money and necessaries for the relief of the poor and distressed, more particularly to be applied to the aid and support of families whose distress is immediately occasioned by the calling off the chief supporters of their families on public service; therefore:

Resolved, That James Ellicott, William W. Taylor, Elisha Tyson, Richard H. Jones, Levin Wethered, Luke Tiernan, William Riley, James Mosher, Joseph Townsend, Peter Diffenderfer, William Brown, Daniel Diffenderfer, William Trimble, William Mundle, William Proctor and John Ogden, be and they are hereby appointed a *Committee of Relief,* requiring them in such manner as they shall think proper to adopt, to solicit subscriptions in money or other necessary supplies for the poor, and that they appoint a committee or committees, to ascertain by the best possible means, the situation and wants of the families of those called out on the present emergency, as well as all others who may probably need assistance, and that they distribute from time to time, with judicious care, such aid and comforts as they shall think proper. The committee then adjourned.

[The minutes of September 1 to 10 are epitomized, but all the essential facts are set out.]

On the 1st of September the case of William Presbury, a justice of the peace at Fells Point, accused of disloyalty was considered, and the governor was requested to remove the offender from office. General Smith reported that orders had been received from the War Department for the removal of some 18-pounder guns on travelling carriages. The guns were the property of the United States, the carriages of the city of Baltimore and as the committee deemed the guns to be indispensably necessary for the defence of the city, they ordered that the carriages be retained and that a remonstrance against the removal of the guns be sent to the War Department.

On the second a further detail of workmen was called out to work on the defences on Camp Look Out Hill; a committee was appointed to provide hospital accommodations for the sick and wounded; money was appropriated for regimental music and Mr. Beatty was ordered to set up and prepare for service, the guns in his care.

On the third a contract was made with Francis W. Bolgiano to bake bread for the troops. The committee on hospital reported that they had appointed Dr. Colin McKenzie hospital surgeon and had authorized him to appoint Doctors James Middleton, Horatio Jamison, William Turner, George Frick and Charles Richardson, assistants, who were to be called into the hospital as needed.

A bridge of scows was ordered to be built from Patterson's Wharf, Fells Point to the nearest land on the opposite shore, and a note is inserted facing the proceedings of the 5th, showing that thirty scows were in service from September 5 until November 30. At this meeting a further call for laborers was made and the city was divided into two districts each of which was placed in charge of a committee of superintendents.

On the 5th a horse was procured for Captain Babcock, one of the engineers in charge of the works; orders were issued for the erection of breast works on the North Point road, the laborers to be hired and furnished with provisions and other

11

necessaries—the other necessaries being apparently liquor. The superintendent was authorized to hire 150 men for work at the fort at not more than a dollar per day, the laborers to furnish their own provisions and liquors. Carpenters and mechanics were allowed a dollar and a quarter a day, but were also required to provide themselves with victuals and drink.

On the 7th the resolutions in regard to the laborers and mechanics were rescinded, and the superintendent authorized to hire men on such terms as he thought best. On the 9th twenty-five dollars was voted to Edward Miles for his trouble in assisting and bringing home Charles Ernest, a soldier, who was wounded in the Battle of Bladensburg.

On the 10th the following address was moved and assented to:

" Those who feel interested in the safety of Baltimore and who have omitted to subscribe to the fund which is placed at the disposal of this committee, are respectfully reminded that the subscription paper is still open at the Mayor's office; that the expenses to be defrayed by the committee are unavoidably large and are for objects deemed by the military authorities indispensable to our safety.

" The committee acknowledge with thanks the liberality of those who have contributed so freely to this important fund, but they deem it their duty to state that although the subscriptions have been liberal, yet that from estimates it is apprehended they will be inadequate to our wants, and that the subscription list comprises only about five hundred names.

" The committee are preparing for publication an alphabetical list of those who have aided them with their funds and that they may appear as speedily and be as respectable as possible, they beg their countrymen to be prompt in their subscriptions."

On the 10th of September the following notice appeared in *Niles' Register:* " At the recommendation of the Committee of Vigilance and Safety the people commenced their labors to fortify the city on Sunday, the 27th ultimo. The work done demonstrates their power and zeal, to the astonishment of all who behold it. Baltimore has long been remarkable for the patriotism and liberal spirit of her citizens; and her high character for these qualities is fully maintained by the free offering of *men* and *money* for the purposes of defence. In the meantime, volunteers and militia from the adjacent parts of Maryland, Pennsylvania and Virginia have flocked in to our aid. We are restrained by the request of the Committee of Vigilance from mentioning any particulars, but the honorable record shall yet be made. We restrain the desire to notice these things because enjoined by the committee, for we are very sure the enemy is apprised of almost everything that is transacted here."

On Sunday, September 11, the news was received of the arrival of the enemy's squadron off North Point. The intelligence was announced to the citizens by the firing of three alarm guns from the courthouse green. When the signal guns were fired and the bells were rung to call the militia to arms, services were in progress in many churches. The congregations were immediately dismissed and the wildest excitement and confusion prevailed. At the Light Street Methodist Church, the Reverend Jacob Gruber prayed that " The Lord would bless King George, convert him, and take him to heaven as we want no more of him." At the Wilke's Street Methodist Church a number of defenders were in attendance, with arms stacked in front of the church, when the preacher suddenly closed the Bible and said " My brethren and friends, the alarm guns have just fired. The British are approaching, and commending you to God and the word of His Grace, I pronounce the benediction, and may the God of battles accompany you." The Reverend John Glendy stood on the steps of his residence on Baltimore street, and, as the soldiers passed, he blessed them and prayed for their safety and success.

Major-General Samuel Smith, who had been selected to command all the forces gathered for the defence of the city, decided to send out a reconnoitering party, the command of which was entrusted to General John Stricker, his brigade consisting almost entirely of Baltimore militia. About three o'clock in the afternoon he marched with his brigade, out Baltimore street to the Philadelphia road. His force consisted of five hundred and fifty of the 5th regiment, under Lieutenant-Colonel Joseph Sterrett; six hundred and twenty of the 6th, under Lieutenant-Colonel William McDonald; five hundred of the 27th under Lieutenant-Colonel Kennedy Long; four hundred and fifty of the 39th, under

Lieutenant-Colonel Benjamin Fowler; seven hundred of the 51st, under Lieutenant-Colonel Henry Amey; one hundred and fifty riflemen under Captain William B. Dyer; one hundred and forty cavalry under Lieutenant-Colonel James Biays; and the Union artillery of seventy-five men, with six 4-pounders, under Captain John Montgomery, an aggregate of three thousand, one hundred and eighty-five effective men.

The route of the march was by the old Philadelphia road to Long Log lane (now the North Point road), and thence to the Methodist meeting house near the head of Bear Creek, seven miles from the city. Here the troops bivouacked for the night, with the exception of the riflemen who were posted along the skirts of a pine wood near a blacksmith's shop, two miles further on; while the cavalry was pushed still further on and stationed near Gorsuch's farm, with orders to place videttes in the vicinity of the enemy and to report promptly to headquarters every movement of the enemy.

Again taking up Gleig's narrative:

"On the 11th we came in sight of the headland where it was designed to land the troops. It was a promontory washed by the Patapsco on one side, and a curvature of the bay itself on the other. It was determined to land here, rather than to ascend the river, because the Patapsco, though broad, is far from deep. It is, in fact, too shallow to admit a line-of-battle ship; and, as no one could guess what impediments might be thrown in the way to obstruct the navigation, prudence forbade that five thousand men should be entrusted to the convoy of the smaller vessels alone. Besides the distance from the point to Baltimore did not exceed fourteen or fifteen miles, a space which might easily be traversed in a day.

"But while the land forces moved in this direction upon Baltimore, it was resolved that the frigates and bomb-ships should endeavor to force their way through every obstacle, and to obtain possession of the navigation of the river, so as, if possible, to cooperate with the army by bombarding the place from the water. A frigate was accordingly dispatched to try the depth, and to take soundings of the channel, whilst the remainder of the fleet came to an anchor off the point. In the meantime all was again bustle and preparation on board the troop-ships and transports. Three days' provisions were cooked, as before, and given to the men; and as we were now to carry everything by a *coup-de-main*, twenty rounds of ammunition were added to the sixty with which soldiers are usually loaded; whilst a smaller quantity of other baggage was directed to be taken on shore. A blanket, with a spare shirt and pair of shoes, was considered enough for each man on an expedition of so rapid a nature; whilst brushes and other articles of that description were divided between comrades, one carrying what would suffice for both. Thus the additional load of twenty cartridges was more than counterbalanced by the clothing and necessaries left behind.

" It was dusk when we reached the anchorage, consequently no landing could take place before the morrow. But as the boats were ordered to be in readiness at dawn, every man slept in his clothes, that he might be prepared to start at a moment's warning . . . . At three o'clock in the morning every ship in the fleet began to lower her boats, and the soldiers were roused from their slumbers . . . . It was seven o'clock before the whole army was disembarked in order for marching. The light brigade, now commanded by Major Jones of the 4th regiment, led the advance; then followed the artillery, amounting to six field-pieces and two howitzers, all of them drawn by horses; next came the second brigade, then the sailors, and last of all the third brigade.

" The column being put in motion, advanced, without the occurrence of any incident deserving of notice, for about an hour, when it arrived at a piece of ground which appeared as if it had been lately in possession of the enemy. It was a narrow neck of land, confined between the river on one side, and the head of a creek on the other, measuring, perhaps, a mile across. From the river to the creek a breastwork had been begun, and was partly completed. In front of it there were lines drawn, apparently for the purpose of marking out the width of a ditch; in some places the ditch itself was dug, and the commencement of what resembled an enfilading battery in the centre, showed that a considerable degree of science had been displayed in the choice of this spot as a military position. Both flanks were completely protected, not only by water, but by a thick wood, while a gentle eminence in the very middle of the line offered the most desirable situation for the projecting battery which had been begun. In its present state, however, it was untenable, unless by a force as able to attack as to defend; consequently the Americans, who acted solely on the defensive, did wisely in choosing another.

"But the aspect of the ground was such as led us to conclude that the enemy could not be very distant. The troops were accordingly halted, that the rear might be well up, and the men fresh and ready for action. Whilst this was done part of the flank patrol came in bringing with them three light-horsemen as prisoners. These were young gentlemen belonging to a corps of volunteers, furnished by the town of Baltimore, who had been sent out to watch our motions and convey intelligence to the American general. Being but little accustomed to such service, they had suffered themselves to be surprised, and instead of reporting to their own general as to the number and dispositions of their adversaries, they were now catechized by General Ross respecting the strength and preparations of their friends. From them we learned that a force of no less than twenty thousand men was embodied for the defense of Baltimore; but as the accounts of prisoners are generally over-rated, we took it for granted that they made their report only to intimidate.[5]

[5] A picket guard composed of William B. Buchanan, James Gittings, and Richard Dorsey, stationed in front of the American forces, chanced to become separated from their friends, with the British army between them. Upon attempting to make their way back, they found the woods full of the enemy, and coming upon a detachment of troops, were ordered to surrender. They refused and leaping their horses over the fences, escaped. Nearing a church they saw a negro going to a spring and offered him five dollars to show them the road to Baltimore. He promised that he would, as soon as he performed a service for some gentlemen and soon returned followed by British soldiers, who covered them with their muskets and forced them to surrender. Mr. Buchanan with great difficulty prevented Mr. Gittings from shooting the negro who had betrayed them. The prisoners were taken before General Ross, to whom they gave an exaggerated account of the strength of the American forces. 'But they are mainly militia I presume' observed General Ross. They replied in the affirmative and General Ross said that he would take Baltimore 'if it rains militia.'" *Oration of H. Clay Dallam, 1878.*

"Having rested for the space of an hour, we again moved forward, but had not proceeded above a mile when a sharp fire of musketry was heard in front, and shortly afterwards a mounted officer came galloping to the rear, who desired us to quicken our pace, for that the advance guard was engaged. At this intelligence the ranks were closed, and the troops advanced at a brisk rate, and in profound silence. The firing still continued, though from its running and irregular sound, it promised little else than a skirmish; but whether it was kept up by detached parties alone, or by the outposts of a regular army, we could not tell, because from the quantity of wood with which the country abounded, and the total absence of all hills or eminences, it was impossible to discern what was going on at the distance of half a mile from the spot where we stood.

"We were already drawing near to the scene of action, when another officer came at full speed towards us, with horror and dismay in his countenance, and calling loudly for a surgeon. Every man felt within himself that all was not right, though none was willing to believe the whispers of his own terror. But what at first we would not guess at, because we dreaded it so much, was soon realized; for the aide-de-camp had scarcely passed, when the general's horse, without its rider, and with the saddle and housings stained with blood, came plunging onwards. In a few moments we reached the ground where the skirmishing had taken place, and beheld General Ross laid by the side of the road, under a canopy of blankets, and apparently in the agonies of death. As soon as the firing began he had ridden to the front, that he might ascertain from whence it originated, and, mingling with the skirmishers, was shot in the side by a rifleman. The wound was mortal; he fell into the arms of his aide-de-camp, and lived only long enough to name his wife, and to commend his family to the protection of his country. He was removed towards the fleet, but expired before his bearers could reach the boats.

"It is impossible to conceive the effect which this melancholy spectacle produced throughout the army. By the courteousness and condescension of his manners, General Ross had secured the absolute love of all who served under him, from the highest to the lowest; and his success on a former occasion, as well as his judicious arrangements on the present, had inspired every one with the most perfect confidence in his abilities. All eyes were turned upon him as we passed, and a sort of involuntary groan ran from rank to rank from the front to the rear of the column.

"By the fall of our gallant leader, the command now devolved upon Colonel Brook, of the 44th regiment, an officer of decided personal courage, but, perhaps, better calculated to lead a battalion, than to guide an army. Being informed of his unexpected and undesired elevation, he came to the front, and under him we continued to move on; sorrowful, indeed, but not dejected. The skirmishing had now ceased, for the American riflemen were driven in; and in a few minutes we found ourselves opposite to a considerable force, drawn up with some skill, and occupying a strong position. Judging from appearances, I should say that the corps now opposed to us amounted to six or seven thousand men. They covered a neck of land, very much resembling that which we had passed; having both flanks defended by little inland lakes; the whole of their position was well wooded, and in front of their line was a range of high palings, similar to those which intersected the field of Bladensburg. About the center, though some way advanced, was a farm-house, with its outbuildings and stack-yard; and near to the right ran the main road. Their artillery, which could not greatly exceed our own, either in weight of metal or number of guns, was scattered along the line of infantry in nearly the same order as had been preserved at Bladensburg, and their reserve was partly seen, and partly hid by a thick wood.

"The whole of this country is flat and unbroken. About half a mile in the rear of the enemy's position were some heights, but to occupy these as they should be occupied would have required a much greater number of men than the American army could muster. Their general, therefore, exhibited some judgment in his choice of ground, but, perhaps, he would have exhibited more had he declined a pitched battle altogether. Yet to do him justice, I repeat that the ground was well chosen; for besides the covering of wood which he secured for his own people, he took care to leave open fields in his front; by which means we were of necessity exposed to a galling fire, as soon as we came within range.

Of one error, however, he was guilty. Either he did not possess himself of the farm-house at all, or he suffered it to be taken from him with very little resistance; for on the arrival of the column at the ground where it was to form, it was in the occupation of our advanced guard. He was likewise to blame in not filling the wood upon our left with skirmishers. In short, he acted unwisely in merely attempting to repel attacks, without ever dreaming that the most effectual mode of so doing is to turn the tables, and attack the assailants.

" As our troops came up they filed off to the right and left, and drew up just within cannon shot in the following order. The light brigade consisting of the 85th regiment, and the light companies of the other corps, in extended order, threatened the whole front of the American army. The 21st remained in column upon the road; the 4th moved off to the right, and advanced through a thicket to turn the enemy's left, and the 44th, the seamen and marines, formed a line in rear of the light brigade.

" While this formation was going on, the artillery being brought up, opened upon the American army, and a smart cannonade ensued on both sides. That our guns were well served I myself can bear witness; for I saw the Shrapnel shells which were thrown from them strike among the enemy, and make fearful gaps in the line. Our rockets likewise began to play, one of which falling short, lighted upon a haystack in the barn-yard belonging to the farm-house, and immediately set it on fire. The house itself, the stables, barns and outhouses, as well as all the other stacks, one after another caught the flames, and were quickly in a state of conflagration; and the smoke and blaze which they emitted, together with the roar of cannon and flashes of the guns, produced together a fine effect.

" In the meantime the American artillery was not idle. Pushing forward two light field-pieces upon the road, they opened a destructive fire of grape upon the 21st regiment, and such of the sailors as occupied that point. Three other guns were directed against our artillery, between which and several of our pieces a sort of duel was maintained; and the rest played without ceasing upon the 85th and the light companies, who had lain down while the other regiments took up their ground. Neither was their infantry altogether quiet. They marched several strong bodies from the right to the left, and withdrew others from the left to the right of their line, though for what end this marching and countermarching was undertaken I am at a loss to conceive. Whilst thus fluctuating it was curious to observe their dread of every spot where a cannon-ball had struck. Having seen the shots fall, I kept my eye upon one or two places, and perceived that each company as it drew near to those points hung back, and then assuming, as it were, a momentary courage, rushed past, leaving a vacancy between it and the company which next succeeded.

"All this while the whole of our infantry, except the 4th regiment, lay or stood in anxious expectation of an order to advance. This, however, was not given till that corps had reached the thicket through which it was to make its way; when Colonel Brook, with his staff, having galloped along the line to see that all was ready, commanded the signal to be made. The charge was accordingly sounded, and echoed back from every bugle in the army, when, starting from the ground where they had lain, the troops moved on in a cool and orderly manner. A dreadful discharge of grape and canister shot, of old locks, pieces of broken muskets, and everything which they could cram into their guns, was now sent forth from the whole of the enemy's artillery, and some loss was on our side experienced. Regardless of this, our men went on without either quickening or retarding their pace, till they came within a hundred yards of the American line. As yet not a musket had been fired, nor a word spoken on either side, but the enemy, now raising a shout, fired a volley from right to left, and then kept up a rapid and ceaseless discharge of musketry. Nor were our people backward in replying to these salutes; for giving them back both their shout and their volley, we pushed on at double-quick, with the intention of bringing them to the charge.

"The bayonet is a weapon peculiarly British; at least it is a weapon which in the hands of a British soldier is irresistible. Though they maintained themselves with great determination, and stood to receive our fire till scarcely twenty yards divided us, the Americans would not hazard a charge. On the left, indeed, where the 21st advanced in column, it was not without much difficulty and a severe loss that any attempt to charge could be made, for in that quarter it seemed to be the flower of the enemy's infantry, as well as the main body of their artillery; towards the right, however, the day was quickly won. The only thing to be regretted, indeed, was that the attack had not been for some time longer deferred, because the Americans were broken and fled just as the 4th regiment began to show itself upon the brink of the water which covered their flank; and before a shallow part could be discovered and the troops were enabled to pass, they had time to escape.

" As soon as their left gave way, the whole American army fell into confusion; nor do I recollect on any occasion to have witnessed a more complete rout. Infantry, cavalry and artillery were huddled together, without the smallest regard to order or regularity. The sole object of anxiety seemed to be, which should escape first from the field of battle; insomuch, that numbers were actually trodden down by their countrymen in the hurry of the flight. Yet, in spite of the short duration of the action, which lasted little more than two hours from its first commencement, the enemy's loss was severe. They stood in some respects better than at Bladensburg, consequently we were more mingled with them when they gave way, and were thus enabled to secure some prisoners, an event which their more immediate flight had on the other occasion prevented. In the capture of guns, however, we were not so fortunate. Their pieces being light,. and well supplied with horses, they contrived to carry off all except two; both of which would have also escaped but for the shooting of the leaders.

" I have said that the number of killed and wounded in the American army was very great; in our, on the other hand, the casualties were fewer by far than might have been expected. The 21st and seamen suffered a good deal, the 85th and light companies a little; but had our gallant general been spared, we should have pronounced this a glorious, because a comparatively bloodless day. In the loss of that one man, however, we felt ourselves more deeply wounded than if the best battalion in the army had been sacrificed.

"In following up the flying enemy the same obstacles which presented themselves at Bladensburg again came in the way. The thick woods quickly screened the fugitives, and as even our mounted drivers were wanting, their horses having been taken for the use of the artillery, no effectual pursuit could be attempted. We accordingly halted upon the field of battle, of necessity content with the success which we had obtained; and having collected the stragglers and called in the pursuers, it was resolved to pass the night in this situation. Fires were speedily lighted, and the troops distributed in such a manner as to secure a tolerable position in case of an attack; and the wounded being removed into two or three houses scattered along the ground, the victors lay down to sleep under the canopy of heaven.

"At an early hour on the 13th, the troops were roused from their lairs, and forming upon the ground, waited until daylight should appear. A heavy rain had come on about midnight, and now fell with so much violence, that some precautions were necessary, in order to prevent the fire-locks from being rendered useless by wet. Such of the men as were fortunate enough to possess leathern cases, wrapped them round the locks of their muskets, whilst the rest held them in the best manner they could, under their elbows; no man thinking of himself, but only how he could best keep his arms in a serviceable condition.

"As soon as the first glimmering of dawn could be discerned, we moved to the road, and took up our wonted order of march; but before we pushed forward, the troops were desired to lighten themselves still further, by throwing off their blankets, which were to be left under a slender guard until their return. This was accordingly done; and being now unencumbered, except by a knapsack now almost empty, every man felt his spirits heightened in proportion to the diminution of his load.

"But our march to-day was not so rapid as our motions generally were. The Americans had at last adopted an expedient, if carried to its proper length, might have entirely stopped our progress. In most of the woods they had felled trees, and thrown them across the road; but as these abattis were without defenders, we experienced no other inconvenience than what arose from loss of time; being obliged to halt on all such occasions till the pioneers had removed the obstacle. So great, however, was even this hindrance, that we did not come in sight of the main army of the Americans till evening, although the distance travelled could not exceed ten miles.

"It now appeared that the corps which we had beaten yesterday was only a detachment, and not a large one, from the force collected for the defence of Baltimore; and that the account given by the volunteer troopers was in every respect correct. Upon a ridge of hills, which concealed the town itself from observation, stood the grand army, consisting of twenty thousand men. Not trusting to his superiority in numbers, their general had there entrenched them in the most formidable manner, having covered the whole face of the heights with breastworks, thrown back his left so as to rest it upon a strong fort erected for the protection of the river, and constructed a chain of field redoubts which covered his right and commanded the entire ascent. Along the line of the hill were likewise *flèches* and other projecting works, from which a cross fire might be kept up; and there were mounted throughout this commanding position no less than one hundred pieces of cannon.

"It would be absurd to suppose that the sight of preparations so warlike did not in some degree damp the ardor of our leader; at least it would have been madness to storm such works without pausing to consider how it might best be attempted. The whole of the country within cannon shot was cleared from wood, and laid out in grass and corn-fields; consequently there was no cover to shelter an attacking army from any part of the deadly fire which would be immediately poured upon it. The most prudent plan, therefore, was to wait till dark, and then, assisted by the frigates and bombs, which he hoped were by this time ready to co-operate, to try the fortune of a battle.

"Having resolved thus to act, Colonel Brook halted his army; and, secured against surprise by a well-connected line of piquets, the troops were permitted to light fires and to cook their provisions. But though the rain still fell in torrents, no shelter could be obtained; and as even their blankets were no longer at hand, with which to form gipsy-tents, this was the reverse of an agreeable bivouac to the whole army.

"Darkness had now come on, and as yet no intelligence had arrived from the shipping. To assail such a position, however, without the aid of the fleet, was deemed impracticable; at least our chance of success would be greatly diminished without their co-operation. As the left of the American army extended to a fort built upon the very brink of the river, it was clear that could the ships be brought to bear upon that point, and the fort be silenced by their fire, that flank of the position would be turned. This once effected, there would be no difficulty in pushing a column within their works; and as soldiers entrenched always place more reliance on the strength of their entrenchments than upon their own personal exertions, the very sight of our people on a level with them would in all probability decide the contest. At all events as the column was to advance under the cover of night, it might easily push forward and crown the hill above the enemy, before any effectual opposition could be offered; by which means they would be enclosed between two fires, and lose the advantage which their present elevated situation bestowed. All, however, depended upon the ability of the fleet to lend their assistance; for without silencing the fort, this flank could scarcely be assailed with any chance of success, and, therefore, the whole plan of operations must be changed. . . . ."

Having established communication with the admiral. it was learned that "no effectual support could be given to the land force; for such was the shallowness of the river, that none except the very lightest craft could make their way within six miles of the town; and even these were stopped by vessels sunk in the channel, and other artificial bars, barely within a shell's longest range of the fort.

"A council of war was instantly summoned to deliberate upon what was best to be done. Without the help of the fleet, it was evident that, adopt what plan of attack we could, our loss must be such as to counterbalance even success itself; whilst success, under existing circumstances, was, to say the least of it, doubtful. And even if we should succeed, what would be gained by it? We could not remove anything from Baltimore for want of proper conveyances. Had the ships been able to reach the town, then, indeed, the quantity of booty might have repaid the survivors for their toil, and consoled them for the loss of comrades. The council of war decided that all idea of storming the enemy's lines should be given up. To draw them from their works would require manœuvreing, and manœuvreing requires time; but delays were all in their favor, and could not possibly advantage us. Every hour brought in re-enforcement to their army, whereas ours had no source from which even to recruit its losses; and it was, therefore, deemed prudent, since we could not fight at once, to lose no time in returning to the shipping.

" About three hours after midnight the troops were accordingly formed upon the road and began their retreat, leaving the piquets to deceive the enemy, and to follow as a rear guard. The rain, which had continued with little interruption since the night before, now ceased, and the moon shone out bright and clear. We marched along, therefore, not in the same spirits as if we had been advancing, but feeling no debasement at having thus relinquished an enterprise so much beyond our strength.

" When the day broke, our piquets, which had withdrawn about an hour before, rejoined us, and we went on in a body. Marching over the field where the battle of the 12th had been fought, we beheld the dead scattered about, and still unburied; but so far different from those which we had seen at Bladensburg, that they were not stripped, every man lying as he had fallen. One object, however, struck me as curious. I saw several men hanging lifeless among the branches of trees, and learnt that they had been riflemen, who chose, during the battle, to fix themselves in these elevated situations, for the combined purposes of securing a good aim and avoiding danger. Whatever might be their success in the first of these designs, in the last they failed; for our men soon discovered them, and, considering the thing as *unfair,* refused to give them quarter, and shot them on their perches.

" Here we paused for about an hour, that the soldiers might collect their blankets and refresh themselves; when we again moved forward, passing the wood where the gallant Ross was killed. It was noon, and as yet all had gone on smoothly without any check or alarm. So little indeed was pursuit dreamt of, that the column began to straggle and to march without much regard to order; when suddenly the bugle sounded from the rear, and immediately after some musket shots were heard. In an instant the men were in their places, and the regiments wheeled into line, facing towards the enemy. The artillery turned round and advanced to the front; indeed I have never seen a manœuvre more coolly or more steadily performed on a parade in England than this rally. The alarm turned out to be groundless, being occasioned only by the sudden appearance of a squadron of horse, which had been sent out by the American general to track our steps. These endeavored to charge the rear guard, and succeeded in making two prisoners; but a single shrapnel checked their farther advance, and sent them back at full speed to boast of the brave exploit which they had performed.

" Seeing that no attack was seriously intended, the army broke once more into the line of march, and proceeded to a favorable piece of ground, near the uncompleted position which I have already described, where we passed the night under little tents made with blankets and ramrods. No alarm occurring, nor any cause of delay appearing, at daybreak we again got under arms, and pushed on towards the shipping, which in two hours were distinguishable.

" The infantry now halted upon a narrow neck of land, while the artillery was lifted into boats, and conveyed on board the fleet. As soon as this was done, brigade after brigade fell back to the water's edge and embarked, till finally all, except the light troops were got off. These being left to cover the embarkation, were extended across the entire space which but a little before contained the whole army; but as no attempt was made to molest them, they had only the honor of being the last to quit the shore. . . . . " On the part of the Americans the same blunders were committed which marked their proceedings during the incursion to Washington, with this exception, that more science was displayed now than formerly in the distribution of their forces along their principal position. At Bladensburg there existed no works, and the troops were badly arranged in an open country: here there were not only fortifications, but fortifications constructed in a scientific manner, and troops drawn up in such order, as that, even without their works, many cross fires would have protected their front. But they neglected numerous favorable opportunities of harassing both our advance and retreat. They felled trees, but left no guards to keep them from being removed, and took no advantage of the delays which their removal created. They risked a battle with a part of their army, when there was no necessity for it; in a word, they committed all those errors which men generally commit who are not soldiers, and yet love war."

"The British loss amounted to one general-staff, one subaltern, two sergeants, and thirty-five rank and file killed; seven captains, four subalterns, eleven sergeants, and two hundred and twenty-nine rank and file wounded, of the army. The navy lost one captain's clerk (Arthur Edmonson), five seamen, and one marine killed; one captain of marines (John Robyns), one lieutenant (Sampson Marshall, severely), one midshipman (Charles Ogle), thirty seamen, and fifteen marines, wounded; making the total loss of the British on shore amount to forty-six killed and three hundred wounded. The great disproportion of wounded arose from the employment, by the enemy, of buck-shot; and the magnitude of the loss altogether, to the enemy's sheltered position. The loss of the Americans upon the field, according to their own account, was twenty killed, ninety wounded, and forty-seven missing. The last item is evidently erroneous, as the British commanding officer carried away with him about two hundred prisoners."[6]

General Stricker's report to General Smith, dated September 15, is as follows: "Sir: I have the honor to report to you, that, in obedience to your orders, I marched from Baltimore on Sunday the 11th instant, with part of my brigade, as the advance corps of the army under your command . . . . I moved towards North Point by the main road, at 8 o'clock P. M. reached the meeting-house near the head of Bear Creek, seven miles from this city. Here the brigade halted, with the exception of the cavalry, who were pushed forward to Gorsuch's farm three miles in advance, and the riflemen who took post near the blacksmith's shop two miles in advance of our encampment. At seven o'clock on the morning of the 12th, I received information from the advanced videttes that the enemy were debarking troops from under cover of their gun vessels which lay off the bluff of North Point, within the mouth of Patapsco river. I immediately ordered back my baggage under a strong guard, moved forward the 5th and 27th regiments, and my artillery to the head of Long Log Lane, resting the 5th with its right at the head of a branch of Bear Creek, and its left on the main North Point road, while the 27th was posted on the other side of the road in line with the 5th, its left extending towards a branch of Back river. The artillery I posted directly at the head of the lane in the interval between the 5th and 27th. The 39th occupied a ground 300 yards in the rear of the 27th, and the 51st the same distance in rear of the 5th, extending each parallel to the front line. The 6th regiment was thrown back to a position a short distance this side of Cook's tavern, and half a mile in the rear of the second line. My orders were, that the 5th and 27th should receive the enemy, and, if necessary, fall back through the 51st and 39th, and form on the right of the 6th or reserve regiment. The riflemen were ordered to the skirts of a thick low pine wood beyond the blacksmith's shop, with a large sedge field in front, that as the cavalry were still in advance who would inform of the enemy's approach, they might take advantage of the covering of the wood and annoy his advance. I soon learned that the enemy's advance party was moving rapidly up the main road, and as the cavalry continually announced their progress, I flattered myself with the hope that the riflemen would soon proclaim by a galling fire their still nearer approach. Imagine my chagrin when I perceived the whole rifle corps falling back on my main position, having too credulously listened to groundless information that the enemy were landing on Back river to cut them off. My hopes of early annoyance to the enemy being thus frustrated, I threw the riflemen on the right flank of my front line, thereby, with the addition of a few cavalry, very well securing that flank. My videttes soon brought information that the enemy in small force was enjoying himself at Gorsuch's farm. Insulted at the idea of a small marauding party thus daringly provoking chastisement, several of my officers volunteered their corps to dislodge it. Captain Levering's and Howard's companies from the 5th, about one hundred and fifty in number, under Major Heath of that regiment; Captain Aisquith's and a few other riflemen, in all about seventy; one 4-pounder with ten men under Lieutenant Stiles, and the cavalry, were immediately pushed forward to punish the insolence of the enemy's advance; or, if his main body appeared, to give evidence of my wish for a general engagement. The latter purpose was soon answered; this small volunteer corps had proceeded scarcely half a mile before the main body of the enemy showed itself, which was immediately attacked. The infantry and riflemen maintained a fire of some minutes, and returned with some loss in killed and wounded; the cavalry and artillery, owing to the disadvantageous ground not being able to support them. In this skirmish, Major Heath's horse was killed under him. At half-past two o'clock, the enemy commenced throwing rockets across my left flank, which seemed harmless, and had no other effect than to prepare my line for the sound of artillery, which soon commenced by us on the enemy's right column then pushing across towards my left, and returned by their 6-pounders and a howitzer upon my left and center. The cannonading was brisk for some minutes, when I ordered my fire to cease until the enemy should get within close range of canister. Seeing that my left flank was the main object of the enemy, I brought up the 39th into line on the left of the 27th, and detached two pieces of artillery to the left of the 39th, still more securely to protect my left flank. Colonel Amey, of the 51st, was ordered to form his regiment at right angles with my line, resting his right near the left of the 39th regiment. The order being badly executed, created for a moment some confusion in that quarter, but was soon rectified by the efforts of my aide-de-camp and brigade majors, who corrected the error of Colonel Amey and posted the 51st in the ordered position. The enemy's right column deployed and advanced upon the 39th and 27th. The 51st, unmindful of my object to use its fire in protection of my left flank in case an attempt should be made to turn it, totally forgetful of the honor of the brigade, and regardless of its own reputation, delivered one random fire and retreated precipitately, and in such confusion, as to render every effort of mine to rally them, ineffective. Some disorder was occasioned in the second battalion of the 39th by the flight of the 51st, and a few gave way. The fire now became general from left to right; my artillery in the center poured forth an incessant volley of canister upon the enemy's left column, who were endeavoring to gain the cover of a small log house, about fifty yards in front of the 5th, which, however, precaution had been taken to fire, so soon as Captain Sadtler's Yagers from the 5th (who were originally posted therein) should be compelled to leave it. The enemy's line advanced about ten minutes before three o'clock, with a severe fire which was well returned by the artillery, the whole 27th, the 5th, except the three companies of Captains Levering, Howard and Sadtler, which were too much exhausted by the advanced skirmish of the two former—and the ordered retreat of the first battalion of the 39th, which maintained its ground in despite of the disgraceful example set by the intended support on the left. The fire was incessant till about fifteen minutes before four o'clock, when, finding that my line, now 1400 strong, was insufficient to withstand the superior numbers of the enemy, and my left flank being exposed by the desertion of the 51st, I was constrained to order a movement back to the reserve regiment, under Colonel M'Donald, which was well posted to receive the retired line, which mostly rallied well. On forming the 6th, the fatigued state of the regiments and corps which had retired, and the probability that my right flank might be turned by a quick movement of the enemy in that direction, induced me, after proper deliberation, to fall back to Worthington's mill; which I was the more persuaded to do, by my desire to have the 6th regiment (whose officers and men were eager to share the dangers of their brother soldiers) perfect and in good order to receive the enemy on his near approach to the city. All retired as I could wish, and were ready to act as circumstances might require it. In this situation you found the brigade on the morning of the 13th, somewhat fatigued, but with increased confidence in ourselves, and renewing our preparations for the annoyance of the enemy, alone, if deemed proper, or in conjunction with any other force.

" I have thought it due to the merits of my brigade, to detail thus fully their whole movement, and I feel a pride in the belief that the stand made on Monday, in no small degree, tended to check the temerity of the foe, daring to invade a country like ours, and designing the destruction of our city, in whose defence some of the best blood of the country has already been spilt, and for whose safety and protection the citizen soldiers of the 3d brigade are ready to suffer every privation, and meet every danger. Should report be true (and I doubt not the fact) that the enemy's commanding officer, *Major-General Ross,* was killed in this action, and that the enemy suffered in proportion to his superior numbers, I shall feel still more the valuable consequences of our fight.

"The conduct of many company officers and privates, was such as I calculated on; that of most of my field officers also merits my particular notice. Major Richard K. Heath, of the 5th, who led on the advance party to bring on the action, behaved as became an officer, the facts of his first horse being killed under him in the first skirmish, his second being badly wounded, and himself receiving a severe contusion on the head, by a musket ball, in the general action, are ample proofs of his bravery and exposure in discharge of his duty. Lieutenant-Colonel Sterett, and Major Barry, of the 5th, gained my highest approbation, and they unite with all in praise of Captain Spangler and his company of volunteers from York, Pa., then attached to their command; also of Adjutant Cheston, who is slightly wounded. Lieutenant-Colonel Long, of the 27th, and his field and company officers did well; this whole regiment was unsurpassed in bravery, resolution and enthusiasm.

"My brigade has to bewail the loss of Adjutant James Lowry Donaldson, who fell in the hottest of the fight, bravely discharging the duties of his commission. Lieutenant-Colonel Fowler, and Major Steiger of the 39th did their duty in every respect; they speak highly of Captain Quantril, from Hagerstown, and Captain Metzgar, from Hanover, Pa., Captain Quantril is wounded. Captain John Montgomery, commander of my artillery, gained for himself and his company lasting honor. Captain Aisquith and his company of riflemen merit my thanks. Ensign Wilmot, commanding the company of United Volunteers of the 5th, and many of his men, distinguished themselves. To brigade Majors Calhoun and Frailey, I am under great obligations for the prompt and zealous performance of their duty. To my aide-de-camp, Major George P. Stevenson, too much praise cannot be given, his industry in every arrangement before the fight, and in animating the whole line was conspicuous; his zeal and courage are of the most ardent kind, the sprightliness of his manners in the most trying scenes had the happiest effect upon all to whom he had to communicate my orders; and the precision with which he delivered my commands, could be exceeded only by the coolness with which he always saw them executed. He was animated, brave and useful. Major William B. Barney and Adjutant Lemuel Taylor of the cavalry, who having no opportunity of distinction in their regiment, owing to the grounds, did me great service, the former aiding Captain Montgomery, the latter in conveying orders through the whole. Mr. Robert Goodloe Harper deserves my thanks. He visited me just before the action; accompanied the advance party, and aided me much throughout. The brave soldiers under my command have suffered many privations, and I recognize among our killed and wounded many valuable men; of which I will make a report in a few days."

While the transports of the British fleet were at anchor off North Point, debarking the troops for the attack on Baltimore, several frigates with the bomb-vessels *Meteor, Aetna, Terror, Volcano,* and *Devastation,* and the rocket-ship *Erebus,* proceeded up the Patapsco and came to anchor off Fort McHenry. On Tuesday morning, the 13th, at daylight, the bombardment commenced upon and was returned by both Fort McHenry, the Star fort and the water batteries on both sides of the entrance. As the vessels of the enemy proved to be out of range of the guns of the fort, their fire was discontinued until 3 p. m., when four of the bomb-vessels and the rocket-ship stood in much nearer the fort. A brisk fire was poured on the attacking vessels, though no serious damage was done them, and a division of boats was sent to tow the *Erebus* out of range.

In the middle of the night of the 13th, a division of twenty boats was detached up the Ferry Branch, but as the rain fell in torrents and the night was extremely dark, eleven of the boats pulled by mistake directly for the harbor, but the lights of the city made the enemy aware of his mistake and enabled him to return in safety to the ships. The remaining nine boats, under the command of Captain Charles Napier, passed up the Ferry Branch to a considerable distance above Fort McHenry, and opened a heavy fire of rockets and shot upon the shore, but accomplished nothing further than to draw some troops down to the beach, while returning to the ships a rocket was fired from the boats and drew on them a shower of round shot, grape and canister from the fort and water batteries below, but James says, "one of the boats was slightly struck and one man mortally wounded. Not another casualty occurred."

Finding that the entrance to the harbor was closed by a line of boats sunken in the channel, and by a heavy iron chain stretched from the Lazaretto to the fort, and that the bombardment of the fort was ineffectual, the British squadron dropped down toward North Point to rejoin the other vessels.

Lieutenant-Colonel Armistead submitted the following report of the bombardment to the Secretary of War:

" . . . . On the night of Saturday the 10th instant, the British fleet, consisting of ships of the line, heavy frigates and bomb-vessels, numbering in all thirty sail, appeared at the mouth of the river Patapsco, with every indication of an attempt on the city of Baltimore. My own force consisted of one company of U. S. Artillery under Captain Frederick Evans, and two companies of Sea Fencibles, under Captains M. S. Bunbury and Wm. H. Addison. Of these three companies, thirty-five men were, unfortunately, on the sick list and unfit for duty. I had been furnished with two companies of volunteer artillery from the city of Baltimore, under Captain John Berry [Washington Artillery], and Captain Charles Pennington [Baltimore Independent Artillerists]. To these I must add another very fine company of volunteer artillerists, under Judge J. H. Nicholson [Baltimore Fencibles], who had proferred their services to aid in the defence of this post whenever an attack might be apprehended; also a detachment from Commodore Barney's Flotilla, under Lieutenant Rodman. Brigadier-General Winder had also furnished me with about six hundred infantry, under the command of Lieutenant-Colonel Steuart and Major Lane, consisting of detachments from the 12th, 14th, 36th, and 38th regiments of U. S. troops—the total amounting to one thousand effective men.

"On Monday morning early it was perceived that the enemy was landing troops on the east side of the Patapsco, distant about ten miles. During that day and the ensuing night he had brought sixteen ships (including five bomb-ships) within about two miles and a half of the fort. I had arranged my force as follows: The regular artillerists under Captain Evans, and the volunteers under Captain Nicholson, manned the bastions in the star fort. Captains Bunbury's, Rodman's, Addison's, Berry's and Pennington's commands were stationed in the lower works, and the infantry under Lieutenant-Colonel Steuart and Major Lane were in the outer ditch, to meet the enemy at his landing should he attempt one.

"On Tuesday morning, about sunrise, the enemy commenced the attack from his five bomb-vessels, at the distance of about two miles, when, finding that his shells reached us, he anchored and kept up an incessant and well-directed bombardment. We immediately opened our batteries, and kept a brisk fire from our guns and mortars, but unfortunately our shot and shells all fell considerably short of him. This was to me a most distressing circumstance, as it left us exposed to a constant and tremendous shower of shells, without the most remote possibility of our doing him the slightest injury. It affords me the highest gratification to state that although we were left thus exposed, and thus inactive, not a man shrunk from the conflict.

"About two o'clock p. m., one of the 24-pounders on the southwest bastion, under the immediate command of Captain Nicholson, was dismounted by a shell, the explosion of which killed his second-lieutenant, and wounded several of his men; the bustle necessarily produced in removing the wounded and remounting the gun probably induced the enemy to suspect that we were in a state of confusion, as he brought in three of his bomb-ships to what I believed to be a good striking distance. I immediately ordered a fire to be opened, which was obeyed with alacrity through the whole garrison, and in half hour those intruders again sheltered themselves by withdrawing beyond our reach. We gave three cheers and again ceased firing. The enemy continued throwing shells, with one or two slight intermissions, till one o'clock in the morning of Wednesday, when it was discovered that he had availed himself of the darkness of the night, and had thrown a considerable force above to our right; they had approached very near to Fort Covington, when they began to throw rockets, intending, I presume, to give them an opportunity of examing the shores, as I have since understood they had detached 1250 picked men, with scaling ladders, for the purpose of storming the fort. We once more had an opportunity of opening our batteries, and kept up a continued blaze for nearly two hours, which had the effect again to drive them off.

"In justice to Lieutenant Newcomb, of the U. S. Navy, who commanded at Fort Covington, with a detachment of sailors, and Lieutenant Webster, of the flotilla, who commanded the six-gun battery near that fort, I ought to state that during this time they kept up an animated, and I believe a very destructive fire, to which, I am persuaded, we are much indebted in repulsing the enemy. One of his sunken barges has since been found with two dead men in it—others have been seen floating in the river. The only means we had of directing our guns was by the blaze of the rockets and flashes of their guns. Had they ventured to the same situation in the day time, not a man would have escaped.

"The bombardment continued, on the part of the enemy, until seven o'clock on Wednesday morning, when it ceased; and about nine, their ships got under way and stood down the river. During the bombardment, which lasted twenty-five hours (with two slight intermissions), from the best calculations I can make, from fifteen to eighteen hundred shells were thrown by the enemy. A few of these fell short. A large proportion burst over us, throwing their fragments among us and threatening destruction. Many passed over and about four hundred fell within the works. Two public buildings were materially injured, others but slightly. I am happy to inform you (wonderful as it may appear) that our loss amounts to only four men killed and twenty-four wounded. The latter will all recover. Among the killed I have to lament the loss of Lieutenant Claggett, and Sergeant Clemm, both of Captain Nicholson's volunteers, two men whose fate is to be deplored, not only for their personal bravery, but for their high standing, amiable demeanor and spotless integrity in private life. Lieutenant Russel, of the company under Lieutenant Pennington, received early in the attack a severe contusion in the heel; notwithstanding which he remained at his post during the whole of the bombardment."

The official British report as to the American losses at North Point brought forth an indignant protest from Brigade Major L. Frailey, in the columns of *Niles' Register,* and his statement of the casualties, in which he says " I pledge myself for its correctness." " List of the killed and wounded of the third brigade, at the late engagement at Long Log Lane, September 12, 1814:

CAPTAIN MONTGOMERY'S ARTILLERY

Wounded—Jos. R. Brookes, 2d Lieutenant,
    1 sergeant,
    12 privates, one since dead.

FIFTH REGIMENT INFANTRY.

Killed—   6 privates.
Wounded—George H. Stewart, Captain,
    John Reese, Lieutenant,
    1 sergeant,
    2 corporals,
    40 privates.

TWENTY-SEVENTH REGIMENT INFANTRY

Killed— . James L. Donaldson, Adjutant,
    8 privates.
Wounded—Samuel Moore, Major,
    2 sergeants,
    2 corporals,
    41 privates.

THIRTY-NINTH REGIMENT INFANTRY

Killed—   3 privates.
Wounded—Thomas Quantrill, Captain,
    2 corporals,
    20 privates.

FIFTY-FIRST REGIMENT INFANTRY

Killed—   3 privates.
Wounded—John Kirby, Ensign,
    3 privates.

RIFLE BATTALION

Killed—   Gregorious Andre, Lieutenant,
    2 privates.

RECAPITULATION

Killed—   1 adjutant,
               1 subaltern.
              22 privates.
Wounded—   1 major,
               2 captains,
               3 subalterns,
              12 non-commissioned officers,
             121 privates.
Made
prisoners —   1 subaltern.
              49 non-commissioned officers and privates.

Total —213.

" The recapitulation contains the aggregate of the prisoners taken by the enemy, excepting those paroled at the meeting-house, included in the wounded."

Dr. James H. McCulloh, Jr., who had been sent to the battle-field to attend to the wounded, signed the following agreement:

" In consequence of the humanity shewn the following American prisoners of war, I do promise upon honor that they shall not directly or indirectly serve against the British until regularly exchanged:

Bryan Allen,	John Jephson,
George Bennett,	William Keane, Jr.,
Thomas Brengman,	John Lamb,
Henry Brice,	James H. McCulloh,
William Collings,	James H. Marriott,
Richard K. Cook,	Walter Muskett (or Muschett)
James Davidson,	Luther A. Norris,
David Davis,	Jacob Noyle,
Conrad Euler,	John Pidgeon,
Benjamin Fleetwood,	George Reintzell,
James Gibson,	George Repert,
Charles Goddard,	John Robinson,
Jacob Hubbard,	Robert Smith.

And I do further engage to get the above twenty-six Americans exchanged as soon as possible for a like number of British left at Bladensburg."

In the memorandum made by John Pendleton Kennedy from the company book of the Baltimore United Volunteers, the following appears: " In the action at North Point, September 12, 1814, Ensign John Wilmot commanding, there were in the battle 78 members of this company and nine volunteers—Thomas Bond and Benedict I. Heard, Richard Dorsey, Hammond Dugan, Gover, Leonard Matthews, James Purse, —— Randolph and John Walsh.

Killed and Wounded

William McClellan, killed on the field,
John C. Byrd, killed on the field,
Jacob Haubert, died on the 14th.

Wounded	Prisoners
Henry Brice,	Henry W. Gray,
Elie Clagett,	George T. Hearsey,
James Gibson,	John G. Pogue.
Reverdy Hays,	
Horatio Hollingsworth,	
Dennis Marsh,	
Walter Muschett,	
Chas. O'Rourke,	
John E. Swann,	
Stedman Van Wyck.	

The official report of the killed and wounded at Fort McHenry is as follows:

Names of the killed and wounded officers, non-commissioned officers and privates, belonging to the 1st regiment of artillery under the command of Lieutenant-Colonel David Harris, on detachment at Fort McHenry, September 13, 1814:

In Captain Joseph H. Nicholson's Company

Killed—   Levi Claggett, 3d Lieutenant,
                 John Clemm, 2d Sergeant,

Slightly wounded—Samuel Harris, 3d Sergeant,
Severely   "   Abraham Lerew, Private,
   "   "   James Granger,   "
Slightly   "   James L. Hawkins,   "
   "   "   Henry Bond,   "
   "   "   Samuel Etting   "

IN CAPTAIN JOHN BERRY'S COMPANY

Killed—   Thomas V. Beeson, Private,
Severely wounded—Samuel Foy,   "
   "   "   Emery Lowman   "
Slightly   "   John Cretzer,   "
   "   "   Cornelius Collins,   "
   "   "   Samuel Gray,   "
   "   "   Jacob Resser,   "
   "   "   Derrick Fahnestock, "

IN CAPTAIN HUGHES' COMPANY [BALTIMORE INDEPENDENT ARTILLERISTS] COMMANDED BY LIEUT. PENNINGTON

Slightly wounded—Thomas Russell, 3d Lieutenant,
   "   "   Marmaduke Wyvill, Private,
   "   "   James Lambie,   "
Severely   "   George Greer,   "
   "   "   Emanuel Kent, Jr.,   "
   "   "   James McNeil, Jr.,   "

IN THE MARINE BATTERY UNDER THE COMMAND OF SAILING-MASTER RODMAN

Killed—   Charles Messenger, Private,
Wounded—   William Jenkins,   "
   "   Joseph Bailey,   "
   "   Joseph Hardy,   "

IN THE COMPANY OF SEA FENCIBLES COMMANDED BY M. S. BUNBURY

Dangerously wounded—Charles Bhare,
Slightly   "   Robert Green.

The following notice appeared in the *Federal Gazette* for October 15, 1814:

Office of Commissary of Prisoners, October 13, 1814.

The officers and privates hereinafter named, belonging to the United States service, having been finally exchanged by an agreement made on the 7th instant, with the proper authorities of the enemy, are hereby declared discharged from parole and are as free to act in all respects as they and either of them may have been before they were made prisoners.

CAPTURED AT BLADENSBURG

Joshua Barney, Captain U. S. Flotilla,
John Reagan, Lieutenant-Colonel Militia,
Samuel Miller, Captain Marine Corps,
Dominic Bader, Captain Militia [Union Yagers],
G. von Hasten, Lieutenant,
Robert M. Hamilton, Master U. S. Navy,
Thomas Dukehart, Acting Master,
Jesse Huffington, Sailing Master,
David Robinson, Acting Midshipman U. S. Flotilla,
John M. Howland, 4th Sergeant [Washington Blues],
J. B. Martin, Surgeon.

PRIVATES

Ammick, George,	Gorsuch, William,
Bell, Brooks,	Goswick, Thomas,
Bennett, Joseph,	Grizel, Joseph,
Bradley, Daniel,	Hoffman, Henry,
Chase, Joseph,	Holbrooks, Thomas,
Claude, Abraham,	Holiday, Thomas,
Cook, John,	Iler, Jacob,
De Grot, John,	Johnson, Christopher,
De Krafft, Edward,	Johnson, Isaac,
Diser, Samuel,	Lambert, Lewis,
Dorse, Patrick,	Leith, John,
Edwards, Jesse,	McCall, Robert,
Fable, Joseph,	Mawe, Michael,
Folks, James,	Montgomery, John,
Gaylor, William,	Morgan, Jeremiah.

Richardson, David K,   Vinemiller, Michael,
Rynehart, Daniel,   Wise, Jacob,
Smith, Charles,   Wysham, William,
Smith, Nathaniel,   Young, Jacob,
Thompson, Barnard,   Zimmerman, Henry.
Tall, Walter,

CAPTURED AT NORTH POINT.

[Here follows the list of twenty-six names of those wounded and paroled by Surgeon James H. McCulloh. *See ante.*]

NOTE.—By the agreement referred to all the prisoners captured in the actions of Bladensburg and Baltimore and now held by either party, are to be released without delay to be exchanged against each other, and the balance against the British government to be carried to the general account of releases.

Subsequent to the attack on Baltimore, the operations of the enemy were of no great importance. Part of the squadron remained in the bay for some months and marauding expeditions were rather frequent. The British took possession of Tilghman's Island and erected extensive barracks thereon. A number of small sailing vessels were captured and used as tenders to the fleet and for purposes of plunder. The people of Baltimore were kept in a state of suspense for months, large re-enforcements of troops from neighboring states were brought in, and the defences of the city were augmented and strengthened. Reports as to the movements of the enemy appear in numerous issues of the local press, and whenever a strange sail was seen headed up the bay, the alarm was given that the British were returning for another attack.

Early in October the exchange of prisoners took place, and Colonels Thornton and Wood, together with about eighty privates who had been wounded at Bladensburg and subsequently removed to the jail at Frederick, were returned to the fleet. Commodore Barney returned to duty and again took command of the flotilla, which he held until after the peace was declared.

On the 14th of October Mayor Johnson issued a proclamation setting aside Tuesday, October 18, as a day of thanksgiving and prayer. The constables were notified to see that nothing took place that might detract from the solemnity of the occasion.

The major portion of the fleet, with the troops on board, sailed away from the Chesapeake to make preparations for the projected attack on New Orleans, but enough vessels were left to patrol the bay and keep a lookout for the troublesome privateers, which frequently slipped into their home port in spite of the close watch kept on their movements. Reports of minor depredations of the enemy were published as late as February 18, 1815, although Christopher Hughes, Jr., the secretary of the peace envoys, arrived in the Chesapeake on his way to Washington with the official news of peace, on the 13th of February, 1815.

ON THE NAVAL ATTACK NEAR BALTIMORE, SEPT., 1814.

By Philip Freneau.

The sons of old ocean advanced from the bay
    To achieve an exploit of renown;
And Cochrane and Cockburn commanded that day,
And meant to exhibit a tragical play,
    Call'd the plunder and burning of Baltimore town.
The scenes to be acted were not very new,
And when they approach'd, with the rat-tat-too,
    As merry as times would allow,
We ran up the colours to liberty true,
And gave them a shot with a tow-row-dow.

By land and by water how many have fail'd
    In attacking an enemy's town,
But Britons, they tell us, have always prevail'd
Wherever they march'd or wherever they sail'd,
    To honour his majesty's sceptre and crown:
Wherever they went with the trumpet and drum,
And the dregs of the world, and the dirt and the scum,
    As soon as the music begun,
The colours were struck, and surrender'd the town
When the summons was given of down, down, down!

But fortune, so fickle, is turning her tide,
    And safe is old Baltimore town,
Though Cockburn and Cochrane, with Ross at their side,
The sons of Columbia despised and defied,
    And determined to batter it down—
Rebuff'd and repulsed in disgrace they withdrew,
With their down, down, down, and their rat-tat-too,
    As well as the times would allow:
And the sight, we expect, will be not very new
When they meet us again with our tow-row-dow.

WEBSTER AND HIS BATTERY.

Captain John A. Webster was born in Harford County, Maryland, on September 19, 1787. A love of adventure took him to sea when only fourteen years of age, and at the outbreak of the War of 1812 he promptly volunteered his services. The following account of his part in the events of the war was prepared by him in July, 1853, and has been furnished by his daughter, Miss Susan A. Webster.

" At the commencement of the war with Great Britain in 1812, I was appointed third-lieutenant of the privateer *Rossie*, by Commodore Barney. We captured and destroyed a great many of the enemy's vessels, one of which, the packet ship *Princess Amelia*, fought hard and did not strike her colors until her commander and two lieutenants were killed. We lost several men, and our first-lieutenant was mortally wounded. At the formation of the flotilla at Baltimore, Commodore Barney procured for me a warrant as sailing master in the navy, and I was placed in charge of one of the barges, where I remained during the whole period of its existence, or until they were burned at Pig Point at the head of the Patuxent river, on the approach of the British towards Washington. I was in all the engagements with Commodore Barney. During an attack on two British frigates at the mouth of St. Leonard's creek, I had two men killed on my barge, Midshipman Aisquith and one seaman. In that engagement we lost nine killed and sixteen wounded.

" At the battle of Bladensburg, I was ordered by Commodore Barney to ride to the field from the Navy Yard at Washington, and take charge of the seamen detached from his ship, the *Scorpion,* and the seamen who had been attached to my barge. We met the enemy about one and a half miles from Bladensburg. Commodore Barney ordered our forces to take position abreast of his cannon, and to the right of an old brick-yard, where the enemy was already advancing. Our army was then in full flight, moving rapidly towards Washington. Our fire was commenced on the enemy both from the long 18-pounders under the immediate command of Commodore Barney, and the different detachments belonging to the flotilla, and commanded by officers of the same grade as myself. An officer named Warner was killed at one of the barge guns, also two petty officers and several seamen. Our seamen who served as infantry, including those under my command, acted nobly and continued to do so until their ammunition gave out and most of us were surrounded. When it became necessary to replenish the ammunition, we discovered that those in charge of the wagons had gone off with them in the general flight. This being the case, we made our escape in double quick time. I passed near by where Commodore Barney's guns had been taken by the enemy, at the time he had been wounded in the thigh. He was being supported by one of the officers of the flotilla, Captain Hamilton, and a British officer. He had upwards of thirty-five killed and as many more wounded. In this engagement I had my horse shot through the head and my hat shot through the crown. I did not take time to pick up my hat. We retreated to Montgomery Court House, where I collected about fifty men. While passing in front of the Capitol, I observed four mounted 18-pounders. I ran down to the Navy Yard and there found eight horses already harnessed. I had with me a petty officer named John Frazier. We took possession of the horses, hitched them to the field pieces and took them with us. On passing the President's house, I found a brass 6-pounder mounted and abandoned. I attached that to the others and continued on. That night at eleven o'clock we halted three miles from Georgetown. One of the 18-pounders broke down near Tenallytown and I had it spiked and left. The others I took to Montgomery Court House. The following morning I ascertained that all the horses had been stolen by our militia men who rode off on them. I therefore had to march to Baltimore with as many men as I could collect. That night at 12 o'clock we arrived at Ellicott's Mills where we laid down on a porch until daylight; we again took up the line of march and breakfasted at Barney's Hotel, on Light street. I then reported myself to Lieutenant Solomon Rutter, next in command to Commodore Barney.

"As soon as the British were known to be approaching Baltimore, September 10, 1814, I was, by request of General Smith, detached by Lieutenant Rutter, and ordered with seventy-five men to take charge of the six gun battery, situated on Ferry Branch, between Fort McHenry and Fort Covington. During the interval between that and the 14th, we were employed in preparing the battery for as effective service as possible. I had two midshipmen, by name Edwards and Andrews. The battery was open and exposed, except for a breastwork of about four feet high; a magazine in the rear about sixty feet off, composed of a hole dug in the side of the hill. When the bomb-vessels were in sight off Fort McHenry, much anxiety and interest was manifested, all hoping to share in the expected conflict. Day and night we were on the alert, until hope was nearly extinct, when on the night of the 13th, about eleven o'clock, the bomb-vessels appeared to renew their fire with redoubled energy. It was raining quite fast, and was cold for the season. The rapid discharge of the bombs from the enemy's shipping excited great vigilance among my officers and men. I had the cannon double shotted with 18-pound balls and grape shot and took a blanket and laid on the breastworks, as I was much exhausted. About midnight I could hear a splashing in the water. The attention of the others was aroused and we were convinced it was the noise of the muffled oars of the British barges. Very soon afterwards we could discern small gleaming lights in different places. I felt sure then that it was the barges, which at that time were not more than two hundred yards off. Some of the lights were above me next to Fort Covington. I mounted the cannon with my breast over the apron of the guns and examined the priming, as it was raining fast. All being right I trained the guns and then opened on them, which caused the boats to cease rowing and a rapid firing followed from the barges, as well as from ourselves. I could distinctly hear the balls from our guns strike the barges. My men stated to me that they could hear the shrieks of the wounded. Soon after I commenced firing, Fort Covington opened on them, although they had not gotten up to it. During the firing of the enemy I could distinctly see their barges by the explosion of their cannon which was a great guide to me to fire by. The enemy had twenty-two barges and a long schooner with them, which they propelled by sweeps. This vessel had an 18-pounder on board, and should have done much execution, but not a man was injured by them, as they fired too high, their shots taking effect in the bank, in front of my cannon (!). Soon after the commencement of the firing, I despatched Midshipman Andrews to Lieutenant Budd, at the circular battery, for thirty of my men I had loaned him the day previous. To my great annoyance and disadvantage, neither Andrews nor the men returned, which reduced my force to forty-five. The officer passed on to Baltimore, and reported that I had abandoned the battery, and the enemy had landed. The following day Lieutenant Budd informed me he had detained my men to work his cannon, in case of my retreat.

" That night's work I had to perform with energy. I had my right shoulder broken by a handspike, and subsequently broken again, which rendered me a complete invalid. During the fight, one of my seamen, an obstinate Englishman, attempted to lay a train of powder to the magazine; without thought, I laid him out for dead with a handspike. He, however, came to and crawled off before the fight ended, and he and Andrews were ever after among the missing. On the return of the barges, which was at one o'clock in the morning of the 14th, rockets were fired from them, and immediately afterwards large fires were made in front of our army and at different points along the line of the Patapsco river. As the barges in retreating passed Fort McHenry, they were again fired on. During the morning of the 15th we were occupied in cleaning up, and preparing for another emergency, and entertained ourselves by digging cannon balls out of the hill in our rear, as well as in the front of my battery. Upwards of twenty 18-pound shot were found, with which I loaded all my cannon, having a wish to return the enemy their own property. I have many times regretted I did not preserve the balls they were so polite to send. I also picked up two barges much shattered by balls, one of which I repaired and sold to Charles and Peter Wirgman. Three men were also picked up, one supposed to be a British officer. About ten days afterwards I was taken seriously ill with bilious fever, which together with the suffering from my injured shoulder, confined me to the house until Christmas following. Soon afterwards the officers were discharged from the navy with three months extra pay.

" When I was sent from the Lazaretto to take charge of the six gun battery, there were but three days provisions issued for us. The consequence was, my officers and men were two days after the battle without rations, and had no alternative but to poach on a garden directly alongside the battery, containing corn, cabbage, etc., belonging to Mr. Presstman, for which his widow has during the last winter called on me to get remuneration for her. Owing to their improper diet, seven men died and I suffered greatly. For my injuries I received a pension of twenty dollars a month. The citizens of Baltimore, and the State of Maryland each presented me with a handsome gold sword, in acknowledgement of my services. Congress also paid me for the loss of my horse, which money I invested in a set of silver and had the figure of my gallant horse " Shoe Tail " put on the larger pieces."

The presentation of the sword, which took place in 1816, was accompanied by the following communication:

" The citizens of Baltimore, with the most lively sentiments of gratitude to you, and the brave men under your command during the attack of the British on this city on the 13th and 14th of September, 1814, appointed us a committee to present you a testimonial for your gallant and successful defense of the Six Gun Battery.

" The committee in discharging this duty have sincere pleasure in now presenting you with a sword bearing an inscription commemorative of the event for which it is presented and beg your acceptance of it in the name of the citizens of Baltimore.

" In common with our fellow citizens we have great pleasure in the remembrance of your gallant conduct and hope it will have a happy influence on others similarly situated to follow so excellent an example. The committee tender you assurances of their highest personal regard and of their best wishes for your health and happiness."

John Eager Howard,
William Lorman,
Thomas Tennant,
Robert Gilmor, Jr.,
Isaac McKim,
Fielding Lucas, Jr.

How the "Star Spangled Banner" Came to be Written.

Several accounts of the events that led up to the writing of the "Star Spangled Banner" have from time to time appeared in print, but that of Chief Justice Roger Brooke Taney, a brother-in-law of Francis Scott Key, may be accepted as authentic. This account in the form of a letter dated at Washington in 1856, and prefixed to the volume of Key's poems, is as follows:

"I promised some time ago to give you an account of the incidents in the life of Mr. F. S. Key, which led him to write the 'Star Spangled Banner,' and of the circumstances under which it was written. The song has become a national one, and will, I think, from its great merit, continue to be so, especially in Maryland; and everything that concerns it author must be a matter of interest to his children and descendants. And I proceed to fulfill my promise with the more pleasure, because while the song shows his genius and taste as a poet, the incidents connected with it, and the circumstances under which it was written, will show his character and worth as a man. The scene he describes, and the warm spirit of patriotism which breathes in the song, were not the offspring of mere fancy, or poetic imagination. He describes what he actually saw. And he tells us what he felt while witnessing the conflict, and what he felt when the battle was over, and the victory won by his countrymen. Every word came warm from his heart, and for that reason, even more than from its poetical merit, it never fails to find a response in the hearts of those who listen to it.

"You will remember that in 1814, when the song was written, I resided in Frederick, and Mr. Key in Georgetown. You will also recollect, that soon after the British troops retired from Washington, a squadron of the enemy's ships made their way up the Potomac, and appeared before Alexandria, which was compelled to capitulate; and the squadron remained there some days, plundering the town of tobacco, and whatever else they wanted. It was rumored, and believed in Frederick, that a marauding attack of the same character would be made on Washington and Georgetown, before the ships left the river. Mr. Key's family were still in Georgetown. He would not, and indeed could not, with honor, leave the place, while it was threatened by the enemy; for he was a volunteer in the Light Artillery, commanded by Major Peter, which was composed of citizens of the District of Columbia, who had uniformed themselves, and offered their services to the government, and who had been employed in active service from the time the British fleet appeared in the Patuxent preparatory to the movement upon Washington. And Mrs. Key refused to leave home, while Mr. Key was thus daily exposed to danger. Believing as we did, that an attack would probably be made on Georgetown, we became very anxious about the situation of his family. For if the attack was made, Mr. Key would be with the troops engaged in the defense; and as it was impossible to forsee what would be the issue of the conflict, his family, by remaining in Georgetown, might be placed in great and useless peril. When I speak of *we*, I mean Mr. Key's father and mother, and Mrs. Taney and myself. But it was agreed among us that I should go to Georgetown and try to persuade Mrs. Key to come away with their children and stay with me or with Mr. Key's father until the danger was over. When I reached Georgetown, I found the English ships still at Alexandria, and a body of militia encamped in Washington, which had been assembled to defend the city. But it was then believed, from information received, that no attack would be made by the enemy on Washington or Georgetown; and preparations were making, on our part, to annoy them by batteries on shore, when they descended the river. The knowledge of these preparations probably hastened their departure; and the second or third day after my arrival, the ships were seen moving down the Potomac.

" On the evening of the day that the enemy disappeared, Mr. Richard West arrived at Mr. Key's and told him that after the British army passed through Upper Marlboro, on their return to their ships, and had encamped some miles below the town, a detachment was sent back, which entered Dr. Beanes's house about midnight, compelled him to rise from his bed, and hurried him off to the British camp, hardly allowing him time to put his clothes on; that he was treated with great harshness, and closely guarded; and that as soon as his friends were apprized of his situation, they hastened to the headquarters of the English army to solicit his release, but it was peremptorily refused, and they were not even permitted to see him; and that he had been carried as a prisoner on board the fleet. And finding their own efforts unavailing, and alarmed for his safety, his friends in and about Marlboro thought it advisable that Mr. West should hasten to Georgetown and request Mr. Key to obtain the sanction of the government to his going on board the admiral's ship, under a flag of truce, and endeavoring to procure the release of Dr. Beanes, before the fleet sailed. It was then lying at the mouth of the Potomac, and its destination was not at that time known with certainty. Dr. Beanes, as perhaps you know, was the leading physician in Upper Marlboro, and an accomplished scholar and gentleman. He was highly respected by all who knew him; was the family physician of Mr. West, and the intimate friend of Mr. Key. He occupied one of the best houses in Upper Marlboro, and lived very handsomely; and his house was selected for the quarters of Admiral Cockburn, and some of the principal officers of the army, when the British troops encamped at Marlboro on their march to Washington. These officers were, of course, furnished with everything that the house could offer; and they in return treated him with much courtesy, and placed guards around his grounds and outhouses, to prevent depredations by their troops.

" But on the return of the army to the ships, after the main body had passed through the town, stragglers who had left the ranks to plunder, or from some other motive, made their appearance from time to time, singly or in small squads, and Dr. Beanes put himself at the head of a small body of citizens, to pursue and make prisoners of them. Information of this proceeding was by some means or other conveyed to the English camp, and the detachment of which I have spoken was sent back to release the prisoners and seize Dr. Beanes. They did not seem to regard him, and certainly did not treat him, as a prisoner of war, but as one who had deceived, and broken his faith to them.

" Mr. Key readily agreed to undertake the mission in his favor, and the President promptly gave his sanction to it. Orders were immediately issued to the vessel usually employed as a cartel, in the communications with the fleet in the Chesapeake, to be made ready without delay; and Mr. John S. Skinner, who was agent for the government for flags of truce and exchange of prisoners, and who was well known as such to the officers of the fleet, was directed to accompany Mr. Key. And as soon as the arrangements were made, he hastened to Baltimore, where the vessel was, to embark; and Mrs. Key and the children went with me to Frederick, and thence to his father's on Pipe Creek, where she remained until he returned.

" We heard nothing from him until the enemy retreated from Baltimore, which, as well as I can now recollect, was a week or ten days after he left us, and we were becoming uneasy about him, when, to our great joy, he made his appearance at my house on his way to join his family.

" He told me that he found the British fleet, at the mouth of the Potomac, preparing for the expedition against Baltimore. He was courteously received by Admiral Cochrane, and the officers of the army, as well as the navy. But when he made known his business, his application was received so coldly that he feared it would fail. General Ross and Admiral Cockburn—who accompanied the expedition to Washington—particularly the latter, spoke of Dr. Beanes in very harsh terms, and seemed at first not disposed to release him. It, however, happened, fortunately, that Mr. Skinner carried letters from the wounded British officers left at Bladensburg; and in these letters to their friends on board the fleet, they all spoke of the humanity and kindness with which they had been treated after they had fallen into our hands. And after a good deal of conversation, and strong representations from Mr. Key, as to the character and standing of Dr. Beanes, and of the deep interest which the community in which he lived took in his fate, General Ross said that Dr. Beanes deserved much more punishment than he had received, but that he felt himself bound to make a return for the kindness which had been shown to his wounded officers, whom he had been compelled to leave at Bladensburg, and upon that ground, and that only, he would release him. But Mr. Key was at the same time informed that neither he, nor any one else would be permitted to leave the fleet for some days; and must be detained until the attack on Baltimore, which was then about to be made, was over. But he was assured that they would make him and Mr. Skinner as comfortable as possible while they detained them. Admiral Cochrane, with whom they dined on the day of their arrival, apologized for not accommodating them in his own ship, saying that it was crowded already with officers of the army, but that they would be well taken care of in the frigate *Surprise*, commanded by his son, Sir Thomas Cochrane. And to this frigate they were accordingly transferred.

" Mr. Key had an interview with Dr. Beanes before General Ross consented to release him. I do not recollect whether he was on board the admiral's ship, or the *Surprise*, but I believe it was the former. He found him in the forward part of the ship among the sailors and soldiers; he had not had a change of clothes from the time he was seized; was constantly treated with indignity by those around him, and no officer would speak to him. He was treated as a culprit and not as a prisoner of war. And this harsh and humiliating treatment continued until he was placed on board the cartel.

" Something must have passed, when the officers were quartered at his house on the march to Washington, which in the judgment of General Ross bound him not to take up arms against the English forces, until the troops had re-embarked. It is impossible on any other ground to account for the manner in which he was spoken of, and treated. But whatever General Ross and the other officers may have thought, I am quite sure that Dr. Beanes did not think he was in any way pledged to abstain from active hostilities against the public enemy. And when he made prisoners of the stragglers, he did not consider himself as a prisoner on parole, nor suppose himself to be violating any obligation he had incurred. For he was a gentleman of untainted character, and a nice sense of honor, and incapable of doing anything that could have justified such treatment. Mr. Key imputed the ill usage he received to the influence of Admiral Cockburn, who it will be remembered, while he commanded in the Chesapeake, carried on hostilities in a vindictive temper, assailing and plundering defenceless villages; or countenancing such proceedings by those under his command.

" Mr. Key and Mr. Skinner continued on board the *Surprise*, where they were very kindly treated by Sir Thomas Cochrane, until the fleet reached the Patapsco, and preparations were making for landing the troops. Admiral Cochrane then shifted his flag to the frigate, in order that he might be able to move further up the river, and superintend in person the attack by water, on the fort. And Mr. Key and Mr. Skinner were then sent on board their own vessel, with a guard of sailors or marines to prevent them from landing. They were permitted to take Dr. Beanes with them, and they thought themselves fortunate in being anchored in a position which enabled them to see distinctly the flag of Fort McHenry from the deck of the vessel. He then proceeded with much animation to describe the scene on the night of the bombardment. He and Mr. Skinner remained on deck during the night, watching every shell from the moment it was fired, until it fell, listening with breathless interest to hear if an explosion followed. While the bombardment continued, it was sufficient proof that the fort had not surrendered. But it suddenly ceased some time before day; and as they had no communication with any of the enemy's ships, they did not know whether the fort had surrendered, or the attack upon it had been abandoned. They paced the deck for the residue of the night in painful suspense, watching with intense anxiety for the return of day, and looking every few minutes at their watches to see how long they must wait for it; and as soon as it dawned, and before it was light enough to see objects at a distance, their glasses were turned to the fort, uncertain whether they should see the stars and stripes or the flag of the enemy. At length the light came and they saw that " our flag was still there." And as the day advanced, they discovered from the movements of the boats between the shore and the fleet, that the troops had been roughly handled, and that many wounded men were carried to the ships. At length he was informed that the attack on Baltimore had failed, and the British army was re-embarking, and that he and Mr. Skinner and Dr. Beanes would be permitted to leave them and go where they pleased, as soon as the troops were on board and the fleet ready to sail.

" He then told me that under the excitement of the time, he had written a song, and handed me a printed copy of the ' Star Spangled Banner.' When I read it, and expressed my admiration, I asked him how he found the time in the scenes he had been passing through, to compose such a song? He said he commenced it on the deck of their vessel, in the fervor of the moment, when he saw the enemy hastily retreating to their ships, and looked at the flag they had watched for so anxiously as the morning opened; that he had written some lines, or brief notes that would aid him in calling them to mind, upon the back of a letter which he happened to have in his pocket; and for some of the lines, as he proceeded, he was obliged to rely altogether on his memory; and that he finished it in the boat on his way to the shore and wrote it out as it now stands, at the hotel, on the night he reached Baltimore, and immediately after he arrived. He said that on the next morning he took it to Judge Nicholson, to ask him what he thought of it, that he was so much pleased with it, that he immediately sent it to a printer, and directed copies to be struck off in hand-bill form; and that he, Mr. Key, believed it to have been favorably received by the Baltimore public . . . ."[7] Judge Nicholson sent the manuscript of the song to the *American* office, then published by W. Pechin, G. Dobbin and Thomas Murphy. Publication of the *American* was suspended between September 10 and 20, as the publishers and all the printers were engaged doing military duty, and Samuel Sands, then an apprentice of fourteen years of age, was the only person in charge of the premises. Thomas Murphy secured leave of absence from his company in order to resume publication of the paper, and to him the manuscript was confided, but the type-setting was done by young Sands. The poem appears in the issue of the *American* for the 21st, under the caption " The defence of Baltimore," followed by a short account of how the song came to be written. It was sung at the theatres, an advertisement of November 12 of a brilliant military entertainment, says " The Star Spangled Banner " will be sung for the second time. It is probable that the song was issued as a broadside in a number of editions; one of the early ones that has survived is set in an elaborate double border and embellished with small cuts in the four corners.

[7] Compare account in "Early days of Washington" by S. S. Mackall, p. 189.

Concerning the affair at Marlborough, Chaplain Gleig says: " The cavalry was sent back as far as Marlborough to discover whether there were any American forces in pursuit; and it was well for the few stragglers we had left behind that this recognizance was made. Though there appeared to be no disposition on the part of the American general to follow our steps and to harass our retreat, the inhabitants of that village, at the instigation of a medical practitioner called Bain, had risen in arms as soon as we departed; and falling upon such individuals as strayed from the column, put some of them to death, and made others prisoners. A soldier whom they had taken, and who escaped, gave information of these proceedings to the troopers, just as they were about to return to headquarters; upon which they immediately wheeled about, and galloping into the village, pulled the doctor out of his bed (for it was early morning), compelled him by threat of instant death, to liberate his prisoners; and mounting him before one of the party, brought him in triumph to the camp."

The following letters are on file in the executive department of the State of Maryland, the second of which shows that Dr. Beanes was not the only person taken at Marlborough, and confirms in part, the statement of Miss Mackall, cited above.

ANNAPOLIS, August 31, 1814.

General Ross.

SIR: I am informed that a party from your army a few nights ago, took Dr. Beanes, a respectable and aged old man, out of his house, treated him with great rudeness and indignity, carried him to your camp, and that he is now on ship board.

The bearer of this, Mr. ——, goes to your camp for the purpose of conveying some necessaries to the doctor for his accommodation, and to ascertain what has occasioned this procedure, so unusual, in warfare amongst civilized nations.

I am persuaded it will only be necessary to enquire into this case, to cause the doctor to be released. I am informed he is an honorable man, and would not have been guilty of any act intentionally and knowingly, contrary to the usages of war, or derogatory to the character of a man of honor.

I hope sir, on enquiry, justice and humanity will induce you to permit the doctor to return to his family and friends as speedily as may be.

I am with great respect yours,

LEV WINDER.

GENERAL ROSS,
  Commander of His Britannic
  Majesty's forces on the Patuxent.

The second document is marked "Enclosure" and bears the same date.

"The bearer hereof. Mr. Richard West, has permission to pass to the enemy's camp for the purpose of carrying a despatch to General Ross and some necessaries to Doctor Beans, Doct Hill and Phillip Weems,[8] a prisoner with the enemy."

LEV WINDER.

The mission was unsuccessful, so far as Dr. Beanes was concerned, but Doctor William Hill and Mr. Philip Weems were promptly released; but what the actual offence of Dr. Beanes was, remains a profound mystery.

WELLS AND McCOMAS

On September 13, 1858, the bodies of Daniel Wells and Henry G. McComas were removed from a vault in Greenmount Cemetery and reinterred with full military honors in Ashland Square, where the monument now stands. There was a large military parade and the speakers of the occasion were Mayor Swann and Judge John C. Legrand. These unusual honors were paid to the remains of Wells and McComas on the supposition that these two young volunteers had been responsible for the death of General Ross, in the skirmish at North Point, forty-four years before. Subscriptions were started for a monument to cover the remains, but it remained uncompleted until 1872, when provision was made by the City Council for its completion. Resolution 348, sess. 1872, is as follows:

"*Resolved*, By the Mayor and City Council of Baltimore, That John W. Colley, Inspector of Public Buildings, be, and he is hereby

[8] The names of Doct Hill and Phillip Weems are interlined.

authorized and directed to complete the unfinished monument on Ashland Square, at the intersection of Gay and Aisquith streets, to the memory of those gallant young heroes Wells and McComas, who on the 12th of September, 1814, sacrificed their lives in defending the city from the brutal battle cry of 'Booty and Beauty.'"

Chaplain Gleig says: "General Ross was shot in the side by a rifleman." Dr. S. B. Martin and John H. W. Hawkins were members of Captain Aisquith's company of sharp shooters, to which command Wells and McComas also belonged. In the life of John H. W. Hawkins, by William George Hawkins, this passage occurs: " This company had been sent in advance of the volunteers, to ascertain the position of the enemy and to report the condition of their forces. It was soon ascertained that they had deployed in the form of the letter V, and before they were aware of the danger, they found themselves nearly surrounded. Most of them effected a safe retreat; Dr. Martin's horse was shot under him.

" Early in the day the word had passed along the lines, ' Remember boys, General Ross rides a white horse to-day.' The two young men had declared, that morning, their intention of selling their lives dearly. Instead of retreating with their comrades, they penetrated the British advance forces, and discovering General Ross, mounted on his white charger, they aimed the fatal shots. The enemy was thrown in confusion, and some moments were consumed in preparing a litter for the removal of their general weltering in his blood.

" Dr. Martin, a few days after the battle, rode down to North Point, to the residence of Mr. Gorsuch, at whose house General Ross and his officers had breakfasted on the morning of the twelfth, and learned from him the following facts: On their departure for the field of battle, Mr. Gorsuch asked the general if he should prepare supper for them upon their return. ' No,' said he; ' I shall sup in Baltimore to-night, or in hell.' It is believed that this account bears upon its face much stronger evidence of authenticity than any of the other numerous versions that have hitherto been published."

William Sannford, of the Enniskillen Dragoons, who was chief of couriers at the headquarters of General Ross, stated that General Ross, on landing, established his headquarters in a planters house built of English brick, remaining there over night. Angus Nesbitt was brought in as a prisoner. He had declined to fight against the British, and while Ross was conversing with him, the head of the column came to a halt in consequence of the skirmish with the American troops. General Ross, accompanied by Colonel McNamara and Lieutenant Hamilton and two couriers (Sergeant Sannford being one of them) rode forward to ascertain the situation. Four hundred yards in their front were discovered three men, one of whom was in a tree. The others had guns and canteens, having the appearance of a detail sent for water. It was afterwards explained that the man in the tree was gathering peaches. By the aid of a glass it was ascertained that the men belonged to separate organizations, one of them being an artillerymen. As soon as the British were discovered, the man jumped down from the tree, and all three fired simultaneously. Ross fell into McNamara's arms; and Hamilton, though prostrated to the ground, was up immediately. McNamara's coat was shot through in three places, and it was found on examination that the guns were loaded with buck-shot and ball cartridges. One of the horses received no less than five buck-shot in his breast. One of the Americans had on a high hat, such as is worn by citizens, and known in London as a castor hat. The skirmish line of the British fired and killed the three men beneath the tree where they were first discovered.[*]

In a letter to General James M. Anderson, Mr. Thomas J. Wilson wrote: " My brother Henry was in England in 1846, and at Ullswater, in the lake district, he met a gentleman at the dinner table. In the course of conversation he asked my brother where he was from. When he told him Baltimore, in America, he said ' I was once near there but did not get in as your soldiers killed our General Ross and we retired to our ships. I was aide-de-camp to the General and he fell into my arms.' On being asked the nature of his wound, he said that it was caused by a musket ball and a buck-shot. The Independent Blues' guns were loaded that way.

[*] Sannford, " The experiences of a Sergeant in the King's service in America," London, 1817.

"This company belonged to the then 5th regiment, and was commanded by Captain Aaron R. Levering. My two uncles, Thomas and William were members, the latter ensign. The company was in the front and Captain L. saw an officer ride up to the head of the British line, and said 'take good aim, there's an officer,' and he saw him fall from his horse. From the description of his dress, it must have been Ross."

The tradition in the Wells family was, that Wells and McComas concealed themselves in a clump of bushes near a spring and that Ross stopping there to get a drink of water, was shot by the two boys, and thereupon their bodies were riddled with bullets.

The company of Captain Aisquith was present at the battle of Bladensburg, and McComas had a plume shot out of his hat. There he saw General Ross, and on his return to Baltimore remarked, that should he see him again he would know him. The tradition of the McComas family was that when Henry bade his family good bye on leaving home, he said: "Here goes for a golden epaulette or a wooden leg." When the sharpshooters were ordered to retreat, he and Wells lagged behind and McComas said: "I see a mark," to which Wells replied, "So do I." Each took shelter behind separate trees and fired simultaneously. As the officer fell, the British fired several volleys in the direction of the tell-tale smoke and both youths fell dead. McComas was apparently reloading his gun, as when found, the ramrod was half way down the barrel. It is probable that he had stepped from behind the tree in order to ram home the charge, when a bullet struck him and passed through his heart. Wells, who was only a few paces off, was shot through the back of the head. Both were buried in the same grave in a churchyard on Broadway, where Johns Hopkins Hospital now stands, and the bodies were subsequently removed, in 1858, to their present resting place.

In Brackenridge's history of the war of 1812 (published in 1817), it was said that Ross was killed by some one in Captain Howard's company, the Mechanical Volunteers, which was in the front of the skirmish line. A military expert, after going over the field at North Point, and locating the positions of the various companies, arrived at the conclusion that a volley from the Mechanical Volunteers brought the unfortunate Ross' career to an end.

14

The remains of General Ross were removed to Halifax, and there, on September 29, 1814, were interred in St. Paul's church-yard, with impressive military honors. The inscription on his monument is as follows: " Here on the 29th of September, 1814, was committed to the earth, the body of Major-General Ross, who after having distinguished himself in all ranks as an officer in Egypt, Italy, Portugal, France and America, was killed at the commencement of an action which terminated in the defeat and rout of the troops of the United States, near Baltimore, on the 12th of September, 1814." At Rosstrevoir, the seat of the family in Ireland, a monument more worthy of his memory has been erected by the noblemen and gentlemen of his country, and the officers of a grateful army, which under his conduct attacked and dispersed the Americans at Bladensburg on the 24th of August, 1814, and victoriously entered Washington, the Capital of the United States. In St. Paul's Cathedral a monument has also been erected to his memory by his country." The inscription on this latter tablet is as follows: " Erected at the public expense to the memory of Major-General Robert Ross, who having under-taken and executed an enterprize against the city of Washington, the Capital of the United States of America, which was crowned with complete success, was killed shortly afterwards while direct-ing a successful attack upon a superior force, near the city of Baltimore, on the 12th of September, 1814."

MARYLAND ROSTER, WAR OF 1812.

The following roster is offered as a contribution to the history of the War of 1812. It has been compiled from original sources, public and private; and while it is by no means complete, it contains all of the information in regard to the " Citizen Soldiers " now available. Arranged alphabetically may be found, as they occur on original muster or pay rolls and in the State Archives, the names of soldiers and sailors, natives or citizens of Maryland, who took part in the last war with Great Britain. The names followed by dates in parentheses have been taken from the commission book of the Maryland adjutant-general's office or from the minutes of the governor and council, the date being that of the commission. Owing to the different forms of entry and the character and diversity of the sources, uniformity in the record of service or the reference to the military organizations has not been possible; and for the same reasons, added to the illiteracy of the military scribes, mistakes and inaccuracies must necessarily be numerous. Many names are repeated, it being impossible to determine whether they refer to different persons of the same name or to different services or tours of duty performed by one person. Reference to the name of commanding officers or to the following list of regiments and brigades may serve to make clear the exact location from which any given person enlisted.

From the data now available it is not possible to reconstruct the Maryland militia system exactly as it was in 1812-1814. Under the Act of 1793 the militia was organized into three divisions, each commanded by a major-general; a fourth division was added in 1824. In 1812 the first division was commanded by Maj.-Gen'l. Robert Cumming; the second by Maj.-Gen'l Levin Winder and the third by Maj.-Gen'l. Samuel Smith.

The twelve brigades were distributed as follows.

First Brigade, Harford and Cecil counties, composed of the 30th, 40th, 42d, and 49th regiments and extra battalion.

Second Brigade, Allegany and Washington counties, 8th, 10th, 24th and 50th regiments.

Third Brigade, Baltimore City, 5th, 6th, 27th, 39th and 51st regiments; 1st artillery regiment; 1st rifle battalion and 5th regiment of cavalry.

Fourth Brigade, Prince George's and Lower Montgomery county, 14th, 17th, 18th and 34th regiments.

Fifth Brigade, St. Mary's and Charles counties, 1st, 12th, 43d and 45th regiments.

Sixth Brigade, Kent and Queen Anne's counties, 21st, 33d, 35th and 38th regiments.

Seventh Brigade, Lower Frederick and Upper Montgomery counties, 3d, 13th, 29th and 44th regiments.

Eighth Brigade, Calvert and Anne Arundel counties, 2d, 22d, 31st and 32d regiments.

Ninth Brigade, Upper Frederick County, 16th, 20th and 47th regiments.

Tenth Brigade, Somerset and Worcester counties, 9th, 23d, 25th and 37th regiments; extra battalion.

Eleventh Brigade, Baltimore County, 7th, 15th, 36th, 41st and 46th regiments.

Twelfth Brigade, Dorchester, Caroline and Talbot counties, 4th, 11th, 19th, 26th and 48th regiments; extra battalions.

The fifty-one regiments were distributed as follows:

1. Charles Co.	18. Montgomery Co.	35. Queen Anne's Co.
2. Anne Arundel Co.	19. Caroline Co.	36. Baltimore Co.
3. Montgomery Co.	20. Frederick Co.	37. Worcester Co.
4. Talbot Co.	21. Kent Co.	38. Queen Anne's Co.
5. Baltimore City.	22. Anne Arundel Co.	39. Baltimore City.
6. Baltimore City.	23. Somerset Co.	40. Harford Co.
7. Baltimore Co.	24. Washington Co.	41. Baltimore Co.
8. Washington Co.	25. Somerset Co.	42. Harford Co.
9. Worcester Co.	26. Talbot Co.	43. Charles Co.
10. Washington Co.	27. Baltimore City.	44. Montgomery Co.
11. Dorchester Co.	28. Frederick Co.	45. St. Mary's Co.
12. St. Mary's Co.	29. Frederick Co.	46. Baltimore Co.
13. Frederick Co.	30. Cecil Co.	47. Frederick Co.
14. Prince George's Co.	31. Calvert Co.	48. Dorchester Co.
15. Baltimore Co.	32. Anne Arundel Co.	49. Cecil Co.
16. Frederick Co.	33. Kent Co.	50. Alleghany Co.
17. Prince George's Co.	34. Prince George's Co.	51. Baltimore City.

The " Regimental Cavalry Districts " were as follows:

1. Washington and Frederick counties.
2. Montgomery and Prince George's counties.
3. Calvert and Anne Arundel counties.
4. Charles and St. Mary's counties.
5. Baltimore City.
6. Baltimore County.
7. Harford County and Howard's Troop from Baltimore County.
8. Cecil and Kent counties.
9. Queen Anne's and Talbot counties.
10. Caroline and Dorchester counties.
11. Somerset and Worcester counties.
    Alleghany County extra squadron for the time being attached to the first district.

The military organization of the state was established by the Act of 1793, modified and supplemented by the Act of 1811, but actual organization of military companies was greatly forwarded by the attack on the *Chesapeake* in 1807, which thoroughly aroused the spirit of the people and resulted in the enrollment of thousands of volunteers and the re-organization of " dead " regiments.

The records in the office of the adjutant-general of the United States, though formidable in mass, are far from complete; many Maryland regiments and detachments performed military service under the orders of the governor and council and were not considered to be in the service of the United States and in consequence payment in many instances, if made at all, was delayed for years. The commission book of the Maryland adjutant-general's office is incomplete and perplexing to work with, and the muster and pay rolls are widely scattered, many of them being in private hands.

By chapter 432 of the Acts of the General Assembly of Maryland for 1868 and chapter 320 of 1876, pensions were granted to the persons therein named for services in the War of 1812, provided that proof of service of the claimant be given the comptroller. Several hundred names appear in these acts, but as no record of their services is given they have not been included here.

The writer is under great obligations to Mr. Julian Brewer of Annapolis for the use of thirty or more pay-rolls of the twenty-second regiment, probably the most complete existing record of any of the military organizations of the period ; to Mrs. George W. Sadtler of this city for the use of a muster roll of the " Baltimore Yägers "; and to Mr. Andrew E. Warner for the use of several contemporary documents. Transcripts have been made from the State Executive Archives, the so-called " Scharf Papers " and other rolls and documents in the possession of the Maryland Historical Society.

LOUIS HENRY DIELMAN.

BALTIMORE, APRIL 21, 1913.

APPENDIX

A

Aaron, Charles. Private in Capt. Travers' co. 48th rgt.

Aaron, John. Corporal in Capt. Brohawn's co. 48th rgt.

Abbey, Jacob. Private in Capt. Rogers' co. 51st. rgt.

Abbey, Joseph. Private in Capt. Rogers' co. 51st. rgt.

Abbot, Michael. Private in Capt. Wilson's co. 6th rgt.

Abbot, William. Private in Capt. Wilson's co. 6th rgt.

Abbott, Edward. Private in Capt. Brohawn's co. 48th rgt.

Abbott, Francis A. Private in Capt. Stapleton's co. 39th rgt.

Abbott, George. Private in Capt. Brohawn's co. 48th rgt.

Abbott, Samuel. Private in Capt. Shryock's co. 24th rgt.

Abbott, Wesley. Private in Capt. Stapleton's co. 39th rgt.

Abel, Philemon. Veterinary surgeon in 9th Regimental Cavalry Dist. (D. 11, 1813).

Abell, James. Private in Capt. Millard's co. 12th rgt.

Abell, Jonathan. Ensign in Capt. Hammitt's co. 12th rgt. (Je. 27, 1811). Court martialed Feb., 1814, for "rude and unofficerlike conduct." Found guilty and ordered cashiered, but re-instated.

Abell, Stanfield. Private in Capt. Rogers' co. 51st rgt.

Abercrombie, James. Private in Capt. Moale's co. Columbian Artillery.

Abert, John James [-1863]. Brevet Major Top. Engineers U. S. (N. 22, 1814).

Abigail, Richard. Private in Capt. Crawford's co. 17th rgt.

Able, Christian. Private in Capt. Haubert's co. 51st rgt.

Aborn, John. Private in Capt. Edes' co. 27th rgt.

Abrams, John. Sergeant in Capt. Patton's co. 30th rgt.

Abry, Christopher. Private in Capt. Lawrence's co. 6th rgt.

Achlan, James. Corporal in Capt. Schwarzauer's co. 27th rgt.

Ackerman, —. Sail-maker of the privateer *Surprise*. Drowned Ap. 15, 1815.

Acton, John. Private in Capt. Dent's co. 43d rgt.

Acworth, Beacham. Captain in 25th rgt. (Ap. 16, 1812).

Adam, William. Private in Capt. Conway's co. 6th rgt.

Adams, Alexander. Captain of the privateer *Amelia*.

Adams, Benedict L. Lieutenant in Capt. Riley's co. 18th rgt. (Ag. 13, 1813).

Adams, Benjamin. Private in Capt. Shrim's co. Balto. Light Infantry.

Adams, Cornelius. Sergeant in Capt. Williams' co. 12th rgt.

Adams, George. Ensign in Capt. Johnson's co. (My. 27, 1811).

Adams, George. Private in Capt. Warfield's co. Balto. United Volunteers.

Adams, George. Private in Capt. Williams' co. 12th rgt.

Adams, Gustavus A. Private in Capt. Burgess' co. 43d rgt.

Adams, Jacob. Private in Capt. Barr's Cavalry co. 1st dist.

Adams, James. Private in Capt. Shryock's co. 24th rgt.

Adams, Joseph. Private in Capt. Thos. Warner's co. 39th rgt.

Adams, Lyman. 1st Lieutenant in Capt. Myers' co. Franklin Artillery (Jy. 28, 1812).

Adams, Minos. Captain in 11th rgt. Resigned Ja. 25, 1814.

Adams, Nathaniel. Private in Capt. Wilson's co. 6th rgt.

Adams, Nathaniel. Private in Capt. Travers' co. 48th rgt.

Adams, Otto. Sergeant in Capt. Barr's Cavalry co. 1st dist.

Adams, Robert. Private in Capt. McDonald's co. 6th rgt.

Adams, Stephen. Private in Capt. William's co. 12th rgt.

Adams, Thomas. Private in Capt. Smith's co. 51st rgt.

Adams, William. Private in Capt. Barr's Cavalry co. 1st dist.

Adams, William of Charles. Private in Capt. Dent's co. 43d rgt.

Adams, William of Wm. Private in Capt. Burgess' co. 43d rgt.

Addison, Francis. Private in Capt. Beall's co. 34th rgt.

Addison, Isaac. Private in Capt. Stewart's co. 51st rgt.

Addison, John. Private in Capt. Dyer's co. 17th rgt.

Addison, William H. [-1814]. Captain, Sea Fencibles (Ap. 27, 1814).

Aderton, Joseph. Private in Capt. Posey's co. 1st rgt.

Aderton, Joseph. Private in Capt. Robey's co. 43d rgt.

Adgate, Andrew. Private in Capt. Warfield's co. Balto. United Volunteers.

Adie, Edmond. Private in Capt. Howard's co. Mechanical Volunteers.

Adlum, John. Captain in Artillery co. 1st Brigade Harford Co. (My. 31, 1808).

Adlum, John. Lieutenant in Capt. Hempstone's co. 3d rgt. (O. 12, 1807).

Adreon, Christian. Captain in Union Volunteers [5th rgt.] (Ag. 5, 1814), vice Conn.

Adreon, George. Private in Capt. Montgomery's co. Balto. Union Artillery.

Adrey, Levin. Private in Capt. Watson's co. 39th rgt.

Adrey, William. Private in Capt. Watson's co. 39th rgt.

Ady, Solomon. Ensign in Capt. Love's co. 40th rgt. (F. 14, 1815).

Agnew, William. Private in Capt. Dyer's co. Fells Point Riflemen.

Aiken, Robert. Private in Capt. Sterett's co. First Balto. Hussars.

Aiken, William. Private in Capt. Faster's co. 51st rgt.

Airs, Samuel. Private in Capt. Conway's co. 6th rgt.

Airy, John. Private in Capt. Wickes' co. 21st rgt.

Aisquith, Augustus. 3d Lieutenant in 2d U. S. Artillery (Mr. 30, 1814) ; 2d Lieutenant (My. 1, 1814).

Aisquith, Edward. Captain, Sharp Shooters in 1st Rifle Bat. Died Ap., 1815.

Aisquith, Robert C. Private in Capt. Berry's co. Washington Artillery.

Albaugh, Isaac. Cornet in Capt. Tayler's co. 2d rgt. 1st Regimental Cavalry Dist. (Je. 15, 1813).

Albaugh, Jacob. Captain in 20th rgt. Resigned Ja. 22, 1814.

Albaugh, Samuel. Captain in 28th rgt.

Albaugh, Solomon. Private in Capt. Getzendanner's co. 16th rgt.

Albaugh, William [1782-1868]. Color bearer in Baltimore Co. rgt.

Alberger, Samuel. Sergeant in Capt. Bouldin's co. Independent Light Dragoons.

Albers, Solomon, G. 1st Major in 1st rgt. Artillery (Je. 12, 1812).

Albert, Jacob. Captain in Extra Battalion Harford Co. Died 1814.

Albert, Jacob. Private in Capt. Levering's co. Independent Blues.

Albert, William. Captain in Extra Battalion Harford Co. (Jy. 8, 1814), vice Jacob Albert.

Albert, William. Corporal in Capt. Getzendanner's co. 16th rgt.

Albertis, William. Private in Capt. Galt's co. 6th rgt.

Alcock, William, Jr. Private in Capt. Levering's co Independent Blues.

Alcorn, George. Private in Capt. Thomas's co. 49th rgt.

Alcorn, Thomas. Private in Capt. Brown's co. 49th rgt.

Aldhausen, William J. Private in Capt. Roney's co. 39th rgt.

Aldnage, James. Private in Capt. Shryock's co. 24th rgt.

Aldnut, James. Private in Capt. Roney's co. 39th rgt.

Aldridge, Andrew. Private in Capt. Warfield's co. Balto. United Volunteers.

Aldridge, Isaac. Captain in 38th U. S. Infantry (My. 20, 1813).

Aldworth, John. Private in Capt. Blizzard's co. 15th rgt.

Alexander, Alexander. Private in Capt. Garrett's co. 49th rgt.

Alexander, Andrew. Private in Capt. Brown's co. 49th rgt.

Alexander, Elie. Private in Capt. Schwarzauer's co. 27th rgt.

Alexander, H. Private in Capt. Sterett's Independent co.

Alexander, Israel. Private in Capt. Sample's co. 49th rgt.

Alexander, Jacob, Jr. Captain in 28th rgt. (Ag. 17, 1808).

Alexander, James. Ensign in Capt. Cozier's co. 30th rgt. (S. 5, 1812).

Alexander, John. Private in Capt. Dillon's co. 27th rgt.

Alexander, Joseph. Private in Capt. Warfield's co. Balto. United Volunteers.

Alexander, Joseph. Private in Capt. Ringgold's co. 6th rgt.

Alexander, Robert. Ensign in Capt. Griffin's co. 36th rgt. (O. 30, 1807).

Alexander, Robert. Private in Capt. Adreon's co. Union Volunteers.

Alexander, Thomas. Private in Capt. Nicholson's co. Balto. Fencibles.

Alexander, Walter S. Private in Capt. Fendall's co. 43d rgt.

Alexander, William. Private in Capt. Maynard's co. 22d rgt.

Alexander, William. Private in Capt. McDonald's co. 6th rgt.

Alexander, William. Private in Capt. Roney's co. 39th rgt.

Alford, Aaron. Private in Capt. Chambers' co 21st rgt.

Alford, Edwin H. Corporal in Capt. Ringgold's co. 6th rgt.

Alford, Jacob. Private in Capt. Addison's co. Sea Fencibles.

Alford, John. Private in Capt. Peters' co. 51st rgt.

Alford, Thomas. Private in Capt. Addison's co. Sea Fencibles.

Alford, Thomas. Private in Capt. Kennedy's co. 27th rgt.

Alfred, James. Private in Capt. Rogers' co. 51st rgt.

Alfriend, Shadrach. Surgeon's mate in 6th Regimental Cavalry Dist. (S. 12, 1814).

All, William. Private in Capt. Stewart's co. 51st rgt.

Allcock, William. Private in Capt. Deems' co. 51st rgt.

Allen, Adam T. Private in Capt. Sheppard's co. 6th rgt.

Allen, Andrew. Private in Capt. Haubert's co. 51st rgt.

Allen, Annis. Private in Capt. Dent's co. 43d rgt.

Allen, Bryan. Command unknown; captured at North Point.

Allen, Benjamin M. Private in Capt. Brooke's co. 34th rgt.

Allen, David. Private in Capt. Dunnington's co. 43d rgt.

Allen, David. Private in Capt. Haubert's co. 51st rgt.

Allen, Henry. Private in Capt. Chalmers' co. 51st rgt.

Allen, Henry. Private in Capt. Snowden's co. 36th rgt.

Allen, Herbert. Private in Capt. Dunnington's co. 43d rgt.

Allen, Holden. Private in Capt. Stiles' Marine Artillery.

Allen, Hugh. Ensign in Capt. McDonald's co. 6th rgt.

Allen, James. Captain in 49th rgt. (Je. 15, 1811).

Allen, James. Captain in Rifle co. Frederick Co.

Allen, James. Ensign in Capt. Burns' co. 10th rgt. (Ag. 2, 1814).

Allen, James. Private in Capt. Magruder's co. American Artillerists.

Allen, John. Private in Capt. Brown's co. 6th rgt.

Allen, John. Private in Capt. Chalmers' co. 51st rgt.

Allen, John. Private in Capt. Blair's co. 50th rgt.

Allen, John. Private in Capt. Edes' co. 27th rgt.

Allen, John. Private in Capt. McConkey's co. 27th rgt.

Allen, John. Private in Capt. Rogers' co. 51st rgt.

Allen, John. Private in Capt. Fowler's co. 46th rgt.

Allen, John C. Private in Capt. Dunnington's co. 43d rgt.

Allen, Meredith. Private in Capt. Dent's co. 43d. rgt.

Allen, Mitchell B. Private in Capt. Burgess' co. 43d rgt.

Allen, Mordecai. Private in Capt. Allen's co. 49th rgt.

Allen, Noah. Prize-master of the privateer *G l o b e.* Severely wounded in action N. 1, 1813.

Allen, Robert. Private in Capt. Snowden's co. 36th rgt.

Allen, Robert D. Lieutenant in Capt. Ringgold's co. 6th rgt. (Jy. 12, 1814).

Allen, Samuel. Private in Capt. Dyer's Fells Point Riflemen.

Allen, Samuel W. Private in Capt. Magruder's co. American Artillerists.

Allen, Thomas. Private in Capt. McConkey's co. 27th rgt.

Allen, Warren. Private in Capt. Dent's co. 43d rgt.

Allender, John. Private in Capt. Ringgold's co. 6th rgt.

Allender, Joseph [1770-1834]. Surgeon 6th rgt. (Ag. 4, 1807).

Allers, John. Private in Capt. Barr's Cavalry co. 1st dist.

Allin, Thomas. Private in Capt. Tilghman's co. 33d rgt.

Allison, William. Private in Capt. Quantrill's co. 24th rgt.

Allman, Henry. Private in Capt. Smith's co. 51st rgt.

Alloway, Gabriel. Private in Capt. Page's co. 21st rgt.

Allston, Jeremiah. Corporal in Capt. Sotheran's co. 45th rgt.

Allston, Thomas. Private in Capt. Blakistone's co. 45th rgt.

Allwell, John. Sergeant in Capt. Hancock's co. 22d rgt.

Almeda, Joseph. Captain of privateer *Caroline,* Oct., 1813, which was captured by the *Medusa* after a very successful cruise; Captain of the *Kemp,* Nov., 1814.

Almony, James. Captain in 41st rgt. (Je. 1, 1813).

Alnutt, Thomas M. Private in Capt. Chew's co. 31st rgt.

Alter, Samuel. Corporal in Capt. Barr's Cavalry co. 1st dist.

Altfather, Henry. Private in Capt. Pike's co. Balto. Volunteer Artillery.

Alvey, Henry. Corporal in Capt. Cawood's co. 45th rgt.

Alvey, James. Private in Capt. Blakistone's co. 45th rgt.

Alvey, John. Private in Capt. Cawood's co. 45th rgt.

Ambler, John. Private in Capt. Stone's co. 31st rgt.

Ambrose, Peter. Private in Capt. Steiner's Frederick Artillery.

Amey, Henry. Lieutenant-Colonel 51st rgt.

Amick, Daniel. Private in Capt. Miller's co. 39th rgt.

Amick, George. Command unknown; captured at Bladensburg.

Amick, Jacob. Private in Capt. Miller's co. 39th rgt.

Amos, John. Private in Capt. Steever's co. 27th rgt.

Amoss, Benjamin S. Ensign in Capt. Amoss' co. 40th rgt. (Jy. 14, 1814).

Amoss, James, Jr. 1st Lieutenant in Capt. Smith's co. 7th Regimental Cavalry Dist. (Mr. 16, 1812).

Amoss, Joshua M. of Robt. Captain 40th rgt. (Mr. 11, 1808).

Amoss, William S. Lieutenant in Capt. Amoss' co 40th rgt. (Mr. 11, 1808).

Anderson, A. M. Private in Capt. Warfield's co. Balto. United Volunteers.

Anderson, Archibald. Private in Capt. Schwarzauer's co. 27th rgt.

Anderson, James. Private in Capt. Snowden's co. 36th rgt.

Anderson, James M. Surgeon 21st rgt. (Ag. 11, 1807).

Anderson, John. Private in Capt. Burke's co. 6th rgt.

Anderson, John. Private in Capt. Quantrill's co. 24th rgt.

Anderson, John. Private in Capt. Howard's co. Mechanical Volunteers.

Anderson, John H. Major in 11th Regimental Cavalry Dist. (F. 28, 1812); Lieutenant-Colonel (Ag. 5, 1814), vice Handy.

Anderson, John J. Private in Capt. Sample's co. 49th rgt.

Anderson, Joseph. Private in Capt. Smith's co. 51st rgt.

Anderson, Nicholas. Private in Capt. Brown's co. Eagle Artillerists.

Anderson, William. Ensign in 1st U. S. Infantry (Ag. 6, 1812); 1st Lieutenant (Je. 16, 1814).

Anderson, William. Private in Capt. Barr's Cavalry co. 1st dist.

Anderson, William. Private in Capt. Lawrence's co. 6th rgt.

Anderson, William. Private in Capt. Watson's co. 39th rgt.

Anderson, William M. Private in Capt. Berry's co. Washington Artillery.

Andre, Gregorius. 1st Lieutenant in Capt. Bader's co. Union Yägers (Jy. 24, 1813). Killed at North Point.

Andrew, George, Jr. Ensign in Capt. Harris' co. 19th rgt. (Ag. 10, 1813).

Andrew, Thomas, Jr. Ensign in Capt. Willis' co. 19th rgt. (My. 18, 1813).

Andrews, Amos. Captain of the privateer *Engineer* (1814).

Andrews, D. Ensign in Capt. Rowan's co. Resigned Ja. 25, 1814.

Andrews, George. Private in Capt. Shrim's co. Balto. Light Infantry.

Andrews, Jacob. Lieutenant in Capt. Upton Norris' co. 20th rgt. (Ja. 24, 1814).

Andrews, John. Private in Capt. Addison's co. Sea Fencibles.

Andrews, John. Private in Capt. Moale's co. Columbian Artillery.

Andrews, Thomas. Ensign in Capt. Wallace's co. 19th rgt.

Andrews, Thomas K. Ensign in 38th U. S. Infantry (My. 20, 1813). Resigned S. 19, 1813.

Andrews, William. Ensign in Capt. Lake's co. 48th rgt. (Jy. 8, 1813).

Andrews, William. Lieutenant in Capt. R. Galloway's co. 46th rgt. Resigned Jy. 8, 1814.

Anthony, Daniel. Corporal in Capt. Dyer's Fells Point Riflemen.

App, John S. Private in Capt. Sadtler's co. Balto. Yägers.

Appleby, John [1790-1834]. Private in Capt. Faster's co. 51st rgt.

Appleby, Rezin. Ensign in Capt. Jos. Marriott's co. 2d rgt. Resigned Jy., 1814.

Appleby, Thomas. Private in Capt. Myers' co. 39th rgt.

Applegarth, John. Sergeant in Capt. Hayward's co. 4th rgt.

Appleton, Charles. Private in Capt. Snowden's co. 36th rgt.

Appold, George. Corporal in Capt. Chalmers' co. 51st rgt.

Apprecht, Jacob. Private in Capt. Shryock's co. 24th rgt.

Aprice, Thomas. Ensign in Capt. Cawood's co. 45th rgt.

Apsley, Dulaney. Private in Capt. Usselton's Artillery co. 6th Brigade.

Apsley, George. Private in Capt. Page's co. 21st rgt.

Apsley, William, Jr. Private in Capt. Usselton's Artillery co. 6th Brigade.

Archer, John. Surgeon in 42d rgt. (Je. 10, 1809).

Archer, Robert H. Surgeon 30th rgt. (My. 17, 1811).

Archer, Stevenson. Paymaster in 40th rgt. (Ap. 22, 1808).

Ardinger, Peter. Lieutenant in Capt. Wolfe's co. 10th rgt. (S. 20, 1813).

Ardrery, John E. Private in Capt. Dyer's co. Fells Point Riflemen.

Armands, James. Private in Capt. Warfield's co. Balto. United Volunteers.

Armiger, Benjamin. Private in Capt. Bader's co. Union Yägers.

Armiger, Richard. Private in Capt. Ireland's co. 31st rgt.

Armistead, George [1780-1818]. 2d Lieutenant in 7th U. S. Infantry (Ja. 8, 1799); 1st Lieutenant (Ap. 1800); Captain (N. 1, 1806); Major 3d Artillery, (Mr. 3, 1813); Transferred to Corps Artillery (My. 12, 1814); Brvt. Lieutenant-Colonel (S. 12, 1814) for gallant conduct in defence of Fort Mc-Henry.

Armitage, Benjamin. Private in Capt. Pike's Balto. Volunteer Artillery.

Armitage, John. Private in Capt. Stewart's co. 51st rgt.

Armitage, Jonas Osborn [1791-1814]. Private in Capt. Sheppard's co. 6th rgt.

Armitage, William. Private in Capt. Chalmers' co. 51st rgt.

Armor, John. Private in Capt. Adreon's co. Union Volunteers.

Armour, David. Private in Capt. Warfield's co. Balto. United Volunteers.

Armour, William. Private in Capt. Quantrill's co. 24th rgt.

Arms, Austin. Private in Capt. Smith's co. 51st rgt.

Armstrong, H. Corporal in Capt. Nicholson's co. Balto. Fencibles.

Armstrong, John. Private in Capt. Montgomery's co. Balto. Union Artillery.

Armstrong, John. Private in Capt. Levering's co. Independent Blues.

Armstrong, John. Private in Capt. Bader's co. Union Yägers.

Armstrong, Joshua. Private in Capt. Thos. Warner's co. 39th rgt.

Armstrong, Peter [1777-1837]. Private in 36th U. S. Infantry; stationed at Ft. McHenry.

Armstrong, Robert. Private in Capt. McKane's co. 27th rgt.

Armstrong, Robert C. Private in Capt. Thompson's co. 1st Baltimore Horse Artillery.

Armstrong, Robert W. Brigade Major, 1st Brigade, M. M.

Armstrong, Solomon. Private in Capt. Wilson's co. 6th rgt.

Armstrong, T. Private in Capt. Sterett's Independent co.

Armstrong, Thomas [-1824]. Private in Capt. Montgomery's co. Balto. Union Artillery.

Armstrong, William. Private in Capt. Shryock's co. 24th rgt.

Arnest, John. Surgeon's mate 51st rgt. (Ag. 20, 1813).

Arnold, Benjamin. Corporal in Capt. Brown's co. Eagle Artillerists.

Arnold, Francis. Private in Capt. Pinney's co. 27th rgt.

Arnold, J. Seaman of the privateer *Globe*. Wounded in action, Nov. 1, 1813.

Arnold, John. Private in Capt. Green's co. 46th rgt.

Arnold, John. Private in Capt. Boone's co. 22d rgt.

Arnold, John. Private in Capt. McDonald's co. 6th rgt.

Arnold, Peter. Private in Capt. Snowden's co. 36th rgt.

Arnold, Peter. Private in Capt. Pinney's co. 27th rgt.

Arnold, Seth S. Sergeant in Capt. Veitch's co. 34th rgt.

Arnold, Thomas. Private in Capt. Brohawn's co. 48th rgt.

Arnold, William. Private in Capt. Sheppard's co. 6th rgt.

Arpold, Frederick. Private in Capt. Snowden's co. 36th rgt.

Arquith, Clay. Corporal in Capt. Brown's co. 6th rgt.

Arsters, Alexander. Private in Capt. Lawson's co. Balto Patriots.

Arthey, William F. Private in Capt. Nicholson's co. Balto. Fencibles.

Arthur, David. Sergeant in Capt. Spry's co. 33d rgt.

Artz, David. 2d Lieutenant in Capt. Shryock's co. 24th rgt.

Arvin, Edward. Private in Capt. Robey's co. 43d rgt. Deserted.

Ash, Jesse. Sergeant in Capt. Sample's co. 49th rgt.

Ash, John. Private in Capt. Pike's co. Balto. Volunteer Artillery.

Ash, Joseph. Lieutenant in Capt. Sample's co. 49th rgt. (Jy. 29, 1811).

Ash, Lewis. Private in Capt. McConkey's co. 27th rgt.

Ashberry, John. Captain 10th rgt. (My. 9, 1808).

Ashcroft, Thomas. Private in Capt. Dyer's co. Fells Point Riflemen.

Asher, Walter. Private in Capt. Galloway's co. 46th rgt.

Ashley, John. Lieutenant in Capt. Comegys' co. 21st rgt. (S. 2, 1811).

Ashmead, Hosea. Private in Capt. McConkey's co. 27th rgt.

Ashton, Henry. Major in 4th Regimental Cavalry Dist. (F. 13, 1812) ; Lieutenant-Colonel 45th rgt.

Ashton, Joseph K. Lieutenant in Capt. Love's co. 40th rgt. (F. 14, 1815).

Askew, Campbell S. Ensign in Capt. Stewart's co. Washington Blues.

Askew, Charles. Private in Capt. Addison's co. Sea Fencibles.

Askew, Robert. Private in Capt. McConkey's co. 27th rgt.

Askew, William. Corporal in Capt. McDonald's co. 6th rgt.

Askridge, William. Private in Capt. Brohawn's co. 48th rgt.

Atkins, Charles. Private in Capt. Getzendanner's co. 16th rgt.

Atkins, Riley. Drummer in Capt. Travers' co. 48th rgt.

Atkinson, Angel. Private in Capt. Berry's co. Washington Artillery.

Atkinson, George D. Captain Artillery co. 10th Brig. Somerset Co. (Jy. 31, 1811).

Atkinson, Isaac. Ensign in Capt. Wilson's co. 6th rgt.

Atkinson, John. Private in Capt. Brown's co. 6th rgt.

Atkinson, Joshua. Ensign in Capt. Lawrence's co. 6th rgt.

Atkinson, Joshua C. Corporal in Capt. Peters' co. 51st rgt.

Atmos, William H. Private in Capt. Peters' co. 51st rgt.

Atterbury, W. B. Sergeant in Capt. Warfield's co. Balto. United Volunteers.

Attergy, James. Private in Capt. Thomas's co. 49th rgt.

Attix, Aquila. Sergeant in Capt. Fowler's co. 33d rgt.

Atwell, Daniel. Private in Capt. Waters' co. 22d rgt.

Atwell, John. Private in Capt. Galt's co. 6th rgt.

Atwell, Nathaniel. Private in Capt. Sheppard's co. 6th rgt.

Atwell, William. Private in Capt. McDonald's co. 6th rgt.

Aubert, Jacob. Private in Capt. Getzendanner's co. 16th rgt.

Audoun, Lewis. Sergeant in Capt. Conway's co. 6th rgt.

Augustine, Samuel. Private in Capt. Stewart's co. Washington Blues.

Auld, Hugh. Lieutenant-Colonel of 26th rgt.

Auld, Ignatius. Private in Capt. Williams' co. 12th rgt.

Auld, John. Private in Capt. Shrim's co. Balto. Light Infantry.

Auld, William. Ensign in Capt. Fiddeman's co. 26th rgt. (Je. 26, 1812).

Austin, Benjamin. Private in Capt. Dyer's Fells Point Riflemen.

Austin, John. Private in Capt. Mc-Conkey's co. 27th rgt.

Austin, John. Captain 44th rgt. (Ag. 22, 1812).

Austin, Lawless. Private in Capt. Roney's co. 39th rgt.

Austin, Purnel. Prize-master of the privateer *Comet*.

Austin, Richard. Lieutenant in Capt. Ray's co. 26th rgt. (Jy. 8, 1813).

Austin, William. Lieutenant in Capt. Jordan's co. 26th rgt. (Je. 26, 1812).

Austin, William. Private in Capt. Oldham's co. 49th rgt.

Austin, William. Private in Capt. Hayward's co. 4th rgt.

Auten, Thomas. Captain of the privateer *Resolution*.

Avery, Jonathan. Private in Capt. McKane's co. 27th rgt.

Ayler, Amon. Private in Capt. Ducker's co. 7th rgt.

Ayler, Thomas. Private in Capt. Ducker's co. 7th rgt.

Ayres, Joshua. Ensign in Capt. Turner's co. 40th rgt. (Je. 16, 1812).

Ayton, Beal. Sergeant in Capt. Crawford's co. 17th rgt.

B

Baar, Jacob. Private in Capt. Shryock's co. 24th rgt.

Baar, Samuel. Sergeant in Capt. Shryock's co. 24th rgt.

Bachelder, William. Private in Capt. McConckin's co. 38th rgt.

Bacon, John. Surgeon's mate 27th rgt. (N. 8, 1814).

Bacon, Martin. Lieutenant in Capt. Hutchins' co. 41st rgt. (Ap. 20, 1808).

Baden, Clement. Lieutenant in Capt. Dyer's co. 17th rgt.

Baden, John T. Ensign in Capt. Dyer's co. 17th rgt.

Baden, Joseph N. Private in Capt. Haden's co. 17th rgt.

Baden, Nehemiah [-1836]. Assistant Deputy Commissary of Ordnance (Ag. 6, 1813).

Baden, Thomas N. Private in Capt. Crawford's co. 17th rgt.

Bader, Dominic. Captain Union Yägers (Jy. 24, 1813), vice Norris. Captured at Bladensburg.

Baer, Jacob. Surgeon's mate 16th rgt. (F. 14, 1815).

Baer, Michael of John. Private in Capt. Steiner's Frederick Artillery.

Bagg, Andrew. Captain Extra Battalion Caroline co. (D. 2, 1808).

Bagwell, Elie. Private in Capt. Smith's co. 51st rgt.

Baifield, James. Private in Capt. Steever's co. 27th rgt.

Bailer, Hezekiah. Private in Capt. Kennedy's co. 27th rgt.

Bailey, Emory. Lieutenant Extra Battalion Caroline co. (Jy. 8, 1813).

Bailey, Esma. Private in Capt. Bunbury's co. Sea Fencibles.

Bailey, George W. Private in Capt. Berry's co. Washington Artillery.

Bailey, John H. Private in Capt. Magruder's American Artillerists.

Bailey, Joseph. Gunner in Capt. Rodman's Marine Battery; wounded Sept. 13, 1814.

Bailey, Robert. Corporal in Capt. Dent's co. 43d rgt.

Bailey, Thomas. Private in Capt. Sterett's Independent Co.

Bailor, John. Private in Capt. Deems' co 51st rgt.

Baily, William. Private in Capt. Shryock's co. 24th rgt.

Bain, James. Private in Capt. Chalmers' co. 51st rgt.

Baine, Andrew. Private in Capt. Dobbin's co. 39th rgt.

Baine, Hope. Private in Capt. Sterett's Independent co.

Baine, John. Private in Capt. McDonald's co. 6th rgt.

Bainer, William. Private in Capt. Howard's co. Mechanical Volunteers.

Baird, Richard. Ensign in Capt. Barr's co. 24th rgt. (F. 10, 1809).

Baker, Benjamin. Private in Capt. Sheppard's co. 6th rgt.

Baker, Charles. Private in Capt. Pennington's co. Balto. Independent Artillerists.

Baker, Charles. Sergeant in Capt. Brown's co. Eagle Artillerists.

Baker, David. Lieutenant in Capt. Rutlidge's co. 40th rgt. (Jy. 19, 1808).

Baker, David. Private in Capt. Steever's co. 27th rgt.

Baker, Ernest. Private in Capt. Thos. Warner's co. 39th rgt.

Baker, Frederick. Corporal in Capt. Steever's co. 27th rgt.

Baker, George J. Private in Capt. Warfield's co. Balto. United Volunteers.

Baker, Giddie. Private in Capt. Brown's co. 6th rgt.

Baker, Isaac. Corporal in Capt. Myers' co. Franklin Artillery.

Baker, Jacob. Private in Capt. Shryock's co. 24th rgt.

Baker, Jacob. Private in Capt. Smith's co. 51st rgt.

Baker, James. Private in Capt. Sheppard's co. 6th rgt.

Baker, John. Private in Capt. Levering's co. Independent Blues.

Baker, John. Private in Capt. Warfield's co. Balto. United Volunteers.

Baker, Joseph. Corporal in Capt. Warfield's co. Balto. United Volunteers.

Baker, Luke. Private in Capt. John Miller's co., 2d D. I.; b. Washington Co., Md.; age 22; blacksmith; drafted.

Baker, Nathan. Major in 15th rgt.

Baker, Peter. Private in Capt. Bader's co. Union Yägers.

Baker, Rathbone. Private in Capt. Stiles' co. Marine Artillery.

Baker, Samuel. Private in Capt. Griffith's co. 21st rgt.

Baker, Samuel H. Private in Capt. Brooke's co. 34th rgt.

Baker, Thomas B. Private in Capt. Sterett's Independent co.

Baker, William, Jr. Private in Capt. Sterett's Independent co.

Balderson, Isaiah. Private in Capt. Howard's Mechanical Volunteers.

Baldwin, Abram. Private in Capt. Sheppard's co. 6th rgt.

Baldwin, Andrew. Private in Capt. Waters' co. 22d rgt.

Baldwin, Edward. Private in Capt. Waters' co. 22d rgt.

Baldwin, Rezin D. Private in Capt. Maynard's co. 22d rgt.

Baldwin, Samuel. Private in Capt. Weems' co. 22d rgt.

Baldwin, William. Ensign in Capt. Veitch's co. 34th rgt. (Je. 27, 1812).

Ball, James. Private in Capt. Pinney's co. 27th rgt.

Ball, John. Private in Capt. Levering's co. Independent Blues.

Ball, Richard. Private in Capt. Brooke's co. 34th rgt.

Ball, Walter. Private in Capt. Shrim's co. Balto. Light Infantry.

Ball, William. Lieutenant in Capt. Linthicum's co. 22d rgt. (S. 11, 1809).

Ballard, James Hudson. 2d Lieutenant 36th U. S. Infantry (Ap. 30, 1813); Regimental Adjutant (Mr., 1814).

Ballard, Levin, Jr. Captain 25th rgt. (Je. 1, 1813).

Ballard, William. Private in Capt. Thompson's co. 1st Baltimore Horse Artillery.

Ballinger [Balinger], Samuel. Private in Capt. A. E. Warner's co. 39th rgt.

Baloon, Pasquel. Private in Capt. Faster's co. 51st rgt.

Baltzell, Charles. Corporal in Capt. Stapleton's co. 39th rgt.

Baltzell, Jacob. Private in Capt. Stapleton's co. 39th rgt.

Baltzell, John. Surgeon 16th rgt. (F. 14, 1815).

Baltzell, Lewis. Private in Capt. Dobbin's co. 39th rgt.

Baltzell, Thomas. Lieutenant and Adjutant 39th rgt.

Baltzell, William. Ensign in Capt. Watson's co. 39th rgt.

Bambell, George. 1st Lieutenant 38th U. S. Infantry (My. 20, 1813). Resigned Ag. 28, 1813.

Bameyalo, Nathaniel. Private in Capt. Stewart's co. 51st rgt.

Bandell, George. Private in Capt. Sheppard's co. 6th rgt. Ensign, same co. Resigned Jy. 13, 1814.

Bandell, John. Private in Capt. Sheppard's co. 6th rgt.

Bandell, William [1786-1871]. Private in Capt. Sheppard's co. 6th rgt.

Bandle, Frederick. Private in Capt. Burke's co. 6th rgt.

Bandle, Michael. Ensign in Capt. Burke's co. 6th rgt. (Jy. 12, 1814).

Bangs, John. Private in Capt. Myers' co. Franklin Artillery.

Banier, Frederick. Private in Capt. Bader's Union Yägers.

Bankard, Jacob. Sergeant in Capt. Getzendanner's co. 16th rgt.

Bankard, Jacob. Private in Capt. Horton's co. Maryland Chasseurs.

Bankard, John. Private in Capt. Getzendanner's co. 16th rgt.

Bankert, Peter. Captain in 20th rgt. (F. 28, 1812).

Bankert, Samuel. Lieutenant in Capt. Simmons' co. 13th rgt. (Je. 26, 1812).

Banks, Daniel. Private in Capt. Stapleton's co 39th rgt.

Banks, Gamaliel. Lieutenant in in Capt. Lynch's co. 11th rgt. (Je. 1, 1813).

Banks, John. Private in Capt. Snowden's co. 36th rgt.

Banks, Samuel. Private in Capt. McLaughlin's co. 50th rgt.

Bankson, James. Private in Capt. Ringgold's co. 6th rgt.

Bankson, John. Private in Capt. Warfield's co. Balto. United Volunteers.

Banning, Robert. Captain in 9th Regimental Cavalry Dist. (Mr. 25, 1812).

Barall, Lewis. Private in Capt. Addison's co. Sea Fencibles.

Barber, George. Captain in 45th rgt.

Barber, Ignatius. Private in Capt. John Miller's co., 2d D. I.; b. Md.; age 22; cooper; subs. for Edward Ebb.

Barber, James. Private in Capt. Haubert's co. 51st rgt.

Barber, Walter. Private in Capt. Cawood's co. 45th rgt.

Barbine, Charles. Quartermaster Gunner in Capt. Bunbury's co. Sea Fencibles.

Barckley, Joseph. Sergeant Major in 39th rgt.

Barcklie, Thomas. Private in Capt. Magruder's co. American Artillerists.

Barclay, James. Ensign in Capt. Hurley's co. 11th rgt. (Ag. 20, 1814) vice Thomas Slight.

Barcroft, Ralph. Private in Capt. Montgomery's co. Balto. Union Artillery.

Barcroft, William. Private in Capt. Fowler's co. 46th rgt.

Bard, Daniel. Private in Capt. Haubert's co. 51st rgt.

Bare, George. Private in Capt. Howard's Mechanical Volunteers.

Bare, Henry. Private in Capt. Chalmers' co. 51st rgt.

Bare, John. Private in Capt. A. E. Warner's co. 39th rgt.

Bare, Samuel. Private in Capt. Levering's co. Independent Blues.

Bargan, Joseph. Private in Capt. Stiles' co. Marine Artillery.

Barge, William. Private in Capt. Haubert's co. 51st rgt.

Barger, George. Private in Capt. Montgomery's co. Balto. Union Artillery.

Barger, John. Private in Capt. Montgomery's co. Balto. Union Artillery.

Barker, Charles. Sergeant in Capt. McConkey's co. 27th rgt.

Barker, Gilbert. Private in Capt. Brown's co. 43d rgt.

Barker, James. Corporal in Capt. Shrim's co. 1st Balto. Light Infantry.

Barker, John. Private in Capt. Burgess' co. 43d rgt.

Barker, Robert M. Lieutenant in Capt. Johnson's co. Extra Batallion, Worcester Co. (O. 21, 1812).

Barkley, Samuel. 3d Lieutenant 38th U. S. Infantry (My. 20, 1813); 2d Lieutenant (My. 1, 1814).

Barkman, Conrad. Private in Capt. Bader's co. Union Yägers.

Barkman, John. Private in Capt. Pennington's co. Balto. Independent Artillerists.

Barkman, John. Private in Capt. Watson's co. 39th rgt.

Barling, Joseph. Corporal in Capt. Warfield's co. Balto. United Volunteers.

Barlow, John. Private in Capt. Lawrence's co. 6th rgt.

Barme, John. Private in Capt. Smith's co. 51st rgt.

Barnes, Adam. Captain in 32d rgt. (Ap. 21, 1809).

Barnes, Andrew. Private in Capt. Cawood's co. 45th rgt.

Barnes, Bennet H. Private in Capt. Dillon's co. 27th rgt.

Barnes, George. Captain in 32d rgt. Resigned Jy. 7, 1814.

Barnes, James. Captain of the privateer *Surprise*.

Barnes, James. Corporal in Capt. Dunnington's co. 43d rgt.

Barnes, John. Captain in Artillery co. 5th Brigade, Charles Co. (Ja. 21, 1814).

Barnes, John. Private in Capt. Montgomery's co Balto. Union Artillery.

Barnes, John. Private in Capt. Brown's co. 49th rgt.

Barnes, Matthew. Private in Capt. Gray's co. 43d rgt.

Barnes, Nathaniel. Private in Capt. McLaughlin's co. 50th rgt.

Barnes, Noble. Private in Capt. Burgess' co. 43d rgt.

Barnes, Oliver. Ensign in Capt. Waring's co. 14th rgt. (Je. 18, 1794).

Barnes, Robert. Private in Capt. Hands' co 21st rgt.

Barnes, Samuel. Sergeant in Capt. Marshall's co. 34th rgt.

Barnes, Samuel. Private in Capt. Steiner's Frederick Artillery.

Barnes, Samuel W. Private in Capt. Quantrill's co. 24th rgt.

Barnes, W. P. Private in Capt. Stiles' co. Marine Artillery.

Barnes, William. Private in Capt. Dent's co. 43d rgt.

Barnes, William. Private in Capt. Shrim's co. Balto. Light Infantry.

Barnett, David. Ensign in Capt. Schnebly's co. 8th rgt. (F. 9, 1814).

Barnett, Joseph. Private in Capt. Adreon's co. Union Volunteers.

Barnett, Perry. Drummer in Capt. Colston's co. 48th rgt.

Barnett, Richard. Sergeant in Capt. Lawson's co. Balto. Patriots.

Barnett, William. 2d Lieutenant in Capt. Walters' co. 6th Regimental Cavalry Dist. (Ap. 26, 1812).

Barney, John. Captain, Assistant Deputy Quartermaster General (Aug. 15, 1814).

Barney, Joshua [1759-1818]. Lieutenant U. S. Navy, 1776; Captain of the privateer *Rossie,* June, 1812; Captain of flotilla service (Ap. 25, 1814).

Barney, Lewis. 1st Lieutenant in Capt. Piper's co. United Maryland Artillery (Jy. 11, 1814) vice Reintzel.

Barney, Wheaton J. Private in Capt. Edes' co. 27th rgt.

Barney, William B. Major in 5th Regimental Cavalry Dist. (F. 13, 1812).

Barnhart, Henry. Private in Capt. Addison's co. Sea Fencibles.

Barnhisel, Martin. Private in Capt. John Miller's co. 2d D. I.; b. York Co., Pa.; age 30; collier.

Barnover, David. Ensign in Capt. John Brown's co. 49th rgt. (Jy. 13, 1814).

Barnsides, Henry. Private in Capt. Winsor's troop, 2d Regimental Cavalry Dist.

Barr, David. Private in Capt. McLaughlin's co. 50th rgt.

Barr, Jacob. 1st Lieutenant in Capt. Tabb's co. 1st Cavalry Dist. (F. 28, 1812); Captain (S. 12, 1814) vice Tabb.

Barr, John. Captain in 24th rgt. (F. 10, 1809).

Barrar, John, Jr. Private in Capt. Stiles' co. Marine Artillery.

Barrett, John M. [-1819]. 2d Lieutenant 38th U. S. Infantry (My. 20, 1813); 1st Lieutenant (My., 1814.)

Barrett, Patrick. Private in Capt. Barnes' co. 32d rgt.

Barrett, Thomas. Private in Capt. McConkey's co. 27th rgt.

Barrey, Louis. 1st Lieutenant in Capt. Piper's co. United Maryland Artillery (Jy. 11, 1814).

Barrick, Henry. Brigadier-General 7th Brigade (D. 28, 1812).

Barrick, Joseph. Private in Capt. John Miller's co. 2d D. I.; b. Washington co., Md.; age 25; distiller.

Barrick, Lewis. 2d Lieutenant in Capt. Clemson's Artillery co. 7th Brigade (Ap. 23, 1808).

Barritt, Solomon. Private in Capt. A. C. Smith's co. 49th rgt.

Barroll, James. Cornet in Capt. Sterett's co. 1st Balto. Hussars.

Barron, William H. Sergeant in Capt. Thompson's co. 1s rgt.

Barrott, William. Private in Capt. Hayward's co. 4th rgt.

Barrow, Denwood H. 2d Lieutenant in Capt. Hooper's co. 10th Regimental Cavalry Dist. (Mr. 23, 1814) vice John Pitt.

Barrow, James B. Private in Capt. Rogers' co 51st rgt.

Barrows, Elijah. Private in Capt. Dobbin's co. 39th rgt.

Barry, Elisha. Ensign in Capt. Marriott's co. 2d rgt. (Jy. 7, 1814).

Barry, Garrett [-1815]. Surgeon's mate 38th U. S. Infantry (Ap. 8, 1814).

Barry, John. Private in Capt. Levering's co. Independent Blues.

Barry, John Jones. Lieutenant of the privateer Torpedo, Jan. 1815.

Barry, Standish. 2d Major 5th rgt.

Barry, Thomas. Private in Capt. Levering's co. Independent Blues.

Barry, William. Private in Capt. Wells' Artillery co.

Bart, Cornelius. Ensign in Capt. Upton Norris' co. 20th rgt. (Ja. 24, 1814).

Bartgis, Benjamin F. Lieutenant in Capt. Kemp's co. 16th rgt. (Je. 26, 1812).

Bartgis, Matthias E. Captain in 16th rgt. (Jy. 24, 1813).

Bartholomew, Joseph. Corporal in Capt. Barnes' co. 22d rgt.

Bartlering, Charles. Lieutenant of the privateer Chasseur, Dec., 1813.

Bartlett, William. Private in Capt. Montgomery's co. Balto. Union Artillery.

Bartling, Daniel. Private in Capt. Berry's co. Washington Artillery.

Bartol, George. Corporal in Capt. Montgomery's co. Balto. Union Artillery.

Barton, Isaac. Private in Capt. Dillon's co. 27th rgt.

Barton, Isaac. Private in Capt. John Miller's co. 2d D. I.; b. Washington co.; age 27; painter. Deserted from Patapsco encampment June 26, 1813.

Barton, Joshua. Private in Capt. Chalmers' co. 51st rgt.

Barton, Samuel. Ensign in 41st rgt. (My. 22, 1812).

Barton, Thomas. 3d Lieutenant in 14th U. S. Infantry (Mr. 13, 1813); 2d Lieutenant (N. 14, 1813).

Barton, William. Private in Capt. Peter's co. 51st rgt.

Basdey, James. Private in Capt. Myers' co. Franklin Artillery.

Baseman, John. 2d Lieutenant in Capt. Ducker's co. 7th rgt.

Baseman, Joshua. Captain in 36th rgt. (O. 12, 1814).

Baseman, Thomas. Private in Capt. Ducker's co. 7th rg.

Baseman, William. Private in Capt. Ducker's co. 7th rgt.; captured at Bladensburg.

Basford, Henry. Private in Capt. Hall's co. 3d Cavalry rgt.

Basford, Jacob. Private in Capt. Belmear's co. 2d rgt. (1813).

Basil, John. Private in Capt. Waters' co. 22d rgt.

Basil, [Bazil], Ralph. Private in Capt. Wells' Artillery co.; Private in Capt. Chase's co. 22d rgt.

Bass, Thomas A. Lieutenant of the privateer *Grampus;* Captain, vice Murphy who was killed in action, Sept. 4, 1814.

Bassett, Isaac. Private in Capt. Stewart's co. Washington Blues.

Bassford, Thomas. Private in Capt. Chase's co. 22d rgt.; Sergeant in Capt. Sand's co. 22d rgt.

Bastin, Hezekiah. Private in Capt. Dent's co. 43d rgt.

Bastin, William. Private in Capt. Dent's co. 43 rgt.

Batchela, William. Private in Capt. Chalmers' co. 51st rgt.

Batchelor, Joshua P. Lieutenant in Capt. Schwartzauer's co. 27th rgt. (S. 23, 1813).

Batchelor, Nathaniel. Private in Capt. Ringgold's co. 6th rgt.

Batchelor, Smith. Private in Capt. Aisquith's co. Sharp Shooters.

Bateman, Amzi. Private in Capt. Sheppard's co. 6th rgt.

Bateman, Aquila. Sergeant in Capt. Posey's co. 1st rgt.

Bateman, Benjamin. Private in Capt. Gray's co. 43d rgt.

Bateman, Nat. Sergeant in Capt. Shryock's co. 24th rgt.

Bateman, Nicholas. Sergeant in 36th U. S. Infantry (My. 24, 1813) ; Ensign (My. 3, 1814).

Bateman, Walter. Private in Gray's co. 43d rgt.

Bates, Jacob. Private in Capt. Stewart's co. 51st rgt.

Bates, Joseph. Private in Capt. Miller's co. 39th rgt.

Bates, William. Assistant Adjutant General, 3d div M. M.

Bates, William. Private in Capt. Maynard's co. 22 rgt.

Battan, Robert. Private in Capt. Travers' co. 48th rgt.

Batteau, Christian. Private in Capt. Pinney's co. 27th rgt.

Battee, John. Private in Capt. Green's co. 46th rgt.

Battie, Richard H. Lieutenant in Capt. Hall's co. 2d rgt. (My. 9, 1808).

Battimore, Thomas. Private in Capt. Smith's co. 51st rgt.

Batty, Philip. Private in Capt. Kennedy's co. 27th rgt.

Baty, Oliver. Private in Capt. Steever's co. 27th rgt.

Baughan, Augustus. Sergeant Major 1st rgt. Artillery.

Baughman, Francis. Sergeant in Capt. Ducker's co. 7th rgt.

Baughman, Frederick. Private in Capt. Howard's co. Mechanical Volunteers.

Baughman, Harry. Private in Capt. Ducker's co. 7th rgt.

Baughman, John. Private in Capt. Ducker's co. 7th rgt.

Baum, Archibald. Private in Capt. Smith's co. 51st rgt.

Baum, Christian. 1st Lieutenant in Capt. Pike's co. 1st Balto. Volunteer Artillery (Je. 26, 1812).

Baum, Samuel. Sergeant in Capt. Pike's co. 1st Balto. Volunteer Artillery.

Baumgarten, Jacob. Lieutenant in Capt. Galt's co. 47th rgt. (Ja. 23, 1808).

Bausman, Joseph. Private in Capt. Myers' co. 39th rgt.

Baxley, George. Private in Capt. Berry's co. Washington Artillery.

Baxley, Joseph M. [-1839]. Ensign in 38th U. S. Infantry (Jy. 7, 1814); 3d Lieutenant (O. 1, 1814).

Baxter, Colin. Private in Capt. Conway's co. 6th rgt.

Baxter, James. Private in Capt. Stewart's co. 51st rgt.

Baxter, John. Private in Capt. Mackey's co. 49th rgt.

Baxter, Samuel. Private in Capt. Dent's co. 43d rgt.

Bay, Thomas [c1789-c1874]. Private in Capt. John Turner's co. 42 rgt., Aug. 28 to Sept. 26, 1814; Private in Capt. John Smithson's co. 49th rgt., Oct. 19, to Oct. 27, 1814.

Bayard, Stephen. 2d Lieutenant in Capt. Ford's co. 8th Regimental Cavalry Dist. (Je. 12, 1812); 1st Lieutenant (Jy. 7, 1814).

Bayless, John B. Captain in 42 rgt. (Jy. 14, 1814) vice Caldwell.

Bayley, James. Captain in 25th rgt. (N. 26, 1807).

Bayley, Jesse. Ensign in Capt. Corcoran's co. 18th rgt. (Ag. 16, 1799).

Bayley, Samuel. Private in Capt. Quantrill's co. 24th rgt.

Bayley, Thomas. Captain in 25th rgt. (Je. 9, 1809).

Baynard, Henry. Private in Capt. McConckin's co. 38th rgt.

Baynard, John. Private in Capt. Warfield's co. Balto. United Volunteers.

Bayne, Horatio. Ensign in Capt. Tolson's co. 14th rgt. (F. 4, 1808).

Beacham, James. 3d Lieutenant in Capt. Berry's co. Washington Artillery (Ag. 22, 1814).

Beacham, Nathaniel. Private in Capt. Oldham's co. 49th rgt.

Beachly, John. Corporal in Capt. John Miller's co. 2d D. I. (b. Washington Co., Md.; age 20; carpenter); subs. for John Keplinger).

Beackly, Edward. Corporal in Capt. Edes' co. 27th rgt.

Beade, George. Private in Capt. Kennedy's co. 27th rgt.

Beale, Nathan. Private in Capt. McKane's co. 27th rgt.

Beall, Alpheus B. Private in Capt. Blair's co. 50th rgt.

Beall, Azael. Captain in 34th rgt. (Jy. 7, 1814).

Beall, Dennis. Captain in 50th rgt. (Jy. 8, 1813).

Beall, Francis. Private in Capt. Dunnington's co. 43d rgt.

Beall, George. Lieutenant in Capt. Beall's co. 34th rgt. (Jy. 7, 1814) vice Jonathan Beall.

Beall, George M. Ensign in 17th U. S. Infantry (Ap. 6, 1813); 3d Lieutenant (Ja. 19, 1814).

Beall, Horatio. Ensign in Capt. Duvall's co. 18th rgt. (S. 30, 1797).

Beall, John H. Private in Capt. Dyer's co. 17th rgt.

Beall, John Hamilton. Surgeon's mate 36th U. S. Infantry (Jy. 31, 1813); Resigned Mr. 24, 1814.

Beall, John L. Lieutenant in Capt. Higgins' co. 44th rgt. (Je. 17, 1813).

Beall, John W. Private in Capt. Nicholson's Balto. Fencibles.

Beall, Jonathan. Lieutenant in Capt. Beall's co. 34th rgt. Resigned Jy. 7, 1814.

Beall, Lloyd [-1817]. Major in U. S. Artillery (Bvt. Jy. 10, 1812).

Beall, Richard B. Private in Capt. Magruder's co. American Artillerists.

Beall, Robert. 3d Lieutenant in 14th U. S. Infantry (Mr. 30, 1813); 2d Lieutenant (N. 14, 1813).

Beall, Robert O. Sergeant in 7th U. S. Infantry; Ensign (Mr. 30, 1814); 3d Lieutenant (My. 1, 1814).

Beall, Thomas Jones [-1832]. 1st Lieutenant in U. S. Artillery (Mr. 3, 1813); Captain in 4th U. S. Rifles (Mr. 17, 1814).

Beall, Walter T. G. Ensign in 36th U. S. Infantry (Ap. 30, 1813). Resigned N. 8, 1813.

Beall, William. Private in Capt. Brooke's co. 34th rgt.

Beall, William Dent. Colonel 17th rgt. (D. 9, 1813) vice Elisha Jones, deceased.

Bealmear [Belmear], Francis. Captain in 2d rgt. (Jy. 6, 1814) vice Benjamin Mullikin, resigned.

Beam, Elijah. 2d Lieutenant in Capt. Horton's co. Maryland Chasseurs (F. 28, 1812).

Beam, George, Jr. Private in Capt. Stiles' co. Marine Artillery.

Beam, William. Private in Capt. Horton's co. Maryland Chasseurs.

Bean, William. Captain in 12th rgt. (O. 3, 1807).

Bean, William. Corporal in Capt. Jackson's co. 34th rgt.

Beanes, William B. Lieutenant-Colonel in 2d Regimental Cavalry Dist. (F. 13, 1812).

Bear, Joseph. Private in Capt. Smith's co. 51st rgt.

Bear, William. Private in Capt. Miller's co. 39th rgt.

Bearbrown, Casper. Ensign in Capt. Stephens' co. 8th rgt. (S. 2, 1811).

Beard, Alexander. Lieutenant of the privateer *Revenge*, Sept., 1812.

Beard, Alexander. Private in Capt. Kennedy's co. 27th rgt.

Beard, Henry. Private in Capt. Galt's co. 6th rgt.

Beard, Hugh. Private in Capt. Brown's co. Eagle Artillerists.

Beard, John [1790-1857]. Sergeant in Capt. Schwarzauer's co. 27th rgt.

Beard, John. Private in Capt. Hall's co. 3d Cavalry rgt.

Beard, Stephen, Jr. Sergeant in Capt. Hall's co. 3d Cavalry rgt.

Beard, William C. [-1837]. 2d Lieutenant in U. S. Rifles (My. 19, 1812); Captain (Ag. 20, 1814).

Bears, Moses. Lieutenant of the privateer *Decatur*, June, 1814.

Beasin, Charles. Private in Capt. Robey's co. 43d rgt.

Beasly, William. Ensign in Capt. Ramply's co. 40th rgt. (Je. 16, 1812).

Beatley, William, Jr. Private in Capt. Magruder's co. American Artillerists.

Beattee, Richard H. Lieutenant in Capt. Hall's co. 2d rgt., 1813.

Beatty, Henry. Private in Capt. Warfield's co. Balto. United Volunteers.

Beatty, J. Seaman of the privateer *Globe*, wounded in action, Nov. 1, 1813.

Beatty, Lewis A. 2d Lieutenant in Capt. Gist's co. 2d rgt. 1st Regimental Cavalry Dist. (My. 31, 1813); 1st Lieutenant (Jy. 28, 1813).

Beatty, Samuel. Private in Capt. Pinney's co. 27th rgt.

Beauly, Thomas. Lieutenant in Capt. Scott's co. 35th rgt. (Ap. 29, 1814).

Beavin, Charles. Private in Capt. Robey's co. 43d rgt.

Bebee, Edward. Private in Capt. Addison's co. Sea Fencibles.

Beck, Elisha. Private in Capt. Page's co. 21st rgt.

Beck, John. Ensign in Capt. Wickes' co. 21st rgt. (Ja. 25, 1814).

Beck, John. Private in Capt. Wickes' co. 21st rgt.; 2d Lieutenant (Ja. 25, 1814).

Beck, John. Private in Capt. Deems' co. 51st rgt.

Beck, John. Private in Capt. Dobbin's co. 39th rgt.

Beck, Peregrine. Private in Capt. Wickes' co. 21st rgt.

Becket, Humphrey. Private in Capt. Crawford's co. 17th rgt.

Beckett, John [-1850]. 2d Lieutenant in 14th U. S. Infantry (Mr. 12, 1812); 1st Lieutenant (Mr. 13, 1813).

Beckly, John. Sergeant in Capt. Ducker's co. 7th rgt.

Beckwith, Jennings. Ensign in 14th U. S. Infantry (Ap. 15, 1814); 2d Lieutenant (D. 2, 1814).

Beckwith, William. Ensign in Capt. Lambden's co. Extra Battalion Dorchester Co. (O. 13, 1814).

Beecham, Thomas. Private in Capt. Pinney's co. 27th rgt.

Beehart, Jacob. Private in Capt. Quantrill's co. 24th rgt.

Beemer, Henry. Private in Capt. Rogers' co. 51st rgt.

Beeston, Thomas V. Private in Capt. Berry's co. Washington Artillery. Killed at Fort McHenry.

Behoo, James. Private in Capt. Roney's co. 39th rgt.

Beigler, Henry. Sergeant in Capt. Shryock's co. 24th rgt.

Bell, —. Captain in 23d rgt. Resigned D. 10, 1813.

Bell, Brooks. Command unknown; captured at Bladensburg.

Bell, Cornelius. Private in Capt. Haubert's co. 51st rgt.

Bell, Ezekiel. Private in Capt. Roney's co. 39th rgt.

Bell, Hugh. Private in Capt. Magruder's co. American Artillery.

Bell, James. Private in Capt. Sheppard's co. 6th rgt.

Bell, James. Private in Capt. Shrim's co. Balto. Light Infantry.

Bell, John. Ensign in Capt. Biddle's co. 49th rgt. (Ag. 2, 1814) vice Boulden.

Bell, John. Sergeant in Capt. Thomas's co. 49th rgt.

Bell, John H. Private in Capt. Stapleton's co. 39th rgt.

Bell, Peter. Ensign in Capt. Dashiell's co. 25th rgt. (N. 15, 1809).

Bell, Richard. Sergeant in Capt. Galt's co. 6th rgt.

Bell, Robert. Sergeant in Capt. Edes' co. 27th rgt.

Bell, Selby. Captain in Extra Battalion Caroline Co. (My. 8, 1812).

Bell, Thomas. Private in Capt. Howard's co. Mechanical Volunteers.

Bell, William. Ensign in Capt. Carter's co. 19th rgt. (Ag. 20, 1814).

APPENDIX 217

Bell, William. Private in Capt. Heath's co. 23d rgt.
Bell, William. Private in Capt. Shrim's co. Balto. Light Infantry.
Bellison, William. Private in Capt. Snowden's co. 36th rgt.
Belmire, Gabriel. Ensign in Capt. Rohrer's co. 10th rgt. (Jy. 13, 1812).
Belott, William. Private in Capt. Addison's co. Sea Fencibles.
Belt, George. Private in Capt. Smith's co. 51st rgt.
Belt, Humphrey. Lieutenant in Capt. Bowie's co. 14th rgt. (Je. 18, 1794).
Belt, James, Jr. Private in Capt. Stiles' co. Marine Artillery.
Belt, Joseph. Private in Capt. McKane's co. 27th rgt.
Belt, Lloyd. Private in Capt. Steiner's Frederick Artillery.
Belt, Osborn. Sergeant in Capt. Beall's co. 34th rgt.
Belt, Richard G. Paymaster in 8th rgt. (N. 8, 1814).
Belt, Thomas H. Private in Capt. Sterett's co. 1st Balto. Hussars.
Belt, Thomas W. Private in Capt. Levering's co. Independent Blues.
Belt, Tobias J. Private in Capt. Stiles' co. Marine Artillery.
Belt, William. Cornet in Capt. Winsor's co. 2d Regimental Cavalry Dist. (Jy. 14, 1814).
Belton, Francis Smith [-1861]. 2d Lieutenant 1st U. S. Light Dragoons (Mr. 27, 1812); Major Assistant Adjutant General (O. 18, 1814).
Belton, John. Private in Capt. Lawrence's co. 6th rgt.
Bend, William B. Corporal in Capt. Warfield's co. Balto. United Volunteers.

Benedick, George G. Lieutenant of the privateer Express, July, 1812.
Benner, James. Private in Capt. Kennedy's co. 27th rgt.
Benner, John. Private in Capt. Schwarzauer's co. 27th rgt.
Benner, John B. T. Captain in 10th rgt. Resigned Ag. 2, 1814.
Bennet, Anthony. Ensign in Capt. Jas. Bayley's co. 25th rgt. (Je. 1, 1813).
Bennett, Bonipart. Private in Capt. Travers' co. 48th rgt.
Bennett, Field F. Private in Capt. Stiles' co. Marine Artillery.
Bennett, Freeman. Private in Capt. Bunbury's co. Sea Fencibles.
Bennett, George. Private in Capt. Adreon's co. Union Volunteers. Wounded at North Point.
Bennett, John. Private in Capt. Deems' co. 51st rgt.
Bennett, Joseph. Private in Capt. Moale's co. Columbian Artillery. Captured at Bladensburg.
Bennett, Matthew. Private in Capt. Brown's co. 6th rgt.
Bennett, Richard [-1843]. 3d Lieutenant 14th U. S. Infantry (Mr. 12, 1813); 1st Lieutenant (D. 1, 1814).
Bennett, Robert. Ensign in Capt. Baseman's co. 36th rgt. (O. 22, 1807).
Bennett, Samuel. Private in Capt. Quantrill's co. 24th rgt.
Bennett, Thomas B. Captain of privateer Osprey (1812); Private in Capt. Stiles' co. Marine Artillery.
Bennett, Thomas I. Lieutenant in Capt. Langley's co. 12th rgt. (N. 7, 1812).
Bennett, William. Lieutenant in Capt. Vincent's co. 3d rgt. (Je. 17, 1813).

Benson, Eden. Ensign in Capt. Hempstone's co. 3d rgt. (O. 12, 1807).

Benson, John. Private in Capt. Peters' co. 51st rgt.

Benson, John P. Private in Capt. Pike's co. 1st Balto. Volunteer Artillery.

Benson, Perry. Brigadier-General 12th Brigade (Je. 27, 1798).

Benson, Robert. Private in Capt. Sterett's co. 1st Balto. Hussars.

Benson, Samuel. Private in Capt. Linthicum's co. 22d rgt.

Benson, Stephen. Private in Capt. Kierstead's co. 6th rgt.

Benson, Thomas. Private in Capt. Jos. Jones's co. 34th rgt.

Benson, William. Private in Capt. Dade's co. 3d rgt.

Bentalou, Paul [-1826]. Major Deputy Quarter-master General (Je. 29, 1813) ; Colonel Quartermaster General (Ag. 17, 1814).

Benton, Benjamin. Lieutenant in Capt. Sturgis' co. 35th rgt. (N. 3, 1812).

Benton, Benjamin. Private in Capt. Chambers's co. 21st rgt.

Benton, Francis. Private in Capt. Page's co. 21st rgt.

Benton, Thomas. Private in Capt. Page's co. 21st rgt.

Benton, Vincent. Cornet in Capt. Osborn's co. 9th Regimental Cavalry Dist. (Ap. 24, 1813).

Bentzle, Frederick. Private in Capt. Dillon's co. 27th rgt.

Berger, John. Private in Capt. McConkey's co. 27th rgt.

Bernard, James. Private in Capt. Blair's co. 50th rgt.

Berrige, Robert. Private in Capt. Rogers' co. 51st rgt.

Berry, Benjamin. Private in Capt. Brooke's co. 34th rgt.

Berry, Benjamin. Private in Capt. Snowden's co. 36th rgt.

Berry, Benjamin F. Private in Capt. Berry's co. Washington Artillery.

Berry, Horatio. Private in Capt. Nicholson's co. Balto. Fencibles.

Berry, James. Private in Capt. Barr's Cavalry co. 1st dist.

Berry, James. Private in Capt. Dobbin's co. 39th rgt.

Berry, John [1791-1856]. 1st Lieutenant Washington Artillery (Jy. 4, 1812) ; Captain (Ag. 15, 1812).

Berry, John. Sergeant in Capt. Sample's co. 49th rgt.

Berry, John N. Private in Capt. Dent's co. 43d rgt.

Berry, John W. Private in Capt. Berry's co. Washington Artillery.

Berry, Philip. Private in Capt. Barnes' co. 32d rgt.

Berry, Philip. Private in Capt. Myers' co. 39th rgt.

Berry, Samuel. Private in Capt. Chalmers' co. 51st rgt.

Berry, Thomas. Ensign in Capt. Magruder's co. 34th rgt. (S. 17, 1807).

Berry, Thomas. Private in Capt. Dyer's co. 17th rgt.

Berry, Thomas D. Private in Capt. Myers' co. Franklin Artillery.

Berry, William. Private in Capt. Smoot's co. 43d rgt.

Berteau, F. C. Private in Capt. Levering's co. Independent Blues.

Berton, Nicholas. Private in Capt. McDonald's co. 6th rgt.

Berwick, John. Private in Capt. Roney's co. 39th rgt.

Bets, Frederick. Private in Capt. Shryock's co. 24th rgt.

Betson, Joseph. Private in Capt. Snowden's co. 36th rgt.

Betton, Nathan. Captain in 38th rgt. (Jy. 28, 1812).

Betts, George W. Corporal in Capt. Myers' co. 39th rgt.

Bevan, James. Lieutenant in Capt. Galloway's co. 46th rgt. (Jy. 8, 1814) vice Andrews.

Bevan, Thomas S. Lieutenant of the privateer Orb, Dec., 1813.

Beven, Walter. Captain in 50th rgt. (O. 16, 1810).

Beverly, Charles. Private in Capt. Hance's co. 31st rgt.

Bevin, Henry. Private in Capt. Crawford's co. 17th rgt.

Bevins, Michael. Private in Capt. McLaughlin's co. 50th rgt.

Bhare, Charles. Private in Capt. Bunbury's co. Sea Fencibles. Severely wounded at Ft. McHenry.

Biays, James [1760-1822]. Lieutenant Colonel 5th Regimental Cavalry Dist. (F. 13, 1812).

Biays, James, Jr. Lieutenant in Capt. McDonald's co. 6th rgt.; Adjutant.

Biays, Joseph, Jr. [1792-1814]. Private in Capt. Sheppard's co. 6th rgt.

Biays, Philip. Private in Capt. Sterett's co. 1st Balto. Hussars.

Bickford, James. Private in Capt. Levering's co. Independent Blues.

Biddison, Abraham. Private in Capt. Shrim's co. Balto. Light Infantry.

Biddle, Abraham. Private in Capt. McConkey's co. 27th rgt.

Biddle, Abram. Private in Capt. Sample's co. 49th rgt.

Biddle, Andrew. Private in Capt. Thomas's co. 49th rgt.

Biddle, Benoni. Private in Capt. Brown's co. 49th rgt.

Biddle, Frisby. Cornet in Capt. Ford's co. 8th Regimental Cavalry Dist. (Jy. 7, 1814) vice Simpson.

Biddle, Hezekiah. Private in Capt. Thomas's co. 49th rgt.

Biddle, Jesse. Private in Capt. Brown's co. 49th rgt.

Biddle, Samuel. Private in Capt. Morgan's co. 49th rgt.

Biddle, Spencer. Captain in 49th rgt. (Mr. 25, 1814).

Biddle, Thomas. Ensign in Capt. Marker's co. 28th rgt.

Biddle, Thomas. Private in Capt. Moore's co. 49th rgt.

Biddle, Thomas A. Private in Capt. Thomas's co. 49th rgt.

Biddle, Tobias. Private in Capt. Oldham's co. 49th rgt.

Bier, John G. Quarter-master in Capt. Stiles' co. Marine Artillery.

Biggs, Joseph. Private in Capt. Morgan's co. 49th rgt.

Biggs, Thomas. Private in Capt. Dyer's co. 17th rgt.

Biggs, William. Private in Capt. Morgan's co. 49th rgt.

Bilby, Stanley. Private in Capt. Travers' co. 48th rgt.

Bill, Thomas. Private in Capt. Oldham's co. 49th rgt.

Billenger, John. Private in Capt. Quantrill's co. 24th rgt.

Billingsly, Thomas. Captain in 31st rgt. (Ag. 20, 1814).

Billington, James. Private in Capt. Ringgold's co. 6th rgt.

Billson, Joseph. Private in Capt. Smith's co. 51st rgt.

Billup, Robert. Private in Capt. Stiles' co. Marine Artillery.

Bilmeyer, Jacob. Private in Capt. Schwarzauer's co. 27th rgt.

Bilson, John. Private in Capt. Piper's co. United Maryland Artillery.

Bingey, John W. [-1837]. Ensign in 12th U. S. Infantry (Jy. 9, 1814); 3d Lieutenant (D. 17, 1814).

Binkley, Jacob. Private in Capt. Barr's Cavalry co. 1st Dist.

Bintzell, Baltzer. Private in Capt. Edes' co. 27th rgt.

Binyon, Thomas. Private in Capt. Brown's co. Eagle Artillerists.

Birckhead, Hugh [1788-1853]. Private in Capt. Sterett's Independent co.

Bird, William C. 2d Lieutenant 5th U. S. Infantry (Ja. 3, 1812); 1st Lieutenant (S. 1, 1812). Resigned Ag. 1, 1814.

Birely, Valentine. Sergeant in Capt. A. E. Warner's co. 39th rgt.

Birkhead, James. Private in Capt. Moale's co. Columbian Artillery.

Birkhead, Lenox. Private in Capt. Pennington's co. Balto. Independent Artillerists.

Birkhead, Richard. Private in Capt. Wilson's co. 31st rgt.

Birmingham, John. Private in Capt. Steever's co. 27th rgt.

Biscoe, Walter. Private in Capt. Warfield's co. Balto. United Volunteers.

Bishop, John. Corporal in Capt. Fowler's co. 46th rgt.

Bishop, Richard. Private in Capt. Dyer's co. Fells Point Riflemen.

Bishop, Richard R. Private in Capt. Dyer's co. Fells Point Riflemen.

Bishop, Thomas. Ensign in Capt. Cornelius' co. 35th rgt. (Jy. 7, 1814).

Bishop, William. Ensign in Capt. Fowler's co. 46th rgt. (Jy. 29, 1811).

Bitty, Elie. Paymaster 24th rgt. (Mr. 9, 1808).

Biven, Horatio. Private in Capt. Howard's co. Mechanical Volunteers.

Bivens, James. Lieutenant in Capt. Galloway's co. 46th rgt.

Bivens, Timothy. Private in Capt. Galloway's co. 46th rgt.

Bixler, David. Private in Capt. Pike's co. 1st Balto. Volunteer Artillery.

Black, Frederick. Private in Capt. Schwarzauer's co. 27th rgt.

Black, John N. Captain in 30th rgt. (My. 6, 1809).

Black, Joseph. Private in Capt. Barnes' co. 32d rgt.

Black, Joseph. Private in Capt. Schwarzauer's co. 27th rgt.

Black, Joshua. Lieutenant in Capt. Burgess's co. 32d rgt. (O. 21, 1812).

Black, Philip. Private in Capt. Morgan's co. 49th rgt.

Black, Robert. Private in Capt. Morgan's co. 49th rgt.

Black, Samuel. Private in Capt. Pennington's co. Balto. Independent Artillerists.

Black, Thomas. Private in Capt. Pike's co. Balto. Volunteer Artillery.

Black, William. Fifer in Capt. Barnes' co. 32d rgt.

Blackburn, John. Private in Capt. Shryock's co. 24th rgt.

Blackford, Thomas. Private in Capt. Steiner's Frederick Artillery.

Blackistone, see Blakistone.

Blacklock, Nicholas F. Lieutenant in Capt. McElderry's co. 17th rgt. (F. 9, 1814).

Blackwell, Francis. Corporal in Capt. Stiles' co. Marine Artillery.

Blades, Benjamin. Private in Capt. Dyer's co. Fells Point Riflemen.

Blades, Garrettson. Captain in 19th rgt. (O. 15, 1811).

Blades, George. Private in Capt. McDonald's co. 6th rgt.

Blades, John. Private in Capt. Conway's co. 6th rgt.

Blades, Perry. Private in Capt. Dyer's co. Fells Point Riflemen.

Blair, James. Sergeant Major in 5th Cavalry rgt.

Blair, Joseph. Private in Capt. Blakistone's co. 45th rgt.

Blair, Richard. Seaman of the privateer *Globe*. Killed in action Nov., 1, 1813.

Blair, Thomas. Captain in 50th rgt. (My. 28, 1808).

Blair, William. Private in Capt. Warfield's co. Balto. United Volunteers.

Blake, —. Major in 38th rgt.

Blake, Benson. Surgeon's mate 21st rgt. (Jy. 8, 1813).

Blake, Charles P. 2d Lieutenant in Capt. Ridgeway's co. 9th Regimental Cavalry Dist. (My. 25, 1812).

Blake, John. Private in Capt. Hayward's co. 4th rgt.

Blake, Oliver. Ensign in 34th U. S. Infantry (Ap. 2, 1813); Lieutenant (My. 30, 1814).

Blake, William H. 1st Lieutenant in Capt. Ridgeway's co. 9th Regimental Cavalry Dist. (My. 25, 1812); Captain (My. 31, 1813).

Blakistone, Dent. Adjutant 45th rgt. (Ag. 13, 1813) vice Kilgour.

Blakistone, Joseph. Corporal in Capt. Foreman's co. 33d rgt.

Blakistone, Kenelm. Private in Capt. Blakistone's co. 45th rgt.

Blakistone, Lewis. Captain in 33d rgt. (S. 24, 1807).

Blakistone, Thomas. Captain in 45th rgt. Rifle co. (Ag. 10, 1813).

Blanch, Thomas. Private in Capt. Edes' co. 27th rgt.

Blandford, Walter. Private in Capt. Dunnington's co. 43d rgt.

Blane, Alexander. Private in Capt. Crawford's co. 17th rg.

Blaney, Daniel. Private in Capt. Stewart's co. 51st rgt.

Blentlinger, Conrad. Private in Capt. Shryock's co. 24th rgt.

Blessing, Abraham. Lieutenant in Capt. Hackney's co. 28th rgt. (S. 2, 1811).

Blight, George G. Lieutenant of the privateer *Revenge*, Feb., 1814.

Blizzard, Isaac. Private in Capt. Blizzard's co. 15th rgt.

Blizzard, John. Ensign in Capt. Blizzard's co. 15th rgt. (O. 22, 1807).

Blizzard, William. Captain in 15th rgt. (O. 22, 1807).

Blondell, John M. Private in Capt. Sadtler's co. Balto. Yägers.

Blotner, Matthais. Private in Capt. Haubert's co. 51st rgt.

Blundle, William. Private in Capt. Roney's co. 39th rgt.

Blunt, Benjamin. Ensign in Capt. McConcking's co. 38th rgt. Died 1814.

Blunt, John. Private in Capt. Rogers' co. 51st rgt.

Blunt, Joseph. Private in Capt. Bunbury's co. Sea Fencibles.

Blunt, Samuel. Private in Capt. McConkey's co. 27th rgt.

Boarman, Benedict L. Sergeant in Capt. Causin's co. 4th Cavalry Dist.

Boarman, Ignatius. Sergeant in Capt. Haubert's co. 51st rgt.

Boarman, Michael. Private in Capt. Causin's co. 4th Cavalry Dist.

Boarman, Raphael H. Private in Capt. Thompson's co. 1st rgt.

Bobart, Charles Carroll [1789-1869]. Corporal in Capt. Lawrence's co. 6th rgt.

Bodensick, Henry. Private in Capt. Watson's co. 39th rgt.

Boehme, Charles L. Private in Capt. Sterett's co. 1st Balto. Hussars.

Boerstler, Charles G. Lieutenant-Colonel 14th U. S. Infantry (Mr. 12, 1812); Colonel (Je. 20, 1813).

Boerstler, Daniel. Ensign in Capt. Lowra's co. 24th rgt. (Je. 16, 1812).

Boggs, Alexander Lowry [1792-1856]. Private in Capt. James Sterett's 1st Balto. Hussars.

Boggus, Robert. Private Capt. A. E. Warner's co. 39th rgt.

Bohannon, Henry. Ensign in Capt. Stevenson's co. 9th rgt. (Mr. 23, 1814).

Bohannon, James. Sergeant in Capt. Jarboe's co. 12th rgt.

Bohn, Charles, Jr. Private in Capt. Levering's co. Independent Blues.

Bolin, Benjamin. Private in Capt. Barnes' co. 32d rgt. Deserted.

Bollman, Thomas. Private in Capt. McKane's co. 27th rgt.

Bolton, Henry. Private in Capt. Stiles' co. Marine Artillery.

Bond, A. Paoli. Private in Capt. Ducker's co. 7th rgt.

Bond, Alexander. Private in Capt. Marker's co. 28th rgt.

Bond, Benjamin. Private in Capt. Haubert's co. 51st rgt.

Bond, Charles. Private in Capt. Pinney's co. 27th rgt.

Bond, Charles M. Private in Capt. Cawood's co. 45th rgt.

Bond, Elijah. Lieutenant in Capt. Magee's co. 20th rgt. Resigned Ag. 1, 1814.

Bond, Henry. Private in Capt. Nicholson's co. Balto. Fencibles. Wounded at Ft. McHenry.

Bond, J. T. Private in Capt. Pennington's co. Balto. Independent Artillerists.

Bond, James. Ensign in Capt. Wherrett's co. 24th rgt. (Je. 1, 1813).

Bond, John, Jr. Captain in 7th rgt. (Je. 26, 1812).

Bond, Joshua. Private in Capt. Magruder's co. American Artillerists.

Bond, Josias. Private in Capt. Green's co. 46th rgt.

Bond, Lambert. Private in Capt. Brown's co. Eagle Artillerists.

Bond, Richard G. B. Ensign in Capt. McWilliams' co. 45th rgt. (D. 22, 1812).

Bond, Samuel. Private in Capt. Blakistone's co. 45th rgt.

Bond, Thomas. Surgeon in 7th Regimental Cavalry Dist. (Ja. 18, 1814) vice Street.

Bond, Thomas. Private (volunteer) in Capt. Warfield's co. Balto. United Volunteers.

Bond, Thomas. Private in Capt. Shryock's co. 24th rgt.

Bond, Thomas. Private in Capt. Green's co. 46th rgt.

Bond, Thomas of John. Lieutenant in Capt. Woodburn's co. 45th rgt. (Jy. 11, 1814).

Bond, Thomas E. [-1855]. Surgeon's mate 40th rgt. (Je. 1, 1813); Surgeon 7th Cavalry rgt.

Bond, William. Private in Capt. Pinney's co. 27th rgt.

Bond, Zachariah. Lieutenant in Capt. Parnham's co. 1st rgt. (Jy. 4, 1812).

Bonfield, Thomas. Private in Capt. Brown's co. 6th rgt.

Bongers' Peter C. Private in Capt. Addison's co. Sea Fencibles.

Bonne, Andrew. Lieutenant of the privateer *Fox*, Mar., 1813.

Bonne, John Jacques. Lieutenant of the privateer *Fox*, Feb., 1813; Captain, Mar., 1813.

Bonner, Hugh. Ensign in Capt. Woods' co. 27th rgt. (D. 2, 1814).

Bonner, John. Private in Capt. McKane's co. 27th rgt.

Boon, Benjamin. Private in Capt. Pinney's co. 27th rgt.

Boon, William. Private in Capt. John Miller's co. 2d D. I.; b. Washington Co., Md.; hatter; drafted.

Boone, Burley. Private in Capt. Pumphrey's co. 22d rgt.

Boone, Charles. Lieutenant in Capt. Boone's co. 22d rgt. (O. 17, 1810).

Boone, James. Captain in 22d rgt. (O. 17, 1810).

Boone, John. Adjutant in Extra Battalion Caroline co. (Ja. 20, 1808).

Boone, Joseph. Ensign in Capt. Clarke's co. 14th rgt. (Je. 18, 1794).

Boone, Oswald. Lieutenant in Capt. Marshall's co. 34th rgt. (Ap. 30, 1813).

Boone, Robert. Private in Capt. Steiner's Frederick Artillery.

Boone, Stephen. Ensign in Capt. Boone's co. 22d rgt. (O. 17, 1810).

Boone, William. Major in 10th Regimental Cavalry Dist. (N. 9, 1812).

Booth, Addison. Private in Capt. Peters' co. 51st rgt.

Booth, John. Paymaster 10th rgt. (O. 10, 1798). Resigned N. 10, 1814.

Booth, Joseph. Private in Capt. Shrim's co. Balto. Light Infantry.

Booth, Michael. Private in Capt. A. E. Warner's co. 39th rgt.

Booth, Sylvester. Cornet in 2d U. S. Light Dragoons (Jy. 19, 1813); 3d Lieutenant 4th U. S. Rifles (Mr. 17, 1814).

Booth, William. Adjutant in 36th rgt. (Je. 1, 1808).

Booth, William. Cornet in Capt. Williams' co. 1st Regimental Cavalry Dist. (S. 12, 1814).

Booth, William. Paymaster 10th rgt. (D. 17, 1814).

Booth, William. Corporal in Capt. Shrim's co. Balto. Light Infantry.

Booth, William. Private in Capt. Ringgold's co. 6th rgt.

Booze, Leonard. Private in Capt. Travers' co. 48th rgt.

Booze, Thomas. Private in Capt. Travers' co. 48th rgt.

Boreland, John. Private in Capt. Garrett's co. 49th rgt.

Boren, George. Private in Capt. Howard's co. Mechanical Volunteers.

Boring, Ely. Corporal in Capt. Blizzard's co. 15th rgt.

Bose, William. Private in Capt. Magruder's co. American Artilerists.

Bosley, John. Private in Capt. Snowden's co. 36th rgt.

Bosley, Nicholas M. Captain in 6th Cavalry Dist. (Jy. 30, 1812); Major (N. 8, 1814).

Bosley, William. Private in Capt. Thompson's co. 1st Baltimore Horse Artillery.

Boss, George. Private in Capt. Brown's co. Eagle Artillerists.

Boss, George. Fifer in Capt. Moale's co. Columbian Artillery.

Boss, John. Private Capt. Sheppard's co. 6th rgt.

Boston, Charles. Private in Capt. Brown's co. Eagle Artillerists.

Boston, Isaac. Private in Capt. Lawrence's co. 6th rgt.

Boston, Jesse. Corporal in Capt. Brown's co. 6th rgt.

Boswell, George. Sergeant in Capt. Dyer's co. 17th rgt.

Botelar, William. Private in Capt. Brooke's co. 34th rgt.

Boteler, Charles. Private in Capt. Naylor's co. 17th rgt.

Boteler, Charles L. Private in Capt. Naylor's co. 17th rgt. Declined appointment as Ensign.

Boteler, Lugen. 1st Lieutenant in Capt. Cost's co. 1st rgt. 1st Cavalry Dist. (Mr. 16, 1812).

Boughan, August. Sergeant in Capt. Magruder's co. American Artillerists.

Boulden, Andrew. Ensign in Capt. Biddle's co. 49th rgt. Resigned Ag. 1, 1814.

Boulden, William. Major in 49th rgt. (N. 3, 1812).

Bouldin, Jehu. Captain Independent Light Dragoons in 5th Regimental Cavalry Dist. (F. 13, 1812).

Bouldin, Samuel. Private in Capt. Thomas's co. 49th rgt.

Bourne, George. 2d Lieutenant in Capt. Mackall's co. 3d Cavalry Dist. (Jy. 28, 1812).

Bousmon, Herbert. Private in Capt. Ducker's co. 7th rgt.

Bousmon, John. Private in Capt. Ducker's co. 7th rgt.

Bowdle, Isaac. 2d Lieutenant in Capt. Martin's co. 9th Cavalry Dist. (My. 8, 1812); 1st Lieutenant (D. 2, 1812); Captain (Jy. 24, 1813).

Bowen, Benjamin. 1st Lieutenant in Capt. Thompson's co. of Artillery 1st Brigade (S. 10, 1814).

Bowen, Charles. Ensign in Capt. Davis' co. 7th rgt. (S. 5, 1812).

Bowen, Martin. Private in Capt. Brown's co. 6th rgt.

Bowen, Oswell. Private in Capt. Sample's co. 49th rgt.

Bowen, Richard. Private in Capt. Dyer's co. Fells Point Riflemen.

Bower, Christian. Major in 20th rgt. (Ap. 18, 1808).

Bower, Jacob. Private in Capt. Horton's co. Maryland Chasseurs.

Bower, Moses. Private in Capt. Shryock's co. 24th rgt.

Bower, Richard. 2d Lieutenant in Capt. Stansbury's Rifle co. 3d Brigade (Ap. 4, 1812).

Bowers, David. Private in Capt. Stapleton's co. 39th rgt.

Bowers, George. Private in Capt. Sadtler's co. Balto. Yägers.

Bowers, John. Private in Capt. McKane's co. 27th rgt.

Bowers, John. Private in Capt. Pinkney's Artillery co. 22d rgt.

Bowers, Martin. Private in Capt. Montgomery's co. Balto. Union Artillery.

Bowers, William. Private in U. S. Light Dragoons (1813); Cornet (Jy. 19, 1814).

Bowie, Allen. Division Quartermaster of 2d Division (D. 22, 1814).

Bowie, Charles. Private in Capt. Brooke's co. 34th rgt.

Bowie, Hezekiah. Private in Capt. Brown's co. 43d rgt.

Bowie, James. Private in Capt. Stiles' co. Marine Artillery.

Bowie, John. Surgeon 18th rgt. (Je. 22, 1808).

Bowie, John B. Lieutenant in Capt. Brooke's co. 34th rgt. (Je. 27, 1812).

Bowie, Joseph. Private in Capt. Burgess' co. 43d rgt.

Bowie, Thomas. Captain in 14th rgt. (Je. 18, 1794).

Bowie, Thomas. Colonel in 34th rgt.

Bowie, Thomas H. Private in Capt. Maynard's co. 22d rgt.

Bowles, David. Paymaster in 28th rgt. (O. 9, 1814).

Bowles, Nicholas. Ensign in Capt. Byers' co. 8th rgt. (S. 20, 1813).

Bowley, Samuel. Private in Capt. Sterett's co. 1st Balto Hussars.

Bowlie, Jacob. Private in Capt. Blair's co. 50th rgt.

Bowline, Roger. Private in Capt. McDonald's co. 6th rgt.

Bowling, Basil. Assistant Deputy Quarter-master General in drafted militia (Ag. 2, 1814).

Bowling, Francis. Private in Capt. Smoot's co. 43d rgt.

Bowly, William L. Adjutant 46th rgt. Resigned Ag. 1, 1814.

Bowman, Israel. Captain in 40th rgt. (Jy. 14, 1814) vice Jones.

Bowman, James O. Captain in 18th rgt. (O. 10, 1799).

Bowman, Joseph. Private in Capt. Shryock's co. 24th rgt.

Boyce, Benjamin. Private in Capt. Schwarzauer's co. 27th rgt.

Boyce, Charles. Private in Capt. McConkey's co. 27th rgt.

Boyce, T. R. S. Private in Capt. Thompson's co. 1st Baltimore Horse Artillery.

Boyd, Alexander. Corporal in Capt. Montgomery's co. Balto. Union Artillery.

Boyd, Alexander H. Lieutenant and Paymaster in 5th rgt. (My. 13, 1813).

Boyd, Andrew. Private in Capt. Nicholson's co. Balto. Fencibles.

Boyd, David. Private in Capt. Steiner's Frederick Artillery co.

Boyd, Dennis. Private in Capt. Hall's co. 34th rgt.

Boyd, Edmund. Quarter-master in 50th rgt. (My. 25, 1812).

Boyd, Jeremiah. Lieutenant in Capt. Stewart's co. 51st rgt.

Boyd, Joseph. Private in Capt. Myers' co. Franklin Artillery.

Boyd, Mathew. Private in Capt. Lawrence's co. 6th rgt.

Boyd, Richard D. Private in Capt. Hall's co. 34th rgt.

Boyd, William. Private in Capt. Hance's co. 31st rgt.

Boyd, William. Private in Capt. Rogers' co. 51st rgt.

Boyde, Samuel. Sergeant in Capt. Burke's co. 6th rgt.

Boyer, Frederick. Captain in 8th Cavalry Dist. (My. 22, 1812).

Boyer, Jacob. Private in Capt. Levering's co. Independent Blues.

Boyer, James. Ensign in Capt. Massey's co. 35th rgt. (N. 23, 1814).

Boyer, James. Private in Capt. McLaughlin's co. 50th rgt.

Boyer, John. Private in Capt. Rogers' co. 51st rgt.

Boyer, Peter. Ensign in Capt. Hauser's co. 10th rgt. (S. 20, 1813).

16

Boyer, William H. Captain in 33d rgt. (Jy. 11, 1814) vice Konky.

Boyle, Benjamin. Corporal in Capt. Lawrence's co. 6th rgt.

Boyle, George S. Corporal in Capt. Aisquith's co. Sharp Shooters.

Boyle, Hugh. Private in Capt. Sterett's co. 1st Balto. Hussars.

Boyle, James. Aid-de-camp to Brig. Genl. Williams (Ag. 5, 1814).

Boyle, James. Private in Capt. Maynard's co. 22d rgt.

Boyle, Thomas [1776-1825]. Captain of the privateer *Comet*, July, 1812; of the *Chasseur*, 1814.

Boyle, William. Private in Capt. Haubert's co. 51st rgt.

Boyton, Thomas. Quarter-gunner of the privateer *Surprise*. Drowned, April 15, 1815.

Boza, John. Private in Capt. Kierstead's co. 6th rgt.

Bracco, Bennet. Paymaster 26th rgt. (S. 4, 1809).

Bradbury, Francis. Private in Capt. Williams' co. 12th rgt.

Bradbury, Stephen. Private in Capt. Galt's co. 6th rgt.

Bradenbaugh, Jacob. Private in Capt. Pike's co. Balto. Volunteer Artillery.

Bradenbaugh, John. Lieutenant in Capt. Levering's co. Independent Blues.

Bradford, George. Ensign in Capt. Bradford's co. 42d rgt. (Ag. 19, 1809).

Bradford, George W. Captain in 42d rgt. (Ag. 19, 1809).

Bradford, John. 2d Lieutenant in Capt. Magruder's co. American Artillerists (Jy. 4, 1812); 1st Lieutenant (Ag. 11, 1813).

Bradford, Samuel. Brigade Quarter-master in 1st Brigade.

Bradford, Samuel. Private in Capt. Hall's co. 3d Cavalry rgt.

Bradford, William. Corporal in Capt. Stewart's co. Washington Blues.

Bradford, William. Private in Capt. Green's co. 46th rgt.

Bradley, Daniel. Command unknown. Captured at Bladensburg.

Bradley, Isaac. Private in Capt. Pike's co. Balto. Volunteer Artillery.

Bradley, James. Private in Capt. Chalmers' co. 51st rgt.

Bradley, Lewis. Private in Capt. Stapleton's co. 39th rgt.

Bradley, Philip. Private in Capt. Brown's co. 49th rgt.

Bradley, William. Private in Capt. Faster's co. 51st rgt.

Bradley, William. Private in Capt. Linthicum's co. 22d rgt.

Bradshaw, John. Private in Capt. Hayward's co. 4th rgt.

Bradshaw, Joseph. Private in Capt. Shryock's co. 24th rgt.

Bradshaw, Richard. Sergeant in Capt. Edes' co. 27th rgt.

Bradshaw, Thomas. Private in Capt. Burke's co. 6th rgt.

Bradshaw, Uriah. Private in Capt. Dent's co. 43d rgt.

Brady, Alexander. Drummer in Capt. Stapleton's co. 39th rgt.

Brady, John. Private in Capt. Thompson's co. 1st rgt.

Brady, Michael. Private in Capt. Dillon's co. 27th rgt.

Brady, Owen. Private in Capt. Veitch's co. 34th rgt.

Braggen, Henry. Private in Capt. Stiles' co. Marine Artillery.

Bramble, Esias. Private in Capt. Travers' co. 48th rgt.

Bramble, Moses. Private in Capt. Fallin's co. 48th rgt.

Bramble, Thomas. Private in Capt. Fallin's co. 48th rgt.

Bramble, William. Corporal in Capt. Foreman's co. 33d rgt.

Brand, David. Corporal in Capt. Haubert's co. 51st rgt

Brandon, Charles. Private in Capt. Adreon's co. Union Volunteers.

Brandt, Jacob. Private in Capt. Stewart's co. Washington Blues.

Branhan, Thomas. Sergeant in Capt. McDonald's co. 6th rgt.

Brannan, Thomas. Sergeant in Capt. Galloway's co. 46th rgt.

Brannen, William. Private in Capt. Watson's co. 39th rgt.

Brannock, Thomas. Private in Capt. Travers' co. 48th rgt.

Brannon, John. Sergeant in Capt. Peters' co. 51st rgt.

Branson, Joseph. Private in Capt. Pennington's co. Balto. Independent Artillerists.

Brant, William. Private in Capt. Wells' Artillery co. 22d rgt.

Brashears, Benedict. Ensign in Capt. Beall's co. 34th rgt. (Jy. 7, 1814) vice Geo. Beall.

Brashears, Ely. Captain in 13th rgt. (S. 16, 1799).

Brashears, Franey. Private in Capt. Brooke's co. 34th rgt.

Brashears, Jeremiah. Private in Capt. Brooke's co. 34th rgt.

Brashears, William. Private in Capt. John Miller's co. 2d D. I.; b. Pr. George's Co., Md.; age 27; wagoner; drafted.

Bratcher, William. Private in Capt. Sheppard's co. 6th rgt.

Brawner, Daniel. Private in Capt. Peters' co. 51st rgt.

Brawner, Henry. Lieutenant in Capt. Brown's co. 43d rgt.

Brawner, Henry. Ensign in Capt. Matthews' co. 1st rgt. (D. 7, 1813) ; Lieutenant (Jy. 11, 1814).

Brawner, John S. Corporal in Capt. Dent's co. 43d rgt.

Brawner, Theophilus. Private in Capt. Dunnington's co. 43. rgt.

Brawner, William of Edward. Private in Capt. Gray's co. 43d rgt.

Brawner, William of Wm. Private in Capt. Dunnington's co. 43d rgt.

Bready, Israel. Private in Capt. Sheppard's co. 6th rgt.

Bready, Jason. Private in Capt. Sheppard's co. 6th rgt.

Bready, John. Private in Capt. Getzendanner's co. 16th rgt.

Breant, Samuel. Private in Capt. Steiner's Frederick Artillery co.

Breeman, Thomas. Private in Capt. McLaughlin's co. 50th rgt.

Breerwood, Jonathan. Captain in Extra Battalion, Dorchester co. (Ap. 23, 1812).

Breevard, James. Captain in Extra Battalion, Worcester co. (Je. 18, 1812).

Brengle, Nicholas. 2d Lieutenant in Capt. Hauer's co. 1st Cavalry Dist. (Je. 16, 1812).

Brengman, Thomas. Command unknown. Captured at North Point.

Brennan, John F. Private in Capt. Stiles' co. Marine Artillery.

Brent, Robert [-1819]. Paymaster of U. S. Army (Jy. 1, 1808).

Brent, William C. Private in Capt. Causin's co. 4th Cavalry Dist.

Breuning, Chas. Private in Capt. Sadtler's co. Balto. Yägers.

Brewer, Allen T. Private in Capt. Pinkney's Artillery co. 22d rgt.

Brewer, Brice. Private in Capt. Sands' co. 22d rgt.

Brewer, Daniel. Lieutenant in Capt. Brewer's co. 8th rgt. (Ap. 21, 1814).

Brewer, Enos. Private in Capt. Pinkney's Artillery co.; 4th Sergeant under Capt. Wells (Ag., 1814).

Brewer, Henry. Private in Capt. Pumphrey's co. 22d rgt.

Brewer, John. Captain in 1st rgt. (Ragan's).

Brewer, John. Captain in 8th rgt. (Ap. 21, 1814).

Brewer, John R. Private in Capt. Pinney's co. 27th rgt.

Brewer, Nicholas [1789-   ]. Lieutenant in Capt. Galt's co. 6th rgt.

Brewer, Nicholas. Paymaster in 22d rgt. (S. 3, 1807).

Brewer, Nicholas, Jr. Private in Capt. Pinkney's Artillery co.; Sergeant in Capt. Slicer's co.

Brewer, William. Surgeon in 3d rgt. (Ag. 30, 1808).

Brewer, William. Private in Capt. Sands' co. 22d. rgt.; Ensign in Capt. Slicer's co. 22d rgt. (Ap. 22, 1814); in command of a detachment of the 36th rgt. at Bladensburg.

Brian, Thomas. Private in Capt. Chalmers' co. 51st rgt.

Briar, Emanuel. Private in Capt. McKane's co. 27th rgt.

Brice, Edmund. Private in Capt. Boone's co. 22d rgt.

Brice, Henry. Private in Capt. Warfield's co. Balto. United Volunteers. Wounded at North Point.

Brice, James E. Private in Capt. Nicholson's co. Balto. Fencibles.

Brice, James F. Private in Capt. Maynard's co. 22d rgt.

Brice, John. Private in Capt. Moale's co. Columbian Artillery.

Brice, John, Jr. Private in Capt. Magruder's co. American Artillerists.

Brice, John P. Private in Capt. Hall's co. 3d Cavalry rgt.

Brice, Joseph. Lieutenant in Capt. Hynson's co. 21st rgt. (F. 9, 1814).

Brice, Nicholas. Private in Capt. Sterett's Independent co.

Brice, Thomas I. Private in Capt. Chase's co. 22d rgt.

Bride, Henry. Private in Capt. Levering's co. Independent Blues.

Brien, Henry. Ensign in Capt. McPherson's co. 10th rgt. (S. 20, 1813).

Briggs, Richard. Private in Capt. Deems' co. 51st rgt.

Bright, Ignatius. Private in Capt. Boone's co. 22d rgt.

Bright, James. Private in Capt. Wells' Artillery co. 22 rgt.

Bright, John. Private in Capt. Hancock's co. 22d rgt.

Brightman, Israel. Sergeant in Capt. Brown's co. 43d rgt.

Brightwell, John L. Lieutenant in Capt. Skinner's co. 17th rgt. (Ag. 10, 1807).

Bringman, Thomas. Private in Capt. Edes' co. 27th rgt.

Brinkman, John. Private in Capt. Bunbury's co. Sea Fencibles.

Briscoe, Alexander. Private in Capt. Moale's co. Columbian Artillery.

Briscoe, Benjamin. Private in Capt. Kennedy's co. 27th rgt.

Briscoe, Bennett. Private in Capt. Cawood's co. 45th rgt.

Briscoe, David. Lieutenant in Capt. Spry's co. 33d rgt.

Briscoe, James. Private in Capt. Tilghman's co. 33d rgt.

Briscoe, James. Private in Capt. Lawrence's co. 6th rgt.

Briscoe, John H. Captain in 45th rgt. (My. 23, 1812); Major (1814).

Briscoe, Philip. Adjutant 4th Cavalry Dist. (Jy. 20, 1812).

Briscoe, Thomas. Private in Capt. Tilghman's co. 33d rgt.

Briscoe, Thomas B. Ensign in 14th U. S. Infantry (S. 15, 1814).

Britt, Robert. Private in Capt. Blair's co. 50th rgt.

Britt, Severn. Private in Capt. Faster's co. 51st rgt.

Britton, James. Captain in 14th U. S. Infantry (Mr. 12, 1812). Resigned O. 1, 1813.

Britton, John. Private in Capt. Dobbin's co. 39th rgt.

Britton, Nathaniel. Private in Capt. Blair's co. 50th rgt.

Broadwater, Charles. Private in Capt. Blair's co. 50th rgt.

Broadwater, William. Private in Capt. McLaughlin's co. 50th rgt.

Brocas, John. Private in Capt. Kennedy's co. 27th rgt.

Brohawn, John. Captain in 48th rgt. (S. 12, 1807).

Bromley, David. Private in Capt. Heath's co. 23d rgt.

Bromley, Lewis [1787-1834]. Sergeant in Capt. John Buck's co. 38th U. S. Infantry.

Bromwell, Henry T. Private in Capt. Aisquith's co. Sharp Shooters.

Bromwell, Jacob. Private in Capt. Chalmers' co. 51st rgt.

Bromwell, Jacob. Private in Capt. Aisquith's co. Sharp Shooters.

Brook, John C. Private in Capt. Barnes' co. 32d rgt.

Brook, Joseph. Private in Capt. Snowden's co. 36th rgt.

Brookbank, John. Captain in 10th rgt. (O. 10, 1798).

Brooke, Clement. Paymaster in 34th rgt. (My. 13, 1813).

Brooke, Richard. Brigade Inspector 9th Brigade (Ja. 6, 1812).

Brooke, Thomas. Captain in 34th rgt. (Je. 27, 1812).

Brooke, Thomas. Surgeon's mate in 50th rgt. (N. 3, 1812).

Brookes, John. Lieutenant in Capt. Hall's co. 34th rgt.; Captain in 38th U. S. Infantry (My. 20, 1813).

Brookes, Robert. Private in Capt. Crawford's co. 17th rgt.

Brooks, Benjamin. Sergeant in Capt. Pennington's co. Balto. Independent Artillerists.

Brooks, George. Private in Capt. Snowden's co. 36th rgt.

Brooks, Henry. 3d Lieutenant in 36th U. S. Infantry (Ap. 30, 1813). Resigned Je., 1813.

Brooks, Joseph. Private in Capt. Brohawn's co. 48th rgt.

Brooks, Joseph R. [1778-1852]. 2d Lieutenant in Capt. Montgomery's co. Balto. Union Artillery (Mr. 25, 1814) vice Pentz. Wounded at North Point. d. July 7, 1852.

Brooks, Robert. Private in Capt. Smith's co. 51st rgt.

Brooks, William. Private in Capt. Heath's co. 23d rgt.

Brooks, William. Private in Capt. Berry's co. Washington Artillery.

Broom, Henry. Private in Capt. Conway's co. 6th rgt.

Broom, John. Private in Capt. Conway's co. 6th rgt.

Broom, Thomas. Private in Capt. McDonald's co. 6th rgt.

Broom, Thomas. Quarter Gunner in Capt. Bunbury's co. Sea Fencibles.

Broome, John. Captain in 31st rgt. (F. 25, 1811).

Brosius, Michael. Private in Capt. Levering's co. Independent Blues.

Brotherton, T. W. Sergeant in Capt. Wilson's co. 6th rgt.

Brotherton, William. Private in Capt. Stiles' co. Marine Artillery.

Broughton, Isaac. Private in Capt. Stewart's co. 51st rgt.

Broughton, Noah. Private in Capt. Haubert's co. 51st rgt.

Brown, Basil. Private in Capt. Sands' co. 22d rgt.

Brown, Benjamin. Private in Capt. Hall's co. 3d Cavalry rgt.

Brown, Benjamin. Private in Capt. McLaughlin's co. 50th rgt.

Brown, Brice. Private in Capt. Snowden's co. 36th rgt.

Brown, Charles. Ensign in Capt. Rogers' co. 51st rgt.

Brown, Charles C. Quarter-master in 38th rgt.

Brown, Christian. Private in Capt. Miller's co. 39th rgt.

Brown, Elias. 1st Lieutenant in Capt. Snowden's co. 6th Cavalry Dist. (Ja. 29, 1814).

Brown, Francis. Private in Capt. Brooke's co. 34th rgt.

Brown, Garrett. Private in Capt. Sheppard's co. 6th rgt.

Brown, George. Private in Capt. Thompson's co. 1st Baltimore Horse Artillery.

Brown, George J. Captain in Eagle Artillerists (Ag. 1, 1814) vice McLaughlin.

Brown, Gustavus. Captain in 43d rgt.

Brown, Hezekiah. Private in Capt. Burgess's co. 43d rgt.

Brown, Hiram. Private in Capt. Griffith's co. 21st rgt.

Brown, Hugh. Lieutenant in Capt. Black's co. 30th rgt. (My. 6, 1809).

Brown, Hugh. Private in Capt. Wilson's co. 6th rgt.

Brown, Hugh. Corporal in Capt. Cozier's co. 30th rgt.

Brown, Isaac. Lieutenant of the privateer Burrows, Sept., 1814.

Brown, Jacob S. Private in Capt. Haubert's co. 51st rgt.

Brown, James. Private in Capt. Dillon's co. 27th rgt.

Brown, James. Sergeant in Capt. Blakistone's co. 45th rgt.

Brown, James F. Private in Capt. Hands' co. 21st rgt.

Brown, James R. M. Private in Capt. Posey's co. 1st rgt.

Brown, Jarvis. Lieutenant in Capt. Marshall's co. 9th rgt. (Je. 19, 1812).

Brown, John. 1st Lieutenant in Capt. King's Artillery co. 49th rgt. (S. 19, 1812) ; Captain (Jy. 13, 1814).

Brown, John. Sergeant in Capt. Snowden's co. 36th rgt.

Brown, John. Seaman of the privateer Comet.

Brown, John. 2d Lieutenant in Capt. Montgomery's co. Balto. Union Artillery (Ag. 15, 1812).

Brown, John. Private in Capt. Moale's co. Columbian Artillery.

Brown, John [1st]. Private in Capt. Bunbury's co. Sea Fencibles.

Brown, John. [2d]. Private in Capt. Bunbury's co. Sea Fencibles.

Brown, John. Private in Capt. Hall's co. 3d Cavalry rgt.

Brown, John. Private in Capt. Pinney's co. 27th rgt.

Brown, John. Private in Capt. Rogers' co. 51st rgt.
Brown, John. Private in Capt. Baders' co. Union Yägers.
Brown, John. Private in Capt. Wilson's co. 6th rgt.
Brown, John C. Private in Capt. Watson's co. 39th rgt.
Brown, John E. Private in Capt. Faster's co. 51st rgt.
Brown, John G. Private in Capt. Thompson's co. 1st Baltimore Horse Artillery.
Brown, John J. 1st Lieutenant in Capt. Chenoweth's co. 6th Cavalry Dist. (Je. 12, 1812).
Brown, John M. Private in Capt. Berry's co. Washington Artillery.
Brown, John R. 2d Lieutenant in Capt. Hammond's co. 3d Cavalry Dist. (Jy. 6, 1814) vice Ridgely.
Brown, John S. Private in Capt. Dent's co. 43d rgt.
Brown, Joseph. Private in Capt. Deems' co. 51st rgt.
Brown, Joseph [3d]. Lieutenant in Capt. Wickes' co. 21st rgt. (Ja. 25, 1814).
Brown, Joshua. Seaman of the privateer Globe. Killed in action, Nov. 1, 1813.
Brown, Josiah. Private in Capt. Snowden's co. 36th rgt.
Brown, Obed. Private in Capt. Miller's co. 39th rgt.
Brown, Paoli. Private in Capt. Pinney's co. 27th rgt.
Brown, Robert. Private in Capt. Snowden's co. 36th rgt.
Brown, Samuel. Sergeant in Capt. Beall's co. 34th rgt.
Brown, Samuel, Jr. 1st Lieutenant in Capt. Hammond's co. 3d Cavalry Dist. (Ap. 23, 1812); Adjutant (Jy. 12, 1814).

Brown, Thomas. Adjutant in 7th Cavalry Dist. (S. 5, 1812).
Brown, Thomas. Private in Capt. Heath's co. 23d rgt.
Brown, Thomas. Private in Capt. Aisquith's co. Sharp Shooters.
Brown, Thomas. Corporal in Capt. Maynard's co. 22d rgt.
Brown, Thomas. Lieutenant in Capt. Kelly's co. 36th rgt. (O. 12, 1814).
Brown, Thomas. Wagon master in 1st Brigade.
Brown, Thomas C. Ensign in Capt. Snowden's co. 36th rgt. (D. 24, 1810).
Brown, Tubman. Private in Capt. Heath's co. 23d rgt.
Brown, William. Lieutenant in Capt. Coats' co. 36th rgt. Resigned Jy. 13, 1814.
Brown, William. Lieutenant in Capt. Shapleigh's co. 24th rgt. Resigned Jy. 12, 1814.
Brown, William. Lieutenant in Capt. Stewart's co. 42d rgt. (Jy. 20, 1812).
Brown, William. Private in Capt. Barnes' co. 32d rgt.
Brown, William, Jr. Captain in 6th rgt. (Je. 12, 1812).
Browne, Charles C. Quarter-master in 38th rgt. (My. 19, 1813).
Browne, Morgan. 2d Lieutenant in Capt. Usselton's Artillery co. 6th Brigade (Ap. 21, 1814).
Browning, Levi. Private in Capt. Piper's co. United Maryland Artillery.
Browning, Meshack. Captain in 50th rgt. (S. 12, 1814).
Browning, Ritson. Sergeant in Capt. Miller's co. 39th rgt.
Browning, William. Private in Capt. Steever's co. 27th rgt.

Brownley, Joseph. Surgeon in 40th rgt. (Ap. 7, 1810).

Bruce, Alexander. Private in Capt. Burgess' co. 43d rgt.

Bruce, Charles Jones. Surgeon's mate in 4th Cavalry Dist. (Ag. 13, 1813).

Bruce, Francis. Private in Capt. Blair's co. 50th rgt.

Bruce, Robert. Private in Capt. Roney's co. 39th rgt.

Bruff, Benj. Private in Capt. Aisquith's co. Sharp Shooters.

Bruff, James. Captain in Artillery co. (Queen Anne Co.) 6th Brigade (My. 19, 1813).

Bruff, James. Surgeon's mate in Extra Battalion, Worcester co.

Bruff, Joseph. Ensign in Capt. Earle's co. 4th rgt. (Se. 21, 1796).

Bruff, William. Private in Capt. Warfield's co. Balto. United Volunteers.

Bruington, John. Ensign in Capt. Parson's co. 37th rgt. (Jy. 11, 1814) vice Powell.

Brukborn, Peter. Lieutenant in Capt. Holtzman's co. 50th rgt. (D. 26, 1810).

Brumbaugh, Henry. Captain in 8th rgt. (Ag. 17, 1808).

Brumfield, William [1776-1841]. Private in Capt. Andrew Porter's co. 30th rgt., Apr., 1813; Private in Capt. James Garry's co. 49th rgt. Aug.-Oct., 1814.

Brunelot, Francis. Lieutenant of the privateer Bordeaux Packet Feb., 1813.

Bruner, Elias. Private in Capt. Kennedy's co. 27th rgt.

Brunett, Andrew. Private in Capt. Montgomery's co. Balto. Union Artillery.

Brunket, William. Private in Capt. Wilson's co. 6th rgt.

Brunner, John. Jr. Lieutenant in Capt. Samuel Albaugh's co. 28th rgt. (Jy. 13, 1812); Captain in 28th rgt. (Ap. 22, 1814).

Brushweller, Ferdinand. Sergeant in Capt. Bouldin's co. Independent Light Dragoons.

Bryan, Allen. Command unknown. Captured at Bladensburg.

Bryan, Charles. Private in Capt. Hanna's co. Fells Point Light Dragoons.

Bryan, Charles K. Captain in Artillery co., 12th Brigade Dorset co. (Ap. 30, 1813).

Bryan, James. Private in Capt. McLaughlin's co. 50th rgt.

Bryan, James. Private in Capt. Travers' co. 48th rgt.

Bryan, Joseph. Private in Capt. Brown's co. 6th rgt.

Bryan, Nathaniel. Private in Capt. McLaughlin's co. 50th rgt.

Bryan, Osborn. Lieutenant in Capt. Dyer's co. 17th rgt. (S. 7, 1810).

Bryan, Stephen. Private in Capt. Page's co. 21st rgt.

Bryan, William. Sergeant in Capt. Dyer's co. 17th rgt.

Bryan, Wrightson. Private in Capt. Maynard's co. 22d rgt.

Bryant, William. Private in Capt. Wells' Artillery co. 22d rgt.

Bryson, James. 1st Lieutenant in Capt. Codd's Rifle co. 3d Brigade (Jy. 24, 1813).

Bryson, James. Private in Capt. Dyer's co. Fells Point Riflemen.

Buchanan, Edward. Private in Capt. Stewart's co. 51st rgt.

Buchanan, Francis. Private in Capt. Edes's co. 27th rgt.

Buchanan, George. Private in Capt. Roney's co. 39th rgt.

Buchanan, James. Lieutenant in 21st rgt. (Je. 18, 1794); Captain (Ag. 21, 1807).

Buchanan, John. 2d Lieutenant in Capt. King's Artillery co. 1st Brigade (S. 19, 1812).

Buchanan, John. Private in Capt. Thomas's co. 49th rgt.

Buchanan, Lloyd. Private in Capt. Stewart's co. Washington Blues.

Buchanan, William B. Sergeant in Capt. Sterett's co. 1st Balto. Hussars.

Bucher, Charles. Private in Capt. Stewart's co. 51st rgt.

Buck, Benjamin. Cornet in Capt. Stansbury's co. 6th Cavalry Dist. (Jy. 14, 1812). Declined promotion.

Buck, Benjamin [1776-1848]. 1st Lieutenant in Capt. Berry's co. Washington Artillery (F. 12, 1813) vice Hipsey.

Buck, Henry. Private in Capt. John Miller's co. 2d D. I.; b. Berkley, Co., Va.; age 21; shoemaker; subs. for John Burbarger.

Buck, John. 2d Lieutenant in Capt. Bader's co. Union Yägers (Ap. 4, 1812); Captain 38th U. S. Infantry (My. 20, 1813).

Buck, John. Trumpeter in Capt. Bouldin's co. Independent Light Dragoons.

Buck, Samuel. Private in Capt. Wilson's co. 6th rgt.

Buck, William. Ensign in Capt. Kennedy's co. 27th rgt.

Buckannan, William. Private in Capt. Fendall's co. 43d rgt.

Bucker, John. Private in Capt. Blair's co. 50th rgt.

Buckey, George. Lieutenant in Capt. Freshour's co. 16th rgt. (Je. 9, 1809).

Buckey, John. Sergeant in Capt. Steiner's Frederick Artillery co.

Buckey, Michael. Cornet in Capt. Hauer's co. 1st Cavalry Dist. (Je. 16, 1812).

Buckingham, Barsell. Private in Capt. Blizzard's co. 15th rgt.

Buckingham, Caleb. Private in Capt. Snowden's co. 36th rgt.

Buckingham, Isaiah. 4th Sergeant in Capt. Myers' co. Franklin Artillery.

Buckingham, Israel. Private in Capt. Frizzell's co. 15th rgt.

Buckingham, Levi [1786-1831]. Private in Capt. Shrim's co. Balto. Light Infantry.

Buckingham, Meshack. Private in Capt. Bizzard's co. 15th rgt.

Buckingham, Thomas. Private in Capt. Schwartzauer's co. 27th rgt.

Buckler, John C. Private in Capt. Nicholson's co. Balto. Fencibles.

Buckler, William. Private in Capt. Brohawn's co. 48th rgt.

Buckley, James. Private in Capt. Dillon's co. 27th rgt.

Buckley, Joseph [-1832]. Ensign in 38th U. S. Infantry (Ag. 12, 1813); 2d Lieutenant (Jy. 22, 1814); Ensign in Capt. Foy's co. 6th rgt. Resigned Jy., 1814.

Buckman, Edward. Lieutenant in Capt. J. B. Burgess's co. 32d rgt. (Ag. 27, 1807).

Buckwith, Samuel. Private in Capt. Oldham's co. 49th rgt.

Budd, William. Corporal in Capt. Gray's co. 43d rgt.

Buell, Albert D. Private in Capt. Aisquith's co. Sharp Shooters.

Buffum, John. Captain in 1st Balto. Volunteer Artillery (Je. 26, 1812).

Buhring, Frederick. Private in Capt. Sadtler's co. Balto. Yägers.

Bull, Aquilla. Private in Capt. Snowden's co. 36th rgt.

Bull, Aquilla. Private in Capt. Roney's co. 39th rgt.

Bull, Isaac. Corporal in Capt. Piper's co. United Maryland Artillery.

Bull, John. Sergeant in Capt. Howard's co. Mechanical Volunteers.

Bullard, Levin W. 2d Lieutenant in Capt. Carcaud's co. 3d Cavalry Dist. (Mr. 26, 1812).

Bumsby, William B. Private in Capt. Blair's co. 50th rgt.

Bunbury, H. A. Private in Capt. Warfield's co. Balto. United Volunteers.

Bunbury, Henry. Private in Capt. Brown's co. 6th rgt.

Bunbury, M. Simmones. Captain in Sea Fencibles (O. 1, 1813).

Bundick, George J. Lieutenant of the privateer *Revenge*, Mar., 1813.

Bunting, John [1782-1847]. Private in Capt. Peters' co. 51st rgt.

Burch, George. Private in Capt. Faster's co. 51st rgt.

Burch, Jonathan T. Private in Capt. Brooke's co. 34th rgt.

Burchell, Warren. Private in Capt. Dent's co. 43d rgt.

Burckhead, Daniel. Ensign in Capt. Kemp's co. 16th rgt. (S. 18, 1812).

Burden, Samuel. Private in Capt. McKane's co. 27th rgt.

Burgain, Joseph. Sergeant in Capt. Fowler's co. 46th rgt.

Burgee, Elisha. Private in Capt. Beall's co. 34th rgt.

Burgee, Thomas, Jr. Cornet in Capt. Cook's co. 2d rgt. 1st Cavalry Dist. (N. 16, 1812); 1st Lieutenant (D. 22, 1812).

Burgess, Alfred. Private in Capt. Blair's co. 50th rgt.

Burgess, Asa. Sergeant in Capt. Dunnington's co. 43d rgt.

Burgess, Benjamin. Private in Capt. Brown's co. 43d rgt.

Burgess, James. Private in Capt. G. W. Smith's co. 4th rgt.

Burgess, John. Private in Capt. Dunnington's co. 43d rgt.

Burgess, John B. Captain in 32d rgt. (Ag. 27, 1807).

Burgess, John M. 3d Lieutenant in 36th U. S. Infantry (Ap. 30, 1813); 2d Lieutenant (My. 1, 1814).

Burgess, Michael. Captain in 32d rgt.

Burgess, Michael. Private in Capt. Dyer's co. 17th rgt.

Burgess, Nathaniel. Private in Capt. Crawford's co. 17th rgt.

Burgess, Peregrine. Ensign in Capt. Adam Barnes' co. 32 rgt. (N. 30, 1811).

Burgess, Roderick. Captain in 32d rgt. (O. 21, 1812).

Burgess, Thomas. Captain in 43d rgt. (Je. 5, 1812).

Burgis, John. Private in Capt. Kierstead's co. 6th rgt.

Burgoine, Keron. Private in Capt. King's co. 49th rgt.

Burk, Edward. Private in Capt. McConckin's co. 38th rgt.

Burk, Greenberry. Seaman of the privateer *High Flyer*. Wounded in action, Dec., 1812.

Burk, James. Corporal in Capt. McConckin's co. 38th rgt.

Burk, John. Corporal in Capt. Aisquith's co. Sharp Shooters.

Burk, John. Lieutenant in Capt. Lawrence's co. 6th rgt.

Burk, Richard. Private in Capt. Steever's co. 27th rgt.

Burk, William. Private in Capt. Schwarzauer's co. 27th rgt.

Burke, David, Jr. Private in Capt. Lawrence's co. 6th rgt.

Burke, Isaac. Sergeant in Capt. Steever's co. 27th rgt.

Burke, Jacob. Corporal in Capt. Burke's co. 6th rgt.

Burke, Jacob. Private in Capt. Stewart's co. Washington Blues.

Burke, John. Lieutenant in Capt. Galt's co. 6th rgt. (Jy. 13, 1814).

Burke, John. Private in Capt. Mc-Donald's co. 6th rgt.

Burke, Joshua. Private in Capt. Edes' co. 27th rgt.

Burke, Nicholas [1781-1858]. Captain in 6th rgt. (Jy. 12, 1814).

Burke, Thomas. 1st Lieutenant in Capt. Larrimore's Artillery Co. 6th Brigade (S. 2, 1811).

Burke, Thomas. Sergeant in Capt. Conway's co. 6th rgt.

Burkhardt, Daniel. Private in Capt. Steiner's Frederick Artillery co.

Burkhead, Thomas H. Major in 7th Cavalry Dist. (F. 13, 1812).

Burkley, Philip. Quarter-master Sergeant in Capt. Barr's Cavalry co. 1st Dist.

Burland, James. Private in Capt. Peters' co. 51st rgt.

Burman, Henry. Private in Capt. Dyer's co. Fells Point Riflemen.

Burnar, George, Jr. Private in Capt. Thomas's co. 49th rgt.

Burnes, Charles. Private in Capt. Dillon's co. 27th rgt.

Burnes, Samuel. Corporal in Capt. Ringgold's co. 6th rgt.

Burnes, Timothy. Private in Capt. Dobbin's co. 39th rgt.

Burneston, Joseph, Jr. Private in Capt. McKane's co. 27th rgt.

Burneston, William. Lieutenant in Capt. Watt's co. 36th rgt. (O. 12, 1814).

Burns, Andrew. Private in Capt. Shryock's co. 24th rgt.

Burns, Dennis. Captain in 10th rgt. (My. 23, 1812).

Burns, James [c1785-1814]. Private in Capt. McConkey's co. 27th rgt.

Burns, James. Private in Capt. Blair's co. 50th rgt.

Burris, Edward. Lieutenant in Capt. Orr's co. 30th rgt. (Je. 26, 1812).

Burris, Henry. Sergeant in Capt. Fowler's co. 33d rgt.

Burroughs, Basil. Private in Capt. Cawood's co. 45th rgt.

Burroughs, George. Sergeant in Capt. Sotheran's co. 45th rgt.

Burroughs, Hanson. Private in Capt. Cawood's co. 45th rgt.

Burroughs, Philip. Private in Capt. Cawood's co. 45th rgt.

Burroughs, William. Private in Capt. Cawood's co. 45th rgt.

Burrows, Elias. Private in Capt. McLaughlin's co. 50th rgt.

Burt, Andrew. Private in Capt. Sterett's Independent co.

Burton, Elijah. Private in Capt. Green's co. 46th rgt.

Burton, Isaac. Lieutenant in Capt. Holmes' co. 18th rgt. (Je. 12, 1812).

Burton, William. Captain of the privateer *Kemp*, July, 1812.

Burton, William. Private in Capt. Fowler's co. 46th rgt.

Burull, Theophilus. Private in Capt. Montgomery's co. Balto. Union Artillery.

Busby, Abraham. Ensign in Capt. Gill's co. 7th rgt. (Je. 26, 1812).

Busey, Charles. Private in Capt. McLaughlin's co. 50th rgt.

Busey, Charles. Private in Capt. Kennedy's co. 27th rgt.

Busey, John. Ensign in Capt. Riley's co. 18th rgt. (Ag. 13, 1813).

Busey, John. Private in Capt. McLaughlin's co. 50th rgt.

Busey, Paul. Ensign in Capt. Beall's co. 50th rgt. (Mr. 9, 1808).

Busey, Samuel. Private in Capt. Rogers' co. 51st rgt.

Bush, John. Lieutenant of the privateer *Ultor,* Nov., 1814.

Bush, John F. Private in Capt. Myers' co. Franklin Artillery.

Bush, William S. Lieutenant in U. S. Marine Corps, killed in the action between the *Constitution* and the *Guerrierre.*

Bushey, George. Private in Capt. Rogers' co. 51st rgt.

Bushy, Jacob. Private in Capt. Haubert's co. 51st rgt.

Busick, John. Private in Capt. Rogers' co. 51st rgt.

Busick, Thomas. Private in Capt. Brohawn's co. 48th rgt.

Bussard, John R. Quarter-master in 18th rgt. (Ap. 27, 1814).

Bussel, George. Gunner in Capt. Bunbury's co. Sea Fencibles.

Bussey, Henry G. Captain in 40th rgt. (Je. 16, 1812).

Butcher, Joseph. Private in Capt. Rogers' co. 51st rgt.

Butcher, Samuel. Lieutenant in Capt. Pumphrey's co. 22d rgt. (My. 27, 1811).

Buterbaugh, Henry. Private in Capt. Shryock's co. 24th rgt.

Buterbaugh, John. Private in Capt. Shryock's co. 24th rgt.

Butler, Absalom. Private in Capt. Edes' co. 27th rgt.

Butler, Alexander. Private in Capt. Sample's co. 49th rgt.

Butler, James. Private in Capt. Horton's co. Maryland Chasseurs.

Butler, John. Private in Capt. Conway's co. 6th rgt.

Butler, Moses. Private in Capt. Thos. Warner's co. 39th rgt.

Butler, Osmand. Ensign in Capt. Markey's co. 16th rgt. (S. 19, 1809).

Butler, Richard. 2d Lieutenant in Capt. Piper's co. United Maryland Artillery (Ap. 30, 1813).

Butler, Richard. Private in Capt. Pike's co. Balto Volunteers Artillery.

Butler, William. Private in Capt. McConkey's co. 27th rgt.

Buxton, George. Ensign in Capt. Austin's co. 44th rgt. Resigned D. 16, 1813.

Byard, Peter. Private in Capt. Roney's co. 39th rgt.; killed at North Point.

Byerley, Lewis. Ensign in Capt. Waltz's co. 16th rgt. (Jy. 15, 1814.

Byers, John. Captain in 8th rgt. (S. 20, 1813).

Byrd, John C. Private in Capt. Warfield's co. Balto. United Volunteers. Killed at North Point.

Byrn, John. Lieutenant in 3d rgt. (Fe. 19, 1813).

Byrn, Wilson. Ensign in 3d rgt. (Fe. 19, 1813).

Byrne, Lawrence. Private in Capt. Ringgold's co. 6th rgt.

Byus, Joseph. Private in Capt. Smith's co. 51st rgt.

C

Cable, Jacob. Corporal in Capt. Pinney's co. 27th rgt.
Cadel, John. Private in Capt. Brown's co. 6th rgt.
Cadle, Daniel. Private in Capt. Edes' co. 27th rgt.
Caffery, John R. Private in Capt. Addison's co. Sea Fencibles.
Cage, Thomas S. Private in Capt. Crawford's co. 17th rgt.
Cain, Claiburn. Private in Capt. McConkey's co. 27th rgt.
Cain, James. Ensign in Capt. Goldsborough's co. 4th rgt. (Mr. 23, 1814).
Cain, Matthew. Cornet in Capt. Macatee's co. 7th Cavalry Dist. (Ap. 16, 1812).
Calder, James. Ensign in Capt. Casey's co. 18th rgt. (O. 10, 1799).
Calder, William. Lieutenant of the privateer Engineer, Sept. 1814.
Caldwell, James. Private in Capt. Sterett's Independent co.
Caldwell, James P. Private in Capt. Magruder's co. American Artillerists.
Caldwell, John A. Private in Capt. Moale's co. Columbian Artillery.
Caldwell, John R. Private in Capt. Magruder's co. American Artillerists.
Caldwell, Joseph. Ensign in Capt. Stapleton's co. 39th rgt.
Caldwell, Timothy. Surgeon's mate in Extra Battalion Caroline co. (Ja. 20, 1808).
Caldwell, William. Major in 42d rgt. Died Dec., 1814.
Cale, Daniel. Private in Capt. Pinney's co. 27th rgt.

Calhoun, Benjamin. Private in Capt. Stapleton's co. 39th rgt.
Calhoun, James, Jr. Brigade Major in 3d Brigade; Deputy Commissary of purchases, U. S. Army (Je. 29, 1813).
Calif, James. Private in Capt. McDonald's co. 6th rgt.
Calif, John. Private in Capt. McDonald's co. 6th rgt.
Callahan, Charles. Private in Capt. Haubert's co. 51st rgt.
Callahan, James. Private in Capt. Maynard's co. 22d rgt.
Callahan, Peter. Private in Capt. Haubert's co. 51st rgt.
Callander, J. A. Private in Capt. Pennington's co. Balto. Independent Artillerists.
Callender, James. Private in Capt. Burke's co. 6th rgt.
Callihan, Joseph. Private in Capt. Massey's co. 38th rgt.
Callihan, Peter. Private in Capt. Kennedy's co. 27th rgt.
Callis, Daniel. Private in Capt. Brohawn's co. 48th rgt.
Calmerry, James. Ensign in Capt. Oldham's co. 30th rgt. (Jy. 31, 1812).
Calvert, William. Private in Capt. Kennedy's co. 27th rgt.
Calvin, Richard. Private in Capt. Ringgold's co. 6th rgt.
Camaham, James. Private in Capt. Montgomery's co. Balto. Union Artillery.
Camden, James. Private in Capt. Rogers' co. 51st rgt.
Camden, John. Sergeant in Capt. Waters' co. 22d rgt.
Camden, William. Private in Capt. Veitch's co. 34th rgt.
Camerly, John. Private in Capt. Wilson's co. 6th rgt.

Camerly, Peter. Private in Capt. Wilson's co. 6th rgt.

Cameron, Charles C. Sergeant in Capt. John Miller's co. 2d D. I.; b. Jefferson Co., Va.; age 24; joiner.

Cammel, John R. Lieutenant in Capt. Litton's co. 44th rgt. Died 1814.

Cammeron, John. Private in Capt. Lawrence's co. 6th rgt.

Camp, Joseph. Private in Capt. Myers' co. 39th rgt.

Camp, William. Private in Capt. Sterett's Independent co.

Camp, William. Private in Capt. Aisquith's co. Sharp Shooters.

Camp, William, Jr. Ensign in 38th U. S. Infantry (My. 20, 1813). Resigned My. 1, 1814.

Campbell, Alexander. Sergeant in Capt. Linthicum's co. 22d rgt.

Campbell, Bernard U. 1st Lieutenant in Capt. Bader's co. Union Yägers; Sergeant-major and Adjutant in 1st Rifle Battalion.

Campbell, George W. Pr. Capt. Stapleton's co. 39th rgt.

Campbell, Henry M. [-1824]. 3d Lieutenant in 2d U. S. Artillery (Jy. 19, 1813). Bvt'd. 1st; Lieutenant (Jy. 5, 1814) for distinguished services at battle of Chippewa, U. C. and Capt. (Jy. 25, 1814) for distinguished services at battle of Niagara Falls.

Campbell, Hugh. Private in Capt. Montgomery's co. Balto. Union Artillery.

Campbell, James. Private in Capt. Burke's co. 6th rgt.

Campbell, John. Private in Capt. Warner's co. 39th rgt.

Campbell, John R. Private in Capt. Thompson's co. 1st Baltimore Horse Artillery.

Campbell, Samuel. Private in Capt. Brown's Artillery co. 49th rgt.

Campble, Francis. Private in Capt. Ducker's co. 7th rgt.; enlisted Sept. 8, 1814.

Canby, Benjamin. Private in Capt. Howard's co. Mechanical Volunteers.

Cannada, Ebenezer. Private in Capt. Lawrence's co. 6th rgt.

Canney, John. Private in Capt. Ringgold's co. 6th rgt.

Cannon, Edward. Private in Capt. Usselton's Artillery co. 6th Brigade.

Cannon, Gustavus. Private in Capt. Fallin's co. 48th rgt.

Cannon, Jacob. Private in Capt. Getzendanner's co. 16th rgt.

Cannon, John. Private in Capt. Heath's co. 23d rgt.

Cantwell, John. Private in Capt. Heath's co. 23d rgt.

Cantwell, Matthew. Private in Capt. Sample's co. 49th rgt.

Capito, Peter. Private in Capt. Schwarzauer's co. 27th rgt.

Caples, Jacob. Lieutenant in Capt. Gill's co. 7th rgt. (Je. 26, 1812).

Caples, Samuel. Ensign in Capt. Frizzell's co. 15th rgt. (O. 22, 1807).

Cappuch, William. Private in Capt. Dillon's co. 27th rgt.

Caprice, Joseph. Private in Capt. Kierstead's co. 6th rgt.

Carback, Ephraim. Private in Capt. Galloway's co. 46th rgt.

Carback, William. Corporal in Capt. Galloway's co. 46th rgt.

* Carberry, Henry [1757-1822]. " Gentleman Cadet " in St. Mary's Co., Independent co., 1776; 2d Lieutenant in Col. Hartley's rgt. (Ja. 24, 1777); Captain (N. 30, 1778); wounded Aug. 13, 1779;

Captain of levies under Gen. St.
Clair in 1791; Captain U. S. Infantry (Mr. 16, 1792); resigned
Feb. 10, 1794; Adjutant-General
of Md. (O. 6, 1794) and served 13
years; Colonel 36th U. S. Infantry
(Mr. 22, 1813); resigned March
4, 1815; died at Georgetown, D. C.,
May 26, 1822.
Carberry, Nicholas. Sergeant in
Capt. Blakistone's co. 45th rgt.
Carberry, Thomas. Captain in 36th
U. S. Infantry (Ap. 30, 1813).
Carberry, Thomas P. Private in
Capt. Blakistone's co. 45th rgt.
Carberry, Uriah. Private in Capt.
Blakistone's co. 45th rgt.
Carcaud, William M. Captain in
3d Cavalry Dist. (F. 13, 1812).
Carey, Joseph. Private in Capt.
Lawrence's co. 6th rgt.
Carlin, Cornelius. Private in Capt.
Getzendanner's co. 16th rgt.
Carlisle, Amos. Ensign in Capt.
Coats' co. 36th rgt. (Jy. 13, 1814).
Carlton, Jonathan. Ensign in Capt.
Brewer's co. 8th rgt. (Ap. 21,
1814).
Carlton, Thomas. Captain in 16th
rgt. (S. 20, 1813).
Carlton, Thomas. 1st Lieutenant
and Quarter-master in 39th rgt.
Carman, Greenberry. Private in
Capt. Lowman's co. 35th rgt.
Carman, Jacob. Private in Capt.
Berry's co. Washington Artillery.
Carman, John. Private in Capt.
Hall's co. 3d Cavalry rgt.
Carman, William. Private in Capt.
Chase's co. 22d rgt.
Carmichael, —. Captain in 38th
rgt.
Carmine, Samuel. Private in Capt.
Brohawn's co. 48th rgt.
Carmine, Thomas. Private in Capt.
Brohawn's co. 48th rgt.

Carnahan, John. Private in Capt.
King's Artillery co. 49th rgt.
Carnan, Christopher. Captain in 6th
Cavalry Dist. (Je. 5, 1812).
Carnes, William. Private in Capt.
Dillon's co. 27th rgt.
Carnighan, James. Private in Capt.
Shrim's co. Balto. Light Infantry.
Carnoles, John. Sergeant in Capt.
Bouldin's co. Independent Light
Dragoons.
Carns, Benjamin. Private in Capt.
John Miller's co. 2d D. I.; b. Culpepper Co., Va.; age 27; wagoner.
Carpenter, Abraham. Private in
Capt. Taylor's co. 46th rgt.
Carpenter, George. Private in Capt.
Gault's co. 6th rgt.
Carpenter, John. Private in Capt.
Burgess' co. 43d rgt.
Carpenter, Richard. Sergeant in
Capt. Thomas's co. 49th rgt.
Carpenter, Robert W. Private in
Capt. Mackey's co. 49th rgt.
Carpenter, Samuel. Lieutenant in
Capt. T. G. Neale's co. 45th rgt.
(O. 31, 1812).
Carpenter, William. Private in
Capt. Dunnington's co. 43d rgt.
Carr, George. Private in Capt. Addison's co. Sea Fencibles.
Carr, Henry. Private in Capt.
Hall's co. 3d Cavalry rgt.
Carr, Jacob. Lieutenant in Capt.
Maulsby's co. 40th rgt. (Jy. 14,
1814).
Carr, John. Ensign in 14th U. S.
Infantry (Ap. 15, 1813); 3d Lieutenant (My. 2, 1814).
Carr, John. Private Capt. Ringgold's co. 6th rgt.
Carr, John. Private in Capt. Barnes'
co. 32d rgt.
Carr, John. Private in Capt. Dobbin's co. 39th rgt.

Carr, Nicholas. Private in Capt. Lawrence's co. 6th rgt.

Carr, Teague. Private in Capt. Stewart's co. 51st rgt.

Carr, Thomas. Private in Capt. Sterett's co. 1st Balto. Hussars.

Carr, William. Private in Capt. John Miller's co. 2d D. I.; b. Philadelphia, Pa.; age 22; tailor; subs. for John Stonebraker.

Carroll, Aquila. Private in Capt. Ringgold's co. 6th rgt.

Carroll, Charles. Corporal in Capt. Galloway's co. 46th rgt.

Carroll, H. D. G. Private in Capt. Sterett's co. 1st Balto. Hussars.

Carroll, Henry James. Lieutenant-Colonel in 11th Cavalry Dist. (F. 28, 1812); Major in 23d rgt. (1814). Died Dec., 1814.

Carroll, Ignatius. Corporal in Capt. Blakistone's co. 45th rgt.

Carroll, James. Ensign in Capt. Rowan's co. 11th rgt. (Ja. 25, 1814); Lieutenant in Capt. Low's co. (Ag. 20, 1814).

Carroll, James. Private in Capt. Pinney's co. 27th rgt.

Carroll, John. Captain in 26th rgt. (Je. 22, 1808).

Carroll, John. Ensign in Capt. Haubert's co. 51st rgt.

Carroll, John. Private in Capt. McDonald's co. 6th rgt.

Carroll, Mark. Private in Capt. Brown's co. Eagle Artillerists.

Carroll, N. C. Private in Capt. Dillon's co. 27th rgt.

Carroll, Patrick. Private in Capt. Hanna's Fells Point Light Dragoons.

Carroll, Philip. Private in Capt. Usselton's Artillery co. 6th Brigade.

Carroll, Robert. Private in Capt. Brown's co. 6th rgt.

Carroll, Simon. Private in Capt. Veitch's co. 34th rgt.

Carroll, William. Private in Capt. Dillon's co. 27th rgt.

Carrs, John. Private in Capt. Snowden's co. 36th rgt.

Carson, David. Private in Capt. Peters' co. 51st rgt.

Carson, John. Private in Capt. Shrim's co. Balto. Light Infantry.

Carson, Morgan. Private in Capt. Peters' co. 51st rgt.

Carson, Robert. Private in Capt. Faster's co. 51st rgt.

Carson, William. Private in Capt. Berry's co. Washington Artillery.

Carter, Abraham. Private in Capt. Fowler's co. 46th rgt.

Carter, Charles. Private in Capt. Boone's co. 22d rgt.

Carter, Charles. Private in Capt. Steever's co. 27th rgt.

Carter, Clement. Private in Capt. Faster's co. 51st rgt.

Carter, Jesse. Private in Capt. Thompson's co. 1st rgt.

Carter, Jesse. Private in Capt. Dillon's co. 27th rgt.

Carter, John. Captain in 17th rgt. (Ag. 1, 1814) vice Eversfield.

Carter, John. Ensign in Capt. Dermott's co. 14th rgt. (Ap. 26, 1799).

Carter, John. Private in Capt. Steever's co. 27th rgt.

Carter, John S. Private in Capt. Burke's co. 6th rgt.

Carter, Solomon. Private in Capt. Taylor's co. 46th rgt.

Carter, Thomas. Captain in 19th rgt. (Jy. 15, 1814) vice Rich.

Carter, Thomas. Private in Capt. Dyer's co. Fells Point Riflemen.

Carter, William. Private in Capt. Roney's co. 39th rgt.

Carter, William. Private in Capt. Rogers' co. 51st rgt.

Carter, William. Private in Capt. Taylor's co. 46th rgt.

Carty, John. Private in Capt. Mc-Conkey's co. 27th rgt.

Carty, Josiah. Private in Capt. Stewart's co. 51st rgt.

Cary, Dennis. Private in Capt. Addison's co. Sea Fencibles.

Cascaden, Robert. Private in Capt. Wilson's co. 6th rgt.

Case, John. Private in Capt. Blair's co. 50th rgt.

Casey, Christopher. Private in Capt. Chalmers' co. 51st rgt.

Casey, John. Corporal in Capt. Magruder's co. American Artillerists.

Casey, William. Captain in 18th rgt. (S. 30, 1797).

Casey, William. Private in Capt. Brown's co. Eagle Artillerists.

Casko, Isaac. Ensign in Capt. Mackey's co. 49th rgt. (Jy. 4, 1812).

Caspari, Jacob. Private in Capt. Sadtler's co. Balto. Yägers.

Casperlinde, Nicholas. Private in Capt. Conway's co. 6th rgt.

Cassard, Gilbert. Private in Capt. Berry's co. Washington Artillery.

Cassard, Lewis. Private in Capt. Edes' co. 27th rgt.

Cassell, William. Private in Capt. Steiner's Frederick Artillery.

Cassen, John. Private in Capt. Brown's co. 6th rgt.

Cassidy, Patrick. Private in Capt. Hanna's Fells Point Light Dragoons.

Castine, Francis. Corporal in Capt. Howard's co. Mechanical Volunteers.

Caswell, John. Private in Capt. Brown's co. 6th rgt.

Cathcart. *See* **Kithcart.**

Cathel, John. Private in Capt. Fookes' co. 37th rgt. Appointed Ensign; refused commission.

Cathell, Clement. Captain of the privateer *Surprise* Mar., 1814.

Cathell, H. P. Prizemaster of the privateer *Chasseur,* 1814-15.

Cathell, William. Lieutenant of the privateer *Daedalus,* Sept., 1813; Private in Capt. Stiles' co. Marine Artillery, Sept., 1814.

Cathrall, Joseph. Private in Capt. Shrim's co. Balto. Light Infantry.

Cathrill, William. Sergeant in Capt. Lawrence's co. 6th rgt.

Catlett, Grandison. Paymaster in 3d rgt. (Je. 5, 1812).

Cato, Robert. Private in Capt. Dent's co. 43d rgt.

Cator, Abel. Private in Capt. Brohawn's co. 48th rgt.

Cator, John. Private in Capt. Montgomery's co. Balto. Union Artillery.

Cator, Joseph. Sergeant in Capt. Brohawn's co. 48th rgt.

Catts, George. Corporal in Capt. Dillon's co. 27th rgt.

Caughry, Bernard. Private in Capt. Wilson's co. 6th rgt.

Caughy, Patrick. Private in Capt. Haubert's co. 51st rgt.

Caulk, Daniel. Lieutenant in Capt. Douglass' co. 19th rgt. (O. 13, 1812).

Causey, —. Ensign in Capt. Fookes' co. 37th rgt. Resigned Jy. 11, 1814.

Causin, Gerard W. Captain in 4th Cavalry Dist. (My. 8, 1812).

Causin, Nathaniel P. 1st Lieutenant in Capt. Stonestreet's co. 4th Cavalry Dist (Mr. 25, 1812); Captain (My. 8, 1812).

17

Causter, William C. Private in Capt. Levering's co. Independent Blues.

Caustin, James H. Private in Capt. Warfield's co. Balto. United Volunteers.

Cavana, Peter. Sergeant in Capt. Hanna's co. Fells Point Light Dragoons.

Cawood, Alexander. Private in Capt. Fendall's co. 43d rgt.

Cawood, James K. Captain in 45th rgt. (Je. 16, 1813).

Cawood, Wilson. Private in Capt. Cawood's co. 45th rgt.

Cecil, Norton. Private in Capt. McConckin's co. 38th rgt.

Cecil, Thomas. Ensign in Capt. Hemand's co. 38th rgt. (S. 24, 1813).

Cellers, Joseph. Corporal in Capt. Quantrill's co. 24th rgt.

Chaffee, Amos. Private in Capt. Levering's co. Independent Blues.

Chaffee, Nathan M. Private in Capt. Warfield's co. Balto. United Volunteers.

Chaffinch, William. Captain in 19th rgt. (Ag. 20, 1814).

Chaille, Peter. Ensign in Capt. Sheppard's co. 6th rgt. (Jy. 13, 1814) vice Bandle.

Chaille, Stephen. Private in Capt. Sheppard's co. 6th rgt.

Chaires, James. Private in Capt. Jas. Massey's co. 38th rgt.

Chalmers, James. Private in Capt. Montgomery's co. Balto. Union Artillery.

Chalmers, John. Private in Capt. Watson's co. 39th rgt.

Chalmers, Philemon. Private in Capt. Roney's co. 39th rgt.

Chalmers, William. Captain in 51st rgt.

Chalunceaux, Charles. Lieutenant of the privateer *Revenge,* Sept., 1813.

Chamberlain, Philip. Private in Capt. Deems' co. 51st rgt.

Chamberlaine, James. Private in Capt. Smith's co. 51st rgt.

Chambers, Alexander. Sergeant in Capt. Chalmers' co. 51st rgt.

Chambers, Benjamin. Brigadier-General, 6th Brigade.

Chambers, Benjamin Lee. Private in Capt. Chambers' co. 21st rgt.

Chambers, David. Private in Capt. Chambers' co. 21st rgt.

Chambers, Ezekiel F. Captain in 21st rgt. (Je. 10, 1809).

Chambers, Henry. Private in Capt. Wilson's co. 31st rgt.

Chambers, James. Ensign in Capt. Seth's co. 4th rgt.

Chambers, John McLaughlin [1790-1838]. Private in Capt. Montgomery's co. Balto. Union Artillery.

Chambers, Joseph. Private in Capt. Chalmers' co. 51st rgt.

Chambers, Levi. Lieutenant in Capt. Gaither's co. 44th rgt. (Ag. 12, 1812).

Chambers, Robert. Private in Capt. Peters' co. 51st rgt.

Chambey, Dennis. Private in Capt. Brown's co. Eagle Artillerists.

Champlin, A. P. Private in Capt. Brown's co. Eagle Artillerists.

Chance, John. Private in Capt. Moale's co. Columbian Artillery.

Chandler, Jacob. Lieutenant Capt. Timanus' co. 36th rgt. (Jy. 28, 1813).

Chandler, Jehu [1784-1822]. Private in Capt. Pinkney's Artillery co. 22d rgt.; Private in Ensign Brewer's detachment of 36th rgt. at Bladensburg.

Chaney, Cornelius. Private in Capt. Dillon's co. 27th rgt.

Chaney, Luke. Ensign in Capt. Scheehter's co. 10th rgt. (Ag. 2, 1814).

Chaney, John. 2d Lieutenant in Capt. Williams' co. 1st Regimental Cavalry Dist. (Mr. 16, 1812).

Chaney, Samuel. Private in Capt. Pumphrey's co. 22d rgt.

Chaney, Thomas. Corporal in Capt. Ireland's co. 31st rgt.

Channel, James. Private in Capt. Dobbin's co. 39th rgt.

Channing, Burton. Private in Capt. Burgess' co. 43d rgt.

Channing, James. Private in Capt. Brown's co. 43d rgt.

Chapman, Amos. Corporal in Capt. Ringgold's co. 6th rgt.

Chapman, Christopher. Private in Capt. Brown's co. Eagle Artillerists.

Chapman, George. Private in Capt. Kennedy's co. 27th rgt.

Chapman, John. Private in Capt. Dobbin's co. 39th rgt.

Chapman, Joseph. Private in Capt. McConkey's co. 27th rgt.

Chapman, Richard. Private in Capt. Rogers' co. 51st rgt.

Chapman, Samuel. Private in Capt. McLaughlin's co. 50th rgt.

Chapman, William. Seaman of the privateer *Surprise*. Drowned April 5, 1815.

Chappelier, John. Major in 45th rgt.

Chappell, John G. Corporal in Capt. Levering's co. Independent Blues.

Chappell, John G. Ensign in Capt. Lawrence's co. 6th rgt.

Chappell, William L. Private in Capt. Levering's co. Independent Blues.

Charlton, John F. Drummer in Capt. Magruder's co. American Artillerists.

Charlton, William. Private in Capt. Aisquith's co. Sharp Shooters.

Chase, Joseph. Command unknown. Captured at Bladensburg.

Chase, Philip W. Private in Capt. Edes' co. 27th rgt.

Chase, Richard M. Ensign in Capt. Maynard's co. 22d rgt.; Captain (Ap. 21, 1814).

Chase, Stephen. Private in Capt. Moale's co. Columbian Artillery.

Chattles, Samuel. Private in Capt. Peters' co. 51st rgt.

Chauncey, John. 1st Lieutenant in 36th U. S. Infantry (Ap. 30, 1813).

Chaytor, David. Sergeant in Capt. Stiles' co. Marine Artillery.

Chaytor, James. Captain of the privateer *Expedition*, June, 1813.

Cheatham, —. Lieutenant in Capt. Fookes' co. 37th rgt. Resigned Jy. 11, 1814.

Chenoweth, Arthur. Private in Capt. Ducker's co. 7th rgt.

Chenoweth, Joshua. Private in Capt. Smith's co. 51st rgt.

Chenoweth, Richard. Captain in 6th Cavalry Dist. (Je. 12, 1812).

Chenoweth, William. Private in Capt. Ducker's co. 7th rgt.; deserted Sept. 4, 1814.

Cheny, Edward. Private in Capt. Stewart's co. 51st rgt.

Cherbert, Charles F. Private in Capt. Galt's co. 6th rgt.

Cherbonnier, Pierre [1781-1866]. Private under General Jackson at battle of New Orleans.

Cherry, Dominick. Private in Capt. Peters' co. 51st rgt.

Cherry, Peter. Private in Capt. Roney's co. 39th rgt.

Cheseldine, Charles. Private in Capt. Blakistone's co. 45th rgt.

Cheseldine, Elijah. Private in Capt. Blakistone's co. 45th rgt.

Cheseldine, John. Private in Capt. Blakistone's co. 45th rgt.

Cheseldine, Kenelm. Corporal in Capt. Blakistone's co. 45th rgt.

Cheseldine, Kenelm G. Private in Capt. Blakistone's co. 45th rgt.

Cheston, James. Lieutenant and Adjutant in 5th rgt.

Cheston, William. Private in Capt. Pinney's co. 27th rgt.

Chestnut, John. Private in Capt. Aisquith's co. Sharp Shooters.

Cheswell, William. Lieutenant in Capt. Fletchall's co. 3d rgt. (O. 12, 1807).

Chew, John. Sergeant in Capt. Jackson's co. 34th rgt.

Chew, John H. Captain in 31st rgt. (D. 23, 1813) vice Reynolds.

Chezrum, Daniel. Ensign in Capt. Blades' co. 19th rgt.

Chezrum, Richard. Lieutenant in Capt. Blades' co. 19th rgt. (O. 15, 1811).

Chick, Josiah. Private in Capt. Thomas's co. 49th rgt.

Chilcoat, Charles. Private in Capt. Schwarzauer's co. 27th rgt.

Child, Henry. Lieutenant of the privateer Female, Feb., 1813.

Child, Samuel C. Captain of the privateer Female, Feb., 1813.

Child, William. Corporal in Capt. Nicholson's co. Balto. Fencibles.

Childerson, Levin. Lieutenant in Capt. Lambden's co. Extra Battalion Dorchester co. (O. 13, 1814).

Childs, Benjamin. Private in Capt. Maynard's co. 22d rgt.; Corporal

in Capt. Chase's co. (1814); Sergeant in Capt. Chase's co. (1814).

Childs, James. Gunner in Capt. Addison's co. Sea Fencibles.

Childs, John. Private in Capt. Maynard's co. 22d rgt.; Private in Ensign Brewer's detachment 36th rgt. at Bladensburg.

Childs, Nathaniel. 1st Lieutenant in Capt. Bosley's co. 6th Cavalry Dist. (Jy. 30, 1812); Captain (D. 15, 1814) vice Bosley.

Childs, Samuel. Private in Capt. Montgomery's co. Balto. Union Artillery.

Childs, Thomas. Private in Capt. Kennedy's co. 27th rgt.

Childs, Thomas. Sergeant in Capt. Roney's co. 39th rgt.

Chittenden, Nathaniel. Captain of the privateer Rolla, Aug., 1813.

Choate, Solomon. Private in Capt. Ducker's co. 7th rgt.

Christhilf, Henry. Private in Capt. Myers' co. 39th rgt.

Christie, James. 2d Lieutenant in 14th U. S. Infantry (Mr. 12, 1812); 1st Lieutenant (O. 1, 1813).

Christopher, Baletta. Ensign in Capt. Irving's co. 25th rgt. (Ja. 10, 1814).

Christopher, Charles. Private in Capt. McDonald's co. 6th rgt.

Christopher, Elijah. Lieutenant in Capt. Johnson's co. 37th rgt. (Ap. 20, 1808).

Christopher, John. Lieutenant in Capt. Taylor's co. 46th rgt. Resigned Jy. 8, 1814.

Chronicle, George C. Private in Ensign Brewer's detachment at Bladensburg.

Church, John. Private in Capt. Peters' co. 51st rgt.

Churchman, Alfred W. Private in
Capt. Montgomery's co. Balto.
Union Artillery.

Churchman, Azahel. Private in
Capt. Brown's Artillery co. 49th
rgt.

Churchman, John. Private in Capt.
Maynard's co. 22d rgt.

Chuscha, Israel. Private in Capt.
John Miller's co. 2d D. I.; b. Ply-
mouth, Conn.; age 18; farmer;
subs. for Jacob Waggoner.

Cissel, Peregrine. Private in Capt.
Jarboe's co. 12th rgt.

Cissell, Thomas H. Private in
Capt. Hammett's co. 12th rgt.

Clabaugh, Martin. Private in Capt.
McLaughlin's co. 50th rgt.

Clackner, Joseph. Private in Capt.
Stiles' co. Marine Artillery.

Clagett, David. 2d Lieutenant
Capt. Tabb's co. 1st rgt. 1st Regimental Cavalry Dist. (F. 28,
1812).

Clagett, David. Private in Capt.
Barr's Cavalry co. 1st Dist.

Clagett, Elie. Private in Capt. Warfield's co. Balto. United Volunteers. Wounded at North Point.

Clagett, Horatio. Lieutenant in
Capt. Burns' co. 10th rgt. (My.
23, 1812).

Clagett, Horatio. Captain in 17th
rgt. (N. 7, 1812).

Clagett, Horatio. Cornet in Capt.
N. P. Causin's co. 4th Cavalry
Dist. (Je. 12, 1812); 2d Lieu-
tenant (F. 19, 1813) vice Morris.

Clagett, John of Joseph. Captain in
44th rgt. (D. 2, 1808).

Clagett, Levi. Lieutenant in Capt.
Nicholson's co. Balto. Fencibles.
Killed at Fort McHenry.

Clagett, Samuel. Paymaster in 17th
rgt. (Ap. 21, 1813).

Clagett, Thomas. Private in Capt.
Nicholson's co. Balto. Fencibles.

Clagett, Thomas D. Captain in 43d
rgt. vice Fendall.

Clagett, Thomas J. Surgeon 44th
rgt. (Ag. 20, 1814).

Clagett, William D. Lieutenant in
Capt. Hall's co. 34th rgt. (Ag. 10,
1813) vice Brookes.

Clapsaddle, Daniel. Private in Capt.
Snowden's co. 36th rgt.

Clarck, George. Private in Capt.
Conway's co. 6th rgt.

Clarck, John. Private in Capt. Conway's co. 6th rgt.

Clare, John. Cornet Capt. Mackall's
Co. 3d Cavalry Dist. (Jy. 28,
1812); 2d Lieutenant (Ja. 31,
1814).

Clare, William. Lieutenant in Capt.
Parran's co. 31st rgt. (Jy. 12,
1814); Captain (Ag. 20, 1814).

Claridge, Edward. Private in Capt.
Brohawn's co. 48th rgt.

Claridge, Henry. Private in Capt.
Burke's co. 6th rgt.

Claridge, Levin. Private in Capt.
Brown's co. 6th rgt.

Clark, Abraham [-1839]. Ensign in 14th U. S. Infantry (Mr.
12, 1812); 2d Lieutenant (O. 1,
1813); Reg. Quarter-master (M.,
1814).

Clark, Baley E. 1st Lieutenant
in Captain Cross's co. 2d Cavalry
Dist. (Ap. 16, 1812).

Clark, Benjamin H. Ensign in Capt.
Brooke's co. 34th rgt.

Clark, David. Ensign in Capt. J.
B. Burgess' co. 32d rgt. (Ag. 27,
1807).

Clark, Edward. Private in Capt.
Williams' co. 12th rgt.

Clark, Henry. Corporal in Capt.
Ducker's co. 7th rgt.

Clark, Henry. Private in Capt. Graves' co. 21st rgt.

Clark, Hooper. Private in Capt. Moale's co. Columbian Artillery.

Clark, Ignatius. Private in Capt. Dent's co. 43d rgt.

Clark, Jacob. Private in Capt. McLaughlin's co. 50th rgt.

Clark, James. Corporal in Capt. Berry's co. Washington Artillery.

Clark, James M. Private in Capt. Addison's co. Sea Fencibles.

Clark, Jesse. Private in Capt. Page's co. 21st rgt.

Clark, John [-1820]. Ensign in 36th U. S. Infantry (Ap. 30, 1813); 2d Lieutenant (My. 1, 1814).

Clark, John. Private in Capt. Chambers' co. 21st rgt.; captured at Caulk's Field.

Clark, John. Private in Capt. Dyer's co. Fells Point Riflemen.

Clark, John. Private in Capt. Kennedy's co. 27th rgt.

Clark, John. Private in Capt. Heath's co. 23d rgt.

Clark, Joseph. Corporal in Capt. Brown's co. Eagle Artillerists.

Clark, Joseph. Private in Capt. Aisquith's co. Sharp Shooters.

Clark, Joseph. Private in Capt. Chalmers' co. 51st rgt.

Clark, Mills. Private in Capt. Faster's co. 51st rgt.

Clark, Nathaniel. Private in Capt. Stewart's co. 51st rgt.

Clark, Richard. Captain in 12th rgt. (1813).

Clark, Richard. Ensign in Capt. Darby's co. 13th rgt. (D. 10, 1813); Lieutenant (S. 10, 1814).

Clark, Richard. Private in Capt. Barnes' co. 32d rgt. Deserted.

Clark, Robert. Ensign in Capt. Rutlidge's co. 40th rgt. (My. 20, 1809).

Clark, Samuel. Private in Capt. Ducker's co. 7th rgt.

Clark, Walter S. Lieutenant in Isaacs' co. 34th rgt. (Jy. 13, 1814).

Clark, William. Captain in 31st rgt.

Clark, William. Corporal in Capt. Ducker's co. 7th rgt.

Clark, William. Private in Capt. Myers' co. Franklin Artillery.

Clark, William. Private in Capt. Aisquith's co. Sharp Shooters.

Clark, Zadock. Private in Capt. Blair's co. 50th rgt.

Clarke, Benjamin H. Ensign in Capt. Brookes' co. 34th rgt. (Je. 27, 1812).

Clarke, George W. Private in Capt. Warfield's co. Balto. United Volunteers. Wounded at Bladensburg.

Clarke, John. Private in Capt. Linthicum's co. 22d rgt.

Clarke, Johnson. Captain in 7th rgt. (My. 17, 1811).

Clarke, Joseph. Captain in 14th rgt. (Je. 18, 1794).

Clarke, Peregrine. Private in Capt. Combs' co. 12th rgt.

Clarke, Staley N. Sergeant-Major in 34th rgt.

Clarke, Thomas. Lieutenant in 12th rgt. (O. 3, 1807).

Clarke, Thomas P. Private in Capt. Brooke's co. 34th rgt.

Clarke, William. Private in Capt. Blakistone's co. 45th rgt.

Clarke, William. Private in Capt. McKane's co. 27th rgt.

Clarke, William H. Sergeant in Capt. Spry's co. 33d rgt.

Claro, Bennett H. Lieutenant in Capt. Lamden's co. 9th rgt. (Mr. 23, 1814).

Clary, Michael. Private in Capt. Brown's co. 6th rgt.

Classon, John. Private in Capt. Brown's co. Eagle Artillerists.

Claude, Abram. Corporal in Capt. Pinkney's Artillery co. 22d rgt.; Private in Ensign Brewer's detachment, 36th rgt., captured at Bladensburg.

Claude, Dennis. Surgeon in 22d rgt. (Je. 19, 1812).

Claude, John. Private in Capt. Sands' co. 22d rgt.

Claude, John. Ensign in 13th U. S. Infantry (Ap. 15, 1814); 3d Lieutenant (Je. 30, 1814).

Clayland, James. Cornet in Capt. Martin's co. 9th Cavalry Dist. (My. 8, 1812); 2d Lieutenant (D. 2, 1812); 1st Lieutenant (Jy. 24, 1813).

Clayland, Lambert. Armorer at Easton (1812).

Clayton, Edward. Lieutenant in Capt. Earle's co. 4th rgt. (S. 21, 1796).

Clayton, John. Ensign in Capt. Hall's co. 34th rgt. (Jy. 13, 1814).

Clayton, John. Drummer in Capt. John Miller's co. 2d D. I.; b. Md.; age 19; shoemaker; volunteer.

Clayton, Philip. Corporal in Capt. Slicer's co. 22d rgt.

Clayton, Samuel. Private in Capt. Miller's co. 39th rgt.

Clayton, Samuel. Private in Capt. Ringgold's co. 6th rgt.

Clein, George. Private in Capt. Roney's co. 39th rgt.

Clemens, Edward. Sergeant in Capt. Conway's co. 6th rgt.

Clements, Francis A. Sergeant in Capt. McPherson's co. 43d rgt.

Clements, Francis T. Private in Capt. Maynard's co. 22d rgt.

Clements, Henry H. Private in Capt. Blakistone's co. 45th rgt.

Clements, Jacob. Private in Capt. Burgess' co. 43d rgt.

Clements, James. Private in Capt. McPherson's co. 43d rgt.

Clements, John. Private in Capt. Dunnington's co. 43d rgt.

Clements, John H. Ensign in Capt. Thompson's co. 43d rgt. (Ap. 20, 1813).

Clements, Robert. Private in Capt. Dent's co. 43d rgt.

Clements, Robert H. Private in Capt. Haubert's co. 51st rgt.

Clemm, John. Sergeant in Capt. Nicholson's co. Balto. Fencibles. Killed at Fort McHenry.

Clemm, Joseph E. 3d Lieutenant in Capt. Pennington's co. Balto. Independent Artillerists (Mr. 23, 1814).

Clemm, William. Private in Capt. Levering's co. Independent Blues.

Clemmer, Lewis. Private in Capt. McLaughlin's co. 50th rgt.

Clemmins, John. Private in Capt. Adreon's co. Union Volunteers.

Clemson, James. Captain in Artillery co. 7th Brigade Frederick Co. (Ap. 23, 1808).

Clerey, James. Private in Capt. Sands' co. 22d rgt.

Clever, Derrick. Private in Capt. Haubert's co. 51st rgt.

Clifford, Sylvester. Private in Capt. Myer's co. Franklin Artillery.

Cliffton, Jesse. Private in Capt. Massey's co. 38th rgt.

Cline, David. Private in Capt. Kierstead's co. 6th rgt.

Cline, John. Private in Capt. Snowden's co. 36th rgt.

Cline, Philip. Captain in 10th rgt. Resigned S. 20, 1813.

Clinedienst, John. Private in Capt. Piper's co. United Maryland Artillery.

Clinton, Thomas. Fifer in Capt. Blair's co. 50th rgt.

Clocker, Daniel. Sergeant in Capt. Combs' co. 12th rgt.

Clopper, Andrew. 2d Lieutenant in Capt. Nicholson's co. Balto. Fencibles.

Cloud, Abner. Lieutenant in Capt. Parker's co. 18th rgt. (S. 30, 1797).

Club, Brice. Private in Capt. Dyer's co. 17th rgt.

Clyne, Daniel D. Private in Capt. Lawrence's co. 6th rgt.

Coale, Edward J. Sergeant in Capt. Stewart's co. Washington Blues.

Coalman, Henry. Surgeon's mate 49th rgt. (Ap. 23, 1813).

Coats, Frederick. Private in Capt. Bouldin's co. Independent Light Dragoons.

Coats, John. Captain in 36th rgt. (My. 22, 1812).

Coats, Searson. Private in Capt. Rogers' co. 51st rgt.

Cobb, G. K. Private in Capt. Pennington's co. Balto. Independent Artillery.

Coburn, Spencer. Drummer in Capt. Miller's co. 39th rgt.

Coburne, William. 1st Lieutenant in Capt. Wilson's co. 8th Cavalry Dist. (My. 16, 1812).

Cochran, George. Private in Capt. Dillon's co. 27th rgt.

Cochran, George. Private in Capt. Maynard's co. 22d rgt.

Cochran, Michael. Private in Capt. Brown's co. 6th rgt.

Cochran, William. Private in Capt. Roney's co. 39th rgt.

Cochran, William A. Private in Capt. Myers' co. Franklin Artillery.

Cochran, William G. Private in Capt. Warfield's co. Balto. United Volunteers.

Cochrane, James. Ensign in 38th U. S. Infantry (Mr. 2, 1814).

Cock, John. Captain of the privateer *Vesta*, Apr., 1813; of the *Ultor*, Sept., 1813; Lieutenant of the *Lawrence*, 1814; Private in Capt. Stiles' co. Marine Artillery.

Cock, Solomon. Private in Capt. Kierstead's co. 6th rgt.

Cockey, Andrew. Private in Capt. Ducker's co. 7th rgt.

Cockey, William. Private in Capt. Ducker's co. 7th rgt.

Cockrill, Thomas. 1st Lieutenant in Capt. Brown's co. Eagle Artillerists (F. 12, 1812).

Cocur, John. Private in Capt. Myers' co. Franklin Artillery.

Codd, George. Private in Capt. Linthicum's co. 22d rgt.

Codd, William. Captain Rifle co. 3d Brigade (Jy. 24, 1813) vice Stansbury.

Coddington, John. Private in Capt. Blair's co. 50th rgt.

Codshall, Andrew. Private in Capt. Snowden's co. 36th rgt.

Coe, Isaac. Private in Capt. Taylor's co. 46th rgt.

Coe, James. Ensign in Capt. Darnall's co. 14th rgt. (S. 9, 1807).

Coe, James D. Adjutant in 34th rgt. (S. 21, 1813).

Coe, Nathan. Private in Capt. Taylor's co. 46th rgt.

Coe, Samuel. Captain in 17th rgt. [In service in 1813.]

Coe, Samuel, Jr. Captain in 17th rgt. Rifle co. (Jy. 11, 1814).

Coffin, Godshall. Private in Capt. Dent's co. 43d rgt.

Coffman, Christian. Private in Capt. Galloway's co. 46th rgt.

Cogswell, James F. 1st Lieutenant in Capt. Atkinson's Artillery co. 10th Brigade (Mr. 16, 1812).

Cohagan, Joshua. Private in Capt. Haubert's co. 51st rgt.

Cohen, Mendes I. Private in Capt. Nicholson's co. Balto. Fencibles.

Cohen, Philip I. Private in Capt. Nicholson's co. Balto. Fencibles.

Cohen, Samuel, Jr. Sergeant in Capt. Magruder's co. American Artillerists.

Coke, Alexander. Private in Capt. Quantrill's co. 24th rgt.

Cole, Abraham. Ensign in Capt Taylor's co. 46th rgt. Broke, 1814.

Cole, Andrew. Private in Capt. Kennedy's co. 27th rgt.

Cole, Benjamin G. Captain in Rifle co. 10th rgt. (Ag. 24, 1814).

Cole, Edward. Seaman of the privateer High Flyer. Wounded in action, Dec., 1812.

Cole, Elsey. Private in Capt. Watson's co. 39th rgt.

Cole, Frederick. Corporal in Capt. Edes's co. 27th rgt.

Cole, Frederick. Private in Capt. Lawrence's co. 6th rgt.

Cole, Frederick. Sergeant in Capt. Burke's co. 6th rgt.

Cole, George. Private in Capt. Myers' co. 39th rgt.

Cole, James Alexander [1782-1822]. Private in Capt. Wilson's co. 6th rgt.

Cole, John. Private in Capt. Levering's co. Independent Blues.

Cole, John. Private in Capt. Kennedy's co. 27th rgt.

Cole, John. Private in Capt. Williams' co. 12th rgt.

Cole, Nathaniel. Private in Capt. Hanna's co. Fells Point Light Dragoons.

Cole, Richard. Private in Capt. Fowler's co. 46th rgt.

Cole, Samuel. Private in Capt. Levering's co. Independent Blues.

Cole, Thomas. Lieutenant in Capt. Dobbin's co. 39th rgt.

Cole, Thomas. Private in Capt. Kierstead's co. 6th rgt.

Cole, William [1784-1844]. Private in Capt. Burke's co. 6th rgt.

Coleby, Edward. Private in Capt. Chambers' co. 21st rgt.

Colegate, George. Surgeon's mate 20th rgt. (N. 15, 1809); Surgeon 2d rgt. 1st Cavalry Dist. (Ap. 23, 1813).

Coleman, Alexander. Private in Capt. Stewart's co. 51st rgt.

Coleman, Charles. Lieutenant of the privateer Sylph, Oct., 1812.

Coleman, Christopher. Private in Capt. Stiles' co. Marine Artillery.

Coleman, Ezekiel. Private in Capt. Page's co. 21st rgt.

Coleman, Isaiah. Private in Capt. Chambers' co. 21st rgt.

Coleman, John. Captain of the privateer Perry, Sept., 1813.

Coleman, John. Private in Capt. Sterett's Independent co.

Coleman, Joseph. Private in Capt. Lawrence's co. 6th rgt.

Coleman, Richard. Private in Capt. Wilson's co. 6th rgt.

Coleman, Rizdon B. Private in Capt. Hayward's co. 4th rgt.

Coleman, Samuel. Corporal in Capt. Wilson's co. 6th rgt.

Coleman, Samuel. Private in Capt. Wickes' co. 21st rgt.

Colley, William. Private in Capt. Burgess' co. 43d rgt.

Collin, Robert. Private in Capt. Page's co. 21st rgt.

Collings, Banister. Private in Capt. Hancock's co. 22d rgt.

Collings, Richard. Private in Capt. Hancock's co. 22d rgt.

Collins, Andrew. Private in Capt. Quantrill's co. 24th rgt.

Collins, Cornelius. Private in Capt. Berry's co. Washington Artillery. Wounded at Fort McHenry.

Collins, Ebenezer. Private in Capt. Travers' co. 48th rgt.

Collins, George. Private in Capt. Adreon's co. Union Volunteers.

Collins, George C. Captain in Balto. Union Artillery (Je. 18, 1812).

Collins, George E. Captain, 39th rgt.

Collins, Isaac. Private in Capt. Dyers' co. Fells Point Riflemen.

Collins, James W. Private in Capt. Nicholson's co. Balto. Fencibles.

Collins, Jesse. Lieutenant in Capt. Harris' co. 19th rgt. (Ag. 10, 1813).

Collins, John. Private in Capt. Burke's co. 6th rgt.

Collins, John. Ensign in Capt. Hodges' co. 21st rgt. (My. 8, 1812).

Collins, Joseph. Private in Capt. Howard's co. Mechanical Volunteers.

Collins, Josias. Private in Capt. Rogers' co. 51st rgt.

Collins, Lee. Private in Capt. Pennington's co. Balto. Independent Artillerists.

Collins, Thomas. Private in Capt. Edes' co. 27th rgt.

Collins, William. Private in Capt. McConkey's co. 27th rgt.

Collins, William. Private in Capt. McKane's co. 27th rgt.; captured at North Point.

Collinson, Edward. Lieutenant in Capt. Norman's co. 2d rgt. (My. 23, 1812).

Collmus, Levi [1786-1856]. Private in Capt. Piper's United Maryland Artillery.

Collyer, James. Private in Capt. Massey's co. 38th rgt.

Colson, James. Captain in Extra Battalion Caroline Co. (S. 2, 1811).

Colston, James. Lieutenant in Capt. Wayman's co. 26th rgt. (Jy. 8, 1813).

Colston, Jesse. Cornet in Capt. Manning's co. 10th Cavalry Dist. (D. 22, 1814).

Colston, Levin. Captain in 48th rgt. (My. 17, 1811).

Colston, William. Captain in 48th rgt. (Je. 26, 1812).

Combs, Cornelius. Captain in 12th rgt. (Je. 27, 1811).

Combs, Ignatius. Private in Capt. Williams' co. 12th rgt.

Combs, John. Captain, 10th rgt. (Promoted S. 20, 1813).

Combs, Joseph. Private in Capt. Williams' co. 12th rgt.

Combs, Nathaniel. Private in Capt. Bean's co. 12th rgt.

Combs, Raphael. Quarter-master Sergeant 12th rgt.

Combs, Stanislaus. Surgeon's mate 1st rgt. (Je. 28, 1812).

Comegys, Benjamin. Corporal in Capt. Deems' co. 51st rgt.

Comegys, Cornelius. Private in Capt. Ringgold's co. 6th rgt.

Comegys, Cornelius, Jr. [-1815]. 3d Lieutenant in 14th U. S. Infantry (My. 10, 1813); 2d Lieutenant (N. 14, 1814).

Comegys, Edward W. Captain in 21st rgt. (S. 2, 1811).

Comegys, George. Cornet in Capt. Boyer's co. 8th Cavalry Dist. (Ap. 30, 1813); Adjutant (Ag. 20, 1813).

Comegys, Jesse. Private in Capt. Ringgold's co. 6th rgt.

Comegys, John G. Corporal in Moale's co. Columbian Artillery.

Comegys, Jonathan. Sergeant in Capt. Vansant's co. 33d rgt.

Comegys, Lemuel. Private in Capt. Chambers' co. 21st rgt.

Compte, Julius. Private in Capt. Moale's co. Columbian Artillery.

Compton, John. Private in Capt. Faster's co. 51st rgt.

Conaway, Edward. Private in Capt. Maynard's co. 22d rgt.; 2d Corporal Chase's co.; Private in Ensign Brewer's detachment 36th rgt. at Bladensburg.

Condon, Robert. Lieutenant in Capt. Orrick's co. 41st (Jy. 11, 1814) vice Wheeler.

Cone, Spencer H. Captain in Union Artillery co. (S. 21, 1813) vice Collins.

Cone, Spencer H. 3d Lieutenant in Capt. Aisquith's co. Sharp Shooters.

Conklin, Elijah. Private in Capt. Stewart's co. 51st rgt.

Conkling, Thomas C. Private in Capt. Nicholson's co. Balto. Fencibles.

Conly, John. Private in Capt. John Miller's co. 2d D. I.; b Washington Co.; age 20; farmer; subs. for John Malott.

Conly, Michael. Private in Capt. Stewart's co. 51st rgt.

Conn, Jacob. 1st Lieutenant in Capt. Stansbury's Rifle co. 3d Brigade (Ap. 4, 1812); Capt. 5th rgt. Resigned Ag. 5, 1814.

Conn, Jacob. Private in Capt. Schwarzauer's co. 27th rgt.

Conn, Thomas. Private in Capt. Garrett's co. 49th rgt.

Connard, Frederick. Private in Capt. McConkey's co. 27th rgt.

Connaway, John. Captain in 15th rgt. (D. 24, 1810).

Connell, Bartholomew. Private in Capt. Edes' co. 27th rgt.

Connell, Robert. Ensign in Capt. Litton's co. 44th rgt. (A. 22, 1812).

Connelly, Bernard. Private in Capt. McKane's co. 27th rgt.

Connelly, Bernard. Private in Capt. McLaughlin's co. 50th rgt.

Connelly, Edward. Private in Capt. McLaughlin's co. 50th rgt.

Connelly, Henry. Private in Capt. Morgan's co. 49th rgt.

Connelly, John. Private in Capt. Bunbury's co. Sea Fencibles.

Connelly, Thomas. Private in Capt. Shrim's co. Balto. Light Infantry.

Conner, Abraham. Private in Capt. Edes' co. 27th rgt.

Conner, Edward. Private in Capt. Kennedy's co. 27th rgt.

Conner, John. Sergeant in Capt. Steever's co. 27th rgt.

Conner, Levin. Lieutenant in Capt. Scarborough's co. 9th rgt. (Jy. 8, 1814).

Connokin, W. M. Corporal in Capt. Burke's co. 6th rgt.

Connor, Martin. Private in Capt. Sample's co. 49th rgt.

Conor, Hugh. Private in Capt. John Miller's co. 2d D. I.; b. Md.; age 34; miller.

Conrad, John. Lieutenant in Capt. Harry's co. 24th rgt. Died 1814.

Conrad, John. Private in Capt. Bunbury's co. Sea Fencibles.

Conrade, Michael. Private in Capt. Blair's co. 50th rgt.

Constable, George P. Private in Capt. Piper's co. United Maryland Artillery.

Constable, Robert. Private in Capt. Chambers' co. 21st rgt.

Contee, John. 2d Lieutenant in U. S. Marine Corps (Ap. 17, 1812); 1st Lieutenant (Jy. 24, 1812). Resigned S. 15, 1813; served on U. S. Frigate *Constitution*.

Converse, Elijah. Private in Capt. Rogers' co. 51st rgt.

Conway, Matthew. Private in Capt. Brown's Artillery co. 49th rgt.

Conway, Robert. Captain in 6th rgt. (Jy. 13, 1814) vice Foy.

Conway, Robert. Private in Capt. McKane's co. 27th rgt.

Conway, Thomas. Private in Capt. Berry's co. Washington Artillery.

Cooch, Zebulon. Private in Capt. Montgomery's co. American Artillerists.

Cook, Anthony L. Private in Capt. Berry's co. Washington Artillery.

Cook, Caleb. Private in Capt. Adreon's co. Union Volunteers.

Cook, Donaldson. Private in Capt. Posey's co. 1st rgt.

Cook, Elisha. 2d Lieutenant in Capt. Reynolds' Rifle co. 3d Brigade (Ap. 4, 1812).

Cook, Elisha. Private in Capt. Haubert's co. 51st rgt.

Cook, Ephraim. Lieutenant in Capt. Gorsuch's co. 15th rgt. (O. 21, 1812).

Cook, Frederick. Private in Capt. Roney's co. 39th rgt.

Cook, George. Private in Capt. Shrim's co. Balto. Light Infantry.

Cook, Hudson. Private in Capt. Brohawn's co. 48th rgt.

Cook, Jerry. Private in Capt. Ducker's co. 7th rgt.

Cook, John. Captain in 2d rgt. 1st Cavalry Dist. (F. 13, 1812); Major (S. 18, 1812); Lieutenant-Colonel (D. 21, 1814) vice Kemp.

Cook, John. Captain 13th rgt. (O. 13, 1807).

Cook, John. Private in Capt. Shryock's co. 24th rgt.

Cook, John F. Private in Capt. Adreon's co. Union Volunteers. Captured at Bladensburg.

Cook, John L. Quarter-master Sergeant in 27th rgt.

Cook, John L. Private in Capt. Pinney's co. 27th rgt.

Cook, John T. Private in Capt. Quantrill's co. 24th rgt.

Cook, John W. Private in Capt. Steever's co. 27th rgt.

Cook, Joseph. Private in Capt. Smith's co. 51st rgt.

Cook, Levin. Private in Capt. Burke's co. 6th rgt.

Cook, Nathan. Private in Capt. Jos. Jones' co. 34th rgt.

Cook, Richard. Private in Capt. Dent's co. 43d rgt.

Cook, Samuel. Private in Capt. Addison's co. Sea Fencibles.

Cook, Thomas. Lieutenant in Capt. Hobbs' co. 32d rgt. (Ag. 20, 1814).

Cook, Thomas. Ensign in Capt. Spedden's co. Extra Battalion Dorchester Co. (Ag. 27, 1810).

Cook, W. G. Private in Capt. Pennington's co. Balto. Independent Artillerists.

Cook, William. Major in 26th rgt. Resigned Ja. 24, 1815.

Cook, William. Lieutenant in Capt. Perrigo's co. 46th rgt. (Jy. 8, 1814).

Cooke, Bernard H. Quarter-master in 46th rgt. (Ja. 22, 1811).

Cooke, Francis. Corporal in Capt. Sterett's co. 1st Balto. Hussars.

Cooke, George. Corporal in Capt. Warfield's co. Balto. United Volunteers.

Cooke, William. Lieutenant in Capt. Warfield's co. Balto. United Volunteers. Wounded at Bladensburg. In command of co. at Bladensburg and North Point. Commissioned Captain N. 8, 1814.

Cooksey, Francis. Surgeon in 4th Regimental Cavalry Dist. (Jy. 20, 1812).

Cooksey, John V. Private in Capt. Edelin's co. 1st rgt.

Cooksey, Richard K. Private in Capt. Stewart's co. Washington Blues.

Cooksey, Samuel. Private in Capt. Crawford's co. 17th rgt.

Cooley, Daniel. Quarter-master of 30th rgt.

Cooley, James. Private in Capt. Crawford's co. 17th rgt.

Coomes, Aloysius. Lieutenant in Capt. Thompson's co. 43d rgt. (Ap. 20, 1813).

Coomes, John. Gunner in Capt. Bunbury's co. Sea Fencibles.

Cooney, Patrick. Corporal in Capt. Sheppard's co. 6th rgt.

Cooper, Ambrose. Private in Capt. Deems' co. 51st rgt.

Cooper, Calvin. Sergeant in Capt. Hanna's co. Fells Point Light Dragoons.

Cooper, Elisha. Private in Capt. Conway's co. 6th rgt.

Cooper, Henry. Private in Capt. Hands' co. 21st rgt.

Cooper, Hezekiah. Private in Capt. Addison's co. Sea Fencibles.

Cooper, John. Private in Capt. Bunbury's co. Sea Fencibles.

Cooper, John. Private in Capt. Sheppard's co. 6th rgt.

Cooper, Johnson [1788-1820]. Sergeant in Capt. Jos. Kemp's co. 26th rgt. "St. Michael's Light Infantry."

Cooper, Peregrine. Ensign in Capt. Scott's co. 33d rgt. (Ag. 27, 1810).

Cooper, Robert [-1817]. Sergeant in Capt. Brown's co. 6th rgt.; Port Warden of Baltimore.

Cooper, Samuel. Private in Capt. Watson's co. 39th rgt.

Cooper, Thomas. Lieutenant in Capt. Hall's co. 4th rgt. (O. 1, 1811).

Cooper, Thomas. Sergeant in Capt. Oldham's co. 30th rgt.

Cooper, Thomas. Private in Capt. Massey's co. 38th rgt.

Cooper, Wells. Sergeant in Capt. Berry's co. Washington Artillery.

Cooper, William. Sergeant in Capt. Hayward's co. 4th rgt.

Cooper, William A. Lieutenant in Capt. Taylor's co. 19th rgt. (Jy. 29, 1811).

Cooper, William S. Private in Capt. Nicholson's co. Balto. Fencibles.

Coppage, Edward. Lieutenant in Capt. Merchant's co. 35th rgt. (Ap. 30, 1813).

Copenhaver, Jacob. Lieutenant in Capt. John Brown's co. 49th rgt. (Jy. 13, 1814).

Copper, George. Private in Capt. Roney's co. 39th rgt.

Copper, William. Captain in 21st rgt. (1813).

Corbin, Amos. Surgeon's mate in 39th rgt.

Corbin, Henry. Private in Capt. Peters' co. 51st rgt.

Corboley, John R. 2d Lieutenant in 5th U. S. Infantry (Ja. 3, 1812); Captain (Je. 28, 1814).

Corcoran, Thomas [-1846]. Captain in 18th rgt. (Ag. 16, 1799); Captain in 36th U. S. Infantry (Ap. 30, 1813).

Cordery, James. Private in Capt. Stiles' co. Marine Artillery.

Cork, John. Private in Capt. Wilson's co. 6th rgt.

Cormacul, John. Private in Capt. Dyers' Fells Point Riflemen.

Cornelius, Campbell J. Captain in 35th rgt. (Jy. 7, 1814).

Cornell, Smith. Captain in 47th rgt. (My. 22, 1812).

Corner, James. Private in Capt. Brown's co. Eagle Artillerists.

Cornthwait, Thomas. Ensign in Capt. Conway's co. 6th rgt. (Jy. 12, 1814).

Correll, Nathan. Private in Capt. Myers' co. 39th rgt.

Corsey, H. Edward. Sergeant in Capt. Brown's co. 6th rgt.

Corwine, Jehu. Private in Capt. Stewart's co. 51st rgt.

Cosden, William. Private in Capt. Moore's co. 49th rgt.

Cose, Richard G. Private in Capt. Magruder's co. American Artillerists.

Cost, Christian. Captain in 1st rgt. 1st Cavalry Dist. (F. 13, 1812).

Costole [Costolo], Andrew. Private in Capt. Sheppard's co. 6th rgt.

Costole, James I. Sergeant in Capt. Sheppard's co. 6th rgt.

Cottingham, Isaac. Captain in 9th rgt. Resigned Jy. 8, 1814.

Cottingham, Lyttleton. Ensign in Capt. Scarborough's co. 9th rgt. (Jy. 8, 1814).

Cougle, John. 1st Lieutenant in Capt. Walter's co. 6th Cavalry Dist. (Ap. 26, 1812).

Coulbourn, John. Lieutenant in Capt. Johnson's co. 23d rgt. (Jy. 14, 1814).

Couley, John. Private in Capt. Quantrill's co. 24th rgt.

Coulson, George. Private in Capt. Sterett's 1st Balto. Hussars.

Coulter, Henry. 2d Lieutenant in 38th U. S. Infantry (My. 20, 1813). Resigned O. 5, 1813.

Coulter, Henry. Private in Capt. Chase's co. 22d rgt.; Sergeant in Ensign Brewer's detachment 36th rgt. at Bladensburg.

Coulter, James. Musician in Capt. Maynard's co. 22d rgt.

Coulter, John P. Private in Capt. Stewart's co. Washington Blues.

Council, James. Ensign in Capt. A. C. Smith's co. 49th rgt. (S. 10, 1814).

Councilman, George. Private in Capt. Fowler's co. 46th rgt.

Councilman, Jacob. Paymaster in 36th rgt. (Ag. 29, 1812).

Councilman, John F. Lieutenant in Capt. Grate's co. 7th rgt. Resigned Ag. 1, 1814.

Counsell, James. Sergeant in Capt. A. C. Smith's co. 49th rgt.

Coursey, William. Lieutenant in Capt. Colson's co. Extra Battalon Caroline Co. (S. 2, 1811).

Courtnay, Thomas. Captain in 42d rgt. (N. 6, 1811).

Courtnay, William. Private in Capt. Warfield's co. Balto. United Volunteers.

Covey, Jacob. Ensign in Capt. Douglass' co. 19th rgt. (O. 13, 1812).

Covington, Henry. 2d Lieutenant in Capt. Blake's co. 9th Cavalry Dist. (My. 31, 1813).

Covington, Jesse. Private in Capt. Page's co. 21st rgt.

*Covington, Leonard [-1813]. Brigadier General U. S. (Ag. 1, 1813). Died N. 14, 1813 of wounds received in battle of Chrystler's Field, N. 11, 1813.

Covington, Philip. Ensign in Capt. Watters' co. 25th rgt. Resigned Jy. 14, 1815.

Covington, Thomas. Private in Capt. Page's co. 21st rgt.

Cowan, —. 2d Mate of the privateer *Surprise.* Drowned Ap. 5, 1815.

Coward, Thomas. Captain of the privateer *Tyro,* Sept., 1812.

Cowarden, James. Corporal in Capt. Miller's co. 2d D. I.; b. Eastern Shore, Md.; age 24; sadler.

Cowden, Samuel. Lieutenant in Capt. Davidson's co. 49th rgt. (S. 16, 1811).

Cowdery, Isaac. Private in Capt. Bunbury's co. Sea Fencibles.

Cowhem, William. Musician in Capt. Schwarzauer's co. 27th rgt.

Cowles, William. Private in Capt. Kierstead's co. 6th rgt.

Cowley, Edward. Private in Capt. Rogers' co. 51st rgt.

Cox, Benjamin. Private in Capt. Morgan's co. 49th rgt.

Cox, Charles B. Private in Capt. Dyer's co. 17th rgt.

Cox, David. Private in Capt. McLaughlin's co. 50th rgt.

Cox, Edward. Private in Capt. Peters' co. 51st rgt.

Cox, Elisha. Private in Capt. Blizzard's co. 15th rgt.

Cox, Hugh. Captain 1st rgt. (Jy. 15, 1814).

Cox, James, Jr. Ensign in Capt. Hackett's co. 35th rgt. (Je. 17, 1812).

Cox, James, Jr. Private in Capt. Sterett's co. 1st Balto. Hussars.

Cox, John. Private in Capt. Blair's co. 50th rgt.

Cox, Jonathan. Private in Capt. Steever's co. 27th rgt.

Cox, Joseph. Ensign in Capt. Howard's co. Mechanical Volunteers.

Cox, Kelly. Private in Capt. John Miller's co. 2d D. I.; b. Md.; age 30; cooper; volunteer. Deserted May 30, 1813, from Patapsco encampment.

Cox, Kempson. Private in Capt. Haubert's co. 51st rgt.

Cox, Peregrine. Private in Capt. Morgan's co. 49th rgt.

Cox, Peter. Private in Capt. Magruder's co. American Artillerists.

Cox, Thomas. Private in Capt. Jas. Massey's co. 38th rgt.

Cox, Thomas, Jr. Private in Capt. Morgan's co. 49th rgt.

Cox, William. Captain Assistant Deputy Quarter-master U. S. (Ag. 31, 1813).

Cox, William. Private in Capt. Hall's co. 3d Cavalry rgt.

Cox, Williamson. Corporal in Capt. Posey's co. 1st rgt.

Coyle, David. Private in Capt. Roney's co. 39th rgt.

Cozier, Thomas. Captain in 30th rgt. (N. 9, 1809).

Crabbin, Hynson. 3d Lieutenant in 38th U. S. Infantry (My. 20, 1913). Resigned Ja. 7, 1814.

Craddick, Joseph [1778-1849]. Private in Capt. Schwarzauer's co. 27th rgt.

Craddock, Benedict. Private in Capt. A. C. Smith's co. 49th rgt.

Craddock, James. Private in Capt. A. C. Smith's co. 49th rgt.

Craddock, William. Private in Capt. A. C. Smith's co. 49th rgt.

Craft, Jacob. Sergeant in Capt. Kennedy's co. 27th rgt.

Craft, William. Captain in 11th rgt. (Ja. 25, 1814).

Craggs, John. Corporal in Capt. Horton's co. Maryland Chasseurs.

Craggs, Robert. Private in Capt. Sheppard's co. 6th rgt.

Craig, Benjamin. Private in Capt. Morgan's co. 49th rgt.

Craig, George. Sergeant-Major in 27th rgt.

Craig, James. Private in Capt. Mc-Kane's co. 27th rgt.

Craig, John. Corporal in Capt. Hanna's co. Fells Point Light Dragoons.

Craig, John. Private in Capt. Bunbury's co. Sea Fencibles.

Craig, Washington M. Surgeon Extra Battalion Dorchester Co. (My. 10, 1808).

Craig, William. Private in Capt. Slicer's co. 22d rgt.

Craig, William, Jr. Private in Capt. Oldham's co. 49th rgt.

Crain, Thomas. Quarter-master in 35th rgt. (My. 7, 1810).

Cramer, George W. Private in Capt. Stewart's co. Washington Blues.

Cramer, John. Private in Capt. Quantrill's co. 24th rgt.

Cramer, William. Private in Capt. Rogers' co. 51st rgt.

Cramphin, Richard. Captain in 14th rgt. (Je. 18, 1794).

Crampton, Moses. Private in Capt. John Miller's co. 2d D. I.; b. Washington Co., Md.; age 25; blacksmith; volunteer.

Crandle, James. Private in Capt. John Miller's co. 2d D. I.; b. Ireland; age 25; miller.

Crane, John. Private in Capt. Stiles' co. Marine Artillery.

Crane, Joseph. Private in Capt. Bader's co. Union Yägers.

Crane, Philip. Private in Capt. Chambers' co. 21st rgt. Wounded at Caulk's Field.

Crane [Crain], William. Paymaster 21st rgt. (N. 26, 1807).

Crangle, James. Private in Capt. Roney's co. 39th rgt.

Crangle, Henry. Private in Capt. Roney's co. 39th rgt.

Crangle, William. Private in Capt. Roney's co. 39th rgt.

Crapster, Peter. Ensign in Capt. Farquar's co. 47th rgt. (Ap. 27, 1813).

Craul, George. Private in Capt. Shryock's co. 24th rgt.

Crawford, David. Captain in 17th rgt. (Je. 27, 1812).

Crawford, David. Private in Capt. Chase's co. 22d rgt.

Crawford, John. Ensign in Capt. Shapleigh's co. 24th rgt. Resigned Jy. 12, 1814.

Crawford, John. Private in Capt. Wilson's co. 6th rgt.

Crawford, Parker. Ensign in Capt. Wiggins' co. Extra Battalion Harford Co. (Jy. 8, 1814).

Crawford, Samuel. Private in Capt. McLaughlin's co. 50th rgt.

Crawford, William. Private in Capt. Aisquith's co. Sharp Shooters.

Crawford, William B. Private in Capt. Magruder's co. American Artillerists.

Crawfurd, Robert. Lieutenant in Capt. Austin's co. 44th rgt. (Ag. 22, 1812).

Crawley, Samuel. Private in Capt. McKane's co. 27th rgt.

Craycroft, Clement. Private in Capt. Naylor's co. 17th rgt.

Craycroft, R. Captain of the privateer *Adeline*.

Crea, Hugh. Gunner in Capt. Bunbury's co. Sea Fencibles.

Crea, Hugh. Private in Capt. Galt's co. 6th rgt.

Crea, James. Private in Capt. Galt's co. 6th rgt.

Creager, Henry. Drummer in Capt. Shryock's co. 24th rgt.

Creager, John. Private in Capt. Shryock's co. 24th rgt.

Creager, John of Lawrence. Cornet in Capt. Johnson's co. 2d rgt. 1st Regimental Cavalry Dist. (Ja. 1, 1813).

Creager, Lewis. Surgeon's mate in 28th rgt. (S. 13, 1814).

Creager, William. Private in Capt. Shryock's co. 24th rgt.

Creagh, James. Private in Capt. Aisquith's co. Sharp Shooters.

Creamer, Barney. Private in Capt. Snowden's co. 36th rgt.

Creamer, John. Private in Capt. McLaughlin's co. 50th rgt.

Creaver, Nathaniel. Corporal in Capt. Dillon's co. 27th rgt.

Creemer, Joshua. Private in Capt. Burke's co. 6th rgt.

Cregg, William. Private in Capt. Sands' co. 22d rgt.

Creighton, Elias. Private in Capt. Travers' co. 48th rgt.

Creighton, Henry. Private in Capt. Travers' co. 48th rgt.

Creighton, Jeremiah. Private in Capt. Travers' co. 48th rgt.

Creighton, John. Private in Capt. Travers' co. 48th rgt.

Creighton, Thomas. Private in Capt. Travers' co. 48th rgt.

Creighton, Varnall. Private in Capt. Brohawn's co. 48th rgt.

Cretzer, John. Private in Capt. Berry's co. Washington Artillery. Wounded at Fort McHenry.

Crew, Jonathan. Private in Capt. Tilghman's co. 33 rgt.

Crey, Frederick [1778-]. Private in Capt. Sadtler's co. Balto. Yägers.

Crisfield, Perry. Private in Capt. McConkey's co. 27th rgt.

Crisfield, Samuel. Private in Capt. Ringgold's co. 6th rgt.

Criswell, Harford. Private in Capt. Blizzard's co. 15th rgt.

Crist, John. Lieutenant in Capt. Carlton's co. 16th rgt. (S. 20, 1813).

Crist, William. Sergeant. in Capt. Peters' co. 51st rgt.

Cristmond, Thomas. Private in Capt. Bouldin's co. Independent Light Dragoons.

Crocker, James. Private in Capt. Addison's co. Sea Fencibles.

Crombacker, Jacob. Lieutenant in Capt. Turbett's co. 16th rgt. (Ap. 28, 1813).

Cromwell, Benjamin. Sergeant in Capt. Ducker's co. 7th rgt.

Cromwell, George. Private in Capt. Linthicum's co. 22d rgt.

Cromwell, Jacob G. Corporal in Capt. Haubert's co. 51st rgt.

18

Cromwell, John. Private in Capt. Linthicum's co. 22d rgt.

Cromwell, Nathan. Adjutant in 8th rgt. (Ag. 9, 1808).

Cromwell, O'Neal. Private in Capt. Hancock's co. 22d rgt.

Cromwell, Philemon. Ensign in Capt. Cushwa's co. 8th rgt. (Ag. 22, 1812).

Cromwell, Richard. Private in Capt. Linthicum's co. 22d rgt.

Cromwell, Richard, Sr. Private in Capt. Linthicum's co. 22d rgt.

Cromwell, Thomas. Private in Capt. Linthicum's co. 22d rgt.

Cromwell, Zachariah. Lieutenant in Capt. Hancock's co. 22d rgt. (Ag. 12, 1812).

Crook, Charles, Jr. Private in Capt. Levering's co. Independent Blues.

Crook, Daniel. Lieutenant in Capt. McKane's co. 27th rgt.

Crook, John. Private in Capt. Thompson's co. 1st rgt.

Crook, Nathan. Private in Capt. Crawford's co. 17th rgt.

Crooks, William. Lieutenant in Capt. John Owings' co. 36th rgt. (Ag. 29, 1812).

Croslin, Richard. Private in Capt. Barnes' co. 32d rgt. Deserted.

Cross, Andrew. Private in Capt. Ringgold's co. 6th rgt.

Cross, Christian A. Private in Capt. Adreon's co. Union Volunteers.

Cross, Howerton. 2d Lieutenant in 42d U. S. Infantry (Ag. 4, 1813); 1st Lieutenant (My. 1, 1814).

Cross, John. Ensign in Capt. Fletchall's co. 3d rgt. (O. 12, 1807).

Cross, John. Private in Capt. Shrim's co. Balto. Light Infantry.

Cross, John. Private in Capt. Boone's co. 22d rgt.

Cross, John. Private in Capt. Dillon's co. 27th rgt.

Cross, Joseph [-1834]. Midshipman, U. S. N. (Je. 8, 1811); Lieutenant (Ap. 27, 1817); attached to the frigate *Constitution* at the time of action with the *Java*.

Cross, Joseph. Captain "Bladensburg Troop of Horse" in 2d Cavalry Dist. (Ap. 16, 1812); Lieutenant-Colonel (Jy. 4, 1812) vice Beanes.

Cross, Michael. Private in Capt. Ducker's co. 7th rgt.

Cross, Trueman [-1846]. Ensign in 42d U. S. Infantry (Ap. 27, 1814); 2d Lieutenant (O. 1, 1814).

Cross, William S. Private in Capt. Bouldin's co. Independent Light Dragoons.

Crossan, John. Private in Capt. Montgomery's co. Balto. Union Artillery.

Crossgrove, Levi. Corporal in Capt. Deems' co. 51st rgt.

Crossley, Walter. Private in Capt. Stone's co. 31st rgt.

Crossly, Garrett. Sergeant in Capt. Spry's co. 33d rgt.

Crossmore, William L. Sergeant in Capt. Smith's co. 51st rgt.

Crouch, James. Private in Capt. Griffith's co. 21st rgt.

Crouch, James. Private in Capt. Aisquith's co. Sharp Shooters.

Crouch, John. Private in Capt. Griffith's co. 21st rgt.

Crouch, Thomas. Private in Capt. Page's co. 21st rgt.

Crow, Richard B. Private in Capt. Jos. Jones's co. 34th rgt.

Crow, William, Jr. Private in Capt. Oldham's co. 49th rgt.

Croxall, Charles. Private in Capt. Miller's co. 39th rgt.

Croxall, James. Private in Capt. Stewart's co. Washington Blues.

Croxall, Richard. Private in Capt. Levering's co. Independent Blues.

Crozier, William. Private in Capt. Galt's co. 6th rgt.

Crumbacker, Samuel. Lieutenant in Capt. Quantrill's co. 24th rgt. (N. 8, 1814).

Crump, Alfred. Sergeant in Capt. Deems' co. 51st rgt.

Crump, George. Private in Capt. Haubert's co. 51st rgt.

Crumwell, Michael. Private in Capt. McKane's co. 27th rgt.

Cruse, William O. Private in Capt. Moale's co. Columbian Artillery.

Crush, Frederick. Lieutenant in Capt. Wherrett's co. 24th rgt. (S. 2, 1811).

Crussen, Francis. Private in Capt. Deems' co. 51st rgt.

Cryer, Jacob. Private in Capt. Brohawn's co. 48th rgt.

Cuddy, Lawson. Lieutenant in Capt. Merryman's co. 41st rgt. (Je. 2, 1813).

Culbert, Lewin. Private in Capt. Adreon's co. Union Volunteers.

Culley, George. Corporal in Capt. Patton's co. 30th rgt.

Cullison, John. Corporal in Capt. Blakistone's co. 45th rgt.

Cully, Robert. Private in Capt. Dyer's co. Fells Point Riflemen.

Culverwell, Stephen. Sergeant in Capt. Deems' co. 51st rgt.

Cumming, John. Aid-de-camp to Genl. Cumming in 1st Division (My. 13, 1813).

Cumming, Robert. Major-General in 1st Division (D. 9, 1812).

Cumming, Samuel. Sergeant in Capt. Mackey's co. 49th rgt.

Cummings, David. 1st Lieutenant in 14th U. S. Infantry (Mr. 12, 1812); Captain (Mr. 13, 1813).

Cummings, James. Private in Capt. Garrett's co. 49th rgt.

Cummings, Robert. Private in Capt. McDonald's co. 6th rgt.

Cummins, Alexander. Quartermaster in 6th rgt.

Cummins, Alexander. Quartermaster Sergeant in Capt. Brown's co. 6th rgt.

Cummins, Robert. Ensign in Capt. Dobbin's co. 39th rgt.

Cunningham, Aquila. Private in Capt. Fowler's co. 46th rgt.

Cunningham, George. Private in Capt. Schwarzauer's co. 27th rgt.

Cunningham, James. Private in Capt. Snowden's co. 36th rgt.

Cunningham, John. Private in Capt. Stiles' co. Marine Artillery.

Cunningham, Joseph. Private in Capt. Lawrence's co. 6th rgt.

Cuppold, Hartman. Private in Capt. Rogers' co. 51st rgt.

Curbey, James. Private in Capt. Schwarzauer's co. 27th rgt.

Curlett, James. Private in Capt. Montgomery's Balto. Union Artillery.

Curlett, Robert. Private in Capt. Stewart's co. 51st rgt.

Curlett, Thomas. Private in Capt. Montgomery's co. Balto. Union Artillery.

Curley, James. Private in Capt. Thos. Warner's co. 39th rgt.

Curran, Barney. 1st Lieutenant in Capt. Hall's co. 3d Cavalry Dist. (Jy. 28, 1812).

Curry, Isaac. Private in Capt. Dillon's co. 27th rgt.

Curry, James. Private in Capt. Shryock's co. 24th rgt.

Curry, John. Private in Capt. Aisquith's co. Sharp Shooters.

Curry, William. Private in Capt. Roney's co. 39th rgt.

Curtain, James. Private in Capt. Faster's co. 51st rgt.

Curteau, William. Private in Capt. Galt's co. 6th rgt.

Curtis, J. L. Private in Capt. Moale's co. Columbian Artillery.

Curtis, James. Private in Capt. Stiles' co. Marine Artillery.

Curtis, John. Private in Capt. Addison's co. Sea Fencibles.'

Curty, Clowdsbury. Private in Capt. Smith's co. 51st rgt.

Cushwa, David. Captain in 8th rgt. (Jy. 4, 1812).

Cusick, Ignatius. Private in Capt. Walker's co. 45th rgt.

Cusick, James. Private in Capt. Cawood's co. 45th rgt.

Cutcher, Samuel. Private in Capt. Deems' co. 51st rgt.

Cuzeanse, Bernard. Private in Capt. Magruder's co. American Artillerists.

D

Dadds, William. Private in Capt. Wells' Artillery co.

Dade, Robert T. Captain in 3d rgt. (My. 17, 1811).

Daffin, James. Ensign in Capt. Combs' co. 12th rgt. (Je. 27, 1811).

Dail, Christian. Private in Capt. Sadtler's co. Balto. Yägers.

Daily, Christian. Private in Capt. Stapleton's co. 39th rgt.

Daily, Elijah. Private in Capt. Stapleton's co. 39th rgt.

Daily, William. Private in Capt. Myers' co. 39th rgt.

Dalck, Andrew. Corporal in Capt. Hanna's co. Fells Point Light Dragoons.

Dale, Daniel. Private in Capt. Magruder's co. American Artillerists.

Daly, Benjamin S. Private in Capt. Magruder's co. American Artillerists.

Daly, John. Private in Capt. Brown's co. Eagle Artillerists.

Daley, John. Private in Capt. Dillon's co. 27th rgt.

Daley, Joseph. Private in Capt. Slicer's co. 22d rgt.

Dallam, Josias M., Jr. Paymaster in 42d rgt. (Jy. 14, 1814).

Dallam, William. Surgeon's mate 42d rgt. Resigned Jy. 14, 1814.

Dalrymple, George. Private in Capt. Nicholson's co. Balto. Fencibles.

Dalrymple, James. Corporal in Capt. Pinney's co. 27th rgt.

Dalrymple, William. Private in Capt. Howard's co. Mechanical Volunteers.

Dalrymple, William P. Private in Capt. Moale's co. Columbian Artillery.

Dalton, Edward. Private in Capt. Addison's co. Sea Fencibles.

Dameron, John. Captain of privateer *Bona*, July, 1812.

Damsell, William. Sergeant in Capt. King's co. 49th rgt.; Captain (D. 10, 1813).

Damute, Peter. Private in Capt. Smith's co. 51st rgt.

Daneker, John J. [1798-1882]. Private in Capt. Schwarzauer's co. 27th rgt.

Danerson, Richard. Private in Capt. Wilson's co. 6th rgt.

Dangerfield, Henry. Private in Capt. Dyer's co. 17th rgt.

Daniel, James. Private in Capt. Kennedy's co. 27th rgt.

Daniels, Peter. Seaman of the privateer *Surprise.* Drowned Ap. 5, 1813.

Danneman, C. H. Private in Capt. Nicholson's co. Balto. Fencibles.

Danse, Leopold. Private in Capt. Stapleton's co. 39th rgt.

Darby, Aden. Lieutenant in Capt. Griffith's co. 44th rgt. (Ag. 20, 1814).

Darby, Denton. Captain in 13th rgt. (Ag. 20, 1813).

Darden, Samuel B. [-1813]. Lieutenant in Capt. Hewitt's co. 4th rgt.

Dare, John. Surgeon in 31st rgt. (Ja. 25, 1815).

Dare, Nathaniel C. Private in Capt. Berry's co. Washington Artillery.

Darling, James. Corporal in Capt. Chalmers' co. 51st rgt.

Darnall, John. Captain in 14th rgt. (My. 23, 1799).

Darnall, John, Jr. Ensign in 5th U. S. Infantry (N. 13, 1812) ; 2d Lieutenant in 2d U. S. Infantry (My. 1, 1814).

Darnall, John of John. Private in Capt. Brooke's co. 34th rgt.

Darnall, Nicholas L. Private in Capt. Hall's co. 34th rgt.

Darnall, William. Private in Capt. Brooke's co. 34th rgt.

Darnell, Henry. Private in Capt. Maynard's co. 22d rgt.

Darnes, Augustus. Private in Capt. Bader's co. Union Yägers.

Darrell, Sampson. Private in Capt. Stiles' co. Marine Artillery.

Darrington, W. Private in Capt. Sterett's Independent co.

Dart, John. Private in Capt. Blair's co. 50th rgt.

Dashields, William. Private in Capt. Kennedy's co. 27th rgt.

Dashiell, George. Captain in 25th rgt. (N. 15, 1809).

Dashiell, George W. Private in Capt. Thompson's co. 1st Baltimore Horse Artillery.

Dashiell, Henry [1769-1830]. Private in Capt. Stiles' co. Marine Artillery.

Dashiell, James. Captain in 25th rgt. [1813].

Dashiell, John. Cornet in Capt. A. E. Jones' co. 11th Cavalry Dist. (Je. 16, 1812).

Dashiell, John. Ensign in Capt. Dennis' co. 37th rgt.

Dashiell, Matthias. Major in 25th rgt. (Je. 6, 1811).

Dashiell, Peter. Quarter-master in 25th rgt. (F. 5, 1808).

Datest, Lewis. Corporal in Capt. Duvall's co. 34th rgt.

Daub, Daniel. Private in Capt. Quantrill's co. 24th rgt.

Daugherty, Charles. Private in Capt. Steever's co. 27th rgt.

Daugherty, Hugh. Private in Capt. Taylor's co. 46th rgt.

Daugherty, Samuel. Private in Capt. Edes's co. 27th rgt.

Davey, Hugh [1776-1849]. Private in Capt. Stiles' co. Marine Artillery.

Davidge, Francis H. Private in Capt. Warfield's co. Balto. United Volunteers.

Davidge, Thomas. Ensign in 14th U. S. Infantry (My. 12, 1813) ; 3d Lieutenant (N. 11, 1813). Resigned F. 1, 1814.

Davids, John. Private in Capt. Deems' co. 51st rgt.

Davidson, Israel. Private in Capt. Hall's co. 3d Cavalry rgt.

*Davidson, James [1760-1841]. Enlisted Jy. 20, 1776; Sergeant 1778; taken prisoner Ja., 1780; Private in Capt. Montgomery's co. Balto. Union Artillery, 1814; captured at North Point.

Davidson, Nelson. Private in Capt. Kennedy's co. 27th rgt.

Davidson, Robert. Private in Capt. Shrim's co. Balto. Light Infantry.

Davidson, Samuel. Private in Capt. Shrim's co. Balto. Light Infantry.

Davidson, Samuel. Private in Capt. Levering's co. Independent Blues.

Davidson, William. Private in Capt. Sheppard's co. 6th rgt.

Davies, Samuel. Private in Capt. McConkey's co. 27th rgt.

Davis, Abraham. Private in Capt. Brown's co. 6th rgt.

Davis, Amos. Private in Capt. Bouldin's co. Independent Light Dragoons.

Davis, Benjamin. Private in Capt. Smith's co. 51st rgt.

Davis, Caleb. Ensign in Capt. Watts' co. 36th rgt. (O. 12, 1814).

Davis, Charles. Private in Capt. Pinney's co. 27th rgt.

Davis, Charles S. Surgeon's mate in 15th rgt.

Davis, David. Private in Capt. Adreon's co. Union Volunteers. Wounded at North Point.

Davis, David. Private in Capt. Berry's co. Washington Artillery.

Davis, Ebenezer. Captain in 50th rgt. (My. 28, 1808).

Davis, Edward. Private in Capt. Moale's co. Columbian Artillery.

Davis, Elijah. Private in Capt. Morgan's co. 49th rgt.

Davis, Francis. Private in Capt. Brown's co. 43d rgt.

Davis, George. Corporal in Capt. Cawood's co. 45th rgt.

Davis, George. Private in Capt. Morgan's co. 49th rgt.

Davis, George W. D. Private in Capt. Brown's co. 43d rgt.

Davis, Gerard. Private in Capt. Cawood's co. 45th rgt.

Davis, Gideon. 2d Lieutenant in Capt. Bruff's co. Artillery 6th Brigade (My. 19, 1813).

Davis, Henry. Private in Capt. Massey's co. 38th rgt.

Davis, Hezekiah of J. Private in Capt. Dunnington's co. 43d rgt.

Davis, Isaiah. Private in Capt. McLaughlin's co. 50th rgt.

Davis, Jacob. 3d Lieutenant in 2d U. S. Infantry (D. 10, 1814).

Davis, Jacob G. Private in Capt. Magruder's co. American Artillerists.

Davis, James. Paymaster in 27th rgt.

Davis, James. Private in Capt. Hall's co. 3d Cavalry rgt.

Davis, James C. Lieutenant in Capt. Brown's co. 49th rgt.

Davis, James G. Private in Capt. Maynard's co. 22d rgt.

Davis, Jenifer. Private in Capt. Dunnington's co. 43d rgt.

Davis, John. Major in 7th rgt. Resigned Ag. 1, 1814.

Davis, John. Captain in 11th Cavalry Dist. (O. 6, 1812).

Davis, John. Lieutenant in Capt. Davis's co. 9th rgt. (N. 30, 1811).

Davis, John. Sergeant in Capt. Haubert's co. 51st rgt.

Davis, John. Lieutenant in Capt. Storey's co. 38th rgt. (Jy. 24, 1813).

Davis, John. Private in Capt. Shrim's co. Balto. Light Infantry.

Davis, John. Corporal in Capt. Ducker's co. 7th rgt.

Davis, John A. Corporal in Capt. Dunnington's co. 43d rgt.

Davis, John B. Lieutenant in Capt. Combs' co. 12th rgt.(Je. 27, 1811).

Davis, John G. Private in Capt. Aisquith's co. Sharp Shooters.

Davis, Joseph. Private in Capt. Dunnington's co. 43d rgt.

Davis, Joseph. Sergeant in Capt. Morgan's co. 49th rgt.

Davis, Joseph, Jr. Private in Capt. Morgan's co. 49th rgt.

Davis, Joshua. Private in Capt. Lawrence's co. 6th rgt.

Davis, Josiah. Lieutenant in Capt. Taylor's co. Extra Battalion Worcester Co. (F. 11, 1809).

Davis, Josias. Private in Capt. Crawford's co. 17th rgt.

Davis, Lancelot. Private in Capt. Burgess' co. 43d rgt.

Davis, Mitchell. Private in Capt. Brown's co. 43d rgt.

Davis, Noble. Private in Capt. Morgan's co. 49th rgt.

Davis, Richard. Private in Capt. Burgess' co. 43d rgt.

Davis, Robert. Private in Capt. Stiles' co. Marine Artillery.

Davis, Robert. Sergeant in Capt. Hall's co. 3d Cavalry rgt.

Davis, Robert. Private in Capt. Wells' Artillery co.; 4th Sergeant (O., 1814).

Davis, Samuel. Private in Capt. Snowden's co. 36th rgt.

Davis, Samuel. Corporal in Capt. Sample's co. 49th rgt.

Davis, Solomon. Captain in 11th rgt. (Ja. 25, 1814) vice Minos Adams.

Davis, Thomas. Private in Capt. Lawrence's co. 6th rgt.

Davis, Thomas. Ensign in 2d rgt. (Je. 26, 1812).

Davis, Thomas. Private in Capt. Aisquith's co. Sharp Shooters.

Davis, Thomas. Seaman of privateer *Chasseur*, severely wounded in action with H. M. Schr. *Lawrence*, Feb. 27, 1815.

Davis, Thomas A. Adjutant in 43d rgt. (Ag. 4, 1801).

Davis, William. Captain in 9th rgt. (N. 30, 1811).

Davis, William. Private in Capt. A. C. Smith's co. 49th rgt.

Davis, William. Private in Capt. Adreon's co. Union Volunteers.

Davison, John. Captain in 49th rgt. (S. 16, 1811).

Davison, Robert. Sergeant in Capt. Moore's co. 49th rgt.

Davison, Thomas. 2d Lieutenant of the privateer *Perry*, Sept., 1814.

Davitt, William. Private in Capt. Ringgold's co. 6th rgt.

Davy, Henry. Private in Capt. McDonald's co. 6th rgt.

Davy, William. Private in Capt. Dyer's co. Fells Point Riflemen.

Dawes, Edward. 3d Lieutenant in U. S. Artillery Corps (S. 15, 1814).

Dawes, James G. Private in Capt. Warfield's co. Balto. United Volunteers.

Dawes, James L. Lieutenant and Paymaster in 27th rgt.

Dawes, Richard. Private in Capt. Smith's co. 51st rgt.

Dawkins, William C. Lieutenant in Capt. Griffis' co. 31st rgt. (Je. 15, 1811).

Dawson, Edward, Jr. Ensign in Capt. Davis' co. 50th rgt. (Ag. 11, 1813).

Dawson, James. Quarter Gunner in Capt. Addison's co. Sea Fencibles.

Dawson, John. Major in 26th rgt. vice Cook.

Dawson, John. Private in Capt. Aisquith's co. Sharp Shooters.

Dawson, Joseph. Private in Capt. Stiles' co. Marine Artillery.

Dawson, Joseph. Private in Capt. Dyer's co. Fells Point Riflemen.

Dawson, Nicholas L. Paymaster in 49th rgt.

Dawson, Robert. 2d Lieutenant of the privateer *Ultor*, Mar, 1814.

Dawson, Samuel. Captain in 28th rgt.

Dawson, Thomas. Private in Capt. Schwarzauer's co. 27th rgt.

Dawson, William. Private in Capt. Bader's co. Union Yägers.

Dawson, William. Private in Capt. Ringgold's co. 6th rgt.

Dawson, William. Private in Capt. Pumphrey's co. 22d rgt.

Day, Cornelius. Private in Capt. Addison's co. Sea Fencibles.

Day, Ishmael. Lieutenant in Capt. Howard's co 46th rgt. (Je. 1, 1813).

Day, John. Private in Capt. Boone's co. 22d rgt.

Day, Lerey. Private in Capt. Sheppard's co. 6th rgt.

Day, Richard. Private in Capt. Boone's co. 22d rgt.

Dayley, John. Private in Capt. Brown's co. 6th rgt.

Deaking, John. Private in Capt. Blair's co. 50th rgt.

Deakins, George. Private in Capt. Brooke's co. 34th rgt.

Deal, George. Private in Capt. Hanna's co. Fells Point Light Dragoons.

Deal, Jacob. Private in Capt. Moale's co. Columbian Artillery.

Deal, John. Private in Capt. Lawson's co. Balto. Patriots.

Deal, Michael. Private in Capt. Stapleton's co. 39th rgt.

Deal, Nathaniel. Corporal in Capt. Foreman's co. 33d rgt.

Deal, Samuel. Private in Capt. Chambers' co. 21st rgt.

Deal, William. Private in Capt. Galt's co. 6th rgt.

Deale, James. Private in Capt. Stiles' co. Marine Artillery.

Deale, Richard. Corporal in Capt. Chew's co. 31st rgt.

Deale, Samuel. Lieutenant of the privateer *Halcyon*, Jan., 1813.

Dean, Charles. Private in Capt. Gray's co. 43d rgt.

Dean, James. Private in Capt. Miller's co. 39th rgt.

Dean, James. Corporal in Capt. Getzendanner's co. 16th rgt.

Dean, John A. Lieutenant in Capt. Getzendanner's co. 16th rgt. (S. 18, 1812).

Dean, Richard. Private in Capt. Barnes' co. 32d rgt.

Dean, Richard. Private in Capt. Snowden's co. 36th rgt.

Dean, Robert. Corporal in Capt. Getzendanner's co. 16th rgt.

Dean, Thomas. Private in Capt. Steiner's Frederick Artillery co.

Dean, William. Private in Capt. Travers' co. 48th rgt.

Deane, William. Private in Capt. Burgess' co. 43d rgt.

Dear, Isaac. Private in Capt. Bunbury's co. Sea Fencibles.

Deatley, Thomas. Private in Capt. Dent's co. 43d rgt.

Deaver, Aquila T. Ensign in Capt. Ruff's co. 42d rgt. (Ag. 11, 1813).

Deaver, Benjamin. Ensign in Capt. Hackney's co. 28th rgt. (My. 22, 1812).

Deaver, Thomas. Private in Capt. Chalmers' co. 51st rgt.

Deblestine, John. Private in Capt. Sands, co. 22d rgt.

DeButts, Elisha. Private in Capt. Thompson's co. 1st Baltimore Horse Artillery.

Decker, George J. Captain in 7th rgt. (Ap. 27, 1813).

Decker, Jacob F. Private in Capt. Levering's co. Independent Blues.

DeCourse, Barney. Private in Capt. Griffith's co. 21st rgt.

Dedie, Solomon. Captain in 10th rgt. Resigned S. 20, 1813.

Deems, Frederick. Sergeant in Capt. McLaughlin's co. 50th rgt.

Deems, Jacob. Captain in 51st rgt.

Deems, John. Private in Capt. Dillon's co. 27th rgt.

Deer, John. Private in Capt. Mackey's co. 49th rgt.

Deer, Thomas. Private in Capt. King's co. 49th rgt.

Deets, Gottlieb. Private in Capt. Shrim's co. Balto. Light Infantry.

Degilver, John. Private in Capt. Brown's co. 6th rgt.

DeGoy, Bartholomew. Private in Capt. Bader's co. Union Yägers.

Degraft, Abraham. Private in Capt. Barr's Cavalry co. 1st Dist.

Degroff, Richard. Private in Capt. A. E. Warner's co. 39th rgt.

DeGrot, John. Command unknown; captured at Bladensburg.

Dehaff, Peter. Ensign in Capt. Showers' co. 15th rgt. (D. 24, 1810).

Deitz, John. Private in Capt. Quantrill's co. 24th rgt.

De Krafft, Edward. Command unknown; captured at Bladensburg.

Delacour, James. Private in Capt. Warfield's co. Balto. United Volunteers.

Delaha, Henry. Corporal in Capt. Wilson's co. 6th rgt.

Delano, Judah. Private in Capt. Kennedy's co. 27th rgt.

Delany, William. Private in Capt. Brown's co. Eagle Artillerists.

Delaware, Thomas. Private in Capt. Brown's co. Eagle Artillerists.

Delawder, Daniel. Private in Capt. Marker's co. 28th rgt.

Delawder, David. Corporal in Capt. Marker's co. 28th rgt.

Delawder, Frederick. Private in Capt. Marker's co. 28th rgt.

Delawder, Jacob. Private in Capt. Barnes' co. 32d rgt. Deserted.

Delcher, George. Private in Capt. Montgomery's co. Balto. Union Artillery.

Delcher, John. Private in Capt. Hanna's co. Fells Point Light Dragoons.

Delcher, Thomas. Private in Capt. Chalmers' co. 51st rgt.

Delmas, Alenis A. Private in Capt. Magruder's co. American Artillerists.

Deloste, Francis. Private in Capt. Levering's co. Independent Blues.

DeLoughrey, T. Sergeant in Capt. Piper's co. United Maryland Artillery.

Delouhrey, John. Corporal in Capt. Blair's co. 50th rgt.

Delozier, Daniel. Sergeant in Capt. Brown's co. 43d rgt.

Delsher, James. Private in Capt. Pinkney's Artillery co.

Delsher, William. Private in Capt. Steever's co. 27th rgt.

Delvachio, Peter. Sergeant in Capt. Sterett's co. 1st Balto. Hussars.

Demar, Thomas. Private in Capt. Naylor's co. 17th rgt.

Dempsey, John. Private in Capt. Burke's co. 6th rgt.

Dempsey, John. Private in Capt. Dobbin's co. 39th rgt.

Dempsey, John. Private in Capt. Lawrence's co. 6th rgt.

Dempsey, Robert. Sergeant in Capt. McDonald's co. 6th rgt.

Demsford, John. Private in Capt. Stiles' co. Marine Artillery.

Demuth, John. Private in Capt. Shim's co. Balto. Light Infantry.

Deneale, Hugh W. Captain in 36th U. S. Infantry (Ap. 30, 1813).

Denison, Edward. Captain in Washington Artillery. (Jy. 4, 1812).

Denning, Spry. Private in Capt. Kierstead's co. 6th rgt.

Dennis, James. Captain in 37th rgt.

Dennis, John. Private in Capt. McDonald's co. 6th rgt.

Dennis, John. Private in Capt. Smith's co. 51st rgt.

Dennis, Wheatly. Lieutenant in Capt. Dennis' co. 37th rgt. Died 1814.

Denny, David G. Private in Capt. Bouldin's co. Independent Light Dragoons.

Denny, James. Private in Capt. Massey's co. 38th rgt.

Denny, John. Private in Capt. McDonald's co. 6th rgt.

Denny, John. Seaman of Barney's flotilla ; wounded and captured at Bladensburg.

Denny, Joseph. Private in Capt. Dyer's co. Fells Point Riflemen.

Denny, Richard A. Private in Capt. Stiles' co. Marine Artillery.

Denny, Theodore. Surgeon in 9th Cavalry Dist. (Jy. 4, 1812).

Denny, William. Private in Capt. Maynard's co. 22d rgt.

Denny, William. Private in Capt. Sheppard's co. 6th rgt.

Denson, James. Private in Capt. Brown's co. 6th rgt.

Denson, Parker. Private in Capt. Heath's co. 23d rgt.

Dent, Alexander. Captain in 1st rgt.

Dent, Hatch. Private in Capt. Thompson's co. 1st rgt.

Dent, James Thomas. Judge-Advocate U. S. (Jy. 19, 1813).

Dent, John. Private in Capt. Hall's co. 3d Cavalry rgt.

Dent, John T. Quarter-master Sergeant in 1st rgt.

Dent, Lewis W. Sergeant in Capt. Dent's co. 43d rgt.

Dent, Nathan S. Ensign in 1st rgt. (Jy. 28, 1812).

Dent, Theophilus. Lieutenant in 1st rgt. (Jy. 4, 1812).

Dent, Walter. Private in Capt. Thos. Warner's co. 39th rgt.

Dent, William. Captain in 43d rgt. [1813].

Dent, William S. Private in Capt. Posey's co. 1st rgt.

Derby, Benedict H. Ensign in Capt. Higgins' co. 44th rgt. (S. 10, 1814).

Dermott, James C. Captain in 14th rgt. (Ap. 26, 1799).

Derne, Frederick. Captain in 47th rgt. (F. 1, 1814).

Deroncery, Charles. Private in Capt. Sadtler's co. Balto. Yägers.

Dersachbroom, Thomas. Private in Capt. Jas. Massey's co. 38th rgt.

Dertzback, George. Sergeant in Capt. Steiner's Frederick Artillery co.

Derumple, Rezin. Private in Capt. Shryock's co. 24th rgt.

Descande, Andrew. Private in Capt. Sadtler's co. Balto. Yägers.

Desent, George. Private in Capt. Kierstead's co. 6th rgt.

Desent, Moses. Corporal in Capt. Kierstead's co. 6th rgt.

Deshner, Jacob. Private in Capt. Getzendanner's co. 16th rgt.

Deshong, James. Private in Capt. Watson's co. 39th rgt.

Desk, Michael. Private in Capt. Pinney's co. 27th rgt.

Desk, Thomas. Private in Capt. Schwarzauer's co. 27th rgt.

Desney, Benjamin. Private in Capt. Thomas Warner's co. 39th rgt.

Despaux, Elie. Private in Capt. Stiles' co. Marine Artilley.

Despaux, John [1796-1826]. Private in Capt. Stiles' co. Marine Artillery.

Detro, Levi. Private in Capt. Smith's co. 51st rgt.

Dettmar, Henry W. Ensign in Capt. Adreon's co. Union Volunteers.

Devatur, Jacob. Private in Capt. Berry's co. Washington Artillery.

Devenie, James. Private in Capt. Sterett's Independent co.

Deverbaugh, Benjamin. Private in Capt. McLaughlin's co. 50th rgt.

Deverix, John. Private in Capt. Steever's co. 27th rgt.

Devilbiss, Charles. Lieutenant in Capt. Bankert's co. 20th rgt. (Jy. 13, 1814) vice Messenheimer.

Devilbiss, George. Lieutenant in Capt. Eckman's co. 20th rgt. (Je. 12, 1812).

Devone, Frederick. Private in Capt. Shrim's co. Balto. Light Infantry.

Devore, Aaron. Private in Capt. Blair's co. 50th rgt.

Devos, John. Private in Capt. Edes' co. 27th rgt.

Devou, I. William. Private in Capt. Bunbury's co. Sea Fencibles.

Dew, Edward. Lieutenant of the privateer Globe, Jan., 1813.

Dew, James C. Corporal in Capt. Bouldin's Independent Light Dragoons.

Dew, William. Sergeant in Capt. Magruder's co. American Artillerists.

Dewees, Andrew. Private in Capt. Sterett's Independent co.

*Dewees, Samuel. Fife Major in Nace's 15th rgt.

Dewling, William. Private in Capt. Pinney's co. 27th rgt.

Diamond, John C. Private in Capt. McConckin's co. 38th rgt.

Dibert, Christian. Private in Capt. John Miller's co. 2d D. I.; b. Md.; age 33; cooper.

Dibert, Henry. Private in Capt. John Miller's co. 2d D. I.; b. Sharpsburg, Md.; cooper; volunteer.

Dick, Henry. Private in Capt. John Miller's co. 2d D. I.; b. Washington Co.; age 29; weaver; subs. for Jacob Summers.

Dickens, John. Private in Capt. Magruder's co. American Artillerists.

Dickenson, David P. Captain of the privateer Midas, Jan., 1815.

Dickerson, Daniel. Lieutenant of the privateer Expedition, Oct., 1812.

Dickinson, P. Private in Capt. Stiles' co. Marine Artillery.

Dickinson, Peter S. Cornet Capt. Bowdle's co. 9th Cavalry Dist. (Jy. 24, 1813).

268 APPENDIX

Dickinson, Samuel S. Quarter-master in 4th rgt. (N. 8, 1811).
Dickinson, Solomon. Brigade Major in 12th Brigade (1813).
Dickinson, William. 1st Lieutenant in Capt. Martin's co. 9th Cavalry Dist. (My. 8, 1812); Captain (D. 2, 1812).
Dickson, Harrison. Surgeon's mate 48th rgt. (Jy. 8, 1813).
Dickson, John, Jr. Sergeant in Capt. Hall's co. 30th rgt.
Dickson, Richard. Seaman of the privateer High Flyer. Wounded in action Dec., 1812.
Dieter, John. 1st officer of the privateer Chasseur.
Diffenderfer, John. Private in Capt. Nicholson's co. Balto. Fencibles.
Diffenderffer, John. 2d Lieutenant in Capt. Thompson's co. 5th Cavalry Dist. (My. 3, 1813); Horse Artillery (D. 9, 1813).
Diffenderffer, Michael. Surgeon's mate 1st rgt. Artillery (Je. 16, 1812).
Diffenderffer, Richard. Corporal in Capt. Edes's co. 27th rgt.
Diffenderffer, William. Sergeant Major in 5th rgt.
Diffendoffer, Charles. Private in Capt. Levering's co. Independent Blues.
Diggs, Beverly [1784-1862]. Commander of Barge in Barney's flotilla.
Dillahunt, Thomas. Private in Capt. Steever's co. 27th rgt.
Dillaway, James. Private in Capt. Garret's co. 49th rgt.
Dillihunt, James. Private in Capt. Barr's Cavalry co. 1st Dist.
Dilling, Christopher. Private in Capt. Frizzell's co. 15th rgt.
Dillman, Peter. Private in Capt. Deems' co. 51st rgt.

Dillon, David. Private in Capt. Deems' co. 51st rgt.
Dillon, James. Captain in 27th rgt.
Dillon, Joseph. Captain Assistant Deputy Quarter-master General U. S. (Mr. 3, 1814).
Dinsmore, John. Private in Capt. Ringgold's co. 6th rgt.
Dinsmore, Patrick. Private in Capt. Dobbin's co. 39th rgt.
Dinsmore, Samuel. Private in Capt. Pennington's co. Balto. Independent Artillerists.
Diser, Samuel. Command unknown; captured at Bladensburg.
Disney, James. Private in Capt. Bader's co. Union Yägers.
Disney, John. Private in Capt. Roney's co. 39th rgt.
Disney, Mordecai. Corporal in Capt. Shrim's co. Balto. Light Infantry.
Disney, Richard. Private in Capt. Snowden's co. 36th rgt.
Disney, Wesley. Private in Capt. Bader's co. Union Yägers.
Disney, William. Private in Capt. Shrim's Balto. Light Infantry.
Disney, William. Private in Capt. McDonald's co. 6th rgt.
Disney, William J. Lieutenant in Capt. Marriott's co. 2d rgt. (Jy. 7, 1814).
Ditman, John. Private in Capt. Peters' co. 51st rgt.
Ditten, David. Private in Capt. Dillon's co. 27th rgt.
Diver, Samuel. Lieutenant in Capt. Herbert's co. 42d rgt. (Ap. 4, 1808).
Divers, Ananias. Lieutenant in Capt. Elliott's co. 41st rgt. (My. 22, 1812).
Dixen, William. Private in Capt. Snowden's co. 36th rgt.
Dixon, Francis. Private in Capt. Hance's co. 31st rgt.

Dixon, James. Private in Capt. Steiner's Frederick Artillery co.

Dixon, Jonas. Private in Capt. Allen's co. 49th rgt.

Dixon, Thomas. Private in Capt. King's co. 49th rgt.

Dixon, Walter G. Private in Capt. Burgess' co. 43d rgt.

Dixon, William. Private in Capt. Pinney's co. 27th rgt.

Dobbin, Archibald [-1830]. Captain in 39th rgt.; Assistant District Paymaster U. S. (N. 8, 1814).

Dobbins, William. Private in Capt. Shrim's co. Balto. Light Infantry.

Dodd, James. Private in Capt. Massey's co. 38th rgt.

Dodd, John. Private in Capt. Massey's co. 38th rgt.

Doddrell, J. C. Private in Capt. Dillon's co. 27th rgt.

Dodds, Robert. Surgeon in 20th rgt. (Je. 12, 1812).

Dodge, Alpheus. Private in Capt. Deems' co. 51st rgt.

Dodge, John. Private in Capt. Travers' co. 48th rgt.

Dodson, Henry. Lieutenant in Capt. Tolson's co. 14th rgt. (F. 4, 1808).

Dodson, James. Acting Quartermaster 26th rgt.

Dodson, John S. Sergeant in Capt. Brooke's co. 34th rgt.

Dodson, Robert. Private in Capt. Brooke's co. 34th rgt.

Dodson, William. Adjutant in 26th rgt. (Je. 26, 1812).

Dome, John. Private in Capt. A. E. Warner's co. 39th rgt.

Donaldson, Aaron. Private in Capt. Schwarzauer's co. 27th rgt.

Donaldson, James Lowrie. Lieutenant and Adjutant in 27th rgt. Killed at North Point.

Donaldson, Jesse. Private in Capt. Lawrence's co. 6th rgt.

Donaldson, John Johnson. Paymaster in 2d Cavalry Dist. (F. 19, 1813).

Donaldson, Joseph. Private in Capt. Thompson's co. 1st Baltimore Horse Artillery.

Donaldson, Robert. Private in Capt. Thomas's co. 49th rgt.

Donaldson, Stephen F. Ensign in 14th U. S. Infantry (Mr. 12, 1812); 1st Lieutenant (N. 14, 1814).

Donlin, Eliphan. Private in Capt. Wickes' co. 21st rgt.

Donnals, Isaac. Private in Capt. Roney's co. 39th rgt.

Donnell, John. Private in Capt. McKane's co. 27th rgt.

Donnelly, Daniel. Private in Capt. Wilson's co. 6th rgt.

Donnelly, John. Private in Capt. Brown's co. Eagle Artillerists.

Donnelly, Simon. Private in Capt. Brown's co. 6th rgt.

Donoho, Barney. Private in Capt. Brown's co. Eagle Artillerists.

Donohoe, Patrick. Private in Capt. Stapleton's co. 39th rgt.

Donovan, Jeremiah. Private in Capt. Deems' co. 51st rgt.

Dooghman, Peter. Private in Capt. Smith's co. 51st rgt.

Dooley, James. Lieutenant of the privateer Dolphin, June, 1812; Captain of the Rolla, Oct, 1812.

Dooly, Rhoady. Private in Capt. Stapleton's co. 39th rgt.

Dopt, George. Private in Capt. Ringgold's co. 6th rgt.

Dorbecker, Adam. Private in Capt. Schwarzauer's co. 27th rgt.

Dorman, William. Private in Capt. Kierstead's co. 6th rgt.

Dorney, Bartholemew. Private in Capt. Brown's co. Eagle Artillerists.

Dorr, Leonard. Private in Capt. McConkey's co. 27th rgt.

Dorry, Henry. Sergeant in Capt. Hanna's co. Fells Point Light Dragoons.

Dorse, Patrick. Command unknown; captured at Bladensburg.

Dorset, Thomas R. Private in Capt. Baden's co. 17th rgt.

Dorsey, Archibald, *M. D.* Quartermaster in 32d rgt. (S. 20, 1808).

Dorsey, Basil. Sergeant in Capt. Snowden's co. 36th rgt.

Dorsey, Basil of Evan. Captain in 13th rgt. (My. 12, 1812).

Dorsey, Caleb of John. Lieutenant in Capt. Hudson's co. 32d rgt. (Ap. 21, 1809).

Dorsey, Charles. Corporal in Capt. Levering's co. Independent Blues.

Dorsey, Charles. Private in Capt. Barnes' co. 32d rgt.

Dorsey, Charles G. 1st Lieutenant in Capt. Saunders' co. 1st Rifle Battalion (S. 20, 1813).

Dorsey, Charles W. Captain in 32d rgt. (Ag. 20, 1814); Major in 32d rgt. vice Hood.

Dorsey, Clement. Appointed by the Executive to collect all arms belonging to the state, in Charles Co. (Je. 27, 1812).

Dorsey, Daniel. Ensign in Capt. Weems' co. 22d rgt. Resigned Jy. 15, 1814.

Dorsey, Edward. Private in Capt. Brooke's co. 34th rgt.

Dorsey, Edward of Vachel. Captain in 32d rgt.

Dorsey, Edward H. Private in Capt. Sterett's co. 1st Balto. Hussars.

Dorsey, Edward W. Corporal in Capt. Owings' co. 32d rgt.

Dorsey, Hammond. Private in Capt. Moale's co. Columbian Artillery.

Dorsey, Henry C. Lieutenant in Capt. Jonathan Norris' co. 20th rgt. (Ap. 27, 1813).

Dorsey, John. Private in Capt. Snowden's co. 36th rgt.

Dorsey, John W. Aid-de-camp to Genl. Cumming 1st Division (My. 13, 1813).

Dorsey, John W. of Caleb. Captain in 32d rgt. (My. 14, 1813).

Dorsey, Jonathan. Lieutenant in Capt. S. C. Owings' co. 36th rgt. (Jy. 28, 1813).

Dorsey, Joshua. Corporal in Capt. Nicholson's co. Balto. Fencibles.

Dorsey, N. Private in Capt. Thompson's co. 1st Baltimore Horse Artillery.

Dorsey, Nicholas. Corporal in Capt. Snowden's co. 36th rgt.

Dorsey, Owen. Lieutenant and Paymaster in 39th rgt. (Ap. 22, 1800).

Dorsey, Ralph. Lieutenant in Capt. Dorsey's co. 32d rgt. (S. 26, 1807).

Dorsey, Richard. Private in Capt. Warfield's co. Balto. United Volunteers, at Bladensburg.

Dorsey, Richard B. Private in Capt. Sterett's co. 1st Balto. Hussars.

Dorsey, Roderick. Paymaster in 3d Cavalry Dist. (Jy. 11, 1814).

Dorsey, Samuel. Private in Capt. Sterett's co. 1st Balto. Hussars.

Dorsey, Samuel. Private in Capt. Snowden's co. 36th rgt.

Dorsey, Samuel J. Private in Capt. Dobbin's co. 39th rgt.

Dorsey, Stephen B. Cornet in Capt. Hammond's co. 3d Cavalry Dist. (Ap. 23, 1812). Resigned 1814.

Dorsey, Thomas. Private in Capt. Stone's co. 31st rgt.

Dorsey, Thomas H. Major, command unknown (Jy. 28, 1813).

Dorsey, Vachel. Private in Capt. Dillon's co. 27th rgt.

Dougherty, Barney. Private in Capt. Wilson's co. 6th rgt.

Dougherty, Charles. Private in Capt. Chalmers' co. 51st rgt.

Dougherty, James. Private in Capt. Stewart's co. Washington Blues.

Dougherty, James. Private in Capt. Kennedy's co. 27th rgt.

Dougherty, John. Private in Capt. Chalmers' co. 51st rgt.

Dougherty, John. Private in Capt. Brown's co. Eagle Artillerists.

Dougherty, John. Private in Capt. Stewart's co. Washington Blues.

Dougherty, John. Private in Capt. McKane's co. 27th rgt.

Dougherty, Neal. Private in Capt. Deems' co. 51st rgt.

Dougherty, Philip. Private in Capt. Peters' co. 51st rgt.

Dougherty, Samuel. Seaman of the privateer *Comet*.

Douglas, George [1790-1869]. Private in Capt. Nicholson's co. Balto. Fencibles.

Douglas, William. Sergeant in Capt. Nicholson's co. Balto. Fencibles.

Douglass, John. Private in Capt. Umsted's co. 25th rgt.

Douglass, Thomas H. Captain in 19th rgt. (O. 13, 1812).

Dove, William G. Lieutenant in Capt. Sheckle's co. 42d rgt. (S. 21, 1813) vice Waters.

Dover, Henry. Private in Capt. Sadtler's co. Balto. Yägers.

Dowden, Zachariah. Private in Capt. Heater's co. 32d rgt.

Dowell, Henry, Jr. Lieutenant in Capt. Chew's co. 31st rgt. (D. 23, 1813). Resigned Jy. 15, 1814.

Dowel, John H. Sergeant in Capt. Chew's co. 31st rgt.

Dowell, Richard. Sergeant in Capt. Chew's co. 31st rgt.

Dowlan, Daniel. Private in Capt. Schwarzauer's co. 27th rgt.

Dowling, William. Private in Capt. Wilson's co. 6th rgt.

Downes, Edward. Sergeant in Capt. McConckin's co. 38th rgt.

Downes, James. Private in Capt. Thos. Warner's co. 39th rgt.

Downes, Nathan. Private in Capt. Massey's co. 38th rgt.

Downes, Richard C. Surgeon's mate in 14th U. S. Infantry (My. 12, 1813). Resigned F. 7, 1814.

Downes, Robert. Private in Capt. McConckin's co. 38th rgt.

Downes, Samuel. Private in Capt. McConckin's co. 38th rgt.

Downey, Edmund. Private in Capt. Smith's co. 51st rgt.

Downey, James. Private in Capt. Page's co. 21st rgt.

Downing, Howell [1790-1845]. Private in Capt. Stewart's co. 51st rgt.

Downs, Isaiah. Private in Capt. Snowden's co. 36th rgt.

Downs, Isaiah. Private in Capt. Haubert's co. 51st rgt.

Downs, William. Private in Capt. Williams' co. 12th rgt.

Doyl, John. Private in Capt. Snowden's co. 36th rgt.

Doyle, David. Private in Capt. Brown's co. 43d rgt.

Doyle, Patrick. Private in Capt. Lawrence's co. 6th rgt.

Drain, James. Private in Capt. Blair's co. 50th rgt.

Drain, Thomas. Private in Capt. Blair's co. 50th rgt.

Drake, William. Sergeant in Capt. Piper's co. United Maryland Artillery.

Drane, Gustavus S. [-1846].
Private, Corporal and Sergeant in
U. S. Light Artillery (1812) ; 2d
Lieutenant (Mr. 17, 1814).

Draper, William. Ensign in Capt.
Smelser's co. 28th rgt. (Je. 15,
1813).

Draver, Nicholas. Private in Capt.
Green's co. 46th rgt.

Drear, Joseph. Private in Capt.
Bunbury's co. Sea Fencibles.

Drummond, James. Private in Capt.
Galt's co. 6th rgt.

Drummond, Richard. Private in
Capt. Dyer's co. Fells Point Riflemen.

Drury, Benedict. Corporal in Capt.
Cawood's co. 45th rgt.

Drury, Enoch. Private in Capt.
Millard's co. 12th rgt.

Drury, Ignatius. 2d Lieutenant in
Capt. John Miller's co. 2d Detached Infantry ; Captain in 10th
rgt. (S. 20, 1813).

Drury, Peter. Sergeant in Cawood's
co. 45th rgt.

Drury, Thomas H. Ensign in Capt.
Snider's co. 8th rgt. (Ap. 21,
1814).

Drury, Wilfred. Private in Capt.
Blakistone's co. 45th rgt.

Drury, William. Ensign in Capt.
Sprigg's co. 10th rgt. (F. 1, 1814).

Dryden, Joshua [1792-1897]. Corporal in Capt. Adreon's co. Union
Volunteers ; Major 6th Md. Artillery ; President of Old Defender's Association, 1883-1897.

Dryden, Littleton W. Private in
Capt. Edes's co. 27th rgt.

Dryden, Thomas. Corporal in Capt.
Edes' co. 27th rgt.

Dryden, Tubman. Private in Capt.
Heath's co. 23d rgt.

Dryden, William. Private in Capt.
Dobbin's co. 39th rgt.

Dryden, William. Private in Capt.
Heath's co. 23d rgt.

Dubois, Nicholas. Sergeant in Capt.
Warfield's co. Balto. United Volunteers.

Duboise, James. Private in Capt.
Levering's co. Independent Blues.

Ducatel, J. F. Private in Capt.
Moale's co. Columbian Artillery.

Ducker, Jeremiah. Captain in 7th
rgt. (F. 9, 1814).

Duckett, Basil. Quarter-master in
34th rgt. (Ag. 1, 1814).

Duckett, John. Private in Capt.
Crawford's co. 17th rgt.

Duckett, Richard. Surgeon's mate
34th rgt. (Jy. 4, 1812).

Duckett, Samuel. Private in Capt.
Crawford's co. 17th rgt.

Duclo, Marshel. Seaman of the privateer Comet.

Duddy, Henry. Private in Capt. Pinney's co. 27th rgt.

Dudley, George. Private in Capt.
Howard's co. Mechanical Volunteers.

Dudley, John. Lieutenant in Capt.
Parrott's co. 4th rgt.

Dudley, Nicholas. Private in Capt.
Page's co. 21st rgt.

Duel, William. Private in Capt.
Briscoe's co. 45th rgt.

Duer, Charles. Private in Capt.
Pennington's co. Balto. Independent Artillery.

Duffee, Hugh. Private in Capt.
Snowden's co. 36th rgt.

Duffy, Henry. Private in Capt. Mc-
Kane's co. 27th rgt.

Duffy, Hugh. Private in Capt. Kennedy's co. 27th rgt.

Dugan, George. Private in Capt.
Adreon's co. Union Volunteers.

Dugan, Hammond. Private in Capt. Warfield's co. Balto. United Volunteers at Bladensburg.

Dugan, John. Private in Capt. Usselton's co. Artillery 6th Brigade.

Dugan, Thomas. Private in Capt. Chambers' co. 21st rgt.

Duke, Basil. Corporal in Capt. Berry's co. Washington Artillery.

Dukehart, Henry [1793-1866]. Private in Capt. Aisquith's co. Sharp Shooters.

Dulany, Samuel [1790-1840]. Private in Capt. Howard's co. Mechanical Volunteers.

Dulsher, Samuel. Private in Capt. Wells' Artillery co. (A. A. Co.)

Duluc, Andrew. Corporal in Capt. Sadtler's co. Balto. Yägers.

Duly, Charles. Private in Capt. Hungerford's co. 1st rgt.

Dumiste, George. Private in Capt. Smith's co. 51st rgt.

Dunbar, George T. Private in Capt. Warfield's co. Balto. United Volunteers.

Dunbar, Henry. Private in Capt. Hancock's co. 22d rgt.

Duncan, Christian. Private in Capt. Haubert's co. 51st rgt.

Duncan, D. W. Ensign in Capt. Kiersted's co. 6th rgt. Resigned Jy., 1814.

Duncan, J. W. Private in Capt. Brown's co. Eagle Artillery.

Duncan, John. Private in Capt. Chalmers' co. 51st rgt.

Duncan, Joseph. Private in Capt. Pennington's co. Balto. Independent Artillerists.

Duncan, Perry. Private in Capt. Stiles' co. Marine Artillery.

Dungan, William. Private in Capt. Steever's co. 27th rgt.

Dunham, Jacob. Private in Capt. Sheppard's co. 6th rgt.

Dunk, Alexander. Private in Capt. Chambers' co. 21st rgt.

Dunk, Henry. Private in Capt. Griffith's co. 21st rgt.

Dunkel, E. A. Private in Capt. Moale's co. Columbian Artillery.

Dunlop, Abraham. Private in Capt. Taylor's co. 46th rgt.

Dunn, Curtis. Corporal in Capt. Kierstead's co. 6th rgt.

Dunn, George. Private in Capt. Slicer's co. 22d rgt.; private in Ensign Brewer's detachment 36th rgt. at Bladensburg.

Dunn, James. Private in Capt. Kennedy's co. 27th rgt.

Dunn, James. Private in Capt. Kierstead's co. 6th rgt.

Dunn, John. Private in Capt. Shrim's co. Balto. Light Infantry.

Dunn, John. Private in Capt. Page's co. 21st rgt.

Dunn, Patrick. Private in Capt. Pinkney's Artillery co. (A. A. Co.)

Dunn, Robert. Lieutenant in Capt. Hodge's co. 21st rgt. (My. 8, 1812).

Dunning, Samuel. Private in Capt. Aisquith's co. Sharp Shooters.

Dunning, William. Private in Capt. Montgomery's co. Balto. Union Artillery.

Dunnington, Francis E. Ensign in Capt. Dunnington's co. 43d rgt.

Dunnington, James B. Sergeant in Capt. Dunnington's co. 43d rgt.

Dunnington, John B. Drummer in Capt. Dunnington's co. 43d rgt.

Dunnington, John P. M. Sergeant in Capt. Dunnington's co. 43d rgt.

Dunnington, Jonathan F. Sergeant in Capt. Dent's co. 43d rgt.

19

Dunnington, Nathan. Private in Capt. Burgess' co. 43d rgt.

Dunnington, Peter. Private in Capt. Dunnington's co. 43d rgt.

Dunnington, Roger. Captain in 43d rgt.

Dunnington, Thomas. Sergeant in Capt. Dent's co. 43d rgt.

Dunnington, William W. Paymaster in 43d rgt. (Ag. 13, 1813).

Dunnock, John. Corporal in Capt. Travers' co. 48th rgt.

Dunnock, Thomas. Corporal in Taylor's co. 48th rgt.

Dunnock, Thomas, Jr. Private in Capt. Travers' co. 48th rgt.

DuPois, Christopher. Private in Capt. Myers' co. 39th rgt.

Dupuy, Bernard. Corporal in Capt. McKane's co. 27th rgt.

Durand, John. Private in Capt. Stiles' co. Marine Artillery.

Durbin, William, Jr. Captain in 20th rgt. (Ap. 4, 1808).

Dureling, John T. Private in Capt. Faster's co. 51st rgt.

Durf, Samuel. Private in Capt. John Miller's co. 2d D. I.; b. Loudon Co., Va.; age 47; tailor; subs. for John Baker.

Durfell, Joseph. Private in Capt. Blizzard's co. 15th rgt.

Durham, John. Corporal in Capt. Horton's co. Maryland Chasseurs.

During, James. Private in Capt. Kennedy's co. 27th rgt.

Durkee, Pearl. Captain of the privateer *Chasseur*, Feb., 1813; Sergeant in Capt. Stiles' co. Marine Artillery, 1814.

Durst, Felix J. Private in Capt. Bader's co. Union Yägers.

Dushane, Valentine. Sergeant in Capt. Deems' co. 51st rgt.

Dutterow, David. Captain in 20th rgt. (Ap. 27, 1813).

Dutton, John. Private in Capt. Ringgold's co. 6th rgt.

Dutton, Notley. Private in Capt. Posey's co. 1st rgt.

Duval, Edmund B. Capt. 42d U. S. Infantry (Ag. 4, 1813).

Duvall, A. Private in Capt. Pinkney's Artillery co. (A. A. Co.)

Duvall, Barton [c1776-1831]. Private in Capt. Brooke's co. 34th rgt.

Duvall, Benjamin. Sergeant in Capt. Marshall's co. 34th rgt.

Duvall, Daniel. Ensign in Capt. Riggs' co. 13th rgt. (D. 28, 1808). Later Captain in 28th rgt.

Duvall, Dennis. Ensign in Capt. Isaacs' co. 34th rgt. (Jy. 13, 1814).

Duvall, Edward. Private in Capt. Snowden's co. 36th rgt.

Duvall, Henry. Adjutant in 22d rgt. (My. 31, 1808).

Duvall, Henry. Private in Capt. Beall's co. 34th rgt.

Duvall, Isaac. Sergeant in Capt. Boone's co. 22d rgt.

Duvall, Jacob. Private in Capt. Hall's co. 3d Cavalry rgt.

Duvall, Jacob. Private in Capt. Boone's co. 22d rgt.

Duvall, John. Private in Capt. Boone's co. 22d rgt.

Duvall, Joseph H. Sergeant in Capt. Boone's co. 22d rgt.

Duvall, Lewis. Lieutenant-Colonel in 3d Cavalry Dist. (F. 13, 1812).

Duvall, Mareen. Private in Capt. Jos. Jones's co. 34th rgt.

Duvall, Marsh M. Private in Capt. Berry's co. Washington Artillery.

Duvall, Nathan. Private in Capt. Deems' co. 51st rgt.

Duvall, Ralph. Private in Capt. Linthicum's co. 22d rgt.

Duvall, Samuel. Private in Capt. Boone's co. 22d rgt.

Duvall, Trueman. Captain in 34th rgt. Died 1814.

Duvall, Washington. Private in Capt. Burke's co. 6th rgt.

Duvall, William. Captain in 18th rgt. (S. 30, 1797).

Duvall, Zachariah. Lieutenant-Colonel in 22d rgt.

Duwasser, Charles. Musician in Capt. Quantrill's co. 24th rgt.

Dwyer, John. Private in Capt. Tilghman's co. 33d rgt.

Dwyer, William. Private in Capt. Montgomery's co. Balto. Union Artillery.

Dycass, Nathan. Sergeant in Capt. Linthicum's co. 22d rgt.

Dye, William. Private in Capt. Brown's co. Eagle Artillerists.

Dyer, Elijah. Corporal in Capt. Dyer's co. Fells Point Riflemen.

Dyer, Ezekiel. Private in Capt. Dyer's co. Fells Point Riflemen.

Dyer, Ignatius. Private in Capt. Rogers' co. 51st rgt.

Dyer, John. Private in Capt. Williams' co. 12th rgt.

Dyer, John A. Lieutenant in Capt. Thompson's co. 1st rgt.

Dyer, John E. Lieutenant in Capt. Clagett's co. 17th rgt. (N. 7, 1812).

Dyer, John R. Captain in 17th rgt. (S. 7, 1810).

Dyer, William B. Captain in Fells Point Riflemen, 3d Brigade (Ap. 4, 1812).

Dyer, William C. Sergeant in Capt. McPherson's co. 43d rgt.

Dykes, James. Private in Capt. Stewart's co. 51st rgt.

Dykes, John. Private in Capt. Stapleton's co. 39th rgt.

Dykes, Joseph. Private in Capt. McConkey's co. 27th rgt.

Dykes, Killim. Ensign in Capt. Johnson's co. 37th rgt. (Ap. 15, 1811).

Dykes, Thomas. Private in Capt. Stapleton's co. 39th rgt.

Dynock, Edward. Cornet in Capt. White's co. 11th Cavalry Dist. (My. 1812); 2d Lieutenant (O. 15, 1814).

Dyron, Gustavus. Private in Capt. Thompson's co. 1st rgt.

Dyron, Oswald. Private in Capt. Thompson's co. 1st rgt.

Dyson, Dr. Bennett. Surgeon's mate 43d rgt. vice Dr. Mungo Mitchett.

Dyson, John A. Lieutenant in Capt. Smoot's co. 43d rgt. (Ap. 27, 1813).

Dyson, Samuel. Private in Capt. Cawood's co. 45th rgt.

Dyson, Samuel. Sergeant in Capt. Parnham's co. 1st rgt.

E

Eady, Jonathan. Quarter-master in 7th Cavalry Dist. (S. 5, 1812).

Eagle, James. Private in Capt. Page's co. 21st rgt.

Eagleston, John. Private in Capt. McDonald's co. 6th rgt.

Eakle, Christian. Lieutenant in Capt. Shauman's co. 10th rgt. (Ag. 23, 1809).

Eakle, Jacob. Private in Capt. Barr's Cavalry co. 1st Dist.

Eakle, Joseph. Trumpeter in Capt. Barr's Cavalry co. 1st Dist.

Earbaugh, John. Private in Capt. Blizzard's co. 15th rgt.

Earle, Caleb. Captain Assistant Deputy Quarter-master General U. S. (Ag. 2, 1814). Resigned Ag. 18, 1814.

Earle, James, Jr. Captain in 4th rgt. (Jy. 24, 1799).

Earle, Thomas, Jr. Private in Capt. Wells' Artillery co. (A. A. Co.)

Earle, Thomas, Sr. Private in Capt. Pinkney's Artillery co. (A. A. Co.)

Earle, Thomas C. Paymaster in 38th rgt. (Mr. 25, 1808).

Earle, William Nelson. 2d Lieutenant in 36th U. S. Infantry (Ap. 30, 1813); 1st Lieutenant (Ag. 15, 1813).

Earley, John. Private in Capt. Edes' co. 27th rgt.

Early, Leonard H. Sergeant in Capt. Eversfield's co. 17th rgt.

Early, Thomas. Private in Capt. Crawford's co. 17th rgt.

Earnest, Charles. Private in Capt. Dyer's co. Fells Point Riflemen. Wounded at North Point.

Earp, Joshua. Private in Capt. Snowden's co. 36th rgt.

Earp, William W. Private in Capt. Snowden's co. 36th rgt.

Easterbrook, David. Private in Capt. Warfield's co. Balto. United Volunteers.

Easterday, Abraham. Captain in 28th rgt. (Ap. 28, 1808).

Easton, Nicholas. Private in Capt. Lawrence's co. 6th rgt.

Easton, William. Lieutenant in Capt. Rohrer's co. 10th rgt. (Ap. 30, 1811).

Eaverson, George. Sergeant in Capt. Montgomery's co. Balto. Union Artillery.

Ebervine, William. Sergeant in Bader's co. Union Yägers.

Eccles, John. Private in Capt. Ringgold's co. 6th rgt.

Eccleston, James. Private in Capt. Levering's co. Independent Blues.

Eccleston, John B. Private in Capt. Hands' co. 21st rgt.

Eccleston, Thomas J. H. Captain in Extra Battalion Dorchester Co. vice Mackey (D. 16, 1814).

Eccleston, William W. Captain in 11th rgt. (O. 3, 1807).

Echburger, Jacob. Private in Capt. Lawrence's co. 6th rgt.

Echburger, John. Sergeant in Capt. Galt's co. 6th rgt.

Eckel, William. Ensign in Capt. A. E. Warner's co. 39th rgt. (S. 10, 1814).

Eckington, John. Private in Capt. Allen's co. 49th rgt.

Eckman, Jacob. Captain in 20th rgt. (Ag. 16, 1808).

Eddy, Rufus. Private in Capt. Dillon's co. 27th rgt.

Edelin, Aloysias. Captain in 1st rgt. (Ja. 10, 1814).

Edelin, Edward. Private in Capt. Burgess's co. 43d rgt.

Edelin, Edward C. Lieutenant in Capt. Wheeler's co. 14th rgt. (F. 4, 1808).

Edelin, Francis. Ensign in Capt. Hamilton's co. 17th rgt. (D. 7, 1813).

Edelin, Horatio. Private in Capt. Burgess' co. 43d rgt.

Edelin, John. Private in Capt. Causin's co. 4th Cavalry Dist.

Edelin, Joseph. Private in Capt. Dent's co. 43d rgt.

Edelin, Lewis. Private in Capt. Brown's co. 43d rgt.

Edelin, Raphael. Ensign in Capt. Clagett's co. 17th rgt. (Je. 15, 1813).

Edelin, Thomas. Private in Capt. Naylor's co. 17th rgt.

Edelin, Thomas H. Private in Capt. Chase's co. 22d rgt.; Ensign in

Capt. Hamilton's co. 17th rgt. Resigned Dec. 7, 1813.

Eden, William. Private in Capt. Dillon's co. 27th rgt.

Edes, —. Ensign in Capt. Ford's co. 6th rgt. Resigned Jy., 1814.

Edes, Benjamin. Captain in 27th rgt.

Edes, John. Private in Capt. Steever's co. 27th rgt.

Edes, Thomas. Private in Capt. Ringgold's co. 6th rgt.

Edgar, Arnold. Sergeant in Capt. Taylor's co. 48th rgt.

Edgar, David. Private in Capt. Dobbin's co. 39th rgt.

Edler, John. Private in Capt. Rogers' co. 51st rgt.

Edmonson, Franklin. Corporal in Capt. McConkey's co. 27th rgt.

Edmonson, Henry H. 2d Lieutenant in Capt. Tootle's co. 10th Cavalry Dist. (S. 26, 1812).

Edmonson, John [1781-1860]. Captain in 10th cavalry dist.; Major in 1813.

Edmonson, Robert. Ensign in Capt. Hillery's co. 13th rgt. (O. 24, 1800).

Edmonson, Samuel. Private in Capt. Brohawn's co. 48th rgt.

Edmonston, Archibald. Sergeant in Capt. Jos. Jones's co. 34th rgt.

Edmonston, Basil. Lieutenant in Capt. Jones' co. 34th rgt. (Ag. 20, 1814).

Edmonston, James. Private in Capt. Jos. Jones' co. 34th rgt.

Edmonston, James. Sergeant Major in Extra Battalion 4th Brigade.

Edmunds, Abijah. Private in Capt. Bunbury's co. Sea Fencibles.

Edwards, Abraham. Sergeant in Capt. Peters' co. 51st rgt.

Edwards, Benjamin. Lieutenant in Capt. Ashberry's co. 10th rgt. (My. 9, 1808).

Edwards, Daniel. Private in Capt. John Miller's co. 2d D. I.; b. Washington Co., Md.; age 20; joiner; volunteer.

Edwards, Jesse. Command unknown; captured at Bladensburg.

Edwards, John. Private in Capt. Hands' co. 21st rgt.

Edwards, Samuel. Private in Capt. Magruder's co. American Artillerists.

Edwards, Thomas. Private in Capt. Fowler's co. 46th rgt.

Edwards, William. Private in Taylor's co. 46th rgt.

Edwards, William. Sergeant in Capt. Colston's co. 48th rgt.

Edwards, William. Sergeant in Capt. Peters' co. 51st rgt.

Egan, Robert. Lieutenant in Capt. Krouss' co. 30th rgt. (Je. 26, 1812).

Egerton, Charles Calvert [-1862]. Ensign in 36th U. S. Infantry (D. 12, 1814).

Egerton, Richard B. 1st Lieutenant in Capt. Maddox's Artillery co. 5th Brigade Charles Co. (N. 3, 1812).

Eggleston, Benjamin. Private in Capt. Deems' co. 51st rgt.

Eggleston, Joseph. Private in Capt. Deems' co. 51st rgt.

Egner, Jacob. Veterinary Surgeon in 8th Cavalry Dist. (D. 9, 1813).

Egnor, John. Ensign in Capt. Davison's co. 49th rgt. (S. 17, 1811).

Eich, Philip. Private in Capt. Stewart's co. 51st rgt.

Eichelberger, George. Private in Capt. Levering's co. Independent Blues.

Eichelberger, George S. 1st Lieutenant in 38th U. S. Infantry (My. 20, 1813); Regimental Quarter-master (1813). Resigned Ap. 22, 1814; Corporal in Capt. Levering's co. Independent Blues.

Eichelberger, Jesse. 1st Lieutenant in Capt. Nicholson's co. Balto. Fencibles.

Eichelberger, Lewis. Private in Capt. Nicholson's co. Balto. Fencibles.

Eichelberger, Martin. Corporal in Capt. Peters' co. 51st rgt.

Eichelberger, Peter. Sergeant in Capt. Smith's co. 51st rgt.

Eichelberger, Samuel. Private in Capt. Watson's co. 39th rgt.

Eichelberger, William. Private in Capt. Nicholson's co. Balto. Fencibles.

Eichelberger, William. Private in Capt. Levering's co. Independent Blues.

Eisenbray, Peter. Sergeant in Capt. Roney's co. 39th rgt.

Eisenhart, J. D. Private in Capt. Dillon's co. 27th rgt.

Elbert, Henry C. 1st Lieutenant in Capt. Woolford's co. 10th Cavalry Dist. (S. 26, 1812).

Elbert, John L. Cornet 2d U. S. Light Dragoons (Ap. 28, 1813); 2d Lieutenant (Jy. 18, 1814).

Elbert, Samuel. Private in Capt. Hands' co. 21st rgt.

Elbert, Samuel [-1815]. Private in Capt. McKane's co. 27th rgt.

Elbin, Reuben. Private in Capt. Blair's co. 50th rgt.

Elburn, William. Private in Capt. Allen's co. 49th rgt.

Elder, Basil S. Private in Capt. Pike's co. Balto. Volunteer Artillery.

Elder, Hillery. Sergeant in Capt. Kennedy's co. 27th rgt.

Elder, Owen. Private in Capt. Snowden's co. 36th rgt.

Elder, Samuel. Private in Capt. Kennedy's co. 27th rgt.

Elderkin, William G. Sergeant in Capt. Magruder's co. American Artillerists.

Elgin, Hezekiah R. Private in Capt. Brown's co. 43d rgt.

Eli, George [1777-   ]. Private in Capt. Steever's co. 27th rgt.

Eliott, Benjamin. Private in Capt. Addison's co. Sea Fencibles.

Ellender, Frederick. Private in Capt. Burke's co. 6th rgt.

Ellery, Epes. Private in Capt. Pennington's Balto. Independent Artillerists.

Ellicott, Nathaniel. Private in Capt. Snowden's co. 36th rgt.

Ellicott, William. Private in Capt. Snowden's co. 36th rgt.

Elligood, Thomas. Corporal in Capt. Aisquith's co. Sharp Shooters.

Elliot, John B. Private in Capt. Montgomery's co. Balto. Union Artillery.

Elliot, Joseph B. Private in Capt. Montgomery's co. Balto. Union Artillery.

Elliott, Benjamin. Ensign in Capt. Hall's co. 2d rgt. (My. 9, 1808).

Elliott, George. Private in Capt. Levering's co. Independent Blues.

Elliott, Jesse Duncan [1782-1845]. Midshipman U. S. N., April, 1804; Lieutenant (Ap. 23, 1810); Master (Jy. 24, 1813); Captain (Mr. 27, 1818).

Elliott, John. Private in Capt. Peters' co. 51st rgt.

Elliott, John. Private in Capt. Burke's co. 6th rgt.

Elliott, John of William. Captain in 38th rgt. (Ag. 1, 1808).

Elliott, John P. Private in Capt. Burke's co. 6th rgt.

Elliott, Lemuel. Corporal in Capt. Taylor's co. 48th rgt.

Elliott, Nicholas. Lieutenant in Capt. Shrim's co. Balto. Light Infantry.

Elliott, Planner. Ensign in Capt. Wm. Craft's co. (Ja. 25, 1814).

Elliott, Richard. Private in Capt. Hall's co. 3d Cavalry rgt.

Elliott, Thomas. Private in Capt. Hall's co. 3d Cavalry rgt.

Elliott, Thomas. Private in Capt. Deems' co. 51st rgt.

Elliott, Thomas W. Private in Capt. Burke's co. 6th rgt.

Elliott, William. Private in Capt. Chambers' co. 21st rgt.

Elliott, William. Private in Capt. Chase's co. 22d rgt.

Elliott, William A. Captain in 41st rgt. (My. 7, 1810).

Ellis, George. Private in Capt. Stiles' co. Marine Artillery.

Ellis, John. Corporal in Capt. Conway's co. 6th rgt.

Ellis, John. Private in Capt. Naylor's co. 17th rgt.

Ellis, John. Private in Capt. Stewart's co. 51st rgt.

Ellis, Lewis. Corporal in Capt. Conway's co. 6th rgt.

Ellis, Owen. Private in Capt. Crawford's co. 17th rgt.

Ellis, Thomas. Private in Capt. Ringgold's co. 6th rgt.

Ellis, William. Private in Capt. Chalmers' co. 51st rgt.

Elmore, James. Private in Capt. Peters' co. 51st rgt.

Elzey, Arnold [-1818]. Garrison Surgeon's mate, U. S. (Ap. 15, 1814).

Elzey, Robert C. 1st Lieutenant in Capt. A. E. Jones' co. 11th Cavalry Dist. (Je. 16, 1812).

Emerling, Christian. Private in Capt. Chalmers' co. 51st rgt.

Emerson, James. Private in Capt. Stewart's co. 51st rgt.

Emerson, William. Private in Capt. Jas. Massey's co. 38th rgt.

Emory, Gideon. Private in Capt. Levering's co. Independent Blues.

Emory, Henry. Private in Capt. Massey's co. 38th rgt.

Emory, John D. Private in Capt. Jas. Massey's co. 38th rgt.

Emory, John M. G. Ensign in Capt. Smith's co. 4th rgt. (N. 6, 1811).

Emory, John R. B. Captain in 38th rgt. (Ag. 16, 1808).

Emory, Lot. Private in Capt. Myers' co. 39th rgt.

Emory, Thomas. Major in 9th Cavalry Dist. (F. 13, 1812).

Emory, Thomas L. Private in Capt. Warfield's co. Balto. United Volunteers; Division Quarter-master in 3d Division (N. 8, 1814).

Emory, William. Private in Capt. McConckin's co. 38th rgt.

Emrich, Jacob. Private in Capt. Shryock's co. 24th rgt.

Engle, Frederick. Private in Capt. Getzendanner's co. 16th rgt.

English, Marshal. 2d Lieutenant in Capt. Pike's co. 1st Balto. Volunteers Artillery (Je. 26, 1812).

Ennalls, Joseph of Henry. Captain in 10th Cavalry Dist. (Jy. 29, 1812); Major (D. 6, 1813). Died Jy., 1814.

Ennalls, Thomas. Lieutenant-Colonel in 10th Cavalry Dist. (My. 13, 1812).

Ennis, John. Private in Capt. Oldham's co. 49th rgt.

Ensminger, Christian. Private in Capt. John Miller's co. 2d D. I.; b. Md.; age 28; blacksmith.

Ensor, George. Private in Capt. Frizzell's co. 15th rgt.

Ensor, J. Quarter-master in Extra Battalion Dorchester Co.

Ensor, William. Private in Capt. Peters' co. 51st rgt.

Ent [Ernt], George W. Captain in 16th rgt. (Ag. 1, 1814) vice Stephen Steiner.

Entler, Michael. Private in Capt. McLaughlin's co. 50th rgt.

Epaugh, Jacob. Lieutenant in Capt. Showers' co. 15th rgt. (D. 24, 1810).

Erb, Joseph. Private in Capt. McLaughlin's co. 50th rgt.

Erickson, Thomas. Private in Capt. Faster's co. 51st rgt.

Ernest, Charles. Command unknown. Wounded at Bladensburg.

Erwin, Gerard. Private in Capt. Berry's co. Washington Artillery.

Erwin, John. Private in Capt. Montgomery's co. Balto. Union Artillery.

Essender, John. Private in Capt. Shrim's co. Balto. Light Infantry.

Essender, Thomas. Private in Capt. Stewart's co. 51st rgt.

Essex, Samuel, Jr. Lieutenant in Capt. Wilson's co. 31st rgt. (D. 23, 1813) vice Isaac.

Estel, James B. Private in Capt. McConkey's co. 27th rgt.

Estell, John. Private in Capt. Edes' co. 27th rgt.

Estep, —. Lieutenant in 2d rgt. 1814.

Estep, Joshua. Private in Capt. Cawood's co. 45th rgt.

Estis, Thomas. Private in Capt. Edes' co. 27th rgt.

Etchberger, John. Private in Capt. Montgomery's co. Balto. Union Artillery.

Etchberger, William [-1830]. Private in Capt. Sheppard's co. 6th rgt.

Etchison, Elisha. Lieutenant in Capt. Etchison's co. 3d rgt. (Je. 12, 1812).

Etchison, Ephraim. Captain in 3d rgt. (My. 7, 1811).

Etherington, John W. Lieutenant in Capt. Allen's co. 49th rgt. (Mr. 25, 1814).

Etherington, Joseph. Private in Capt. Morgan's co. 49th rgt.

Etherington, William. Private in Capt. Morgan's co. 49th rgt.

Etherington, William. Private in Capt. Travers' co. 48th rgt.

Etsberger, William. Private in Capt. Kennedy's co. 27th rgt.

Etting, Samuel. Private in Capt. Nicholson's co. Balto. Fencibles. Wounded at Fort McHenry.

Euler, Conrad. Private in Capt. Bader's co. Union Yägers. Captured at North Point.

Euler, Jacob. 1st Sergeant in Capt. Bader's co. Union Yägers. Wounded at North Point.

Eulon, Philip. Private in Capt. Levering's co. Independent Blues.

Eunick, Thomas. Lieutenant in Capt. Chambers' co. 21st rgt.

Evans, Amos A. Private in Capt. Moore's co. 49th rgt.

Evans, Daniel. Lieutenant in Capt. Chas. Jones' co. 7th rgt. (Ap. 23, 1808).

Evans, Daniel. Sergeant in Capt. Sheppard's co. 6th rgt.

Evans, David. Private in Capt. Addison's co. Sea Fencibles.

Evans, Elias. Private in Capt. Dyer's co. Fells Point Riflemen.

Evans, Elisha. Private in Capt. Getzendanner's co. 16th rgt.

Evans, George. Private in Capt. Adreon's co. Union Volunteers.

Evans, George W. Sergeant in Capt. Faster's co. 51st rgt.

Evans, Henry F. Ensign in 22d U. S. Infantry (Mr. 31, 1814); 2d Lieutenant (Je. 2, 1814).

Evans, Hugh W. Private in Capt. Sterett's co. 1st Balto. Hussars.

Evans, James. Sergeant in Capt. Mackey's co. 49th rgt.

Evans, Jeremiah. Private in Capt. Faster's co. 51st rgt.

Evans, John. Private in Capt. Roney's co. 39th rgt.

Evans, John. Private in Capt. Pinney's co. 27th rgt.

Evans, John, Sr. Captain in Artillery co. 1st Brigade Cecil Co. (O. 21, 1808).

Evans, John R. Captain in 8th Cavalry Dist. "Elkton Troop" (Ap. 23, 1812).

Evans, Jonathan. Sergeant in Capt. McConckin's co. 38th rgt.

Evans, Joseph. Private in Capt. Edes's co. 27th rgt.

Evans, Joseph. Private in Capt. Pinkney's Artillery co. (A. A. Co.)

Evans, Joshua. Private in Capt. A. E. Warner's co. 39th rgt.

Evans, Patrick. Private in Capt. Bunbury's co. Sea Fencibles.

Evans, Richard. Lieutenant in Capt. Hammitt's co. 12th rgt. (Je. 27, 1811).

Evans, Robert. Private in Capt. Mackey's co. 49th rgt.

Evans, Robert. Private in Capt. Roney's co. 39th rgt.

Evans, Thomas. Private in Capt. Roney's co. 39th rgt.

Evans, Thomas. Private in Capt. Lawrence's co. 6th rgt.

Evans, Wesley. Private in Capt. Sheppard's co. 6th rgt.

Evans, William. Lieutenant in Capt. Sheppard's co. 6th rgt.

Evard, Andrew. Private in Capt. Snowden's co. 36th rgt.

Ever, Abraham. Private in Capt. Schwarzauer's co. 27th rgt.

Everet, Thomas. Private in Capt. Bouldin's co. Independent Light Dragoons.

Everett, Edward. Private in Capt. Pennington's co. Balto. Independent Artillerists.

Everett, James. Private in Capt. Snowden's co. 36th rgt.

Everett, Samuel. Private in Capt. Snowden's co. 36th rgt.

Eversfield, John. Private in Capt. Eversfield's co. 17th rgt.

Eversfield, Thomas. Captain in 17th rgt. Resigned Ag. 1, 1814.

Everson, Joseph. Corporal in Capt. Horton's co. Maryland Chasseurs.

Evett, George. Private in Capt. Steiner's Frederick Artillery co.

Ewaldt, J. H. Private in Capt. Pennington's co. Balto. Independent Artillerists.

Ewing, James of Henry. Lieutenant in Capt. Oldham's co. 30th rgt. (Je. 26, 1812).

Ewing, James P. Ensign in Capt. Porter's co. 30th rgt. (S. 11, 1807).

Ewing, John W. Ensign in Capt. Hall's co. 30th rgt. (Jy. 3, 1812).

Ewing, Samuel. Private in Capt. Watson's co. 39th rgt.

F

Fable, John. Command unknown; captured at Bladensburg.

Fable, Jesse. Command unknown; captured at Bladensburg.

Fague, Michael. Private in Capt. Shryock's co. 24th rgt.

Fahnestock, Derrick. Private in Capt. Berry's co. Washington Artillery. Wounded at Fort McHenry.

Fahnestock, Henry. Private in Capt. Warfield's co. Balto. United Volunteers.

Fahnestock, Peter. Private in Capt. Berry's co. Washington Artillery.

Fahs, Caspar. Private in Capt. Sadtler's co. Balto. Yägers.

Fair, Michael. Private in Capt. Marker's co. 28th rgt.

Fairall, Horace. Private in Capt. Crawford's co. 17th rgt.

Fairbain, Thomas H. Sergeant in Capt. Pike's Balto. Volunteer Artillery.

Fairbanks, William. Private in Capt. Kennedy's co. 27th rgt.

Fairburn, James. Private in Capt. Levering's co. Independent Blues.

Faithful, William. Corporal in Capt. Deems' co. 51st rgt.

Falconer, Elisha. Ensign in Capt. Dorsey's co. 13th rgt. (My. 12, 1812).

Falconer, Jonathan. Private in Capt. Pennington's co. Balto. Independent Artillerists.

Falconer, Jonathan H. 3d Lieutenant in 14th U. S. Infantry (My. 4, 1813); 2d Lieutenant (N. 14, 1813). Resigned Mr. 4, 1814.

Falconer, Pere. Private in Capt. Thompson's co. 1st Baltimore Horse Artillery.

Fales, Benjamin. Private in Capt. Ringgold's co. 6th rgt.

Falkner, Abraham. Private in Capt. Magruder's co. American Artillerists.

Falknier, Abraham. Private in Capt. Pinney's co. 27th rgt.

Fallier, George. Private in Capt. Roney's co. 39th rgt.; wounded at North Point and died Sept. 19.

Fallin, Daniel. Captain in 48th rgt. (S. 2, 1807).

Falls, David. Private in Capt. Chambers' co. 21st rgt.

Fango, Matthew. Quarter Gunner of the privateer *Surprise*. Drowned Ap. 5, 1815.

Fanning, Zephaniah. Private in Capt. Cawood's co. 45th rgt.

Fannon, William. Private in Capt. McConkey's co. 27th rgt.

Fansbrimer, Daniel. Private in Capt. Horton's co. Maryland Chasseurs.

Farber, Christian. Private in Capt. John Miller's co. 2d D. I.; b. Germany; age 35; weaver; volunteer.

Farland, John. Private in Capt. Burke's co. 6th rgt.

Farquar, William P. Captain in 47th rgt. (F. 20, 1813).

Farr, John B. Lieutenant in Capt. Cawood's co. 45th rgt. (Je. 16, 1813).

Farrall, Charles. Private in Capt. Thompson's co. 43d rgt.

Farrall, James W. Private in Capt. Montgomery's co. Balto. Union Artillery.

Farrall, John. Private in Capt. Burgess's co. 43d rgt.

Farrell, Holly. Private in Capt. Brown's co. 43d rgt.

Farrell, Thomas. Private in Capt. Deems' co. 51st rgt.

Farrell, William. Lieutenant in Capt. Foreman's co. 33d rgt.

Faster, James. Captain in 51st rgt.

Faster, Peter. Sergeant in Capt. Massey's co. 38th rgt.

Faulac, Anthony. Private in Capt. Stewart's co. Washington Blues.

Faulkner, Benjamin. Private in Capt. Massey's co. 38th rgt.

Faulkner, Henry B. Private in Capt. Hayward's co. 4th rgt.

Fauce, John. 2d Lieutenant in Capt. Thompson's Artillery co. 1st Brigade (S. 10, 1814).

Fave, Joseph. Private in Capt. Sadtler's co. Balto. Yägers.

Fawsbrenner, Andrew. Private in Capt. Peters' co. 51st rgt.

Feagler, Jacob. Private in Capt. Steiner's Frederick Artillery.

Fear, John C. Private in Capt. Burgess' co. 43d rgt.

Fechtig, Christopher. Ensign in Capt. Wise's co. 24th rgt. (Jy. 12, 1814).

Fefle, Joseph. Private in Capt. Rogers' co. 51st rgt.

Feguet, Dominick. Corporal in Capt. Rogers' co. 51st rgt.

Feigley, Samuel. Private in Capt. Shryock's co. 24th rgt.

Feishel, Anthony. Private in Capt. Stewart's co. 51st rgt.

Felinefer, Francis. Ensign in Capt. Kelly's co. 36th rgt. (O. 12, 1814).

Fellingham, Robert. Private in Capt. Wickes' co. 21st rgt.

Fenby, Peter, Jr. Private in Capt. Sheppard's co. 6th rgt.

Fenby, Samuel. Private in Capt. Sheppard's co. 6th rgt.

Fendall, Benjamin. Captain in 43d rgt.

Fendall, Edward. Private in Capt. Edes' co. 27th rgt.

Fendall, John. Ensign in 5th U. S. Infantry (My. 27, 1812); 1st Lieutenant (Je. 28, 1814).

Fendall, Philip R. Lieutenant in Capt. Stonestreet's co. 4th Cavalry Dist.

Fenning, Dennis. Private in Capt. Lawson's co. Balto. Patriots.

Fenton, John. Private in Capt. McDonald's co. 6th rgt.

Fenton, William. Private in Capt. Thos. Warner's co. 39th rgt.

Fenwick, Athanasius. Lieutenant-Colonel in 12th rgt.

Fenwick, Edward. Ensign in Capt. Fendall's co. 43d rgt.

Fenwick, Enoch. Private in Capt. G. N. Causin's co. 4th Cavalry Dist.

Fenwick, Martin. Surgeon in 1st rgt. Artillery (Je. 16, 1812).

Fenwick, Philip. Private in Capt. Cawood's co. 45th rgt.

Fenwick, Richard. Private in Capt. Jarboe's co. 12th rgt.

Ferguson, George. Private in Capt. Schwarzauer's co. 27th rgt.

Fernandis, Anthony. Private in Capt. Galt's co. 6th rgt.

Fernandis, Samuel. Private in Capt. Pike's co. Balto. Volunteer Artillery.

Fernandis, Walter. Private in Capt. Nicholson's co. Balto. Fencibles.

Ferrall, William. Lieutenant in Capt. Foreman's co. 33d rgt. (Ap. 30, 1813).

Ferrel, Francis. Private in Capt. Kennedy's co. 27th rgt.

Fessler, John. Lieutenant in Capt. Waltz's co. 16th rgt. (Jy. 15, 1814).

Fetz, Frederick. Private in Capt. Levering's co. Independent Blues.

Fiddeman, Daniel. Captain in 26th rgt. (S. 7, 1810).

Fields, James. Private in Capt. Green's co. 46th rgt.

Fields, James. Private in Capt. Sheppard's co. 6th rgt.

Fife, Andrew H. Gunner in Capt. Addison's co. Sea Fencibles.

File, John. Private in Capt. Stapleton's co. 39th rgt.

Fimister, Alexander. Private in Capt. Sterett's Independent co.

Fingan, James. Private in Capt. Kierstead's co. 6th rgt.

Finlay, Hugh. Private in Capt. Moale's co. Columbian Artillery.

Finlay, John. Private in Capt. Magruder's co. American Artillerists.

Finley, Ebenezer L. Private in Capt. Moale's co. Columbian Artillery.

Finley, John M. Corporal in Capt. Warfield's co. Balto. United Volunteers.

Finley, Thomas. Private in Capt. Pike's co. Balto. Volunteer Artillery.

Finn, John W. Private in Capt. Montgomery's co. Balto. Union Artillery.

Finney, Lewis. Private in Capt. Pinney's co. 27th rgt.

Finny, Daniel P. Private in Capt. Burgess' co. 43d rgt.

Fish, Allen. Lieutenant of the privateer *Bona,* July, 1812.

Fish, Allen. Private in Capt. Edes' co. 27th rgt.

Fish, James. Private in Capt. Brown's co. 6th rgt.

Fish, William. Sergeant in Capt. Adreon's co. Union Volunteers.

Fisher, Abraham. Private in Capt. Bader's co. Union Yägers.

Fisher, Caleb. Private in Capt. Conway's co. 6th rgt.

Fisher, Caleb. Private in Capt. Blizzard's co. 15th rgt.

Fisher, George. Private in Capt. Ducker's co. 7th rgt.; Wagon Master in 11th Brigade, Aug. 20, 1814.

Fisher, Henry M. Lieutenant and Quarter-master in 27th rgt. (Ap. 28, 1813)

Fisher, Jacob. Private in Capt. Berry's co. Washington Artillery.

Fisher, James. Corporal in Capt. Bader's co. Union Yägers.

Fisher, James. Private in Capt. Burke's co. 6th rgt.

Fisher, James. Sergeant in Capt. A. C. Smith's co. 49th rgt.

Fisher, John. Quarter-master in 20th rgt. (My. 2, 1808).

Fisher, John. Private in Capt. Blair's co. 50th rgt.

Fisher, John. Private in Capt. Pike's co. Balto. Volunteer Artillery.

Fisher, John. Private in Capt. Bader's co. Union Yägers.

Fisher, John. Corporal in Capt. Miller's co. 39th rgt.

Fisher, Martin. Private in Capt. Roney's co. 39th rgt.

Fisher, Philip. Ensign in 36th U. S. Infantry (Ap. 30, 1813); 2d Lieutenant (My. 1, 1814).

Fisher, Purnell. Captain in 19th rgt. (My. 18, 1813) vice Richardson.

Fisher, Robert. Ensign in Capt. Hall's co. 4th rgt. (O. 1, 1811).

Fisher, Stephen. Cornet in Capt. Goldsborough's co. 10th Cavalry Dist. (My. 20, 1813).

Fisher, Thomas A. 2d Lieutenant in Capt. Thomas' Artillery co. 12th Brigade (Ap. 20, 1808); 1st Lieutenant (Jy. 12, 1814).

Fisher, William. Private in Capt. Dillon's co. 27th rgt.

Fishpaw, John. Major in 7th rgt. (Ag. 1, 1814).

Fishwick, John. Private in Capt. Burke's co. 6th rgt.

Fisk, Richard. Private in Capt. Pumphrey's co. 22d rgt.

Fitch, Daniel. Captain of the privateer *Arab* which was captured by boats of the British squadron in the Chesapeake April 3, 1813, after she had been chased on shore and abandoned.

Fitch, David. Lieutenant of the privateer *Globe,* July, 1812.

Fitch, Jonathan. 3d Lieutenant in Balto. Union Artillery (Jy. 15, 1814).

Fitch, William. 1st Lieutenant in Capt. Stansbury's co. 6th Cavalry Dist. (Jy. 8, 1814) vice Wyley.

Fitchew, Ezekiel. Private in Capt. Travers' co. 48th rgt.

Fitchew, Shenton. Private in Capt. Travers' co. 48th rgt.

Fitzgerald, Austin. Private in Capt. Rogers' co. 51st rgt.

Fitzgerald, James. Sergeant in Capt. Brooke's co. 34th rgt.

Fitzgerald, John. 1st Lieutenant in U. S. Artillery (Mr. 14, 1812). Resigned Je. 14, 1814.

Fitzhugh, Daniel. Surgeon's mate 24th rgt. (Jy. 12, 1814).

Flaherty, Bartley. Private in Capt. Piper's co. United Maryland Artillery.

Flaherty, John R. Private in Capt. Stewart's co. Washington Blues.

Flanagan, Hugh. Private in Capt. Conway's co. 6th rgt.

Flanagan, John R. Private in Capt. Warfield's co. Balto. United Volunteers.

Flannagan, Gamaliel. Private in Capt. Burgess' co. 43d rgt.

Flannagan, Samuel. Private in Capt. Dent's co. 43d rgt.

Flant, George. Captain in 47th rgt. (Ap. 22, 1808).

Flee, Christian. Private in Capt. Haubert's co. 51st rgt.

Fleetwood, Benjamin. Private in Capt. Schwarzauer's co. 27th rgt.; captured at North Point.

Fleming, Cephas. Ensign in Capt. Wade's co. 44th rgt. (Ag. 22, 1812).

Fleming, Frederick. Private in Capt. Watson's co. 39th rgt.

Fleming, James. Captain in 37th rgt. Resigned Ja. 21, 1814.

Fleming, James. Private in Capt. Steever's co. 27th rgt.

Fleming, William. Private in Capt. Heath's co. 23d rgt.

Fletchall, James. Captain in 3d rgt. (O. 12, 1807).

Fletcher, George. Ensign in Capt. Hammond's co. 32d rgt. (Ap. 5, 1808).

Fletcher, George. 2d Lieutenant in 38th U. S. Infantry (My. 20, 1813); 1st Lieutenant (My. 20, 1814).

Fletcher, James. Private in Capt. Chalmers' co. 51st rgt.

Fletcher, James. Ensign in Capt. Harper's co. 11th rgt. (Ag. 20, 1813).

Fletcher, John. Private in Capt. Bunbury's co. Sea Fencibles.

Fletcher, John. Private in Capt. Faster's co. 51st rgt.

Fletcher, Thomas. Private in Capt. Rogers' co. 51st rgt.

Fletcher, William. Private in Capt. Chalmers' co. 51st rgt.

Flick, Adam. Lieutenant in Capt. Andrew Smith's co. 47th rgt. (My. 8, 1812).

Fling, John. Private in Capt. Blair's co. 50th rgt.

Flora, Conrad. Captain in 24th rgt.

Flower, Augustine. Private in Capt. Williams' co. 12th rgt.

Flower, Augustus. Private in Capt. Williams' co. 12th rgt.

Flower, Gustavus [c1795-c1830]. Private in Capt. Burgess' co. 43d rgt.

Flower, John. Private in Capt. Dent's co. 43d rgt.

Flower, William. Sergeant in Capt. Dunnington's co. 43d rgt.

Flowers, Benjamin. Private in Capt. Sadtler's co. Balto. Yägers. Wounded at North Point.

Floyd, Joseph P. Private in Capt. Thompson's co. 1st Baltimore Horse Artillery.

Floyd, Samuel. Private in Capt. Chambers' co. 21st rgt.

Floyd, William. Captain in 12th rgt. (Ap. 4, 1812).

Foard, Joseph R. 2d Lieutenant in Capt. Bouldin's co. Independent Light Dragoons; 5th Cavalry Dist. (My. 18, 1813).

Foard, Richard. Private in Capt. Oldham's co. 49th rgt.

Foard, Zebulon. Private in Capt. Oldham's co. 49th rgt.

Foble, Daniel. Private in Capt. Dyer's co. Fells Point Riflemen.

Fockler, George. Private in Capt. Shryock's co. 24th rgt.

Fogleman, George. Private in Capt. Bader's co. Union Yägers.

Fogwill, Aquila. Ensign in Capt. Merchant's co. 35th rgt. (Ap. 30, 1813).

Folay, Dennis. Private in Capt. Piper's co. United Maryland Artillery.

Foley, John. Private in Capt. Blair's co. 50th rgt.

Folk, Jacob. Private in Capt. Pinkney's Artillery co. (A. A. Co.)

Folks, James. Command unknown; captured at Bladensburg.

Follin, James. Private in Capt. Massey's co. 38th rgt.

Foltz, William. Private in Capt. Levering's co. Independent Blues.

Fonder, Peter. Private in Capt. Shrim's co. Balto. Light Infantry.

Fonerdon, William H. Corporal in Capt. Montgomery's co. Balto. Union Artillery.

Fookes, Charles. Lieutenant in Capt. Fookes' co. (Jy. 11, 1814) vice Cheatham.

Fookes, James. Captain in 37th rgt. (S. 26, 1807).

Forbes, Sandy. Seaman of the privateer *Globe*. Killed in action N. 1, 1813.

Ford, George W. [1795-1887] Private in Capt. Pennington's co. Independent Artillerists.

Ford, James. Private in Capt. Snowden's co. 36th rgt.

Ford, John. Private in Capt. Haubert's co. 51st rgt.

Ford, John. Private in Capt. Lawson's co. Balto. Patriots.

Ford, John F. 2d Lieutenant in Capt. G. N. Causin's co. 4th Cavalry Dist. (My. 8, 1812).

Ford, Levi G. Captain in 8th Cavalry Dist. (Je. 12, 1812). Died 1814.

Ford, Nicholas. Private in Capt. Dobbin's co. 39th rgt.

Ford, Richard. 1st Lieutenant in Capt. Ford's co. 8th Cavalry. Dist. (Je. 12, 1812); Captain (Jy. 7, 1814).

Ford, Stephen. Private in Capt. Stewart's co. 51st rgt.

Ford, Thomas. Cornet in Capt. Tootle's co. 10th Cavalry Dist. (S. 26, 1812).

Ford, Thomas. Private in Capt.
Peters' co. 51st rgt.
Ford, Walter. Private in Capt.
Smith's co. 51st rgt.
Ford, William. Captain in 6th rgt.
Resigned Jy. 1814.
Ford, William [-1834]. 1st
Lieutenant in 38th U. S. Infantry
(My. 20, 1813).
Ford, William. Private in Capt.
Tilghman's co. 33d rgt.
Fordice, John. Private in Capt.
Kennedy's co. 27th rgt.
Foreman, Christian. Private in
Capt. Shrim's co. Balto. Light
Infantry.
Foreman, Elijah. Private in Capt.
Horton's co. Maryland Chasseurs.
Foreman, Ezekiel. Captain in 33d
rgt. (Ap. 30, 1813); A. D. C. to
General Foreman.
Foreman, Ezekiel. Private in Capt.
Usselton's Artillery co. 6th Brigade.
Foreman, Francis. Private in Capt.
Rogers' co. 51st rgt.
Foreman, George. Lieutenant in
Capt. Mann's co. 33d rgt. (S. 2,
1811).
Foreman, Henry. Ensign in Capt.
Hancock's co. 22d rgt. (Ag. 12,
1812).
Foreman, Joseph. Private in Capt.
Pumphrey's co. 22d rgt.
Foreman, Thomas M. Brigadier-
General in 1st Brigade (D. 11,
1810).
Foreman, Valentine. Private in
Capt. Shrim's co. Balto. Light
Infantry.
Forester, George. Private in Capt.
Wilson's co. 6th rgt.
Forman, Andrew. Private in Capt.
Blizzard's co. 15th rgt.
Forman, George. Private in Capt.
Fowler's co. 46th rgt.

Forman, Thomas. Private in Capt.
Fowler's co. 46th rgt.
Forney, George. Private in Capt.
Snowden's co. 36th rgt.
Forney, Michael. Private in Capt.
Ducker's co. 7th rgt.
Fornshill, John. Private in Capt.
Steever's co. 27th rgt.
Forrest, Allen. Private in Capt.
Linthicum's co. 22d rgt.
Forrest, Allen. Private in Capt.
Roney's co. 39th rgt.
Forrest, James. Captain in 4th Cavalry Dist. (My. 8, 1812).
Forrest, Lancelot. Private in Capt.
Linthicum's co. 22d rgt.
Forrest, Nicholas. Private in Capt.
Roney's co. 39th rgt.
Forrest, Thomas. 2d officer of the
privateer Dolphin.
Forrester, John. Private in Capt.
Roney's co. 39th rgt.
Forrester, Leonard. Private in
Capt. Myer's co. Franklin Artillery.
Forrester, Ralph E. Private in Capt.
Shrim's co. Balto. Light Infantry.
Forsey, P. Elias. Private in Capt.
Bunbury's co. Sea Fencibles.
Forster, Francis. Lieutenant in
Capt. Stewart's co. Washington
Blues.
Forsyth, Joseph. Private in Capt.
Blair's co. 50th rgt.
Fort, Joshua. Private in Capt.
Deems' co. 51st rgt.
Fort, Samuel. Lieutenant in Capt.
Grate's co. 7th rgt. (Ag. 1, 1814).
Forwood, William. Lieutenant in
Capt. Albert's co. Extra Battalion
Harford Co. (Jy. 8, 1814) vice
Silvers.
Fosler, George. Private in Capt.
Schwarzauer's co. 27th rgt.
Foss, Daniel. Corporal in Capt.
Stewart's co. 51st rgt.

Foss, George, Jr. Private in Capt. Pike's co. Balto. Volunteer Artillery.

Foss, Jacob. Corporal in Capt. Chalmers' co. 51st rgt.

Foss, Jacob. Private in Capt. Pike's co. Balto. Volunteer Artilery.

Foss, Joseph. Ensign in 38th U. S. Infantry (My. 20, 1813).

Foss, Joseph. Sergeant in Capt. Stewart's co. 51st rgt.

Fosset, John. Sergeant in Capt. Wilson's co. 6th rgt.

Fossett, Thomas S. Surgeon in 9th rgt. (Je. 18, 1794).

Foster, Jacob. Private in Capt. Wilson's co. 6th rgt.

Foster, James. Private in Capt. McConkey's co. 27th rgt.

Foster, Joseph. Private in Capt. Galt's co. 6th rgt.

Fouke [Fauck], Henry. Captain in 8th rgt. (S. 20, 1813).

Foulds, William. Private in Capt. Galt's co. 6th rgt.

Fountain [Fontain], Henry. 1st Lieutenant in Capt. Atkinson's Artillery co. 10th Brigade (Ja. 7, 1814) vice Cogswell.

Fous, Jacob. Private in Capt. Peters' co. 51st rgt.

Foutz, Henry. Private in Capt. Myers' co. Franklin Artillery.

Foutz, William. Ensign in Capt. Fouke's co. 8th rgt. (S. 20, 1813).

Fowble, Jacob. Musician in Capt. Steiner's Frederick Artillery.

Fowble, Peter. Sergeant in Capt. Rogers' co. 51st rgt.

Fowble, Peter, Jr. Private in Capt. Rogers' co. 51st rgt.

Fowble, William. Private in Capt. Bader's co. Union Yägers.

Fowke, Gerard. Private in Capt. Burgess' co. 43d rgt.

Fowke, James. Ensign in Capt. Burgess' co. 43d rgt. (Je. 5, 1812).

Fowler, Archibald. Captain in 33d rgt. (O. 13, 1814).

Fowler, Benjamin. Lieutenant-Colonel in 39th rgt.

Fowler, Henry. Captain in 46th rgt. (Jy. 29, 1811).

Fowler, Isaac D. Private in Capt. Peters' co. 51st rgt.

Fowler, James. Lieutenant of the privateer *Express,* June, 1814.

Fowler, James. Private in Capt. Dobbin's co. 39th rgt.

Fowler, John. Private in Capt. Frizzell's co. 15th rgt.

Fowler, John. Private in Capt. McConkey's co. 27th rgt.

Fowler, Perry. Private in Capt. Dobbin's co. 39th rgt.

Fowler, Richard. Private in Capt. Pinkney's Artillery co. (A. A. Co.)

Fowler, Samuel. Private in Capt. Schwarzauer's co. 27th rgt.

Fowler, William. Ensign in Capt. Blakistone's co. 33d rgt. (Ag. 27, 1810).

Fowler, William. Corporal in Capt. Fowler's co. 46th rgt.

Fowler, William. Private in Capt. Magruder's co. American Artillerists.

Fowler, William, Jr. Private in Capt. Maynard's co. 22d rgt.; drummer in Capt. Chase's co.

Fox, Charles. Corporal in Capt. Galt's co. 6th rgt.

Fox, George. Lieutenant in Capt. C. W. Dorsey's co. 32d rgt. (My. 24, 1808).

Fox, John. Ensign in Capt. Foreman's co. 33d rgt. (O. 13, 1814)

Fox, Joshua. 2d Lieutenant in Capt. Owings' co. 32d rgt.

Fox, Thomas. Corporal in Capt. Pinney's co. 27th rgt.

Foxcroft, James. Private in Capt. Chase's co. 22d rgt.

Foxcroft, Samuel. Private in Capt. Maynard's co. 22d rgt.

Foxcroft, William. Private in Capt. Slicer's co. 22d rgt.

Foxwell, Abram. Private in Capt. Travers' co. 48th rgt.

Foxwell, Joseph of R. Private in Capt. Travers' co. 48th rgt.

Foxwell, Labin. Private in Capt. McNamara's co. 48th rgt.

Foy, Frederick. Private in Capt. Smith's co. 51st rgt.

Foy, Gregory. Captain in 6th rgt. Resigned Jy., 1813; 1st Lieutenant in Capt. Bunbury's co. Sea Fencibles (O. 1, 1813).

Foy, James. Private in Capt. Berry's co. Washington Artillery.

Foy, Peter. 1st Lieutenant in Capt. Dyer's co. Fells Point Riflemen (Ap. 4, 1812).

Foy, Samuel. Private in Capt. Snowden's co. 36th rgt.

Foy, Samuel. Private in Capt. Berry's co. Washington Artillery. Wounded at Fort McHenry.

Frailey, Leonard [-1864]. Major in 38th U. S. Infantry (My. 19, 1813). Resigned My. 1, 1814; Brigade Major in 3d Brigade M. M.

France, Thomas. Private in Capt. Watson's co. 39th rgt.

France, William. Private in Capt. Fowler's co. 46th rgt.

Francis, Ephraim. Sergeant in Capt. Deems' co. 51st rgt.

Franciscus, George. Private in Capt. Montgomery's co. Balto. Union Artillery.

20

Franciscus, William. Private in Capt. Shrim's co. Balto. Light Infantry.

Frank, Nicholas. Private in Capt. Morgan's co. 49th rgt.

Franklin, Benjamin. Private in Capt. Stiles' co. Marine Artillery.

Franklin, Garrat. Private in Capt. Fowler's co. 46th rgt.

Franklin, George. Private in Capt. Bader's co. Union Yägers.

Franklin, Henry, Jr. Lieutenant in Capt. Williams' co. Extra Battalion Worcester Co. (S. 26, 1807).

Franklin, Hezekiah. Private in Capt. Dunnington's co. 43d rgt.

Franklin, Jacob. Captain in 2d rgt. (Ag. 14, 1807).

Franklin, Lloyd. Private in Capt. Dent's co. 43d rgt.

Franklin, Nehemiah. Private in Capt. Brown's co. 43d rgt.

Franklin, S. W. Lieutenant in Capt. Gray's co. 43d rgt. Died 1814.

Franklin, Thomas. Lieutenant in Capt. Chase's co. 22d rgt. (Ap. 22, 1814).

Franklin, Thomas G. B. Private in Capt. Dent's co. 43d rgt.

Franklin, William. Private in Capt. Dent's co. 43d rgt.

Fray, George. Private in Capt. Graves' co. 21st rgt.

Frazee, Elisha. Private in Capt. Blair's co. 50th rgt.

Frazer, John. Seaman of the privateer *Surprise*. Drowned Ap. 5, 1815.

Frazier, Alexander. Private in Capt. Maynard's co. 22d rgt.

Frazier, Alfred. Cornet in Capt. Cost's co. 1st rgt. 1st Regimental Cavalry Dist. (Je. 14, 1812) vice Late.

Frazier, Charles. Private in Capt. Slicer's co. 22d rgt.

Frazier, Frederick. Private in Capt. Tilghman's co. 33d rgt.

Frazier, Horatio. Private in Capt. Brooke's co. 34th rgt.

Frazier, James. Private in Capt. Stiles' co. Marine Artillery.

Frazier, John. Petty officer of Barney's flotilla.

Frazier, William. Private in Capt. Peters' co. 51st rgt.

Frazier, Zachariah. Private in Capt. Wells' Artillery co. (A. A. Co.)

Frazure, Jeremiah. Private in Capt. Sheppard's co. 6th rgt.

Freberger, Henry. Private in Capt. Schwarzauer's co. 27th rgt.

Freburger, Peter. Private in Capt. Steiner's Frederick Artillery.

Frederick, Lawrence. Private in Capt. Bader's co. Union Yägers.

Frederick, Paul. Private in Capt. Bunbury's co. Sea Fencibles.

Freeburger, Henry. Sergeant in Capt. Kennedy's co. 27th rgt.

Freeland, Alfred. Captain in 31st rgt. (Je. 12, 1812).

Freeland, Egbert. Private in Capt. Warfield's co. Balto. United Volunteers.

Freeland, Peregrine F. Lieutenant in Capt. Freeland's co. 31st rgt. (Jy. 14, 1812).

Freeland, William [-1813]. Ensign in Capt. Hewitt's co. 4th rgt., 1813.

Freeman, Charles. Private in Capt. Myer's co. Franklin Artillery.

Freeman, Horatio. Private in Capt. Veitch's co. 34th rgt.

Freeman, John. Private in Capt. Lawrence's co. 6th rgt.

Freeman, William. Private in Capt. Addison's co. Sea Fencibles.

Freer, Peter. Private in Capt. Faster's co. 51st rgt.

Freiks, Richard. Private in Capt. Wickes' co. 21st rgt.

Frelett, Augustus. Private in Capt. Warfield's co. Balto. United Volunteers.

French, Ebenezer. Private in Capt. Magruder's co. American Artillerists.

French, Thomas. Private in Capt. Roney's co. 39th rgt.

French, William. Private in Capt. Deems' co. 51st rgt.

Fresh, James. Private in Capt. Ducker's co. 7th rgt.

Freshour, Jacob. Captain in 16th rgt. (Je. 9, 1809).

Frew, James. Private in Capt. Cawood's co. 45th rgt.

Frew, John. Private in Capt. Cawood's co. 45th rgt.

Freyburger, George. Private in Capt. Shrim's co. Balto. Light Infantry.

Freyer, Henry. Private in Capt. Shrim's co. Balto. Light Infantry.

Frick, Christian. Private in Capt. Peters' co. 51st rgt.

Frick, John. Corporal in Capt. Sterett's Independent co.

Frick, William. 2d Lieutenant in Capt. Moale's co. Columbian Artillery (Je. 15, 1813) vice Williams.

Frick, William. Private in Capt. Peters' co. 51st rgt.

Friday, Henry. Private in Capt. Getzendanner's co. 16th rgt.

Frinks, John. Prize-master of the privateer *Globe*. Wounded in action N. 1, 1813.

Frisby, Richard. Private in Capt. Sterett's co. 1st. Balto. Hussars.

Frisby, William. Private in Capt. Page's co. 21st rgt.

Frizell, Jacob. Ensign in Capt. Magee's co. 20th rgt. (Ag. 1, 1814) vice N. D. Frizell.

Frizell, Nimrod D. Ensign in Capt. Magee's co. 20th rgt. Resigned Ag. 1, 1814.

Frizzell, John. Private in Capt. Blizzard's co. 15th rgt.

Frizzell, William. Captain in 15th rgt. (O. 2, 1807).

Frost, John R. Ensign in Capt. C. W. Dorsey's co. 32d rgt. (My. 24, 1808).

Frost, T. Captain of the privateer *Hornet.*

Fry, John. Private in Capt. Berry's co. Washington Artillery.

Fry, Thomas. Private in Capt. Brown's co. 43d rgt.

Fryer, George. Private in Capt. Blair's co. 50th rgt.

Fulford, Henry. Private in Capt. Sterett's Independent co.

Fuller, George. Private in Capt. Fowler's co. 46th rgt.

Fuller, John. 2d Lieutenant in Capt. Wilson's co. 6th Cavalry Dist. (Ap. 4, 1812).

Fuller, John. Private in Capt. Fower's co. 46th rgt.

Fuller, Nicholas. Private in Capt. Horton's co. Maryland Chasseurs.

Fuller, Richard. Private in Capt. Brohawn's co. 48th rgt.

Fuller, Thomas. Private in Capt. Brohawn's co. 48th rgt.

Fulton, Hugh. Private in Capt. Mackey's co. 49th rgt.

Fulton, James. Sergeant in Capt. Cozier's co. 30th rgt.

Fulton, James. Private in Capt. Levering's co. Independent Blues.

Fulton, Robert. 2d Lieutenant in Capt. Phillips' co. 2d rgt. 1st Cavalry Dist. (Mr. 16, 1812); Captain (Je. 15, 1813).

Fulton, William S. Corporal in Capt. Nicholson's co. Balto. Fencibles.

Funk, Jacob. Private in Capt. Haubert's co. 51st rgt.

Funston, John. Lieutenant in Capt. Dutterow's co. 20th rgt. (Ap. 27, 1813).

Furguson, Robert. Private in Capt. McConckin's co. 38th rgt.

Furguson, William. Private in Capt. Lawrence's co. 6th rgt.

Furgusson, Thomas. Private in Capt. Magruder's co. American Artillerists.

Furlong, William. Captain of the privateer *Bordeaux* Packet, Feb., 1813; Private in Capt. Stiles' co. Marine Artillery (1814).

Fury, John. Private in Capt. Sample's co. 49th rgt.

Fuss, John. Private in Capt. Watson's co. 39th rgt.

Fyia, John. Private in Capt. Shrim's co. Balto. Light Infantry.

G

Gable, John. Private in Capt. Roney's co. 39th rgt.

Gable, William. Corporal in Capt. Roney's co. 39th rgt.

Gadd, Benjamin. Private in Capt. Travers' co. 48th rgt.

Gairy, William G. Private in Capt. Peters' co. 51st rgt.

Gaither, Edward. Ensign in 24th rgt. (Je. 26, 1812).

Gaither, George. Captain in 44th rgt. (Ag. 12, 1812).

Gaither, John. Sergeant in Capt. Pinkney's Artillery co. 22d rgt.

Gaither, John of R. Private in Capt. Hall's co. 3d Cavalry rgt.

Gaither, Joshua. Private in Capt. Waters' co. 22d rgt.

Gale, James H. Ensign in 14th U. S. Infantry (Mr. 12, 1812); 1st Lieutenant (Je. 29, 1814).

Gale, Joseph. 2d Lieutenant of the privateer *Ultor*, Nov, 1814.

Gale, Lewis. Private in Capt. McKane's co. 27th rgt.

Gale, William. Private in Capt. Lawrence's co. 6th rgt.

Gales, James, Jr. Private in Capt. Robey's co. 43d rgt.

Gall, Jacob. Private in Capt. Rogers' co. 51st rgt.

Gall, John. Private in Capt. Barr's Cavalry co. 1st Dist.

Gallagher, Hugh. Private in Capt. Faster's co. 51st rgt.

Gallaspy, Patrick. Sergeant in Capt. Lawrence's co. 6th rgt.

Gallaway, Thomas. Sergeant in Capt. Brown's co. 6th rgt.

Gallegher, Leslie. Private in Capt. Levering's co. Independent Blues.

Galloway, E. Sergeant in Capt. Hanna's co. Fells Point Light Dragoons.

Galloway, John. Private in Capt. Wilson's co. 6th rgt.

Galloway, Robert. Ensign in Capt. Oldham's co. 49th rgt. (Ap. 23, 1813).

Galloway, Robert C. Captain in 46th rgt. (Ap. 19, 1810).

Galt, James. Private in Capt. Massey's co. 38th rgt.

Galt, John. Captain in 47th rgt. (Ja. 8, 1808).

Galt, Mathew. Ensign in 5th U. S. Infantry (D. 4, 1812); 2d Lieutenant (D. 7, 1813). Resigned Ja. 1, 1814.

Galt, Peter. Captain in 6th rgt. (Mr. 16, 1812).

Galt, Richardson. Sergeant in Capt. Stewart's co. Washington Blues.

Gamble, Alexander. Private in Capt. Chalmers' co. 51st rgt.

Gamble, Darius. Private in Capt. Pinney's co. 27th rgt.

Gamble, John. Private in Capt. Burke's co. 6th rgt.

Gamble, Robert. Private in Capt. Rogers' co. 51st rgt.

Gamble, Stansbury. Lieutenant in Capt. Lowman's co. 35th rgt. Died 1815.

Gamble, Stephen. Private in Capt. Rogers' co. 51st rgt.

Gambra, Domingado. Lieutenant in Capt. McPherson's co. 43d rgt. (Jy. 7, 1814).

Gambrall, John. Private in Capt. Magruder's co. American Artillerists.

Gambriel, George. Private in Capt. Hall's co. 3d Cavalry rgt.

Gambrill, Amos. Lieutenant in Capt. Hatherly's co. 22d rgt. (Ap. 28, 1814).

Gambrill, John. Private in Capt. Bouldin's co. Independent Light Dragoons.

Gambrill, Joseph. Sergeant in Capt. Pumphrey's co. 22d rgt.

Gambrill, Thomas. Private in Capt. Pumphrey's co. 22d rgt.

Gantt, Charles. Captain in 31st rgt. Resigned Jy. 12, 1814.

Gantt, Charles L. 2d Lieutenant in Capt. Cross' co. 2d Cavalry Dist. (Ap. 16, 1812). Resigned Jy., 1814.

Gantt, George. Private in Capt. Fendall's co. 43d rgt.

Gantt, James. Corporal in Capt. Lawson's co. Balto. Patriots.

Gardener, William. Private in Capt. Dobbin's co. 39th rgt.

Gardiner, George. Lieutenant in Capt. Middleton's co. 1st rgt. (Jy. 4, 1812); Captain (Jy. 15, 1814).

Gardiner, Ignatius F. Captain in 1st rgt. (Jy. 28, 1812).

Gardiner, James. Private in Capt. Brown's co. Eagle Artillerists.

Gardiner, John. Private in Capt. Boone's co. 22d rgt.

Gardiner, Richard. Private in Capt. Boone's co. 22d rgt.

Gardiner, Thomas. Private in Capt. Waters' co. 22d rgt.

Gardiner, Timothy. 3d Lieutenant in Capt. Stiles' co. Marine Artillery (S. 10, 1814).

Gardner, George. Private in Capt. Shrim's co. Balto. Light Infantry.

Gardner, George. Private in Capt. Lawrence's co. 6th rgt.

Gardner, Henry. Private in Capt. Faster's co. 51st rgt.

Gardner, John. Private in Capt. Pumphrey's co. 22d rgt.

Gardner, John of William. Private in Capt. Pumphrey's co. 22d rgt.

Gardner, Kensey. Private in Capt. Galt's co. 6th rgt.

Gardner, Peter. Private in Capt. McKane's co. 27th rgt.

Gardner, Samuel. Private in Capt. Stiles' co. Marine Artillery.

Gardner, Samuel. Private in Capt. Addison's co. Sea Fencibles.

Gardner, Samuel. Private in Capt. Maynard's co. 22d rgt.

Gardner, W. H. Private in Capt. Stiles' co. Marine Artillery.

Gardner, William. Private in Capt. Snowden's co. 36th rgt.

Garey, Frederick. Private in Capt. McLaughlin's co. 50th rgt.

Garey, Samuel Y. Acting Adjutant in 26th rgt.

Garland, John B. Private in Capt. Pike's co. Balto. Volunteer Artillery.

Garner, Charles. Private in Capt. Burgess' co. 43d rgt. Wounded Jy. 14, 1814.

Garner, Henry G. Quarter-master Sergeant in 45th rgt.

Garner, Joseph. Sergeant in Capt. Brown's co. 43d rgt.

Garner, Thomas. Ensign in Capt. McPherson's co. 43d rgt. (Jy. 7, 1814).

Garnett, James. Quarter-master Sergeant in 33d rgt.

Garretson, R. W. Private in Capt. Stiles' co. Marine Artillery.

Garrett, Erasmus. 1st Lieutenant in Capt. Philpott's co. 2d rgt. 1st Cavalry Dist. (Ja. 1, 1813).

Garrett, John. Lieutenant in Capt. Owings' co. 32d rgt. (Ap. 23, 1812).

Garrett, John. Lieutenant in Capt. Garrett's co. 49th rgt. (Ap. 23, 1813).

Garrett, John. Sergeant in Capt. A. E. Warner's co. 39th rgt.

Garrett, John. Private in Capt. Smith's co. 51st rgt.

Garrett, Samuel. Ensign in Capt. Merryman's co. 41st rgt. (Je. 2, 1813).

Garrett, Thomas. Private in Capt. Deems' co. 51st rgt.

Garrett, William. Captain in 49th rgt. (O. 5, 1807).

Garrey, Jeremiah. Private in Capt. A. E. Warner's co. 39th rgt.

Garvin, Thomas. Private in Capt. Lawson's co. Balto. Patriots.

* Gassaway, John [1754-1820]. Sergeant in Capt. Ramsey's co., Smallwood's battalion (Ja. 2, 1776); Ensign in Capt. Tillard's co., 3d Md. bat. (Jy. 1776); 2d Lieutenant in Smallwood's bat. (D. 10, 1776); 1st Lieutenant, 2d Md. rgt. (Ap. 17, 1777); Cap-

tain-Lieutenant (Jy 1, 1779);
Captain (Ap. 2, 1780); taken
prisoner at Camden, Aug. 16,
1780; Adjutant-General of Md.
(Je. 6, 1811) and served six years.
Died, June 25, 1820.
Gassaway, John. Private in Capt.
Deems' co. 51st rgt.
Gassaway, John. Ensign and 2d
Lieutenant in 5th U. S. Infantry
(Ja. 3, 1812); 1st Lieutenant (Ag.
15, 1813).
Gassaway, Lewis. Private in Capt.
Maynard's co. 22d rgt.
Gassaway, Thomas. Lieutenant in
Capt. Clagett's co. 44th rgt. Re-
signed D. 16, 1813.
Gatch, Philip. Private in Capt. Tay-
lor's co. 46th rgt.
Gatch, Philip. Sergeant in Capt.
Steever's co. 27th rgt.
Gatchaire, Francis. Lieutenant of
the privateer *Burrows*, Sept.,
1813; Captain, Sept., 1814.
Gates, James. Private in Capt. Mc-
Pherson's co. 43d rgt.
Gates, James, Jr. Private in Capt.
Robey's co. 43d rgt.
Gates, John. Private in Capt. Dent's
co. 43d rgt.
Gatterell, Francis. Private in Capt.
Barnes' co. 32d rgt.
Gattig, Jacob. Private in Capt.
Deems' co. 51st rgt.
Gaver, George. Private in Capt.
Marker's co. 28th rgt.
Gaver, John. Private in Capt.
Marker's co. 28th rgt.
Gavett, John. Captain of the priva-
teer *High Flyer* (Jy., 1812); Priv-
ate in Capt. Stiles' co. Marine Ar-
tillery.
Gawthorp, Thomas. Private in
Capt. Stewart's co. 51st rgt.
Gay, Samuel. Lieutenant in Capt.
Gerry's co. 30th rgt.

Gaylor, William. Command un-
known; captured at Bladensburg.
Geddes, David R. Private in Capt.
Chase's co. 22d rgt.
Geese, George. Private in Capt.
Haubert's co. 51st rgt.
Gehring, John George [-1843].
Private in Capt. Sadtler's co.
Balto. Yägers.
Geiger, Jacob. Private in Capt.
Shryock's co. 24th rgt.
Geiger, John. Corporal in Capt.
Bader's co. Union Yägers.
Geiser, Peter. Private in Capt.
Shryock's co. 24th rgt.
Gelaspy, John. Lieutenant in Capt.
Brookbank's co. 10th rgt. (O. 10,
1798).
Geltz, John. Musician in Capt. Get-
zendanner's co. 16th rgt.
Gennam, William. Private in Capt.
John Miller's co. 2d D. I.; b.
Kent Co., Md.; age 22; sailor;
subs. for Ludwick Ensminger.
Geoghegan, Moses. Private in Capt.
Brohawn's co. 48th rgt.
Geoghegan, Philemon. Private in
Capt. Brohawn's co. 48th rgt.
Geoghegan, William. Lieutenant in
Capt. Woolford's co. 48th rgt. (S.
2, 1811).
Geoghegan, William. Private in
Capt. Brohawn's co. 48th rgt.
George, Ezekiel. Private in Capt.
Addison's co. Sea Fencibles.
George, James. Private in Capt. Ad-
dison's co. Sea Fencibles.
Germain, Benjamin. Sergeant in
Capt. Piper's co. United Maryland
Artillery.
German, Jonathan. Private in Capt.
Montgomery's co. Balto. Union
Artillery.
German, Philip. Private in Capt.
Piper's co. United Maryland Ar-
tillery.

Germane, Julius. Ensign in 36th
U. S. Infantry (Ap. 30, 1813).
Resigned N. 23, 1813.

Germon, Vincent. Private in Capt.
Maynard's co. 22d rgt.

Gerrand, Ibram. Private in Capt.
Kierstead's co. 6th rgt.

Gerry, James. Captain in 30th rgt.

Getinger, Jacob. Cornet in Capt.
Chenoweth's co. 6th Cavalry
Dist. (Je. 12, 1812).

Gettings, Thomas. Adjutant in 18th
rgt. (Ap. 27, 1814).

Getzendanner, Adam. Sergeant in
Capt. Getzendanner's co. 16th rgt.

Getzendanner, Henry. Private in
Capt. Getzendanner's co. 16th rgt.

Getzendanner, Jacob of Ad. Captain
in 16th rgt. (Je. 26, 1812).

Getzendanner, Solomon. Musician
in Capt. Getzendanner's co. 16th
rgt.

Geyer, Henry S. 1st Lieutenant
in 38th U. S. Infantry (My. 20,
1813).

Gibben, Hugh. Private in Capt.
King's co. 49th rgt.

Gibbeny, John. Paymaster in 47th
rgt. (Ja. 8, 1808).

Gibbins, Josias. Private in Capt.
Baden's co. 17th rgt.

Gibbons, John. Private in Capt.
Faster's co. 51st rgt.

Gibbons, Reuben. Private in Capt.
Heath's co. 23d rgt.

Gibbons, Thomas. Private in Capt.
Chalmers' co. 51st rgt.

Gibbons, Walter. Private in Capt.
Haden's co. 17th rgt.

Gibbons, William. Private in Capt.
Naylor's co. 17th rgt.

Gibbs, John. Private in Capt.
Schwarzauer's co. 27th rgt.

Gibbs, John. Private in Capt.
Smith's co. 51st rgt.

Gibbs, John. Sergeant in Capt.
Myers' co. 39th rgt.

Gibbs, Joseph. Private in Capt.
Hands' co. 21st rgt.

Gibbs, Nicholas. Private in Capt.
Schwarzauer's co. 27th rgt.

Gibson, Edward R. Quarter-master
in 26th rgt. (N. 11, 1811).

Gibson, James [-1814]. Major
Assistant Inspector General (Ap.
2, 1813) ; Colonel 4th U. S. Rifles
(F. 21, 1814). Killed S, 17, 1814,
in action at Ft. Erie U. C.

Gibson, James. Private in Capt.
Warfield's co. Balto. United Vol-
unteers. Wounded at North
Point.

Gibson, John. Private in Capt.
Sterett's co. 1st Balto. Hussars.

Gibson, John. Lieutenant in Capt.
Caldwell's co. 42d rgt. (Ap. 27,
1813).

Gibson, Joshua. Corporal in Capt.
Pike's co. Balto. Volunteer Artillery.

Gibson, Samuel. Corporal in Capt.
Ireland's co. 31st rgt.

Gibson, Samuel. Private in Capt.
Dillon's co. 27th rgt.

Gibson, Thomas. Private in Capt.
Bunbury's co. Sea Fencibles.

Gibson, William. 2d Lieutenant in
36th U. S. Infantry (Ap. 30,
1813). Resigned O. 22, 1813.

Gibson, Dr. William. Private in
Capt. Thompson's co. 1st Baltimore Horse Artillery.

Giddings, Benjamin. Private in
Capt. Edes' co. 27th rgt.

Giddings, Benjamin. Private in
Capt. Thompson's co. 43d rgt.

Gidley, Joseph. Private in Capt.
Usselton's Artillery co. 6th Brigade.

Gifford, Alexander. Private in Capt. Lawson's co. Balto. Patriots.

Gilbach, Charles. Private in Capt. Sadtler's co. Balto. Yägers.

Gilbert, David. Private in Capt. Peters' co. 51st rgt.

Gilbert, George. Private in Capt. Stiles' co. Marine Artillery.

Gilberthorp, William. Sergeant in Capt. Brown's co. Eagle Artillerists.

Gilder, Reuben. 1st Lieutenant in 14th U. S. Infantry (Mr. 12, 1812) ; Captain (Je. 26, 1813).

Giles, John. Private in Capt. Sample's co. 49th rgt.

Giles, Joseph. Private in Capt. Deems' co. 51st rgt.

Giles, Thomas. Private in Capt. King's co. 49th rgt.

Gill, Bennet C. Private in Capt. Bouldin's co. Independent Light Dragoons.

Gill, Ezekiel C. Private in Capt. Montgomery's co. Balto. Union Artillery.

Gill, John. Private in Capt. Haubert's co. 51st rgt.

Gill, John. Captain in Sea Fencibles (N. 25, 1813).

Gill, John B. Private in Capt. Moale's co. Columbian Artillery.

Gill, Nicholas C. Private in Capt. Bouldin's co. Independent Light Dragoons.

Gill, Selmon. Private in Capt. Ringgold's co. 6th rgt.

Gill, Stephen [1781-1846]. Captain in 41st rgt.

Gill, Stephen, Jr. Captain in 7th rgt. (Je. 26, 1812).

Gill, William Lowry [1797-1880]. Midshipman, U. S. S. *Superior* (1814).

Gillen, Lakey. Private in Capt. Stewart's co. 51st rgt.

Gillis, William R. Lieutenant in Capt. Almoney's co. 41st rgt. (Je. 1, 1813).

Gillispie, George. Sergeant in Lieut. Egan's detachment 30th rgt.

Gillum, Simon. Private in Capt. Kennedy's co. 27th rgt.

Gilman, John. Private in Capt. Burke's co. 6th rgt.

Gilmor, William. Private in Capt. Warfield's co. Balto. United Volunteers.

Gilmore, James. Private in Capt. Galloway's co. 46th rgt.

Ginn, John. Private in Capt. Mackey's co. 49th rgt.

Giscy, Jacob. Ensign in Capt. Carlton's co. 16th rgt. (S. 20, 1813).

Gist, Joshua C. Cornet in Capt. Hollingsworth's co. 2d rgt. 1st Cavalry Dist. (Je. 17, 1812) ; 2d Lieutenant (Ap. 27, 1814).

Gist, Thomas. 1st Lieutenant in 12th U. S. Infantry (Mr. 12, 1812).

Gist, Thomas C. Captain in 2d rgt. 1st Cavalry Dist. (My. 31, 1813).

Gist, William. 2d Lieutenant in Capt. Woolford's co. 10th Cavalry Dist. (S. 26, 1812).

Gitchell, J. Private in Capt. Sterett's Independent co.

Gittinger, Francis. Ensign in Capt. Miller's co. 15th rgt. (Ap. 22, 1813).

Gittings, James, Jr. Private in Capt. Sterett's co. 1st Balto. Hussars.

Gittings, James C. Private in Capt. Sterett's co. 1st Balto. Hussars.

Gittings, Thomas. Captain in 34th rgt.

Givan, James. Cornet in Capt. Handy's co. 11h Cavalry Dist. (O. 15, 1814).

Given, James. Quarter-master Sergeant in 49th rgt.

Gladding, Samuel. Private in Capt. Edes' co. 27th rgt.

Gladson, Michael. Private in Capt. Chalmers' co. 51st rgt.

Glanson, Solomon. Private in Capt. Massey's co. 38th rgt.

Glanville, John. Private in Capt. Page's co. 21st rgt., and in Capt. Chambers' co. Wounded at battle of Caulk's Field.

Glasby, John. Private in Capt. Kierstead's co. 6th rgt.

Glass, John. Private in Capt. Kierstead's co. 6th rgt.

Glassbrenner, Peter. Private in Capt. Quantrill's co. 24th rgt.

Glassco, John. Private in Capt. Linthicum's co. 22d rgt.

Glaucer, Jacob. Private in Capt. Schwarzauer's co. 27th rgt.

Gleaves, John W. Paymaster in 35th rgt. (N. 3, 1814).

Gleaves, Nathan. Private in Capt. Page's co. 21st rgt.

Gleaves, William F. Lieutenant in Capt. Scott's co. 33d rgt. (Ag. 27, 1810).

Glen, Walter. Private in Capt. Snowden's co. 36th rgt.

Glenn, Elijah. Private in Capt. Pinney's co. 27th rgt.

Glenn, James. Private in Capt. Magruder's co. American Artillerists.

Glenn, James. Private in Capt. Jas. Massey's co. 38th rgt.

Glenn, John, Jr. Private in Capt. Magruder's co. American Artillerists.

Glenn, John W. Private in Capt. Magruder's co. American Artillerists.

Glenn, Robert W. Lieutenant of the privateer Express, June, 1813; Private in Capt. Stiles' co. Marine Artillery (1814).

Glenn, Samuel T. [1794-1875]. Private in Capt. Dillon's co. 27th rgt.

Glover, Philip. Private in Capt. Posey's co. 1st rgt.

Glover, William. Private in Capt. Chase's co. 22d rgt.

Glover, William. Private in Capt. Shrim's co. Balto. Light Infantry.

Gobright, William. Private in Capt. Watson's co. 39th rgt.

Gochear, Anthony. Private in Capt. Galt's co. 6th rgt.

Goddard, Charles [1794-1872]. Private in Capt. McConkey's co. 27th rgt. Severely wounded at North Point.

Goddard, John. Private in Capt. Dyer's co. 17th rgt.

Godwin, George. 1st Lieutenant in Capt. Jones' co. 9th Cavalry Dist. (Je. 1, 1813); Captain (Jy. 8, 1813).

Godwin, Kimmel. Ensign in 14th U. S. Infantry (Mr. 12, 1812); 1st Lieutenant (Ag. 31, 1814).

Godwin, Thomas. Private in Capt. Massey's co. 38th rgt.

Gold, John. Private in Capt. Smith's co. 51st rgt.

Gold, Joseph. Captain of the privateer Cora; of the Burrows, Sept., 1813; 1st Lieutenant in Capt. Stiles' co. Marine Artillery (S. 10, 1814).

Golden, Alexander. Private in Capt. Burgess' co. 43d rgt.

Golder, Archibald. Private in Capt. Moale's co. Columbian Artillery.

Golder, George. Private in Capt. Warfield's co. Balto. United Volunteers. Wounded at Bladensburg.

Golder, John. Corporal in Capt. Pinkney's Artillery co. 22d rgt.

Golder, Robert. Private in Capt. Magruder's co. American Artillerists.

Golding, William. Private in Capt. Blair's co. 50th rgt.

Goldsberry, William. Private in Capt. Williams' co. 12th rgt.

Goldsborough, Nicholas. Capt. in 4th rgt. (S. 18, 1812).

Goldsborough, Nicholas. Private in Capt. Steiner's Frederick Artillery.

Goldsborough, Robert H. Captain in 9th Cavalry Dist. (My. 8, 1812); Major (F. 13, 1813).

Goldsborough, Thomas. Captain in 10th Cavalry Dist. (My. 20, 1813).

Goldsborough, William. Ensign in Capt. Jordan's co. 26th rgt. (Je. 26, 1812).

Goldsbury, Bennet. Private in Capt. Williams' co. 12th rgt.

Goldsbury, Ignatius. Private in Capt. Williams' co. 12th rgt.

Goldsbury, William. Private in Capt. Williams' co. 12th rgt.

Goldsmith, John. Private in Capt. McKane's co. 27th rgt.

Goldsmith, Townley. Private in Capt. Thompson's co. 1st rgt.

Gollibert, Joseph. Corporal in Capt. Brown's co. 6th rgt.

Gombey, George. Private in Capt. Smith's co. 51st rgt.

Gomley, Richard. Private in Capt. Dillon's co. 27th rgt.

Gooden, John. Private in Capt. Brooke's co. 34th rgt.

Gooding, James. Private in Capt. Chambers' co. 21st rgt.

Gooding, Jonas. Private in Capt. Ringgold's co. 6th rgt.

Gooding, Marmaduke. Private in Capt. Ringgold's co. 6th rgt.

Goodmanson, Peter. Private in Capt. Bunbury's co. Sea Fencibles.

Goodrich, John. Private in Capt. Cawood's co. 45th rgt.

Goodrich, Sylvester. Private in Capt. Posey's co. 1st rgt.

Goodrich, William. Command unknown; captured at Bladensburg.

Goodrick, Eli. Private in Capt. Pennington's co. Balto. Independent Artillerists.

Goodwin, Caleb. Private in Capt. McDonald's co. 6th rgt.

Goodwin, Caleb Dorsey. Private in Capt. Sterett's Independent co.

Goodwin, Edward. 2d Lieutenant in Capt. Bosley's co. 6th Cavalry Dist. (Jy. 30, 1812); 1st Lieutenant (D. 15, 1814).

Goodwin, Edward. Ensign in Capt. Sparks' co. 35th rgt. (My. 6, 1807).

Goodwin, Jacob. Private in Capt. Rogers' co. 51st rgt.

Goodwin, John. Private in Capt. Brown's co. 6th rgt.

Goodwin, Lyde. 1st Lieutenant in Capt. Wilson's co. 6th Cavalry Dist. (Ap. 4, 1812).

Goodwin, Robert Morris [1796-1861]. Ensign in 5th U. S. Infantry (Ap. 14, 1812); transferred to 3d U. S. Infantry (My. 1, 1812); 3d Lieutenant (Mr. 12, 1813); 2d Lieutenant (Ag. 15, 1813); resigned Jy. 31, 1814; 2d Lieutenant in 27th Infantry (F. 11, 1815); honorably discharged (Je. 15, 1815).

Goodwin, William. Lieutenant in Capt. Sparks' co. 35th rgt. (My. 6, 1807).

Gordon, James. Private in Capt. Chalmers' co. 51st rgt.

Gordon, John. Private in Capt. Addison's co. Sea Fencibles.

Gordon, John. Private in Capt. Dyer's co. Fells Point Riflemen.

Gordon, Joseph. Private in Capt. McConkey's co. 27th rgt.

Gordon, Joseph. Private in Capt. Stewart's co. 51st rgt.

Gordon, Joseph N. Surgeon in 21st rgt. (Ap. 16, 1813).

Gordon, Richard. Private in Capt. Dyer's co. Fells Point Riflemen.

Gordon, Walton. Private in Capt. Stiles' co. Marine Artillery.

Gordon, William. Private in Capt. Blair's co. 50th rgt.

Gordy, Benjamin H. Lieutenant in Capt. Milson's co. 37th rgt. (Jy. 8, 1813).

Gore, Charles. Captain in 41st rgt. (Ap. 20, 1808).

Gore, George [1791-1861]. Private in Capt. Carnan's co. 6th Cavalry Dist.

Gore, Henry. Corporal in Capt. Snowden's co. 36th rgt.

Gore, Michael. Private in Capt. Ducker's co. 7th rgt.

Gorham, John. Lieutenant of the privateer *Midas*, Jan., 1815.

Gorsic, Thomas. Private in Capt. Wilson's co. 6th rgt.

Gorsuch, Benjamin. Captain in 15th rgt. Rifle co. (O. 21, 1812).

Gorsuch, Gerard. 3d Lieutenant in Capt. Bunbury's Sea Fencibles (O. 1, 1813).

Gorsuch, George. Corporal in Capt. Frizzell's co. 15th rgt.

Gorsuch, John. Private in Capt. Piper's co. United Maryland Artilery.

Gorsuch, John. Ensign in Capt. Dyer's co. Fells Point Riflemen.

Gorsuch, Joshua. Private in Capt. Dillon's co. 27th rgt.

Gorsuch, Nicholas. Private in Capt. Edes's co. 27th rgt.

Gorsuch, Robert. Private in Capt. Sterett's co. 1st Balto. Hussars.

Gorsuch, Thomas. Private in Capt. Steever's co. 27th rgt.

Gorsuch, William. Command unknown; captured at Bladensburg.

Gosler, John. Lieutenant in Capt. Corcoran's co. 18th rgt. (Ag. 16, 1799).

Goslin, John. Private in Capt. Heath's co. 23d rgt.

Gosling, Joshua. Private in Capt. Chalmers' co. 51st rgt.

Gosmann, James. Private in Capt. Stewart's co. 51st rgt.

Gosnell, Anthony. Private in Capt. Ducker's co. 7th rgt.

Gosnell, Barsell. Private in Capt. Blizzard's co. 15th rgt

Gosnell, Charles. Private in Capt. Ducker's co. 7th rgt.

Gosnell, Ezekiel. Private in Capt. Ducker's co. 7th rgt.

Gosnell, Greenberry. Private in Capt. Ducker's co. 7th rgt.

Gosnell, Jasper. Private in Capt. Ducker's co. 7th rgt.

Gosnell, Jerry. Private in Capt. Ducker's co. 7th rgt.

Gosnell, Jesse. Captain in 7th rgt. (Ap. 27, 1813).

Gosnell, Joshua. Ensign in Capt. Grate's co. 7th rgt. (Ag. 1, 1814).

Gosnell. Moses. Private in Capt. Ducker's co. 7th rgt.

Gosnell, Philip. Private in Capt. Ducker's co. 7th rgt.

Gosnell, Philip. Private in Capt. Blizzard's co. 15th rgt.

Gosnell, William. Private in Capt. Ducker's co. 7th rgt.

Gosnell, William. Ensign in Capt. Gorsuch's co. 15th rgt. (O. 21, 1812).

Gosnell, Zebediah. Private in Capt. Ducker's co. 7th rgt.

Gossen, Henry. Private in Capt. McConkey's co. 27th rgt.

Goswick, Thomas. Command unknown; captured at Bladensburg.

Gott, Richard. Lieutenant in Capt. Dade's co. 3d rgt. (My. 17, 1811).

Gough, Bennett. Paymaster in 4th Cavalry Dist.

Gough, Harry Dorsey. Private in Capt. Lee's co. 7th Cavalry Dist.

Gough, Joseph. Paymaster in 12th rgt. (Je. 12, 1812).

Gough, Stephen. Brigade Quartermaster 5th Brigade (O. 13, 1814).

Gough, Stephen. Private in Capt. Causin's troop, attached to 12th rgt.

Gould, —. Ensign in Capt. Sturgis' co. 35th rgt.

Gould, Alexander. Private in Capt. Stewart's co. Washington Blues.

Gould, James. Private in Capt. Pike's co. Balto. Volunteer Artillery.

Gould, William. Cornet in Capt. Blake's co. 9th Cavalry Dist. (My. 31, 1813).

Gove, Edward. Private in Capt. Brohawn's co. 48th rgt.

Gover, Philip. Private in Capt. Levering's co. Independent Blues.

Gowan, John. Private in Capt. Horton's Maryland Chasseurs.

Gowen, George. Private in Capt. Myers' co. Franklin Artillery.

Gower, Adam. Ensign in Capt. Gower's co. 50th rgt. (N. 3, 1812).

Gower, Jacob. Private in Capt. Shryock's co. 24th rgt.

Gower, Nicholas. Private in Capt. McLaughlin's co. 50th rgt.

Gower, Nicholas, Sr. Captain in 50th rgt. (N. 3, 1812).

Goxdwait, E. Private in Capt. Stiles' co. Marine Artillery.

Goyer, Jacob. Private in Capt. Quantrill's co. 24th rgt.

Grace, Alexander. Private in Capt. Morgan's co. 49th rgt.

Grace, John. Private in Capt. Piper's co. United Maryland Artillery.

Grace, John. Private in Capt. Galt's co. 6th rgt.

Grace, Skinner. Ensign in Capt. Haddaway's co. 26th rgt. (Jy. 8, 1813).

Grady, Anthony. Private in Capt. Chalmers' co. 51st rgt.

Graff, F. C. Private in Capt. Sterett's Independent co.

Graff, George. 2d Lieutenant in Capt. Steiner's Frederick Artillery 9th Brigade (O. 1, 1811). Resigned Jy., 1814.

Graff, Jacob. Private in Capt. Sheppard's co. 6th rgt.

Graff, John. Private in Capt. Sheppard's co. 6th rgt.

Graff, Joseph. Lieutenant in Capt. Derne's co. 47th rgt. (Ap. 21, 1814).

Graff, Marcus Y. Corporal in Capt. Steiner's Frederick Artillery.

Graff, Sebastian. Paymaster in 29th rgt. (N. 5, 1801).

Grafton, Corbin. Ensign in Capt. Little's co. 40th rgt. (Je. 16, 1812).

Grafton, Mark. Private in Capt. Moale's co. Columbian Artillery.

Grafton, Nathan. Private in Capt. Moale's co. Columbian Artillery.

Graham, David. Private in Capt. Lawson's co. Balto. Patriots.

Graham, Edward. Sergeant in Capt. Taylor's co. 48th rgt.

Graham, Henry. Lieutenant of the privateer *Decatur*, Mar, 1813.

Graham, James. Sergeant in Capt. Taylor's co. 46th rgt.

Graham, James. Private in Capt. Chalmers' co. 51st rgt.

Graham, Joseph. Sergeant in Capt. McDonald's co. 6th rgt.

Graham, Owen. Private in Capt. Brown's co. Eagle Artillerists.

Graham, William. Private in Capt. Brown's co. 6th rgt.

Graham, William. Private in Capt. Ringgold's co. 6th rgt.

Graham, Zachariah. Private in Capt. Blizzard's co. 15th rgt.

Grahame, Thomas. Private in Capt. Steiner's Frederick Artillery.

Grainer, William. Private in Capt. Stapleton's co. 39th rgt.

Grainger, Matthew. Private in Capt. Watson's co. 39th rgt.

Grammar, Benjamin. Corporal in Capt. Dobbin's co. 39th rgt.

Grammar, H. of G. Private in Capt. Chase's co. 22d rgt.

Grandshamp, William. Private in Capt. Levering's co. Independent Blues.

Granger, Clement. Private in Capt. Linthicum's co. 22d rgt.

Granger, James. Private in Capt. Nicholson's co. Balto. Fencibles. Wounded at Fort McHenry.

Granger, Nathan. Private in Capt. Linthicum's co. 22d rgt.

Granger, Samuel. Private in Capt. Shrim's co. Balto. Light Infantry.

Grant, Elijah. Private in Capt. Thos. Warner's co. 39th rgt.

Grant, Henry. Private in Capt. Stiles' co. Marine Artillery.

Grant, Jeremiah. Captain of the privateer *High Flyer*, Oct, 1812. Killed in action.

Grantt, Richard. Ensign in Capt. Hynson's co. 21st rgt. (F. 9, 1814).

Grary, Samuel. Private in Capt. Berry's co. Washington Artillery. Wounded at Fort McHenry.

Grason, George W. Private in Capt. Brown's co. 43d rgt.

Grate, Michael. Captain in 7th rgt. (Je. 26, 1812).

Graves, Jeremiah. Private in Capt. Blakistone's co. 45th rgt.

Graves, John. Private in Capt. Steever's co. 27th rgt.

Graves, Richard. Major in 21st rgt.; Brigade Major, 6th Brigade.

Graves, Robert. Lieutenant in Capt. Conway's co. 6th rgt. (Jy. 12, 1814).

Graves, William. Captain in 21st rgt.[1814].

Gravy, William. Private in Capt. Dyer's co. Fells Point Riflemen.

Gray, Alexander. Corporal in Capt. Brown's co. 43d rgt.

Gray, Allen. Private in Capt. Peters' co. 51st rgt.

Gray, Andrew. Private in Capt. Kierstead's co. 6th rgt.

Gray, Benjamin. Captain in 31st rgt. (My. 22, 1812).

Gray, Callender. Private in Capt. Snowden's co. 36th rgt.

Gray, Callender. Private in Capt. Smith's co. 51st rgt.

Gray, Charles R. Private in Capt. Burgess' co. 43d rgt.

Gray, Edward. Private in Capt. Thompson's co. 1st Baltimore Horse Artillery.

Gray, Eli. Private in Capt. Brown's co. 43d rgt.

Gray, Henley. Private in Capt. Burgess' co. 43d rgt.

Gray, Henry W. Private in Capt. Warfield's co. Balto. United Volunteers. Captured at North Point.

Gray, James. Private in Capt. Dillon's co. 27th rgt.
Gray, John. Private in Capt. Pumphrey's co. 22d rgt.
Gray, John. Private in Capt. Lawrence's co. 6th rgt.
Gray, John. Private in Capt. McDonald's co. 6th rgt.
Gray, John. Private in Capt. Shryock's co. 24th rgt.
Gray, John. Private in Capt. Berry's co. Washington's Artilery.
Gray, John F. Captain in 43d rgt.
Gray, Johnson. Ensign in Capt. Breevard's co. Extra Battalion Worcester Co. (Je. 18, 1812).
Gray, Joseph. Private in Capt. Dunnington's co. 43d rgt.
Gray, Joshua. Fifer in Capt. Hancock's co. 22d rgt.
Gray, Nicholas. Private in Capt. McKane's co. 27th rgt.
Gray, Robert. Sergeant in Capt. Dunnington's co. 43d rgt.
Gray, Walter. Private in Capt. Sheppard's co. 6th rgt.
Gray, William. Private in Capt. Pinney's co. 27th rgt.
Gray, William. Private in Capt. Berry's co. Washington Artillery.
Gray, William S. 1st Lieutenant in 35th U. S. Rifles (Mr. 17, 1814).
Gray, William W. Ensign in Capt. Selby's co. 9th rgt. (Jy. 13, 1814).
Gray, Zachariah. Private in Capt. Haubert's co. 51st rgt.
Gray, Zachariah R. Private in Capt. McConkey's co. 27th rgt.
Graybell, Philip. Private in Capt. Nicholson's co. Balto. Fencibles.
Grayham, John. Lieutenant in Capt. Kemp's co. 26th rgt. (N. 6, 1811).
Grayham, John. Lieutenant in Capt. McNamara's co. 48th rgt. (Ag. 8, 1809).

Grayham, Thomas. Ensign in Capt. Kemp's co. 26th rgt. (N. 6, 1811).
Grayson, John. Ensign in 6th U. S. Infantry (O. 27, 1813); Regimental Adjutant (Je., 1814).
Grayson, Marcellus. Private in Capt. Travers' co. 48th rgt.
Grayson, Thomas. Private in Capt. Maynard's co. 22d rgt.
Grayson, William. 2d Lieutenant in Capt. Wright's Artillery Co. 6th Brigade (O. 13, 1814) vice James Smith.
Greary, William. Private in Capt. Pike's co. Balto. Volunteer Artillery.
Greaves, David. Corporal in Capt. Brown's co. Eagle Artillerists.
Green, Abel. Private in Capt. Bouldin's co. Independent Light Dragoons.
Green, Anthony. Private in Capt. Bunbury's co. Sea Fencibles.
Green, Armistead. Private in Capt. Faster's co. 51st rgt.
Green, Caleb. Sergeant in Capt. Thompson's co. 43d rgt.
Green, Charles Bosley [1793-1871]. Private in Capt. Guyton's co. 2d rgt.
Green, Clement. Private in Capt. McPherson's co. 43d rgt.
Green, Dorsey. Private in Capt. Blizzard's co. 15th rgt.
Green, Edward. Private in Capt. Edes' co. 27th rgt.
Green, Eli. Sergeant in Capt. Bouldin's co. Independent Light Dragoons.
Green, George W. 1st Lieutenant Sea Fencibles (Mr. 17, 1814).
Green, Henry. Private in Capt. Maynard's co. 22d rgt.
Green, James. Ensign in Capt. Chase's co. 22d rgt. (Ap. 22, 1814).

Green, Jeremiah. Ensign in Capt. Steever's co. 27th rgt.

Green, Jeremiah. 2d Lieutenant in 38th U. S. Infantry (My. 20, 1813); 1st Lieutenant (My. 1, 1814). Resigned Jy. 9, 1814.

Green, Joel [-1814]. Captain in 46th rgt.

Green, John. Sergeant in Capt. Massey's co. 38th rgt.

Green, John. Private in Capt. Mc-Conckin's co. 38th rgt.

Green, John. Private in Capt. A. E. Warner's co. 39th rgt.

Green, John. Private in Capt. Bunbury's co. Sea Fencibles.

Green, Jonas. Captain in 6th Cavalry Dist. (F. 13, 1812) Major (Ap. 21, 1814) vice Lyon.

Green, Jonas. Private in Capt. Maynard's co. 22d rgt.

Green, Joseph. Lieutenant in Capt. Ogle's co. 47th rgt. (My. 22, 1812).

Green, Lewis. 2d Lieutenant in Capt. Steiner's Frederick Artillery co. (S. 10. 1814).

Green, Peter. Private in Capt. Sheppard's co. 6th rgt.

Green, Robert. Private in Capt. Bunbury's co. Sea Fencibles. Slightly wounded at Fort McHenry.

Green, Samuel. Private in Capt. Adreon's co. Union Volunteers.

Green, Samuel, Jr. Ensign in Capt. Andrew Smith's co. 47th rgt. (N. 28, 1808).

Green, Thomas. Private in Capt. Magruder's co. American Artillerists.

Green, Thomas B. Private in Capt. Moale's co. Columbian Artillery.

Green, William S. Lieutenant in Capt. Sands' co. 22d rgt; Captain, vice Sands.

Greenfield, Francis. Private in Capt. Haden's co. 17th rgt.

Greenfield, John. Private in Capt. Shrim's co. Balto. Light Infantry.

Greenfield, Neilson. Private in Capt. Dobbin's co. 39th rgt.

Greenfield, Thomas. Corporal in Capt. Sotheran's co. 45th rgt.

Greentree, Benjamin. Lieutenant in Capt. Duvall's co. 18th rgt. (S. 30, 1797).

Greenwald, Christian. Sergeant in Capt. Getzendanner's co. 16th rgt.

Greenway, Thomas [1775-1814]. 2d Lieutenant of the privateer Fox.

Greenwell, Athanasius. Private in Capt. Millard's co. 12th rgt.

Greenwell, Charles G. Private in Capt. Williams' co. 12th rgt.

Greenwell, Charles G. Ensign in 12th rgt. (Je. 12, 1812).

Greenwell, John. Lieutenant of the privateer Caroline, Oct, 1813.

Greenwell, Samuel. 1st Lieutenant in Capt. G. N. Causin's co. 4th Cavalry Dist. (My. 8, 1812).

Greenwell, Samuel. Private in Capt. Millard's co. 12th rgt.

Greenwell, Thomas. Lieutenant-Colonel in 50th rgt. (Jy. 8, 1813).

Greenwood, William. Private in Capt. Tilghman's co. 33d rgt.

Greer, George [-1826]. Private in Capt. Pennington's co. Balto. Independent Artillerists. Wounded at Fort McHenry.

Greer, Levin B. Private in Capt. Crawford's co. 17th rgt.

Greetham, William. Private in Capt. Warfield's co. Balto. United Volunteers.

Gregg, A. P. Private in Capt. Stiles' co. Marine Artillery.

Gregg, Alexander. Private in Capt. Pennington's co. Balto. Independent Artillerists.

Gregg, Andrew. Private in Capt. Levering's co. Independent Blues.

Gregg, James. Private in Capt. Lawson's co. Balto. Patriots.

Greggs, Eben. Private in Capt. Peters' co. 51st rgt.

Grenville [Greenwell], Henry. Private in Capt. Sands' co. 22d rgt.

Grewe, Henry W. Private in Capt. Edes' co. 27th rgt.

Grezell, Francis. Private in Capt. Lawson's co. Balto. Patriots.

Grier, Levin B. Private in Capt. Haden's co. 17th rgt.

Grieves, James. Private in Capt. Sheppard's co. 6th rgt.

Grieves, John. Private in Capt. Lawson's co. Balto. Patriots.

Griffey, John. Private in Capt. Blair's co. 50th rgt.

Griffin, Abraham. Private in Capt. Galloway's co. 46th rgt.

Griffin, Benjamin. 1st Lieutenant in Capt. Ducker's co. 7th rgt.

Griffin, Benjamin. Private in Capt. Brown's co. 6th rgt.

Griffin, Caleb. Private in Capt. Brohawn's co. 48th rgt.

Griffin, Charles. Captain in 36th rgt. (O. 30, 1807).

Griffin, Charles K. Private in Capt. Smith's co. 51st rgt.

Griffin, George. Private in Capt. Faster's co. 51st rgt.

Griffin, Henry. Private in Capt. Brown's co. 6th rgt.

Griffin, James S. 2d Lieutenant in 38th U. S. Infantry (My. 20, 1813); 1st Lieutenant (My. 20, 1814).

Griffin, Levin. Private in Capt. Brohawn's co. 48th rgt.

Griffin, Luther. Private in Capt. McConkey's co. 27th rgt.

Griffin, Martin. Private in Capt. Deems' co. 51st rgt.

Griffin, Nathan. Private in Capt. Haubert's co. 51st rgt.

Griffin, Robert. Private in Capt. Haubert's co. 51st rgt.

Griffin, Thomas. Private in Capt. John Miller's co. 2d D. I.; b. Baltimore, Md.; age 39; cooper; subs. for Valentine Thomas.

Griffin, William. Corporal in Capt. Snowden's co. 36th rgt.

Griffin, William. Private in Capt. Crawford's co. 17th rgt.

Griffis, Edward. Private in Capt. Faster's co. 51st rgt.

Griffis, Joseph [Griffith]. Captain in 31st rgt. (Je. 22, 1808).

Griffith, Anthony. Private in Capt. Piper's co. United Maryland Artillery.

Griffith, Caleb. Ensign in Capt. Waters' co. 13th rgt. (Ap. 15, 1795).

Griffith, David. Private in Capt. Lawrence's co. 6th rgt.

Griffith, David. 2d Lieutenant in Capt. Magruder's co. American Artillerists (Ag. 10, 1813) vice Bradford.

Griffith, Edward. Private in Capt. Sands' co. 22d rgt.; in Capt. Wells Artillery co.; in Ensign Brewer's detachment, 36th rgt. at Bladensburg.

Griffith, George. Lieutenant in Capt. Taylor's co. 48th rgt. (S. 21, 1813).

Griffith, Henry B. Private in Capt. Edes' co. 27th rgt.

Griffith, Howard, Jr. [1794-1866]. Private in Capt. Levering's co. Independent Blues.

Griffith, Isaac. 2d Lieutenant in U. S. Light Dragoons (Mr. 18, 1813).

Griffith, Jacob. Private in Capt. Piper's co. United Maryland Artillery.

Griffith, John. Lieutenant in Capt. Hillery's co. 13th rgt. (O. 24, 1800).

Griffith, John. Private in Capt. Kennedy's co. 27th rgt.

Griffith, John. Ensign in Capt. Travers' co. 48th rgt. (D. 10, 1813).

Griffith, John H. Private in Capt. Haubert's co. 51st rgt.

Griffith, Joseph. Captain in 31st rgt.

Griffith, Joshua. Lieutenant in Capt. Wm. Jones' co. 7th rgt. (Ag. 1, 1814).

Griffith, Joshua. Private in Capt. Barnes' co. 32d rgt. Died 1813.

Griffith, Lyde. Captain in 44th rgt. (Ag. 20, 1814).

Griffith, Mathew. Private in Capt. Magruder's co. American Artillerists.

Griffith, Perry. Private in Capt. Dunnington's co. 43d rgt.

Griffith, Samuel. Captain in 21st rgt. (Je. 6, 1811).

Griffith, Samuel. Surgeon's mate 11th rgt. Died 1814.

Griffith, Samuel. Private in Capt. Chambers' co. 21st rgt.

Griffith, Samuel G. Private in Capt. Sterett's co. 1st Balto. Hussars.

Griffith, Sandy. Surgeon's mate 42d rgt. (Jy. 14, 1814) vice Dallam.

Griffith, Stephen [-1818]. 3d Lieutenant in 1st U. S. Infantry (S. 16, 1814).

Griffith, Stephen. Private in Capt. Roney's co. 39th rgt.

Griffith, Sylvanus. Lieutenant in Capt. Dedie's co. 10th rgt. Died, Sept. 20, 1813.

Griffith, Thomas. Captain in 32d rgt. (O. 21, 1812).

Griffith, Thomas. Lieutenant in Capt. Griffith's co. 21st rgt. (Ap. 22, 1813).

Griffith, William. Private in Capt. Snowden's co. 36th rgt.

Griffith [Griffis], William. Private in Capt. Dunnington's co. 43d rgt.

Griffiths, Thomas B. Private in Capt. Addison's co. Sea Fencibles.

Grigg, Alexander P. Lieutenant of the privateer *Inca*, Aug, 1812; Captain May, 1813.

Grimes, Edward. Ensign in Capt. Randall's co. 36th rgt. (N. 7, 1812).

Grimes, James. Lieutenant in Capt. Drury's co. 10th rgt. (S. 20, 1813).

Grimes, James. Private in Capt. Brown's co. 49th rgt.

Grimes, John. Private in Capt. Haden's co. 17th rgt.

Grimes, Joseph. Private in Capt. Magruder's co. American Artillerists.

Grimes, Levi. Private in Capt. Brown's co. 6th rgt.

Grimes, Nicholas. Ensign in Capt. Ravon's co. 46th rgt. (Je. 1, 1813).

Grimes, Noah. Private in Capt. Pumphrey's co. 22d rgt.

Grimes, Richard. Sergeant in Capt. Horton's co. Maryland Chasseurs.

Grimes, William. Private in Capt. Green's co. 46th rgt.

Grindall, William. Private in Cawood's co. 45th rgt.

Grinnell, William. Private in Capt.
Stapleton's co. 39th rgt.
Griswold, Livy. Private in Capt.
Kennedy's co. 27th rgt.
Grizel, Joseph L. Command un-
known; captured at Bladensburg.
Groom, William. Private in Capt.
Brown's co. Eagle Artillerists.
Groome, John. Surgeon in 49th rgt.
(Mr. 9, 1808).
Groome, William H. Lieutenant in
Capt. Hayward's co. 4th rgt. (S.
10, 1814).
Grooms, William. Private in Capt.
Peters' co. 51st rgt.
Groover, Charles. Private in Capt.
Faster's co. 51st rgt.
Gross, Adam. Private in Capt.
Blair's co. 50th rgt.
Gross, Francis. Private in Capt.
Snowden's co. 36th rgt.
Grossh, John. Private in Capt.
Brown's co. Eagle Artillerists.
Grove, Jacob. Private in Capt. Hau-
bert's co. 51st rgt.
Grove, John. 2d Lieutenant in Capt.
Cost's co. 1st rgt. 1st Cavalry
Dist. (Mr. 16, 1812).
Grover, William. Sergeant in Capt.
Gantt's co. 31st rgt.
Groves, Gordon. Private in Capt.
Dunnington's co. 43d rgt.
Groves, Isaac. Private in Capt.
Shrim's co. Balto. Light Infantry.
Groves, John. Private in Capt.
Dunnington's co. 43d rgt.
Groves, Solomon. Lieutenant in
Capt. Sanders' co. 2d rgt. (Ag.
14, 1807).
Grubb, George. Private in Capt.
Shrim's co. Balto. Light Infantry.
Grubb, George. Private in Capt.
Shryock's co. 24th rgt.
Grubb, Michael, Jr. Private in Capt.
Pike's co. Balto. Volunteer Ar-
tillery.

Grubb, Michael. Private in Capt.
Bader's co. Union Yägers.
Grubb, William. Private in Capt.
Smith's co. 51st rgt.
Grundy, George Carr. Private in
Capt. Thompson's co. 1st Balti-
more Horse Artillery.
Grundy, Thomas B. Private in Capt.
Warfield's co. Balto. United Vol-
unteers.
Gruver, John. Private in Capt. Ais-
quith's co. Sharp Shooters.
Guarnego, Louis. Private in Capt.
Stiles' co. Marine Artillery.
Guest, Richard. Private in Capt.
Smith's co. 51st rgt.
Guest, Thomas. Private in Capt.
Edes' co. 27th rgt.
Guildener, Charles. Private in Capt.
Nicholson's co. Balto. Fencibles.
Gunby, George S. Surgeon's mate
37th rgt. (Ag. 5, 1814) vice Sav-
age.
Gunby, Stephen. Private in Capt.
Lawrence's co. 6th rgt.
Gurlaugh, Henry. Private in Capt.
Barr's Cavalry co. 1st Dist.
Gusenderffer, John. Private in Capt.
Bader's co. Union Yägers.
Guthrow, Stephen. Private in Capt.
Pennington's co. Balto. Independ-
ent Artillerists.
Gutrow, James. Private in Capt.
Watson's co. 39th rgt.
Guy, John R. Ensign in 16th U. S.
Infantry (Ap. 8, 1814) ; 2d Lieu-
tenant (Jy. 22, 1814).
Guyton, Benjamin. 1st Lieutenant
in Capt. Lee's co. 7th Cavalry
Dist. (Ap. 16, 1812) vice Robin-
son.
Gwinn, Benjamin. Private in Capt.
Levering's co. Independent Blues.
Gwinn, Edward. Private in Capt.
Warfield's co. Balto. United Vol-
unteers.

Gwinn, William R. 1st Lieutenant in 38th U. S. Infantry (My. 20, 1813). Resigned D. 31, 1813.

Gwynn, James. Private in Capt. Fowler's co. 33d rgt.

Gwynn, John, Jr. Private in Capt. Maynard's co. 22d rgt.

Gwynn, William. Private in Capt. McKane's co. 27th rgt.

Gwynne, David [-1849]. 1st Lieutenant in 19th U. S. Infantry (Mr. 12, 1812) ; Major 2d Rifles (F. 21, 1814).

H

Habskiss, S. H. Private in Capt. Stiles' co. Marine Artillery.

Hacke, Nicholas. Sergeant in Capt. Sadtler's co. Balto. Yägers.

Hackett, Henry. Ensign in Capt. Storey's co. 38th rgt. (F. 1, 1814).

Hackett, John, Jr. Captain in 35th rgt. (My. 8, 1812).

Hackney, Barton. Captain in 28th rgt. (S. 2, 1811).

Hackney, William. Private in Capt. Deems' co. 51st rgt.

Haddaway, James. Lieutenant in Capt. Carroll's co. 26th rgt. (Je. 26, 1812).

Haddaway, James. Private in Capt. Adreon's co. Union Volunteers.

Haddaway, Okley. Captain in 26th rgt. (N. 6, 1811).

Haddaway, Robert. Private in Capt. Edes' co. 27th rgt.

Haddaway, William. Private in Capt. Myers' co. Franklin Artillery.

Haden, Francis. Private in Capt. Edelin's so. 1st rgt.

Hadley, Joseph. Private in Capt. Addison's co. Sea Fencibles.

Hadley, Samuel. Sergeant in Capt. Pinney's co. 27th rgt.

Haeffer, Joel. Private in Capt. Hanna's co. Fells Point Light Dragoons.

Hafernagle, John. Private in Capt. Burke's co. 6th rgt.

Haftey, Jacob. Private in Capt. Smith's co. 51st rgt.

Hagan, Edward. Private in Capt. Crawford's co. 17th rgt.

Hagen, Michael. Private in Capt. McConkey's co. 27th rgt.

Hager, George. Private in Capt. McLaughlin's co. 50th rgt.

Hagg, John. Private in Capt. Stapleton's co. 39th rgt.

Haglen, Isaac. Private in Capt. Getzendanner's co. 16th rgt.

Hagner, George. Private in Capt. Adreon's co. Union Volunteers.

Hagner, John. Private in Capt. Watson's co. 39th rgt.

Hagthorp, Thomas. Private in Capt. Dyer's co. Fells Point Riflemen.

Hague, Joseph. Private in Capt. McDonald's co. 6th rgt.

Hague, William. Private in Capt. Hands' co. 21st rgt.

Hague, William. Private in Capt. Hynson's co. 21st rgt.

Hahn, David. Ensign in Capt. Hunter's co. 8th rgt. (Ag. 14, 1810).

Hahn, John. Sergeant in Capt. Berry's co. Washington Artillery.

Haislip, Charles. Corporal in Capt. Dunnington's co. 43d rgt.

Haislip, Hezekiah. Ensign in Capt. Burgess' co. 43d rgt.

Haislip, Humphrey B. Private in Capt. Piper's co. United Maryland Artillery.

Hale, Stephen. Private in Capt. Snowden's co. 36th rgt.

Hales, John A. Private in Capt. Dent's co. 43d rgt.

Haley, James. Private in Capt. Chambers' co. 21st rgt.

Halfpenny, John. Private in Capt. Faster's co. 51st rgt.

Hall, Amos. Captain in 4th rgt. (O. 1, 1811).

Hall, Andrew. Captain in 30th rgt. (Je. 26, 1812).

Hall, Andrew. Private in Capt. Thompson's co. 1st Baltimore Horse Artillery.

Hall, Baruch. Cornet in Capt. Hall's co. 2d rgt. 1st Cavalry Dist. (D. 22, 1812).

Hall, Benedict W. 3d Lieutenant in Capt. Thompson's Independent Artillery co. (D. 20, 1814) vice Patterson.

Hall, Benjamin. Private in Capt. Beall's co. 34th rgt.

Hall, Caleb. Private in Capt. Bouldin's co. Independent Light Dragoons.

Hall, Daniel. Private in Capt. Pumphrey's co. 22d rgt.

Hall, Edward. Private in Capt. Hancock's co. 22d rgt.

Hall, Edward. Private in Capt. Moale's co. Columbian Artillery.

Hall, Elijah. Private in Capt. Myers' co. Franklin Artillery.

Hall, Francis M. Major in 34th rgt. (Ja. 11, 1815).

Hall, George. Private in Capt. McKane's co. 27th rgt.

Hall, Grafton [1784-1822]. Private in Capt. Jackson's co. 34th rgt.; in Duvall's co.; in Capt. Isaac's co. in Capt. Beall's co.; in Capt. Marshall's co.

Hall, Dr. H. Surgeon in 2d rgt. Resigned Ja. 11, 1815.

Hall, Henry. 2d Lieutenant in Capt. Smith's co. 7th Cavalry Dist. (Mr. 16, 1812).

Hall, Henry. Private in Capt. Dyers' Fells Point Riflemen.

Hall, Henry. Private in Capt. McKane's co. 27th rgt.

Hall, Henry. Captain in 2d U. S. Light Dragoons (Mr. 12, 1812).

Hall, Henry F. Surgeon's mate in 32d U. S. Infantry (My. 17, 1813) ; Surgeon (Ap. 15, 1814).

Hall, Henry T. Private in Capt. Maynard's co. 22d rgt.

Hall, James. Private in Capt. Smith's co. 51st rgt.

Hall, James. Captain in 35th rgt. (My. 8, 1812).

Hall, James J. Private in Capt. Faster's co. 51st rgt.

Hall, John. Captain in 3d Cavalry Dist. (Jy. 28, 1812).

Hall, John. Private in Capt. McKane's co. 27th rgt.

Hall, John. Private in Capt. Pumphrey's co. 22d rgt.

Hall, John. Private in Capt. Stiles' Co. Marine Artillery.

Hall, John B. Sergeant, in Capt. Ringgold's co. 6th rgt.

Hall, John C. 1st Lieutenant in Capt. Evans' Artillery co. 1st Brigade (O. 21, 1808).

Hall, Joseph. Surgeon in 2d rgt. vice Dr. H. Hall resd.

Hall, Joseph. Private in Capt. Bunbury's co. Sea Fencibles.

Hall, Josiah. Private in Capt. Faster's co. 51st rgt.

Hall, Leonard. Lieutenant of the privateer *High Flyer,* July 1812; Capt. of the *Wasp,* Feb., 1813.

Hall, Lewis. Private in Capt. Kierstead's co. 6th rgt.

Hall, Mordecai. Private in Capt. Pumphrey's co. 22d rgt.

Hall, Mortimer D. Captain in 36th U. S. Infantry (Ap. 30, 1813).

Hall, Nathaniel. Private in Capt. Pumphrey's co. 22d rgt.

Hall, Nelson. Private in Capt. Waters' co. 22d rgt.

Hall, Nicholas, Jr. 2d Lieutenant in Capt. Cook's co. 2d rgt. 1st Cavalry Dist. (N. 16, 1812); Captain (D. 22, 1812).

Hall, Nicholas, Jr. Lieutenant in Capt. Cook's co. 13th rgt. (O. 3, 1807).

Hall, Richard. Ensign in Capt. Cook's co. 13th rgt. (O. 3, 1807).

Hall, Richard, Jr. Private in Capt. Waters' co. 22d rgt.

Hall, Richard, Sr. Private in Capt. Waters' co. 22d rgt.

Hall, Richard L. Captain in 34th rgt.

Hall, Richard M. Private in Capt. Levering's co. Independent Blues.

Hall, Richard T. Surgeon in 2d rgt., 1814.

Hall, Richard Wilmott [1785-1847]. Surgeon in 51st rgt. (Ja. 18, 1812).

Hall, Robert L. Paymaster in 41st rgt. (D. 22, 1808).

Hall, Solomon. Private in Capt. Blair's co. 50th rgt.

Hall, Thomas. Corporal in Capt. Dyer's co. Fells Point Riflemen.

Hall, Thomas B. Adjutant in 1st Cavalry Dist. (My. 8, 1812).

Hall, Thomas H. Captain in 2d rgt. (My. 9, 1808).

Hall, Thomas H. Private in Capt. Hall's co. 3d Cavalry rgt.

Hall, Thomas L. Ensign in Capt. Langley's co. 12th rgt. (Je. 27, 1812).

Hall, Thomas P. [1789-1825]. Surgeon in 36th rgt. U. S. Infantry (Jy. 10, 1813).

Hall, Washington. Quarter-master 6th rgt. (N. 9, 1814).

Hall, William. 1st Lieutenant in 38th U. S. Infantry (My. 20, 1813).

Hall, William. Private in Capt. Crawfurd's co. 17th rgt.

Hall, William. Private in Capt. McConckin's co. 38th rgt.

Hall, William J. Private in Capt. Hall's co. 3d Cavalry rgt.

Hall, William Wilmott [1787-   ]. Surgeon U. S. Rifles (Mr. 24, 1812).

Hall, Wright. 3d Lieutenant in 36th U. S. Infantry (Ap. 30, 1813); 2d Lieutenant (F. 21, 1814)

Haller, Tobias. 1st Lieutenant in Capt. Steiner's Frederick Artillery co. 9th Brigade (Ap. 4, 1808).

Halmon, Philemon. Private in Capt. Snowden's co. 36th rgt.

Halsy, Michael. Private in Capt. Rogers' co. 51st rgt.

Hambleton, Bates. Sergeant in Capt. Sample's co. 49th rgt.

Hambleton, Edward N. 2d Lieutenant in Capt. Goldsborough's co. 9th Cavalry Dist. (My. 8, 1812).

Hambleton, James. Cornet in Capt. Banning's co. 9th Cavalry Dist. (Mr. 25, 1812).

Hambley, James. Private in Capt. Addison's co. Sea Fencibles.

Hamer, Daniel. Sergeant in Capt. Miller's co. 39th rgt.

Hamilton, Gavin. Captain in 17th rgt.

Hamilton, James. Private in Capt. Pinney's co. 27th rgt.

Hamilton, James, Jr. Private in Capt. Levering's co. Independent Blues.

Hamilton, John. Ensign in Capt. Brashears' co. 13th rgt. (Ag. 20, 1814).

Hamilton, John. Private in Capt. Ringgold's co. 6th rgt.

Hamilton, John. Private in Capt. Lawrence's co. 6th rgt.

Hamilton, John. Private in Capt. Addison's co. Sea Fencibles.

Hamilton, John. Private in Capt. Miller's co. 39th rgt.

Hamilton, John A. Private in Capt. Watson's co. 39th rgt.

Hamilton, Lancelot C. Sergeant in Capt. Dent's co. 43d rgt.

Hamilton, Pliny. Private in Capt. Stiles' co. Marine Artillery.

Hamilton, Robert. Private in Capt. Dillon's co. 27th rgt.

Hamilton, Thomas. Surgeon in 27th rgt. (Ag. 28, 1807); in 39th rgt. 1813.

Hamilton, William. Lieutenant-Colonel in 43d rgt. [1813].

Hamilton, William. Sergeant in Capt. Dent's co. 43d rgt.

Hamilton, William. Private in Capt. Warfield's co. Balto. United Volunteers.

Hammell, Samuel. Private in Capt. Stiles' co. Marine Artillery.

Hammer, August. Private in Capt. Sadtler's co. Balto. Yägers.

Hammer, Daniel. Private in Capt. Stapleton's co. 39th rgt.

Hammer, George. Private in Capt. Horton's co. Maryland Chasseurs.

Hammer, Jacob. Private in Capt. Berry's co. Washington Artillery.

Hammer, William. Private in Capt. Blizzard's co. 15th rgt.

Hammet, Jesse. Private in Capt. Wilson's co. 6th rgt.

Hammett, Ignatius. Private in Capt. Hammett's co. 12th rgt.

Hammitt [Hammett], Robert. Captain in 12th rgt. (Je. 27, 1811).

Hammon, Joshua. Private in Capt. John Miller's co. 2d D. I.; b. Washington Co., Md.; age 22; farmer.

Hammond, Andrew. Private in Capt. Linthicum's co. 22d rgt.

Hammond, James. Captain in 32d rgt. (Ap. 5, 1808).

Hammond, John. Seaman of the privateer High Flyer, wounded in action, Dec., 1812.

Hammond, John. Private in Capt. Maynard's co. 22d rgt.

Hammond, Joseph. Private in Capt. Lawrence's co. 6th rgt.

Hammond, Larkin. Captain in 3d Cavalry Dist. (F. 13, 1812).

Hammond, Lloyd T. Paymaster in 32d rgt. (Je. 28, 1808).

Hammond, Rezin. Private in Capt. Hall's co. 3d Cavalry rgt.

Hammond, Rezin. Private in Capt. Linthicum's co. 22d rgt.

Hammond, William. Ensign in Capt. Marshall's co. 9th rgt. (Je. 19, 1812).

Hammond, William. Surgeon in 1st Cavalry Dist. (My. 8, 1812).

Hanawalt, Jacob. Private in Capt. Stewart's co. 51st rgt.

Hance, Francis, Jr. Ensign in Capt. Wilson's co. 31st rgt. (Je. 18, 1812).

Hance, Jacob B. Captain in 31st rgt.

Hance, James. Private in Capt. Levering's co. Independent Blues.

Hancock, Francis. Captain in 22d rgt. (Jy. 4, 1812).

Hancock, John. Private in Capt. Hancock's co. 22d rgt.

Hancock, Robert. Private in Capt. Stiles' co. Marine Artillery.

Hancock, Stephen. Private in Capt. Hancock's co. 22d rgt.

Hancock, Thomas G. Private in Capt. Posey's co. 1st rgt.

Hand, Bedingfield. Captain in 21st rgt. (Je. 12, 1812).

Handlin, Patrick. Gunner in Capt. Addison's co. Sea Fencibles.

Hands, Alexander. Adjutant in 9th Cavalry Dist. (D. 11, 1813).

Hands, Ephraim. Private in Capt. Addison's co. Sea Fencibles.

Hands, Nicholas. Private in Capt. Addison's co. Sea Fencibles.

Hands, P. G. Private in Capt. Sadtler's co. Balto. Yägers.

Hands, William G. Private in Capt. Magruder's co. American Artillerists.

Handy, George, Jr. Lieutenant in Capt. Walters' co. 23d rgt. (D. 7, 1813); Captain (S. 10, 1814).

Handy, Henry. Captain in 23d rgt. Resigned Jy. 14, 1814.

Handy, Robert J. H. 1st Lieutenant in Capt. White's co. 11th Cavalry Dist. (Je. 19, 1812) vice Holland; Captain (Ag 5, 1814); Colonel.

Handy, Robert J. H. Lieutenant-Colonel in 11th Cavalry Dist. (Je. 5, 1812).

Handy, Thomas. Captain in 23d rgt. (D. 10, 1813) vice Bell.

Handy, Thomas R. Colonel in 37th rgt. (1813); Brigadier-General in 10th Brigade (Mr. 29, 1813).

Handy, Thomas W. Surgeon's mate in 25th rgt. (D. 7, 1813); Surgeon vice McCrea (Jy. 15, 1814).

Handy, William S. 2d Lieutenant in Capt. A. E. Jones' co. 11th Cavalry Dist. (Je. 16, 1812).

Hane, Jacob, Jr. Private in Capt. Addison's co. Sea Fencibles.

Hanes, David. Private in Capt. Rogers' co. 51st rgt.

Hanes, James. Private in Capt. Bunbury's co. Sea Fencibles.

Haney, Charles. Private in Capt. Roney's co. 39th rgt.

Haney, Charles. Private in Capt. Shrim's co. Balto. Light Infantry.

Hanham, James R. [-1865]. Capt. U. S. Artillery Corps. (My. 12, 1814).

Hanks, Lewis. Private in Capt. Haubert's co. 51st rgt.

Hanlon, David. Private in Capt. Pinkney's Artillery co. 22d rgt.

Hanna, John. Captain in Fells Point Light Dragoons 5th Cavalry Dist. (Ag. 12, 1813).

Hanna, William. Ensign in Capt. McAdow's co. 42d rgt. (Je. 19, 1812).

Hanney, Jacob. Sergeant in Capt. Horton's co. Maryland Chasseurs; Cornet (D. 2, 1814).

Hanshaw, Charles. Private in Capt. Hancock's co. 22d rgt.

Hanshaw, John. Private in Capt. Snowden's co. 36th rgt.

Hanshaw, John. Private in Capt. Hancock's co. 22d rgt.

Hanshaw, Lloyd. Private in Capt. Hancock's co. 22d rgt.

Hanshew, Henry. Private in Capt. Steiner's Frederick Artillery.

Hansman, Henry. Private in Capt. Haubert's co. 51st rgt.

Hanson, Benedict H. Private in Capt. Dyer's co. Fells Point Riflemen.

Hanson, Henry. Private in Capt. Shrim's co. Balto. Light Infantry.

Hanson, Josiah H. 3d Lieutenant in U. S. Artillery Corps (D. 12, 1814).

Hanson, Nicholas. Private in Capt. Burke's co. 6th rgt.

Hanson, Samuel. Private in Capt. Dyer's co. 17th rgt.

Hanson, Samuel. Private in Capt. Dent's co. 43d rgt.

Hanson, Samuel, Jr. Private in Capt. Dent's co. 43d rgt.

Hanson, Thomas. Captain in 42d U. S. Infantry (Ag. 4, 1813).

Hanson, Thomas. Private in Capt. Maynard's co. 22d rgt.

Hanson, Thomas M. Private in Capt. Dent's co. 43d rgt.

Hanson, William. Private in Capt. Dent's co. 43d rgt.

Hanson, William. Private in Capt. Magruder's co. American Artillerists.

Hanson, William. Quarter-master Gunner in Capt. Addison's co. Sea Fencibles.

Hanson, William H. Lieutenant and Adjutant in 39th rgt. (D. 20, 1808).

Harbaugh, Daniel. Private in Capt. Smith's co. 51st rgt.

Harberger, George. 3d Lieutenant in 4th U. S. Infantry (D. 1, 1813); 1st Lieutenant (Je. 30, 1814).

Harbert, Zebedee. Private in Capt. Chambers' co. 21st rgt.

Harbin, Samuel P. Private in Capt. Posey's co. 1st rgt.

Harbison, Robert. Private in Capt. Haubert's co. 51st rgt.

Harbst, David. Ensign in Capt. Hievely's co. 15th rgt. (Ag. 22, 1812).

Hardacre, Mordecai. Private in Capt. Crawford's co. 17th rgt.

Hardacre, Moses. Private in Capt. Haden's co. 17th rgt.

Hardcastle, Henry P. Ensign in Capt. Hennix's co. 4th rgt. (Ag. 11, 1813).

Hardcastle, Peter. 2d Lieutenant in Capt. Goldsborough's co. 10th Cavalry Dist. (My. 20, 1813).

Hardcastle, William. 1st Lieutenant in Capt. Goldsborough's co. 10th Cavalry Dist. (My. 20, 1813).

Harden, Charles. Private in Capt. Blakistone's co. 45th rgt.

Harden, Samuel. Private in Capt. Sterett's Independent co.

Harden, Thomas. Private in Capt. Kierstead's co. 6th rgt.

Harden, Vachel. Private in Capt. Barnes' co. 32d rgt.

Harden, Walter. Sergeant in Capt. Dunnington's co. 43d rgt.

Hardesty, Henry. Private in Capt. Levering's co. Independent Blues.

Hardesty, Richard. Private in Capt. Wilson's co. 31st rgt.

Hardesty, Richard. Private in Capt. Cawood's co. 45th rgt.

Hardie, Robert [1798-1881]. Seaman on the privateer Nonsuch; captured and sent to Dartmoor prison.

Harding, Christopher. Private in Capt. Dyer's co. Fells Point Riflemen.

Harding, John. Private in Capt. Blair's co. 50th rgt.

Harding, John L. Private in Capt. Steiner's Frederick Artillery.

Harding, Nicholas. Lieutenant in Capt. Snowden's co. 36th rgt. (D. 24, 1810).

Harding, Stephen. Private in Capt. Piper's co. United Maryland Artillery.

Harding, Thomas. Sergeant in Capt. in Owings' co. 32d rgt.

Hardman, John. Musician in Capt. Schwartzauer's co. 27th rgt.

Hardy, Henry W. Sergeant in Capt. Smoot's co. 43d rgt.

Hardy, John F. Captain in 17th rgt. (O. 6, 1803).

Hardy, Joseph. Gunner in Rodman's Marine Battery; wounded Sept. 13, 1814.

Hardy, William. Corporal in Capt. Thos. Warner's co. 39th rgt.

Hare, Jesse. Private in Capt. McConkey's co. 27th rgt.

Hargrove, Theophilus. Private in Capt. Burgess' co. 43d rgt.; Quarter-master in 43d rgt. (Ag. 13, 1813).

Harker, John. Private in Capt. Pipers' co. United Maryland Artillery.

Harker, William. Private in Capt. Chalmers' co. 51st rgt.

Harkins, Giles. Private in Capt. Stapleton's co. 39th rgt.

Harley, Joseph. Private in Capt. Snowden's co. 36th rgt.

Harman, Daniel H. Private in Capt. Faster's co. 51st rgt.

Harman, Jacob. Private in Capt. Waters' co. 22d rgt.

Harman, John. Private in Capt. Shrim's co. Balto. Light Infantry.

Harmange, Peter. Private in Capt. Watson's co. 39th rgt.

Harn, John. Ensign in Capt. Pumphrey's co. 22d rgt. (S. 16, 1811).

Harn, Overton. Lieutenant in Capt. Magee's co. 20th rgt. (Ag. 1, 1814) vice Bond.

Harper, David. Private in Capt. Travers' co. 48th rgt.

Harper, John. Private in Capt. Deems' co. 51st rgt.

Harper, Peter. Private in Capt. Brown's co. 6th rgt.

Harper, Robert Goodloe [1765-1825]. Major-General in 3d Division (N. 8, 1814).

Harper, Samuel A. Lieutenant-Colonel in 9th rgt.

Harper, William. Captain in 11th rgt. (Je. 5, 1812).

Harr, William. Private in Capt. Dillon's co. 27th rgt.

Harrington, Edmond. Private in Capt. Travers' co. 48th rgt.

Harrington, Nicholas. Lieutenant in Capt. Fiddeman's co. 26th rgt. (Je. 26, 1812).

Harrington, Peter. Ensign in Capt. Woolford's co. 48th rgt. (S. 2, 1811).

Harrington, Samuel. Private in Capt. Crawfurd's co. 17th rgt.

Harrington, Samuel. Private in Capt. Travers' co. 48th rgt.

Harrington, Stuart. Private in Capt. Travers' co. 48th rgt.

Harrington, Thomas. Sergeant in Capt. Burke's co. 6th rgt.

Harris, Andrew. Sergeant in Capt. Gerry's co. 30th rgt.

Harris, Charles. Sergeant in Capt. Patton's co. 30th rgt.

Harris, David [1770-1845]. Lieutenant-Colonel in 1st rgt. Artillery (Je. 12, 1812); Attached to 3d Brigade.

Harris, Elijah. Private in Capt. Mackey's co. 49th rgt.

Harris, Firbin. Ensign in Capt. Elliott's co. 41st rgt. (My. 22, 1812).

Harris, George S. Private in Capt. Thompson's co. 43d rgt.

Harris, Henry of Amos. Captain in 19th rgt. (Ag. 10, 1813).

Harris, John. Private in Capt. Addison's co. Sea Fencibles.

Harris, Jonathan. Ensign in Capt. Griffith's co. 21st rgt. (Ag. 27, 1810).

Harris, Jonathan. Private in Capt. Griffith's co. 21st rgt.

Harris, Joseph. Major in 12th rgt.

Harris, Joseph. Private in Capt. Dobbin's co. 39th rgt.

Harris, Levin. Private in Capt. Brohawn's co. 48th rgt.

Harris, Levin. Private in Capt. Heath's co. 23d rgt.

Harris, Nathan. Lieutenant in Capt. Millard's co. 12th rgt.

Harris, Nehemiah. Private in Capt. Dyer's co. Fells Point Riflemen.

Harris, Runyon. Private in Capt. Thompson's co. 1st Baltimore Horse Artillery.

Harris, S. W. Private in Capt. McKane's co. 27th rgt.

Harris, Samuel. Private in Capt. Brown's co. Eagle Artillerists.

Harris, Samuel. Sergeant in Capt. Lawson's co. Balto. Patriots.

Harris, Samuel. Sergeant in Capt. Nicholson's co. Balto. Fencibles. Wounded at Fort McHenry.

Harris, Samuel H. Private in Capt. Moale's co. Columbian Artillery.

Harris, Thomas, Jr. Private in Capt. Maynard's co. 22d rgt.

Harris, Thomas W. Ensign in Capt. Leach's co. 31st rgt. (D. 23, 1813) vice Parran.

Harris, Tubman. Ensign in Capt. Heath's co. 23d rgt.

Harris, William. 2d Lieutenant in Capt. Atkinson's Artillery co. 10th Brigade (S. 26, 1812).

Harrison, Benjamin. Private in Capt. Steuart's co. Washington Blues.

Harrison, Charles. Private in Capt. Dyer's co. Fells Point Riflemen.

Harrison, George. Private in Capt. Shryock's co. 24th rgt.

Harrison, H. D. Private in Capt. Dent's co. 1st rgt.

Harrison, Henry. Private in Capt. Brown's co. 6th rgt.

Harrison, Henry. Sergeant in Capt. Thompson's co. 1st rgt.

Harrison, James. Private in Capt. Massey's co. 38th rgt.

Harrison, John. 1st Lieutenant of the privateer *Globe*, killed in action, Nov. 1, 1813.

Harrison, Joseph. Quarter-master in 1st rgt.

Harrison, Joseph. Private in Capt. McDonald's co. 6th rgt.

Harrison, Joseph G. Ensign in Capt. Simmons' co. 2d rgt. (Mr. 29, 1813).

Harrison, Nathan. Private in Capt. Cawood's co. 45th rgt.

Harrison, Nicholas. Private in Capt. McDonald's co. 6th rgt.

Harrison, Nicholas H. Private in Capt. Thompson's co. 1st rgt.

Harrison, Samuel. Private in Capt. McDonald's co. 6th rgt.

Harrison, Samuel. Sergeant in Capt. Lawrence's co. 6th rgt.

Harrison, Samuel of Jacob. Private in Capt. Wilson's co. 31st rgt.

Harrison, Stephen. Private in Capt. Smith's co. 51st rgt.

Harrison, Thomas. Private in Capt. Lawrence's co. 6th rgt.

Harrison, Thomas. Private in Capt. McDonald's co. 6th rgt.

Harrison, Thomas. Private in Capt. Maynard's co. 22d rgt.

Harrison, Thomas E. Sergeant in Capt. Sotheran's co. 45th rgt.

Harrison, William. Private in Capt. Galt's co. 6th rgt.

Harrison, William. Private in Capt. Massey's co. 38th rgt.

Harrison, William, Jr. 1st Lieutenant in Capt. Goldsborough's co. 9th Cavalry Dist. (My. 8, 1812).

Harrison, William S. 2d Lieutenant in Capt. Larrimore's Artillery co. 6th Brigade (S. 2, 1811); Private in Capt. Hayward's co. 4th rgt.

Harrison, Williamson. Private in Capt. Barnes' co. 32d rgt.

Harry, George. 2d Lieutenant in Capt. Quantrill's co. 24th rgt.

Harry, John. Private in Capt. Burgess' co. 43d rgt.

Harry, John. Sergeant in Capt. Quantrill's co. 24th rgt.

Harry, John. Captain in 24th rgt. Resigned Jy. 12, 1814.

Harry, Samuel. Private in Capt. Quantrill's co. 24th rgt.

Harry, William. Private in Capt. Quantrill's co. 24th rgt.

Harryman, George. Quarter-master in 7th rgt. (D. 2, 1807); Brigade Quarter-master in 11th Brigade.

Harryman, S. Private in Capt. Dillon's co. 27th rgt.

Harryman, Stephen. Private in Capt. Hanna's co. Fells Point Light Dragoons.

Harsnipe, William. Surgeon in 15th rgt. (My. 13, 1813).

Hart, Asa. Seaman of the privateer Globe, wounded in action Nov. 1, 1813, and died of his wounds.

Hart, Daniel. Private in Capt. Maynard's co. 22d rgt.

Hart, Henry. Private in Capt. Levering's co. Independent Blues.

Hart, Joseph. Ensign in Capt. Ringgold's co. 6th rgt. (Jy. 12, 1814).

Hart, Joseph. Private in Capt. Smith's co. 51st rgt.

Hart, Michael. Private in Capt. Marker's co. 28th rgt.

Hart, Richard. Private in Capt. Crawford's co. 17th rgt.

Hart, Robert. Capt. of the privateer Orb, Dec., 1813.

Hart, Robert. Quarter-master in 48th rgt. (Je. 29, 1808).

Hart, William. Private in Capt. Levering's co. Independent Blues.

Hart, William. Private in Capt. Snowden's co. 36th rgt.

Hartley, Thomas. Private in Capt. Wickes' co. 21st rgt.

Harvey, Andrew. 1st Lieutenant in Capt. Damsell's Artillery co. 1st Brigade (D. 10, 1813).

Harvey, Arthur. Private in Capt. Sample's co. 49th rgt.

Harvey, Benjamin. Private in Capt. King's co. 49th rgt.

Harvey, James. Captain in Extra Battalion Harford Co. (S. 2, 1811).

Harvey, Nathan. Private in Capt. Travers' co. 48th rgt.

Harvey, William. Private in Capt. Crawford's co. 17th rgt.

Harwood, Benjamin. Private in Capt. Lawrence's co. 6th rgt.

Harwood, Charles. Private in Capt. Pennington's co. Balto. Independent Artillerists.

Harwood, Edward. Quarter-master in 17th rgt.

Harwood, Frederick. Private in Capt. Chase's co. 22d rgt.

Harwood, Henry Hall. Quarter-master in 22d rgt. (Ag. 4, 1807).

Harwood, Henry S. Private in Capt. Maynard's co. 22d rgt.; Corporal in Capt. Chase's co. 1814.

Harwood, J. T. Private in Capt. Pinkney's Artillery co. 22d rgt.

Harwood, James. Private in Capt. Dobbin's co. 39th rgt.

Harwood, Joseph. Paymaster in 2d rgt. (O. 12, 1807).

Harwood, Richard of Thomas. Private in Capt. Maynard's co. 22d rgt.

Harwood, Thomas. Sergeant in Capt. Dobbin's co. 39th rgt.

Harwood, Thomas. Private in Capt. Wells' Artillery co. 22d rgt.

Harwood, William. 3d Lieutenant in 38th U. S. Infantry (My. 20, 1813); 2d Lieutenant (My. 1, 1814); Regimental Quartermaster June, 1814.

Haseltine, Charles. Captain in 8th rgt. Rsd. S. 20, 1813.

Hash, Peter. Private in Capt. Bunbury's co. Sea Fencibles.

Haslam, John. Veterinary Surgeon in 5th Cavalry rgt.

Haslet, James. Private in Capt. Myers' co. 39th rgt.

Haslett, Charles. Private in Capt. Kennedy's co. 27th rgt.

Haslett, James. Brigade Major in 11th Brigade.

Hasley, Samuel. Private in Capt. Watson's co. 39th rgt.

Haslup, Jesse. Sergeant in Capt. Montgomery's co. Balto. Union Artillery.

Hass, William. Private in Capt. Shrim's co. Balto. Light Infantry.

Hassard, Ralph. Private in Capt. Smith's co. 51st rgt.

Hasselman, Lewis. Private in Capt. Sadtler's co. Balto. Yägers.

Hassen, Alexander. Private in Capt. Mackey's co. 49th rgt.

Hassett, John. Private in Capt. Massey's co. 38th rgt.

Hatch, Samuel. Private in Capt. Galt's co. 6th rgt.

Hatcher, John. Private in Capt. Dent's co. 43d rgt.

Hatcherson, James. Private in Capt. Usselton's Artillery co. 6th Brigade.

Hatcherson, Thomas. Private in Capt. Brown's co. 6th rgt.

Hatchison [Hatcherson], John. Captain in 9th rgt. (Jy. 8, 1814).

Hatfield, Edward. Private in Capt. Linthicum's co. 22d rgt.

Hatfield, Jacob. Private in Capt. Jacob Miller's co. 2d D. I.; b. Washington Co. Md.; age 23; shoe-maker; subs. for William Vanlier.

Hatfield, Samuel. Private in Capt. Barnes' co. 32d rgt.

Hatherly, John. Captain in 22d rgt. (Ap. 28, 1814).

Hatten, Aquila. Private in Capt. Steever's co. 27th rgt.

Hatten, Caleb. Private in Capt. Steever's co. 27th rgt.

Hatton, Hagerty. Private in Capt. Ringgold's co. 6th rgt.

Hatton, John. Private in Capt. Peters' co. 51st rgt.

Hatton, Joshua. Private in Capt. Chalmers' co. 51st rgt.

Haubert, Jacob. Private in Capt. Warfield's co. Balto. United Volunteers. Killed at North Point.

Haubert, Michael [1779-1814]. Captain in 51st rgt. Resigned Dec., 1814.

Hauer, Daniel, Jr. Captain in 1st Cavalry Dist. (Mr. 16, 1812); Major (My. 13, 1813).

Hauer, George. Private in Capt. Steiner's Frederick Artillery.

Hauer, Henry. 3d Corporal in Capt. Steiner's Frederick Artillery.

Haughey, William. Lieutenant in Capt. Moore's co. 49th rgt.

Haulman [Hollman], William. Private in Capt. Pinkney's Artillery co. 22d rgt.

Hauptman, Daniel. Private in Capt. Moale's co. Columbian Artillery.

Hauptman, John. Private in Capt. Pinney's co. 27th rgt.

Hauser, Isaac, Jr. Captain in 10th rgt. (S. 20, 1813).

Havener, Benedict. Private in Capt. Crawfurd's co. 17th rgt.

Hawder, George. Seaman of Barney's flotilla; captured at Bladensburg.

Hawes, Frederick. Private in Capt. A. E. Warner's co. 39th rgt.

Hawes, James. Private in Capt. Heath's co. 23d rgt.

Hawkey, Samuel. Private in Capt. Shryock's co. 24th rgt.

Hawkins, Aaron. Private in Capt. Linthicum's co. 22d rgt.

Hawkins, Aaron of Aaron. Private in Capt. Linthicum's co. 22d rgt.

Hawkins, Caleb. Brigadier-General (Charles Co.) April, 1813.

Hawkins, Daniel. Private in Capt. Quantrill's co. 24th rgt.

Hawkins, Daniel. Private in Capt. Dyer's co. Fells Point Riflemen.

Hawkins, George. Lieutenant in Capt. Suddon's co. 46th rgt. (Ja. 22, 1811).

Hawkins, Isaac. Lieutenant in Capt. Harvey's co. Extra Battalion Harford Co. (S. 2, 1811).

Hawkins, James. Private in Capt. Aisquith's co. Sharp Shooters.

Hawkins, James L. Private in Capt. Nicholson's co. Balto. Fencibles. Wounded at Fort McHenry.

Hawkins, Joseph. Private in Capt. Linthicum's co. 22d rgt.

Hawkins, Ralph. Private in Capt. Linthicum's co. 22d rgt.

Hawkins, Robert. Lieutenant in Capt. Stephenson's co. 42d rgt. (D. 10, 1807).

Hawkins, Samuel. Lieutenant-Colonel in 1st rgt.

Hawkins, Samuel. Private in Capt. Linthicum's co. 22d rgt.

Hawkins, Thomas. Private in Capt. Posey's co. 1st rgt.

Hawley, Irza. Private in Capt. McKane's co. 27th rgt.

Hawney, Samuel. Corporal in Capt. Lawrence's co. 6th rgt.

Hay, David. Private in Capt. Watson's co. 39th rgt.

Hay, George. Private in Capt. Myers' co. Franklin Artillery.

Hay, John. Sergeant in Capt. Scott's co. 35th rgt.

Hayden, Azariah. Private in Capt. Cawood's co. 45th rgt.

Hayden, Bartholomew. Private in Capt. Melton's co. 45th rgt.

Hayden, Dennis. Private in Capt. Howard's co. Mechanical Volunteers.

Hayden, George. Sergeant in Capt. Briscoe's co. 45th rgt.

Hayden, Horace H. Sergeant in Capt. Thos. Warner's co. 39th rgt.

Hayden, Joseph. Private in Capt. Melton's co. 45th rgt.

Hayden, Stephen K. Private in Capt. Burgess' co. 43d rgt.

Hayden, William of Wm. Private in Capt. Millard's co. 12th rgt.

Hayes, Abraham. Private in Capt. Chalmers' co. 51st rgt.

Hayes, Adam. Private in Capt. Bunbury's co. Sea Fencibles.

Hayes, Bartholomew. Private in Capt. Travers' co. 48th rgt.

Hayes, George. Private in Capt. Morgan's co. 49th rgt.

Hayes, John. Private in Capt. Morgan's co. 49th rgt.

Hayes, John. Private in Capt. Adreon's co. Union Volunteers.

Hayes, Nathan W. Sergeant in Capt. John Miller's co. 2d D. I.; b. Sharpsburg, Md.; age 22; joiner; subs. for Gabriel Thomas.

Hayes, Robert. Private in Capt. Morgan's co. 49th rgt.

Hayes, Walter Cody [1778-1826]. Private in Capt. Stiles' co. Marine Artillery.

Hayes, William. Private in Capt. Brown's co. 49th rgt.

Hayes, William. Private in Capt. Faster's co. 51st rgt.

Hayley, Henry. Private in Capt. Pinney's co. 27th rgt.

Hayman, Isaiah. Private in Capt. Heath's co. 23d rgt.

Hayman, William. Private in Capt. Heath's co. 23d rgt.

Hayne, George. Private in Capt. Pennington's co. Balto. Independent Artillerists.

Hays, Henry. Private in Capt. Travers' co. 48th rgt.

Hays, John. Lieutenant in Capt. McAdow's co. 42d rgt. (O. 3, 1807).

Hays, Reverdy. Private in Capt. Warfield's co. Balto. United Colunteers. Wounded at North Point.

Hays, Robert. Lieutenant in Capt. Wise's co. 24th rgt. (Jy. 12, 1814) vice Brown.

Hays, Robert. Private in Capt. Edes' co. 27th rgt.

Hays, Samuel. Private in Capt. Travers' co. 48th rgt.

Hays, Simeon. Seaman of the letter of-marque brig *Matilda;* captured and sent to Dartmoor; exchanged; seaman of the privateer *Surprise;* again captured and sent to Dartmoor.

Hays, Thomas A. Quarter-master in 40th rgt. (Ap. 22, 1808).

Hays, William. Private in Capt. Snowden's co. 36th rgt.

Hayward, John. Private in Capt. Fallin's co. 48th rgt.

Hayward, John. Private in Capt. McKane's co. 27th rgt.

Hayward, William, Jr. Captain in 4th rgt. (S. 10, 1814).

Haywood ,John. Private in Capt. Williams' co. 12th rgt.

Hazledine, John. Private in Capt. Aisquith's co. Sharp Shooters.

Hazletine, David. Private in Capt. Montgomery's co. Balto. Union Artillery.

Head, Benjamin P. Ensign in 38th U. S. Infantry (My. 20, 1813).

Head, John. 2d Lieutenant in Capt. Johnson's co. 2d rgt. 1st Cavalry Dist. (Ja. 1, 1813).

Headington, Laban. Sergeant in Capt. Frizzell's co. 15th rgt.

Headington, Nicholas [1789-1856]. Private in Capt. Gorsuch's co., Randall's Battalion of Riflemen, 2d rgt.

Heard, Benedict I. Ensign in 14th U. S. Infantry (S. 16, 1814); 3d Lieutenant (O. 1, 1814).

Heard, Benjamin I. Sergeant-Major in 45th rgt.

Heard, John. Private in Capt. Conway's co. 6th rgt.

Heard, Joseph. Lieutenant in Capt. Williams' co. 12th rgt.

Hearn, Isaac. Ensign in Capt. Owings' co. 32d rgt. (S. 19, 1899).

Hearsey, George T. Private in Capt. Warfield's co. Balto. United Volunteers. Captured at North Point.

Hearth, J. T. Private in Capt. Stiles' co. Marine Artillery.

Heary, David. Private in Capt. Mc-Donald's co. 6th rgt.

Heater, George. Ensign in Capt. Heater's co. 44th rgt. Resigned D. 16, 1813.

Heater, John. Captain in 44th rgt. (Ag. 22, 1812).

Heath, John. Private in Capt. Blizzard's co. 15th rgt.

Heath, Josiah Wilson. Captain in 23d rgt.; Major (D. 16, 1814) vice Carroll.

Heath, Richard Key [-1821]. 1st Major in 5th rgt.; Lieutenant-Colonel 5th rgt.; vice Sterett (D. 20, 1814).

Heath, Samuel. Lieutenant in 23d rgt.

Heath, Upton S. 1st Lieutenant in Columbian Artillery (My. 22, 1812); 1st Lieutenant and Adjutant in 1st rgt. Artillery (Ap. 23, 1813); 1st Lieutenant United Maryland Artillery (O. 15, 1814) vice Barney.

Heath, William. Private in Capt. Shryock's co. 24th rgt.

Heathers, Samuel. Private in Capt. McConckin's co. 38th rgt.

Hebb, Henry. Private in Capt. McKane's co. 27th rgt.

Hedges, Joseph. Adjutant in 29th rgt. (S. 20, 1802).

Hedges, Moses. 1st Lieutenant in Capt. Fulton's co. 2d rgt. 1st Cavalry Dist. (Mr. 23, 1814).

Hedges, Peter. Private in Capt. Rogers' co. 51st rgt.

Hedrick, Joseph. Private in Capt. Miller's co. 2d D. I.; b. Washington Co., Md.; age 25; wheelwright; subs. for Dr. Fauny Prentice.

Heffner, Jacob. Private in Capt. Getzendanner's co. 16th rgt.

Heffner, John of Fr. Lieutenant in Capt. Mantz's co. 16th rgt. (Jy. 15, 1814).

Heffner, Lawrence. Private in Capt. Getzendanner's co. 16th rgt.

Heffner, Michael. Private in Capt. Steiner's Frederick Artillery.

Heflebower, John. Private in 24th rgt.

Heidelbaugh, George. Private in Capt. Levering's co. Independent Blues.

Heislet, Hezekiah. Ensign in Capt. Gray's co. 43d rgt. (Jy. 7, 1814).

Helm, Leonard. Private in Capt. Berry's co. Washington Artillery.

Helms, Henry. Surgeon's mate 10th Cavalry Dist. (D. 11, 1812).

Helms, John A. Lieutenant in Capt. Coats' co. 36th rgt. (Jy. 13, 1814) vice Wm. Brown.

Helms, Richard. Fifer in Capt. Rogers' co. 51st rgt.

Helser, Philip. Private in Capt. Quantrill's co. 24th rgt.

Heltebridle, Jacob. Private in Capt. Frizzell's co. 15th rgt.

Heltebridle, John. Private in Capt. Frizzell's co. 15th rgt.

Hemand, Joseph. Captain in 38th rgt.

Hemling, Anthony. Private in Capt. Watson's co. 39th rgt.

Hemphill, James. Private in Capt. Moore's co. 49th rgt.

Hemphill, Joseph. Private in Capt. Quantrill's co. 24th rgt.

Hempstone, Christian. Captain in 3d rgt. (O. 12, 1807).

Hemsley, Jabez. Private in Capt. Massey's co. 38th rgt.

Hemsley, Philemon W. Cornet in Capt. Goldsborough's co. 9th Cavalry Dist. (My. 8, 1812).

Henck, F. W. Sergeant in Capt. Sadtler's co. Balto. Yägers.

Henderson, Andrew. Cornet in Capt. Evans' co. 8th Cavalry Dist. (Ap. 23, 1812).

Henderson, Andrew F. Sergeant-Major in 49th rgt.; Adjutant.

Henderson, Benjamin. Private in Capt. Haubert's co. 51st rgt.

Henderson, David. Private in Capt. Haubert's co. 51st rgt.

Henderson, George. 2d Lieutenant in Capt. Smith's co. 7th Regimental Cavalry Dist. (Ap. 25, 1812) vice Hall.

Henderson, John. Lieutenant in Capt. Allen's co. 49th rgt.

Henderson, John. Private in Capt. Edes' co. 27th rgt.

Henderson, John. Private in Capt. Thompson's co. 1st Baltimore Horse Artillery.

Henderson, Peter [1790-1845]. Private in Capt. Haubert's co. 51st rgt.

Henderson, Robert. Private in Capt. Stiles' co. Marine Artillery.

Henderson, Robert. Private in Capt. Deems' co. 51st rgt.

Henderson, Zachariah. Private in Capt. Haubert's co. 51st rgt.

Hendrick, Daniel. Lieutenant in Capt. Oldham's co. 49th rgt.

Hendrick, Zecheriah. Private in Capt. Fowler's co. 46th rgt.

Hendrickson, Jeremiah. Private in Capt. Brown's co. 49th rgt.

Hendrixon, Thomas. Private in Capt. Blair's co. 50th rgt.

Hendry, Thomas, Jr. Private in Capt. Pinkney's Artillery co. 22d rgt.

Henegar, Frederick. Private in Capt. Peters' co. 51st rgt.

Heneker, Peter. Private in Capt. Stewart's co. 51st rgt.

Henneman, Isaac. Private in Capt. Myers' co. Franklin Artillery.

Henneman, Jacob. Private in Capt. Myers' co. Franklin Artillery.

Hennessy, Thomas. Private in Capt. Nicholson's co. Balto. Fencibles.

Hennick, George. Major in 39th rgt. (Mr. 24, 1814).

Hennicks, Joseph. Private in Capt. Snowden's co. 36th rgt.

Henning, Frederick. Private in Jarboe's co. 12th rgt.

Henning, George. Private in Capt. Shrim's co. Balto. Light Infantry.

Hennix, Thomas. Captain in 4th rgt. (My. 8, 1812).

Henricks, Thomas. Ensign in Capt. Shock's co. 41st rgt. (Je. 22, 1808).

Henry, Francis. Private in Capt. Deems' co. 51st rgt.

Henry, Hugh. Private in Capt. Deems' co. 51st rgt.

Henry, John. Private in Capt. Bunbury's co. Sea Fencibles.

Henry, John. Private in Capt. Shryock's co. 24th rgt.

Henry, Thomas. Private in Ensign Brewer's detachment, 36th rgt.; Private in Capt. Slicer's co. 22d rgt.

Henry, William. Cornet in Capt. Linthicum's co. 2d Cavalry Dist. (Je. 12, 1812).

Henry, William. Privateersman of the *Joseph and Mary* captured by the frigate *Narcissus* and sent into Jamaica.

Henry, William. Private in Capt. Aisquith's co. Sharp Shooters.

Henshaw, John. Sergeant in Capt. Smith's co. 51st rgt.

Henwood, Joshua. Private in Capt. Bouldin's co. Independent Light Dragoons.

Hepborn, Thomas. Sergeant in Capt. Tilghman's co. 33d rgt.

Hepburn, Samuel. Surgeon's mate 14th rgt. (F. 4, 1808).

Herbert, Charles. Private in Capt. Myers' co. Franklin Artillery.

Herbert, James. Sergeant in Capt. Melton's co. 45th rgt.; Ensign (Jy. 7, 1814) vice Price.

Herbert, John. Captain in 42d rgt. (Ap. 4, 1808).

Herbert, John. Private in Capt. Sterett's Independent co.

Herbert, John C. Captain "Bladensburg Troop of Horse" in 2d Cavalry Dist. (Ag. 11, 1813) vice Cross.

Herbert, Robert. Private in Capt. Blakistone's co. 45th rgt.

Herbert, Stewart. Ensign in Capt. Quantrill's co. 24th rgt. (Je. 16, 1812).

Herbert, Thomas. Private in Capt. Ringgold's co. 6th rgt.

Herbert, Warren. Private in Capt. Posey's co. 1st rgt.

Herbert, William P. Private in Capt. McKane's co. 27th rgt.

Herman, John. Private in Capt. Getzendanner's co. 16th rgt.

Hermitage, James. Private in Capt. Snowden's co. 36th rgt.

Heron, Alexander. Private in Capt. McConkey's co. 27th rgt.

Herring, George. 2d Lieutenant in Capt. Berry's co. Washington Artillery (Mr. 24, 1814) vice Taylor.

Herring, Henry. Private in Capt. Sterett's co. 1st Balto. Hussars.

Herring, Jacob. Ensign in Capt. Alexander's co. 28th rgt. (Jy. 24, 1814).

Herrington, Richard. Private in Capt. Comegys' co. 21st rgt.

Heslip, John. Private in Capt. McConkey's co. 27th rgt.

Hess, Charles. Lieutenant in Capt. Cornell's co. 47th rgt. (My. 22, 1812).

Hess, Jacob. Corporal in Capt. Shryock's co. 24th rgt.

Hess, Jesse. Private in Capt. Magruder's co. American Artillerists.

Hess, Joseph. Private in Capt. Magruder's co. American Artillerists.

Hessey, Henry. Ensign in Capt. John Owings' co. 36th rgt. (Ag. 29, 1812).

Hetzelberger, John. Private in in Capt. Piper's co. United Maryland Artillery.

Hetzler, John. Private in Capt. Bader's co. Union Yägers.

Hewett, Michael. Private in Capt. Dobbin's co. 39th rgt.

Hewitt, Edmund. Private in Capt. Chase's co. 22d rgt. [Nov., 1814]. Private in Capt. Pinkney's Artillery co. [Aug., 1813].

Hewitt, Elmer. Private in Capt. Ringgold's co. 6th rgt.

Hewitt, Jacob R. Sergeant in Capt. Moore's co. 49th rgt.

Hewitt, Joseph. Private in Capt. Travers' co. 48th rgt.

Hewitt, William. Gun-Captain in Capt. Brown's co. 49th rgt.

Hewitt, William. Private in Capt. Montgomery's co. Balto. Union Artillery.

Hews, Henry. Private in Capt. Galloway's co. 46th rgt.

Heyat, William. Ensign in Capt. Phillips' co. 3d rgt. (O. 12, 1807).

Hibbert, Solomon. Private in Capt. Pinney's co. 27th rgt.

Hickinbottom, James. Private in Capt. Chambers' co. 21st rgt.

22

Hickman, David. Private in Capt. Green's co. 46th rgt.
Hickman, Jacob. Ensign in Capt. Fisher's co. 19th rgt. (My. 10, 1813).
Hickman, John. Private in Capt. Green's co. 46th rgt.
Hicks, Elijah. Private in Capt. Dillon's co. 27th rgt.
Hicks, John. Private in Capt. Magruder's co. American Artillerists.
Hicks, John. Private in Capt. Roney's co. 39th rgt.
Hicks, John. Sergeant in Capt. McConkey's co. 27th rgt.
Hievely, John. Captain in 15th rgt. (Ag. 22, 1812).
Highbarger, David. 2d Sergeant in Capt. Miller's co. 2d D. I.; b. Sharpsburgh, Md.; age 20; joiner; volunteer.
Higby, Noah. Quarter-Gunner in Capt. Bunbury's co. Sea Fencibles.
Higden, Ralph. Private in Capt. Roney's co. 39th rgt.
Higdon, Benjamin D. Sergeant in Capt. Sterett's Independent co.
Higdon, Francis, Jr. Private in Capt. Posey's co. 1st rgt.
Higdon, Leonard. Private in Capt. Posey's co. 1st rgt.
Higginbottom, John. Private in Capt. Nicholson's co. Balto. Fencibles.
Higginbottom, Thomas. Private in Capt. Moale's co. Columbian Artillery.
Higgins, Benjamin. Captain in 44th rgt. (Jy. 20, 1812).
Higgins, James. Private in Capt. Massey's co. 38th rgt.
Higgins, John. Private in Capt. McConckin's co. 38th rgt.

Higgins, Joshua C. Major in 2d rgt. Died 1815.
Higgs, Alexander. Private in Capt. Cawood's co. 45th rgt.
Higgs, Thomas. Private in Capt. John Miller's co. 2d D. I.; b. Washington Co., Md.; age 33; laborer.
High, David. Private in Capt. Smith's co. 51st rgt.
High, James. Private in Capt. Dobbin's co. 39th rgt.
Hilbert, Henry. Corporal in Capt. Berry's co. Washington Artillery.
Hilbert, John. Private in Capt. Berry's co. Washington Artillery.
Hildebrand, John. Ensign in Capt. Getzendanner's co. 16th rgt. (S. 18, 1812).
Hildebrandt, Andrew. Private in Capt. Adreon's co. Union Volunteers.
Hildebrandt, Christian. Private in Capt. Adreon's co. Union Volunteers.
Hildt, John [1775-1862]. Ensign in Capt. Stewart's co. 51st rgt.
Hill, Alexander. Private in Capt. McConkey's co. 27th rgt.
Hill, Arthur. Private in Capt. Montgomery's co. Balto. Union Artillery.
Hill, George, Jr. Private in Capt. Pike's co. Balto. Volunteer Artillery.
Hill, Henry Oswell. 2d Lieutenant in 5th U. S. Infantry (Ja. 3, 1812); 1st Lieutenant (Ja. 31, 1814).
Hill, John. Private in Capt. Getzendanner's co. 16th rgt.
Hill, John. Private in Capt. Stiles' co. Marine Artillery.
Hill, Joseph. Sergeant in Capt. Burke's co. 6th rgt.

Hill, Peter. Private in Capt. John Miller's co. 2d D. I.; b. Washington Co., Md.; age 22; shoemaker; volunteer.

Hill, Richard. Lieutenant in Capt. Waring's co. 14th rgt. (Je. 18, 1794).

Hill, Thomas. Private in Capt. Tilghman's co. 33d rgt.

Hill, Thomas. Private in Capt. Steuart's co. Washington Blues.

Hill, Thomas F. Cornet in Capt. Hooper's co. 10th Cavalry Dist. (D. 22, 1814) vice Robert Pitt.

Hill, Thomas Gardner [1793-1849]. Sergeant in Capt. McKane's co. 27th rgt.

Hill, William. Lieutenant in Capt. Crawford's co. 17th rgt. (Jy. 10, 1812).

Hilleary, Lloyd. 3d Lieutenant in U. S. Light Artillery (Ag. 1, 1813).

Hillen, John. Lieutenant in Capt. Sterett's Independent co.

Hillen, John J. Quartermaster in 31st rgt. (F. 25, 1811).

Hillen, Solomon [1770-1841]. Private in Capt. Magruder's co. American Artillerists.

Hillert, John A. Private in Capt. Stiles' co. Marine Artillery.

Hillery, Osborn. Captain in 13th rgt. (O. 24, 1800).

Hillery, William. Surgeon in 28th rgt. (O. 15, 1801).

Hilton, Abraham. Private in Capt. Fowler's co. 46th rgt.

Hilton, Henry. Private in Capt. Cawood's co. 45th rgt.

Hilton, Henry. Private in Capt. Edelin's co. 1st rgt.

Hilton, James G. Sergeant in Capt. Thos. Warner's co. 39th rgt.

Hindes, John. Private in Capt. Ringgold's co. 6th rgt.

Hindes, M. Private in Capt. Sterett's Independent co.

Hindman, Jacob [-1827]. Captain in 2d U. S. Artillery (Jy. 2, 1812); Major (Je. 26, 1813); bvt. Lieutenant-Colonel for distinguished services in defense of Ft. Erie, U. C.

Hindman, William, Jr. 3d Lieutenant in 36th U. S. Infantry (Ap. 30, 1813); 1st Lieutenant in 3d U. S. Rifles (Mr. 17, 1814).

Hinds, John. Sergeant in Capt. Roney's co. 39th rgt.

Hinds, William. Private in Capt. Shrim's co. Balto. Light Infantry.

Hines, George. Private in Capt. John Miller's co. 2d D. I.; b. Washington Co., Md.; age 22; laborer; volunteer; deserted from Patapsco encampment Jy. 1, 1813.

Hines, Peter. Cornet in Capt. Gist's co. 2d rgt. 1st Cavalry Dist. (My. 31, 1813); 2d Lieutenant (Jy. 28, 1813).

Hinhart, Abraham. Seaman of the privateer *Globe*, wounded in action Nov. 1, 1813, and died of his wounds.

Hinkle, Alpheus. Sergeant in Capt. Blair's co. 50th rgt.

Hinkley, William. Private in Capt. McConkey's co. 27th rgt.

Hinneman, William. Private in Capt. Stewart's co. 51st rgt.

Hins, Anthony. Lieutenant in Capt. Hievely's co. 15th rgt. (Ag. 22, 1812).

Hinton, Dennis. Private in Capt. Galt's co. 6th rgt.

Hinton, Dennis. Private in Capt. Pumphrey's co. 22d rgt.

Hinton, James. Private in Capt. Deems' co. 51st rgt.

Hinton, Robert. Private in Capt. Veitch's co. 34th rgt.

Hinton, Robert W. Private in Capt. Burke's co. 6th rgt.

Hinton, Thomas. Private in Capt. Dillon's co. 27th rgt.

Hipsey, George, Jr. 1st Lieutenant in Capt. Berry's co. Washington Artillery (Ag. 15, 1812) vice Myers.

Hirsch, Martin. Corporal in Capt. Bader's co. Union Yägers.

Hiser, John. Private in Capt. Watson's co. 39th rgt.

Hiss, Jacob. Private in Capt. Peters' co. 51st rgt.

Hiss, Philip. Private in Capt. Steever's co. 27th rgt.

Hissey, Archibald. Private in Capt. Haubert's co. 51st rgt.

Hissey, Archibald. Private in Capt. Roney's co. 39th rgt.

Hissey, Caleb. Private in Capt. Haubert's co. 51st rgt.

Hitchcock, Nathaniel. Cornet in Capt. Bouldin's co. Independent Light Dragoons 5th Cavalry Dist. (N. 8, 1814).

Hitchcock, William. Captain in 41st rgt. (O. 15, 1795).

Hites, Abraham. 1st Lieutenant in Capt. Thompson's co. 2d rgt. 1st Cavalry Dist. (D. 22, 1812).

Hitzelberger Anthony. Private in Capt. Howard's co. Mechanical Volunteers.

Hitzelberger, John. Private in Capt. Sadtler's co. Balto. Yägers.

Hix, William. Private in Capt. Myers' co. 39th rgt.

Hoake, John. Private in Capt. Blizzard's co. 15th rgt.

Hoar, Elias. Private in Capt. Howard's co. Mechanical Volunteers.

Hobbs, Charles. Captain in 38th rgt. (Ag. 27, 1810).

Hobbs, Daniel. Private in Capt. Snowden's co. 36th rgt.

Hobbs, George W. Captain in 32d rgt. (Jy. 6, 1814) vice George Barnes.

Hobbs, Lanvac. Private in Capt. Ducker's co. 7th rgt.

Hobbs, Patrick. Private in Capt. Barnes' co. 32d rgt.

Hobbs, William. Private in Capt. Ducker's co. 7th rgt.

Hobbs, William. Corporal in Capt. Barnes' co. 32d rgt.

Hobbs, William. Private in Capt. Smith's co. 51st rgt.

Hobbs, William C. [-1815]. 1st Lieutenant in 36th U. S. Infantry (Ap. 30, 1813); Captain (S. 30, 1814).

Hoblitzell, Samuel. Private in Capt. McLaughlin's co. 50th rgt.

Hoburg, Harman. Private in Capt. Shrim's co. Balto. Light Infantry.

Hoburg, John. Sergeant in Capt. Shrim's co. Balto. Light Infantry.

Hockensmith, George. Lieutenant in Capt. Sluss' co. 47th rgt. (O. 13, 1807).

Hockensmith, John. Ensign in Capt. Ogle's co. 47th rgt. (Je. 12, 1812).

Hodges, Benjamin. 2d Lieutenant and Pay Master in 1st rgt. Artillery (Je. 16, 1812).

Hodges, Benjamin. Ensign in Capt. Crawford's co. 17th rgt. (Jy. 10, 1812).

Hodges, John. Private in Capt. Pumphrey's co. 22d rgt.

Hodges, Joseph. Private in Capt. Pumphrey's co. 22d rgt.

Hodges, Robert. Captain in 21st rgt. (Ap. 7, 1810).

Hodges, Thomas R. Surgeon in 17th rgt. (Ap. 21, 1813).

Hodgkin, Theodore. Lieutenant-Colonel in 31st rgt.

Hodgkin, William C. Ensign in Capt. Ireland's co. 31st rgt.

Hodkin, Samuel. Private in Capt. Snowden's co. 36th rgt.

Hodson, Charles. 2d Lieutenant in Capt. Tootle's co. 10th Cavalry Dist. (Ja. 17, 1814) vice Edmonson.

Hodson, William. Captain in Extra Battalion Dorchester Co. (Ap. 21, 1814).

Hoey, John. Sergeant in Capt. Lawson's co. Balto. Patriots.

Hoff, Frederick. Private in Capt. Blair's co. 50th rgt.

Hoffman, Andrew. Sergeant in Capt. Shrim's co. Balto. Light Infantry.

Hoffman, Caspar. Ensign in Capt. Bader's co. Union Yägers.

Hoffman, David. Private in Capt. Moale's co. Columbian Artillery.

Hoffman, Frederick W. 3d Lieutenant in 38th U. S. Infantry (My. 20, 1813); 2d Lieutenant (My. 1, 1814).

Hoffman, George. Ensign in Capt. Bartgis' co. 16th rgt. (Jy. 15, 1814).

Hoffman, George. Private in Capt. Thompson's co. 1st Baltimore Horse Artillery.

Hoffman, George W. Private in Capt. Pinney's co. 27th rgt.

Hoffman, Gotleib. Sergeant in Capt. Pike's co. Balto. Volunteer Artillery.

Hoffman, Henry. Private in Capt. Sadtler's co. Balto. Yägers; prisoner at Bladensburg.

Hoffman, Henry. Private in Capt. John Miller's co. 2d D. I.; b. Washington Co., Md.; age 20; farmer.

Hoffman, Jacob. Sergeant in Capt. Watson's co. 39th rgt.

Hoffman, Jacob. Private in Capt. Blair's co. 50th rgt.

Hoffman, John. Private in Capt. Pike's Balto. Volunteer Artillery.

Hoffman, John J. Private in Capt. Blair's co. 50th rgt.

Hoffman, Lawrence. Private in Capt. Bader's co. Union Yägers.

Hoffman, Peter, Jr. Private in Capt. Thompson's co. 1st Baltimore Horse Artillery.

Hoffman, Samuel. Private in Capt. Thompson's co. 1st Baltimore Horse Artillery.

Hoffmaster, George. Private in Capt. John Miller's co. 2d D. I.; b. Md.; age 20; farmer.

Hogg, Charles. Sergeant in Capt. Stapleton's co. 39th rgt.

Hogg, James. Private in Capt. Deems' co. 51st rgt.

Hogmire, Andrew. Ensign in Capt. Mills' co. 10th rgt. (Jy. 13, 1812).

Hogner, William. Private in Capt. Smith's co. 51st rgt.

Hohn, Henry. Private in Capt. Dobbin's co. 39th rgt.

Hohne, Christopher. 1st Sergeant in Capt. Pinkney's Artillery co. 8th Brigade; 2d Lieutenant (Ap. 22, 1814).

Hohne, Wesley. Drummer in Capt. Chase's co. 22d rgt.

Holbrooks, John. Private in Capt. Chalmers' co. 51st rgt.

Holbrooks, Thomas. Command unknown; prisoner at Bladensburg.

Holding, John W. [-1821]. Ensign in 21st U. S. Infantry (Ag. 5, 1813); bvt. Captain (Jy. 25, 1814) for gallant conduct at battle of Niagara.

Holiday, Thomas. Command unknown; prisoner at Bladensburg.

Holladay, Clement. Sergeant in Capt. Eversfield's co. 17th rgt.

Holland, Charles. Private in Capt. Pinkney's Artillery co. 22d rgt.

Holland, Edward. Musician in Capt. Pinkney's Artillery co. 22d rgt.

Holland, Henry S. Private in Capt. Chase's co. 22d rgt.

Holland, Isaac. Ensign in Capt. Gaither's co. 44th rgt. (Ag. 12, 1812).

Holland, Isaac. Private in Capt. Slicer's co. 22d rgt.; Private in Ensign Brewer's detachment, 36th rgt. at Bladensburg.

Holland, Isaac, Jr. Private in Capt. Pinkney's Artillery co. 22d rgt.

Holland, James. 1st Lieutenant in Capt. White's co. 11th Cavalry Dist. (My., 1812).

Holland, James. Ensign in Capt. Taylor's co. 37th rgt. (Jy. 11, 1814).

Holland, James. Private in Capt. Montgomery's co. Balto. Union Artillery.

Holland, James. Private in Capt. Maynard's co. 22d rgt.

Holland, John. Private in Capt. Haubert's co. 51st rgt.

Holland, Joseph. Private in Capt. Steuart's co. Washington Blues.

Holland, Littleton. Lieutenant in Capt. Deems' co. 51st rgt.

Holland, Thomas. Private in Capt. Chalmers' co. 51st rgt.

Holland, W. R. Private in Capt. Warfield's co. Balto. United Volunteers.

Holland, William. Captain in 9th rgt. (Rsd. Jy. 8, 1814.)

Holland, William G. Sergeant in Capt. Stapleton's co. 39th rgt.

Hollandshead, James. Private in Capt. Wilson's co. 31st rgt.

Holler, Henry. Private in Capt. Steiner's Frederick Artillery.

Holliday, Henry. Paymaster in 9th Cavalry Dist. (D. 11, 1813).

Holliday, John. Private in Capt. King's co. 49th rgt.

Holliday, William. Private in Capt. Haubert's co. 51st rgt.

Hollidayoke, John. Private in Capt. Chase's co. 22d rgt.

Hollings, John. Private in Capt. Addison's co. Sea Fencibles.

Hollingsworth, Francis. Captain in 2d rgt. 1st Cavalry Dist. (Je. 17, 1812); Adjutant (Ap. 23, 1813).

Hollingsworth, Horatio. Private in Capt. Warfield's co. Balto. United Volunteers. Wounded at North Point.

Hollingsworth, Jacob. 1st Lieutenant in Capt. Thompson's co. 5th Cavalry Dist. (My. 3, 1813); Horse Artillery (D. 9, 1813).

Hollingsworth, L. Private in Capt. Sterett's Independent co.

Hollingsworth, Saml., Jr. Private in Capt. Sterett's co. 1st Balto. Hussars.

Hollingsworth, Thomas. Private in Capt. Roney's co. 39th rgt.

Hollins, John. Corporal in Capt. Rogers' co. 51st rgt.

Hollins, John Smith. 1st Lieutenant in Capt. Sterett's co. 1st Balto. Hussars (Ap. 23, 1812).

Hollins, Robert S. Secretary to Genl. Smith in 3d Division M. M.

Hollins, William. Private in Capt. Sterett's co. 1st Balto. Hussars.

Hollis, W. C. Private in Capt. Stiles' co. Marine Artillery.

Hollis, William G. Lieutenant in Capt. Ruff's co. 42d rgt. (Ag. 12, 1813).

Holloway, Hezekiah. Private in Capt. Hancock's co. 22d rgt.

Holloway, John. Private in Capt. Hancock's co. 22d rgt.

Holloway, Nicholas. Private in Capt. Hancock's co. 22d rgt.

Holmes, James. 2d Lieutenant in 38th U. S. Infantry (My. 20, 1813); 1st Lieutenant (D. 31, 1813).

Holmes, James. Private in Capt. Stiles's co. Marine Artillery.

Holmes, James. Private in Capt. Stewart's co. 51st rgt.

Holmes, Joseph. Private in Capt. Rogers' co. 51st rgt.

Holmes, Richard. Captain in 18th rgt. (D. 4, 1810).

Holmes, Thomas. Private in Capt. Rogers' co. 51st rgt.

Holmes, Thomas. Private in Capt. Wilson's co. 6th rgt.

Holmes, Vincent. Private in Capt. Wilson's co. 6th rgt.

Holmes, William. Ensign in Capt. Posey's co. 1st rgt. (Jy. 24, 1813).

Holt, Andrew. Corporal in Capt. Cozier's co. 30th rgt.

Holt, Ennels. Private in Capt. Frizzell's co. 15th rgt.

Holt, John. Private in Capt. Wilson's co. 31st rgt.

Holter, Daniel. Private in Capt. Steiner's Frederick Artillery.

Holton, David. Private in Capt. Burke's co. 6th rgt.

Holtz, Peter. Private in Capt. Peters' co. 51st rgt.

Holtzman, George. Private in Capt. Chambers' co. 21st rgt.

Holztman, John. Captain in 50th rgt. (D. 26, 1810).

Hone, Joseph. Private in Capt. Thos. Warner's co. 39th rgt.

Hood, Thomas. Lieutenant-Colonel in 32d rgt. (Jy. 7, 1814) vice Watkins.

Hook, Conrad. Captain in 2d rgt.

Hook, James. Lieutenant in Capt. Osborn's co. 50th rgt. (My. 17, 1811). [Later McLaughlin's co.]

Hook, James Harvey [-1841]. Ensign in 5th U. S. Infantry (Ap. 30, 1812); Capt. 38th U. S. Infantry (My. 20, 1813).

Hook, Joseph [-1837]. 2d Lieutenant in 2d U. S. Artillery (Mr. 12, 1812); Captain in 36th U. S. Infantry (Ap. 30, 1813).

Hook, Michael. Private in Capt. Adreon's co. Union Volunteers.

Hook, Rezin. Corporal in Capt. McLaughlin's co. 50th rgt.

Hooker, James. Private in Capt. Wilson's co. 6th rgt.

Hooker, Jesse. Private in Capt. Chalmers' co. 51st rgt.

Hooker, Samuel. Lieutenant in Capt. Stocksdale's co. 15th rgt. (O. 1, 1811).

Hooper, Henry. 1st Lieutenant in Capt. Ennals' co. 10th Cavalry Dist. (Jy. 29, 1812); Captain (Mr. 23, 1814) vice Ennalls.

Hooper, James [1804-]. Powder monkey of privateer *Comet*, under Capt. Boyle.

Hooper, James. Private in Capt. Lawrence's co. 6th rgt.

Hooper, James. Seaman of Barney's flotilla; wounded and captured at Bladensburg.

Hooper, John. Private in Capt. Brohawn's co. 48th rgt.

Hooper, John H. Surgeon's mate in 11th rgt. (Jy. 8, 1814).

Hooper, Roger. Private in Capt. Wilson's co. 31st rgt.

Hooper, Thomas. Lieutenant in Capt. Parsons' co. 37th rgt. Resigned Jy. 11, 1814.

Hooper, William. Private in Capt. Brohawn's co. 48th rgt.

Hoopes, John. Cornet in Capt. Boyer's co. 8th Cavalry Dist. (D. 7, 1813).

Hoopman, John. Private in Capt. Howard's co. Mechanical Volunteers.

Hoover, Henry. Musician in Capt. Marker's co. 28th rgt.

Hope, Daniel. Private in Capt. Thos. Warner's co. 39th rgt.

Hopewell, Hugh. Private in Capt. Edes' co. 27th rgt.

Hopkins, Edward [-1814]. Ensign in 36th U. S. Infantry (Ap. 30, 1813).

Hopkins, Greenbury. Private in Capt. Burke's co. 6th rgt.

Hopkins, Joshua. Private in Capt. Shrim's co. Balto. Light Infantry.

Hopkins, Philip. Private in Capt. Sands' co. 22d rgt.

Hopkins, Rezin. Captain in 22d rgt. (My. 18, 1813).

Hopkins, Richard. Private in Capt. Kennedy's co. 27th rgt.

Hopkins, Samuel. Private in Capt. Hayward's co. 4th rgt.

Hopkins, Samuel. Private in Capt. Linthicum's co. 22d rgt.

Hopkins, William. Lieutenant in Capt. Thos. Bayley's co. 25th rgt. (D. 4, 1810).

Hopkinson, Francis. Private in Capt. Moale's co. Columbian Artillery.

Hopper, Thomas. Surgeon's mate in 38th rgt. (Ag. 14, 1807).

Horner, Benjamin. Private in Capt. Hancock's co. 22d rgt.

Horner, Francis. Private in Capt. Nicholson's co. Balto. Fencibles.

Horner, Samuel. Private in Capt. Hancock's co. 22d rgt.

Horseman, Charles. Private in Capt. Wilson's co. 6th rgt.

Horsey, Lazarus. Surgeon in 23d rgt. (Jy. 14, 1814).

Horsey, Morris. Private in Capt. Aisquith's co. Sharp Shooters.

Horsnep, see Harsnipe.

Horten, William. Seaman of the privateer *Baltimore*.

Horton, Chester. Private in Capt. Moore's co. 49th rgt.

Horton, James. Captain Mayland Chasseurs in 5th Cavalry Dist. (F. 28, 1812).

Horton, Peter. Private in Capt. Gray's co. 43d rgt.

Horze, William. Private in Capt. Shrim's co. Balto. Light Infantry.

Hossefross, John. Private in Capt. Pinkney's Artillery co. 22d rgt.

Houk, William. Captain in 6th Cavalry Dist. (Ap. 22, 1814) vice Chenoweth.

Houlton, John. Private in Capt. Sheppard's co. 6th rgt.

Houlton, Robert. Private in Capt. Frizell's co. 15th rgt.

Houlton, William. Sergeant-Major in 6th rgt.

House, Henry. Private in Capt. Shryock's co. 24th rgt.

House, John. Ensign in Capt. Griffith's co. 44th rgt. (S. 10, 1814).

House, Samuel. Ensign in Capt. Coe's co. 17th rgt. (D. 6, 1813).

House, Samuel. Corporal in Capt. Montgomery's co. Balto. Union Artillery.

Houser, William. Sergeant in Capt. Steiner's Frederick Artillery.

Houx, George M. Sergeant in Capt. Blair's co. 50th rgt.

Howard, Beale [1770-1835]. Private in Capt. Weems' co. 22d rgt.

Howard, Benjamin Chew [1791-1872]. Captain in Mechanical Volunteers (Ap. 21, 1814).

Howard, Brice. Private in Capt. Nicholson's co. Balto. Fencibles.

Howard, Cornelius. Private in Capt. Barnes' co. 32d rgt.

Howard, David. Private in Capt. Montgomery's co. Balto. Union Artillery.

Howard, George. Adjutant in 3d Cavalry Dist. (F. 19, 1813); Adjutant in 15th rgt. (D. 21, 1813).

Howard, George. Private in Capt. Thompson's co. 1st Baltimore Horse Artillery.

Howard, George W. Sergeant in Capt. Aisquith's co. Sharp Shooters.

Howard, Henry. Private in Capt. Warfield's co. Balto. United Volunteers.

Howard, Henry. Surgeon in 39th rgt.

Howard, Jacob. Private in Capt. Moale's co. Columbian Artillery.

Howard, Jacob. Private in Capt. Aisquith's co. Sharp Shooters.

Howard, John. Captain in 46th rgt. (Je. 1, 1813).

Howard, John. Private in Capt. Tilghman's co. 33d rgt.

Howard, John. Sergeant in Capt. Briscoe's co. 45th rgt.

Howard, John. Private in Capt. Aisquith's co. Sharp Shooters.

Howard, John. Private in Capt. Barr's Cavalry co. 1st Dist.

Howard, John B. Major in 7th Cavalry Dist. (F. 13, 1812).

Howard, John Eager, Jr. Cornet in Capt. Thompson's co. 5th Cavalry Dist. (My. 3, 1813); 3d Lieutenant Horse Artillery in 3d Brigade (D. 9, 1813); 2d Lieutenant (D. 20, 1814).

Howard, Perry. Private in Capt. Rogers' co. 51st rgt.

Howard, Richard. Ensign in Capt. Eckman's co. 20th rgt. (Jy. 7, 1814).

Howard, Robert. Private in Capt. Dent's co. 43d rgt.

Howard, Thomas. Ensign in Capt. Sample's co. 49th rgt. (D. 3, 1799).

Howard, William. Private in Capt. Pinney's co. 27th rgt.

Howel, Abraham. Private in Capt. Myer's co. Franklin Artillery.

Howell, James. Private in Capt. A. C. Smith's co. 49th rgt.

Howell, John B. Private in Capt. Magruder's co. American Artillerists.

Howell, William. Corporal in Capt. Lawson's co. Balto. Patriots.

Howell, William, Jr. Private in Capt. Magruder's co. American Artillerists.

Howland, John M. Sergeant in Capt. Steuart's co. Washington Blues; captured at Bladensburg.

Howlet, John. Private in Capt. Ringgold's co. 6th rgt.

Hoxworth, Thomas. Private in Capt. Fowler's co. 33d rgt.

Hoyt, Reuben. Private in Capt. McKane's co. 27th rgt.

Hubball, Ebenezer. Private in Capt. Magruder's co. American Artillerists.

Hubbard, Jacob. Command unknown; prisoner at North Point.

Hubbard, William. Lieutenant in Capt. Kierstead's co. 6th rgt. (Jy. 13, 1814) vice Milholland.

Hubbard, William. Private in Capt. Brohawn's co. 48th rgt.

Hubbard, William B. Surgeon's mate 2d rgt. 1st Cavalry Dist. (Ap. 23, 1813).

Huber, Henry. Corporal in Capt. Kennedy's co. 27th rgt.

Huber, Henry. 3d Lieutenant in 38th U. S. Infantry (My. 20, 1813); 2d Lieutenant (My. 1, 1814).

Huber, Thomas. Private in Capt. Kierstead's co. 6th rgt.

Hudson, Horatio. Captain in 32d rgt. (Ap. 21, 1809).

Hudson, James. Private in Capt. Page's co. 21st rgt.

Hudson, James. Private in Capt. Ringgold's co. 6th rgt.

Hudson, John. Private in Capt. Galt's co. 6th rgt.

Hudson, Robert. Lieutenant in Capt. Baseman's co. 36th rgt. (O. 12, 1814).

Hudson, Robert W. Surgeon in 36th rgt. (Jy. 13, 1814) vice Todd.

Huffington, John. Cornet in Capt. Tootle's co. 10th Cavalry Dist. (Ja. 17, 1814) vice Ford. Resigned S. 24, 1814.

Huffington, Joshua. Private in Capt. Morgan's co. 49th rgt.

Huffington, William. Ensign in Capt. Acworth's co. 25th rgt. (Ap. 16, 1812).

Hugg, Richard. Private in Capt. Pinney's co. 27th rgt.

Hughes, Christopher. Captain in Balto. Independent Artillerists (Ap. 30, 1812).

Hughes, Daniel. Adjutant in 24th rgt. (Je. 16, 1812); Major, Assistant Inspector-General U. S. (Ag. 7, 1813); Major 2d U. S. Infantry (F. 21, 1814).

Hughes, Dennis. Private in Capt. Sterett's Independent co.

Hughes, Edward. Captain in 3d rgt. (Ag. 30, 1808).

Hughes, George A. Quarter-master 1st rgt. Artillery (Je. 16, 1812).

Hughes, George L. Private in Capt. Pike's Balto. Volunteer Artillery.

Hughes, James. Private in Capt. Stiles' co. Marine Artillery.

Hughes, Jeremiah. 2d Lieutenant in Capt. Pinkney's Artillery co. 8th Brigade (S. 18, 1812); 1st Lieutenant (Ap. 22, 1814); Adjutant.

Hughes, John. Private in Capt. Sterett's Independent co.

Hughes, Samuel. Quarter-master in 24th rgt. (O. 9, 1798).

Hughes, Vincent. Private in Capt. Ringgold's co. 6th rgt.

Hughes, William. Private in Capt. Nicholson's co. Balto. Fencibles.

Hughes, William. Private in Capt. Stapleton's co. 39th rgt.

Hughlett, Richard. Cornet in Capt. Slaughter's co. 10th Cavalry Dist. (Ap. 23, 1813).

Hughlett, Richard. Major in Extra Battalion Caroline Co. (Ap. 22, 1814).

Hughlett, William. Captain in 10th Cavalry Dist. (Je. 18, 1812) Major, 1813.

Hughs, Edward. Private in Capt. Getzendanner's co. 16th rgt.

Hughs, Hugh. Private in Capt. Getzendanner's co. 16th rgt.

Hughs, Samuel. Private in Capt. Blizzard's co. 15th rgt.

Hugo, Samuel B. Surgeon's mate in 14th Infantry (Mr. 12, 1812).

Hugues, Aquila. Private in Capt. Smith's co. 51st rgt.

Hukill, Levi [-1813]. Captain in U. S. Light Dragoons (Je. 17, 1813).

Hull, Edward. Private in Capt. Howard's co. Mechanical Volunteers.

Hull, George. Sergeant in Capt. Howard's co. Mechanical Volunteers.

Hull, James. Musician in Capt. Peters' co. 51st rgt.

Hull, John. Sergeant-Major in 4th rgt.

Hull, John C. Private in Capt. Brown's co. 49th rgt.

Hull, William. Private in Capt. Edes' co. 27th rgt.

Hulse, John [1791-1864]. Corporal in Capt. Aisquith's co. Sharp Shooters.

Hulstine, Michael. Private in Capt. Thos. Warner's co. 39th rgt.

Humes, John. Private in Capt. Snowden's co. 36th rgt.

Humphrey, John. Private in Capt. Blair's co. 50th rgt.

Humphreys, M. Private in Capt. Thompson's co. 1st Baltimore Horse Artillery.

Humphries, John. Private in Capt. Brown's co. 6th rgt.

Humphries, John. Private in Capt. Page's co. 21st rgt.

Humphries, Thomas. Lieutenant-Colonel in 25th rgt.

Humrichouse, Frederick. Private in Capt. Quantrill's co. 24th rgt.

Hungerford, John R. Captain in 1st rgt. (F. 9, 1814).

Hungerford, William E. Ensign in Capt. Parran's co. 31st rgt.; Lieutenant in Capt. Clark's co. (Ag. 20, 1814).

Hunt, Benjamin. Private in Capt. Sheppard's co. 6th rgt.

Hunt, Jesse. Private in Capt. Kennedy's co. 27th rgt.

Hunt, Jesse. Private in Capt. Steuart's co. Washington Blues.

Hunt, John. Private in Capt. Hancock's co. 22d rgt.

Hunt, John. Private in Capt. Kierstead's co. 6th rgt.

Hunt, Walter S. Captain in 7th rgt. (Ag. 1, 1814).

Hunt, William of Wm. Private in Capt. Galloway's co. 46th rgt.

Hunt, William S. Lieutenant in Capt. Clarke's co. 7th rgt. (My. 17, 1811).

Hunt, William S. Ensign in Capt. Galloway's co. 46th rgt. (Jy. 8, 1814) vice Sinclair.

Hunt, William T. Sergeant in Capt. Galloway's co. 46th rgt.

Hunter, Andrew. Fifer in Capt. Berry's co. Washington Artillery.

Hunter, Henry. Private in Capt Boone's co. 22d rgt.

Hunter, Isaac. Private in Capt. Sheppard's co. 6th rgt.

Hunter, James. Private in Capt. Hall's co. 3d Cavalry rgt.

Hunter, John. Corporal in Capt. Quantrill's co. 24th rgt.

Hunter, Joseph. Captain in 8th rgt. (Je. 1, 1813).

Hunter, Robert. Private in Capt. Brooke's co. 34th rgt.

Hunterman, Dedrick. Private in Capt. Watson's co. 39th rgt.

Huntington, John. Private in Capt. Melton's co. 45th rgt.

Huntt, Henry. Hospital Surgeon U. S. (Mr. 17, 1814).

Huntzberry, Henry. Private in Capt. Shryock's co. 24th rgt.

Hurdis, James. Private in Capt. Nicholson's co. Balto. Fencibles.

Hurley, George, Sr. Captain in 11th rgt. (Ja. 2, 1813).

Hurley, Job. Lieutenant in Capt. Hurley's co. 11th rgt. Resigned Ja. 25, 1814.

Hurn, Thomas. Private in Capt. Pumphrey's co. 22d rgt.

Hurst, Elijah. Private in Capt. Piper's co. United Maryland Artillery.

Hurst, George. Private in Capt. Brown's co. 6th rgt.

Hurst, John. Private in Capt. Pinkney's Artillery co. 22d rgt.

Hurxthall, Ferdinand. Private in Capt. Sterett's co. 1st Balto. Hussars.

Hush, Samuel [-1814]. Private in Capt. McGee's co. 1st rgt.; wounded at Bladensburg; died from the effects of fatigue and exposure, Dec. 25, 1814.

Hussey, Asabel. Private in Capt. Pike's co. Balto. Volunteer Artillery.

Hussey, George, Jr. Private in Capt. Berry's co. Washington Artillery.

Hussey, Isaac. Private in Capt. Smith's co. 51st rgt.

Hussey, Joseph. Private in Capt. Ringgold's co. 6th rgt.

Huster, Gotleib. Private in Capt. Hanna's Fells Point Light Dragoons.

Huston, James F. Captain in 16th rgt. (Jy. 15, 1814).

Hutchings, Joshua. Cornet in Capt. Jenkins' co. 7th Cavalry Dist. (Ja. 10, 1814) vice Merryman.

Hutchins, James. Captain in 41st rgt. (O. 15, 1795).

Hutchins, James. Private in Capt. Levering's co. Independent Blues.

Hutchins, Jarrett. Private in Capt. Moale's co. Columbian Artillery.

Hutchins, Thomas. Private in Capt. Nicholson's co. Balto. Fencibles.

Hutchinson, Benedick. Private in Capt. Crawfurd's co. 17th rgt.

Hutchinson, William. Private in Capt. Edes' co. 27th rgt.

Hutchison, James. Private in Capt. Mackey's co. 49th rgt.

Hutchison, John. Private in Capt. Crawfurd's co. 17th rgt.

Hutchison, John. Private in Capt. Mackey's co. 49th rgt.

Hutchison, John. Sergeant in Capt. Parnham's co. 1st rgt.

Hutson, John. Private in Capt. Stiles' co. Marine Artillery.

Hutson, Smith. Private in Capt. Oldham's co. 49th rgt.

Hutten, Benjamin. Private in Capt. Waters' co. 22d rgt.

Hutton, Elisha. Private in Capt. Howard's co. Mechanical Volunteers.

Hutton, Jonathan. Private in Capt. Slicer's co. 22d rgt.

Hutton, Joseph. Private in Capt. Ringgold's co. 6th rgt.

Hutton, Samuel. Lieutenant in Capt. Lawson's co. Balto. Patriots.

Hutton, Samuel. Private in Capt. Addison's co. Sea Fencibles.

Huyett, Jacob. Sergeant in Capt. Barr's Cavalry co. 1st Dist.

Huzza, John. Private in Capt. Aisquith's co. Sharp Shooters.

Hyatt, Aquila. Private in Capt. Chase's co. 22d rgt.

Hyde, John. Private in Capt. Sands' co. 22d rgt.

Hyde, Martin. Seaman of the privateer *Baltimore*.

Hyde, Samuel G. Lieutenant in Capt. Edes' co. 27th rgt.

Hyland, Henry. Surgeon's mate in 25th rgt. (Jy. 15, 1814).

Hyland, Henry M. [1796-1851]. Private in Capt. Wickes' co. 21st rgt.

Hyland, John. Private in Capt. Stiles' co. Marine Artillery.

Hyland, John. Private in Capt. Wickes' co. 21st rgt.

Hyland, John of Jacob. Lieutenant in Capt. Cozier's co. 30th rgt. (My. 16, 1812); Captain.

Hyland, Joshua. Ensign in Capt. Williamson's co. 49th rgt. (Je. 26, 1810).

Hyland, William. Private in Capt. Hands' co. 21st rgt.

Hynes, Isaac. Sergeant-Major in 33d rgt.

Hynson, Benjamin. Private in Capt. Page's co. 21st rgt.

Hynson, Joseph. Private in Capt. Oldham's co. 49th rgt.

Hynson, Thomas B. Captain in 21st rgt. (F. 9, 1814).

Hyson, Jacob. Private in Capt. Haubert's co. 51st rgt.

Hyson, Nicholas. Private in Capt. Roney's co. 39th rgt.

I

Ichler, John. Private in Capt. Smith's co. 51st rgt.

Iglehart, Dennis. Private in Capt. Snowden's co. 36th rgt.

Iglehart, Jacob. Ensign in Capt. Griffith's co. 32d rgt. (O. 26, 1812).

Iglehart, James. 3d Sergeant in Capt. Slicer's co. 22d rgt.

Iglehart, James. Private in Capt. Sands' co. 22d rgt.

Iglehart, Thomas. Ensign in Capt. Sanders' co. 2d rgt. (Jy. 28, 1812); Lieutenant (1814).

Iler, Jacob. Command unknown; prisoner at Bladensburg.

Iles, Henry. Private in Capt. Stewart's co. 51st rgt.

Iller, Isaac. Private in Capt. Massey's co. 38th rgt.

Imley, Habbakkuk. Private in Capt. Fallin's co. 48th rgt.

Ing, John. Private in Capt. Addison's co. Sea Fencibles.

Ingelbrits, Daniel. Private in Capt. Chalmers' co. 51st rgt.

Ingram, James. 2d Lieutenant in Capt. Boyer's co. 8th Cavalry Dist. (My. 22, 1812); 1st Lieutenant (Ap. 30, 1813).

Inloes, James. Private in Capt. Pike's co. Balto. Volunteer Artillery.

Inloes, John. Private in Capt. Lawrence's co. 6th rgt.

Inloes, William. Lieutenant in Capt. Wilson's co. 6th rgt.

Intwiler, David. Quarter-master Sergeant in 39th rgt.

Ireland, John F. Private in Capt. Edes' co. 27th rgt.

Ireland, Richard. Captain in 31st rgt.

Ireland, Richard. Private in Capt. Miller's co. 39th rgt.

Ireland, Stephen G. Private in Capt. Freeland's co. 31st rgt.

Ireland, William. Brigade Quarter-master in 6th Brigade.

Ireland, William P. Quarter-master in 33d rgt. (Ag. 20, 1813).

Irons, James. Private in Capt. Blair's co. 50th rgt.

Irons, Thomas. Private in Capt. Blair's co. 50th rgt.

Irvine, Daniel. Private in Capt. Deems' co. 51st rgt.

Irvine, John. Private in Capt. Pike's co. Balto. Volunteer Artillery.

Irving, Handy H. Captain in 25th rgt. (Ja. 10, 1814) vice Umstead.

Irving, V. P. G. Private in Capt. Shryock's co. 24th rgt.

Irwin, John. Private in Capt. Warfield's co. Balto. United Volunteers.

Isaac, Edward. Lieutenant in Capt. Chew's co. 31st rgt. (Jy. 15, 1814) vice Dowell.

Isaac, Sutton. Lieutenant in Capt. Wilson's co. 31st rgt. Resigned D. 23, 1813.

Isaacs, Joseph of Richard. Captain in 34th rgt. (Jy. 13, 1814).

Isenhart, Jacob. Private in Capt. McLaughlin's co. 50th rgt.

Isett, Adam. Private in Capt. Dobbin's co. 39th rgt.

Isinbarger, Jacob. Private in Capt. John Miller's co. 2d D. I.; b. Washington Co., Md.; age 24; farmer; subs. for William Steward.

Israel, Beale. Private in Capt. Ducker's co. 7th rgt.

Israel, Dorsey. Private in Capt. Ducker's co. 7th rgt.

Israel, Fielder. Private in Capt. Moale's co. Columbian Artillery.

Ivry, William. Private in Capt. Page's co. 21st rgt.

Izer, Joshua. Private in Capt. Addison's co. Sea Fencibles.

J

Jackson, Archibald. Private in Capt. Thos. Warner's co. 39th rgt.

Jackson, Christopher. 1st Sergeant in Capt. Maynard's co. 22d rgt.

Jackson, George W. 1st Lieutenant in 19th rgt., U. S. Infantry (Jy. 6, 1812).

Jackson, Isaac. Private in Capt. Brohawn's co. 48th rgt.

Jackson, James. Private in Capt. Jas. Massey's co. 38th rgt.

Jackson, Jasper M. Captain in 34th rgt. (Je. 27, 1812).

Jackson, John. Private in Capt. Bunbury's co. Sea Fencibles.

Jackson, John. Private in Capt. Pinkney's Artillery co. 22d rgt.

Jackson, John. Seaman of the privateer Surprise, drowned, Ap. 5, 1815.

Jackson, John. Private in Capt. Orr's co. 30th rgt.

Jackson, John E. Private in Capt. Warfield's co. Balto. United Volunteers.

Jackson, Joseph. Ensign in Capt. Edes' co. 27th rgt.

Jackson, Major. Private in Capt. Wilson's co. 6th rgt.

Jackson, Peter. Private in Capt. Oldham's co. 49th rgt.

Jackson, Thaddeus. Private in Capt. Stiles' co. Marine Artillery.

Jackson, William. Major in 5th Cavalry Dist. (F. 13, 1812).

Jackson, William. Surgeon in 11th rgt. (Je. 5, 1812).

Jackson, William. Corporal in Capt. McKane's co. 27th rgt.

Jackson, William. Private in Capt. Roney's co. 39th rgt.

Jackson, William. Private in Capt. Horton's co. Maryland Chasseurs.

Jackson, William. Private in Capt. Shryock's co. 24th rgt.

Jacob, John. Private in Capt. Pumphrey's co. 22d rgt.

Jacobs, Benjamin. Private in Capt. Kennedy's co. 27th rgt.

Jacobs, George. Lieutenant in Capt. Frizzell's co. 15th rgt. (O. 22, 1807).

Jacobs, James. Private in Capt. Dillon's co. 27th rgt.

Jacobs, John. Private in Capt. Bader's co. Union Yägers.

Jacobs, Richard. Lieutenant in Capt. McLaughlin's co. 50th rgt. (O. 16, 1810).

Jacobs, Wilson. Captain of the privateer *Father and Sons*, Feb. 1813; of the *Kemp*, April, 1813; Private in Capt. Stiles' co. Marine Artillery.

Jag, Samuel. Private in Capt. Stewart's co. 51st rgt.

Jamart, Michael [1780-1860]. Private in Capt. Sadtler's co. Balto. Yägers.

James, Barton. Private in Capt. Snowden's co. 36th rgt.

James, Charles. Private in Capt. Bader's co. Union Yägers.

James, Daniel. Private in Capt. Stiles' co. Marine Artillery.

James, George. Private in Capt. McKane's co. 27th rgt.

James, Jesse. Sergeant in Capt. Piper's co. United Maryland Artillery.

James, John, Jr. Adjutant in 13th rgt. (Mr. 15, 1813).

James, Joseph. Major in 13th rgt. (Ap. 4, 1812).

James, Levi. Private in Capt. Sheppard's co. 6th rgt.

James, Robert. Private in Capt. Dyers' co. Fells Point Riflemen.

James, Singleton. Private in Capt. Dobbin's co. 39th rgt.

James, Thomas J. Private in Capt. Hands' co. 21st rgt.

Jameson [Jamieson], Joseph. Major in 1st rgt. Artillery (Je. 12, 1812). Resigned Jy., 1814.

Jameson, Samuel. Private in Capt. Snowden's co. 36th rgt.

Jameson, William. Private in Capt. Snowden's co. 36th rgt.

Jamet, Charles. Private in Capt. Sadtler's co. Balto. Yägers.

Jamieson, John. Private in Capt. Steiner's Frederick Artillery.

Jamison, Jesse. Surgeon in 1st rgt. [1813-14].

Jamison, John. Private in Capt. Mackey's co. 49th rgt.

Jamison, Robert. Private in Capt. Brown's co. 49th rgt.

Janvier, Peregrine. Private in Capt. Steuart's co. Washington Blues.

Jarboe, Elisha. Private in Capt. Pinkney's Artillery co. 22d rgt.

Jarboe, Henry. 2d Lieutenant in Capt. Philpott's co. 2d rgt. 1st Cavalry Dist. (Ja. 1, 1813).

Jarboe, James. Captain in 12th rgt. (Je. 12, 1812).

Jarboe, William. Private in Capt. Briscoe's co. 45th rgt.

Jarman, Thomas. Private in Capt. Fowler's co. 46th rgt.

Jarman, Walter. Private in Capt. Galloway's co. 46th rgt.

Jarratt, Bennett. Captain in 7th Cavalry Dist. (My. 8, 1812).

Jarrett, John. Private in Capt. Schwarzauer's co. 27th rgt.

Jarvis, —. Colonel in 8th Cavalry Dist.

Jarvis, William. Corporal in Capt. Adreon's co. Union Volunteers.

Jay, Samuel. 1st Lieutenant in Capt. Adlum's Artillery co. 1st Brigade Harford Co. (My. 31, 1808).

Jeffers, James. Private in Capt. Aisquith's co. Sharp Shooters.

Jefferson, Jesse. Fifer in Capt. Colston's co. 48th rgt.

Jeffrey, Richard. Private in Capt. McConkey's co. 27th rgt.

Jeffrey, Robert. Private in Capt. McConkey's co. 27th rgt.

Jeffries, William. Private in Capt. Steever's co. 27th rgt.

Jeffry, Isaac. Seaman of the privateer *Surprise*, drowned, Ap. 5, 1815.

Jenifer, Daniel. 1st Lieutenant in Capt. N. P. Causin's co. 4th Cavalry Dist. (My. 8, 1812).

Jenifer, Walter. Cornet in Capt. Stonestreet's co. 4th Cavalry Dist. (My. 8, 1812).

Jenkins, Charles. Private in Capt. Steuart's co. Washington Blues.

Jenkins, Edward [1774-1833]. Private in Capt. Sterett's Independent co.

Jenkins, Felix. Private in Capt. Moale's co. Columbian Artillery.

Jenkins, Frederick. Private in Capt. Warfield's co. Balto. United Volunteers.

Jenkins, George. Private in Capt. Steuart's co. Washington Blues.

Jenkins, James. Private in Capt. Levering's co. Independent Blues.

Jenkins, Jason. Private in Capt. Faster's co. 51st rgt.

Jenkins, John I. [1789-1845]. Private in Capt. John Barnes's Artillery co. 5th Brigade.

Jenkins, Josias. 1st Lieutenant in Capt. Jarratt's co. 7th Cavalry Dist. (My. 8, 1812) ; Captain (Ja. 10, 1814) vice Jarratt.

Jenkins, Lewis A. Ensign in Capt. Hungerford's co. 1st rgt. (F. 9, 1814).

Jenkins, Michael. Private in Capt. Steuart's co. Washington Blues.

Jenkins, Oswald. 1st Lieutenant. in Capt. Wilson's co. 6th Cavalry Dist. (Jy. 13, 1814) vice Goodwin.

Jenkins, Richard. Private in Capt. Brown's co. 43d rgt.

Jenkins, Samuel. Private in Capt. Moale's co. Columbian Artillery.

Jenkins, Solomon. Seaman of the privateer *Surprise*, drowned, Apr. 5, 1815.

Jenkins, William. Lieutenant in Capt. Stevens' co. 4th rgt. (S. 20, 1808).

Jenkins, William. Private in Capt. Steiner's Frederick Artillery.

Jenkins, William. Private in Capt. Thompson's co. 1st Baltimore Horse Artillery.

Jenkins, William. Surgeon in Capt. Henry Thompson's co. 5th Cavalry Dist., 3 Brigade.

Jenkins, William. Gunner in Rodman's Marine Artillery; wounded at Fort McHenry.

Jenkins, William C. Private in Capt. Levering's co. Independent Blues.

Jenks, T. W. Private in Capt. Stiles' co. Marine Artillery.

Jennings, Daniel. Private in Capt. Conway's co. 6th rgt.

Jennings, John. Private in Capt. Steever's co. 27th rgt.

Jennings, Samuel. Private in Capt. McConkey's co. 27th rgt.

Jephson, John. Private in Capt. Dillon's co. 27th rgt.; prisoner at North Point.

Jeremiah, John. Private in Capt. Peters' co. 51st rgt.

Jervis, William. Private in Capt. Edes' co. 27th rgt.

Jessop, Charles. Private in Capt. Pennington's co. Balto. Independent Artillerists.

Jifford, T. Seaman of the privateer *Globe,* wounded in action, Nov. 1, 1813.

Jodwin, Thomas. Private in Capt. McLaughlin's co. 50th rgt.

Johanness, William B. Private in Capt. Bader's co. Union Yägers.

Johns, Henry. Quarter-master in 15th rgt.

Johns, Isaac D. Private in Capt. Galt's co. 6th rgt.

Johns, James. Private in Capt. Mc-Kane's co. 27th rgt.

Johns, Kinsey. Quarter-master in 15th rgt. (O. 22, 1807).

Johns, Richard. Ensign in Capt. Whann's co. 18th rgt. (Ag. 16, 1799).

Johns, Richard. Private in Capt. Galt's co. 6th rgt.

Johns, Stephen S. Major in 31st rgt.

Johns, William. Private in Capt. Brown's co. Eagle Artillerists.

Johns, William P. Private in Capt. Moale's co. Columbian Artillery.

Johnson, Abraham. Lieutenant in Capt. Hitchcock's co. 41st rgt. (D. 22, 1808).

Johnson, Archibald. Private in Capt. Brown's co. Eagle Artillerists.

Johnson, Archibald. Private in Capt. Pumphrey's co. 22d rgt.

Johnson, Baker. Captain in 2d rgt. 1st Cavalry Dist. (Ja. 1, 1813).

Johnson, Benjamin. Captain in 37th rgt. (Ap. 20, 1808).

Johnson, Charles. Private in Capt. Myers' co. 39th rgt.

Johnson, Charles. Private in Capt. Lawrence's co. 6th rgt.

Johnson, Christopher. Private in Capt. Pumphrey's co. 22d rgt.

Johnson, David. Private in Capt. Peters' co. 51st rgt.

Johnson, Deter. Private in Capt. McConkey's co. 27th rgt.

Johnson, Elijah. Private in Capt. Rogers' co. 51st rgt.

Johnson, Elisha E. 2d Lieutenant in Capt. Carnan's co. 6th Cavalry Dist. (Jy. 8, 1814) vice Lyon.

Johnson, Ezekiel. Private in Capt. Travers' co. 48th rgt.

Johnson, Frederick. Corporal in Capt. Taylor's co. 48th rgt.

Johnson, George. Ensign in 36th U. S. Infantry (Ap. 30, 1813); 3d Lieutenant (F. 24, 1814).

Johnson, Harman. Private in Capt. Peters' co. 51st rgt.

Johnson, Hezekiah [-1837]. Captain in 1st U. S. Infantry (Ja. 20, 1813).

Johnson, Isaac. Command unknown; captured at Bladensburg.

Johnson, Isaac S. Lieutenant in Capt. Jones' co. 9th rgt. (Jy. 8, 1814).

Johnson, Jacob. Private in Capt. Marker's co. 28th rgt.

Johnson, James. 1st Lieutenant in Capt. Johnson's co. 2d rgt. 1st Cavalry Dist. (Ja. 1, 1813).

Johnson, James. Private in Capt. Stiles' co. Marine Artillery.

Johnson, James. Private in Capt. Myers' co. 39th rgt.

Johnson, James. Private in Capt. Pinney's co. 27th rgt.

Johnson, John. Corporal in Capt. Dyer's co. Fells Point Riflemen.

Johnson, John. Private in Capt. Pinney's co. 27th rgt.

Johnson, John. Seaman of the privateer Surprise, drowned April 5, 1815.

Johnson, John. Private in Capt. McLaughlin's co. 50th rgt.

Johnson, John Griffis. Quartermaster in 1st rgt. Artillery (O. 15, 1814).

Johnson, John M. Ensign in Capt. Jones' co. 9th rgt. (Jy. 8, 1814).

23

Johnson, Joseph. Paymaster in 2d rgt. 1st Cavalry Dist. (Ap. 23, 1813).

Johnson, Josiah. Captain in 23d rgt. (Jy. 14, 1814) vice Handy.

Johnson, Lawson. Private in Capt. Burgess' co. 43d rgt.

Johnson, Leonard. Ensign in Capt. Purnell's co. 9th rgt. (O. 31, 1812).

Johnson, Lloyd. Captain in 22d rgt. (My. 27, 1811).

Johnson, Moses. Lieutenant in Capt. Bussey's co. 40th rgt. (Jy. 14, 1814).

Johnson, Nicholas. Private in Capt. Schwarzauer's co. 27th rgt.

Johnson, Nicholas. Private in Capt. Pumphrey's co. 22d rgt.

Johnson, Reverdy. Private in Ensign Brewer's detachment 36th rgt.; at Bladensburg.

Johnson, Robert. Captain in 13th rgt. (Je. 18, 1794).

Johnson, Robert. Private in Capt. Brown's co. Eagle Artillerists.

Johnson, Robert, Jr. Ensign in Capt. Johnson's co. 28th rgt. (Jy. 8, 1814) vice Murray.

Johnson, Robert B. Captain in Extra Battalion Worcester Co. (O. 21, 1812).

Johnson, Samuel. Surgeon in 29th rgt. (Ag. 22, 1812).

Johnson, Samuel. Private in Capt. Piper's co. United Maryland Artillery.

Johnson, Samuel. Musician in Capt. Slicer's co. 22d rgt.

Johnson, Silas. Private in Capt. Travers' co. 48th rgt.

Johnson, Thomas. Captain in 28th rgt. (Je. 1, 1813).

Johnson, Thomas. Surgeon in 7th rgt. (Je. 29, 1808).

Johnson, Thomas. Lieutenant in Capt. Turner's co. 40th rgt. (Je. 16, 1812).

Johnson, Thomas. Private in Capt. Hall's co. 3d Cavalry rgt.

Johnson, Thomas. Private in Capt. Lawson's co. Balto. Patriots.

Johnson, Vachel. Private in Capt. Sands' co. 22d rgt.

Johnson, Vachel. Private in Capt. Slicer's co. 22d rgt.

Johnson, William. Ensign in Capt. Taylor's co. Extra Battalion Worcester Co. (Je. 18, 1812).

Johnson, William. Private in Capt. Linthicum's co. 22d rgt.

Johnson, William. Private in Capt. Traver's co. 48th rgt.

Johnson, William. Private in Capt. McLaughlin's co. 50th rgt.

Johnson, William. Corporal in Capt. Dunnington's co. 43d rgt.

Johnson, William. Private in Capt. Steiner's Frederick Artillery.

Johnson, William. Private in Capt. Faster's co. 51st rgt.

Johnson, William, Jr. Private in Capt. Pinkney's Artillery co. 22d rgt.

Johnson, William, Sr. Private in Capt. Dent's co. 43d rgt.

Johnson, William H. Private in Capt. Brown's co. Eagle Artillerists.

Johnson, Zachariah. Private in Capt. Slicer's co. 22d rgt.

Johnston, Abijah. Private in Capt. Haubert's co. 51st rgt.

Johnston, Arthur. Private in Capt. Shryock's co. 24th rgt.

Johnston, Henry. Surgeon's mate in 6th rgt. (S. 13, 1814).

Johnston, James. Sergeant-Major in 51st rgt.

Johnston, John. Private in Capt. Quantrill's co. 24th rgt.

Johnston, John G. Quarter-master in 1st rgt. Artillery.

Johnston, Joseph. Private in Capt. Edes' co. 27th rgt.

Johnston, Josiah. Paymaster in Extra Battalion Harford Co. (My. 9, 1808).

Johnston, Mathias. Private in Capt. Galt's co. 6th rgt.

Johnston, Samuel. Private in Capt. Garrett's co. 49th rgt.

Joice, Aaron. Private in Capt. Haubert's co. 51st rgt.

Joice, Jesse. Private in Capt. Stewart's co. 51st rgt.

Joice, John. Private in Capt. Magruder's co. American Artillerists.

Joice, John. Private in Capt. Waters' co. 22d rgt.

Joice, Joshua. Ensign in Capt. Black's co. 30th rgt. (My. 6, 1809).

Joice, Thomas. Private in Capt. Maynard's co. 22d rgt.

Joice, William. Private in Capt. Faster's co. 51st rgt.

Joiner, Dobs. Sergeant in Capt. Graves' co. 21st rgt.

Jolley, Benjamin. Private in Capt. McLaughlin's co. 50th rgt.

Jolley, William. Private in Capt. McLaughlin's co. 50th rgt.

Jolly, Thomas M. Private in Capt. Steiner's Frederick Artillery.

Jonas, Jacob. Private in Capt. Magruder's co. American Artillerists.

Jones, —. Captain in 34th rgt.

Jones, —. Captain in 40th rgt. Resigned Jy. 14, 1814.

Jones, Acquila. Private in Capt. Brohawn's co. 48th rgt.

Jones, Alexander. Ensign in Capt. Ballard's co. 25th rgt. (Je. 1, 1813).

Jones, Arnold E. Captain in 11th Cavalry Dist. (Je. 16, 1812).

Jones, Barren. Private in Capt. Kierstead's co. 6th rgt.

Jones, Caleb. Ensign in 12th rgt. (O. 3, 1807).

Jones, Basil. Surgeon's mate in 3d rgt. (Je. 5, 1812).

Jones, Baynard. Private in Capt. Massey's co. 38th rgt.

Jones, Benjamin J. Adjutant in 25th rgt. (D. 4, 1810).

Jones, Caleb M. Surgeon's mate 12th rgt. (Ag. 1, 1814).

Jones, Charles. Captain in 7th rgt. (Ap. 23, 1808).

Jones, Charles L. Ensign in Capt. Dyer's co. 17th rgt. (S. 7, 1810).

Jones, Dr. D. Surgeon in 23d rgt. Resigned Jy. 14, 1814.

Jones, Daniel. Lieutenant in Capt. Cline's co. 10th rgt. Resigned Sept. 20, 1813.

Jones, Daniel. Private in Capt. McKane's co. 27th rgt.

Jones, David. Private in Capt. Griffith's co. 21st rgt.

Jones, David. Private in Capt. Pinkney's Artillery co. 22d rgt.; Private in Ensign Brewer's detachment, 36th rgt.

Jones, Dorsey. Private in Capt. Deems' co. 51st rgt.

Jones, Edward. Private in Capt. Nicholson's co. Balto. Fencibles.

Jones, Edward. Private in Capt. Aisquith's co. Sharp Shooters.

Jones, Elisha [1813]. Colonel in 17th rgt.

Jones, Ellis. Private in Capt. Sadtler's co. Balto. Yägers.

Jones, Enoch. Private in Capt. Snowden's co. 36th rgt.

Jones, Evan. Private in Capt. Burke's co. 6th rgt.

Jones, George. Private in Capt. Brown's co. Eagle Artillerists.

Jones, Giles. Captain in 9th rgt. (Ap. 28, 1808).

Jones, Griffin. Private in Capt. Haubert's co. 51st rgt.

Jones, Harry. Seaman of Barney's flotilla; wounded and captured at Bladensburg.

Jones, Hugh S. Private in Capt. Steever's co. 27th rgt.

Jones, Jacob. Private in Capt. Graves' co. 21st rgt.

Jones, Jacob, Jr. Sergeant in Capt. Comegys' co. 21st rgt.

Jones, James. Private in Capt. Heath's co. 23d rgt.

Jones, James. Lieutenant in Capt. Haddaway's co. 26th rgt. (Je. 26, 1812).

Jones, James. Private in Capt. Dyers' co. Fells Point Riflemen.

Jones, James D. Private in Capt. Wilson's co. 6th rgt.

Jones, Jeremiah. Private in Capt. Snowden's co. 36th rgt.

Jones, John. Lieutenant-Colonel (Dorchester Co.) in 48th rgt.

Jones, John. Private in Capt. Deems' co. 51st rgt.

Jones, John. Private in Capt. Faster's co. 51st rgt.

Jones, John. Private in Capt. Chambers' co. 21st rgt.

Jones, John. Private in Capt. Wickes' co. 21st rgt.

Jones, John. Private in Capt. John Miller's co. 2d D. I.; b. Balto. Co. Md.; age 20; cooper; subs. for Jacob Snider; deserted from Patapsco encampment June 30, 1813.

Jones, John. Private in Capt. Taylor's co. 46th rgt.

Jones, John. Private in Capt. Allen's co. 49th rgt.

Jones, John. Private in Capt. Conway's co. 6th rgt.

Jones, John W. Private in Capt. Morgan's co. 49th rgt.

Jones, John W. Private in Capt. Brown's co. Eagle Artillerists.

Jones, Jonathan J. Private in Capt. Pike's co. Balto. Volunteer Artillery.

Jones, Joseph. Private in Capt. Fallin's co. 48th rgt.

Jones, Joseph of Josiah. Cornet in Capt. Cross' co. 2d Cavalry Dist. (Ap. 16, 1812); 2d Lieutenant vice Gantt.

Jones, Joseph J. Captain in 34th rgt. (Ag. 20, 1814) vice Waters.

Jones, Joseph J. W. Adjutant in 3d rgt. (D. 9, 1813).

Jones, Joshua. Private in Capt. John Miller's co. 2d D. I.; b. Anne Arundel Co., Md.; age 41; laborer.

Jones, Joshua. Private in Capt. Montgomery's co. Balto. Union Artillery.

Jones, Joshua. Private in Capt. Howard's co. Mechanical Volunteers.

Jones, Josiah. Ensign in Capt. Wheeler's co. 14th rgt. (F. 4, 1808).

Jones, Josiah, Jr. Lieutenant in Capt. Lansdale's co. 18th rgt. (Ap. 27, 1814).

Jones, Lemuel. Private in Capt. Snowden's co. 36th rgt.

Jones, Levin. Sergeant-Major in 21st U. S. Infantry (My. 16, 1812); 2d Lieutenant (O. 1, 1814).

Jones, Luke. Private in Capt. Hancock's co. 22d rgt.

Jones, Malon. Private in Capt. Steever's co. 27th rgt.

Jones, Morris. Captain in 16th rgt. (Jy. 15, 1814).

Jones, Moses U. Lieutenant in Capt. Stevenson's co. 9th rgt. (Mr. 23, 1814).

Jones, Nicholas S. Private in Capt. Magruder's co. American Artillerists.

Jones, R. H. Private in Capt. Sterett's Independent co.

Jones, Richard. Private in Capt. Aisquith's co. Sharp Shooters.

Jones, Richard J. Captain in 9th Cavalry Dist. (F. 13, 1813); Major (Jy. 8, 1813).

Jones, Robinson. Private in Capt. Dillon's co. 27th rgt.

Jones, Samuel. Private in Capt. Dent's co. 43d rgt.

Jones, Solomon. 1st Lieutenant in Capt. Bryan's Artillery co. 12th Brigade (Ap. 30, 1813).

Jones, Stephen. Sergeant in Capt. A. C. Smith's co. 49th rgt.

Jones, T. A. Private in Capt. Warfield's co. Balto. United Volunteers.

Jones, Talbot. Private in Capt. Sterett's Independent co.

Jones, Thomas. Major in 26th rgt.

Jones, Thomas. Captain in 30th rgt. (Je. 26, 1812).

Jones, Thomas. Lieutenant in Capt. Juett's co. 23d rgt. (Jy. 14, 1814) vice Sterling.

Jones, Thomas. Ensign in Capt. Davis' co. 9th rgt. (N. 30, 1811).

Jones, Thomas. Private in Capt. Burgess' co. 43d rgt.

Jones, Uriah [1788-1859]. Private in Capt. Deems' co. 51st rgt.

Jones, William. Captain in 7th rgt. (Ag. 1, 1814).

Jones, William. Lieutenant in Capt. Leach's co. 31st rgt. (Mr. 19, 1813).

Jones, William. 2d Lieutenant in 38th U. S. Infantry (My. 20, 1813); 1st Lieutenant (My. 1, 1814).

Jones, William. Ensign in Capt. Jones' co. 34th, rgt. (Ag. 20 1814).

Jones, William. Hospital Surgeon's mate, U. S. (Jy. 2, 1813).

Jones, William. Seaman of the privateer *High Flyer,* wounded in action, Dec., 1812; Quarter-Gunner in Capt. Bunbury's co. Sea Fencibles, 1814.

Jones, William. Private in Capt. Wilson's co. 6th rg.

Jones, William. Private in Capt. Dent's co. 43d rgt.

Jones, William. Private in Capt. McConkey's co. 27th rgt.

Jones, William M. Private in Capt. Barnes' co. 32d rgt.

Jones, William Robinson [1786-1857]. Purser's steward in U. S. Flotilla service; acted as Ensign to Capt. Barney at Bladenburg; was at Fort Covington during the bombardment.

Jones, William S. Private in Capt. Burgess' co. 43d rgt.

Jones, William W. Lieutenant in Capt. Leitch's co. 31st rgt.

Jordan, Alexander. Sergeant in Capt. Blakistone's co. 45th rgt.

Jordan, Frederick. Private in Capt. Montgomery's co. Balto. Union Artillery.

Jordan, George. Private in Capt. Peters' co. 51st rgt.

Jordan, Henry. Private in Capt. Myers' co. Franklin Artillery.

Jordan, John. 2d Lieutenant in Capt. Forrest's co. 4th Cavalry Dist. (Je. 5, 1812).

Jordan, John. Private in Capt. Stapleton's co. 39th rgt.

Jordan, John. Private in Capt. Baders' co. Union Yägers.

Jordan, Robert. Private in Capt. Edes' co. 27th rgt.

Jordan, Samuel. Quarter-Gunner Capt. Addison's co. Sea Fencibles.

Jordan, William. Captain in 26th rgt. (S. 1, 1807).

Jordon, James. Private in Capt. Adreon's co. Union Volunteers.

Jory, John. Seaman in Barney's flotilla; Private in Capt. Brewer's co. 1st rgt.

Joseph, Manuel. Private in Capt. Montgomery's co. Balto. Union Artillery.

Joy, Edward. Private in Capt. Pinney's co. 27th rgt.

Joy, Peter. Private in Capt. Dobbin's co. 39th rgt.

Joyce, Zachariah. Private in Capt. Linthicum's co. 22d rgt.

Joynes, Leonard. Private in Capt. Wilson's co. 6th rgt.

Juett, —. Captain in 23d rgt.

Jump, Abel N. Private in Capt. Hayward's co. 4th rgt.

Jump, Alemby. Paymaster in Extra Battalion Caroline Co. (Ja. 15, 1814) vice Ridgeway.

Jump, Henry. Lieutenant in Capt. Bell's co. Extra Battalion Caroline Co. (My. 8, 1812).

Jump, John. Ensign in Capt. Bell's co. Extra Battalion Caroline co. (My. 8, 1812).

Justis, Morton. Private in Capt. Brown's co. 6th rgt.

K

Kalbfus, Daniel M. Sergeant in Capt. Stewart's co. 51st rgt.

Kalbfus, William. Private in Capt. Faster's co. 51st rgt.

Kalckbrenner, Ferd. Private in Capt. Sadtler's co. Balto. Yägers.

Kaminskie, John C. Private in Capt. McKane's co. 27th rgt.

Kanes, John M. Captain in 27th rgt. (Mr. 24, 1814).

Karney, Thomas [-1834]. 1st Lieutenant in 14th U. S. Infantry (Mr. 12, 1812); Capt. (My. 13, 1813).

Katy, Samuel. 2d Lieutenant of the privateer *Water Witch*, Aug. 1814.

Kauffman, Christian. Private in Capt. Getzendanner's co. 16th rgt.

Kauffman, Daniel. Private in Capt. Miller's co. 39th rgt.

Kauffman, John. Private in Capt. Miller's co. 39th rgt.

Kauffman, Jonathan [c1796-1850]. Private in Capt. Haubert's co. 51st rgt.

Kaylor, George. Private in Capt. Sadtler's co. Balto. Yägers.

Kealhofer, Henry. Cornet in Capt. Barr's Cavalry co. 1st Dist. (S. 12, 1814).

Kealhofer, John. Saddler in Capt. Barr's co. 1st Dist.

Keallyer, Jesse. Private in Capt. Quantrill's co. 24th rgt.

Kealy, Jacob. Private in Capt. Quantrill's co. 24th rgt.

Keane, William, Jr. Command unknown; captured at North Point.

Keath, James. Corporal in Capt. Blair's co. 50th rgt.

Keatley, Richard. Private in Capt. Galt's co. 6th rgt.

Keatts, John. Private in Capt. Massey's co. 38th rgt.

Keech, John E. Sergeant in Capt. Sotheran's co. 45th rgt.

Keech, Robert. Private in Capt. McConkey's co. 27th rgt.

Keech, Samuel. Private in Capt. Cawood's co. 45th rgt.

Keefer, Henry. Major in 16th rgt. (Je. 5, 1812).

Keem, Thomas W. Private in Capt. Rogers' co. 51st rgt.

Keen, Jesse. Ensign in 14th U. S. Infantry (Jy. 19, 1813); 3d Lieutenant (N. 14, 1813).

Keen, Thomas. Sergeant in Capt. Quantrill's co. 24th rgt.

Keen, William, Jr. Private in Capt. Montgomery's co. Balto. Union Artillery.

Keene, Benjamin. Sergeant in Capt. Brohawn's co. 48th rgt.

Keene, Henry. Paymaster in 48th rgt. (Ag. 1, 1812).

Keene, John. Private in Capt. Brohawn's co. 48th rgt.

Keene, Levin. Private in Capt. Brohawn's co. 48th rgt.

Keene, Marselus. Surgeon in 19th rgt. (Ag. 10, 1807).

Keene, Samuel. Major in 48th rgt. (Jy. 7, 1810).

Keene, Samuel, Jr. Private in Capt. Travers' co. 48th rgt.

Keene, Shadrach. Private in Capt. Travers' co. 48th rgt.

Keener, Christian, Jr. [1795-]. Private in Capt. Warfield's co. Balto. United Volunteers. Wounded at Bladensburg.

Keener, John. Private in Capt. Levering's co. Independent Blues.

Keener, William. Private in Capt. Shrim's co. Balto. Light Infantry.

Keeny, Abel. Private in Capt. Sadtler's co. Balto. Yägers.

Keerl, John C. Private in Capt. Warfield's co. Balto. United Volunteers.

Keerl, Samuel. Private in Capt. Warfield's co. Balto. United Volunteers.

Keichkoff, George. Private in Capt. Edes' co. 27th rgt.

Keilholtz, Henry. Private in Capt. A. E. Warner's co. 39th rgt.

Keilholtz, William. Corporal in Capt. Pike's co. Balto. Volunteer Artillery.

Keiner, Melchoir. Private in Capt. Watson's co. 39th rgt.

Keipple, Henry. Private in Capt. Bader's co. Union Yägers.

Keirl, Matthew. Private in Capt. Pinney's co. 27th rgt.

Keirman, Charles. Private in Capt. Dobbin's co. 39th rgt.

Keiser, Christopher [-1819]. Assistant Deputy Commissioner of Ordnance (Ag. 6, 1813).

Kelby, Samuel. Private in Capt. McDonald's co. 6th rgt.

Kell, Fleming. Private in Capt. Kierstead's co. 6th rgt.

Kell, Thomas [1772-1846]. 1st Lieutenant in Capt. Bouldin's co. Independent Light Dragoons 5th Cavalry Dist. (My. 18, 1813); Clerk of Court of Balto. City; State's Attorney; Attorney-General of Md.; Judge of Circuit Court.

Kelleigh, John. Surgeon's mate in 4th rgt. (S. 1, 1807).

Keller, Conrad. Sergeant in Capt. Kennedy's co. 27th rgt.

Keller, George. Private in Capt. Pike's co. Balto. Volunteer Artillery.

Keller, John. Private in Capt. Nicholson's co. Balto. Fencibles.

Kelley, William. Prvate in Capt. Brohawn's co. 48th rgt.

Kellum, James. Private in Capt. Ringgold's co. 6th rgt.

Kelly, Edward. Sergeant in Capt. Chalmers' co. 51st rgt.

Kelly, James. Private in Capt. Massey's co. 38th rgt.

Kelly, James. Private in Capt. Lawson's co. Balto. Patriots.

Kelly, James. Private in Capt. Stewart's co. 51st rgt.

Kelly, Jarrett. Seaman of the privateer *Comet*.

Kelly, John. 2d Lieutenant in Capt. Chenoweth's co. 6th Cavalry Dist. (Je. 12, 1812).

Kelly, Joseph. Private in Capt. Blair's co. 50th rgt.

Kelly, Mathew. Captain of the privateer *Patapsco*, Nov., 1813; Private in Capt. Stiles' co. Marine Artillery, 1814.

Kelly, Moses Private in Capt. Blair's co. 50th rgt.

Kelly, Nicholas. Lieutenant in Capt. Miller's co. 15th rgt. (Ap. 22, 1813).

Kelly, Perry. Private in Capt. Adreon's co. Union Volunteers.

Kelly, Samuel. Private in Capt. Blair's co. 50th rgt.

Kelly, Thomas. Private in Capt. McKane's co. 27th rgt.

Kelly, William. Captain in 36th rgt. (O. 12, 1814).

Kelly, William. Sergeant in Capt. Dillon's co. 27th rgt.

Kelly, William. Private in Capt. Blair's co. 50th rgt.

Kelner, George. Private in Capt. Chalmers' co. 51st rgt.

Kelsner, John. Private in Capt. Dillon's co. 27th rgt.

Kelsner, William. Private in Capt. Lawson's co. Balto. Patriots.

Kelso, George G. Private in Capt. Moale's co. Columbian Artillery.

Kelso, John R. Corporal in Capt. Steuart's co. Washington Blues.

Kelso, Thomas. Private in Capt. Peters' co. 51st rgt.

Kemberly, Michael. Private in Capt. Smith's co. 51st rgt.

Kemp, David. 1st Lieutenant in Capt. Hauer's co. 1st Cavalry Dist. (Mr. 16, 1812).

Kemp, Frederick. Private in Capt. Getzendanner's co. 16th rgt.

Kemp, Gilbert. Captain in 16th rgt. (Je. 26, 1812).

Kemp, Henry. Major in 1st Cavalry Dist. (F. 13, 1812); Lieutenant-Colonel in 2d rgt. 1st Dist. (My. 8, 1812). Resigned D. 20, 1814.

Kemp, John. 2d Lieutenant in Capt. Vinson's Artillery co. 12th Brigade (D. 10, 1813).

Kemp, John. Drummer in Capt. Chambers' co. 21st rgt.

Kemp, Joseph. Captain in 26th rgt. (Ja. 3, 1810).

Kemp, Joseph. Private in Capt. Kierstead's co. 6th rgt.

Kemp, Thomas. Private in Capt. Kierstead's co. 6th rgt.

Kemp, William. Private in Capt. Myers' co. Franklin Artillery.

Kempton, James. Private in Capt. McLaughlin's co. 50th rgt.

Kendall, William. Private in Capt. Griffith's co. 21st rgt.

Kenly, Edward [1788-1861]. Private in Capt. Schwarzauer's co. 27th rgt.

Kennard, Joseph. Captain in 38th rgt.

Kennard, Patrick P. Private in Capt. Comegys' co. 21st rgt.

Kennard, Richard. Private in Capt. Wickes' co. 21st rgt.

Kennard, Samuel. Ensign in Capt. Merrick's co. 4th rgt. (Ag. 11, 1813).

Kennard, Samuel G. Private in Comegys' co. 21st rgt.

Kennard, Samuel T. Sergeant in Capt. Hayward's co. 4th rgt.

Kennard, Thomas I. Private in Capt. Chambers' co. 21st rgt.

Kennedy, Dennis. Private in Capt. Magruder's American Artillerists.

Kennedy, James. Private in Capt. Edes' co. 27th rgt.

Kennedy, James. Private in Capt. Blair's co. 50th rgt.

Kennedy, John. Captain in 27th rgt.

Kennedy, John. Private in Capt. Thompson's co. 1st Baltimore Horse Artillery.

Kennedy, John. 3d Lieutenant in Capt. Piper's co. United Maryland Artillery.

Kennedy, John Pendleton. Private in Capt. Warfield's co. Balto. United Volunteers.

Kennedy, Mordecai. Private in Capt. Moale's Columbian Artillery.

Kennedy, Richard. Private in Capt. Myers' co. Franklin Artillery.

Kennedy, Robert R. Private in Capt. McLaughlin's co. 50th rgt.

Kennedy, William. Private in Capt. Moale's co. Columbian Artillery.

Kennerly, Joseph. Ensign in Capt. Thos. Bayley's co. 25th rgt. (Jy. 5, 1813).

Kennon, John B. Private in Capt. Kennedy's co. 27th rgt.

Kensy, Peter. Private in Capt. McDonald's co. 6th rgt.

Kent, Emanuel, Jr. Private in Capt. Pennington's co. Balto. Independent Artillerists. Wounded at Fort McHenry.

Kent, John. Private in Capt. Peters' co. 51st rgt.

Kent, Joseph. Major in 2d Cavalry Dist. (F. 13, 1812).

Kent, Robert. Private in Capt. Steever's co. 27th rgt.

Kent, Robert W. Captain in 14th U. S. Infantry (Mr. 12, 1812).

Keplinger, George. Private in Capt. Addison's co. Sea Fencibles.

Keplinger, Michael [1766-1849]. Private in Capt. Chalmers' co. 51st rgt.

Keplinger, Samuel. Private in Capt. Dobbin's co. 39th rgt.

Kerby, George. Private in Capt. Dyer's co. 17th rgt.

Kerby, Nicholas. Private in Capt. Snowden's co. 36th rgt.

Kerby, Samuel. Private in Capt. Kierstead's co. 6th rgt.

Kerby, Thomas. Private in Capt. Brown's co. 6th rgt.

Kerby, William. Private in Capt. Hancock's co. 22d rgt.

Kermichael, William. Private in Capt. Brown's co. 6th rgt.

Kern, Nathan. Private in Capt. Massey's co. 38th rgt.

Kern, William. Sergeant in Capt. Massey's co. 38th rgt.

Kernan, Leonard. Private in Capt. Aisquith's co. Sharp Shooters.

Kerr, Archibald. Paymaster in 5th Cavalry Dist. (Je. 26, 1812).

Kerr, David, Jr. Paymaster in 4th rgt., 1813.

Kerr, James. Ensign in Capt. Harvey's co. Extra Battalion Harford Co. (Jy. 8, 1814) vice McFaddin.

Kerr, John Leeds. Division Inspector 2d Division M. M. (Ag. 14, 1814) ; Captain in 4th rgt. to above date.

Kerr, Robert. Ensign in 30th rgt.

Kerr, Samuel. Sergeant in Capt. Patton's co. 30th rgt.

Kerr, Samuel. Private in Capt. Tilghman's co. 33d rgt.

Kerr, Samuel. Surgeon's mate in 23d rgt. (O. 24, 1800).

Kerr, William. Private in Capt. Garrett's co. 49th rgt.

Kerr, William. Private in Capt. McConkey's co. 27th rgt.

Kersey, Robert. Private in Capt. Hayward's co. 4th rgt.

Kershner, George. Private in Capt. Barr's Cavalry co. 1st Dist.

Kershner, Jacob. Sergeant in Capt. Barr's Cavalry co. 1st Dist.

Kerwell, Samuel. Private in Capt. Chalmers' co. 51st rgt.

Kesler, John. Private in Capt. Rogers' co. 51st rgt.

Kessler, Christian. Private in Capt. Myers' co. 39th rgt.

Key, Abner. Private in Capt. Edes' co. 27th rgt.

Key, Eli. Private in Capt. King's co. 49th rgt.

Key, Henry G. S. Private in Capt. Maynard's co. 22d rgt.

Key, Robert M. Major in 4th Cavalry Dist. (D. 7, 1814).

Keys, John. Sergeant in Capt. Pike's co. Balto. Volunteer Artillery.

Keys, William. Private in Capt. Smith's co. 51st rgt.

Keyser, George. Major in 26th rgt. M. M.; Major in 38th U. S. Infantry (My. 20, 1813).

Keyser, Peter [-1814]. 3d Lieutenant in 38th U. S. Infantry (My. 20, 1813) ; 2d Lieutenant (Ap. 22, 1814).

Keyser, William. Private in Capt. Myers' co. 39th rgt.

Kidd, John. Private in Capt. Chalmers' co. 51st rgt.

Kidd, Joshua. Private in Capt. Chalmers' co. 51st rgt.

Kidwell, Jonas. Private in Capt. Crawfurd's co. 17th rgt.

Kieffer, Jacob. Corporal in Capt. Steiner's Frederick Artillery.

Kieffer, Philip. Ensign in Capt. Freshour's co. 16th rgt. (Je. 9, 1809).

Kierl, John W. Private in Capt. Brown's co. 6th rgt.

Kiernan, John. Private in Capt. Piper's United Maryland Artillery.

Kierstead, Luke. Captain in 6th rgt.

Kight, Cornelius. Private in Capt. Blair's co. 50th rgt.

Kilbourne, Samuel. Private in Capt. Dobbin's co. 39th rgt.

Kilgour, Charles J. Quarter-master in 44th rgt. (Jy. 30, 1814).

Kilgour, John. Adjutant in 45th rgt. Resigned, 1813; Quarter-master in 4th Cavalry Dist. (Ap. 21, 1813).

Killey, John. Ensign in Capt. White's co. 23d rgt. Resigned Jy. 14, 1814.

Killey, William. Ensign in Capt. White's co. 23d rgt. (Jy. 14, 1814).

Killiam, James. Private in Capt. Haubert's co. 51st rgt.

Kilman, John. Private in Capt. Brown's co. 49th rgt.

Kilman, Martin. Private in Capt. Brohawn's co. 48th rgt.

Kimball, Samuel. Lieutenant of the privateer *Ultor*, Nov., 1813.

Kimberly, Nathaniel [1775-1836]. Private in Capt. Stewart's co. Washington Blues.

Kimble, Zachariah. Lieutenant in Capt. Michael's co. 42d rgt. (Je. 19, 1812).

Kimes, Thomas. Private in Capt. Howard's co. Mechanical Volunteers.

Kimmel, Michael. Private in Capt. Pike's co. Balto. Volunteer Artillery.

Kincaid, Myers. Private in Capt. Bunbury's co. Sea Fencibles.

Kincaid, Wallace. Private in Capt. Pennington's co. Balto. Independent Artillerists.

Kindell, Joseph. Private in Capt. Barr's Cavalry co. 1st Dist.

King, Francis. Private in Capt. Brooke's co. 34th rgt.

King, George. Private in Capt. Roney's co. 39th rgt.

King, Henry. Private in Capt. Pike's co. Balto. Volunteer Artillery.

King, James. Private in Capt. Snowden's co. 36th rgt.

King, James. Private in Capt. Galt's co. 6th rgt.

King, James C. Private in Capt. Snowden's co. 36th rgt.

King, Jesse. Private in Capt. Roney's co. 39th rgt.

King, John. Captain in Elkton Artillery co. 49th rgt. (S. 19, 1812) vice Evans; Adjutant in 49th rgt.

King, John. 1st Lieutenant in Capt. Pike's co. First Balto. Volunteer Artillery (Mr. 25, 1814) vice Baum.

King, John. Private in Capt. Myers' co. Franklin Artillery.

King, John S. Sergeant in Capt. Pennington's co. Balto. Independent Artillerists.

King, Joseph. Private in Capt. Posey's co. 1st rgt.

King, Levin. Ensign in Capt. Walters' co. 23d rgt. (D. 7, 1813); Lieutenant in Capt. Handy's co. (S. 10, 1814).

King, Nicholas. Armorer at Frederick, Nov., 1812.

King, Planner F. Private in Capt. Heath's co. 23d rgt.

King, Samuel. Sergeant in Capt. Heath's co. 23d rgt.

King, Thomas. Private in Capt. Heath's co. 23d rgt.

King, Thomas. Private in Ensign Brewer's co. 36th rgt.; in Capt. Slicer's co. 22d rgt.

King, Thomas, Jr. Private in Capt. Lawrence's co. 6th rgt.

King, Thomas E. Adjutant in 31st rgt. (My. 22, 1812).

King, William [-1826]. Captain in 15th U. S. Infantry (Jy. 2, 1812); Major (Mr. 3, 1813); Colonel 3d U. S. Rifles (F. 21, 1814).

King, William. Captain in 23d rgt. [1814].

Kingston, Thomas Jones. Lieutenant in Capt. Miles' co. 23d rgt. (Je. 15, 1813).

Kinkaid, George. Private in Capt. Sample's co. 49th rgt.

Kinkaid, James. Private in Capt. Magruder's co. American Artillerists.

Kinkaid, William. Private in Capt. Moore's co. 49th rgt.

Kinkerly, Jacob. Private in Capt. Quantrill's co. 24th rgt.

Kinkle, Henry. Private in Capt. Shryock's co. 24th rgt.

Kinley, Daniel. Private in Capt. Chalmers' co. 51st rgt.

Kinnamon, Nehemiah S. Private in Capt. Thompson's co. 43d rgt.

Kinsell, Frederick. Fifer in Capt. Shryock's co. 24th rgt.

Kinsey, David. Private in Capt. McLaughlin's co. 50th rgt.

Kinsey, Ezekiel. Private in Capt. Snowden's co. 36th rgt.

Kinsey, Samuel. Private in Capt. Barnes' co. 32d rgt.

Kirby, Amasa. Corporal in Capt. Piper's co. United Maryland Artillery.

Kirby, Cornelius. Sergeant in Capt. Jarboe's co. 12th rgt.

Kirby, Francis. Ensign in Capt. Kirby's co. 14th rgt. (My. 23, 1799).

Kirby, John. Ensign in Capt. Chalmers' co. 51st rgt. Wounded at North Point.

Kirby, John B. Captain in 14th rgt. (My. 23, 1799).

Kirby, Robert. Adjutant in Extra Battalion Worcester Co.

Kirby, William. Private in Capt. Hayward's co. 4th rgt.

Kirk, George Wells. Private in Capt. Stiles' co. Marine Artillery, 1814; Lieutenant of the privateer *Swift*, Jan., 1815.

Kirk, John. Private in Capt. Jos. Jones' co. 34th rgt.

Kirk, Thomas. Private in Capt. Horton's co. Maryland Chasseurs.

Kirkland, Alexander. Private in Capt. Pike's co. Balto. Volunteer Artillery.

Kirkland, David. Private in Capt. Myers' co. 39th rgt.

Kirkpatrick, Daniel. Military storekeeper (My. 9, 1812).

Kislinger, Conrad. Major in 15th rgt. (Ag. 22, 1812).

Kislinger, John. Lieutenant in Capt. Kislinger's co. 15th rgt. (Ag. 22, 1812).

Kislinger, John of George. Captain in 15th rgt. (Ag. 22, 1812).

Kite, James. Private in Capt. Peters' co. 51st rgt.

Kithcart [Cathcart], John. Private in Capt. Ringgold's co. 6th rgt.

Kithcart, Robert [1786-1814]. Private in Capt. Smith's co. 51st rgt.

Kithcart, William. Private in Capt. Stapleton's co. 39th rgt.

Kitz, Frederick. Private in Capt. Barr's Cavalry co. 1st Dist.

Kivens, Samuel. Private in Capt. Lawrence's co. 6th rgt.

Klassen, Christopher. Private in Capt. Sadtler's co. Balto. Yägers.

Klee, John. Sergeant in Capt. Sadtler's co. Balto. Yägers.

Kleinfelter, Michael. Private in Capt. Pennington's co. Balto. Independent Artillerists.

Kline, Charles. Private in Capt. Marker's co. 28th rgt.

Kline, Daniel. Private in Capt. Barr's Cavalry co. 1st Dist.

Kline, Frederick. Corporal in Capt. Getzendanner's co. 16th rgt.

Kline, George. Private in Capt. Marker's co. 28th rgt.

Kline, Jacob. Private in Capt. Shryock's co. 24th rgt.

Kline, John. Private in Capt. Getzendanner's co. 16th rgt.

Kline, Philip. Musician in Capt. Marker's co. 28th rgt.

Klink, John. Private in Capt. Getzendanner's co. 16th rgt.

Klock, John. Private in Capt. Sheppard's co. 6th rgt.

Klockengeter, Diedrich. Private in Capt. Sadtler's co. Balto. Yägers.

Klunk, Peter. Private in Capt. Haubert's co. 51st rgt.

Knease, Frederick. Private in Capt. Quantrill's co. 24th rgt.

Kneeland, Richard. Private in Capt. Dillon's co. 27th rgt.

Kneppenburg, Andrew. Private in Capt. Galt's co. 6th rgt.

Knight, George W. Lieutenant in Capt. Hunt's co. 7th rgt. (Ag. 1, 1814).

Knight, James. Private in Capt. Snowden's co. 36th rgt.

Knight, John. Private in Capt. Dobbin's co. 39th rgt.

Knight, Peregrine. Private in Capt. Piper's co. United Maryland Artillery.

Knight, William. Cornet in Capt. Boyer's co. 8th Cavalry Dist. (My. 22, 1812); 2d Lieutenant (Ap. 30, 1813).

Knile, Jacob. Lieutenant in Capt. Smelser's co. 28th rgt. (Je. 26, 1812).

Knode, Jacob. Private in Capt. Barr's Cavalry co. 1st Dist.

Knode, Jacob. Private in Capt. John Miller's co. 2d D. I.; b. Washington Co., Md.; age 27; shoemaker.

Knode, John of Mathias. 2d Lieutenant in Capt. Cole's co. 10th rgt. vice Swagley (Ag. 2, 1814).

Knodt, Adam. Private in Capt. Sadtler's co. Balto. Yägers.

Knodt, John. Private in Capt. Sadtler's co. Balto. Yägers.

Knorr, William. Private in Capt. Pinney's co. 27th rgt.

Knott, Charles. Private in Capt. Posey's co. 1st rgt.

Knott, Edward [1790-1866]. Ensign in Capt. Wheeler's co. 3d rgt. (Ap. 26, 1813); Lieutenant in Capt. Waile's co.

Knott, Leonard. Major in 3d rgt. (Je. 12, 1812).

Knott, William. Private in Capt. Blair's co. 50th rgt.

Knowlton, Silas. Private in Capt. Myers' co. 39th rgt.

Knox, George. Private in Capt. Burgess' co. 43d rgt.

Knox, James. Private in Capt. Kennedy's co. 27th rgt.

Knox, John. Private in Capt. Kennedy's co. 27th rgt.

Knox, Robert D. Private in Capt. Dent's co. 43d rgt.

Knox, William. Captain in 47th rgt. (Ap. 21, 1814).

Knuff, Abraham. Private in Capt. Miller's co. 39th rgt.

Koch, Henry. Private in Capt. Dillon's co. 27th rgt.

Koellenger, Henry. Private in Capt. Bader's co. Union Yägers.

Koellinger, J. L. Corporal in Capt. Bader's co. Union Yägers.

Kohlstadt, Benjamin. Private in Capt. Horton's co. Maryland Chasseurs.

Kolb, William. Lieutenant in Capt. Markey's co. 16th rgt. (S. 19, 1809).

Kolehouse, Frederick. Private in Capt. Kierstead's co. 6th rgt.

Kolehouse, Lawrence G. Private in Capt. Sheppard's co. 6th rgt.

Kone, Daniel. Private in Capt. Myers' co. 39th rgt.

Konig, F. A. L. Private in Capt. Sadtler's co. Balto. Yägers.

Konig, Samuel. Private in Capt. Berry's co. Washington Artillery.

Konkey, Charles [-1814]. Captain in 33d rgt.

Koog, Martin. Private in Capt. Bunbury's co. Sea Fencibles.

Koontz, John. Private in Capt. Steiner's Frederick Artillery.

Korns, Charles. Private in Capt. Blair's co. 50th rgt.

Koutz, George. Private in Capt. Smith's co. 51st rgt.

Krail, John G. Private in Capt. Horton's co. Maryland Chasseurs.

Kraler, Daniel. Sergeant in Capt. Levering's co. Independent Blues.

Krebbs, George. Private in Capt. Sheppard's co. 6th rgt.

Krebbs, John. Private in Capt. Miller's co. 39th rgt.

Kreigh, Frederick. Private in Capt. Myers' co. Franklin Artillery.

Krems, Reinhart. Private in Capt. Deems' co. 51st rgt

Kreps, George. Sergeant in Capt. Quantrill's co. 24th rgt.

Krider, George. Private in Capt. Barr's Cavalry co. 1st Dist.

Krouse, Jacob. Private in Capt. Smith's co. 51st rgt.

Krouss, Leonard. Captain in 30th rgt. (Je. 26, 1810).

Kuhn, A. C. Private in Capt. Sadtler's co. Balto. Yägers.

Kuinard, Thomas. Private in Capt. Stiles' co. Marine Artillery.

Kummer, Frederick. Private in Capt. Bader's co. Union Yägers.

Kurtz, Charles. Private in Capt. Levering's co. Independent Blues.

Kurtz, Henry. Private in Capt. Rogers' co. 51st rgt.

Kurtz, John. Private in Capt. McConkey's co. 27th rgt.

Kurtz, Robert. Private in Capt. McConkey's co. 27th rgt.

Kyle, Adam B. Corporal in Capt. Magruder's co. American Artillerists.

L

Labborrie, Nicholas. Private in Capt. McConkey's co. 27th rgt.

Labroche, Barnabas. Private in Capt. Edes' co. 27th rgt.

Lacey, William. Private in Capt. Addison's co. Sea Fencibles.

Lackey, John. Corporal in Capt. McConkey's co. 27th rgt.

Lackland, James C. Lieutenant in Capt. Heater's co. 44th rgt. (Ag. 22, 1812).

Lacount, Thomas. Private in Capt. Shrim's co. Balto. Light Infantry.

Lacy, Benj. H. Private in Capt. McLaughlin's co. 50th rgt.

Lacy, John. Private in Capt. Snowden's co. 36th rgt.

Lafavier, Abraham. Private in Capt. Aisquith's co. Sharp Shooters.

Lafferty, William. Lieutenant in Capt. Kennedy's co. 27th rgt.

Lafoot, John. Private in Capt. Blair's co. 50th rgt.

Laivett, Peter. Private in Capt. Haubert's co. 51st rgt.

Lake, George [1776-1831]. Captain in 48th rgt. (S. 2, 1807) ; Delegate to Genl. Assembly for Dorchester Co., 1827-28.

Lake, Washington [1784-1826]. Lieutenant in Capt. Lake's co. 48th rgt. (Jy. 8, 1813).

Lakins, Benjamin. Ensign in Capt. Easterday's co. 28th rgt. (S. 21, 1813) vice Simmons.

Lamas, James. Private in Capt. Brooke's co. 34th rgt.

Lamb, David. Private in Capt. Snowden's co. 36th rgt.

Lamb, George. Private in Capt. Steuart's co. Washington Blues.

Lamb, John. 1st Lieutenant in Capt. Montgomery's co. Balto. Union Artillery (Ag. 15, 1812); Private in same company in Sept., 1814; wounded at North Point and taken prisoner.

Lamb, William. Private in Capt. Wickes' co. 21st rgt.

Lambden, Edward. Captain in 9th rgt. (N. 30, 1811).

Lambden, James M. Paymaster in 4th rgt. (S. 12, 1814).

Lambden, Robert of Robt. Ensign Capt. Carroll's co. 26th rgt. (Je. 26, 1812).

Lambden, Thomas. Captain in Extra Battalion Dorchester Co. (O. 13, 1814).

Lambdin, William K. Private in Capt. Moore's co. 49th rgt.

Lambdon, James. Corporal in Capt. Haubert's co. 51st rgt.

Lambert, John. Lieutenant in Capt. Barr's co. 24th rgt. (Jy. 4, 1812).

Lambert, John. Private in Capt. Deems' co. 51st rgt.

Lambert, Lewis. Private in Capt. Adreon's co. Union Volunteers; captured at Bladensburg.

Lambie, James. Private in Capt. Pennington's co. Balto. Independent Artillerists. Wounded at Fort McHenry.

Lampley, John M. Private in Capt. McKane's co. 27th rgt.

Lamson, Henry. Private in Capt. Moale's co. Columbian Artillery.

Lancaster, Abram. Private in Capt. Oldham's co. 49th rgt.

Lancaster, Enoch. Private in Capt. Faster's co. 51st rgt.

Lancaster, John F. Ensign in Capt. Edelin's co. 1st rgt.

Lancaster, John F. Private in Capt. Posey's co. 1st rgt.

Lancaster, John H. Lieutenant in Capt. Hungerford's co. 1st rgt. (F. 9, 1814).

Lance, Christian. Captain in 8th rgt. (Rsd. S. 20, 1813.)

Landon, Moses. Private in Capt. Fowler's co. 46th rgt.

Landragan, Philip. Private in Capt. Galt's co. 6th rgt.

Landstreet, John [-1855]. Private in Capt. Berry's co. Washington Artillery.

Lane, Samuel [-1822]. Captain in 14th U. S. Infantry (Mr. 12, 1812); Major (Mr. 3, 1813); Lieutenant-Colonel in 32d U. S. Infantry (Je. 15, 1814).

Lane, Thomas A. Captain of the privateer *Decatur*, March, 1813; Private in Capt. Stiles' co. Marine Artillery.

Langdon, Charles. Veterinary Surgeon in 10th Cavalry Dist. (Jy. 8, 1813).

Langford, John. Private in Capt. Green's co. 46th rgt.

Langley, Walter. Captain in 12th rgt. (Je. 12, 1812).

Langrell, James. Lieutenant in Capt. Hurley's co. 11th rgt. (Ja. 25, 1814) vice Job Hurley.

Lanham, Benjamin. Private in Capt. Crawfurd's co. 17th rgt.

Lanham, George. Ensign in Capt. Sewell's co. 17th rgt. (Je. 18, 1794).

Lanham, John. Private in Capt. McConkey's co. 27th rgt.

Lanham, Richard. Lieutenant in Capt. Sewell's co. 17th rgt. (O. 13, 1796).

Lanham, William. Captain in 34th rgt. (Jy. 13, 1814) vice Duvall.

Lankford, Tubman. Private in Capt. Heath's co. 23d rgt.

Lanman, Daniel. Private in Capt. McDonald's co. 6th rgt.

Lansdale, John W. Captain in 18th rgt. (Ap. 27, 1814).

Lansdale, William M. Private in Capt. Moale's Columbian Artillery.

Lape, Samuel. Private in Capt. Getzendanner's co. 16th rgt.

Larens, Samuel. Captain of the privateer *Burrows*, June, 1814.

Larew, James. Corporal in Capt. Peters' co. 51st rgt.

Larkin, William. Private in Capt. Wilson's co. 6th rgt.

Larrimore, Robert. Captain in Artillery co. 6th Brigade Queen Anne Co. (S. 12, 1811).

Larsh, Abraham. Private in Capt. Sterett's co. Independent co.

Larsh, Charles. Private in Capt. Levering's Independent Blues.

Larsh, George. Private in Capt. Taylor's co. 46th rgt.

Larue, George. Private in Capt. Barnes' co. 32d rgt. Deserted.

Lash, George. Private in Capt. Sadtler's co. Balto. Yägers.

Lassell, William C. Private in Capt. Chambers' co. 21st rgt.

Lassell, William S. Private in Capt. Chambers's co. 21st rgt.

Lastie, John. Private in Capt. Galt's co. 6th rgt.

Late, Jacob. Cornet in Capt. Cost's co. 1st rgt. 1st Cavalry Dist. (Mr. 16, 1812).

Lathan, George L. Private in Capt. John Miller's co. 2d D. I.; b. Washington Co., Md.; age 22; tailor; subs.

Latimer, Marcus. Ensign in 36th U. S. Infantry (O. 25, 1813); 2d Lieutenant (S. 30, 1814).

Latimer, Thomas, Jr. Private in Capt. Posey's co. 1st rgt.

Latimer, R. W. Sergeant in Capt. Moale's co. Columbian Artillery.

Laty, John. Private in Capt. Stiles' co. Marine Artillery.

Lauderman, Frederick. Private in Capt. Sheppard's co. 6th rgt.

Lauderman, George. Private in Capt. Brown's co. 6th rgt.

Laudun, Martin. Private in Capt. Sadtler's co. Balto. Yägers.

Lauduslager, Jacob. Private in Capt. Horton's co. Maryland Chasseurs.

Laughridge, John. Private in Capt. McLaughlin's co. 50th rgt.

Laviele, John T. Lieutenant in Capt. Broome's co. 31st rgt. (F. 25, 1811).

Law, Henry. Corporal in Capt. Cozier's co. 30th rgt.

Law, John. Ensign in Capt. Lawrence's co. 20th rgt. (Ag. 9, 1808).

Lawless, John. Private in Capt. Steever's co. 27th rgt.

Lawrence, John M. Surgeon in 46th rgt. (Je. 5, 1812).

Lawrence, John T. Captain in 20th rgt. (Ap. 9, 1808).

Lawrence, Joseph. Private in Capt. Wilson's co. 6th rgt.

Lawrence, Joseph. Corporal in Chalmers' co. 51st rgt.

Lawrence, Thomas L. Captain in 6th rgt. (Jy. 12, 1814).

Lawrence, William [-1841]. Major in 2d U. S. Infantry (Ap. 19, 1814); bvt. Lieutenant-Colonel (S. 15, 1814) for gallant conduct in defense of Ft. Bowyer, Ala. against greatly superior land and naval forces.

Lawrenson, James. Bo'sun in Capt. Bunbury's co. Sea Fencibles.

Laws, James of James. Major in Extra Battalion Worcester Co. (S. 21, 1810).

Lawson, George. Private in Capt. Nicholson's co. Balto. Fencibles.

Lawson, James. Ensign in Capt. Juett's co. 23d rgt. (Jy. 14, 1814) vice Wilson.

Lawson, James. Private in Capt. Eversfield's co. 17th rgt.

Lawson, Richard. Private in Capt. Levering's co. Independent Blues.

Lawson, Robert. Captain in Balto. Patriots.

Lawson, Stephen. Corporal in Capt. Magruder's co. American Artillerists.

Lawton, Jacob H. Corporal in Capt. McConkey's co. 27th rgt.

Lawton, Jacob H. Private in Capt. Adreon's co. Union Volunteers.

Lawton, John. Private in Capt. Hancock's co. 22d rgt.

Lawton, John. Private in Capt. McConkey's co. 27th rgt.

Lawyer, John. Private in Capt. Hayward's co. 4th rgt.

Lawyer, John. Ensign in Capt. Wolfe's co. 10th rgt. (S. 20, 1813).

Layfield, James. Private in Capt. Heath's co. 23d rgt.

Layfield, John. Private in Capt. Heath's co. 23d rgt.

Layfield, Thomas of David. Private in Capt. Heath's co. 23d rgt.

Layfield, Thomas of John. Private in Capt. Heath's co. 23d rgt.

Layman, John C. Ensign in Capt. Wm. Thompson's co. 1st rgt. (Jy. 11, 1814).

Layman, Nicholas. Private in Capt. Rogers' co. 51st rgt.

Lea, George W. 3d Lieutenant in 38th U. S. Infantry (Ag. 15, 1813).

Lea, Isaac. Private in Capt. Massey's co. 38th rgt.

Lea, Isaac C. Sergeant in Capt. Moale's co. Columbian Artillery.

Lea, Samuel John. Lieutenant in Capt. Adreon's co. Union Volunteers (Ja. 10, 1814) vice Taylor.

Leach, Henry. Private in Capt. Kierstead's co. 6th rgt.

Leach, Jesse. Paymaster in 44th rgt. (Ag. 22, 1812).

Leach, John. Private in Capt. McDonald's co. 6th rgt.

Leaf, Johnzie. Private in Capt. Galt's co. 6th rgt.

League, Abraham. Private in Capt. Wilson's co. 6th rgt.

League, James. Drummer in Capt. Lawrence's co. 6th rgt.

League, Nathan. Private in Capt. Steever's co. 27th rgt.

Leahy, John. Private in Capt. Wilson's co. 6th rgt.

Leakin, Sheppard Church. Captain in 38th U. S. Infantry (My. 20, 1813); Mayor of Baltimore, 1838.

Leakin, Thomas J. Private in Capt. Slicer's co. 22d rgt.; 3 Lieutenant in 38th U. S. Infantry (My. 20, 1813).

Leakins, James. Corporal in Capt. Stapleton's co. 39th rgt.

Lear, William W. [-1846]. Private, Corporal and Sergeant in U. S. Light Dragoons My. 18, 1812, to Je. 15, 1815.

Leard, Samuel. Private in Capt. Edes' co. 27th rgt.

Leary, Peter [1781-1871]. Lieutenant in Capt. A. E. Warner's co. 39th rgt.; Judge of the Orphan's Court of Balto, 1844; Judge of Appeal Tax Court; Commissioner of Public Schools; one of the founders of the Md. Institute.

Leas, William A. Private in Capt. Dunnington's co. 43d rgt.

24

Leath, Samuel. Lieutenant in Capt. Smith's co. 51st rgt.

Leatherbury, Thomas. Private in Capt. Burke's co. 6th rgt.

Leatherbury, Willis. Lieutenant in Capt. Ballard's co. 25th rgt. (Je. 1, 1813).

Leatherwood, John. Private in Capt. Bader's co. Union Yägers.

Lebon, Charles. Private in Capt. Pike's co. Balto. Volunteer Artillery.

LeCompte, Benjamin W. Paymaster Extra Battalion Dorchester Co. (Mr. 27, 1813).

Ledwell, Benjamin. Private in Capt. Travers' co. 48th rgt.

Lee, Benjamin. Surgeon's mate in 17th rgt. (Ap. 21, 1813).

Lee, Caleb. Ensign in Capt. Wallace's co. 18th rgt. (D. 4, 1810).

Lee, Charles G. Private in Capt. Blakistone's co. 45th rgt.

Lee, Elias. Private in Capt. Morgan's co. 49th rgt.

Lee, Frederick. Private in Capt. McLaughlin's co. 50th rgt.

Lee, George. Captain of the privateer *Oriental*, Sept., 1812; of the *Bordeaux Packet*, Nov., 1813; Private in Capt. Stiles' co. Marine Artillery.

Lee, George. Corporal in Capt. Conway's co. 6th rgt.

Lee, George. Private in Capt. McConkey's co. 27th rgt.

Lee, George. Private in Capt. Thomas's co. 49th rgt.

Lee, Henry, Jr. [-1837]. Major in 36th U. S. Infantry (Ap. 8, 1813).

Lee, Jacob. Private in Capt. McLaughlin's co. 50th rgt.

Lee, James. Ensign in Capt. Perrigo's co. 46th rgt. (Jy. 8, 1814).

Lee, James. Private in Capt. McLaughlin's co. 50th rgt.

Lee, James A. Private in Capt. Aisquith's co. Sharp Shooters.

Lee, James H. Private in Capt. Levering's co. Independent Blues.

Lee, John. Private in Capt. Hall's co. 3d Cavalry rgt

Lee, John. Private in Capt. McLaughlin's co. 50th rgt.

Lee, John. Private in Capt. Roney's co. 39th rgt.

Lee, Joseph. Private in Capt. Sands' co. 22d rgt.

Lee, Joseph. Corporal in Capt. Slicer's co. 22d rgt.

Lee, Richard Henry. Ensign in 36th U. S. Infantry (Ap. 30, 1813); 3d Lieutenant in Artillery corps; bvt. 2d Lieutenant Ag. 15, 1814, for distinguished services in the defense of Ft. Erie, U. C.

Lee, Samuel John. Lieutenant in Capt. Adreon's co. Union Volunteers.

Lee, Thomas. Private in Capt. McKane's co. 27th rgt.

Lee, William D. Captain in 7th Cavalry Dist. (Mr. 16, 1812).

Lee, William T. Captain in 45th rgt. (My. 23, 1812).

Leeson, John. Private in Capt. Shrim's co. Balto. Light Infantry.

Lefler, George. Private in Capt. Schwarzauer's co. 27th rgt.

Leforge, Clarkson. Private in Capt. Steever's co. 27th rgt.

Legard, Joseph. Sergeant in Capt. Faster's co. 51st rgt.

Legg, James. Private in Capt. Page's co. 21st rgt.

Legg, Richard. Ensign in Capt. Scott's co. 35th rgt. (Ap. 29, 1814).

Legg, William. Lieutenant in Capt. Emory's co. 38th rgt. (Ag. 16, 1808).

Legrand, Samuel. Lieutenant in Capt. Pinney's co. 27th rgt.

Lehea, Morris. Private in Capt. Brown's co. Eagle Artillerists.

Leider, Jacob. Blacksmith in Capt. Barr's Cavalry co. 1st Dist.

Leigh, William. Private in Capt. Levering's co. Independent Blues.

Leinhart, Henry. Private in Capt. Brown's co. Eagle Artillerists.

Leitch, Benjamin. Captain in 31st rgt. (Mr. 19, 1813).

Leith, John. Command unknown; prisoner at Bladensburg.

Lemars, John. Seaman of the privateer *High Flyer*, wounded in action, Dec., 1812.

Lemmon, Alexis. Major in 46th rgt. (Jy. 14, 1812).

Lemmon, Charles. Lieutenant in Capt. Merryman's co. 41st rgt. (Je. 22, 1808).

Lemmon, Henry. Private in Capt. Brown's co. 6th rgt.

Lemmon, Nicholas. Private in Capt. Snowden's co. 36th rgt.

Lemmon, Robert. Private in Capt. Moale's co. Columbian Artillery.

Lemmon, Wm. P. Sergeant in Capt. Moale's co. Columbian Artillery.

Lemmon, William P. 3d Lieutenant in 1st U. S. Infantry (S. 16, 1814).

Lemmonier, A. L. Private in Capt. Warfield's co. Balto. United Volunteers.

Lemonth, Alexander. Private in Capt. Edes' co. 27th rgt.

Lenox, James. Private in Capt. Brown's co. Eagle Artillerists.

Lenox, Richard. Sergeant in Capt. McKane's co. 27th rgt.

Lenox, William. Private in Capt. Galt's co. 6th rgt.

Leonard, Amassa. Private in Capt. Dobbin's co. 39th rgt.

Leonard, Jeremiah. Private in Capt. Shryock's co. 24th rgt.

Leoni, G. C. Private in Capt. Lawrence's co. 6th rgt.

Lepeltier, Francis. Private in Capt. Miller's co. 39th rgt.

Leppo, Jacob. Private in Capt. Blizzard's co. Nace's rgt.

Lerew, Abraham. Private in Capt. Nicholson's co. Balto. Fencibles. Wounded at Fort McHenry.

Lerew, John. Private in Capt. Nicholson's co. Balto. Fencibles.

Lerich, Barney. Sergeant in Capt. Kierstead's co. 6th rgt.

Lester, John. Ensign in Capt. Dillon's co. 27th rgt.

Lester, John. 1st Lieutenant in Capt. Piper's co. United Maryland Artillery (Ap. 30, 1813).

Letherbury, Charles. Private in Capt. Usselton's co. Artillery 6th Brigade.

Letters, Daniel. Private in Capt. McLaughlin's co. 50th rgt.

Levely, H. Captain of the privateer *Nonsuch*.

Levely, John S. Private in Capt. Moale's co. Columbian Artillery.

Levely, William. Private in Capt. Levering's co. Independent Blues.

Levering, Aaron R. [1784-1852]. Captain in Independent Blues.

Levering, Jesse. Private in Capt. Sterett's co. Independent co.

Levering, John. Private in Capt. Sterett's co. Independent co.

Levering, Peter. Private in Capt. A. E. Warner's 39th rgt.

356 APPENDIX

Leverton, Daniel. 1st Lieutenant in Capt. Saulsbury's co. 10th Cavalry Dist. (N. 3, 1812).

Levy, Andrew. Private in Capt. Horton's co. Maryland Chasseurs.

Levy, Peter. Sergeant in Capt. Thompson's co. 1st rgt.

Levy, Thomas. Private in Capt. Howard's co. Mechanical Volunteers.

Levy, Vincent. Private in Capt. McKane's co. 27th rgt.

Lewellin, John. Private in Capt. Kennedy's co. 27th rgt.

Lewis, Abel. Private in Capt. Travers' co. 48th rgt.

Lewis, Elisha. Sergeant in Capt. Pinney's co. 27th rgt.

Lewis, Elisha. Private in Capt. Travers' co. 48th rgt.

Lewis, Elisha J. 1st Lieutenant in Capt. Montgomery's co. Balto. Union Artillery (S. 21, 1813) vice Lamb.

Lewis, James. Private in Capt. Burke's co. 6th rgt.

Lewis, Jesse. Private in Capt. Snowden's co. 36th rgt.

Lewis, Joab. Fifer in Capt. Travers' co. 48th rgt.

Lewis, John. Private in Capt. Smith's co. 51st rgt.

Lewis, John. Private in Capt. McKane's co. 27th rgt.

Lewis, Joseph. Private in Capt. Wells' Artillery co. 22d rgt.

Lewis, Joseph. Ensign. in Capt Holmes' co. 18th rgt. (Je. 12, 1812).

Lewis, Lewis D. Private in Capt. Ringgold's co. 6th rgt.

Lewis, Reuben. Sergeant in Capt. Travers' co. 48th rgt.

Lewis, Robert. Private in Capt. Bean's co. 12th rgt.

Lewis, Samuel. Private in Capt. Pumphrey's co. 22d rgt.

Lewis, Shadrach. Private in Capt. Edes' co. 27th rgt.

Lewis, Stephen. Lieutenant in Capt. Hughes' co. 3d rgt. (Ag. 30, 1808).

Lewis, Thomas. Private in Capt. Sample's co. 49th rgt.

Lewis, William W. 1st Lieutenant in Capt. Barnes' Artillery co. 5th Brigade (Ja. 21, 1814).

Lewis, William W. Private in Capt. Dent's co. 43d rgt.

Lewis, Willoughby. Private in Capt. Faster's co. 51st rgt.

Liams, Jeremiah. Private in Capt. Smith's co. 51st rgt.

Light, John. Private in Capt. Dobbin's co. 39th rgt.

Lightner, George. Private in Capt. Steever's co. 27th rgt.

Lightner, George W. Captain in 30th rgt. Rifle co. (Ap. 22, 1814).

Lightner, Henry. Drummer in Capt. Berry's co. Washington Artllery.

Limner, Laurence. Private in Capt. Addison's co. Sea Fencibles.

Linch, John. Private in Capt. Berry's co. Washington Artillery.

Lindenberger, Jacob. Private in Capt. Nicholson's co. Balto. Fencibles.

Lindenburger, John C. Private in Capt. Smith's co. 51st rgt.

Linderman, William. Private in Capt. Thos. Warner's co. 39th rgt.

Lindsey, Samuel. Sergeant in Capt. Dyer's co. 17th rgt.

Linebargar, Samuel. Private in Capt. Smith's co. 51st rgt.

Lineberger, William. Corporal in Capt. Myers' co. 39th rgt.

Ling, Robert. Private in Capt. Sheppard's co. 6th rgt.

Link, Henry. Private in Capt. Miller's co. 39th rgt.

Linsey, Andrew. Private in Capt. Pike's co. Balto. Volunteer Artillery.

Linsey, Michael. Private in Capt. Pike's co. Balto. Volunteer Artillery.

Linthicum, Abner. Captain in 22d rgt. (S. 11, 1809).

Linthicum, Charles. Adjutant in 32d rgt. (O. 21, 1812).

Linthicum, Francis. Private in Capt. Brohawn's co. 48th rgt.

Linthicum, Frederick. Captain in 2d Cavalry Dist. (My. 22, 1812). Resigned Jy., 1814.

Linthicum, Hezekiah. Private in Capt. Pumphrey's co. 22d rgt.; Sergeant in Capt. Barnes' co. 32d rgt.

Linthicum, John. Private in Capt. Travers' co. 48th rgt.

Linthicum, Richard. Private in Capt. Linthicum's co. 22d rgt.

Linthicum, William. Captain in 48th rgt. (S. 21, 1813).

Linton, John. Ensign in Capt. Patton's co. 30th rgt. (Jy. 8, 1811).

Linvill, John. Private in Capt. Magruder's co. American Artillerists.

Linville, James M. Private in Capt. Moale's co. Columbian Artillery.

Lishar, Thomas. Private in Capt. Griffith's co. 21st rgt.; deserted July 25, 1814.

Lister, Edward. Private in Capt. Morgan's co. 49th rgt.

Litchfield, John. Private in Capt. Pumphrey's co. 22d rgt.

Litsinger, William. Private in Capt. Blizzard's co. Nace's rgt.

Litten, Thomas. Private in Capt. Wilson's co. 6th rgt.

Littig, Philip. Private in Capt. McKane's co. 27th rgt.

Little, George. Captain in 9th Cavalry Dist. (My. 22, 1812).

Little, James. Captain in 40th rgt. (Je. 16, 1812).

Little, James. Private in Capt. Sheppard's co. 6th rgt.

Little, John. Private in Capt. Kennedy's co. 27th rgt.

Little, Joseph. Ensign in Capt. Deems' co. 51st rgt.

Little, Peter [1775-1830]. Colonel in 38th U. S. Infantry (My. 19, 1813); Delegate to General Assembly, 1806; Member of Congress, 1810.

Little, Robert. Sergeant in Capt. McLaughlin's co. 50th rgt.

Little, William. Private in Capt. Steever's co. 27th rgt.

Littlejohn, Leonard M. Lieutenant in Capt. Ent's co. 16th rgt. (Ag. 20, 1814).

Litton, Brice. Captain in 44th rgt. (Ag. 22, 1812).

Livers, Arnold. Private in Capt. Stapleton's co. 39th rgt.

Livers, Thomas. Ensign in Capt. Ogle's co. 47th rgt. (My. 22, 1812).

Livingston, James. Private in Capt. Pinney's co. 27th rgt.

Livres, G. William. Private in Capt. Bunbury's co. Sea Fencibles.

Lizer, Jacob. Private in Capt. Shryock's co. 24th rgt.

Lizer, Jonas. Private in Capt. Shryock's co. 24th rgt.

Lizer, William. Private in Capt. Shryock's co. 24th rgt.

Llewellin, John. Ensign in Capt. Lee's co. 45th rgt. (My. 23, 1812).

Lloyd, Edward. Lieutenant-Colonel in 9th Cavalry Dist. (F. 13, 1812).

Lloyd, Frisby P. Private in Capt. Allen's co. 49th rgt.

Lloyd, James. 2d Lieutenant in Capt. Frisby's co. Kent Co. militia (S. 11, 1776); General in War of 1812.

Lloyd, John. Private in Capt. Conway's co. 6th rgt.

Lloyd, William. Private in Capt. Smith's co. 51st rgt.

Lloyd, William. Private in Capt. Myers' co. Franklin Artillery.

Lloyd, William. Private in Capt. McKane's co. 27th rgt.

Loar, George. Private in Capt. McLaughlin's co. 50th rgt.

Loatz, John. Private in Capt. McLaughlin's co. 50th rgt.

Lobby, Lewis. Private in Capt. Galt's co. 6th rgt.

Locher, John. Private in Capt. Shryock's co. 24th rgt.

Lock, Alexander. Private in Capt. Melton's (later Cawood's) co. 45th rgt.; Baggage master in 5th Brigade (D. 20, 1814).

Lock, Samuel. Private in Capt. Dyer's co. Fells Point Riflemen.

Lock, Washington. Private in Capt. Lawrence's co. 6th rgt.

Lock, William. Private in Capt. Dyer's co. Fells Point Riflemen.

Lockard, John. Private in Capt. Blizzard's co. Nace's rgt.

Locke, Benedict. Private in Capt. Melton's co. 45th rgt.

Locke, Charles J. Private in Capt. Blakistone's co. 45th rgt.

Locke, Thomas M. Sergeant in Capt. Pennington's co. Balto. Independent Artillerists.

Locker, Jacob. Private in Capt. Quantrill's co. 24th rgt.

Lockerman, Richard. Private in Capt. Maynard's co. 22d rgt.

Lockhead, Joseph. Private in Capt. Steuart's co. Washington Blues.

Logan, John B. Private in Capt. Steever's co. 27th rgt.

Logan, Joseph. Private in Capt. Haubert's co. 51st rgt.

Logan, Samuel. Private in Capt. Schwarzauer's co. 27th rgt.

Logue, Francis. Private in Capt. Frizzell's co. 15th rgt.

Logue, Joshua. Private in Capt. Frizzell's co. Nace's rgt.

Lomax, John. Private in Capt. Dunnington's co. 43d rgt.

Lomax, Samuel. Private in Capt. Dunnington's co. 43d rgt.; served also in Capt. Brown's co. 43d rgt.

Loney, Jacob. Private in Capt. Quantrill's co. 24th rgt.

Loney, John. Private in Capt. Moale's co. Columbian Artillery.

Long, Abraham. Private in Capt. Montgomery's co. Balto. Union Artillery.

Long, Conrad. Private in Capt. Blizzard's co. Nace's rgt.

Long, Cornelius B. Sergeant in Capt. Sheppard's co. 6th rgt.

Long, Francis. Private in Capt. Bader's co. Union Yägers.

Long, George. Private in Capt. Blair's co. 50th rgt.

Long, Henry. Private in Capt. Blizzard's co. 15th rgt.

Long, Henry. Private in Capt. Steever's co. 27th rgt.

Long, Jacob. Private in Capt. Brown's co. 6th rgt.

Long, Jesse [1793-1857]. Private in Capt. Stewart's co. Washington Blues.

Long, John. Private in Capt. Galt's co. 6th rgt.

Long, Kennedy. Lieutenant-Colonel in 27th rgt.

Long, Levi. Private in Capt. Mc-Kane's co. 27th rgt.

Long, Nathan. Ensign in Capt. Orrick's co. 41st rgt. (Jy. 11, 1814).

Long, Reuben. Private in Capt. Levering's co. Independent Blues.

Long, Robert W.[-1813]. Ensign in 14th U. S. Infantry (Mr. 12, 1812).

Long, Samuel. Ensign in Capt. Bankert's co. 20th rgt. (Jy. 13, 1814).

Long, Sylvanus. Lieutenant of the privateer *Rossie;* mortally wounded in action with the *Princess Amelia.*

Long, William. Corporal in Capt. Posey's co. 1st rgt.

Long, William C. 3d Lieutenant in Capt. Myers' co. Franklin Artillery (Jy. 15, 1814).

Longellee, Lewis. Private in Capt. Peters' co. 51st rgt.

Longfellow, Edward. Private in Capt. Boyer's co. 33d rgt.

Longford, John. Private in Capt. Edes' co. 27th rgt.

Longman, Jacob. Private in Capt. Marker's co. 28th rgt.

Longwell, John. Private in Capt. Mackey's co. 49th rgt.

Longwell, Walter. Lieutenant in Capt. Mackey's co. 49th rgt. (Ag. 19, 1809).

Lora, John. Private in Capt. Shryock's co. 24th rgt.

Loree, Reuben. Private in Capt. Snowden's co. 36th rgt.

Lorman, Alexander. Private in Capt. Sterett's co. 1st Balto. Hussars.

Lorman, William. Private in Capt. Brown's co. Eagle Artillerists.

Loud, Baltzer. Private in Capt. Schwarzauer's co. 27th rgt.

Love, Archibald. Private in Capt. McLaughlin's co. 50th rgt.

Love, Bennett. Captain in 40th rgt. Rifle co. (F. 14, 1815).

Love, Charles. Private in Capt. Dent's co. 43d rgt.

Love, James. Private in Capt. Rogers' co. 51st rgt.

Love, Joseph. Private in Capt. Steever's co. 27th rgt.

Love, Leonard. Private in Capt. Dunnington's co. 43d rgt.

Love, Robert. Private in Capt. Hynson's co. 21st rgt.

Loveall, Aquilla. Private in Capt. Blizzard's co. Nace's rgt.

Lovedet, John. Private in Capt. Ringgold's co. 6th rgt.

Lovelace, Thomas H. Private in Capt. Brooke's co. 34th rgt.

Lover, Zebulon. Private in Capt. Shryock's co. 24th rgt.

Lovering, Francis. Private in Capt. Sterett's co. 1st Balto. Hussars.

Lovett, Philip. Private in Capt. Ogle's co. 47th rgt.; deserted from Patapsco encampment; court-martialed and ordered to ride the "wooden horse" for ten minutes.

Low, Adam. Private in Capt. Roney's co. 39th rgt.

Low, Arthur. Captain in 11th rgt. (Ag. 20, 1814).

Low, Rezin. Private in Capt. Veitch's co. 34th rgt.

Lowdermilk, Peter. Lieutenant in Capt. Blair's co. 50th rgt. (My. 28, 1808).

Lowdermilk, Samuel, Ensign in Capt. Blair's co. 50th rgt.

Lowe, Edward. Private in Capt. Ducker's co. 7th rgt.

Lowe, Henderson P. Private in Capt. Berry's co. Washington Artillery.

Lowery, John. Private in Capt. Blair's co. 50th rgt.

Lowery, Samuel. Private in Capt. Garrett's co. 49th rgt.

Lowery, William. Private in Capt. Garrett's co. 49th rgt.

Lowman, Emory. Private in Capt. Berry's co. Washington Artillery. Wounded at Fort McHenry.

Lowman, Thomas. Captain in 35th rgt. (My. 27, 1811).

Lowndes, Richard. Lieutenant in Capt. Cramphin's co. 14th rgt. (Je. 18, 1794).

Lowra, Henry. Captain in 24th rgt. (Je. 16, 1812).

Lowry, Robert. Private in Capt. Montgomery's co. Balto. Union Artillery.

Lowrye, Henry. Captain in 1st rgt. (Ragan's).

Luberg, John. Private in Capt. Conway's co. 6th rgt.

Lucas, Fielding, Jr. Private in Capt. McKane's co. 27th rgt.

Lucas, Harrison. Private in Capt. Levering's co. Independent Blues.

Lucas, James. Private in Capt. Frizell's co. 15th rgt.

Lucas, James. Private in Capt. Stewart's co. 51st rgt.

Lucas, Joseph. Private in Capt. Shrim's co. Balto. Light Infantry.

Lucas, Samuel. Private in Capt. Sterett's Independent co.

Luckett, John Roger Nelson [-1813]. Captain in 2d U. S. Infantry (Jy. 6, 1812).

Luckett, Nelson. Major in U. S. Light Dragoons (Ja. 20, 1813); Lieutenant-Colonel (Ag. 1, 1813).

Luckett, Valentine P. Ensign in 14th U. S. Infantry (Mr. 12, 1812); 2d Lieutenant in 1st U. S. Light Dragoons (O. 9, 1812).

Ludden, Lemuel, Jr. Private in Capt. Sterett's co. 1st Balto. Hussars.

Lugenbeel, Moses. Ensign in Capt. Dutterow's co. 20th rgt. (Ap. 27, 1813).

Luke, William. Private in Capt. Heath's co. 23d rgt.

Luley, Charles. Private in Capt. Bunbury's co. Sea Fencibles.

Lum, Michael. Sergeant in Capt. Cozier's co. 30th rgt.

Lusby, Benjamin. Private in Capt. Pinkney's Artillery co. [Ag., 1813]; Private in Capt. Chase's co. 22d rgt. [N., 1814].

Lusby, Henry. Private in Capt. Pumphrey's co. 22d rgt.

Lusby, Henry. Ensign in Capt. Roney's co. 39th rgt.

Lusby, John. Private in Capt. Allen's co. 49th rgt.

Lusby, John of Thomas. Private in Capt. Morgan's co. 49th rgt.

Lusby, John C. Ensign in Capt. A. C. Smith's co. 49th rgt.

Lusby, John H. Private in Capt. Morgan's co. 49th rgt.

Lusby, Robert. Ensign in Capt. Boyer's co. 33d rgt. (Jy. 11, 1814) vice Woodall.

Lusby, Robert C. Lieutenant in Capt. A. C. Smith's co. 49th rgt. (S. 10, 1814).

Lusby, Thomas. Private in Capt. Pinkney's Artillery co. 22d rgt.

Lusby, William. Private in Capt. Pennington's co. Balto. Independent Artillerists.

Luster, Shipley. Private in Capt. Smith's co. 51st rgt.

Lutz, Samuel. Private in Capt. Shryock's co. 24th rgt.

Lyas, Micajah. Ensign in Capt. Reinhart's co. 20th rgt. (Jy. 12, 1814).

Lyles, David C. Private in Capt. Moale's co. Columbian Artillery.

Lyles, Henry. Private in Capt. Ireland's co. 31st rgt.

Lyles, Richard J. Private in Capt. Hall's co. 34th rgt.

Lyles, Zachariah. Private in Capt. Hall's co. 34th rgt.

Lynch, Abraham. Private in Capt. Conway's co. 6th rgt.

Lynch, Amos W. Ensign in Capt. Hall's co. 35th rgt. (Ap. 21, 1814).

Lynch, James. Private in Capt. Lawson's co. Balto. Patriots.

Lynch, Jethro. 2d Lieutenant in Capt. Stansbury's co. 6th Cavalry Dist. (Jy. 8, 1814).

Lynch, John. Captain in 11th rgt. (Je. 1, 1813).

Lynch, John [-1813]. Ensign in 14th U. S. Infantry (O. 9, 1812); 2d Lieutenant (Ag. 15, 1813); killed N. 11, 1813, in battle of Chrystler's Field U. C.

Lynch, John. Private in Capt. Green's co. 46th rgt.

Lynch, Patrick. Private in Capt. Dobbin's co. 39th rgt.

Lynch, Peregrine L. Private in Capt. A. C. Smith's co. 49th rgt.

Lynch, Samuel, Jr. Ensign in Capt. Drury's co. 10th rgt. (S. 20, 1813).

Lynch, William. Private in Capt. Green's co. 46th rgt.

Lynch, William. Private in Capt. Steuart's co. Washington Blues.

Lynes, George. Private in Capt. Quantrill's co. 24th rgt.

Lynes, John. Corporal in Capt. Dobbin's co. 39th rgt.

Lyon, Alexander. Corporal in Capt. Sotheran's co. 45th rgt.

Lyon, Charles. 2d Lieutenant in Capt. Carnan's co. 6th Cavalry Dist. (Je. 26, 1812); 1st Lieutenant (Jy. 8, 1814) vice Williamson.

Lyon, Robert. Major in 6th Cavalry Dist. (F. 13, 1812).

Lyon, Robert, Jr. Private in Capt. Moale's co. Columbian Artillery.

Lyon, William. Private in Capt. Thompson's co. 1st rgt.

Lyon, William. Lieutenant in Capt. Rowe's co. 5th rgt. (Ag. 5, 1814).

Lyon, William. Private in Capt. Watson's co. 39th rgt.

Lyons, John. Private in Capt. Snowden's co. 36th rgt.

Lythe, John. Private in Capt. Aisquith's co. Sharp Shooters.

Lytle, Thomas. Private in Capt. Moale's co. Columbian Artillery.

M

Maas, Andrew. Private in Capt. Roney's co. 39th rgt.

McAdow, Andrew. Captain in 42d rgt. (O. 3, 1807).

McAllister, Richard. Private in Capt. Dyer's co. Fells Point Riflemen.

McAllister, Robert. Sergeant in Capt. Chalmers' co. 51st rgt.

McArdel, Henry. Private in Capt. Rogers' co. 51st rgt.

Macatee, Henry. Captain 7th Cavalry Dist. (Ap. 16, 1812).

McAtee, Walter. Lieutenant in Capt. Blair's co. 50th rgt. (O. 16, 1810).

McAttic, Francis. Private in Capt. Moale's co. Columbian Artilelry.

McBayne, Thomas. Private in Capt. Dent's co. 43d rgt.

McBean, Angus. Private in Capt. Kierstead's co. 6th rgt.

Macbee, Alexander. Private in Capt. Hall's co. 34th rgt.

Macbee, Philip. Private in Capt. Brooke's co. 34th rgt.

McBryde, Samuel. Cornet in Capt. A. E. Jones' co. 11th Cavalry Dist. (D. 17, 1814) vice Dashiell.

McCafferty, John. Private in Capt. Sheppard's co. 6th rgt.

McCain, Charles. Private in Capt. Edes' co. 27th rgt.

McCall, Robert. Command unknown; prisoner at Bladensburg.

McCann, Thomas. Private in Capt. McConkey's co. 27th rgt.

McCanna, William. Private in Capt. Stewart's co. 51st rgt.

McCardell, William. Sergeant in Capt. Quantrill's co. 24th rgt.

McCarter, James. Private in Capt. Adreon's co. Union Volunteers.

McCarthy, Alexander. Private in Deems' co. 51st rgt.

McCartney, James. Private in Capt. Blair's co. 50th rgt.

McCartney, Peter. Private in Capt. Pennington's co. Balto. Independent Artillerists.

McCaughin, Davis. Ensign in Capt. Kierstead's co. 6th rgt. (Jy. 12, 1814).

Macauley, Elijah. Private in Capt. Brooke's co. 34th rgt.

McCauley, Hugh. Ensign in Capt. Stonebraker's co. 24th rgt. (Ag. 1, 1814) vice Williams.

McCauley, James. Private in Capt. Stewart's co. 51st rgt.

McCaully, Arthur. Private in Capt. Chalmers' co. 51st rgt.

McCauly, James. Private in Capt. Waters' co. 22d rgt.

McCausland, George. Major in Extra Battalion Harford Co. (Ap. 5, 1808).

McCeeney, Benjamin. Captain in 1813; command unknown.

McChristal, James. Private in Capt. McConkey's co. 27th rgt.

McChristal, John. Private in Capt. McConkey's co. 27th rgt.

McChristal, Patrick. Private in Capt. McConkey's co. 27th rgt.

McClain, Charles. Private in Capt. Brown's co. Eagle Artillerists.

McClain, George. Private in Capt. Steiner's Frederick Artillery.

McClain, John. Private in Capt. Ringgold's co. 6th rgt.

McClain, John. Private in Capt. Berry's co. Washington Artillery.

McClanahan, Robert. Private in Capt. Quantrill's co. 24th rgt.

McClane, Elias. Private in Capt. McKane's co. 27th rgt.

McCleanley, John. Private in Capt. Kierstead's co. 6th rgt.

McClellan, Matthew. Private in Capt. Ringgold's co. 6th rgt.

McClellan, Samuel. Sergeant in Capt. Sterett's co. 1st Balto. Hussars.

McClellan, William. Private in Capt. Warfield's co. Balto. United Volunteers. Killed at North Point.

McClellen, Andrew. Sergeant in Capt. Myers' co. Franklin Artillery.

McClenahan, James. Private in Capt. Brown's co. 49th rgt.

McClenan, William. 2d Lieutenant in Capt. Damsell's Artillery co. 1st Brigade (D. 10, 1813).

McCloskey, A. Private in Capt. Stiles' co. Marine Artillery.

McCloskey, James. Captain, Asst. Depy. Q. M. U. S. (Je. 24, 1813).

McCluster, Henry. Private in Capt. Brown's co. Eagle Artillerists.

McCollister, Richard. Private in Capt. Wilson's co. 6th rgt.

McColm, Mathew. Private in Capt. Pike's Balto. Volunteer Artillery.

McComas, Aquila. Lieutenant in Capt. Amoss's co. 40th rgt. (Jy. 14, 1814).

McComas, Charles. Private in Capt. Addison's co. Sea Fencibles.

McComas, Harry Gough. Private in Capt. Aisquith's co. Sharp Shooters. Killed at North Point.

McComas, John. Quarter-master in 7th Cavalry Dist. (Ja. 18, 1814) vice Eady.

McComas, Nathaniel. Lieutenant in Capt. Bradford's co. 42d rgt. (Ag. 19, 1809).

McComas, Preston. Ensign in Capt. Amoss' co. 40th rgt. (Mr. 11, 1808).

McComas, Zacheus O. [1792-1867]. Private in Capt. Lowrye's co. 1st rgt.

McCombs, Solo. Private in Capt. Stiles' co. Marine Artillery.

McConchie, Alexander J. Lieutenant in Capt. Burgess' co. 43d rgt.

McConchie, John. Private in Capt. Burgess' co. 43d rgt.

McConchie, John T. S. Private in Capt. Dunnington's co. 43d rgt.

McConchie, Thomas. Private in Capt. Burgess' co. 43d rgt.

McConckie, Walter. Private in Capt. Burgess' co. 43d rgt.

McConcking, William E. Captain in 38th rgt.

McConkey, Alexander T. Lieutenant in Capt. Burgess' co. 43d rgt. (Je. 5, 1812).

McConkey, James. Captain in 27th rgt.

McConkey, William. Private in Capt. Ringgold's co. 6th rgt.

McConkey, William. Private in Capt. Edes' co. 27th rgt.

McCorkle, John. Lieutenant in Capt. Lightner's co. 30th rgt. (Ap. 22, 1814).

McCormack, John. Private in Capt. Chalmers' co. 51st rgt.

McCormack, John, Jr. Private in Capt. Chalmers' co. 51st rgt.

McCormick, Alexander. Lieutenant in Capt. Dermot's co. 14th rgt. (Ap. 26, 1799).

McCormick, James. Private in Capt. Faster's co. 51st rgt.

McCormick, Thomas. Private in Capt. Snowden's co. 36th rgt.

McCormick, Thomas. Private in Capt. Peters' co. 51st rgt.

McCosh, Samuel. Private in Capt. Jas. Massey's co. 38th rgt.

McCotton, Charles. Private in Capt. Brohawn's co. 48th rgt.

McCoul, James. Private in Capt. Lawson's co. Balto. Patriots.

McCoul, Robert. Private in Capt. Lawson's co. Balto. Patriots.

McCoy, Alexander. Private in Capt. Addison's co. Sea Fencibles.

McCoy, Daniel. Lieutenant in Capt. Hunter's co. 8th rgt. (Je. 1, 1813).

McCoy, David. Private in Capt. Pumphrey's co. 22d rgt.

McCoy, James. Private in Capt. Edes's co. 27th rgt.

McCoy, John. Private in Capt. Brown's co. 6th rgt.

McCoy, Joseph. Private in Capt. Mackey's co. 49th rgt.

McCoy, Samuel. Private in Capt. Steever's co. 27th rgt.

McCoy, William. Private in Capt. McKane's co. 27th rgt.

McCracken, John. Quarter-Gunner in Capt. Addison's co. Sea Fencibles.

McCracken, William. Private in Capt. Brown's co. 49th rgt.

McCrea, Robert. Private in Capt. Deems' co. 51st rgt.

McCrie [McCrea], James. Surgeon in 25th rgt. Died, 1814.

McCrimmin, Daniel. Ensign in 14th U. S. Infantry (Ap. 30, 1813); 2d Lieutenant (O. 1, 1814).

McCristal, Patrick. Private in Capt. Pumphrey's co. 22d rgt.

Maccubbin, see also Mackubin.

Maccubbin, Charles C. Private in Capt. Moale's co. Columbian Artillery.

McCubbin, John S. Private in Capt. Berry's co. Washington Artillery.

Maccubbin, Moses. Private in Capt. Nicholson's co. Balto. Fencibles.

McCubbin, Moses. Private in Capt. Adreon's co. Union Volunteers.

McCubbin, Nicholas Z. Private in Capt. Sands' co. 22d rgt.

McCubbin, William. Private in Capt. Conway's co. 6th rgt.

McCubbin, William H. Private in Capt. Warfield's co. Balto. United Volunteers.

McCubbin, Zachariah. Private in Capt. Snowden's co. 36th rgt.

McCuller, James. Private in Capt. Smith's co. 51st rgt.

McCulloch, James W. Corporal in Capt. Warfield's co. Balto. United Volunteers. Wounded at Bladensburg.

McCulloh, James H. Command unknown; captured at North Point.

McCulloh, James H., Jr. Garrison-Surgeon U. S. (Jy. 17, 1814).

McCullough, Andrew. Sergeant in Capt. Patton's co. 30th rgt.

McCullough, James. Private in Capt. Peters' co. 51st rgt.

McCullough, John. Sergeant in Capt. Hall's co. 30th rgt.

McCullough, Jonathan. Ensign in Capt. Krause' co. 30th rgt. (Ja. 21, 1811).

McCully, John J. Ensign in Capt. Ent's co. 16th rgt. (Ag. 20, 1814).

McCurley, Felix [1779-1845]. Private in Capt. Smith's co. 51st rgt.

McCutchen, George. Private in Capt. Watson's co. 39th rgt.

McCutcheon, John D. Private in Capt. Thomas's co. 49th rgt.

McDaniel, Daniel. Private in Capt. Kennedy's co. 27th rgt.

McDaniel, Horatio. Private in Capt. Smoot's co. 43d rgt.

McDaniel, Isaac. Private in Capt. Robey's co. 43d rgt.

McDaniel, James. 1st Lieutenant in Capt. Tayler's co. 2d rgt. 1st Cavalry Dist. (Je. 15, 1813).

McDaniel, John. Sergeant in Capt. Foreman's co. 33d rgt.

McDermitt, James. Private in Capt. Schwarzauer's co. 27th rgt.

McDermitt, Stephen. Private in Capt. Stewart's co. 51st rgt.

McDonald, Charles. Private in Capt. Chalmers' co. 51st rgt.

McDonald, Cornelius. Private in Capt. Thomas's co. 49th rgt.

McDonald, Ebenezer. Assistant Deputy Commissary of Ordnance (D. 26, 1814).

McDonald, George. Private in Capt. Garret's co. 49th rgt.

McDonald, H. Private in Capt. Sterett's Independent co.

McDonald, Hugh. Private in Capt. Hanna's co. Fells Point Light Dragons.

McDonald, James [-1814]. 1st Lieutenant in 14th U. S. Infantry (Mr. 12, 1812); Captain (O. 1, 1813).

McDonald, James. Private in Capt. Kennedy's co. 27th rgt.

McDonald, James. Private in Capt. Dyer's co. Fells Point Riflemen.

McDonald, James. Private in Capt. Stewart's co. 51st rgt.

McDonald, John. Private in Capt. Dobbin's co. 39th rgt.

McDonald, John. Private in Capt. Peters' co. 51st rgt.

McDonald, John. Private in Capt. Stewart's co. 51st rgt.

McDonald, P. Private in Capt. Sterett's Independent co.

McDonald, Samuel. Captain in 6th rgt.

McDonald, Samuel. Quarter-Gunner in Capt. Addison's co. Sea Fencibles.

McDonald, Thomas. Private in Capt. Stewart's co. 51st rgt.

McDonald, William [1758-1845]. Lieutenant-Colonel in 6th rgt.

McDonald, William. Adjutant in 19th rgt. (My. 18, 1813).

McDonoh, Patrick. Private in Capt. Haubert's co. 51st rgt.

McDonoh, Peter. Private in Capt. Haubert's co. 51st rgt.

McDonough, John. Private in Capt. Quantrill's co. 24th rgt.

McDowel, Thomas. Private in Capt. Addison's co. Sea Fencibles.

McDowell, G. Private in Capt. Sterett's Independent co.

McDowell, Maxwell. Private in Capt. Thompson's co. 1st Baltimore Horse Artillery.

Mace, Thomas. Private in Capt. Conway's co. 6th rgt.

Mace, Thomas. Private in Capt. McConkey's co. 27th rgt.

McElderry, Horatio C. Captain in 17th rgt. (F. 9, 1814) vice Hamilton.

McElderry, Hugh. Private in Capt. Stiles' co. Marine Artillery.

McElderry, John. Private in Capt. Faster's co. 51st rgt.

McElderry, Thomas. Private in Capt. Faster's co. 51st rgt.

McElfish, John. Captain in 50th rgt. (Jy. 8, 1813).

McElligott, Pierce G. Private in Capt. Berry's co. Washington Artillery.

McElroy, John. Private in Capt. Wilson's co. 6th rgt.

McElwee, Samuel. Private in Capt. Adreon's co. Union Volunteers.

McEvoy, James. Private in Capt. Deems' co. 51st rgt.

Macey, William. Private in Capt. McDonald's co. 6th rgt.

McFaddin, John. Ensign in Capt. Harvey's co. Extra Battalion Harford Co. Resigned 1814.

McFaden, J., Jr. Private in Capt. Sterett's Independent co.

McFarland, John. Private in Capt. McConkey's co. 27th rgt.

McFarland, Peter. Private in Capt. Steiner's Frederick Artillery.

McFarron [Mc Ferran], John [1793-1868]. Sergeant in Capt. Aisquith's co. Sharp Shooters. Wounded at North Point.

McGaw, John [1797-1864]. 2d Lieutenant in Capt. Jarrett's co. 7th Cavalry Dist. (My. 8, 1812); 1st Lieutenant (Ja. 10, 1814).

McGaw, Richard. Paymaster in 7th Cavalry Dist. (Ja. 18, 1814).

McGee, Charles. Private in Capt. Morgan's co. 49th rgt.

McGee, James. Private in Capt. Heath's co. 23d rgt.

McGee, John. Private in Capt. Edes.
Edes' co. 27th rgt.
McGee, Peter. Private in Capt.
Heath's co. 23d rgt.
McGee, Richard. Private in Capt.
Oldham's co. 49th rgt.
McGenerty, Patrick. Private in
Capt. Dyer's co. Fells, Point Rifle-
men.
McGill, Arthur. Private in Capt.
Myers' Franklin Artillery.
Macgill, Basil. Private in Capt. Ais-
quith's co. Sharp Shooters.
McGill, Robert. Private in Capt.
Brooke's co. 34th rgt.
Macgill, Thomas. Private in Capt.
Aisquith's co. Sharp Shooters.
McGinnis, Casparus. Quarter-Mas-
ter in 21st rgt. (Ja. 4, 1814).
McGinnis, Daniel. Lieutenant in
Capt. Goldsborough's co. 4th rgt.
(Mr. 23, 1814).
McGinnis, John. Lieutenant of the
privateer *Father and Sons*, Feb.
1813; Lieutenant of the *Kemp*,
April, 1813.
McGinnis, John. Private in Capt.
Hanna's co. Fells' Point Light
Dragoons.
McGlennan, James. Private in Capt.
Bouldin's co. Independent Light
Dragoons.
McGloshen, Robert. Private in
Capt. Haubert's co. 51st rgt.
McGoldrick, John. Private in Capt.
McConkey's co. 27th rgt.
McGraw, Thomas. Private in Capt.
McDonald's co. 6th rgt.
McGregor, Archibald. Lieutenant of
the privateer *Water Witch*, Aug.,
1812.
McGrok, Andrew. Private in Capt.
Smith's co. 51st rgt.
McGruder, Samuel. Private in Capt.
Kennedy's co. 27th rgt.

McGuchin, Alexander. Private in
Capt. Lawson's co. Balto. Pa-
triots.
McGuiness, George. 2d Lieutenant
in Capt. Little's co. 9th Cavalry
Dist. (My. 22, 1812); 1st Lieu-
tenant (Ap. 24, 1813).
McGuire, Absalom. Private in Capt.
Blizzard's co. Nace's rgt.
McGuire, John. Private in Capt.
Smith's co. 51st rgt.
McGuire, Philip. 2d Lieutenant in
Capt. Myers' co. Franklin Artil-
lery (Jy. 28, 1812).
McGuire, Robert. Private in Capt.
Hands' co. 21st rgt.
McGurch, John. Private in Capt.
Conway's co. 6th rgt.
McHenry, F. D. Private in Capt.
McKane's co. 27th rgt.
McHenry, John. Adjutant in 5th
rgt. (D. 17, 1814) vice Cheston.
McHenry, John. Sergeant in. Capt.
Warfield's co. Balto. United Vol-
unteers.
McHenry, John P. 1st Lieutenant
in Capt. Davis' co. 11th Cavalry
Dist. (O. 6, 1812).
McIlvain, George. Private in Capt.
McKane's co. 27th rgt.
McInhammer, John. Private in
Capt. Thos. Warner's co. 39th rgt.
McIntire, John. Private in Capt.
Schwarzauer's co. 27th rgt.
McIntire, John. Private in Capt.
McLaughlin's co. 50th rgt.
McIntire, Thomas. Lieutenant in
Capt. Thomas's co. 49th rgt.
McJilton, William. Private in Capt.
Dillon's co. 27th rgt.
Mackall, Benjamin, Jr. Ensign in
Capt. Billingsly's co. 31st rgt. (Je.
12, 1812).
Mackall, E. Private in Capt.
Sterett's Independent co.

Mackall, John. Adjutant in 12th rgt.

Mackall, John G. Captain in 3d Cavalry Dist. (Jy. 28, 1812).

Mackall, William. Ensign in Capt. Hance's co. 31st rgt.

McKane, John. Captain in 27th rgt.

McKay, William. Private in Capt. Fowler's co. 46th rgt.

McKean, Edward. Private in Capt. Brown's co. Eagle Artillerists.

McKearney, John. Private in Capt. Stewart's co. 51st rgt.

McKee, William. Private in Capt. Magruder's co. American Artillerists.

McKeel, John. Private in Capt Magruder's co. American Artillerists.

Mackelfresh, David. Private in Capt. Sands' co. 22d rgt.

Mackelworth, John. Private in Capt. John Miller's co. 2d D. I.; b. New York; age 23; tailor; subs.

McKennian, James. Private in Capt. A. E. Warner's co. 39th rgt.

McKenny, John. Adjutant in 42d rgt. (Mr. 4, 1808).

McKenzie, Alexander. Sergeant in Capt. Aisquith's co. Sharp Shooters. Wounded at North Point.

McKenzie, G. Private in Capt. Sterett's Independent co.

McKenzie, James. Private in Capt. Pinney's co. 27th rgt.

McKenzie, Kenneth [-1817]. Captain in 14th U. S. Infantry (Jy. 6, 1812).

McKenzie, Thomas [1794-1866]. Private in Capt. Kennedy's co. 27th rgt.

Mackerson, Lambert. Private in Capt. Shryock's co. 24th rgt.

McKesseck, John. Private in Capt. Adreon's co. Union Volunteers.

Mackey, David. Private in Capt. Garrett's co. 49th rgt.

Mackey, James. Private in Capt. Edes' co. 27th rgt.

Mackey, John, Jr. Private in Capt. Berry's co. Washington Artillery.

McKey, Michael. Private in Capt. Sadtler's co. Balto. Yägers.

Mackey, Robert. Private in Capt. Addison's co. Sea Fencibles.

Mackey, William. Captain in Extra Battalion Dorchester Co. Resigned D. 16, 1814.

Mackey, William. Private in Capt. Edes' co. 27th rgt.

Mackey, William. Sergeant in Capt. Garrett's co. 49th rgt.

Mackey, William, Jr. Captain in 49th rgt. (Ag. 19, 1809).

McKim, Daniel. Private in Capt. Myers' co. Franklin Artillery.

McKim, Isaac. Aid-de-camp to Genl. Smith in 3d Division M. M.

McKim, William. Private in Capt. Stewart's co. 51st rgt.

Mackin, James. Private in Capt. Pennington's co. Balto. Independent Artillerists.

McKinley, James. Private in Capt. Snowden's co. 36th rgt.

McKinley, William. Private in Capt. McKane's co. 27th rgt.

McKinnon, Hector. Private in Capt. King's co. 49th rgt.

McKinsey, Jesse. Private in Capt. Brown's co. 49th rgt.

McKinsey, Jesse. Private in Capt. Blair's co. 50th rgt.

McKinsey, Moses. Drummer in Capt. Blair's co. 50th rgt.

McKinsey, William. Private in Capt. Barnes' co. 32d rgt.

McKinsey, William. Private in Capt. Snowden's co. 36th rgt.

McKnight, John. Private in Capt. Thos. Warner's co. 39th rgt.

McKnight, John. Private in Capt. Travers' co. 48th rgt.

McKnight, Lewis. Private in Capt. Bunbury's co. Sea Fencibles.

McKubbin, Samuel. Private in Capt. Peters' co. 51st rgt.

Mackubin, George. Private in Capt. Pinkney's Artillery co. 22d rgt.

McKubin, James, Jr. Private in Capt. Boone's co. 22d rgt.

Mackubin, Richard Creagh. Private in Capt. Pinkney's Artillery co. 22d rgt.; Private in Ensign Brewer's detachment in 36th rgt. Killed at Bladensburg.

McLane, Charles. Private in Capt. McDaniel's co. 6th rgt.

McLannahan, J. J. Private in Capt. Sterett's co. 1st Balto. Hussars.

McLaughlin, Daniel. Private in Capt. Bouldin's co. Independent Light Dragoons.

McLaughlin, Francis. Private in Capt. Haubert's co. 51st rgt.

McLaughlin, John. Private in Capt. Schwarzauer's co. 27th rgt.

McLaughlin, Joseph. Private in Capt. Wilson's co. 6th rgt.

McLaughlin, Matthew. Captain in Eagle Artillerists (F. 12, 1812); 2. Major in 1st rgt. Artillery (Je. 15, 1814) vice Jameson.

McLaughlin, Peter. Private in Capt. Pennington's co. Balto. Independent Artillerists.

McLaughlin, Philip. Private in Magruder's co. American Artillerists.

McLaughlin, Thomas. Sergeant in Capt. Foreman's co. 33d rgt.

McLaughlin, William. Captain in 50th rgt. (O. 16, 1810).

McLean, Charles. Private in Capt. Watson's co. 39th rgt.

McLeavy, Henry. Private in Capt. Berry's co. Washington Artillery.

McMackin, William. Private in Capt. Berry's co. Washington Artillery.

McMackon, Alexander. Private in Capt. Sheppard's co. 6th rgt.

McMechen, Samuel. Private in Capt. Haubert's co. 51st rgt.

McMillon, James. Private in Capt. Cawood's co. 45th rgt.

McMon, William. Private in Capt. Shryock's co. 24th rgt.

McMullen, Nathaniel. Private in Capt. Wilson's co. 6th rgt.

McMullen, Samuel. Private in Capt. Marker's co. 28th rgt.

McMullen, Thomas. Private in Capt. Miller's co. 39th rgt.

McMullin, Timothy. Private in Capt. Adreon's co. Union Volunteers.

McMullin, William. Private in Capt. Brown's co. Eagle Artillerists.

McMurray, Samuel [1792-1850]. Sergeant in Capt. Frizell's co. Nace's rgt.; Sergeant in Capt. Murray's co. 36th rgt.

McNamara, Henry. Ensign in Capt. McNamara's co. 48th rgt. (Ag. 8, 1809).

McNamara, John. Lieutenant in Capt. Fallin's co. 48th rgt. (Jy. 8, 1813).

McNamara, John, Jr. Drummer in Capt. Fallin's co. 48th rgt.

McNamara, Levin. Private in Capt. Fallin's co. 48th rgt.

McNamara, Timothy. Fifer in Capt. Fallin's co. 48th rgt.

McNamara, William. Captain in 48th rgt. (Ag. 8, 1809).

McNeal, Daniel. Private in Capt. Stiles' co. Marine Artillery.

APPENDIX 369

McNeal, James [1779-1857]. Private in Capt. Brown's co. Eagle Artillerists.
McNeil, James. Private in Capt. Allen's co. 49th rgt.
McNeil, James, Jr. Private in Capt. Pennington's co. Balto. Independent Artillerists.
McNeilly, Jeremiah. Private in Capt. Dillon's co. 27th rgt.
McNeir, George. 3d Lieutenant in Capt. Addison's co. Sea Fencibles. (Mr. 17, 1814). Resigned N. 24, 1814.
McNeir, George. Private in Capt. Sands' co. 22d rgt.
McNeir, George. Private in Ensign Brewer's co. 36th rgt.
McNeir, Jeremiah. Private in Capt. Jos. Jones' co. 34th rgt.
McNeir, John. Private in Capt. McKane's co. 27th rgt.
McNeir, Thomas. 2d Corporal in Capt. Pinkney's Artillery co. Aug., 1813; Private in Capt. Chase's co. Nov., 1814; Private in Ensign Brewer's detachment in 36th rgt.
McNeir, Walter. Private in Capt. Slicer's co. 22d rgt.
McNeir, William. Private in Capt. Peters' co. 51st rgt.
McNicholls, Isaac. Private in Capt. Watson's co. 39th rgt.
McNulty, Israel. Private in Capt. Smith's co. 51st rgt.
McNulty, John. Private in Capt. Sterett's co. 1st Balto. Hussars.
McParlin, William. Sergeant in Capt. Pinkney's Artillery co. 22d rgt.
McPhail, Daniel. Private in Capt. Thos. Warner's co. 39th rgt.
McPherrin, William. Private in Capt. Quantrill's co. 24th rgt.

McPherson, Henry H. 2d Lieutenant in Capt. Stonestreet's co. 4th Cavalry Dist. (Je. 16, 1812).
McPherson, Henry T. Captain in 43d rgt. (Jy. 7, 1814) vice W. T. McPherson.
McPherson, John. Private in Capt. Deem's co. 51st rgt.
McPherson, John. Private in Capt. Stewart's co. 51st rgt.
McPherson, Jonas. Captain in 10th rgt. (S. 20, 1813).
McPherson, Robert G. 2d Lieutenant in Capt. Steiner's Artillery co. 9th Brigade (Jy. 12, 1814); vice Graff; 1st Lieutenant (S. 10, 1814).
McPherson, Thomas. Private in Capt. McConkey's co. 27th rgt.
McPherson, William. Private in Capt. Steiner's Frederick Artillery.
McPherson, William. Private in Capt. Nailor's co. 17th rgt.
McPherson, William T. Captain in 43d rgt. Resigned Jy. 7, 1814.
McVey, James. Ensign in Capt. Thos. Jones' co. 30th rgt. (My. 17, 1811).
McWilliams, George. Captain in 45th rgt. (O. 31, 1812).
McWilliams, Hugh. Private in Capt. Burke's co. 6th rgt.
McWilliams, M. Private in Capt. Brown's co. Eagle Artillerists.
Madary, William. Private in Capt. Wilson's co. 6th rgt.
Madden, Daniel. Private in Capt. A. E. Warner's co. 39th rgt.
Maddox, Benjamin. Private in Capt. McPherson's co. 43d rgt.
Maddox, Frederick. Private in Capt. McPherson's co. 43d rgt.
Maddox, Gilbert. Private in Capt. Brown's co. 43d rgt.

25

Maddox, James. Ensign in Capt. T. G. Neale's co. 45th rgt. (O. 31, 1812).

Maddox, Marcy. Ensign in Capt. Handy's co. 23d rgt. (S. 10, 1814).

Maddox, Richard. Private in Capt. Dyer's co. Fells Point Riflemen.

Maddox, Samuel J. Captain in Artillery co. 5th Brigade Charles Co. (N. 3, 1812).

Maddox, William. Ensign in Capt. Miles' co. 23d rgt. (Jy. 14, 1814).

Maddox, William R. Private in Capt. Gray's co. 43d rgt.

Maddox, William T. Ensign in Capt. Millard's co. 12th rgt.

Madison, Thomas. Private in Capt. Edes' co. 27th rgt.

Madore, Francis. Private in Capt. McLaughlin's co. 50th rgt.

Magarity, John. Private in Capt. Stewart's co. 51st rgt.

Magauran, Henry. Private in Capt. Steever's co. 27th rgt.

Magee, George W. Captain in 20th rgt. (My. 14, 1812).

Magness, Benjamin. Lieutenant in Capt. Bowman's co. 40th rgt. (Jy. 14, 1814).

Magnor, John. Private in Capt. Chambers' co. 21st rgt. Wounded at Caulk's Field.

Magruder, Dennis F. Private in Capt. Warfield's co. Balto. United Volunteers. Wounded at Bladensburg.

Magruder, Gustavus. Private in Capt. Magruder's American Artillerists.

Magruder, H. B. Sergeant in Capt. Stapleton's co. 39th rgt.

Magruder, Henry B. 1st Lieutenant in 36th U. S. Infantry (Ag. 7, 1813).

Magruder, James A. Paymaster in 14th rgt. (My. 23, 1799).

Magruder, John R. Lieutenant in Capt. Alexander's co. 28th rgt. (Jy. 24, 1814).

Magruder, John R. Private in Capt. Brooke's co. 34th rgt.

Magruder, Jonathan. Ensign in Capt. Wilcoxen's co. 44th rgt. (S. 10, 1814).

Magruder, Middleton B. Private in Capt. Thompson's co. 1st Baltimore Horse Artillery.

Magruder, Ninian. Surgeon's mate in 18th rgt. (Je. 18, 1794).

Magruder, Peter. 2d Lieutenant in 12th U. S. Infantry (Mr. 12, 1812).

Magruder, Richard B. 1st Lieutenant in American Artillery co. (Jy. 4, 1812) ; Captain (Ag. 10, 1813) vice Woodyear.

Magruder, Samuel. Captain in 34th rgt. (S. 17, 1807).

Magruder, Samuel W. Surgeon's mate in 14th U. S. Infantry (Mr. 28, 1813).

Magruder, Thomas. Quarter-master in 14th rgt. (S. 9, 1807).

Magruder, Warren. Paymaster in 18th rgt. (Je. 12, 1812).

Maguire, John. Private in Capt. McConkey's co. 27th rgt.

Maguire, Michael. Private in Capt. Stewart's co. 51st rgt.

Mahaney, John. Private in Capt. Burke's co. 6th rgt.

Mahon, George. Private in Capt. Sample's co. 49th rgt.

Mahoney, Elisha. Private in Capt. Rogers' co. 51st rgt.

Mahoney, Mathias. Private in Capt. Smith's co. 51st rgt.

Mahr, Martin F. Private in Capt. Sterett's co. 1st Balto. Hussars.

Mahue, William. Private in Capt. Galt's co. 6th rgt.

Maidwell, John. Private in Capt. Horton's co. Maryland Chasseurs.

Main, Jacob. Private in Capt. Getzendanner's co. 16th rgt.

Majors, William. Private in Capt. Blair's co. 50th rgt.

Male, Joseph A. Private in Capt. Pike's co. Balto. Volunteer Artillery.

Malloc, John. Private in Capt. Pumphrey's co. 22d rgt.

Mallonee, John. Private in Capt. Steuart's co. Washington Blues.

Mallonnee, John. Private in Capt. Sands' co. 22d rgt.

Malloy, Patrick. Private in Capt. Hanna's co. Fells Point Light Dragoons.

Malony, Owen. Private in Capt. Haubert's co. 51st rgt.

Malot, Theodore. Private in Capt. John Miller's co., 2d D. I.; b. Washington Co., Md.; age 48; carpenter; subs. for Jacob Knutle.

Malott, Daniel. Ensign in Capt. Ashberry's co. 10th rgt. (My. 9, 1808).

Man, Solomon. Private in Capt. Quantrill's co. 24th rgt.

Manly, James. Private in Capt. Faster's co. 51st rgt.

Manly, John. Private in Capt. Cozier's co. 30th rgt.

Mann, Charles. Private in Capt. Maynard's co. 22d rgt.

Mann, George. Private in Capt. Ringgold's co. 6th rgt.

Mann, James. Private in Capt. Ringgold's co. 6th rgt.

Mann, Joseph. Captain in 33d rgt. (S. 2, 1811).

Mann, Wm. H. A. G. Private in Capt. Maynard's co. 22d rgt.

Manna, Francis. Private in Capt. in Linthicum's co. 22d rgt.

Mannering, William. Private in Capt. Foreman's co. 33d rgt.

Manning, Alexander. Private in Capt. Burgess' co. 43d rgt.

Manning, Anthony. 1st Lieutenant in Capt. Tootle's co. 10th Cavalry Dist. (S. 26, 1812); Captain (D. 22, 1814).

Manning, Cornelius. Quarter-master in 17th rgt. (S. 10, 1814).

Manning, Cornelius. Private in Capt. Williams' co. 12th rgt.

Manning, Ignatius. Major in service June and July, 1814.

Manning, Jesse. Sergeant in Capt. Blizzard's co. 15th rgt.

Manning, Jesse. Private in Capt. Dobbin's co. 39th rgt.

Manning, John. Private in Capt. Burgess' co. 43d rgt.

Manning, Samuel. Corporal in Capt. Blizzard's co. Nace's rgt.

Manning, Wilfred. Quarter-master sergeant in Capt. Causin's co. 4th Cavalry Dist.

Manroe, James. Ensign in Capt. Frizell's co. Nace's rgt.

Mansfield, James. Private in Capt. Chambers' co. 21st rgt.

Mansfield, John. Ensign in 36th U. S. Infantry (Ap. 30, 1813); 2d Lieutenant (S. 30, 1814).

Mansfield, John. Sergeant in Capt. Ringgold's co. 6th rgt.

Mansfield, Thomas. Private in Capt. Kemp's co. 26th rgt.

Mansfield, Vachel. Private in Capt. Travers' co. 48th rgt.

Manship, Noah. Private in Capt. Spencer's co. 26th rgt.

Manship, Thomas. Lieutenant in Capt. Chaffinch's co. 19th rgt. (Ag. 20, 1814).

Manson, Henry. Private in Capt. Bunbury's co. Sea Fencibles.

Mantz, David. Sergeant in Capt. Steiner's Frederick Artillery.

Mantz, George. Captain in 16th rgt. (Jy. 15, 1814).

Mapp, William. Private in Capt. Kennedy's co. 27th rgt.

March, Gale. Private in Capt. Dyer's co. Fells Point Riflemen.

Marche, Perry. Private in Capt. Horton's co. Maryland Chasseurs.

Marean, Thomas. Private in Capt. Sterett's co. 1st Balto. Hussars.

Mark, Aaron. Private in Capt. Schwarzauer's co. 27th rgt.

Markee, John. Private in Capt. McLaughlin's co. 50th rgt.

Markell, Jacob. Lieutenant in Capt. Jones' co. 16th rgt. (Jy. 15, 1814).

Marker, Daniel. Captain in 28th rgt. (Je. 26, 1812).

Marker, John. Private in Capt. Marker's co. 28th rgt.

Marker, John. Private in Capt. Rogers' co. 51st rgt.

Marker, Samuel. Private in Capt. Marker's co. 28th rgt.

Markert, Augustin. Private in Capt. Sadtler's co. Balto. Yägers.

Markey, David. Capt. in 16th rgt. (S. 19, 1809).

Markland, James. Private in Capt. McKane's co. 27th rgt.

Markle, John. Quarter-master in 16th rgt (Ag. 23, 1812).

Marlow, Aquila. Private in Capt. Robey's co. 43d rgt.

Marlow, Edward. Ensign in Capt. Lansdale's co. 18th rgt. (Ap. 27, 1814).

Marlowe, Samuel. Private in Capt. Brooke's co. 34th rgt.

Marlowe, William B. Private in Capt. Dent's co. 43d rgt.

Marr, Alexander. Private in Capt. Miller's co. 39th rgt.

Marr, Daniel. Private in Capt. Dent's co. 43d rgt.

Marr, James. Private in Capt. Dunnington's co. 43d rgt.

Marr, William. Private in Capt. Dent's co. 43d rgt.

Marriott, Elisha. Sergeant in Capt. Adreon's co. Union Volunteers.

Marriott, James H. Private in Capt. Adreon's co. Union Volunteers. Wounded at North Point.

Marriott, John. Private in Capt. Waters' co. 22d rgt.

Marriott, Joseph. Captain in 2d rgt. Resigned Jy., 1814.

Marriott, Rezin H. Private in Capt. Chase's co. 22d rgt.

Marriott, Richard. Private in Capt. Maynard's co. 22d rgt.

Marriott, Thomas. Lieutenant in Capt. Marriott's co. 2d rgt. Resigned Jy., 1814.

Marriott, William. Captain in 2d rgt. (Jy. 7, 1814).

Marriott, William H. Brigade Major, 8th Brigade.

Marrow, Hugh. Private in Capt. Stapleton's co. 39th rgt.

Marrow, Isaac. Private in Capt. Stapleton's co. 39th rgt.

Marselas, James. Private in Capt. Dyer's co. Fells Point Riflemen.

Marselas, John E. Private in Capt. Dyer's co. Fells Point Riflemen.

Marser, Bartholomew. Private in Capt. Howard's co. Mechanical Volunteers.

Marsh, Dennis. Private in Capt. Warfield's co. Balto. United Volunteers. Wounded at North Point.

Marsh, John J. Private in Capt. Dobbin's co. 39th rgt.

Marsh, Stephen. Private in Capt. Sterett's co. 1st Balto. Hussars.

Marshal, Thomas. Private in Capt. Massey's co. 38th rgt.

Marshall, —. Ensign in Capt. Selby's co. 9th rgt. (Rsd. Jy. 13, 1814).

Marshall, Andrew. Private in Capt. Pinney's co. 27th rgt.

Marshall, Elias. Private in Capt. Bunbury's co. Sea Fencibles.

Marshall, Hugh R. Corporal in Capt. Faster's co. 51st rgt.

Marshall, Isaac. Lieutenant in Capt. Brevard's co. Extra Battalion Worcester Co. (Je. 18, 1812).

Marshall, Isaiah. Lieutenant in Capt. Gore's co. 41st rgt. (Ap. 20, 1808).

Marshall, Joseph. 1st Lieutenant in 14th U. S. Infantry (Mr. 12, 1812) ; Captain (Ag. 15, 1813).

Marshall, Josias. Ensign in Capt. Marshall's co. 34th rgt. (Ap. 30, 1813).

Marshall, Leonard. Private in Capt. Hancock's co. 22d rgt.

Marshall, Levin. Private in Capt. Brohawn's co. 48th rgt.

Marshall, Matthias. Private in Capt. Burke's co. 6th rgt.

Marshall, Richard H. Captain in 34th rgt. (Ap. 30, 1813).

Marshall, Robert. Private in Capt. Crawfurd's co. 17th rgt.

Marshall, Thomas. Private in Capt. Smith's co. 51st rgt.

Marshall, Thomas of Jas. Captain in 23d rgt. (D. 10, 1813) vice Schoolfield.

Marshall, William. Captain in 9th rgt. (Je. 19, 1812).

Marshall, William. Lieutenant in Capt. Marshall's co. 23d rgt. (D. 10, 1813).

Martin, Anthony B. Private in Capt. Quantrill's co. 24th rgt.

Martin, Benjamin. Ensign in Capt. Young's co. 12th rgt. (O. 3, 1807).

Martin, Charles. Private in Capt. Heath's co. 23d rgt.

Martin, Daniel. Captain in 9th Cavalry Dist. (My. 8, 1812) ; Major (N. 3, 1812).

Martin, Daniel. Sergeant in Capt. Woolford's co. 48th rgt.

Martin, Ennalls, M. D. Surgeon to Talbot co. militia, 1813.

Martin, James. Private in Capt. Levering's co. Independent Blues.

Martin, James E. Private in Capt. Aisquith's co. Sharp Shooters.

Martin, John. Private in Capt. McLaughlin's co. 50th rgt.

Martin, John. Private in Capt. Sterett's Independent co.

Martin, John. Private in Capt. Myers' co. Franklin Artillery.

Martin, John. Private in Capt. Lawrence's co. 6th rgt.

Martin, John. Private in Capt. Dyer's co. 17th rgt.

Martin, John B. Ensign in 38th U. S. Infantry (My. 20, 1813) ; 2d Lieutenant (S. 9, 1814).

Martin, John S. Surgeon in 37th rgt. (S. 26, 1807).

Martin, John T. Sergeant in Capt. Jarboe's co. 12th rgt.

Martin, Jones. Private in Capt. Snowden's co. 36th rgt.

Martin, Joseph. Private in Capt. Lawrence's co. 6th rgt.

Martin, Joseph. Private in Capt. Dillon's co. 27th rgt.

Martin, Joseph. Private in Capt. Blair's co. 50th rgt.

Martin, Mordecai. Private in Capt. Rogers' co. 51st rgt.

Martin, Nicholas. Ensign in Capt. Smith's co. 4th rgt. (Je. 18, 1794).

Martin, Nicholas, Jr. Lieutenant in Capt. Smith's co. 4th rgt. (S. 11, 1794).

Martin, Richard. Musician in Capt. Roney's co. 39th rgt.

Martin, Samuel B. Surgeon in 1st Rifle Battalion. Captured at Bladensburg.

Martin, Solomon. Private in Capt. Blizzard's co. 15th rgt.

Martin, Thomas. Private in Capt. Mackey's co. 49th rgt.

Martin, Thomas. Private in Capt. Deems' co. 51st rgt.

Martin, Thomas. Adjutant in 1st rgt. (Ag. 4, 1814).

Martin, Thomas. Ensign in Capt. Hand's co. 21st rgt. Resigned Jy. 13, 1814.

Martin, Thomas H. B. Lieutenant in Capt. Ecclestone's co. Extra Battalion Dorchester Co. (D. 16, 1814).

Martin, William. Private in Capt. Hand's co. 21st rgt.

Martin, William. Private in Capt. Roney's co. 39th rgt.

Martiney, John. Private in Capt. Quantrill's co. 24th rgt.

Martracy, J. Private in Capt. Sterett's Independent co.

Martz, Henry. Private in Capt. Blair's co. 50th rgt.

Marvin, Clarr. Private in Capt. Edes' co. 27th rgt.

Mask, Marshall. Sergeant in Capt. Stewart's co. 51st rgt.

Mason, Abraham. Private in Capt. Kierstead's co. 6th rgt.

Mason, Horatio. Private in Capt. Dent's co. 43d rgt.

Mason, James. Private in Capt. Kierstead's co. 6th rgt.

Mason, Richard B. Quarter-master in 12th rgt.

Mass, Robert. Private in Capt. Watson's co. 39th rgt.

Mass, Samuel. Private in Capt. Myers' co. 39th rgt.

Massey, Benjamin. Captain in 33d rgt. (My. 28, 1808).

Massey, James. Captain in 38th rgt.

Massey, Joshua W. Captain in 35th rgt. (N. 23, 1814).

Massor, John. Private in Capt. Blair's co. 50th rgt.

Masters, Ezekiel. Corporal in Capt. Jackson's co. 34th rgt.

Matchett, James. Private in Capt. Galloway's co. 46th rgt.

Matchett, Richard J. [1790-1854]. Private in Capt. Peters' co. 51st rgt.

Matere, James. Private in Capt. Shryock's co. 24th rgt.

Mather, Michael. Ensign in Capt. Murray's co. 28th rgt. (Jy. 8, 1814).

Mathews, Cornelius. Seaman of the privateer Baltimore.

Mathews, George. Private in Capt. Umstead's co. 25th rgt.

Mathews, John. 4th Sergeant in Capt. Boone's co. 22d rgt.

Mathews, John. Private in Capt. Heath's co. 23d rgt.

Mathews, Luke F. Major in 1st rgt. (Rifle Corps).

Mathews, Patrick. Private in Capt. Faster's co. 51st rgt.

Mathews, William. Private in Capt. Heath's co. 23d rgt.

Mathews, William. Ensign in Capt. Parnham's co. 1st rgt. (Ja. 10, 1814).

Mathias, John. Private in Capt. Haubert's co. 51st rgt.

Mathias, Nicholas. Private in
Capt. Haubert's co. 51st rgt.
Mathiot, Christian. Private in Capt.
Howard's co. Mechanical Volun-
teers.
Mathiot, George. Sergeant in Capt.
Howard's co. Mechanical Volun-
teers.
Matlock, John. Private in Capt. A.
E. Warner's co. 39th rgt.
Matsabaugh, John. Private in Capt.
Shryock's co. 24th rgt.
Matthews, Elias. Private in Capt.
Shrim's co. Balto. Light Infantry.
Matthews, James. Lieutenant of
the privateer Ultor, Sept., 1813;
Captain, Nov., 1813.
Matthews, James. Private in Capt.
Brown's co. Eagle Artillerists.
Matthews, John. Private in Capt.
McDonald's co. 6th rgt.
Matthews, John. 2d Major in 51st
rgt.
Matthews, John. Sergeant in Capt.
Pumphrey's co. 22d rgt. [August,
1813].
Matthews, John. Captain in 1st rgt.
(D. 7, 1813); Major (Jy. 11,
1814).
Matthews, Leonard. Private in
Capt. Warfield's co. Balto. United
Volunteers.
Matthews, Samuel. Private in
Capt. Wells' Artillery co. 22d rgt.
Matthews, Thomas L. Private in
Capt. Myers' co. Franklin Artil-
lery.
Matthews, William [1781-1857].
Ensign in 1st rgt. (Charles Co.).
Matthews, William. Surgeon in
35th rgt. (Jy. 24, 1813).
Matthews, William. Private in
Capt. Ringgold's co. 6th rgt.
Matthews, William. Private in
Capt. Brohawn's co. 48th rgt.

Matthias, Jacob. Paymaster in 20th
rgt. (Je. 1, 1813).
Matthias, John. Adjutant in 20th
rgt. Resigned Ag. 1, 1814.
Mattingley, Henry. Private in Capt.
Blakistone's co. 45th rgt.
Mattingley, John. Private in Capt.
Blakistone's co. 45th rgt.
Mattingley, Sylvester. Private in
Capt. Blakistone's co. 45th rgt.
Mattingly, Francis. Private in
Capt. Cawood's co. 45th rgt.
Mattingly, John. Lieutenant in
Capt. Porter's co. 50th rgt. (S. 2,
1811).
Mattingly, Zachariah. Private in
Capt. Cawood's co. 45th rgt.
Mattocks, George. Private in Capt.
McConkey's co. 27th rgt.
Mattocks, John. Private in Capt.
Myers' co. 39th rgt.
Mattocks, William. Private in
Capt. McKane's co. 27th rgt.
Mattox, Edward. Private in Capt.
Dobbin's co. 39th rgt.
Mattox, James. Private in Capt.
Snowden's co. 36th rgt.
Mattox, William. 4th Sergeant in
Capt. Snowden's co. 36th rgt.
Mauldin, John. Private in Capt.
Warfield's co. Balto. United Vol-
unteers.
Maulsby, Isaac D. Adjutant in 40th
rgt. (Ag. 5, 1808).
Maulsby, Israel D. Ensign in Capt.
Bowman's co. 40th rgt. (Jy. 14,
1814).
Maulsby, Israel D. Private in Capt.
Levering's co. Independent Blues.
Maulsby, Morris. Captain in 40th
rgt. (Jy. 16, 1814) vice Richard-
son.
Maurice, John. Private in Capt.
Barnes' co. 32d rgt.

Mauro, Philip. Private in Capt. Nicholson's co. Balto. Fencibles.

Mawe, Michael. Command unknown; captured at North Point.

Maxfield, John. Private in Capt. Bouldin's co. Independent Light Dragoons.

Maxwell, George. Private in Capt. Moore's co. 49th rgt.

Maxwell, James. Quarter-master in 30th rgt. (N. 7, 1812).

Maxwell, John. Corporal in Capt. Dobbin's co. 39th rgt.

Maxwell, John. Private in Capt. Taylor's co. 46th rgt.

Maxwell, Joshua. Private in Capt. Ringgold's co. 6th rgt.

Maxwell, Robert H. Corporal in Capt. A. C. Smith's co. 49th rgt.

Maxwell, William, Jr. Lieutenant in Capt. Blakistone's co. 33d rgt. (Ag. 27, 1810).

May, Benjamin. Private in Capt. Getzendanner's co. 16th rgt.

May, James. Lieutenant in Capt. Steever's co. 27th rgt. (Ap. 28, 1813).

May, Jonas. Private in Capt. Deems' co. 51st rgt.

May, Thomas. Private in Capt. Rogers' co. 51st rgt.

Maydwell, James. Private in Capt. Peters' co. 51st rgt.

Mayer, Charles F. Private in Capt. Nicholson's co. Balto. Fencibles.

Mayer, Lewis. Private in Capt. Pennington's co. Balto. Independent Artillerists.

Mayher, Timothy D. Private in Capt. Lawrence's co. 6th rgt.

Maynadier, D. Private in Capt. Stiles' co. Marine Artillery.

Maynard, Foster. Lieutenant in Capt. Haubert's co. 51st rgt.

Maynard, Samuel. Captain in 22d rgt. [1813]; Major [1814].

Maynarn, Quincy. Private in Capt. Piper's co. United Maryland Artillery.

Mayo, John. Private in Capt. Sands' co. 22d rgt.; Corporal in Ensign Brewer's detachment, 36th rgt.

Mayo, Joseph. Private in Capt. Chase's co. 22d rgt.

Mead, Benjamin. Private in Capt. Maynard's co. 22d rgt.

Meads, Daniel. Private in Capt. Bader's co. Union Yägers.

Means, Robert. Ensign in 5th U. S. Infantry (Jy. 29, 1813); 1st Lieutenant (My. 1, 1814).

Mearis, Jacob. Private in Capt. Pinney's co. 27th rgt.

Mearle, Nicholas. Sergeant in Capt. Marker's co. 28th rgt.

Medby, Lewis. Private in Capt. G. N. Causin's co. 4th Cavalry Dist.

Medcalf, George. Private in Capt. Pinkney's Artillery co.; 1st Corporal under Capt. Wells, August, 1814.

Medcalf, William. Private in Capt. Pinney's co. 27th rgt.

Medders, John. Lieutenant in Capt. Vansant's co. 33d rgt.

Mediary, Jacob. Corporal in Capt. Adreon's co. Union Volunteers.

Mediary, John. Private in Capt. Adreon's co. Union Volunteers.

Medley, Lewis. Quarter-master-Sergeant in 45th rgt.

Medley, Philip. Private in Capt. Walker's co. 45th rgt.

Medtart, Joshua. 2d Lieutenant in 38th U. S. Infantry (My. 20, 1813); 1st Lieutenant (Ag. 15, 1813).

Meed, Isaiah. Private in Capt. Peters' co. 51st rgt.

Meed, Jesse. Sergeant in Capt. Massey's co. 38th rgt.

Meek, Joseph H. Private in Capt. Dent's co. 43d rgt.

Meekins, Henry. Private in Capt. Travers' co. 48th rgt.

Meekins, John. Private in Capt. Travers' co. 48th rgt.

Meekins, John of J. Private in Capt. Travers' co. 48th rgt.

Meekins, John R. Sergeant in Capt. Travers' co. 48th rgt.

Meekins, Joseph. Private in Capt. Travers' co. 48th rgt.

Meekins, Matthias. Private in Capt. Travers' co. 48th rgt.

Meekins, Richard. Private in Capt. Travers' co. 48th rgt.

Meeks, P. James. Private in Capt. Bunbury's co. Sea Fencibles.

Meeks, William. Private in Capt. Pennington's co. Balto. Independent Artillerists.

Meeks, William. Private in Capt. Dobbins' co. 39th rgt.

Meeley, Lewis. Quarter-master-Sergeant in 45th rgt.

Meeteer, William. 2d Lieutenant in Capt. Aisquith's co. Sharp Shooters (Jy. 24, 1812).

Megee, William. Private in Capt. Wells' Artillery co. 22d rgt.

Meholm, Thomas. Private in Capt. Oldham's co. 49th rgt.

Melliss, William. Private in Capt. Aisquith's co. Sharp Shooters.

Meloney, John. Private in Capt. Massey's co. 38th rgt.

Melton *see also* **Milton.**

Melton, John. Lieutenant in Capt. Barber's co. 45th rgt.

Melton, Philip. Private in Capt. Briscoe's co. 45th rgt.

Melton, Richard. Captain in 45th rgt.

Melvill, Thomas. Lieutenant in Capt. Carter's co. 19th rgt. (Ag. 20, 1814).

Mercer, Edward. Private in Capt. Morgan's co. 49th rgt.

Mercer, James. Private in Capt. Horton's co. Maryland Chasseurs.

Mercer, John. Cornet in U. S. Light Dragoons. (N. 22, 1814).

Mercer, Robert T. Cornet in Capt. Snowden's co. 6th Cavalry Dist. (Ja. 29, 1814).

Merchant, Noah. Captain in 35th rgt. (My. 17, 1811).

Mercier, Archibald. Ensign in Capt. S. C. Owings, co. 36th rgt. (S. 13, 1814).

Meredith, Benjamin. Private in Capt. Lawson's co. Balto. Patriots.

Meredith, James, Jr. Ensign in Capt. Roe's co. 35th rgt. (N. 3, 1812).

Meredith, John. Major, militia accountant M. M.

Meredith, Jonathan. Division Inspector in 3d Division (S. 10, 1814).

Meredith, Jonathan. Private in Capt. Warfield's co. Balto. United Volunteers.

Meredith, Joshua. Major in 41st rgt. (O. 1, 1811).

Meriken, Joseph. Private in Capt. Watson's co. 39th rgt.

Merrican, John. Private in Capt. Thos. Warner's co. 39th rgt.

Merrick, John. Captain in 4th rgt. (Jy. 7, 1810).

Merrick, Joseph J. Captain in 36th U. S. Infantry (Ap. 30, 1813).

Merrick, William D. 3d Lieutenant in 36th U. S. Infantry (Ap. 30, 1813); Regimental Adjutant, Ap., 1814; 1st Lieutenant (S. 30, 1814).

Merriken, Jacob. Private in Capt. Adreon's co. Union Volunteers.

Merriken, James. Sergeant in Capt. Adreon's co. Union Volunteers.

Merriken, Joseph R. Private in Capt. Watson's co. 39th rgt.

Merrikin, William D. Lieutenant in Capt. Bealmear's co. 2d rgt. (Jy. 6, 1814).

Merrill, William. Ensign in Capt. Marshall's co. 23d rgt. (D. 10, 1813).

Merritt, Benjamin [1779-1833]. Private in Capt. Boyer's co. 8th Cavalry rgt.

Merritt, John. Private in Capt. Schwarzauer's co. 27th rgt.

Merritt, Samuel. Private in Capt. Ringgold's co. 6th rgt.

Merryman, John, Jr. Private in Capt. Warfield's co. Balto. United Volunteers.

Merryman, John B. 3d Lieutenant in U. S. Artillery Corps. (Jy. 25, 1814); 2d Lieutenant (O. 11, 1814).

Merryman, Micajah. Cornet in Capt. Jarratt's co. 7th Cavalry Dist. (My. 8, 1812); 2d Lieutenant (Ja. 10, 1814).

Merryman, Moses. Surgeon's mate in 7th rgt. (F. 9, 1814).

Merryman, Nicholas. Captain in 41st rgt. (Ap. 20, 1808).

Merryman, Nicholas of Benjamin. Captain in 41st rgt. (O. 11, 1811).

Merryman, Nicholas R. Cornet in Capt. Bosley's co. 6th Cavalry Dist. (Jy. 30, 1812); 2d Lieutenant (D. 15, 1814).

Merryman, Philemon. Quartermaster-Sergeant in 15th rgt.

Merryman, Samuel. Private in Capt. Ringgold's co. 6th rgt.

Messenger, Charles. Gunner in Rodman's Marine Battery; killed Sept. 13, 1814.

Messenger, Simpson. Private in Capt. Dobbin's co. 39th rgt.

Messenheimer, Peter. Lieutenant in Capt. Bankert's co. 20th rgt. Resigned Jy. 13, 1814.

Mestler, Conrad. Private in Capt. Addison's co. Sea Fencibles.

Metler, John M. Sergeant in Capt. Bader's co. Union Yägers.

Mettee, Charles A. Corporal in Capt. Schwarzauer's co. 27th rgt.

Mettee, Joseph. Private in Capt. Peters' co. 51st rgt.

Mettee, Martin. Private in Capt. Wilson's co. 6th rgt.

Metz, George. Private in Capt. Wilson's co. 6th rgt.

Metz, Peter. Private in Capt. Bader's co. Union Yägers.

Metzger, Daniel. Sergeant in Capt. Dyer's co. Fells Point Riflemen.

Metzger, Daniel. Quarter-masterSergeant in 1st Rifle Battalion.

Metzger, Jacob. Armorer at Frederick, 1813.

Metzger, William. Private in Capt. Myers' co. Franklin Artillery.

Meyer, Adam. Private in Capt. Bader's co Union Yägers.

Meyer, Andrew. Private in Capt. Sadtler's co. Balto. Yägers.

Meyer, Godfrey. Private in Capt. Sadtler's co. Balto. Yägers.

Meyer, Jacob. Private in Capt. Howard's co. Mechanical Volunteers.

Meyer, John. Private in Capt. Bader's co. Union Yägers.

Mezick, Baptist. 2d Lieutenant. in Capt. Stiles' co. Marine Artillery (S. 10, 1814).

Mezick, George. Private in Capt. Umsted's co. 25th rgt.

Mezick, Joshua. Private in Capt. Stiles' co. Marine Artillery.

Michael, Jacob. Captain in 42d rgt. (O. 3, 1807).

Michaels, Abraham. Private in Capt. McLaughlin's co. 50th rgt.

Mickle, Conrad. Private in Capt. Marker's co. 28th rgt.

Mickle, John. Private in Capt. Lawrence's co. 6th rgt.

Mickle, Robert. Private in Capt. McKane's co. 27th rgt.

Middleton, Henry. Corporal in Capt. McDonald's co. 6th rgt.

Middleton, James. Surgeon's mate in 46th rgt. (Je. 5, 1812).

Middleton, James. Private in Capt. Hands' co. 21st rgt.

Middleton, James H. A. Captain in 1st rgt. (Jy. 4, 1812).

Middleton, Richard [1786-1869]. Private in Capt. Levering's co. Independent Blues.

Middleton, Theodore. Lieutenant in Capt. Kirby's co. 14th rgt. (My. 23, 1799).

Milburn, John. Lieutenant in Capt. Jarboe's co. 12th rgt. (Je. 12, 1812).

Milburn, Samuel. Private in Capt. Stapleton's co. 39th rgt.

Mildews, Nathan. Private in Capt. Chalmers' co. 51st rgt.

Miles, Benjamin. Private in Capt. McDonald's co. 6th rgt.

Miles, Benjamin. Private in Capt. Pinkney's Artillery co. 22d rgt.

Miles, John. Private in Capt. Addison's co. Sea Fencibles.

Miles, Joshua. Private in Capt. Kennedy's co. 27th rgt.

Miles, Nathaniel. Corporal in Capt. Fowler's co. 46th rgt.

Miles, Thomas. Private in Capt. Fowler's co. 46th rgt.

Miles, William. Captain in 23d rgt. (Jy. 4, 1812).

Miles, William. Corporal in Capt. Shryock's co. 24th rgt.

Millar, Walter M. Lieutenant in Capt. Gray's co. 43d rgt. (Jy. 7, 1814) vice Franklin. Bvt. Captain after the suspension of Capt. Burgess.

Millard, Enoch J. Captain in 12th rgt. (Ag. 17, 1804).

Millard, J. L. Private in Capt. Brown's co. Eagle Artillerists.

Millard, John L. Lieutenant in Capt. Floyd's co. 12th rgt.

Miller, Adam. Captain in 15th rgt. (Ap. 22, 1813).

Miller, Adam. Private in Capt. Smith's co. 51st rgt.

Miller, Adam. 4th Sergeant in Capt. Maynard's co. 22d rgt.; 2d Sergeant in Capt. Chase's co. 1814.

Miller, Andrew. Private in Capt. Deems' co. 51st rgt.; captured at North Point and taken to Barbadoes.

Miller, Benjamin H. Private in Capt. Levering's co. Independent Blues.

Miller, Charles. Private in Capt. Shrim's co. Balto. Light Infantry.

Miller, Charles. Private in Capt. Peters' co. 51st rgt.

Miller, Christopher. Private in Capt. Horton's co. Maryland Chasseurs.

Miller, Daniel. Private in Capt. Barr's Cavalry co. 1st Dist.

Miller, Edward. Lieutenant in Capt. Quarles' co. Extra Battalion Harford Co. Resigned Jy., 1814.

Miller, Francis A. Employed in making cartridges at North Point.

Miller, Frederick. Private in Capt. Montgomery's co. Balto. Union Artillery.

Miller, George. Corporal in Capt. Sands' co. 22d rgt.

Miller, George. Private in Capt. Magruder's co. American Artillerists.

Miller, George. Private in Ensign Brewer's co. 36th rgt.; mortally wounded at Bladensburg.

Miller, George. Private in Capt. McLaughlin's co. 50th rgt.

Miller, George W. Private in Capt. Berry's co. Washington Artillery.

Miller, Godfrey. Private in Capt. Blair's co. 50th rgt.

Miller, Henry. Private in Capt. Barr's Cavalry co. 1st Dist.

Miller, Henry W. Private in Capt. Moore's co. 49th rgt.

Miller, Jacob. Private in Capt. Marker's co. 28th rgt.

Miller, Jacob. Private in Capt. Haubert's co. 51st rgt.

Miller, James. Ensign in Capt. Spry's co. 33d rgt. (Jy. 12, 1814) vice Stavils.

Miller, James. Sergeant in Capt. Barnes' co. 32d rgt.

Miller, James. Private in Capt. Brown's co. 6th rgt.

Miller, James D. Private in Capt. Chambers' co. 21st rgt.

Miller, John. Captain in 10th rgt. (Ap. 30, 1811). In command of co. of 2d detached infantry at Baltimore, 1813.

Miller, John. Captain in 2d U. S. Infantry (Mr. 12, 1812).

Miller, John. Lieutenant in Capt. Murray's co. 28th rgt. (Jy. 8, 1814).

Miller, John. Fifer in Capt. Stiles' co. Marine Artillery.

Miller, John. Private in Capt. Barr's Cavalry co. 1st Dist.

Miller, John. Private in Capt. Peters' co. 51st rgt.

Miller, John. Private in Capt. Steever's co. 27th rgt.

Miller, John. Private in Capt. Schwarzauer's co. 27th rgt.

Miller, John. Private in Capt. Steiner's Frederick Artillery.

Miller, John. Private in Capt. Rogers' co. 51st rgt.

Miller, John, Jr. Private in Capt. Maynard's co. 22d rgt.; 4th Corporal in Capt. Chase's co., 1814.

Miller, John D. Captain in 39th rgt.

Miller, John N. Private in Capt. Quantrill's co. 24th rgt.

Miller, Joseph. Lieutenant in Capt. Seth's co. 26th rgt. (N. 5, 1812).

Miller, Joseph. Ensign in Capt. Tull's co. Extra Battalion Worcester co. (Je. 18, 1812).

Miller, Joseph. Lieutenant in Capt. Bagg's co. Extra Battalion Caroline Co. (Jy. 11, 1814).

Miller, Lewis. Private in Capt. Moore's co. 49th rgt.

Miller, Matthew. Private in Capt. Berry's co. Washington Artillery.

Miller, Merritt. Ensign in Capt. Page's co. 21st rgt.

Miller, Philip. Private in Capt. Schwarzauer's co. 27th rgt.

Miller, Philip. Private in Capt. Bader's co. Union Yägers.

Miller, Robert. Captain of the privateer Revenge, Sept., 1812.

Miller, Robert, Jr. Private in Capt. Warfield's co. Balto. United Volunteers.

Miller, Thomas. Private in Capt. Haubert's co. 51st rgt.

Miller, William. 2d Lieutenant in Capt. Stuart's co. Artillery 12th Brigade (Ja. 2, 1815) vice Kemp.

Miller, William. 3d Lieutenant in Capt. Myers' co. Franklin Artillery.

Miller, William. Private in Capt. Page's co. 21st rgt.

Miller, William E. Lieutenant-Colonel in 30th rgt.

Miller, William F. Veterinary Surgeon in 7th Cavalry Dist. (Ja. 18, 1814).

Millholland, Robert Douglass. Lieutenant in Capt. Brown's co. 6th rgt. (Jy. 12, 1814) vice Biays.

Millholland, Stephen. Private in Capt. Blair's co. 50th rgt.

Milliman, George. Sergeant in Capt. Haubert's co. 51st rgt.

Mills, Anthony. Private in Capt. Burgess's co. 43d rgt.

Mills, Cornelius. Lieutenant in Capt. Clarke's co. 14th rgt. (Je. 18, 1794).

Mills, Ezekiel [1757-1847]. Private in Capt. Montgomery's co. Balto. Union Artillery.

Mills, George. Private in Capt. Stiles' co. Marine Artillery.

Mills, Henry. Private in Capt. Rogers' co. 51st rgt.

Mills, James. Ensign in Capt. Hunter's co. 8th rgt. (Je. 1, 1813).

Mills, James F. 2d Lieutenant in Capt. Davis' co. 11th Cavalry Dist. (O. 6, 1812).

Mills, Levin. Private in Capt. Howard's co. Mechanical Volunteers.

Mills, Theodore. Captain in 10th rgt. (Jy. 13, 1812).

Mills, William. Private in Capt. Fallin's co. 48th rgt.

Mills, William G. Ensign in 14th U. S. Infantry (Ap. 30, 1812) ; 1st Lieutenant (N. 14, 1813).

Mills, William P. Private in Capt. Montgomery's co. Balto. Union Artillery.

Milson, Benjamin. Captain in 37th rgt. (Jy. 21, 1810).

Milstead, Edward. Private in Capt. Dent's co. 43d rgt.

Milstead, George K. Sergeant in Capt. Dent's co. 43d rgt.

Milstead, Peter. Private in Capt. Dunnington's co. 43d rgt.

Miltenberger, Anthony. Captain in 38th U. S. Infantry (My. 20, 1813).

Miltenberger, Anthony. Private in Capt. Levering's co. Independent Blues; Captain in 51st rgt. (D. 2, 1814) vice Haubert.

Miltenberger, George. Sergeant in Capt. McConkey's co. 27th rgt.

Milton, *see also* Melton.

Milton, Daniel. Seaman of the privateer *Globe*, wounded in action, Nov. 1, 1813.

Milton, John. Lieutenant in Capt. Milton's co. 45th rgt. Resigned 1814.

Milton, Richard. Captain in 45th rgt. (My. 23, 1798).

Milward, Samuel. Ensign in Capt. Spry's co. 33d rgt.

Mincher, John. Private in Capt. Smith's co. 51st rgt.

Mincher, Joseph. Private in Capt. Smith's co. 51st rgt.

Minnis, George. Private in Capt. Dyer's co. 17th rgt.

Mintz, Seth. Private in Capt. Dillon's co. 27th rgt.

Miskelly, Peter. Private in Capt. McConkey's co. 27th rgt.

Mitchela, James W. Quarter-master in 1st Rifle Battalion.

Mitchell, Abraham D. Cornet in Capt. Evans' co. 8th Cavalry Dist. (Ag. 12, 1813).

Mitchell, Alexander. Private in Capt. Wells' Artillery co. 22d rgt.

Mitchell, Alexander. Private in Capt. Aisquith's co. Sharp Shooters.

Mitchell, Francis I. Private in Capt. Thompson's co. 1st Baltimore Horse Artillery.

Mitchell, G. C. Captain of the "Elkton Volunteers."

Mitchell, George E. [-1832]. Major in 3d U. S. Artillery (My. 1, 1812); bvt. Colonel (My. 5, 1814) for gallant conduct in repelling attack of British forces on Ft. Oswego, N. Y.

Mitchell, Henrick. Private in Capt. Crawfurd's co. 17th rgt.

Mitchell, Hendrick. Private in Capt. Brooke's co. 34th rgt.

Mitchell, James. Private in Capt. Allen's co. 49th rgt.

Mitchell, John. Cornet in Capt. N. P. Causin's co. 4th Cavalry Dist. (F. 19, 1813) vice Morris.

Mitchell, John. Seaman of the privateer Globe, wounded in action, Nov. 1, 1813.

Mitchell, John. Private in Capt. Chalmers' co. 51st rgt.

Mitchell, John. Private in Capt. Ringgold's co. 6th rgt.

Mitchell, John H. T. S. [-1815]. Lieutenant in Capt. Dent's co. 43d rgt.

Mitchell, Joseph. Ensign in Capt. Courtnay's co. 42d rgt. (Ap. 27, 1813).

Mitchell, Joseph. Private in Capt. Thomas' co. 49th rgt.

Mitchell, Matthew P. Corporal in Capt. Magruder's co. American Artillerists.

Mitchell, Richard. Private in Capt. Ringgold's co. 6th rgt.

Mitchell, Richard B. Private in Capt. Thompson's co. 1st Baltimore Horse Artillery.

Mitchell, Samuel. Private in Capt. Haden's co. 17th rgt.

Mitchell, Thomas. Sergeant in Capt. Dyer's co. Fells Point Riflemen.

Mitchell, Thomas. Private in Capt. Crawfurd's co. 17th rgt.

Mitchell, Thomas. Private in Capt. Stone's co. 31st rgt.

Mitchell, Thomas. Private in Capt. Snowden's co. 36th rgt.

Mitchell, William. Private in Capt. Wilson's co. 6th rgt.

Mitchell, Zephaniah. Sergeant in Capt. Jos. Jones' co. 34th rgt.

Mitchett, Dr. Mungo. Surgeon's mate in 43d rgt.

Mitten, William. Lieutenant in Capt. Durbin's co. 20th rgt. (S. 12, 1814).

Mix, Lewis. Private in Capt. Stewart's co. 51st rgt.

Mixter, Ezra. Private in Capt. Schwarzauer's co. 27th rgt.

Moale, Randall H. Private in Columbian Artillery Quarter-master in 1st rgt. Artillery (Ag. 10, 1813).

Moale, Robert N. Quarter-master in 6th Cavalry Dist. (Jy. 8, 1813).

Moale, Samuel. Captain in Columbian Artillery co. (My. 22, 1812).

Moberry, James. Corporal in Capt. Schwarzauer's co. 27th rgt.

Mobley, Edward. Private in Capt. Snowden's co. 36th rgt.

Mobly, Edward. Lieutenant in Capt. Waters' co. 13th rgt. (Ap. 15, 1795).

Mocksby, Nehemiah. Private in Capt. Barnes' co. 32d rgt.

Mocksby, Nehemiah, Sr. Private in Capt. Barnes' co. 32d rgt.

Moellinger, Jacob. Private in Capt. Piper's co. United Maryland Artillery.

Moffit, John. Private in Capt. Chalmers' co. 51st rgt.

Moffit, Noah. Private in Capt. Mc-Kane's co. 27th rgt.

Moffit, William. Adjutant in 30th rgt. (Je. 26, 1812).

Moffitt, George. Lieutenant in Capt. Spencer's co. 26th rgt. (Je. 6, 1809).

Moland, Edward. Private in Capt. Getzendanner's co. 16th rgt.

Moland, Samuel. Private in Capt. Dyer's co. 17th rgt.

Monahan, Michael. Private in Capt. Shryock's co. 24th rgt.

Monett, Abram. Sergeant in Capt. Hance's co. 31st rgt.

Money, Jesse. Private in Capt. Morgan's co. 49th rgt.

Monk, George. Private in Capt. Warfield's co. Balto. United Volunteers.

Monmonier, Francis [1790-1876]. Sergeant in Capt. Dyer's co. Fells Point Riflemen.

Monroe, Alvin. Private in Capt. Steuart's co. Washington Blues.

Monroe, Isaac. Private in Capt. Nicholson's co. Balto. Fencibles.

Monsarrat, David. Captain of the privateer *Express*, June 1813; Private in Capt. Stiles' co. Marine Artillery, 1814.

Monsarrat, Nicholas. Private in Capt. McKane's co. 27th rgt.

Montgomery, Archibald. Private in Capt. Bunbury's co. Sea Fencibles.

Montgomery, Archibald. Private in Capt. Blizzard's co. 15th rgt.

Montgomery, George. Captain of the privateer *Decatur*, Dec., 1813.

Montgomery, James. Private in Capt. Warfield's co. Balto. United Volunteers.

Montgomery, John. Private in Capt. Edes' co. 27th rgt.

Montgomery, John. Captain in Balto. Union Artillery (Mr. 25, 1814) vice Cone.

Montgomery, Joseph. Private in Capt. Thompson's co. 1st rgt.

Montgomery, Thomas [-1816]. Captain in 14th U. S. Infantry (Mr. 12, 1812) ; Major in 19th Infantry (D. 21, 1814).

Montieth, John. Private in Capt. Levering's co. Independent Blues.

Moody, Isaac. Private in Capt. Myers' co. Franklin Artillery.

Moody, John. Private in Capt. Brown's co. 49th rgt.

Moon, Allen. Private in Capt. Lawrence's co. 6th rgt.

Moon, Richard. Captain of the privateer *Globe*, Jan., 1813.

Moor, John. Private in Capt. Blair's co. 50th rgt.

Moor, Nathaniel. Private in Capt. Brown's co. Eagle Artillerists.

Moor, Thomas. Private in Capt. Chalmers' co. 51st rgt.

Moore, Daniel M. Surgeon in 47th rgt. (F. 1, 1814).

Moore, Dennis. Private in Capt. Fallin's co. 48th rgt.

Moore, Ezekiel. Private in Capt. Moore's co. 49th rgt.

Moore, Gabriel M. Private in Capt. Blair's co. 50th rgt.

Moore, Henry. Private in Capt. Pike's co. Balto. Volunteer Artillery.

Moore, James. Adjutant in 47th rgt. (Ap. 21, 1814).

Moore, James. Private in Capt. Snowden's co. 36th rgt.

Moore, James. Corporal in Capt. Fallin's co. 48th rgt.

Moore, James. Private in Capt. McLaughlin's co. 50th rgt.

Moore, John. Private in Capt. Getzendanner's co. 16th rgt.

Moore, John. Private in Capt. Haubert's co. 51st rgt.

Moore, John B. Private in Capt. Berry's co. Washington Artillery.

Moore, John C. Lieutenant in Capt. Darnall's co. 14th rgt. (S. 9, 1807).

Moore, Joshua. Private in Capt. Peters' co. 51st rgt.

Moore, Levin. Private in Capt. Brohawn's co. 48th rgt.

Moore, Nicholas. Captain in 49th rgt.

Moore, Nicholas Ruxton [1754-1816]. Lieutenant-Colonel in 6th Cavalry Dist. (F. 13, 1812).

Moore, Robert. Corporal in Capt. John Miller's co. 2d D. I.; b. Georgetown, Md.; age 22; printer; subs.; deserted from Patapsco encampment June 15, 1813.

Moore, Robert S. 3d Lieutenant in Capt. Pennington's co. Balto. Independent Artillerists.

Moore, Robert S. Private in Capt. Levering's co. Independent Blues.

Moore, Samuel. 1st Major in 27th rgt. Wounded at North Point.

Moore, Stephen H. [-1841]. Captain in Canadian campaign.

Moore, Thomas. Captain in Artillery co. 49th rgt.

Moore, Thomas. Private in Capt. Shryock's co. 24th rgt.

Moore, Thomas. Private in Capt. John Miller's co. 2d D. I.; b. St. Mary's Co., Md.; age 20; shoemaker; subs. for Jacob Whiteman.

Moore, Warren F. Private in Capt. Causin's troop, attached to 12th rgt.

Moore, William. Lieutenant of the privateer *Express*, June, 1813.

Moore, William. Quarter-master in 29th rgt. (S. 12, 1807).

Moore, William. Private in Capt. Massey's co. 38th rgt.

Moore, William. Fifer in Capt. Magruder's co. American Artillerists.

Moore, William M. Private in Capt. Shryock's co. 24th rgt.

Moores, James. 2d Lieutenant in Capt. Lee's co. 7th Cavalry Dist. (Ap. 16, 1812).

Moores, Samuel Lee. Surgeon's mate in 7th Cavalry Dist. (Ja. 18, 1814).

Mooses, Parker. Private in Capt. Magruder's co. American Artillerists.

Mopps, Adam. Private in Capt. Montgomery's co. Balto. Union Artillery.

Mopps, Frederick. Private in Capt. Pinney's co. 27th rgt.

Moran, Aquila. Private in Ensign Brewer's detachment in 36th rgt.; Private in Capt. Slicer's co. 22d rgt.

Moran, Charles. Ensign in Capt. Morton's co. 1st rgt. (My. 7, 1810); Captain in 1st rgt.; Major.

Moran, James. Private in Capt. Snowden's co. 36th rgt.

Moran, William. Private in Capt. Pinkney's Artillery co. 22d rgt.

More, John. Private in Capt. Kennedy's co. 27th rgt.

More, Warren. Private in Capt. Williams' co. 12th rgt.

Morehead, Henry. Private in Capt. Pennington's co. Balto. Independent Artillerists.

Morehead, John. Private in Capt. Lawson's co. Balto. Patriots.

Morehead, Turner. Private in Capt. Warfield's co. Balto. United Volunteers.

Moreland, Horatio. Private in Capt. Thompson's co. 43d rgt. Deserted.

Moreland, Littleton S. Sergeant in Capt. Dent's co. 43d rgt.

Moreland, Matthew. Private in Capt. Robey's co. 43d rgt.

Moreland, Theodore. Private in Capt. Robey's co. 43d rgt.

Morely, Henry. Private in Capt. Massey's co. 38th rgt.

Morgan, Edward. Private in Capt. Nicholson's co. Balto. Fencibles.

Morgan, George. Ensign in Capt. Barber's co. 45th rgt.; Captain (Ja. 23, 15) vice John Stone.

Morgan, Ignatius. Private in Capt. Cawood's co. 45th rgt.

Morgan, James. Captain in 49th rgt. (D. 10, 1813) vice Pennington.

Morgan, Jeremiah. Command unknown; captured at North Point.

Morgan, Jesse. Private in Capt. Pinney's co. 27th rgt.

Morgan, John. Lieutenant in Capt. Satterfield's co. 19th rgt.

Morgan, John. Private in Capt. Addison's co. Sea Fencibles.

Morgan, John W. Private in Capt. Burke's co. 6th rgt.

Morgan, Lodowick [-1814]. Major in 1st U. S. Rifles (Ja. 24, 1814) ; killed Aug. 12, 1814, in action at Ft. Erie, U. C.

Morgan, Thomas. Ensign in Capt. Jones' co. 16th rgt. (Jy. 15, 1814).

Morgan, Thomas. Quarter-master-Sergeant in 39th rgt.

Morgan, Thomas A. Private in Capt. Dent's co. 43d rgt.

Morgan, Thomas W. Ensign in 5th U. S. Infantry (Jy. 17, 1813) ; 3d Lieutenant (My. 1, 1814).

Morgan, William. Captain of the privateer *Tyro,* Jan., 1813; captured Feb. 25, 1813, by the *Laurentius.*

Morgan, William. Ensign in Capt. Schofield's co. 19th rgt. (Ja. 21, 1814).

Morgan, William. Private in Capt. Haubert's co. 51st rgt.

Morgan, William. Private in Capt. Smith's co. 51st rgt.

Morgan, William T. Private in Capt. Blakistone's co. 45th rgt.

Morgentall, George. Private in Capt. Shryock's co. 24th rgt.

Morris, Elisha. Private in Capt. Blair's co. 50th rgt.

Morris, George. Private in Capt. Bunbury's co. Sea Fencibles.

Morris, Jacob. Private in Capt. Heath's co. 23d rgt.

Morris, James. Private in Capt. Kierstead's co. 6th rgt.

Morris, Jesse. Private in Capt. Edes' co. 27th rgt.

Morris, John. Private in Capt. Brown's co. 6th rgt.

Morris, John. Private in Capt. Snowden's co. 36th rgt.

Morris, John B. 2d Lieutenant in Capt. N. P. Causin's co. 4th Cavalry Dist. (Je. 12, 1812) ; Division Inspector, 1st Division, M. M. (Ag. 4, 1814).

Morris, Joseph. Paymaster in 25th rgt. (Je. 16, 1812).

Morris, Joseph. Seaman of the privateer *Comet.*

Morris, Morris. Corporal in Capt. Wilson's co. 6th rgt.

Morris, Owen. Corporal in Capt. Wilson's co. 6th rgt.

Morris, Richard. Private in Capt. Snowden's co. 36th rgt.

Morris, T. C. Private in Capt. Stiles' co. Marine Artillery.

Morrison, Arthur. Private in Capt. Blair's co. 50th rgt.

Morrison, George W. Private in Capt. Blair's co. 50th rgt.

Morrison, James. Captain in Artillery co. 6th Brigade Kent Co. Jy. (14, 1812).

Morrison, James. Private in Capt. Schwarzauer's co. 27th rgt.

Morrison, John. Private in Capt. Stiles' co. Marine Artillery.

Morrison, P. V. Private in Capt. Levering's co. Independent Blues.

Morrison, William V. Corporal in Capt. Myers' co. 39th rgt.

Morrow, James. Private in Capt. McLaughlin's co. 50th rgt.

Morrow, William. Drummer in Capt. Rogers' co. 51st rgt.

Morsell, William S. Ensign in Capt. Freeland's co. 31st rgt. (Jy. 14, 1812).

Morter, Jacob. Private in Capt. Quantrill's co. 24th rgt.

Mortimer, James M. Captain of the privateer *Patapsco*, Sept., 1812.

Mortimer, John. Private in Capt. Faster's co. 51st rgt.

Mortimer, John. Private in Capt. Myers' co. Franklin Artillery.

Mortimer, Thomas. Private in Capt. Pumphrey's co. 22d rgt.

Mortimer, Thomas. Private in Capt. Schwarzauer's co. 27th rgt.

Morton, Francis. Ensign in Capt. McKane's co. 27th rgt. (Ap. 22, 1814).

Morton, John. Corporal in Capt. Pennington's co. Balto. Independent Artillerists.

Morton, John. Captain in 1st rgt. (Jy. 11, 1814) vice Moran.

Morton, Robert. Private in Capt. Hook's co., M. M.

Morton, William. Private in Capt. Thompson's co. 1st rgt.

Morton, William. Private in Capt. Haubert's co. 51st rgt.

Mosburg, John. Private in Capt. Getzendanner's co. 16th rgt.

Mosel, John. Private in Capt. Smith's co. 51st rgt.

Moses, Jacob. Private in Capt. Bader's co. Union Yägers.

Mosher, William. Private in Capt. Shrim's co. Balto. Light Infantry.

Moshur, James, Jr. Private in Capt. Sterett's co. 1st Balto. Hussars.

Moss, Barney. Private in Capt. Wilson's co. 6th rgt.

Moss, Charles. Private in Capt. McConkey's co. 27th rgt.

Moss, James. Private in Capt. Boone's co. 22d rgt.

Moss, Richard of James. Private in Capt. Boone's co. 22d rgt.

Moss, Richard of Robert. Private in Capt. Boone's co. 22d rgt.

Mossiter, Christopher. Lieutenant in Capt. Riggs' co. 13th rgt. (Je. 26, 1804).

Motter, Lewis. Quarter-master in 47th rgt. (O. 31, 1812).

Motter, Michael. Ensign in Capt. Murray's co. 28th rgt. (Jy. 8, 1814).

Mottu, Leonard. Seaman of the privateer *High Flyer,* wounded in action, Dec., 1812.

Mowbray, Henry. Private in Capt. Shrim's co. Balto. Light Infantry.

Mowton, John [-1865]. 1st Lieutenant in 38th U. S. Infantry (My. 20, 1813) ; Captain (My. 1, 1814).

Mozer, John D. Private in Capt. Sadtler's co. Balto. Yägers. Wounded at Bladensburg.

Mudd, Aloysius. Sergeant in Capt. Dyer's co. 17th rgt.

Mudd, Francis L. Ensign in Capt. Robey's co. 43d rgt. (O. 1, 1811).

Mudd, Joshua. Lieutenant in Capt. Robey's co. 43d rgt. (O. 1, 1811).

Mudd, Massom. Ensign in 14th U. S. Infantry (Mr. 13, 1813); 2d Lieutenant (Je. 29, 1814).

Mudd, Michael. Private in Capt. Dent's co. 43d rgt.

Mudd, Theodore. Lieutenant in Capt. Gardiner's co. 1st rgt.

Mudd, Zephaniah. Private in Capt. Posey's co. 1st rgt.

Muderwood, John. Sergeant in Capt. McKane's co. 27th rgt.

Muer, Thomas. Private in Capt. Brown's co. 6th rgt.

Mugg, Peter. Private in Capt. Blakistone's co. 45th rgt.

Mules, Samuel. Private in Capt. Chew's co. 31st rgt.

Mullenhoover, Joshua. Private in Capt. Dobbin's co. 39th rgt.

Muller, Lewis C. Sergeant in Capt. Wilson's co. 6th rgt.

Mulliken, Basil D. Private in Capt. Sterett's co. 1st Balto. Hussars.

Mulliken, Richard D. Private in Capt. Sterett's co. 1st Balto. Hussars.

Mullikin, Barruck. Private in Capt. Warfield's co. Balto. United Volunteers.

Mullikin, Benjamin. Captain in 2d rgt. Resigned Jy. 6, 1814.

Mullikin, Benjamin H. Private in Capt. Thompson's co. 1st Baltimore Horse Artillery.

Mullikin, Francis. Private in Capt. Veitch's co. 34th rgt.

Mullikin, Joseph. Private in Capt. Brooke's co. 34th rgt.

Mullikin, Rignal. Private in Capt. Warfield's co. Balto. United Volunteers.

Mullikin, Solomon. Ensign in Capt. Stevens' co. 4th rgt. (My. 31, 1808).

Mullikin, William. 1st Lieutenant in Capt. Steuart's Artillery co. 12th Brigade (Ja. 2, 1815) vice Shields.

Mullin, John. Private in Capt. Sample's co. 49th rgt.

Muman, David. Private in Capt. Blair's co. 50th rgt.

Mumford, John. 2d Lieutenant in Capt. Tayler's co. 2d rgt. 1st Cavalry Dist. (Je. 15, 1813).

Mumma, Jacob. Private in Capt. Chalmers' co. 51st rgt.

Mumma, John. Private in Capt. Taylor's co. 46th rgt.

Mumma, John. Private in Capt. Bouldin's co. Independent Light Dragoons.

Mumma, Samuel. Private in Capt. Montgomery's co. Balto. Union Artillery.

Mumma, William. Corporal in Capt. Bouldin's co. Independent Light Dragoons.

Mumma, William. Private in Capt. Snowden's co. 36th rgt.

Mumma, William. Private in Capt. Taylor's co. 46th rgt.

Mummy, Thomas. Lieutenant and Quarter-master in 39th rgt.

Mundell, William. 2d Lieutenant in Capt. Brown's co. Eagle Artillerists (F. 12, 1812).

Munn, Eli. Private in Capt. Brohawn's co. 48th rgt.

Munn, John. Private in Capt. Schwarzauer's co. 27th rgt.

Munroe, H. G. Private in Capt. Pinkney's Artillery co. 22d rgt.

Munroe, James. Private in Capt. Myers' co. 39th rgt.

Munroe, James W. Ensign in Capt. Connoway's co. 15th rgt. (Je. 15, 1813).

Muratte, Samuel. Private in Capt. Ringgold's co. 6th rgt.

Murdoch, Alexander. Private in Capt. Dent's co. 43d rgt.

Murdoch, Edward. Private in Capt. Brown's co. 43d rgt.

Murdoch, Francis. Sergeant in Capt. Burgess's co. 43d rgt.

Murdoch, Gilbert. Private in Capt. Slicer's co. 22d rgt.

Murdoch, James. Private in Capt. Burgess's co. 43d rgt.

Murdoch, John. Private in Capt. Dunnington's co. 43d rgt.

Murdoch, Samuel. Private in Capt. Brown's co. 43d rgt.

Murdoch, William of James. Private in Capt. Brown's co. 43d rgt.

Murdock, George. 1st Lieutenant in 14th U. S. Infantry (N. 14, 1813).

Murdock, Richard H. Private in Capt. Steiner's Frederick Artillery.

Murdock, William. Private in Capt. Chase's co. 22d rgt.

Murke, Joseph H. Private in Capt. Dent's co. 43d rgt.

Murphey, Thomas. Ensign in 5th U. S. Infantry (Jy. 2, 1813); 2d Lieutenant (Je. 25, 1814).

Murphy, Basil. Private in Capt. Smith's co. 51st rgt.

Murphy, Charles. Private in Capt. Edelin's co. 1st rgt.

Murphy, James (1). Private in Capt. Blair's co. 50th rgt.

Murphy, James (2). Private in Capt. Blair's co. 50th rgt.

Murphy, John. Captain of privateer *Globe*, 1812; of the *Grampus*, 1814; killed in action, Sept. 4, 1814.

Murphy, John. Corporal in Capt. Burke's co. 6th rgt.

Murphy, John. Private in Capt. McConckin's co. 38th rgt.

Murphy, William. Private in Capt. Massey's co. 38th rgt.

Murray, Edward. Private in Capt. Sterett's Independent co.

Murray, Francis. Ensign in Capt. Peters' co. 51st rgt.

Murray, Henry M. Private in Capt. Maynard's co. 22d rgt.

Murray, John. Private in Capt. Shryock's co. 24th rgt.

Murray, John E. Private in Capt. Aisquith's co. Sharp Shooters.

Murray, Mathew. Ensign in Capt. Johnson's co. 28th rgt. Captain (Jy. 8, 1814).

Murray, Matthew. Private in Capt. Piper's co. United Maryland Artillery.

Murray, Richard. Lieutenant of the privateer *Oriental*, Sept., 1812.

Murray, Thomas [-1817]. Captain U. S. Artillerists (F. 10, 1813).

Murray, William. Private in Capt. Dillon's co. 27th rgt.

Murray, William. Captain in 15th rgt. (D. 24, 1810).

Murray, William H. Sergeant in Capt. Warfield's co. Balto. United Volunteers. Wounded at Bladensburg.

Murry, Mathew. Private in Capt. Levering's co. Independent Blues.

Murry, Matthias. Private in Capt. Getzendanner's co. 16th rgt.

Murry, Thomas. Private in Capt. Kennedy's co. 27th rgt.

Muschett, Walter. Private in Capt. Warfield's co. Balto. United Volunteers. Wounded at North Point.

Muschett, William. Private in Capt. Burgess' co. 43d rgt.

Muse, Joseph E. Quarter-master in Extra Battalion Dorchester co. (My. 18, 1813).

Musgrove, Samuel. Private in Capt. Snowden's co. 36th rgt.

Musgrove, William. Private in Capt. Brown's co. Eagle Artillerists.

Musser, Samuel. Private in Capt. Getzendanner's co. 16th rgt.

Muth, Philip. Private in Capt. Sadtler's co. Balto. Yägers.

Myers, Bernard. Private in Capt. Peters' co. 51st rgt.

Myers, Charles. Private in Capt. Stapleton's co. 39th rgt.

Myers, George. Sergeant in Capt. Levering's co. Independent Blues.

Myers, Henry [1795-1870]. Captain in 39th rgt.

Myers, Henry. Private in Capt. Horton's co. Maryland Chasseurs.

Myers, Henry. Private in Capt. Dillon's co. 27th rgt.

Myers, Jacob. 1st Lieutenant in Capt. Horton's co. Maryland Chasseurs. (F. 28, 1812).

Myers, John. Private in Capt. Allen's co. 49th rgt.

Myers, John. Private in Capt. Myers' co. 39th rgt.

Myers, John. Private in Capt. Chalmers' co. 51st rgt.

Myers, Joseph. Captain in Franklin Artillery (Jy. 28, 1812).

Myers, Joseph. 1st Lieutenant in Capt. Berry's co. Washington Artillery (Jy. 4, 1812).

Myers, Nicholas. Captain of the privateer Oriental, Nov. 1813; 1st Lieutenant of the Kemp, Nov., 1814; Private in Capt. Stiles' co. Marine Artillery.

Myers, Peter. Private in Capt. McLaughlin's co. 50th rgt.

Myers, Robert. Private in Capt. Stewart's co. 51st rgt.

Myers, Samuel. Adjutant in 27th rgt. (N. 4, 1814).

Myers, Samuel. Sergeant-Major in 39th rgt.

Myers, Samuel. Sergeant in Capt. Levering's co. Independent Blues.

Myers, Solomon. Private in Capt. Brown's co. Eagle Artillerists.

Myers, Stephen. Private in Capt. Magruder's American Artillerists.

Myers, Thomas. Private in Capt. Levering's co. Independent Blues.

Myers, William. Lieutenant in Capt. Stapleton's co. 39th rgt.

Myers, William. Private in Capt. Horton's co. Maryland Chasseurs.

N

Nabb, William. Private in Capt. Thos. Warner's co. 39th rgt.

Nace, William. Lieutenant-Colonel in 15th rgt.

Nagle, Anthony. Private in Capt. Levering's co. Independent Blues.

Nagle, Joseph. Private in Capt. Berry's co. Washington Artillery.

Nalley, Raphael. Private in Capt. Thompson's co. 1st rgt.

Nally, Aquila. Private in Capt. Dent's co. 43d rgt.

Nally, Jesse. Private in Capt. Burgess' co. 43d rgt.

Nally, Zachariah. Private in Capt. Dent's co. 43d rgt.

Nary, Michael. Private in Capt. Addison's co. Sea Fencibles.

Nash, Ephraim. Private in Capt. Schwarzauer's co. 27th rgt.

Nash, Thomas. Private in Capt. Hall's co. 34th rgt.

Naskey, John. Private in Capt. Haubert's co. 51st rgt.

Naylor, George. Private in Capt. Smith's co. 51st rgt.

Naylor, James. Sergeant in Capt. Eversfield's co. 17th rgt.

Naylor, James of Joshua. Ensign in Capt. Naylor's co. 17th rgt. (Jy. 11, 1814).

Naylor, Joshua, Sr. Captain in 17th rgt. (O. 21, 1812).

Neaff, Abraham. Private in Capt. Steiner's Frederick Artillery.

Neagle, James. Private in Capt. Thos. Warner's co. 39th rgt.

Neal, James. Private in Capt. Piper's co. United Maryland Artillery.

Neal, John. Private in Capt. Chalmers' co. 51st rgt.

Neal, John. Private in Capt. Dillon's co. 27th rgt.

Neal, Joseph. Private in Capt. Quantrill's co. 24th rgt.

Neal, Richard. Private in Capt. Myers' co. Franklin Artillery.

Neale, —. Captain in 1st rgt.

Neale, Abner P. Ensign in 18th U. S. Infantry (My. 8, 1812).

Neale, Benjamin. Private in Capt. McKane's co. 27th rgt.

Neale, Francis. Ensign in Capt. Briscoe's co. 45th rgt.

Neale, Francis J. 1st Lieutenant in 36th U. S. Infantry (Ap. 30, 1813).

Neale, George W. Private in Capt. Causin's co. 4th Cavalry Dist.

Neale, Henry A. Private in Capt. Causin's co. 4th Cavalry Dist.

Neale, Henry C. Captain in 36th U. S. Infantry (Ap. 30, 1813).

Neale, James. 1st Lieutenant in 36th U. S. Infantry (Ap. 30, 1813).

Neale, James G. W. Private in Capt. McConkey's co. 27th rgt.

Neale, John G. Private in Capt. Nicholson's co. Balto. Fencibles.

Neale, Raphael. Private in Capt. Millard's co. 12th rgt.

Neale, Thomas G. Captain in 45th rgt. (O. 31, 1812).

Neale, William of James. Corporal in Capt. Blakistone's co. 45th rgt.

Neale, William G. Lieutenant in Capt. Lee's co. 45th rgt. (My. 23, 1812); Lieutenant in Capt. Blakiston's Rifle co. 45th rgt. (Ag. 10, 1813).

Neavitt, John. Private in Capt. McConckin's co. 38th rgt.

Needham, Asa. Ensign in Capt. Clare's co. 31st rgt. (Ag. 20, 1814).

Needs, Richard. Private in Capt. McConckin's co. 38th rgt.

Neff, Andrew. Private in Capt. Marker's co. 28th rgt.

Neff, Jacob. Private in Capt. Marker's co. 28th rgt.

Neff, John, Jr. Private in Capt. McLaughlin's co. 50th rgt.

Neighbours, Harrison. Private in Capt. Hayward's co. 4th rgt.

Neighle, Francis. Private in Capt. Stiles' co. Marine Artillery.

Neil, James. Ensign in Capt. Foreman's co. 33d rgt.

Neilson. See also Nelson.

Neilson, Hugh. Private in Capt. Ducker's co. 7th rgt.

Neilson, Robert [1792-1845]. Private in Crook's co. 27th rgt.; Private in Faster's co. 51st rgt.

Neilson, Thomas. Sergeant in Capt. Steuart's co. Washington Blues.

Neilson, William W. 1st Lieutenant in 2d U. S. Light Dragoons (Je. 7, 1813).

Nelms, J. B. Private in Capt. Haubert's co. 51st rgt.

Nelson, Basil. Private in Capt. Wilson's co. 6th rgt.

Nelson, Benjamin. Private in Capt. Magruder's co. American Artillerists.

Nelson, John. 1st Lieutenant and Assistant Aid-de-camp to Genl. Stansbury in 11th Brigade.

Nelson, Joseph, Jr. Private in Capt. Shrim's co. Balto. Light Infantry.

Nelson, Joseph S. [-1843]. Captain in 36th U. S. Infantry (Ap. 30, 1813).

Nelson, Nathaniel. Private in Capt. Smith's co. 51st rgt.

Nelson, Oliver Hugh. Adjutant in 1st rgt. Artillery (Je. 17, 1812); Private in Capt. Warfield's co. Balto. United Volunteers; Quarter-master in 51st rgt.

Nelson, Richard. Private in Capt. Smith's co. 51st rgt.

Nelson, Robert. Private in Capt. Faster's co. 51st rgt.

Neppod, Jacob. Private in Capt. Rogers' co. 51st rgt.

Neptune, William. Private in Capt. Blair's co. 50th rgt.

Neth, Lewis, Jr. Private in Capt. Maynard's co. 22d rgt.

Neuhaus, Carsten. 1st Lieutenant in Capt. Sadtler's co. Balto. Yägers (Ap. 22, 1814).

Neven, Thomas [1796-1845]. Private in Capt. McDonald's co. 6th rgt.

Nevill, John. Ensign in Capt. Albert's co. Extra Battalion Harford Co. (Jy. 8, 1814).

Newbury, John. Private in Capt. Wilson's co. 6th rgt.

Newcomb, John. Sergeant in Capt. Mann's co. 33d rgt.

Newcomer, David. Cornet in Capt. Tabb's co. 1st rgt. 1st Cavalry Dist. (F. 28, 1812); 1st Lieutenant (S. 12, 1814).

Newcomer, John. Private in Capt. Smith's co. 51st rgt.

Newit, Edward. Private in Capt. Addison's co. Sea Fencibles.

Newman, Francis. Captain in 1st U. S. Artillery (Mr. 12, 1812).

Newman, Francis. Lieutenant-Colonel in 4th Cavalry Dist. (F. 13, 1812).

Newman, George A. Ensign in Capt. Tomlinson's co. 50th rgt. (F. 15, 1814).

Newman, Horatio. Private in Capt. Brooke's co. 34th rgt.

Newman, James. Captain in 4th rgt. (S. 18, 1812).

Newman, John C. Private in Capt. Blair's co. 50th rgt.

Newman, John H. Sergeant in Capt. Myers' co. Franklin Artillery.

Newman, John M. Lieutenant in Capt. Massey's co. 33d rgt. (My. 28, 1808).

Newman, Lawson. Private in Capt. Magruder's co. American Artillerists.

Newman, Richard. Private in Capt. Fendall's co. 43d rgt.

Newton, Anthony. Private in Capt. Bouldin's co. Independent Light Dragoons.

Newton, Athanias. Private in Capt. Blair's co. 50th rgt.

Newton, Ignatius. Ensign in Capt. Parker's co. 18th rgt. (S. 30, 1797).

Newton, John. Adjutant in Extra Battalion Dorchester Co. (Ag. 1, 1808).

Newton, John. Private in Capt. Peters' co. 51st rgt.

Newton, Patrick. Private in Capt. Pinney's co. 27th rgt.

Newton, William. Major in Extra Battalion Dorchester Co. (Mr. 25, 1812).

Nicholas, George [-1813]. Surgeon's mate in 14th U. S. Infantry (O. 14, 1812).

Nicholas, Patrick. Private in Capt. Snowden's co. 36th rgt.

Nicholls, Andrew. Ensign in Capt. Waters' co. 22d rgt. (Jy. 15, 1814) vice Dorsey.

Nicholls, Andrew. Sergeant in Capt. Hall's co. 3d Cavalry rgt.

Nicholls, David. Private in Capt. Roney's co. 39th rgt.

Nicholls, David Charles. 3d Lieutenant in 3d U. S. Artillery (Ap. 26, 1814); 2d Lieutenant (Jy. 22, 1814).

Nicholls, Isaac. Lieutenant in Capt. Acworth's co. 25th rgt. (Ap. 16, 1812).

Nicholls, Jacob. Ensign in Capt. Johnson's co. 28th rgt. Resigned Je. 8, 1814.

Nicholls, John. Sergeant in Capt. Hall's co. 34th rgt.

Nicholls, Thomas C. Lieutenant in Capt. Hennix's co. 4th rgt. (Ag. 11, 1813).

Nicholls, William. Sergeant in Capt. Weems' co. 22d rgt.; Ensign in Capt. Waters' co. (Ap. 29, 1814).

Nichols, Adam. Private in Capt. Steiner's Frederick Artillery.

Nichols, Andrew. Private in Capt. Hall's co. 3d Cavalry rgt.

Nichols, Isaiah. Major (Montgomery Co.). Command unkonwn.

Nichols, Nelson. Private in Capt. Slicer's co. 22d rgt.

Nichols, Samuel. Sergeant in Capt. Hatherly's co. 22d rgt.

Nichols, Samuel. Private in Capt. Watson's co. 39th rgt.

Nichols, Thomas C. Major 2d Cavalry Dist. (F. 13, 1812).

Nicholson, Benjamin. Private in Capt. Boone's co. 22d rgt.

Nicholson, Benjamin [-1813]. 1st Lieutenant in 14th U. S. Infantry (Mr. 12, 1812); Captain (Mr. 3, 1813); died My. 13, 1813, of wounds received at the capture of York, U. C.

Nicholson, Charles B. Lieutenant in Capt. Hall's co. 35th rgt. (N. 3, 1814).

Nicholson, Christopher. Private in Capt. Stewart's co. 51st rgt.

Nicholson, Edward. Private in Capt. Usselton's co. Artillery 6th Brigade.

Nicholson, Ezekiel. Private in Capt. Chase's co. 22d rgt.

Nicholson, Josa H. Private in Capt. Adreon's co. Union Volunteers.

Nicholson, Joseph. Private in Capt. Massey's co. 38th rgt.

Nicholson, Joseph H. Captain in Balto. Fencibles.

Nicholson, Joseph H, Jr. Corporal in Capt. Jas. Massey's co. 38th rgt.

Nicholson, Thomas. Private in Capt. Pike's co. Balto. Volunteer Artillery.

Nicholson, Thomas. Private in Capt. Rogers' co. 51st rgt.

Nicholson, Thomas. Private in Capt. Smith's co. 51st rgt.

Nicholson, William. Private in Capt. Myers' co. Franklin Artillery.

Nicholson, William H. Major in 38th rgt.

Nicolas, Henry. Private in Capt. John Miller's co. 2d D. I.; b. Md.; age 25; farmer.

Nicolason, Thomas. Corporal in Capt. John Miller's co. 2d D. I.; b. Ireland; age 33; coachmaker; subs for Jonathan Hager.

Nicoll, Thomas. Private in Capt. Dyers' co. Fells Point Riflemen.

Nicolls, Edward. Cornet in Capt. Saulsbury's co. 10th Cavalry Dist. (N. 3, 1812).

Nicolls, Henry. 2d Lieutenant in Capt. Saulsbury's co. 10th Cavalry Dist. (N. 3, 1812).

Nicols, Jeremiah. Private in Capt. Hands' co. 21st rgt.

Nicols, Joseph. Surgeon in 10th Cavalry Dist. (Ag. 22, 1812).

Nielson, Oliver H. 1st Lieutenant in 38th U. S. Infantry (My. 20, 1813).

Night, John. Private in Capt. Rogers' co. 51st rgt.

Niles, Hezekiah. Private in Capt. Pinney's co. 27th rgt.

Ninde, Isaac. Private in Capt. Stiles' co. Marine Artillery.

Nippard, George. Private in Capt. Montgomery's co. Balto. Artillery.

Nippard, George. Private in Capt. Pinney's co. 27th rgt.

Nixdorff, Henry. Private in Capt. Steiner's Frederick Artillery.

Nizor, Thomas. Sergeant in Capt. Perrigo's co. 46th rgt.

Noah, Lowry. Private in Capt. Thos. Warner's co. 39th rgt.

Noble, Alexander. Private in Capt. Berry's co. Washington Artillery.

Noble, James. Private in Capt. Quantrill's co. 24th rgt.

Noble, Richard. Private in Capt. Aisquith's co. Sharp Shooters.

Noble, Roswell. Private in Capt. Snowden's co. 36th rgt.

Noone, John. Private in Capt. Deems' co. 51st rgt.

Norfolk, John. Sergeant in Capt. Stone's co. 31st rgt.

Norfolk, John of John. Private in Capt. Wilson's co. 31st rgt.

Norfolk, Thomas. Private in Capt. Gray's co. 31st rgt.

Norfolk, Thomas of Thos. Private in Capt. Wilson's co. 31st rgt.

Norfolk, William. Private in Capt. Wilson's co. 31st rgt.

Norman, Solomon. Private in Capt. Hall's co. 3d Cavalry rgt.

Norman, William. Captain in 2d rgt. (My. 23, 1812).

Norris, Alexander. Cornet in Capt. Lee's co. 7th Cavalry Dist. (Ap. 16, 1812).

Norris, Aquila. Private in Capt. Levering's co. Independent Blues.

Norris, Benjamin. Private in Capt. Levering's co. Independent Blues.

Norris, Charles. Private in Capt. Williams' co. 12th rgt.

Norris, Edward. Private in Capt. Steuart's co. Washington Blues.

Norris, James. Captain in Union Yägers (Ap. 4, 1812).

Norris, James. Private in Capt. Williams' co. 12th rgt.

Norris, John. Sergeant in Capt. Sands' co. 22d rgt.; Ensign (Ag. 20, 1813).

Norris, John R. Sergeant in Capt. Dent's co. 43d rgt.

Norris, Jonathan. Captain in 20th rgt. Rifle co. (Ap. 27, 1813).

Norris, Luther A. Private in Capt. Levering's co. Independent Blues; captured at North Point.

Norris, Richard. Private in Capt. Thompson's co. 1st Baltimore Horse Artillery.

Norris, Samuel. Private in Capt. Levering's co. Independent Blues.

Norris, Silas C. Private in Capt. Levering's co. Independent Blues.

Norris, Thomas. Private in Capt. Sterett's Independent co.

Norris, Upton. Captain in 20th rgt. (Ja. 24, 1814) vice Albaugh.

Norris, Vachel. Private in Capt. Chase's co. 22d rgt.

Norris, William. Private in Capt. Sterett's Independent co.

Norris, William. Private in Capt. Snowden's co. 36th rgt.

Norris, William, Jr. Private in Capt. Snowden's co. 36th rgt.

Norriss, Ignatius. Private in Capt. Dunnington's co. 43d rgt.

Norriss, Thomas. Private in Capt. Burgess' co. 43d rgt.

North, Edward. Private in Capt. Kierstead's co. 6th rgt.

North, Hicks. Private in Capt. Brohawn's co. 48th rgt.

North, John. Corporal in Capt. McLaughlin's co. 50th rgt.

North, Richard. Private in Capt. Brohawn's co. 48th rgt.

North, William. Private in Capt. Brohawn's co. 48th rgt.

Northcraft, Edward. Private in Capt. Blair's co. 50th rgt.

Northcraft, M. Private in Capt. McLaughlin's co. 50th rgt.

Northcroft, Hezekiah. 1st Lieutenant in Capt. Winsor's co. 2d Cavalry Dist. (Jy. 4, 1814).

Norvell, John [1789-1850]. Private in Capt. Nicholson's co. Baltimore Fencibles; later, U. S. Senator from Michigan.

Norwood, Edward. Private in Capt. Magruder's American Artillerists.

Norwood, John. Private in Capt. Snowden's co. 36th rgt.

Norwood, John. Private in Capt. Dobbin's co. 39th rgt.

Norwood, John B. 2d Lieutenant in Capt. Snowden's co. 6th Cavalry Dist. (Ja. 29, 1814).

Norwood, Nicholas. Corporal in Capt. Ducker's co. 7th rgt.

Notherman, George. Private in Capt. Myers' co. Franklin Artillery.

Nottingham, William. Private in Capt. Burgess' co. 43d rgt.

Notts, William. Private in Capt. Chambers' co. 21st rgt.

Nouvell, Michael. Private in Capt. Leverings' co. Independent Blues.

Nowland, Benedict. Sergeant in Capt. Boyer's co. 33d rgt.

Nowland, Benjamin. Major in 42d rgt. (D. 29, 1814) vice Calwell.

Nowland, James. Lieutenant in Capt. A. C. Smith's co. 49th rgt.

Nowland, Lambert. Private in Capt. Pennington's co. Balto. Independent Artillerists.

Noyle, Jacob. Command unknown; captured at North Point.

Nugent, J. B. Private in Capt. Gardiner's co. 1st rgt.

Nugent, Neal. Private in Capt. Dillon's co. 27th rgt.

Nussear, Jesse. Private in Capt. Myers' co. 39th rgt.

Nussear, Joseph. Private in Capt. Myers' co. 39th rgt.

Nutton, —. Surgeon in 25th rgt. Died, 1813.

O

Oakley, Asa. Private in Capt. Posey's co. 1st rgt.

Oakley, Isaac. Private in Capt. Posey's co. 1st rgt.

Oakley, Richard. Private in Capt. Posey's co. 1st rgt.

O'Brien, Francis. Private in Capt. Ringgold's co. 6th rgt.

O'Brien, James. Private in Capt. McKane's co. 27th rgt.

O'Brien, Patrick. Private in Capt. Stewart's co. 51st rgt.

O'Bryan, Thomas N. Private in Capt. McConckin's co. 38th rgt.

O'Conner, John. Surgeon's mate in 5th Cavalry Dist. (Je. 26, 1812); Surgeon's mate in 3d U. S. Rifles (Mr. 31, 1814).

O'Connor, Lewis. Private in Capt. Brown's co. Eagle Artillerists.

O'Dean, Kendle. Private in Capt. Heath's co. 23d rgt.

Oden, Lewis. Private in Capt. Sample's co. 49th rgt.

Odenton, Joseph. Private in Capt. Robey's co. 43d rgt.

O'Donnell, Barney. Private in Capt. McConkey's co. 27th rgt.

O'Donnell, Columbus. Private in Capt. Sterett's co. 1st Balto. Hussars.

O'Donnell, Patrick. Private in Capt. McKane's co. 27th rgt.

O'Ferrall, John. Private in Capt. Quantrill's co. 24th rgt.

Offley, Vincent. Lieutenant in Capt. Massey's co. 35th rgt. (N. 23, 1814).

Offutt, Basil. Lieutenant in Capt. Clagett's co. 44th rgt. (D. 16, 1813) vice Gassaway.

Ogden, Benjamin. Private in Capt. Ireland's co. 31st rgt.

Ogden, David. Private in Capt. Pinney's co. 27th rgt.

Ogden, James I. Sergeant in Capt. Chase's co. 22d rgt.

Ogden, John. Private in Capt. Gray's co. 31st rgt.

Ogden, Jonathan. Private in Capt. Stapleton's co. 39th rgt.

Ogden, Joseph J. Private in Capt. Maynard's co. 22d rgt.

Ogden, Nathaniel J. Private in Capt. Burke's co. 6th rgt.

Ogden, William. Private in Capt. Gray's co. 31st rgt.

Ogle, Samuel. Captain in 47th rgt. (My. 22, 1812).

O'Harro, Arthur. Private in Capt. Stewart's co. 51st rgt.

O'Harro, William. Ensign in Capt. Norman's co. 2d rgt. (My. 23, 1812).

Ohr, Conrad. Ensign in Capt. Flora's co. 24th rgt. (Ag. 1, 1814).

Olcott, Joel. Private in Capt. Dobbin's co. 39th rgt.

Oldham, Cyrus. Captain in 30th rgt. (O. 10, 1807).

Oldham, Edward. Captain in 49th rgt. (Mr. 25, 1811).

Oldham, Elisha. Private in Capt. McKane's co. 27th rgt.

Oldham, George W. Captain in 49th rgt.

Oldson, Robert. Lieutenant in Capt. Cornelius' co. 35th rgt. (Jy. 7, 1814).

Oldson, Samuel. Private in Capt. Lawson's co. Balto. Patriots; in Capt. Adreon's Union Volunteers.

Oler, George. Private in Capt. Myers' co. Franklin Artillery.

Oliver, Amos. Private in Capt. McConkey's co. 27th rgt.

Oliver, John. Private in Capt. Stapleton's co. 39th rgt.

Oliver, John C. Sergeant in Capt. Heath's co. 23d rgt.

Oliver, Joseph C. Private in Capt. Heath's co. 23d rgt.

O'Neal, Henry. Captain in 38th U. S. Infantry (My. 20, 1813).

O'Neal, John. 2d Lieutenant in Capt Linthicum's co. 2d Cavalry Dist. (Je. 12, 1812).

O'Neale, Henry. Adjutant in 3d rgt.

O'Neale, Thomas. Private in Capt. Crawfurd's co. 17th rgt.

O'Neale, William. Private in Capt. Crawfurd's co. 17th rgt.

O'Neill, John [1768-1838]. "The Hero of Havre de Grace." See pages 33, 42.

O'Neill, Joseph. Private in Capt. Stewart's co. 51st rgt.

Onshippin, Peter. Private in Capt. John Miller's co. 2d D. I.; b. Germany; age 46; weaver; subs. for John Snively.

Opperman, Lewis. Private in Capt. Sadtler's co. Balto. Yägers.

Oram, John. Private in Capt. Bunbury's co. Sea Fencibles.

Oram, Levy. Ensign in Capt. Craft's co. 11th rgt. (Ja. 25, 1814).

Oram, Lloyd. Private in Capt. Thos. Warner's co. 39th rgt.

Oram, William. Lieutenant in Capt. Ravon's co. 46th rgt. (Ag. 29, 1812).

Orchard, John. Private in Capt. Steuart's co. Washington Blues.

Ord, James. 1st Lieutenant in 36th U. S. Infantry (Ap. 30, 1813).

Ordronaux, John [1778-1841]. Captain of the privateer *Prince of Neufchatel.*

O'Reily, Joseph C. Private in Capt. Bouldin's co. Independent Light Dragoons.

Orem, Rezin. Private in Capt. A. E. Warner's co. 39th rgt.

Orielly, Pollydore E. Surgeon's mate 22d rgt. (Ap. 4, 1812).

Orme, Archibald E. Private in Capt. Pike's co. Balto. Volunteer Artillery.

O'Rourke, Charles. Private in Capt. Warfield's co. Balto. United Volunteers. Wounded at North Point.

Orr, Jacob. Lieutenant in Capt. Lowra's co. 24th rgt. (Je. 16, 1812).

Orr, Thomas. Captain in 30th rgt. (Ag. 14, 1810).

Orr, William. Sergeant in Capt. Hall's co. 30th rgt.

Orrell, William. Cornet in Capt. Hughlett's co. 10th Cavalry Dist. (Je. 18, 1812); 2d Lieutenant (Ap. 23, 1813).

Orrick, Daniel. Ensign in Capt. Orrick's co. 41st rgt. Resigned Jy. 11, 1814.

Orrick, Edward. Captain in 41st rgt. (My. 22, 1812) Rifle co.

Orrick, James. Surgeon in 6th Cavalry Dist. (Jy. 8, 1813).

Orrick, John. Private in Capt. Stiles' co. Marine Artillery.

Orsler, John. Sergeant in Capt. Blizzard's co. 15th rgt.

Ortman, Daniel. Private in Capt. John Miller's co. 2d D. I.; b. Washington Co., Md.; age 25; cooper; subs. for John Mulendore.

Orum, Edward. Private in Capt. McConkey's co. 27th rgt.

Osborn, John W. Lieutenant in Capt. Parks' co. 35th rgt. (My. 22, 1812).

Osborn, Joshua. Sergeant in Capt. Jackson's co. 34th rgt.

Osborn, Joshua. Sergeant in Capt.
Brooke's co. 34th rgt.

Osborn, Samuel G. 1st Lieutenant
in Capt. Little's co. 9th Cavalry
Dist. (My. 22, 1812); Captain
(Ap. 24, 1813).

Osborn, William. Captain in 50th
rgt. (O. 15, 1814).

Osborne, Alexander. Corporal in
Capt. Pennington's co. Balto. Volunteer Artillerists.

Osborne, H. P. Private in Capt.
Pennington's co. Balto. Independent Artillerists.

Osbourn, Charles. Private in Capt.
Dyer's co. 17th rgt.

Osbourn, Thomas. Sergeant in
Capt. Crawfurd's co. 17th rgt.

Osburn, John. Private in Capt.
Brooke's co. 34th rgt.

Osburn, Joseph. Private in Capt.
Brooke's co. 34th rgt.

Osburn, Michael. Private in Capt.
Taylor's co. 46th rgt.

Osburn, Thomas. Private in Capt.
Brooke's co. 34th rgt.

Oshel, John. Ensign in Capt. Gore's
co. 41st rgt. (Je. 26, 1812).

Oster, Samuel. Lieutenant in Capt.
Fouke's co. 8th rgt. (S. 20, 1813).

Otto, Jacob. Lieutenant in Capt.
Farquar's co. 47th rgt.

Oursler, Stephen. Sergeant in Capt.
Frizzell's co. Nace's rgt.

Ouvacre, John. Private in Capt.
Roney's co. 39th rgt.

Overhoff, Frederick. Private in
Capt. Chalmers' co. 51st rgt.

Owen, John. Surgeon in 5th rgt.
(Jy. 24, 1807).

Owen, R. H. Private in Capt. Warfield's co. Balto. United Volunteers.

Owen, Richard. Private in Capt.
Burgess' co. 43d rgt.

Owen, Washington. Adjutant in
44th rgt. (Jy. 20, 1812).

Owen, William. Private in Capt.
Stiles' co. Marine Artillery.

Owens, Edward. Private in Capt.
Brohawn's co. 48th rgt.

Owens, Isaac. Private in Capt.
Pennington's co. Balto Independent Artillerists.

Owens, James. Private in Capt.
Burke's co. 6th rgt.

Owens, John. Private in Capt. Brohawn's co. 48th rgt.

Owens, Joseph. 1st Lieutenant in
5th U. S. Infantry. (Ja. 3, 1812);
Capt. (My. 1, 1814).

Owens, Joseph [1780-1849]. Private in Capt. Sterett's Independent co. Wounded at North Point.

Owens, Thomas. Private in Capt.
Hall's co. 3d Cavalry rgt.

Owens, William. Private in Capt.
Levering's co. Independent Blues.

Owings, Beal. Private in Capt.
Sterett's co. 1st Balto. Hussars.

Owings, Beale. Private in Capt.
Snowden's co. 36th rgt.

Owings, Beale of Saml. Cornet in
Capt. Carnan's co. 6th Cavalry
Dist. (Je. 26, 1812).

Owings, Edward. Cornet in Capt.
Gist's co. 2d rgt. 1st Cavalry
Dist. (Jy. 28, 1813) vice Hines.

Owings, Francis. Lieutenant in
Capt. Orr's co. 30th rgt.

Owings, George of Richard. Private
in Capt. Williams' co. 12th rgt.

Owings, John. Captain in 36th rgt.
(D. 27, 1811).

Owings, John. Private in Capt.
Pike's co. Balto. Volunteer Artillery.

Owings, Samuel. Paymaster in 6th
Cavalry Dist. (Jy. 8, 1813).

Owings, Samuel C. Captain in 36th rgt. (S. 10, 1814).

Owings, Thomas. Captain in 32d rgt. (Ap. 23, 1812).

Oxinham, Mordecai. Ensign in Capt. Wayman's co. 26th rgt. (Jy. 8, 1813).

Oyler, John. Ensign in Capt. Flant's co. 47th rgt. (Mr. 15, 1809).

Oyster, Daniel. Corporal in Capt. Quantrill's co. 24th rgt.

P

Padgett, Henry. Private in Capt. Thompson's co. 1st rgt.

Padgett, Henry. Private in Capt. Smoot's co. 43d rgt.

Padgett, John. Private in Capt. Dent's co. 43d rgt.

Padgett, Josias. Private in Capt. Dyer's co. 17th rgt.

Padgett, Thomas. Private in Capt. Smoot's co. 43d rgt.

Padgett, William. Private in Capt. Brooke's co. 34th rgt.

Pagan, William. Private in Capt. Brohawn's co. 48th rgt.

Page, Henry. Capt. in 21st rgt. (1813-14).

Page, James, M. D., [1783-1832]. Surgeon at Baltimore Station, 1813.

Page, Jenkin. Private in Capt. Bunbury's co. Sea Fencibles.

Page, John. Ensign in 1st U. S. Rifles (Mr. 18, 1814).

Pain, Richard. Private in Capt. Kennedy's co. 27th rgt.

Palmer, Edward [1787-1864]. Private in Capt. Sterett's co. 1st Balto. Hussars.

Palmer, Isaac. Private in Capt. Wilson's co. 6th rgt.

Palmer, John. Private in Capt. Mackey's co. 49th rgt.

Palmer, Joseph. Private in Capt. Shryock's co. 24th rgt.

Palmetary, John H. Private in Capt. McConkey's co. 27th rgt.

Palmetery, John. Private in Capt. Kennedy's co. 27th rgt.

Palmore, Charles. Fifer in Capt. Travers' co. 48th rgt.

Pamphilion, Edward. Private in Capt. Brown's oo. 6th rgt.

Pane, Samuel. Captain in Extra Battalion Caroline co. (S. 12, 1814).

Pantry, John. Private in Capt. McDonald's co. 6th rgt.

Papyon, John. Private in Capt. McDonald's co. 6th rgt.

Parish, Edward. Private in Capt. Ducker's co. 7th rgt.

Parish, John. Private in Capt. Snowden's co. 36th rgt.

Parish, William. Private in Capt. Slicer's co. 22d rgt.

Parker, Charles. Corporal in Capt. Pinkney's Artillery co. 22d rgt.

Parker, Charles. Lieutenant in Capt. Dennis' co. 37th rgt. (Jy. 11, 1814) vice Wheatly Dennis.

Parker, Charles. Private in Capt. Adreon's co. Union Volunteers.

Parker, David. Captain in 18th rgt. (S. 30, 1797).

Parker, Elisha. Lieutenant in Capt. Jos. Bayley's co. 25th rgt. (Je. 1, 1813).

Parker, Evan. Private in Capt. Montgomery's co. Balto. Union Artillery.

Parker, G. W. Private in Capt. Pinkney's Artillery co. 22d rgt.

Parker, George. Corporal in Capt. Slicer's co. 22d rgt.; Corporal in Ensign Brewer's detachment, 36th rgt. at Bladensburg.

Parker, George. Private in Capt. Haubert's co. 51st rgt.

Parker, George, Jr. Private in Capt. Sands' co. 22d rgt.

Parker, Henry. Private in Capt. Travers' co. 48th rgt.

Parker, Hix. Private in Capt. Travers' co. 48th rgt.

Parker, Isaac. Private in Capt. Chase's co. 22d rgt.

Parker, James. Major in 33d rgt.

Parker, James. Private in Capt. Levering's co. Independent Blues.

Parker, John. Private in Capt. Travers' co. 48th rgt.

Parker, John of Levin. Private in Capt. Travers' co. 48th rgt.

Parker, Marsham. Paymaster in 31st rgt. (Ap. 1, 1809).

Parker, Philip. Private in Capt. Pinkney's Artillery co. 22d rgt.

Parker, Resin B. Private in Capt. Posey's co. 1st rgt.

Parker, Richard. Private in Capt. Travers' co. 48th rgt.

Parker, Richard B. Private in Capt. McConkey's co. 27th rgt.

Parker, Samuel. Private in Capt. Getzendanner's co. 16th rgt.

Parker, Thomas. Private in Capt. Stewart's co. 51st rgt.

Parker, William. Private in Capt. Ducker's co. 7th rgt.

Parker, Zebediah. Private in Capt Ducker's co. 7th rgt.

Parkerson, Richard. Private in Capt. Wells' Artillery co. 22d rgt.

Parkerson, William. Private in Capt. Sands' co. 22d rgt.

Parkes, Thomas. Private in Capt. Shryock's co. 24th rgt.

Parkeson, William. Private in Capt. Blair's co. 50th rgt.

Parkinson, Abraham. Private in Capt. Wells' Artillery co. 22d rgt.

Parks, Abraham. Sergeant in Capt. Dyer's co. Fells Point Riflemen.

Parks, Elisha. Private in Capt. Galloway's co. 46th rgt.

Parks, James. Private in Capt. Massey's co. 38th rgt.

Parks, William. Captain in 35th rgt. (My. 22, 1812).

Parks, William. Private in Capt. Brown's co. Eagle Artillerists.

Parlett, Isaac. Corporal in Capt. Fowler's co. 46th rgt.

Parlett, Mordecai. Private in Capt. Sadtler's co. Balto. Yagers.

Parlett, Thomas. Private in Capt. Deems' co. 51st rgt.

Parlett, William. Sergeant in Capt. Fowler's co. 46th rgt.

Parlett, Zacharias. Private in Capt. Taylor's co. 46th rgt.

Parnham, George D. Paymaster in 1st rgt. (Ag. 1, 1808).

Parnham, John P. Captain in 1st rgt. (Ja. 10, 1814).

Parr, David. Private in Capt. Peters' co. 51st rgt.

Parr, Elisha. Private in Capt. Peters' co. 51st rgt.

Parran, James M. Cornet in Capt. Carcaud's co. 3d Cavalry Dist. (Mr. 26, 1812).

Parran, Richard. Captain in 31st rgt. (Jy. 12, 1814) vice Gantt.

Parran, Thomas. Ensign in Capt. Leach's co. 31st rgt. Resigned D. 23, 1813.

Parrish, Isaac. Private in Capt. Pinney's co. 27th rgt.

Parrish, William [1794-1833]. Private in Capt. Aisquith's co. Sharp Shooters.

Parrott, David. Private in Capt. Stiles' co. Marine Artillery.

Parrott, George. Captain in 4th rgt.

Parrott, Richard. Sergeant in Capt. Galt's co. 6th rgt.

Parrott, Samuel. Private in Capt. Chase's co. 22d rgt.

Parrott, Thomas. 2d Lieutenant in Capt. Vickers' co. 12th Brigade (Jy. 12, 1814).

Parsley, Arthur. Private in Capt. Hands' co. 21st rgt.

Parsons, Benjamin. Lieutenant in Capt. Parsons' co. 37th rgt. (Jy. 11, 1814) vice Hooper.

Parsons, John. Corporal in Capt. Kierstead's co. 6th rgt.

Parsons, John D. Private in Capt. Galt's co. 6th rgt.

Parsons, John W. B. Captain in 37th rgt. (Jy. 21, 1810).

Parsons, Jonathan. Private in Capt. Dyer's co. Fells Point Riflemen.

Parsons, Joseph. Private in Capt. Schwarzauer's co. 27th rgt.

Parsons, Joseph. Corporal in Capt. Tilghman's co. 33d rgt.

Parsons, Thomas. Private in Capt. Chalmers' co. 51st rgt.

Parston, William. Ensign in Capt. Cornell's co. 47th rgt. (My. 22, 1812).

Partridge, *see also* **Patridge.**

Partridge, Eaton R. Private in Capt. Moore's co. 49th rgt.

Partridge, James. Private in Capt. Sterett's co. 1st Balto. Hussars.

Pascault, Francis. Private in Capt. Pennington's co. Balto. Independent Artillerists.

Paschal, Jeremiah. Private in Capt. Kennedy's co. 27th rgt.

Pasterfield, Caleb. Corporal in Capt. Dillon's co. 27th rgt.

Pastorias, Samuel. Private in Capt. Stewart's co. 51st rgt.

Patdurf, Henry. Private in Capt. Shryock's co. 24th rgt.

Pater, Stephen. Fifer in Capt. Miller's co. 39th rgt.

Pater, Stephen A. Private in Capt. Maynard's co. 22d rgt.

Patillo, Henry H. Private in Capt. Pennington's co. Balto. Independent Artillerists.

Patrick, L. C. Private in Capt. Sterett's Independent co.

Patrick, Matthew A. [-1834]. Ensign in 29th U. S. Infantry (Mr. 30, 1814); 3d Lieutenant (My. 1, 1814).

Patridge, Daubner B. Private in Capt. Hanna's co. Fells Point Light Dragoons.

Patridge, Eaton R. Private in Capt. Moale's co. Columbian Artillery.

Patridge, Job. Private in Capt. Pinney's co. 27th rgt.

Patterson, Andrew. Private in Capt. Stewart's co. 51st rgt.

Patterson, Edward. Aid-de-camp to Genl. Smith in 3d Division M. M.

Patterson, George. Private in Capt. Dobbin's co. 39th rgt.

Patterson, Gerard. Private in Capt. Stiles' co. Marine Artillery.

Patterson, James. Ensign in Capt. Porter's co. 30th rgt. (S. 11, 1807).

Patterson, James. Ensign in Capt. Lightner's co. 30th rgt. (Ap. 22, 1814).

Patterson, John. Private in Capt. Dobbin's co. 39th rgt.

Patterson, John. Private in Capt. Smith's co. 51st rgt.

Patterson, John. Private in Capt. Sterett's Independent co.

Patterson, Joshua W. 2d Lieutenant in Capt. Thompson's co. Independent Horse Artillery (D. 20, 1814) vice Howard.

Patterson, Nathan. Sergeant in Capt. Rogers' co. 51st rgt.

Patterson, Robert. Assistant Division Inspector in 3d Division M. M.

Patterson, Robert. Private in Capt. Thompson's co. 1st Baltimore Horse Artillery.

Patterson, Samuel. Private in Capt. John Miller's co. 2d D. I.; b. Pennsylvania; age 29; stage-driver; subs. for Patrick Boyle.

Patterson, Thomas. Private in Capt. Rogers' co. 51st rgt.

Patterson, Thomas. Private in Capt. Adreon's co. Union Volunteers.

Patterson, William. Private in Capt. Bunbury's co. Sea Fencibles.

Patterson, William. Private in Capt. Ringgold's co. 6th rgt.

Patterson, William. Private in Capt. Myers' co. Franklin Artillery.

Pattison, Henry. Ensign in Capt. Brohawn's co. 48th rgt. (S. 2, 1807).

Pattison, James J. Ensign in Capt. Griffis' co. 31st rgt. (D. 23, 1813).

Pattison, Thomas J. Major in 48th rgt.

Patton, Columbus. Private in Capt. Quantrill's co. 24th rgt.

Patton, James. Private in Capt. Garrett's co. 49th rgt.

Patton, John. Corporal in Capt. Patton's co. 30th rgt.

Patton, Robert. Private in Capt. Chalmers' co. 51st rgt.

Patton, Thomas. Captain in 30th rgt. (Jy. 8, 1811).

Pattridge, James. Private in Capt. McKane's co. 27th rgt.

Paul, Thomas. Private in Capt. McConkey's co. 27th rgt.

Pawley, John. Private in Capt. A. E. Warner's co. 39th rgt.

Paxton, Joseph. Private in Capt. McLaughlin's co. 50th rgt.

Paxton, William. Private in Capt. McLaughlin's co. 50th rgt.

Payne, Joseph. Private in Capt. Walker's co. 45th rgt.

Payne, Thomas. Private in Capt. Cawood's co. 45th rgt.

Peach, Isaac. Private in Capt. Crawfurd's co. 17th rgt.

Peach, Joseph. Private in Capt. Jos. Jones' co. 34th rgt.

Peach, Philip. Private in Capt. Haubert's co. 51st rgt.

Peacock, Jacob. Private in Capt. Snowden's co. 36th rgt.

Peacock, William. Private in Capt. Kierstead's co. 6th rgt.

Peake, John. Private in Capt. Williams' co. 12th rgt.

Peal, John. Musician in Capt. Sheppard's co. 6th rgt.

Pearce, Gideon. Adjutant in 33d rgt. (S. 20, 1813).

Pearce, Israel. Private in Capt. Wells' Artillery co. 22d rgt.

Pearce, James. Major in 10th Cavalry Dist. (Je. 16, 1812).

Pearce, John. Private in Capt. Wickes' co. 21st rgt.

Pearce, Joshua. Ensign in Capt. Hutchins' co. 41st rgt. (Ap. 20, 1808).

Pearce, Nathaniel. Sergeant-Major in 1st rgt. Artillery; 2d Lieutenant in Capt. Piper's co. United Maryland Artillery (O. 15, 1814).

Pearce, William. Private in Capt. Pinney's co. 27th rgt.

Pearson, Edward. Sergeant in Capt. Taylor's co. 48th rgt

Pearson, Elias. Private in Capt. Steuart's co. Washington Blues.

Pearson, Joseph. Corporal in Capt. Shrim's co. Balto. Light Infantry.

Pearson, Levin. Corporal in Capt. Taylor's co. 48th rgt.

Pearson, Thomas. Private in Capt. Edes' co. 27th rgt.

Pechin, William [1773-1849]. 2d Major in 6th rgt.

Peck, Jacob. Private in Capt. Smith's co. 51st rgt.

Pecock, John. Private in Capt. Dillon's co. 27th rgt.

Peddicord, Humphrey. Private in Capt. Ducker's co. 7th rgt.

Peddicord, Jasper. Private in Capt. Snowden's co. 36th rgt.

Peduse, Peter. Cornet in Fells Point Light Dragoons (Jy. 28, 1812) ; 2d Lieutenant (Ag. 12, 1813).

Peel, George. Private in Capt. Kierstead's co. 6th rgt.

Pell, Thomas. Private in Capt. Deems' co. 51st rgt.

Pencast, Asa. Private in Capt. Dillon's co. 27th rgt.

Pence, Joseph. Private in Capt. Levering's co. Independent Blues.

Pendigrast, Patrick. Private in Capt. Brown's co. Eagle Artillerists.

Pendleton, Daniel. Private in Capt. Berry's co. Washington Artillery.

Penfield, Samuel. Private in Capt. McConckin's co. 38th rgt.

Penman, John. Private in Capt. Montgomery's co. Balto. Union Artillery.

Penn, George. Private in Capt. Roney's co. 39th rgt.

Penn, John. Private in Capt. Smith's co. 51st rgt.

Penn, John. Private in Capt. Posey's co. 1st rgt.

Penn, William. Private in Capt. Causin's co. 4th Cavalry Dist.

Pennington, —. Captain in 49th rgt. Resigned 1813.

Pennington, Benjamin. Private in Capt. Oldham's co. 49th rgt.

Pennington, Charles [-1817]. 1st Lieutenant in Balto. Independent Artillery (Ap. 30, 1812) ; Captain (1814).

Pennington, Elijah. Lieutenant in Capt. Johnson's co. 22d rgt. (My. 27, 1811).

Pennington, George. Private in Sample's co. 49th rgt.

Pennington, Henry. Private in Capt. Allen's co. 49th rgt.

Pennington, John. Sergeant in Capt. Mann's co. 33d rgt.

Pennington, Josias [1797-1874]. Private in Capt. Warfield's co. Balto. United Volunteers.

Pennington, Robert B. Sergeant in Capt. Vansant's co. 33d rgt.

Pennington, Samuel P. Private in Capt. A. C. Smith's co. 49th rgt.

Pennington, Thomas. Private in Capt. Morgan's co. 49th rgt.

Pennington, William. Private in Capt. Schwarzauer's co. 27th rgt.

Penny, Thomas. Private in Capt. Ducker's co. 7th rgt.

Pentz, Daniel [1794-1871]. Private in Capt. Piper's co. United Maryland Artillery.

Pentz, Henry. 2d Lieutenant in Balto. Union Artillery (S. 21, 1813) vice John Brown ; 1st Lieutenant United Maryland Artillery.

Pepple, Peter. Private in Capt. Smith's co. 51st rgt.

Perce, Elem. Private in Capt. Ducker's co. 7th rgt. ; wounded at Bladensburg.

Peregoy, Benjamin. Sergeant in Capt. Taylor's co. 46th rgt.
Peregoy, Caleb. Private in Capt. Piper's co. United Maryland Artillery.
Peregoy, William. Gunner in Capt. Addison's co. Sea Fencibles.
Perguson, Abraham. Private in Capt. Well's Artillery co. 22d rgt.
Perigo, Daniel. Corporal in Capt. Sheppards' co. 6th rgt.
Perigo, Jehu. Private in Capt. Rogers' co. 51st rgt.
Perigo, Joel. Private in Capt. Snowden's co. 36th rgt.
Perkins, Ebenezer. Corporal in Capt. Moale's co. Columbian Artillery.
Perkins, John [1781-1840]. Private in Capt. Warfield's co. Balto. United Volunteers.
Perkins, John D. Surgeon's mate in 35th rgt. (Jy. 24, 1813).
Perkins, William. Private in Capt. Crawfurd's co. 17th rgt.
Permer, James. Ensign in Capt. Colson's co. Extra Battalion Caroline Co. (Ag. 11, 1813).
Perrie, Charles S. Private in Capt. Haden's co. 17th rgt.
Perrigo, Charles. Ensign in Capt. Timanus' co. 36th rgt. (Jy. 13, 1814) vice Wilson.
Perrigo, James. Corporal in Capt. Ducker's co. 7th rgt.
Perrigo, Joseph. Captain in 46th rgt. (Jy. 8, 1814) vice Green.
Perrigo, Joseph. Ensign in Capt. Wm. Jones' co. 7th rgt. (Ag. 1, 1814).
Perrigoy, James. Private in Capt. Deems' co. 51st rgt.
Perrin, Joseph. Private in Capt. McLaughlin's co. 50th rgt.

Perrine, D. M. Private in Capt. Magruder's co. American Artillerists.
Perrine, Peter. Private in Capt. Miller's co. 39th rgt.
Perrine, William. Lieutenant in Capt. Fowler's co. 46th rgt. (Jy. 29, 1811).
Perry, Burdet B. Private in Capt. Dunnington's co. 43d rgt.
Perry, Charles G. Private in Capt. Stiles' co. Marine Artillery.
Perry, Herman. Captain of the privateer *Orb*, Nov., 1814.
Perry, James. Private in Capt. Green's co. 46th rgt.
Perry, Jeremiah. Private in Capt. McKane's co. 27th rgt.
Perry, Richard. Private in Capt. Berry's co. Washington Artillery.
Perry, Seneca. Private in Capt. Snowden's co. 36th rgt.
Perry, Thomas. Private in Capt. Burgess' co. 43d rgt.
Perry, Tristram. Lieutenant in Capt. Merrick's co. 4th rgt. (S. 7, 1810).
Peterkin, William. Private in Capt. Stiles' co. Marine Artillery.
Peterman, John. Private in Capt. Blair's co. 50th rgt.
Peters, Adam. Private in Capt. Peters' co. 51st rgt.
Peters, Christian G. Private in Capt. Sheppard's co. 6th rgt.
Peters, Daniel. Private in Capt. Shrim's co. Balto. Light Infantry.
Peters, George. Private in Capt. Blair's co. 50th rgt.
Peters, Henry C. Private in Capt. Howard's co. Mechanical Volunteers.
Peters, James. Private in Capt. McKane's co. 27th rgt.
Peters, John. Seaman of the privateer *Comet*.

Peters, Michael. Captain in 51st rgt. Resigned in Nov., 1814.
Peters, Richard. Private in Capt. Beall's co. 34th rgt.
Peters, William. Private in Capt. Addison's co. Sea Fencibles.
Peters, William. Private in Capt. Roney's co. 39th rgt.
Peterson, John. Private in Capt. Stiles' co. Marine Artillery.
Peterson, John, Jr. Private in Capt. Stiles' co. Marine Artillery.
Petit, Augustus. Private in Capt. Magruder's co. American Artillerists.
Pettebone, Charles. Private in Capt. Boone's co. 22d rgt.
Pettecord, John. Private in Capt. Steever's co. 27th rgt.
Pettygrew, James. Private in Capt. Aisquith's co. Sharp Shooters.
Pewder, George. Private in Capt. Levering's co. Independent Blues.
Phelps, Gardner. Private in Capt. Faster's co. 51st rgt.
Phelps, Greenbury. Private in Capt. Edes' co. 27th rgt.
Phelps, James. Private in Capt. Linthicum's co. 22d rgt.
Phelps, John. Private in Capt. Snowden's co. 36th rgt.
Phelps, Joshua. Private in Capt. Snowden's co. 36th rgt.
Phelps, Richard. Lieutenant in Capt. Hopkins' co. 22d rgt. (My. 18, 1814).
Philips, Charles. Private in Capt. Stewart's co. 51st rgt.
Philips, Edward. Private in Capt. Dillon's co. 27th rgt.
Philips, George. Private in Capt. Lawrence's co. 6th rgt.
Philips, Isaac, Jr. Private in Capt. Warfield's co. Balto. United Volunteers.

Philips, James. Private in Capt. Stiles' co. Marine Artillery.
Philips, John. 2d Lieutenant in Capt. Hall's co. 2d rgt. 1st Cavalry Dist. (D. 22, 1812).
Philips, John. Private in Capt. Pinkney's Artillery co. 22d rgt.
Philips, Nathaniel. Private in Capt. Sheppard's co. 6th rgt.
Phillip, Richard. Private in Capt. Massey's co. 38th rgt.
Phillips, Dennard. Private in Capt. Travers' co. 48th rgt.
Phillips, Elie. Captain in 2d rgt. 1st Cavalry Dist. (F. 13, 1813).
Phillips, Harmon. Private in Capt. Thomas's co. 49th rgt.
Phillips, Holton. Private in Capt. Travers' co. 48th rgt.
Phillips, John. Private in Capt. Dobbin's co. 39th rgt.
Phillips, John. Corporal in Capt. Travers' co. 48th rgt.
Phillips, Levy. Captain in 3d rgt. (O. 12, 1807).
Phillips, Osten. Private in Capt. Travers' co. 48th rgt.
Phillips, Richard. Private in Capt. Travers' co. 48th rgt.
Phillips, Solomon. Private in Capt. Travers' co. 48th rgt.
Phillips, Vachel. 2d Sergeant in Capt. Hancock's co. 22d rgt.
Phillips, William. Private in Capt. Pike's co. Balto. Volunteer Artillery.
Philpot, Alexander. Private in Capt. Crawfurd's co. 17th rgt.
Philpott, Burton. Captain in 2d rgt. 1st Cavalry Dist. (Ja. 1, 1813).
Phipps, Benjamin. Private in Capt. Pumphrey's co. 22d rgt.
Phoenix, Henry. Private in Capt. McConckin's co. 38th rgt.

Phoenix, Thomas. Private in Capt. Levering's co. Independent Blues.

Piat, John. Private in Capt. Levering's co. Independent Blues.

Pickering, John. Private in Capt. Travers' co. 48th rgt.

Pickett, John. Sergeant in Capt. Wilson's co. 6th rgt.

Pickrell, Hendley. Private in Capt. Thompson's co. 1st rgt.

Pidgeon, John. Private in Capt. Adreon's co. Union Volunteers. Wounded at North Point.

Pierce, Edward A. Paymaster in 45th rgt.

Pierce, Elias. Private in Capt. Smith's co. 51st rgt.

Pierce, George. Private in Capt. Crawfurd's co. 17th rgt.

Pierce, Joseph. Private in Capt. Kierstead's co. 6th rgt.

Pierce, Levi, Jr. Private in Capt. Moale's co. Columbian Artillery.

Pierce, Samuel. Private in Capt. Smith's co. 51st rgt.

Pierce, William. Private in Capt. Warfield's co. Balto. United Volunteers.

Pike, Abraham. 2d Lieutenant in 1st Balto. Volunteer Artillery (Ap. 30, 1813) ; Captain (Mr. 25, 1814) vice Buffum.

Pike, Henry. Private in Capt. Warfield's co. Balto. United Volunteers.

Pilch, James. Private in Capt. Hanna's co. Fells Point Light Dragoons.

Pilchard, William. Private in Capt. Dyer's co. Fells Point Riflemen.

Pilcher, Warner. Private in Capt. Faster's co. 51st rgt.

Pilgrim, Nathaniel. Private in Capt. Stewart's co. 51st rgt.

Pilkington, Thomas. Private in Capt. Sheppard's co. 6th rgt.

Pilkinton, Uriah. Private in Capt. Millard's co. 12th rgt.

Pimberden, William. Private in Capt. Ducker's co. 7th rgt.; Quarter-Master, Sept. 10, 1814.

Pindall, Richard. Sergeant in Capt. Pinkney's Artillery co. 22d rgt.

Pindel, John. Private in Capt. Taylor's co. 46th rgt.

Pindell, John. Private in Capt. Shrim's co. Balto. Light Infantry.

Pindell, John. Private in Capt. Peters' co. 51st rgt.

Pindell, Philip. Private in Capt. Hall's co. 3d Cavalry rgt.

Pindell, Richard. Ensign in Capt. Galt's co. 6th rgt. (Jy. 13, 1814) vice Burke.

Pines, Vincent. Private in Capt. Galloway's co. 46th rgt.

Pinkerton, William. Captain in 7th rgt. Resigned Jy., 1814.

Pinkney, Jonathan. Captain in Artillery co. 8th Brigade A. A. co. (My. 9, 1812).

Pinkney, Ninian [-1825]. Major in 5th U. S. Infantry (Ja. 20, 1813) ; Lieutenant-Colonel in 22d Infantry (Ap. 15, 1814).

Pinkney, W. E. Surgeon to 22d rgt., 1814.

Pinkney, William [1764-1822]. Major in 1st Rifle Battalion 3d Brigade (Jy. 8, 1813) ; Attorney-General U. S., 1812.

Pinkney, William, Jr. [1789-1853]. Adjutant in 1st Rifle Battalion (Jy. 24, 1813). Wounded at Bladensburg.

Pinney, Peter. Captain in 27th rgt.

Piper, James. Captain in United Maryland Artillery (My. 19, 1813) vice Walsh.

Piper, Philip. Private in Capt. Smith's co. 51st rgt.

Pirkeybile, Andrew. Ensign in Capt. Kislinger's co. 15th rgt. (Ag. 22, 1812).

Pitch, Samuel. Private in Capt. Wilson's co. 6th rgt.

Pitcher, Thomas. Private in Capt. Linthicum's co. 22d rgt.

Pitcock, Benjamin. Ensign in Capt. Caldwell's co. 42d rgt. (Ap. 27, 1813).

Pitt, John. 2d Lieutenant in Capt. Ennalls' co. 10th Cavalry Dist. (Jy. 29, 1812); 1st Lieutenant (Mr. 23, 1814).

Pitt, Robert. Cornet in Capt. Hooper's co. 10th Cavalry Dist. (Mr. 23, 1814) vice Richardson.

Plains, George. Private in Capt. Faster's co. 51st rgt.

Plate, John. Private in Capt. Snowden's co. 36th rgt.

Plintenberger, Charles. Private in Capt. Dillon's co. 46th rgt.

Plowden, William H. Cornet in Capt. G. N. Causin's co. 4th Cavalry Dist. (Je. 26, 1812).

Plowman, Joshua. Private in Capt. Ducker's co. 7th rgt.; Assistant Quarter-Master, Sept. 10, 1814.

Plumm, Benjamin. Sergeant in Capt. Duvall's co. 34th rgt.

Plumm, Charles H. Sergeant in Capt. Duvall's co. 34th rgt.

Plummer, Benjamin. Sergeant in Capt. Hall's co. 34th rgt.

Plummer, Benjamin. Sergeant in Capt. Jackson's co. 34th rgt.

Plummer, Benjamin C. Private in Capt. Sheppard's co. 6th rgt.

Plummer, James. Private in Capt. Ringgold's co. 6th rgt.

Plummer, Lewis. Private in Capt. Linthicum's co. 22d rgt.

Plummer, Philip. Sergeant in Capt. Oldham's co. 49th rgt.

Plummer, Samuel. Private in Capt. Linthicum's co. 22d rgt.

Plummer, Thomas. Private in Capt. Blair's co. 50th rgt.

Plummer, William of John. Ensign in 3d rgt. (F. 19, 1813).

Plunkett, Peter. Private in Capt. Barnes' co. 32d rgt.

Pochon, Charles. Private in Capt. Warfield's co. Balto. United Volunteers.

Pocock, Joshua. Private in Capt. Snowden's co. 36th rgt.

Poe, David. Private in Capt. Lawson's co. Balto. Patriots.

Poffenbarger, Andrew. Private in Capt. Quantrill's co. 24th rgt.

Pogen, John. Private in Capt. Levering's co. Independent Blues.

Pogue, James, Jr. Private in Capt. Warfield's co. Balto. United Volunteers.

Pogue, John G. Private in Capt. Warfield's co. Balto. United Volunteers. Captured at North Point.

Poland, Daniel. Corporal in Capt. McLaughlin's co. 50th rgt.

Poland, John. Private in Capt. Blair's co. 50th rgt.

Pole, John. Ensign in Capt. Trundle's co. 3d rgt. (Ag. 30, 1808).

Polk, Cordo. Private in Capt. Dyers' co. Fells Point Riflemen.

Polk, David Peale. Ensign in 12th U. S. Infantry (Je. 22, 1812); 1st Lieutenant (Ag. 24, 1814).

Polk, Josiah F. Private in Capt. Heath's co. 23d rgt.

Polk, Whittington. Captain in 23d rgt. (My. 5, 1815).

Polkinghorn, Richard. Private in Capt. Adreon's co. Union Volunteers.

Pollard, Seth. Private in Capt. Montgomery's co. Balto. Union Artillery.

Pollett, J. B. Private in Capt. Nicholson's co. Balto. Fencibles.

Pollitt, James S. Sergeant in Capt. Heath's co. 23d rgt.

Pollitt, William F. Private in Capt. Steuart's co. Washington Blues.

Pollock, Benjamin F. Sergeant in Capt. Dillon's co. 27th rgt.

Polton, Thomas. Corporal in Capt. Owings' co. 32d rgt.

Pomeroy, Ralph. Private in Capt. Faster's co. 51st rgt.

Pontier, Joseph. Private in Capt. Sadtler's co. Balto. Yägers.

Pool, James. Private in Capt. Roney's co. 39th rgt.

Poole, Frederick. Lieutenant in Capt. Lawrence's co. 20th rgt. (Ag. 9, 1808).

Poole, Thomas. Cornet in Capt. Poole's co. 2d rgt. 1st Cavalry Dist. (Ap. 27, 1814).

Poole, William. 1st Lieutenant in Capt. Hollingsworth's co. 2d rgt. 1st Cavalry Dist. (Je. 17, 1812); Captain (Ap. 27, 1814).

Poor, John F. Corporal in Capt. Nicholson's co. Balto. Fencibles.

Poor, John H. Private in Capt. Warfield's co. Balto. United Volunteers.

Pope, Elijah. Private in Capt. Schwarzauer's co. 27th rgt.

Pope, George. Private in Capt. Barnes' co. 32d rgt.

Pope, John. Private in Capt. Posey's co. 1st rgt.

Popp, Charles F. Private in Capt. Shrim's co. Balto. Light Infantry.

Poque, Lowdie J. Private in Capt. Howard's co. Mechanical Volunteers.

Porter, Andrew R. Captain in 30th rgt. (S. 11, 1807).

Porter, Benjamin. Private in Capt. Roney's co. 39th rgt.

Porter, Charles. Sergeant in Capt. Barnes' co. 32d rgt.

Porter, Daniel. Private in Capt. Ducker's co. 7th rgt.

Porter, Henry. Ensign in Capt. Porter's co. 50th rgt. (S. 2, 1811).

Porter, Henry. Private in Capt. McLaughlin's co. 50th rgt.

Porter, James L. Major in 30th rgt.

Porter, Jeptha. Private in Capt. Dobbin's co. 39th rgt.

Porter, John. Sergeant in Capt. McLaughlin's co. 50th rgt.

Porter, Joseph. Private in Capt. Blair's co. 50th rgt.

Porter, Michael. Private in Capt. Sterett's Independent co.

Porter, Samuel. Major in 50th rgt. (D. 26, 1810).

Porter, Thomas. Captain in 50th rgt. (S. 2, 1811).

Porter, Thomas. Private in Capt. Galt's co. 6th rgt.

Porter, William. Private in Capt. A. E. Warner's co. 39th rgt.

Porter, William. Private in Capt. Sterett's Independent co.

Porter, Wrixam L. Private in Capt. Heath's co. 23d rgt.

Posey, Abednego. Private in Capt. Dent's co. 43d rgt.

Posey, Adrian. Private in Capt. Posey's co. 1st rgt.

Posey, Francis. Private in Capt. Dent's co. 43. rgt.

Posey, Gustavus. Private in Capt. Burgess' co. 43d rgt.

Posey, Hanson H. Private in Capt. Burgess' co. 43d rgt.

Posey, Henley. Private in Capt. Dunnington's co. 43d rgt.

Posey, Jeremiah. Private in Capt. Burgess' co. 43d rgt.

Posey, John. Private in Capt. Dunnington's co. 43d rgt.

Posey, Joseph H. Private in Capt. Brown's co. 43d rgt.

Posey, Joseph H. H. Private in Capt. Brown's co. 43d rgt.

Posey, Lawrence. Capt. in 1st rgt. (Jy. 24, 1813).

Posey, Nathaniel. Ensign in Capt. Shryock's co. 24th rgt. (Jy. 12, 1814) vice Crawford.

Posey, Robert. Private in Capt. Dunnington's co. 43d rgt.

Posey, Roger. Private in Capt. Dunnington's co. 43d rgt.

Posey, Thomas. Private in Capt. Dunnington's co. 43d rgt.

Posey, William. Sergeant in Capt. Dunnington's co. 43d rgt.

Post, Thomas. 1st Lieutenant in 12th U. S. Infantry (Ap. 25, 1812) ; Capt. (Mr. 29, 1813).

Potee, Francis. Private in Capt. Roney's co. 39th rgt.

Potee, Peter. Private in Capt. Miller's co. 39th rgt.

Poteet, Jesse. Private in Capt. Peters' co. 51st rgt.

Potter, Benjamin. Private in Capt. John Miller's co. 2d D. I.; b. Montgomery Co., Md.; age 21; farmer; subs. for John Potter.

Potter, David. Private in Capt. Blair's co. 50th rgt.

Potter, David. Private in Capt. Galt's co. 6th rgt.

Potter, John. Private in Capt. Blair's co. 50th rgt.

Potter, Martin. Private in Capt. Dillon's co. 27th rgt.

Potter, Martin. Private in Capt. Fowler's co. 46th rgt.

Potter, Thomas. Private in Capt. John Miller's co. 2d D. I.; b. Shenandoah Co., Va.; age 20; farmer.

Potter, William. Lieutenant-Colonel in 19th rgt. (1813).

Potts, John L. Quarter-master Sergeant in 5th rgt.

Potts, Philip. Private in Capt. Steiner's Frederick Artillery.

Pouge, Loudy I. Private in Capt. McConkey's co. 27th rgt.

Poulnat, John. Private in Capt. McKane's co. 27th rgt.

Poulston, John. Private in Capt. Schwarzauer's co. 27th rgt.

Poulton, Charles. Private in Capt. Pumphrey's co. 22d rgt.

Poulton, Nicholas. Private in Capt. Pumphrey's co. 22d rgt.

Powell, Howell. Corporal in Capt. Faster's co. 51st rgt.

Powell, James. Ensign in Capt. Parson's co. 37th rgt.; Adjutant (Ja. 21, 1814).

Powell, James. Private in Capt. Pinney's co. 27th rgt.

Powell, P. B. Private in Capt. Dillon's co. 27th rgt.

Powell, William. Private in Capt. Galt's co. 6th rgt.

Powell, William. Sergeant in Capt. Pinney's co. 27th rgt.

Powell, Zadock. Ensign in Capt. Johnson's co. Extra Battalion Worcester co. (O. 21, 1812).

Powers, James. Private in Capt. Snowden's co. 36th rgt.

Powers, John. Lieutenant of the privateer *Bordeaux Packet*, Nov., 1813; Prize-master of the *Chasseur*, 1814-15.

Powers, Robert. Private in Capt. Dunnington's co. 43d rgt.

Powers, Thomas. Private in Capt. John Miller's co. 2d D. I.; b. New York; age 28; miller; subs. for John Miller.

Powers, William. Private in Capt. Brohawn's co. 48th rgt.

Pratt, Henry. Private in Capt. Mc-Conckin's co. 38th rgt.

Pratt, John H. Private in Capt. Berry's co. Washington Artillery.

Pratt, Walter. Captain of the privateer *Liberty*, Sept., 1812; Lieutenant of the *Oriental*, Nov., 1813.

Pratt, William, Jr. Private in Capt. Massey's co. 38th rgt.

Presbury, George. Paymaster in 42d rgt.

Presstman, Stephen Wilson. Ensign in 5th U. S. Infantry (Ap. 14, 1812); 1st Lieutenant (My. 1st 1814).

Prettyman, David G. Private in Capt. Aisquith's co. Sharp Shooters.

Prettyman, Thomas G. Private in Capt. Aisquith's co. Sharp Shooters.

Pretzel, Henry. Lieutenant in Capt. Wilheads' co. 29th rgt.

Price, Andrew. Private in Capt. Nicholson's co. Balto. Fencibles.

Price, Archibald. Private in Capt. Williams' co. 12th rgt.

Price, Edward. Ensign in Capt. Spencer's co. 26th rgt. (Je. 6, 1809).

Price, Frederick. Private in Capt. Morgan's co. 49th rgt.

Price, Hezekiah. Quarter-master in 51st rgt. (Ap. 28, 1813).

Price, Hyland. Private in Capt. A. C. Smith's co. 49th rgt.

Price, Jacob. Private in Capt. Jas. Massey's co. 38th rgt.

Price, John C. Sergeant in Capt. Allen's co. 49th rgt.

Price, John V. Ensign in Capt. Allen's co. 49th rgt. (Mr. 25, 1814).

Price, Joseph. Private in Capt. Tilghman's co. 33d rgt.

Price, Lowther. Private in Capt. Heath's co. 23d rgt.

Price, Nehemiah. Private in Capt. Myers' co. Franklin Artillery.

Price, Nicholas. Special Judge Advocate, 3d Division M. M.

Price, Nicodemus. Private in Capt. Levering's co. Independent Blues.

Price, Richard. Private in Capt. Dent's co. 43d rgt.

Price, Robert. Ensign in Capt. Stewart's co. 42d rgt. (Ag. 13, 1811).

Price, Samuel A. Captain in 10th rgt.

Price, Samuel D. Lieutenant in Capt. McPherson's co. 10th rgt. (S. 20, 1813).

Price, Thomas. Lieutenant in Capt. Milton's co. 45th rgt. (Jy. 7, 1814) vice Milton.

Price, Thomas. Sergeant in Capt. Lawrence's co. 6th rgt.

Price, Thomas. Private in Capt. Thomas's co. 49th rgt.

Price, Thomas, Jr. Ensign in Capt. Dent's co. 43d rgt.

Price, Walter. Private in Capt. Peters' co. 51st rgt.

Price, Walter. Private in Capt. Sterett's co 1st Balto. Hussars.

Prichard, Cyrus. Private in Capt. McConkey's co. 27th rgt.

Priest, Richard. Ensign in Capt. Fowler's co. 33d rgt. (O. 13, 1814.)

Priestly, Edward. Private in Capt. Warfield's co. Balto. United Volunteers.

APPENDIX

410

Prill, Henry. Private in Capt. Edes' co. 27th rgt.

Primm, John F. Lieutenant in Capt. Coe's co. 17th rgt. (Jy. 11, 1814).

Prince, Caspar. Private in Capt. Sterett's co. 1st Balto. Hussars.

Pringle, Mark W. Private in Capt. Warfield's co. Balto. United Volunteers.

Prior, John. Private in Capt. Stiles' co. Marine Artillery.

Pritchett, Elijah. Sergeant in Capt. Aisquith's co. Sharp Shooters.

Pritchett, Elijah. Private in Capt. McNamara's co. 48th rgt.

Proctor, Hugh. Private in Capt. Galloway's co. 46th rgt.

Proebsting, Theodore C. 2d Lieutenant in Capt. Sadtler's co. Balto. Yägers. (Ap. 22, 1814).

Prosper, James. Private in Capt. Maynard's co. 22d rgt.; Sergeant in Capt. Chase's co., 1814.

Prosser, Samuel. Private in Capt. Edes' co. 27th rgt.

Prosser, Uriah. Private in Capt. Edes' co. 27th rgt.

Protman, Lodowick. Ensign in Capt. Ridenour's co. 24th rgt. Resigned Ag. 1, 1814.

Protzman, Henry. Sergeant in Capt. Shryock's co. 24th rgt.

Proud, William T. Private in Capt. Warfield's co. Balto. United Volunteers.

Prout, Daniel. Ensign in Capt. Chew's co. 31st rgt. (Jy. 15, 1814).

Pugh, David. Private in Capt. McConkey's co. 27th rgt.

Pumphrey, Aquilla. Private in Capt. Linthicum's co. 22d rgt.

Pumphrey, Charles. Captain in 22d rgt. (My. 27, 1811).

Pumphrey, Cockey. Private in Capt. Pumphrey's co. 22d rgt.

Pumphrey, Ebenezer. Sergeant in Capt. A. E. Warner's co. 39th rgt.

Pumphrey, Thomas. Corporal in Capt. Pumphrey's co. 22d rgt. [Aug., 1813].

Pumphrey, William. Private in Capt. Pumphrey's co. 22d rgt.

Punce, Gasper. Cornet in Fells Point Light Dragoons (Ag. 12, 1813).

Purden, Joseph. Corporal in Capt. Dillon's co. 27th rgt.

Purdom, John. Ensign in 3d rgt. (Je. 5, 1812).

Purdy, James. Private in Capt. Snowden's co. 36th rgt.

Purdy, John. Private in Capt. Sands' co. 22d rgt.

Purdy, Richard. Private in Capt. Dunnington's co. 43d rgt.

Purnell, George W. Quarter-master in Extra Battalion Worcester Co.

Purnell, Lemuel. Captain in 9th rgt. (O. 31, 1812).

Purnell, Richard. Private in Capt. Stewart's co. 51st rgt.

Purse, James. Private in Capt. Warfield's co. Balto. United Volunteers.

Purviance, James. Private in Capt. Sterett's Independent co.

Purviance, Robert. Private in Capt. Warfield's co. Balto. United Volunteers.

Pusey, Parker. Private in Capt. Heath's co. 23d rgt.

Pusey, Planner. Private in Capt. Heath's co. 23d rgt.

Putsar, Martin. Private in Capt. Adreon's co. Union Volunteers.

Putton, David. Sergeant and 3d Lieutenant in Capt. Nicholson's Co. Balto. Fencibles.

Pye, Edward. 1st Lieutenant in Capt. Stonestreet's co. 4th Cavalry Dist. (Je. 12, 1812).

Pyfer, John. Corporal in Capt. McKane's co. 27th rgt.

Pyfer, Philip. Private in Capt. Steiner's Frederick Artillery.

Q

Quantrill, Thomas. Captain in 24th rgt. (Je. 16, 1812). Wounded at North Point.

Quarles, John. Captain in Extra Battalion Harford Co. Resigned Jy., 1814.

Queen, Charles. 2d Lieutenant in 36th U. S. Infantry (Ap. 30, 1813) ; 1st Lieutenant (S. 30, 1814).

Quest, Charles. Private in Capt. Kennedy's co. 27th rgt.

Quin, Edward. Private in Capt. Brown's co. 6th rgt.

Quinton, Littleton. Quarter-master in 37th rgt. (S. 21, 1813) vice Williams.

Quinton, William. Paymaster in 37th rgt. (Je. 5, 1812).

Quistic, John. Private in Capt. Sheppard's co. 6th rgt.

Quynn, John. Private in Capt. Sands' co. 22d rgt.

R

Raborg, Christopher [1779-1862]. Sergeant in Capt. Sterett's Independent co.

Raborg, Samuel. Private in Capt. Sterett's co. 1st Balto. Hussars.

Radcliff, Charles. Prize-master of the privateer *High Flyer*.

Radish, Thomas. Private in Capt. Lawrence's co. 6th rgt,

Ragan, John [1782-1816]. Lieutenant-Colonel of 24th rgt. In command of a regiment at Bladensburg, where he was injured and captured; in command of a company at battle of New Orleans.

Rainer, William. Private in Capt. Linthicum's co. 22d rgt.

Rains, Lewis. Private in Capt. Lawrence's co. 6th rgt.

Raisin, Cyrus. Private in Capt. Usselton's co. Artillery 6th Brigade.

Raisin, Philip, Jr. Private in Capt. Usselton's co. Artillery 6th Brigade.

Ralston, Joseph. Private in Capt. Sample's co. 49th rgt.

Ramage, John. Private in Capt. Mackey's co. 49th rgt.

Ramply, James. Captain in 40th rgt. (Je. 16, 1812).

Ramsay, James. Private in Capt. Stiles' co. Marine Artillery.

Ramsay, Joseph. Private in Capt. Dyer's co. Fells Point Riflemen.

Ramsay, William. Private in Capt. Stewart's co. 51st rgt.

Ramsburg, Joseph. Private in Capt. Shaver's co.

Ramsey, John. Private in Capt. Conway's co. 6th rgt.

Ramsey, John. Private in Capt. Jos. Jones' co. 34th rgt.

Ramsey, Samuel. Lieutenant in Capt. Patton's co. 30th rgt. (Jy. 8, 1811).

Ramsey, Thomas. Private in Capt. Conway's co. 6th rgt.

Randall, Aquila A. Private in Capt. Howard's co. Mechanical Volunteers. Killed at North Point.

Randall, Beale [1782-1853]. Major in 2d rgt. (Jy. 8, 1813) ; Brigade Major 11th Brigade; Major in 15th rgt.; on service July 21 to Sept. 2, 1814; Lieutenant-Colonel (N. 12, 1814).

Randall, Daniel [-1851]. Assistant District Paymaster U. S. (Je. 8, 1814).
Randall, Daniel. Private in Capt. Sands' co. 22d rgt.
Randall, Elisha. Private in Capt. Howard's co. Mechanical Volunteers.
Randall, Henry. Private in Ensign Brewer's detachment in 36th rgt.
Randall, Henry K. Private in Capt. Slicer's co. 22d rgt.
Randall, Jesse. Private in Capt. Rogers' co. 51st rgt.
Randall, John. Private in Capt. Linthicum's co. 22d rgt.
Randall, John T. Captain in 36th rgt. Rifle co. (N. 7, 1812).
Randall, Nathaniel D. Sergeant in Capt. Owings' co. 32d rgt.
Randall, Richard. Private in Capt. Slicer's co. 22d rgt.; Private in Ensign Brewer's detachment in 36th rgt. at Bladensburg.
Randall, Thomas. 2d Lieutenant in 14th U. S. Infantry (Mr. 12, 1812); Captain (D. 1, 1814).
Randall, William. Private in Capt. Chalmers' co. 51st rgt.
Randall, William D. Private in Capt. Snowden's co. 36th rgt.
Randle, Christopher. Private in Capt. Dobbin's co. 39th rgt.
Randle, Jacob. Private in Capt. Smith's co. 51st rgt.
Randolph, Charles C. Captain in 36th U. S. Infantry (Ap. 30, 1813).
Randolph, Thompson. Private in Capt. Myers' co. 39th rgt.
Randolph, Tobias. Quarter-master in 49th rgt.
Rapley, Abraham. Private in Capt. Kennedy's co. 27th rgt.
Rasin, Samuel. Captain in 36th U. S. Infantry (Ap. 30, 1813).

Ratcliff, Courtney. Private in Capt. Posey's co. 1st rgt.
Ratcliff, Robert. Private in Capt. Dunnington's co. 43d rgt. Also served in Capt. Brown's co. 43d rgt.
Ratcliff, Silas. Sergeant in Capt. Dunnington's co. 43d rgt.
Ratcliffe, Joseph. Lieutenant in Capt. Dent's co. 43d rgt.
Ratcliffe, Luther. Private in Capt. Warfield's co. Balto. United Volunteers.
Ratcliffe, Stephen. Private in Capt. Brown's co. 43d rgt.
Ratcliffe, William P. Private in Capt. Dent's co. 43d rgt.
Ratier, Thomas. Private in Capt. Stiles' co. Marine Artillery.
Ratiken, John. Private in Capt. Faster's co. 51st rgt.
Ratliff, Gilbert. Private in Capt. McKane's co. 27th rgt.
Rau, John C. Corporal in Capt. Sadtler's co. Balto. Yägers.
Raven, Thomas. Cornet in Capt. Hanna's co. Fells Point Light Dragoons.
Ravenscraft, James. Private in Capt. Blair's co. 50th rgt.
Ravon, Isaac. Captain in 46th rgt. (Ag. 29, 1812).
Rawleigh, Levin. Captain in Extra Battalion Dorchester Co.
Rawleigh, Stephen. 2d Lieutenant in Capt. Manning's co. 10th Cavalry Dist. (D. 22, 1814).
Rawleigh, Walter. 1st Lieutenant in Capt. Manning's co. 10th Cavalry Dist. (D. 22, 1814).
Rawles, Nicholas. Ensign in Capt. Bryer's co. 8th rgt. (S. 20, 1813).
Rawlings, Benjamin. Lieutenant in Capt. Schwarzauer's co. 27th rgt.

Rawlings, Henry T. Private in Capt. Crawfurd's co. 17th rgt.

Rawlings, John T. Private in Capt. Crawfurd's co. 17th rgt.

Rawlings, Richard. Private in Capt. Linthicum's co. 22d rgt.

Ray, Andrew. Private in Capt. Kennedy's co. 27th rgt.

Ray, Benjamin. Private in Capt. Brooke's co. 34th rgt.

Ray, Enos [1793-1881]. Private in Capt. Heater's co. 32d rgt.

Ray, Francis. Private in Capt. Mc-Conkey's co. 27th rgt.

Ray, John. Private in Capt. Snowden's co. 36th rgt.

Ray, Joseph. 1st Lieutenant in Capt. Owings' co. 32d rgt.

Ray, William. Captain in 26th rgt. (Jy. 8, 1813).

Raymond, Daniel. Private in Capt. Pennington's co. Balto. Independent Artillerists.

Raynals, Caleb. Seaman of the privateer Comet.

Rea, William. Private in Capt. Deems' co. 51st rgt.

Read, John. Private in Capt. Mc-Donald's co. 6th rgt.

Read, John. Coropral in Capt. Gerry's co. 30th rgt.

Reading, John. Private in Capt. Steever's co. 27th rgt.

Ready, John. Sergeant in Capt. Nicholson's co. Balto. Fencibles.

Ready, Joseph. Private in Capt. Shrim's co. Balto. Light Infantry.

Ready, Samuel [1789-1871]. Private in Capt. Conway's co. 6th rgt.

Realer, David. Private in Capt. Pumphrey's co. 22d rgt.

Reanny, Isaac. Private in Capt. Steever's co. 27th rgt.

Reardon, Lambert. Lieutenant in Capt. Smith's co. 4th rgt. (N. 6, 1811).

Reardon, Thomas. Lieutenant in Capt. Burke's co. 6th rgt. (Jy. 13, 1814).

Redding, William. Assistant Quarter-master in 33d rgt.

Reddish, Halton. Private in Capt. Brohawn's co. 48th rgt.

Reddon, George. Private in Capt. Ringgold's co. 6th rgt.

Reddy, William. Private in Capt. Deems' co. 51st rgt.

Redeffer, Jacob. Private in Capt. Thos. Warner's co. 39th rgt.

Redgrave, John. Private in Capt. Comegys' co. 21st rgt.

Redgrave, John. Private in Capt. Howard's co. Mechanical Volunteers.

Redgrave, Samuel. Landsman of the privateer Baltimore.

Redgrave, Samuel Hance. Private in Capt. Thomas Patton's co. 49th rgt.

Redgraves, Samuel. Private in Capt. Conway's co. 6th rgt.

Redgreave, Samuel. Private in Capt. Linthicum's co. 22d rgt.

Rediford, Jesse. Private in Capt. Stapleton's co. 39th rgt.

Redman, Benjamin. Private in Capt. Bean's co. 12th rgt.

Redman, Henry [-1823]. 3d Lieutenant in 36th U. S. Infantry (Ap. 30, 1813) ; 2d Lieutenant (My. 1, 1814).

Redman, James. Private in Capt. Addison's co. Sea Fencibles.

Redman, John. Private in Capt. Schwarzauer's co. 27th rgt.

Redman, Joshua. Private in Capt. Addison's co. Sea Fencibles.

Redman, Zachariah. Private in Capt. Williams' co. 12th rgt.

Redue, Joseph. Private in Capt. Hands' co. 21st rgt.

Reece, Jacob. Musician in Capt. Blizzard's co. 15th rgt.

Reece, John. Lieutenant in Capt. A. C. Smith's co. 49th rgt.

Reed, Amos. Major in 8th Cavalry Dist. (F. 28, 1812).

Reed, Benedict. Private in Capt. Fowler's co. 33d rgt.

Reed, Caleb. Private in Capt. Deems' co. 51st rgt.

Reed, Ezekiel. Lieutenant in Capt. Turpin's co. 11th rgt. (O. 3, 1807).

Reed, John. 2d Lieutenant in Capt. Morrison's Artillery co. 6th Brigade. (Jy. 14, 1812); 1st Lieutenant (Ap. 21, 1814).

Reed, John. Quarter-master in 10th Cavalry Dist. (My. 20, 1813).

Reed, John. Private in Capt. McKane's co. 27th rgt.

Reed, John. Boatswain's mate of the privateer *Surprise*.

Reed, Joshua. Private in Capt. Deem's co. 51st rgt.

Reed, Patrick. Private in Capt. McKane's co. 27th rgt.

***Reed, Philip [1760-1829].** Lieutenant-Colonel of 21st rgt.; Brigadier-General 6th Brigade (Ja. 15, 1815). *See* page 125.

Reed, Robert. Private in Capt. Sheppard's co. 6th rgt.

Reed, Samuel. Private in Capt. Deems' co. 51st rgt.

Reed, William. Lieutenant in Capt. McElfish's co. 50th rgt. (F. 15, 1815).

Reed, William. Paymaster in 30th rgt. (N. 3, 1812).

Reeder, —. Major in 43d rgt.

Reeder, Richard. Lieutenant in Capt. Geo. Morgan's co. 45th rgt.

Reeder, Robert D. Private in Capt. Millard's co. 12th rgt.

Reeder, Thomas. Sergeant-Major in 45th rgt.

Reeder, Thomas. Private in Capt. G. N. Causin's co. 4th Cavalry Dist.

Reeder, William. Cornet in Capt. Forrest's co. 4th Cavalry Dist. (Je. 16, 1812).

Reel, Rezin. Sergeant in Capt. John Miller's co. 2d D. I.; b. Washington Co., Md.; age 21; teacher.

Rees, Jacob. Second Lieutenant of the privateer *Perry*, Sept., 1814.

Rees, John. Private in Capt. Roney's co. 39th rgt.

Reese, George. Private in Capt. Conway's co. 6th rgt.

Reese, Henry. Private in Capt. Bouldin's co. Independent Light Dragoons.

Reese, John. Ensign in Capt. Sterett's Independent co.; Lieutenant (S. 12, 1814). Wounded at North Point.

Reese, John. Private in Capt. Pinney's co. 27th rgt.

Reese, William. Private in Capt. Rogers' co. 51st rgt.

Reeves, Hezekiah J. Private in Capt. Smoot's co. 43d rgt.

Reeves, John. Private in Capt. Galt's co. 6th rgt.

Reeves, Thomas. Private in Capt. McPherson's co. 43d rgt.

Reeves, William. Captain of the privateer *Sylph*, Oct., 1812; of the *Swift*, Jan, 1814.

Reeves, William. Sergeant in Capt. Edes' co. 27th rgt.

Reezer, Samuel C. Private in Capt. Howard's co. Mechanical Volunteers.

Reggin, James. Private in Capt. Berry's co. Washington Artillery.

Rehberg, J. L. Private in Capt. Bader's co. Union Yägers.

Reid, Eliphalet. Ensign in Capt. Taylor's co. 38th rgt. (S. 13, 1814).

Reid, John. Quarter-master in Extra Battalion Dorchester Co. Died 1813.

Reid, Upton S. Private in Capt. Maynard's co. 22d rgt.

Reid, Upton S. Captain in 2d rgt. 1st Cavalry Dist. (S. 10, 1814) vice Thompson.

Reilly, Patrick. Private in Capt. Brown's Eagle Artillerists.

Reinagle, Thomas. Private in Capt. McKane's co. 27th rgt.

Reinhart, George. Captain in 20th rgt. (Ap. 16, 1812).

Reinicker, Henry. Private in Capt. Warfield's co. Balto. United Volunteers.

Reinicker, Samuel. Private in Capt. Myers' co. 39th rgt.

Reintzel, George. 1st Lieutenant in Capt. Piper's co. United Maryland Artillery (My. 19, 1813) vice Lester.

Reintzel, George. Private in Capt. McKane's co. 27th rgt.

Reip, Henry. Private in Capt. Sadtler's co. Balto. Yägers.

Reister, Peter. Sergeant in Capt. Ducker's co. 7th rgt.

Reitzell, John. Lieutenant in Capt. Bartgis' co. 16th rgt. (Jy. 15, 1814).

Remman, Philip. Private in Capt. Conway's co. 6th rgt.

Remmy, Richard. Private in Capt. Faster's co. 51st rgt.

Rench, Daniel. Private in Capt. Shryock's co. 24th rgt.

Rench, John. Lieutenant in Capt. Brumbaugh's co. 8th rgt. (Ag. 17, 1808).

Rench, John. Lieutenant in Capt. Byers' co. 8th rgt. (S. 20, 1813).

Rench, Levy. Corporal in Capt. Barr's Cavalry co. 1st Dist.

Rencher, Richard M. Sergeant in Capt. Posey's co. 1st rgt.

Rennell, John N. Private in Capt. Warfield's co. Balto. United Volunteers.

Renner, John. Private in Capt. Bader's co. Union Yägers.

Renshaw, Thomas S. Private in Capt. Montgomery's co. Balto. Union Artillery.

Renshaw, William. Corporal in Capt. Moale's co. Columbian Artillery.

Repp, John. Private in Capt. Barr's Cavalry co. 1st Dist.

Reppard, Jacob. Private in Capt. Stiles' co. Marine Artillery.

Reppart, George. Private in Capt. Schwarzauer's co. 27th rgt.

Resonor, Arjalon. Private in Capt. McLaughlin's co. 50th rgt.

Resser, Jacob. Private in Capt. Berry's co. Washington Artillery. Wounded at Fort McHenry.

Retew, William. Private in Capt. Myers' co. Franklin Artillery.

Reticker, Jacob. Ensign in 38th U. S. Infantry (Jy. 14, 1814); 3d Lieutenant (O. 1, 1814).

Reune, Peter. Private in Capt. Sadtler's co. Balto. Yägers.

Reyburn, Thomas G. Private in Capt. Levering's co. Independent Blues.

Reyburn, William M. Ensign in U. S. Rangers (O. 1, 1813); 3d Lieutenant (My. 30, 1814).

Reyner, Stephen. Ensign in Capt. Dickinson's co. 9th Cavalry Dist. (D. 2, 1812); 2d Lieutenant (Jy. 24, 1813).

Reynolds, Dennis. Ensign in Capt. Hopkins' co. 22d rgt. (My. 18, 1813).

Reynolds, George. Captain in 1st Rifle Battalion 3d Brigade (Ap. 4, 1812).

Reynolds, James. 1st Lieutenant in Capt. Reynolds' Rifle co. 3d Brigade (Ap. 4, 1812).

Reynolds, Jeremiah. Private in Capt. A. C. Smith's co. 49th rgt.

Reynolds, John [1793-1881]. Private in Capt. Coat's co. 36th rgt.

Reynolds, John. Drummer in Capt. Stiles' co. Marine Artillery.

Reynolds, Joshua. Private in Capt. Brown's co. 49th rgt.

Reynolds, Richard. Private in Capt. Lawson's co. Balto. Patriots.

Reynolds, Samuel. Lieutenant in Capt. Fishpaw's co. 7th rgt. (Resigned Ag. 1, 1814).

Reynolds, Thomas. Captain in 31st rgt. Resigned D. 23, 1813.

Reynolds, William. Private in Capt. Pumphrey's co. 22d rgt.

Reynolds, William B. Corporal in Capt. Smith's co. 51st rgt.

Rhode, John. Cornet in Capt. Philpott's co. 2d rgt. 1st Cavalry Dist. (Ja. 1, 1813).

Rhodes, Daniel. Private in Capt. McLaughlin's co. 50th rgt.

Rhodes, Frederick. Private in Capt. Blizzard's co. 15th rgt.

Rhodes, Zachariah. Private in Capt. Stiles' co. Marine Artillery.

Rhynhart, Ezekiel. Private in Capt. McConkey's co. 27th rgt.

Rial, Absalom. Private in Capt. Pinney's co. 27th rgt.

Ricaud, Benjamin. Private in Capt. Sterett's co. 1st Balto. Hussars.

Ricaud, John. 1st Lieutenant in 36th U. S. Infantry (Ap. 30, 1813).

Ricaud, Thomas P. Corporal in Capt. Pennington's co. Balto. Independent Artillerists.

Rice, Archibald B. Private in Capt. Williams' co. 12th rgt.

Rice, Edward. Private in Capt. Lawrence's co. 6th rgt.

Rice, Frederick. Private in Capt. McLaughlin's co. 50th rgt.

Rice, Frederick of John. Ensign in Capt. Osborn's co. 50th rgt. (My. 17, 1811).

Rice, George. Private in Capt. McLaughlin's co. 50th rgt.

Rice, Joseph. Seaman of the privateer *Comet*.

Rich, George. Private in Capt. Moale's co. Columbian Artillery.

Rich, James. Captain in 19th rgt. Resigned Jy. 15, 1814.

Rich, John. Private in Capt. Moale's co. Columbian Artillery.

Rich, Mathias. Corporal in Capt. Moale's co. Columbian Artillery.

Rich, Peter. 1st Lieutenant in 14th U. S. Infantry (Mr. 12, 1814).

Rich, Thomas. Private in Capt. Heath's co. 23d rgt.

Richards, Benedict. Private in Capt. Dyer's co. Fells Point Riflemen.

Richards, David. Private in Capt. McConkey's co. 27th rgt.

Richards, J. C. Private in Capt. Stapleton's co. 39th rgt.

Richards, John. Private in Capt. Edes' co. 27th rgt.

Richards, John. Private in Capt. Sands' co. 22d rgt.

Richards, Leonard. Fifer in Capt. Smoot's co. 43d rgt.

Richards, Lewis M. Private in Capt. Moale's co. Columbian Artillery.

Richards, William. Private in Capt. Boone's co. 22d rgt.

Richardson, Benjamin. Major in 40th rgt. (F. 12, 1814).

Richardson, Charles. Private in Capt. Jarboe's co. 12th rgt.

Richardson, Daniel. Private in Capt. Levering's co. Independent Blues.

Richardson, David K. Corporal in Capt. Lawson's co. Balto. Patriots.

Richardson, Edward. Private in Capt. Schwarzauer's co. 27th rgt.

Richardson, Ezekiel. Private in Capt. Pike's Balto. Volunteer Artillery.

Richardson, George. Private in Capt. Haubert's co. 51st rgt.

Richardson, George W. Corporal in Capt. Snowden's co. 36th rgt.

Richardson, Henry. Ensign in Capt. Lowman's co. 35th rgt.

Richardson, Jabez. Private in Capt. Dillon's co. 27th rgt.

Richardson, James. Lieutenant in Capt. Fisher's co. 19th rgt. (My. 18, 1813).

Richardson, James. Private in Capt. Crawfurd's co. 17th rgt.

Richardson, James. Private in Capt. Kennedy's co. 27th rgt.

Richardson, James. Private in Capt. Nailor's co. 17th rgt.

Richardson, John. Private in Capt. Myers' co. 39th rgt.

Richardson, John. Private in Capt. Peters' co. 51st rgt.

Richardson, John Thomas. Private in Capt. Franklin's co. 2d rgt.

Richardson, Joseph. Captain of the privateer America; and later of the Chesapeake.

Richardson, Joseph P. W. Cornet in Capt. Hooper's co. 10th Cavalry Dist. (F. 19, 1813).

Richardson, Morgan. 1st Lieutenant in Capt. Macatee's co. 7th Cavalry Dist. (Ap. 16, 1812);

Adjutant (S. 10, 1814) vice Brown.

Richardson, Nathaniel. Private in Capt. Moore's co. 49th rgt.

Richardson, Noah. Ensign in Capt. Colston's co. 48th rgt. (Jy. 8, 1813).

Richardson, Richard. 2d Lieutenant in Capt. Bryan's Artillery co. 12th Brigade (Ap. 30, 1813).

Richardson, Solomon. Major in 19th rgt. (D. 7, 1812).

Richardson, Stephen. Ensign in Capt. Mann's co. 33d rgt. (S. 2, 1811).

Richardson, Thomas. Private in Capt. Naylor's co. 17th rgt.

Richardson, Thomas. Private in Capt. Massey's co. 38th rgt.

Richardson, Thomas A. Sergeant in Capt. Dyer's co. 17th rgt.

Richardson, Thomas Tillard. Ensign in Capt. Maulsby's co. 40th rgt. (Jy. 16, 1814).

Richardson, Tristram. Sergeant in Capt. Brohawn's co. 48th rgt.

Richardson, William. Captain of the privateer Express, July, 1812; Private in Capt. Bunbury's co. Sea Fencibles, 1814.

Richardson, William. Adjutant in Extra Battalion Harford Co. (My. 8, 1812).

Richardson, William. Private in Capt. Snowden's co. 36th rgt.

Richmond, Francis. Lieutenant in Capt. Johnson's co. 28th rgt. (Jy. 8, 1814).

Rick, John. Private in Capt. Addison's co. Sea Fencibles.

Ricketts, George. Quarter-master in 8th Cavalry Dist. (Ag. 20, 1813).

Ricketts, Levering. Private in Capt. Steever's co. 27th rgt.

28

Ricketts, William. 2d Lieutenant in Capt. Evans' co. 8th Cavalry Dist. (Ap. 23, 1812).

Ricketts, William C. Private in Capt. Mackey's co. 49th rgt.

Rickey, William W. Private in Capt. Pike's co. Balto. Volunteer Artillery.

Rickstein, George. Private in Capt. Magruder's co. American Artillerists.

Riddle, Edward. Private in Capt. Stiles' co. Marine Artillery.

Riddle, Samuel. Private in Capt. Crawfurd's co. 17th rgt.

Riddle, Samuel. Corporal in Capt. Duvall's co. 34th rgt.

Ridenour, —. Captain in 24th rgt.

Ridenour, Michael. Private in Capt. Shryock's co. 24th rgt.

Rider, Arthur. Private in Capt. Pike's co. Balto. Volunteer Artillery.

Rider, Joshua. Private in Capt. Conway's co. 6th rgt.

Rider, Mathias. Private in Capt. Ducker's co. 7th rgt.

Rider, Philip. Captain of the privateer *Experiment,* July, 1812; of the *Argo,* 1813.

Ridgate, Benjamin Cornick [1788-1858]. Private in Capt. Sterett's co. 1st Balto. Hussars.

Ridgel, Jonathan. Private in Capt. Williams' co. 12th rgt.

Ridgeley, Thomas. Private in Capt. Magruder's co. American Artillerists.

Ridgely, Charles. Private in Capt. Sands' co. 22d rgt.

Ridgely, Charles C. Lieutenant in Capt. Welling's co. 32d rgt. (Je. 14, 1808).

Ridgely, Charles S. Major in 3d Cavalry Dist. (F. 13, 1812).

Ridgely, Daniel B. 2d Lieutenant in Capt. Hammond's co. 3d Cavalry Dist. (Ap. 23, 1812). Died 1814.

Ridgely, David. Private in Capt. Maynard's co. 22d rgt.

Ridgely, Davidge. Private in Capt. Stewart's co. 51st rgt.

Ridgely, Edward. Private in Capt. Warfield's co. Balto. United Volunteers.

Ridgely, Isaiah. Private in Capt. Moale's Columbian Artillery.

Ridgely, James. Private in Capt. Moale's co. Columbian Artillery.

Ridgely, Dr. John. Private in Capt. Maynard's co. 22d rgt.

Ridgely, John. Cornet in Capt. Carnan's co. 6th Cavalry Dist. (S. 21, 1813) vice Owings.

Ridgely, John. Surgeon in 3d Cavalry Dist. (Ap. 21, 1813) vice Warfield.

Ridgely, John C. 2d Lieutenant in Capt. Thomas' co. 3d Cavalry Dist. (My. 8, 1812); 1st Lieutenant (Jy. 6, 1814).

Ridgely, Nicholas. Corporal in Capt. McConkey's co. 27th rgt.

Ridgely, Nicholas. Private in Capt. Maynard's co. 22d rgt.

Ridgely, Robert. Private in Capt. Barnes' co. 32d rgt.

Ridgely, Samuel N. Cornet in Capt. Warfield's co. 3d Cavalry Dist. (Jy. 6, 1814).

Ridgely, William A. Ensign in Capt. Clarke's co. 7th rgt. (My. 17, 1811).

Ridgeway, James. Paymaster in Extra Battalion Caroline Co.

Ridgeway, William P. Captain in 9th Cavalry Dist. (My. 25, 1812).

Ridgway, Fielder. Captain U. S. Rifles (Jy. 31, 1810); struck off My., 1814.

Ridgway, Levi. Private in Capt. Brooke's co. 34th rgt.

Ridout, Addison. Private in Capt. Chase's co. 22d rgt.

Ridout, John. Private in Capt. Maynard's co. 22d rgt.

Ridout, John. Private in Capt. Boone's co. 22d rgt.

Ridwell, William. Private in Capt. Haden's co. 17th rgt.

Riffle, John. Private in Capt. Getzendanner's co. 16th rgt.

Rigby, Edward. Private in Capt. McConkey's co. 27th rgt.

Rigby, James I. Sergeant in Capt. Sheppard's co. 6th rgt.

Rigby, John. Private in Capt. Pinkney's Artillery co. 22d rgt.

Rigden, John E. Private in Capt. Nicholson's co. Balto. Fencibles.

Rigdon, William. Private in Capt. Ringgold's co. 6th rgt.

Riggen, Benton. Private in Capt. Burke's co. 6th rgt.

Riggen, James. Private in Capt. Dyer's co. Fells Point Riflemen.

Riggin, John. Private in Capt. Heath's co. 23d rgt.

Riggin, Levi. Private in Capt. McKane's co. 27th rgt.

Riggins, Joseph. Private in Capt. Schwarzauer's co. 27th rgt.

Riggs, Elisha. Ensign in Capt. Owing's co. 32d rgt. (Ap. 23, 1812); Private in Capt. Rothrock's co. 38th U. S. Infantry.

Riggs, George. Private in Capt. Levering's co. Independent Blues.

Riggs, George W. Private in Capt. Moale's co. Columbian Artillery.

Riggs, Henry. Captain in 13th rgt. (Ap. 7, 1810).

Riggs, Remus. Lieutenant in Capt. Wilcoxen's co. 44th rgt. (S. 10, 1814).

Righart, Philip. Private in Capt. Nicholson's co. Balto. Fencibles.

Right, Jesse. Private in Capt. Shryock's co. 24th rgt.

Righter, George. Private in Capt. Smith's co. 51st rgt.

Rigney, John. Adjutant in 16th rgt. (Jy. 20, 1812).

Rigo, Clement. Private in Capt. Lawrence's co. 6th rgt.

Riland, Thomas. Private in Capt. Blair's co. 50th rgt.

Riley, Bennet [-1853]. Ensign in U. S. Rifles (Ja. 19, 1813); 2d Lieutenant (Ap. 15, 1814).

Riley, Camden. Captain in 18th rgt. (My., 1808).

Riley, Elisha. Private in Capt. Blair's co. 50th rgt.

Riley, James. Cornet in Capt. Davis' co. 11th Cavalry Dist. (O. 6, 1812).

Riley, John. Sergeant in Capt. Montgomery's co. Balto. Union Artillery.

Riley, John. Private in Capt. Kennedy's co. 27th rgt.

Riley, John S. Private in Capt. McKane's co. 27th rgt.

Riley, Thomas. Private in Capt. McLaughlin's co. 50th rgt.

Riley, Valerius. Private in Capt. Pinney's co. 27th rgt.

Riley, William. Sergeant in Capt. Spry's co. 33d rgt.

Riley, William. Private in Capt. Chalmers' co. 51st rgt.

Rily, Edward. Private in Capt. Haubert's co. 51st rgt.

Rind, William A. 3d Lieutenant in 36th U. S. Infantry (Ap. 30, 1813); 1st Lieutenant (S. 30, 1814).

Rinehart, David. Private in Capt. Faster's co. 51st rgt.

Riner, Peter. Private in Capt. Shryock's co. 24th rgt.

Ring, George. Private in Capt. Haubert's co. 51st rgt.

Ring, Thomas. Lieutenant of the privateer *Comet*, July 1812.

Ringgold, Benjamin. Captain in 6th rgt. (Jy. 12, 1814).

Ringgold, James, Jr. Private in Capt. Hands' co. 21st rgt.

Ringgold, Samuel. Brigadier-General 2d Brigade (Jy. 7, 1810).

Ringgold, Samuel W. Lieutenant in Capt. Watters' co. 38th rgt. (Ap. 18, 1808).

Ringrose, James. Private in Capt. Galt's co. 6th rgt.

Ringrose, John W. Private in Capt. Montgomery's co. Balto. Union Artillery.

Rinoll, George. Private in Capt. Shryock's co. 24th rgt.

Risbrough, John. Captain of the privateer *Vixen*, Nov., 1814.

Riston, George. Private in Capt. Magruder's American Artillerists.

Ritazel, Francis. Private in Capt. Howard's co. Mechanical Volunteers.

Ritchie, Jesse. Private in Capt. Brown's co. 49th rgt.

Ritchie, John. Private in Capt. Moore's co. 49th rgt.

Ritchie, Thomas. 1st Lieutenant in 36th U. S. Infantry (Ap. 30, 1813).

Ritchie, William. Private in Capt. Brown's co. Eagle Artillerists.

Ritter, Jacob. Private in Capt. Wilson's co. 6th rgt.

Rizer, John. Private in Capt. Blair's co. 50th rgt.

Roab, J. P. Private in Capt. Bader's co. Union Yägers.

Roach, Thomas D. Private in Capt. Dobbin's co. 39th rgt.

Roach, William H. Surgeon in 45th rgt. [1813].

Roache, Alexander. Private in Capt. Brown's Eagle Artillerists.

Roads, Jacob. Private in Capt. Blair's co. 50th rgt.

Roads, John. Private in Capt. John Miller's co. 2d D. I.; b. Boonsborough, Md.; age 33; wagoner; subs. for Jacob Scheckter.

Roan, George H. Private in Capt. Steever's co. 27th rgt.

Robb, John. Private in Capt. Myers' co. 39th rgt.

Robb, John. Sergeant and Quartermaster-Sergeant in 7th U. S. Infantry D. 3, 1813, to D., 1814; Ensign (D. 22, 1814).

Robbins, William. Seaman of the privateer *Surprise*, drowned April 5, 1815.

Roberts, Caleb. Fifer in Capt. Taylors' co. 48th rgt.

Roberts, Edward B. Private in Capt. McConkey's co. 27th rgt.

Roberts, Horatio. Cornet in Capt. Little's co. 9th Cavalry Dist. (My. 22, 1812); 2d Lieutenant (Ap. 24, 1813).

Roberts, Hugh. Private in Capt. Brohawn's co. 48th rgt.

Roberts, John. Private in Capt. Warfield's co. Balto. United Volunteers.

Roberts, John. Private in Capt. Rogers' co. 51st rgt.

Roberts, John. Lieutenant in Capt. Morgan's co. 49th rgt. (D. 10, 1813).

Roberts, Lewis. Private in Capt. Morgan's co. 49th rgt.

Roberts, Owen. Private in Capt. Wilson's co. 6th rgt.

Roberts, Thomas. Private in Capt. Deems' co. 51st rgt.

Roberts, William. Ensign in Capt. Clagett's co. 44th rgt. (D. 16, 1813).

Roberts, William. 2d Lieutenant in Capt. Banning's co. 9th Cavalry Dist. (Mr. 25, 1812).

Roberts, William. Private in Capt. Weems' co. 22d rgt.

Roberts, William. Drummer in Capt. Taylor's co. 48th rgt.

Robertson, George. Ensign in Capt. Wm. Dent's co. 43d rgt.; Lieutenant in Capt. Gray's co.

Robertson, George. Private in Capt. Magruder's co. American Artillerists.

Robertson, James. Lieutenant of the privateer *Kemp*, July, 1812.

Robertson, James. Private in Capt. Dent's co. 43d rgt.

Robertson, John. Private in Capt. Dyer's co. Fells Point Riflemen.

Robertson, Joshua O. Lieutenant in Capt. Davis's co. 50th rgt. (Ag. 11, 1813).

Robertson, Thomas. Private in Capt. Bunbury's co. Sea Fencibles.

Robertson, Thomas. Private in Capt. Dent's co. 43d rgt.

Robertson, Thomas. Ensign in Capt. Watters' co. 25th rgt. (Jy. 15, 1814) vice Covington.

Robertson, William. 1st Lieutenant in Capt. Blake's co. 9th Cavalry Dist. (My. 31, 1813).

Robertson, William. Ensign in Capt. Fallin's co. 48th rgt. (Jy. 8, 1813).

Robertson, William. Private in Capt. Dent's co. 43d rgt.

Robey, Aquila. Private in Capt. Thompson's co. 43d rgt.

Robey, Charles. Lieutenant in Capt. Posey's co. 1st rgt. (Jy. 24, 1813).

Robey, Thomas H. Private in Capt. Dent's co. 43d rgt.

Robey, Townley. Captain in 43d rgt. (O. 1, 1811).

Robinette, Elizophr. Private in Capt. McLaughlin's co. 50th rgt.

Robins, Daniel G. Adjutant in 9th rgt. (F. 19, 1813).

Robins, Edward. Paymaster in Extra Battalion Worcester Co.

Robinson, ——. Captain in 17th rgt.

Robinson, Abraham. Private in Capt. Haubert's co. 51st rgt.

Robinson, Andrew. Private in Capt. Schwarzauer's co. 27th rgt.

Robinson, Benjamin. Private in Capt. Pumphrey's co. 22d rgt.

Robinson, Benjamin H. Private in Capt. Levering's co. Independent Blues.

Robinson, Caleb R. [-1815]. 2d Lieutenant in Capt. Addison's co. Sea Fencibles (Mr. 17, 1814).

Robinson, Clement. Private in Capt. Fallin's co. 48th rgt.

Robinson, David. Private in Capt. Ringgold's co. 6th rgt.

Robinson, James. Private in Capt. Boyer's co. 33d rgt.

Robinson, James. Private in Capt. Magruder's co. American Artillerists.

Robinson, James. Private in Capt. Chambers' co. 21st rgt.

Robinson, Jesse. Private in Capt. Schwarzauer's co. 27th rgt.

Robinson, Jesse. Private in Capt. Dobbin's co. 39th rgt.

Robinson, John. Private in Capt. Lawrence's co. 6th rgt.

Robinson, John. 5th Sergeant in Capt. Snowden's co. 36th rgt.

Robinson, John. Private in Capt. Stapleton's co. 39th rgt.

Robinson, John. Private in Capt. Montgomery's co. Balto. Union Artillery. Wounded at North Point and taken prisoner.

Robinson, John. Private in Capt. Myers' co. 39th rgt.

Robinson, John. Fifer in Capt. Fallin's co. 48th rgt.

Robinson, John M. Private in Capt. Pinney's co. 27th rgt.

Robinson, Joseph. 2d Major in 27th rgt.

Robinson, Joseph. Private in Capt. Wilson's co. 6th rgt.

Robinson, Joseph. Sergeant in Capt. Kierstead's co. 6th rgt.

Robinson, Joseph. Major in 26th rgt. (Ja. 24, 1814) vice Keyser.

Robinson, Luke. Private in Capt. Fallin's co. 48th rgt.

Robinson, Richard. Private in Capt. Pumphrey's co. 22d rgt.

Robinson, Samuel. Private in Capt. Moale's co. Columbian Artillery.

Robinson, Samuel. Private in Capt. Fallin's co. 48th rgt.

Robinson, T. G., M. D. Wounded in action on the privateer *Prince of Neufchatel,* Sept. 11, 1814.

Robinson, Thomas. 1st Lieutenant in Capt. Lee's co. 7th Cavalry Dist. (Mr. 16, 1812).

Robinson, Thomas. Private in Capt. Magruder's co. American Artillerists.

Robinson, Thomas. Private in Capt. Pike's Balto. Volunteer Artillery.

Robinson, Thomas. Private in Capt. Lawrence's co. 6th rgt.

Robinson, William. Ensign in Capt. Travers' co. 48th rgt.

Robinson, William. Private in Capt. Thomas's co. 49th rgt.

Robinson, William. Private in Capt. Smith's co. 51st rgt.

Robinson, William. Private in Capt. Pike's co. Balto. Volunteer Artillery.

Robinson, William. Private in Capt. Faster's co. 51st rgt.

Robinson, Zachariah. Private in Capt. Hancock's co. 22d rgt.

Robison, John. Ensign in Capt. Holtzman's co. 50th rgt. (D. 26, 1810).

Robson, William. Private in Capt. Brohawn's co. 48th rgt.

Roche, James. Private in Capt. Piper's co. United Maryland Artillery.

Roche, Joseph. Private in Capt. Piper's co. United Maryland Artillery.

Rock, Francis. Private in Capt. Morgan's co. 49th rgt.

Rockhold, Asel. Private in Capt. Burke's co. 6th rgt.

Rockhold, Charles. Private in Capt. Sheppard's co. 6th rgt.

Roddy, Robert. Private in Capt. Haden's co. 17th rgt.

Rodemeyer, George. Private in Capt. Sadtler's co. Balto. Yägers.

Rodgers, Walter. 3d officer of the privateer *Dolphin.*

Rodman, Robert R. Private in Capt. Edes' co. 27th rgt.

Roe, Archibald. Private in Capt. Jas. Massey's co. 38th rgt.

Roe, Benjamin. Ensign in Capt. Talbot's co. 19th rgt. (O. 30, 1807).

Roe, Charles. Private in Capt. Dobbin's co. 39th rgt.

Roe, James. Captain in 35th rgt. (O. 17, 1810).

Roe, Samuel. Private in Capt. Dobbin's co. 39th rgt.

Roeschen, Bernard. Corporal in Capt. Sadtler's co. Balto. Yägers.

Roesner, John [1768-1814]. Private in Capt. Sadtler's co. Balto. Yägers.

Rogers, Daniel. Private in Capt. Sterett's Independent co.

Rogers, David. Private in Capt. Sheppard's co. 6th rgt.

Rogers, Elisha. Private in Capt. Levering's co. Independent Blues.

Rogers, George. Private in Capt. Pinney's co. 27th rgt.

Rogers, George. Private in Capt. Sterett's Independent co.

Rogers, Harrison G. Quarter-master-Sergeant in 14th U. S. Infantry; Ensign (Ap. 15, 1814).

Rogers, Henry W. Private in Capt. Sterett's co. 1st Balto. Hussars.

Rogers, John. Corporal in Capt. Myers' co. Franklin Artillery.

Rogers, John. Private in Capt. Smith's co. 51st rgt.

Rogers, John H. Captain in 51st rgt.

Rogers, Joseph. Private in Capt. Bunbury's co. Sea Fencibles.

Rogers, Joshua. Ensign in Capt. Taylor's co. 46th rgt. (Jy. 8, 1814) vice Cole.

Rogers, Joshua. Private in Capt. Taylor's co. 46th rgt.

Rogers, Lloyd, N. Private in Capt. Thompson's co. 1st Baltimore Horse Artillery.

Rogers, Patrick. Private in Capt. Conway's co. 6th rgt.

Rogers, Richard. Private in Capt. Levering's co. Independent Blues.

Rogers, Roland. Private in Capt. Smith's co. 51st rgt.

Rogers, Thomas. Private in Capt. Nicholson's co. Balto. Fencibles.

Rogers, William. Private in Capt. McConkey's co. 27th rgt.

Rogers, William. Private in Capt. Sterett's Independent Co.

Rogers, William L. 2d Lieutenant in 36th U. S. Infantry (Ap. 30, 1813); 1st Lieutenant (My. 1, 1814).

Rogge, Charles. Private in Capt. Sadtler's co. Balto. Yägers.

Rohr, Andrew. Sergeant in Capt. Horton's co. Maryland Chasseurs.

Rohrback, Jacob. Lieutenant in Capt. Miller's co. 10th rgt. (Ag. 2, 1814).

Rohrback, William. Ensign in Capt. Miller's co. 10th rgt. (Ag. 2, 1814).

Rohrer, Frederick. Corporal in Capt. Barr's Cavalry co. 1st Dist.

Rohrer, John M. Captain in 10th rgt. (Ap. 30, 1811).

Rohrer, Samuel. 2d Lieutenant in Capt. Barr's co. 1st rgt. 1st Cavalry Dist. (S. 12, 1814).

Roland, Joseph M. Private in Capt. A. E. Warner's co. 39th rgt.

Rolle, Fiddemon. 1st Lieutenant in Capt. Banning's co. 9th Cavalry Dist. (Mr. 25, 1812).

Rollins, James. Private in Capt. Stiles' co. Marine Artillery.

Rollinson, Levin. Private in Capt. Wickes' co. 21st rgt.

Rolph, Neal. Private in Capt. Galt's co. 6th rgt.

Romney, Robert. Private in Capt. Steever's co. 27th rgt.

Roney, William [1782-1844]. Ensign in 39th rgt. (Ag. 5, 1807); Lieutenant in 39th rgt. (F. 24, 1810); Captain of Drafted Infantry (Je. 15, 1813); Captain in 39th rgt. 1814.

Rook, John. Private in Capt. Addison's co. Sea Fencibles.

Rook, Thomas D. 3d Lieutenant in Capt. Dyer's co. Fells Point Riflemen.

Ropp, John. Private in Capt. Shryock's co. 24th rgt.

Rose, Jacob. Private in Capt. Maynard's co. 22d rgt.

Rose, John P. Private in Capt. Magruder's co. American Artillerists.

Rosensteel, Henry. Private in Capt. Haubert's co. 51st rgt.

Rosensteel, William. Private in Capt. Smith's co. 51st rgt.

Ross, Benjamin C. Private in Capt. Levering's co. Independent Blues.

Ross, David. Private in Capt. Sheppard's co. 6th rgt.

Ross, Horatio. Ensign in Capt. Cramphin's co. 14th rgt. (My. 23, 1799).

Ross, James. Private in Capt. Myers' co. 39th rgt.

Ross, James. Private in Capt. McConkey's co. 27th rgt.

Ross, James. Private in Capt. Brown's co. Eagle Artillerists.

Ross, John. Lieutenant of the privateer *Chasseur*, Feb., 1813; Private in Capt. Stiles' co. Marine Artillery.

Ross, Peter. Private in Capt. Jas. Massey's co. 38th rgt.

Ross, Reuben [1781-1830]. 2d Lieutenant in Capt. Pike's co. Balto. Volunteer Artillery.

Ross, S. Samuel. Private in Capt. Bunbury's co. Sea Fencibles.

Ross, Solomon. Private in Capt. Stewart's co. 51st rgt.

Ross, Thomas. Private in Capt. Horton's co. Maryland Chasseurs.

Ross, William. Lieutenant of the privateer *Patapsco*, Sept., 1812.

Ross, William. Private in Capt. Chase's co. 22d rgt.

Rosse, George. Private in Capt. Piper's co. United Maryland Artillery.

Roston, William. Private in Capt. Dillon's co. 27th rgt.

Rote, John. Private in Capt. Howard's co. Mechanical Volunteers.

Rothe, William. Private in Capt. Bader's co. Union Yägers.

Rothemond, Dietrick. Private in Capt. Bader's co. Union Yägers.

Rothrock, Jacob. Private in Capt. Steever's co. 27th rgt.

Rothrock, John. Captain in 38th U. S. Infantry (My. 20, 1813).

Rothrock, Philip. Private in Capt. Shrim's co. Balto. Light Infantry.

Rourk, Peter. Private in Capt. Stewart's co. 51st rgt.

Rouse, Benjamin. Sergeant in Capt. Brown's co. Eagle Artillerists.

Rouse, George. Private in Capt. Pinney's co. 27th rgt.

Rouse, James. Private in Capt. Dyer's co. Fells Point Riflemen.

Rouse, Peregrine. Ensign in Capt. Taylor's co. 19th rgt. (My. 22, 1812).

Roush, William H. Surgeon in 45th rgt. (D. 8, 1813).

Rowan, John. Captain in 11th rgt.

Rowe, Benjamin. Private in Capt. Dent's co. 43d rgt.

Rowe, John K. Captain in 6th rgt.

Rowe, Richard T. Private in Capt. Fendall's co. 43d rgt.

Rowe, Thomas. Private in Capt. Brown's co. 49th rgt.

Rowles, David. Private in Capt. Pumphrey's co. 22d rgt.

Rowles, John. Private in Capt. Montgomery's co. Balto. Union Artillery.

Rowlinson, John. Private in Capt. Jos. Kemp's co. 26th rgt.

Roy, John. Private in Capt. Edes' co. 27th rgt.

Roy, Joseph. Lieutenant in Capt. Griffith's co. 32d rgt. (O. 21, 1812).

Rozen, Jacob. Private in Capt. Stiles' co. Marine Artillery.

Ruark, Dennard. Private in Capt. Travers' co. 48th rgt.

Ruark, Henry. Private in Capt. Travers' co. 48th rgt.

Ruark, Meekins. Private in Capt. Travers' co. 48th rgt.

Ruark, Samuel. Private in Capt. Travers' co. 48th rgt.

Ruark, Thomas. Private in Capt. Travers' co. 48th rgt.

Rubey, Thomas. Ensign in Capt. McLaughlin's co. 50th rgt. (O. 16, 1810).

Ruckle, Samuel. Private in Capt. Steuart's co. Washington Blues.

Ruckle, Thomas. Corporal in Capt. Steuart's co. Washington Blues.

Rudenstein, John M. Private in Capt. Shrim's co. Balto. Light Infantry.

Rudolph, Tobias. Quarter-master in 49th rgt. (D. 29, 1812).

Rudolph, Zebulon. Private in Capt. Magruder's co. American Artillerists.

Rue, Suthy. Lieutenant in Capt. Vinson's co. 11th rgt. (Ap. 7, 1810).

Ruff, Andrew. Private in Capt. Roney's co. 39th rgt.

Ruff, Henry. Private in Capt. Stapleton's co. 39th rgt.

Ruff, Henry P. Captain in 42d rgt. (Ag. 13, 1811).

Rumbaugh, Peter. Private in Capt. Dillon's co. 27th rgt.

Rumney, Samuel. Private in Capt. Chambers' co. 21st rgt.

Rumsey, Charles H. Private in Capt. Aisquith's co. Sharp Shooters.

Rush, John. 1st Lieutenant in Fells Point Light Dragoons (Jy. 28, 1812).

Rusk, David L. Private in Capt. Rogers' co. 51st rgt.

Rusk, George [1790-1838]. Private in Capt. Hanna's co. Fells Point Light Dragoons.

Rusk, John. Private in Capt. Snowden's co. 36th rgt.

Rusk, John. 1st Lieutenant in Capt. Hanna's co. Fells Point Light Dragoons.

Rusk, Paul. Private in Capt. Smith's co. 51st rgt.

Rusk, Thomas. Private in Capt. Aisquith's co. Sharp Shooters.

Rusk, William. Private in Capt. Levering's co. Independent Blues.

Russel, Samuel. Private in Capt. Kennedy's co. 27th rgt.

Russell, James. Sergeant in Capt. Berry's co. Washington Artillery.

Russell, John. Private in Capt. Burgess' co. 43d rgt.

Russell, John. Private in Capt. McLaughlin's co. 50th rgt.

Russell, Joseph. Sergeant in Capt. Shrim's co. Balto. Light Infantry.

Russell, Nathan. Ensign in Capt. Styll's co. 19th rgt. (Ag. 28, 1812).

Russell, Philip. 2d Lieutenant in Capt. Maddox's Artillery co. 5th Brigade Charles co. (N. 3, 1812).

Russell, Samuel. Private in Capt. Stiles' co. Marine Artillery.

Russell, Theophilus. Private in Capt. Chambers' co. 21st rgt.

Russell, Thomas. 1st Lieutenant in Capt. Pennington's co. Balto. Independent Artillerists. Wounded at Fort McHenry.

Russell, Thomas. 2d Lieutenant in Capt. Pennington's co. Balto. Independent Artillerists (Ap. 30, 1812); 1st Lieutenant (1814).

Russell, Thomas. Private in Capt. Garrett's co. 49th rgt.

Russell, William. Private in Capt. Steever's co. 27th rgt.

Russell, William. Private in Capt. Stapleton's co. 39th rgt.

Russom, James. Private in Capt. McConckin's co. 38th rgt.

Russum, Mitchel. Major in 10th Cavalry Dist. (Je. 16, 1812).

Rust, Abraham. Private in Capt. Dillon's co. 27th rgt.

Rust, Charles. Private in Capt. Montgomery's co. Balto. Union Artillery.

Rust, Henry. Corporal in Capt. Kennedy's co. 27th rgt.

Rust, Samuel [1781-1863]. Private in Capt. Hughes (later Pennington's) Balto. Independent Artillery.

Rust, Samuel. Private in Capt. McConkey's co. 27th rgt.

Rust, William. Private in Capt. Steever's co. 27th rgt.

Ruster, Lewis. Private in Capt. Sheppard's co. 6th rgt.

Ruthell, Parrott. Ensign in Capt. Seth's co. 26th rgt. (N. 5, 1812); Lieutenant (1814).

Rutlidge, Jacob. Captain in 40th rgt. (Ja. 16, 1808).

Rutter, John. Ensign in 14th U. S. Infantry (N. 22, 1814).

Rutter, John. Cornet in Capt. Wilson's co. 8th Cavalry Dist. (My. 16, 1812).

Rutter, John. Private in Capt. Haubert's co. 51st rgt.

Rutter, John. Private in Capt. Warfield's co. Balto. United Volunteers.

Rutter, Michael. Sergeant in Capt. Cozier's co. 30th rgt.

Rutter, Solomon. Lieutenant of Barney's flotilla.

Rutter, Thomas G. Private in Capt. Pennington's co. Balto. Independent Artillerists.

Rutter, William. Private in Capt. Ringgold's co. 6th rgt.

Ryan, Amos. Cornet in Capt. Bouldin's co. Independent Light Dragoons 5th Cavalry Dist. (My. 18, 1813).

Ryan, George. Private in Capt. A. E. Warner's co. 39th rgt.

Ryan, James. Private in Capt. Griffith's co. 21st rgt. Deserted Aug. 1, 1814.

Ryan, Joseph. Private in Capt. Blizzard's co. 15th rgt.

Ryan, Joseph C. Ensign in Capt. Orr's co. 30th rgt. (Jy. 8, 1811).

Ryan, William. Private in Capt. Dillon's co. 27th rgt.

Rye, Henry. Private in Capt. Steiner's Frederick Artillery.

Rye, John of John. Private in Capt. Dent's co. 43d rgt.

Rye, John of Raleigh. Private in Capt. Dent's co. 43d rgt.

Rye, John of Warren. Private in Capt. Dent's co. 43d rgt.

Rye, Warren. Private in Capt. Dunnington's co. 43d rgt.

Rye, William. Private in Capt. Dunnington's co. 43d rgt.

Rye, Willis. Private in Capt. Dunnington's co. 43d rgt.

Ryland, Thomas A. Sergeant in Capt. Allen's co. 49th rgt.

Ryson, John. Private in Capt. Dunnington's co. 43d rgt.

Ryson, Middleton M. Private in Capt. Brown's co. 43d rgt.
Ryson, Peter. Private in Capt. Brown's co. 43d rgt.

S

Sablis, Michael. Private in Capt. Kierstead's co. 6th rgt.
Sadler, Augustus. Private in Capt. Addison's co. Sea Fencibles.
Sadler, Joseph. Private in Capt. Thos. Warner's co. 39th rgt.
Sadler, Joseph R. Private in Capt. Stapleton's co. 39th rgt.
Sadtler, Philip Benjamin [1771-1860]. Captain in Balto. Yägers (Ap. 22, 1814).
Saffield, Joshua. Private in Capt. Pumphrey's co. 22d rgt.
Sager, John. Private in Capt. Shryock's co. 24th rgt.
Sailor, Peter. Lieutenant in Capt. Shryock's co. 24th rgt. (Jy. 12, 1814) vice Conrad.
Saiman, Joseph. Private in Capt. Lawrence's co. 6th rgt.
St. Clair, Henry. Private in Capt. Cawood's co. 45th rgt.
St. Clair, James. Private in Capt. Cawood's co. 45th rgt.
St. Clair, Jehu. Private in Capt. Cawood's co. 45th rgt.
Saldge, Conrad. Private in Capt. Burke's co. 6th rgt.
Salmon, Charles. Private in Capt. Steiner's Frederick Artillery.
Salques, Coley. Private in Capt. Schwarzauer's co. 27th rgt.
Salques, Selah. Private in Capt. Ringgold's co. 6th rgt.
Saltenstall, Nathaniel. Corporal in Capt. Sterett's co. 1st Balto. Hussars.
Saltzwedel, John. Private in Capt. Sadtler's co. Balto. Yägers.

Samble, Thomas [1783-]. Seaman in Barney's flotilla.
Sample, John. Captain in 49th rgt. (Jy. 29, 1811).
Sampson, Charles. Private in Capt. Pike's co. Balto. Volunteer Artillery.
Samuels, Samuel. Corporal in Capt. Stewart's co. 51st rgt.
Samuels, William. Corporal in Capt. Myer's co. 39th rgt.
Sanders, Benjamin. Private in Capt. A, E. Warner's co. 39th rgt.
Sanders, Edward. Private in Capt. Taylor's co. 46th rgt.
Sanders, Edward. Private in Capt. Deems' co. 51st rgt.
Sanders, George. Private in Capt. Conway's co. 6th rgt.
Sanders, George. Lieutenant in Capt. Scheehter's co. 10th rgt. (Ag. 2, 1814).
Sanders, Humphrey. Private in Capt. Smith's co. 51st rgt.
Sanders, James. Captain in 2d rgt. (Ag. 14, 1807).
Sanders, John. Private in Capt. Rogers' co. 51st rgt.
Sanders, Joseph. Private in Capt. Roney's co. 39th rgt.
Sanders, Obedia. Private in Capt. Fowler's co. 46th rgt.
Sanders, Thomas. Ensign in Capt. Simmons' co. 13th rgt. (S. 10, 1814).
Sanders, Thomas. Private in Capt. Schwarzauer's co. 27th rgt.
Sanders, William G. [-1845]. Ensign in 14th U. S. Infantry (Mr. 12, 1812); 2d Lieutenant (My. 13, 1813).
Sanderson, Francis. Private in Capt. Smith's co. 51st rgt.
Sanderson, Henry. Private in Capt. Sadtler's co. Balto. Yägers.

Sanderson, Michael. Sergeant in Capt. Sterett's Independent co.

Sands, Benjamin N. Private in Capt. Nicholson's co. Balto. Fencibles.

Sands, Joseph. Captain in 22d rgt.

Sands, Richard Martin [-1836]. Ensign in 38th U. S. Infantry (My. 20, 1813); 2d Lieutenant (Jy. 9, 1814).

Sangrell, James. *See* **Langrell.**

Sangston, James. Paymaster in 19th rgt. (My. 28, 1812) (Commission record gives Samuel).

Sank, George. Private in Capt. Linthicum's co. 22d rgt.

Sankee, William. Sergeant in Capt. Dobbin's co. 39th rgt.

Sanner, John. Private in Capt. Jarboe's co. 12th rgt.

Sanner, Joseph, Jr. Ensign in Capt. Jarboe's co. 12th rgt. (Je. 12, 1812).

Sanner, William. Private in Capt. Jarboe's co. 12th rgt.

Sap, Henry. Private in Capt. Green's co. 46th rgt.

Sap, Oliver. Corporal in Capt. Green's co. 46th rgt.

Sap, William. Private in Capt. Green's co. 46th rgt.

Sapp, Adam. Private in Capt. Blair's co. 50th rgt.

Sappington, Augustin. Private in Capt. Hall's co. 3d Cavalry rgt.

Sappington, Jonathan. Private in Capt. Linthicum's co. 22d rgt.

Sasscer, Underwood. Private in Capt. Crawfurd's co. 17th rgt.

Sasscer, William. Private in Capt. Haden's co. 17th rgt.

Sasscer, Zadoc. Ensign in Capt. Carter's co. 17th rgt. (Ag. 1, 1814).

Satchvell, Isaac. Seaman of the privateer *Comet.*

Satterfield, —. Captain in 19th rgt. [1814].

Sauerwein, Peter [1797-1858]. Private in Capt. Sadtler's co. Balto. Yägers.

Saulsbury, Thomas. Captain in 10th Cavalry Dist. (N. 3, 1812).

Saulsby, John. Private in Capt. Mc-Conkey's co. 27th rgt.

Saunders, Alexander. Private in Capt. Brown's co. Eagle Artillerists.

Saunders, Benedict. Private in Capt. Robey's co. 43d rgt.

Saunders, Benedict J. Private in Capt. Steever's co. 27th rgt.

Saunders, Edward. Ensign in Capt. Sheckle's co. 42d rgt. (Jy. 15, 1814).

Saunders, George. Ensign in Capt. Stake's co. 10th rgt. [1813].

Saunders, Humphrey. Captain in 1st Rifle Battalion (S. 20, 1813) vice Reynolds.

Saunders, James. Private in Capt. Schwarzauer's co. 27th rgt.

Saunders, John F. R. Private in Cap. Brown's co. 43d rgt.

Saunders, Thomas. Lieutenant in Capt. Casey's co. 18th rgt. (S. 30, 1797).

Saunders, Thomas B. Sergeant in Capt. Dent's co. 43d rgt.

Saunders, William. Lieutenant in 2d rgt. (Je. 26, 1812).

Savage, Samuel. Private in Capt. Blair's co. 50th rgt.

Savage, William. Surgeon's mate in 37th rgt. Resigned Ag. 5, 1814.

Savery, John. Ensign in 38th (My. 20, 1813); 2d Lieutenant (My. 23, 1814).

Sawner, George. Private in Capt. Rogers' co. 51st rgt.

Sawner, John. Private in Capt. Rogers' co. 51st rgt.

Saxton, Joseph. Private in Capt. Burgess's co. 43d rgt.

Say, John. Lieutenant in Capt. Gosnell's co. 7th rgt. (Ap. 27, 1813).

Say, John. Private in Capt. Ducker's co. 7th rgt.

Saylor, Jacob. Private in Capt. McLaughlin's co. 50th rgt.

Saylor, Matthias. Private in Capt. Shryock's co. 24th rgt.

Saylor, Samuel. Private in Capt. Shryock's co. 24th rgt.

Scaff, George. Private in Capt. Stewart's co. 51st rgt.

Scanlon, James. Surgeon's mate in 8th Cavalry Dist. (Ag. 20, 1813) ; Surgeon (O. 13, 1814).

Scantling, James. Private in Capt. Rogers' co. 51st rgt.

Scarborough, Edward. Captain in 9th rgt. (Jy. 8, 1814).

Scarborough, John. Sergeant in Capt. Hall's co. 30th rgt.

Scarf, William. Private in Capt. Deems' co. 51st rgt.

Scarfe, William. Paymaster in 46th rgt. (Ag. 1, 1808).

Schaeffer, Christian. Private in Capt. Pennington's co. Balto. Independent Artillerists.

Schaeffer, F. G. Private in Capt. Magruder's co. American Artillerists.

Schaffer, Christian. Private in Capt. Thos. Warner's co. 39th rgt.

Schaffner, Jacob. Private in Capt. Steiner's Frederick Artillery.

Scharffer, William. Private in Cape. Bader's co. Union Yägers.

Schaub, Jacob [1779-1852]. Private in Capt. Bader's co. Union Yägers.

Scheehter, Henry. Captain in 10th rgt. (Ag. 2, 1814).

Schissler, John. Private in Capt. Steiner's Frederick Artillery.

Schleigh, William. Private in Capt. Quantrill's co. 24th rgt.

Schley, Jacob. Private in Capt. Moale's co. Columbian Artillery.

Schmeckpeper, J. R. Private in Capt. Sadtler's co. Balto. Yägers.

Schminke, George [1776-1847]. Private in Capt. Sadtler's co. Balto. Yägers.

Schnebley, John. Private in Capt. Quantrill's co. 24th rgt.

Schnebly, Daniel. Quarter-master in 8th rgt. (Ag. 22, 1812).

Schnebly, James. Captain in 8th rgt. (F. 9, 1814).

Schoffer, Jacob. Private in Capt. McLaughlin's co. 50th rgt.

Schofield, —. Captan in 19th rgt. [1814].

Schofield, J. S. Private in Capt. Brown's co. Eagle Artillerists.

Schoolfield, W. A. Captain in 23d rgt.; Major (D. 10, 1813).

Schorb, Andrew. Private in Capt. Myers' co. 39th rgt.

Schriver, Jacob. Private in Capt. Steiner's Frederick Artillery.

Schroeder, Edward. Private in Capt. Warfield's co. Balto. United Volunteers.

Schroeder, George. Private in Capt. Stewart's co. 51st rgt.

Schroeder, Henry. Private in Capt. Bader's co. Union Yägers.

Schroeder, John. Private in Capt. Ringgold's co. 6th rgt.

Schroeder, William. 3d Lieutenant in Capt. Moale's co. Columbian Artillery (Mr. 23, 1814).

Schroyer, Daniel. Private in Capt. Rogers' co. 51st rgt.

Schryake, Samuel. Private in Capt. Steuart's Washington Blues.

Schryock, David. Private in Capt. Quantrill's co. 24th rgt.

Schuchts, John Henry [1753-1848]. Lieutenant-Colonel in 2d rgt.

Schultz, Conrad. Private in Capt. Pike's co. Balto. Volunteer Artillery.

Schultz, John. Private in Capt. Bader's co. Union Yägers.

Schultz, John H. Lieutenant-Colonel in 46th rgt. (Jy. 14, 1812).

Schunck, John. Private in Capt. Peters' co. 51st rgt.

Schunck, Philip. Private in Capt. Peters' co. 51st rgt.

Schunk, Jacob. Private in Capt. Chalmers' co. 51st rgt.

Schutt, Augustin. Private in Capt. Sadtler's co. Balto. Yägers.

Schwarer, George. Corporal in Capt. Sands' co. 22d rgt.; Private in Capt. Slicer's co. 22d rgt. [1814].

Schwartz, A. J. B. Private in Capt. Pennington's co. Balto. Independent Artillerists.

Schwartzauer, Daniel. Captain in 27th rgt. (My. 14, 1813).

Schwartze, Henry. Private in Capt. Nicholson's co. Balto. Fencibles.

Schwier, Joseph. Private in Capt. Sadtler's co. Balto. Yägers.

Scipe, Michael. Private in Capt. Dobbin's co. 39th rgt.

Scoby, John. Private in Capt. Rogers' co. 51st rgt.

Scott, Abraham. Lieutenant in Capt. McConkey's co. 27th rgt.

Scott, Alexander. Private in Capt. Causin's co. 4th Cavalry Dist.

Scott, Charles. Private in Capt. Snowden's co. 36th rgt.

Scott, Edward. Captain in 33d rgt. (Jy. 25, 1807).

Scott, Edward. Surgeon in 33d rgt. (O. 13, 1814).

Scott, Henry. Private in Capt. Moale's co. Columbian Artillery.

Scott, Henry D. Private in Capt. Sterett's co. 1st Balto. Hussars.

Scott, Jeremiah. Private in Capt. Moale's co. Columbian Artillery.

Scott, John. Private in Capt. Stiles' co. Marine Artillery.

Scott, John. Private in Capt. Snowden's co. 36th rgt.

Scott, John. Private in Capt. Cawood's co. 45th rgt.

Scott, John L. Private in Capt. Faster's co. 51st rgt.

Scott, Joseph. Private in Capt. Addison's co. Sea Fencibles.

Scott, Manoah. Private in Capt. Crawfurd's co. 17th rgt.

Scott, Moses. Private in Capt. Mackey's co. 49th rgt.

Scott, Richard. Private in Capt. Addison's co. Sea Fencibles.

Scott, Richard K. Private in Capt. Crawfurd's co. 17th rgt.

Scott, Robert. Private in Capt. Lawrence's co. 6th rgt.

Scott, Samuel. Corporal in Capt. Sterett's co. 1st Balto. Hussars.

Scott, Solomon, Jr. Captain in 35th rgt. (Mr. 23, 1814).

Scott, Thomas. Private in Capt. Steiner's Frederick Artillery.

*Scott, William. Ensign in 2d sublegion (My. 1, 1795); 1st Lieutenant (Mr. 3, 1799); Captain (N. 8, 1800); Lieutenant-Colonel in 36th U. S. Infantry (Mr. 25, 1813).

Scott, William. Leutenant in Capt. Wade's co. 44th rgt. (Ag. 22, 1812).

Scott, William. Private in Capt. Dent's co. 43d rgt.

Scott, William. Sergeant in Capt. Oldham's co. 30th rgt.

Scott, William B. Paymaster in 4th Cavalry Dist. (D. 18, 1812); Adjutant (Mr. 4, 1813) vice Briscoe.

Scott, Zachariah. Private in Capt. Dunnington's co. 43d rgt.

Scracklin, Lewis. Private in Capt. Bunbury's co. Sea Fencibles.

Scrivan, William. Ensign in Capt. Chambers' co. 21st rgt. (Je. 10, 1809).

Scrivener, John. Lieutenant in Capt. Simmons' co. 2d rgt. (Mr. 29, 1813).

Scroggin, George. Private in Capt. Posey's co. 1st rgt.

Scroggin, James. Corporal in Capt. Posey's co. 1st rgt.

Scroggs, John. Private in Capt. Myers' co. 39th rgt.

Seamons, Charles. Private in Capt. John Miller's co. 2d D. I.; b. Berkeley Co., Va.; age 24; distiller; subs. for John Easton.

Seamons, Joseph. Private in Capt. John Miller's co. 2d D. I.; Berkley Co., Va.; age 20; boatman; subs. for William Murdock.

Sears, George. Sergeant in Capt. Warfield's co. Balto. United Volunteers.

Sears, George. 3d Lieutenant in 1st U. S. Infantry (S. 16, 1814).

Sears, James. Private in Capt. Veitch's co. 34th rgt.

Sears, Jesse. Private in Capt. Veitch's co. 34th rgt.

Seaton, Henry. Private in Capt. Berry's co. Washington Artillery.

Seaton, Robert. Private in Capt. Hanna's co. Fells Point Light Dragoons.

Seavon, William. Private in Capt. Smith's co. 51st rgt.

Sederburgh, Trol. Private in Capt. A. E. Warner's co. 39th rgt.

Sedwick, Joseph C. Private in Capt. Dent's co. 43d rgt.

Seemon, Jacob. Private in Capt. Rogers' co. 51st rgt.

Seers, William, Jr. Lieutenant in Capt. Wallace's co. 18th rgt. (D. 4, 1810).

Seig, Peter. Private in Capt. Pike's co. Balto. Volunteer Artillery.

Selby, John of James. Ensign in Capt. Hatchison's co. 9th rgt. (Jy. 8, 1814).

Selby, John of Parker. Captain in 9th rgt. (Je. 22, 1808).

Sellers, —. Sailing-master of the privateer *Kemp*.

Sellers, John [1794-1879]. Private in Capt. Adam Showers' co. 15th rgt.

Sellers, John. Private in Capt. Deems' co. 51st rgt.

Sellman, Thomas. Lieutenant in Capt. Franklin's co. 2d rgt. (Ag. 26, 1807).

Sellman, William. Lieutenant in Capt. Dorsey's co. 13th rgt. (My. 12, 1812).

Seltzer, Jacob. Private in Capt. Horton's co. Maryland Chasseurs.

Seltzer, Lewis. Private in Capt. Horton's co. Maryland Chasseurs.

Selvey, John S. Private in Capt. Crawfurd's co. 17th rgt.

Semmes, Alexander. Private in Capt. Dent's co. 43d rgt.

Semmes, Joseph M. Private in Capt. Dunnington's co. 43d rgt.

Semmes, Raphael. Private in Capt. Dunnington's co. 43d rgt.

Senseny, Jacob. Private in Capt. Stewart's co. 51st rgt.

Sergeant, Alling. Sergeant in Capt. Pinney's co. 27th rgt.

Seth, Jacob. Cornet in Capt. Godwin's co. 9th Cavalry Dist. (Je. 1, 1813).

Seth, John. Captain in 26th rgt. (Jy. 31, 1812).

Seth, John. Lieutenant in Capt. Jas. Massey's co. 38th rgt.

Seth, William, Jr. Ensign in Capt. Parks' co. 35th rgt. (Je. 15, 1812).

Severson, Thomas. Private in Capt. Faster's co. 51st rgt.

Sewall, Clement. 2d Lieutenant in 36th U. S. Infantry (Ap. 30, 1813); 1st Lieutenant (My. 1, 1814).

Sewall, James. Brigade-Major, 1st Brigade.

Sewall, John R. Private in Capt. Wilson's co. 31st rgt.

Seward, William. Private in Capt. Jas. Massey's co. 38th rgt.

Sewell, Benjamin. Private in Capt. Pinkney's Artillery co. 22d rgt.

Sewell, Elijah. Sergeant in Capt. Weems' co. 22d rgt.

Sewell, Jacob. Private in Capt. Spencer's co. 26th rgt.

Sewell, John. Private in Capt. Maynard's co. 22d rgt. Ag., 1813; Private in Capt. Slicer's co. 22d rgt. N., 1814.

Sewell, John M. Private in Capt. Warfield's co. Balto. United Volunteers.

Sewell, Joseph. Sergeant in Capt. Steever's co. 27th rgt.

Sewell, Reuben. Private in Capt. Stewart's co. 51st rgt.

Sewell, Robert. Captain in 17th rgt. (Ap. 4, 1800).

Sewell, Robert, Jr. Ensign in Capt. Coe's co. 17th rgt. (Jy. 11, 1814).

Sewell, William. Sergeant in Capt. Montgomery's co. Balto. Union Artillery.

Sexton, Charles. Private in Capt. Wilson's co. 6th rgt.

Seyler, Frederick. Private in Capt. Sterett's Independent co.

Seymour, Richard. Private in Capt. Hands' co. 21st rgt.

Shaaff, Arthur. Private in Capt. Maynard's co. 22d rgt.

Shade, John. Private in Capt. Montgomery's co. Balto. Union Artillery.

Shade, William G. Ensign in 14th U. S. Infantry (Mr. 18, 1813); 3d Lieutenant (O. 1, 1813).

Shaeffer, Joseph. Private in Capt. Deems' co. 51st rgt.

Shafer, George. Lieutenant in Capt. Benner's co. 10th rgt. Resigned, Aug. 2, 1814.

Shaffer, David. Private in Capt. Blizzard's co. 15th rgt.

Shaffer, James. Private in Capt. Sheppard's co. 6th rgt.

Shaffer, Martin. Lieutenant in Capt. Murray's co. 15th rgt. (D. 24, 1810).

Shaffer, Nicholas. Sergeant in Capt. Ducker's co. 7th rgt.

Shafner, Jacob. Private in Capt. Schwarzauer's co. 27th rgt.

Shakspear, Jonathan. Private in Capt. Taylor's co. 46th rgt.

Shall, William. Ensign in Capt. Quantrill's co. 24th rgt.

Shamburgh, John. Private in Capt. Pike's co. Balto. Volunteer Artillery.

Shane, Daniel. Private in Capt. Shrim's co. Balto. Light Infantry.

Shane, Dennis. Private in Capt. Pennington's co. Balto. Independent Artillerists.

Shane, Michael. Private in Capt. Wilson's co. 6th rgt.

Shank, John. 1st Lieutenant in Capt. Phillips' co. 2d rgt. 1st Cavalry Dist. (Mr. 16, 1812).

Shank, Samuel. Private in Capt. Quantrill's co. 24th rgt.

Shanks, George. Private in Capt. Blakistone's co. 45th rgt.

Shanks, Peregrine. Ensign in Capt. Blakistone's co. 45th rgt. (Ag. 10, 1813).

Shanna, Burton. Private in Capt. Brown's co. 43d rgt.

Shannon, John. Private in Capt. Rogers' co. 51st rgt.

Shapleigh, John. Captain in 24th rgt. Resigned Jy. 12, 1814.

Sharar, John. Ensign in Capt. Jonathan Norris' co. 20th rgt. (Jy. 7, 1814).

Share, Joseph. Private in Capt. Pike's co. Balto. Volunteer Artillery.

Sharer, Jacob. Private in Capt. Blizzard's co. 15th rgt.

Sharkey, Michael. Private in Capt. Montgomery's co. Balto. Union Artillery.

Sharp, Henry. Lieutenant of the privateer *Vixen,* Nov. 1814.

Sharrer, George. Sergeant in Capt. Roney's co. 39th rgt.

Shartle, Henry. Private in Capt. Addison's co. Sea Fencibles.

Shauman, George. Captain in 10th rgt. (Ap. 30, 1811).

Shaw, Daniel. Private in Capt. Stiles' co. Marine Artillery.

Shaw, George. Private in Capt. Maynard's co. 22d rgt.

Shaw, Isaiah. Private in Capt. Howard's co. Mechanical Volunteers.

Shaw, Jacob. Private in Capt. Shryock's co. 24th rgt.

Shaw, James. Ensign in Capt. Bagg's co. Extra Battalion Caroline Co. (Ap. 28, 1808).

Shaw, James. Private in Capt. Hynson's co. 21st rgt.

Shaw, James. Private in Capt. Maynard's co. 22d rgt.

Shaw, James B. Private in Balto. Union Artillery.

Shaw, Joshua. Private in Capt. Green's co. 46th rgt.

Shaw, Nathan. Private in Capt. Magruder's co. American Artillerists.

Shaw, Samuel. Private in Capt. Pike's co. Balto. Volunteer Artillery.

Shaw, Samuel. Private in Capt. Adreon's co. Union Volunteers.

Shaw, Samuel H. Private in Capt. Sheppard's co. 6th rgt.

Shaw, William. Private in Capt. Shryock's co. 24th rgt.

Shaw, William. Private in Capt. Robey's co. 43d rgt.

Shaw, William. Private in Capt. Green's co. 46th rgt.

Shaw, William. Sergeant in Capt. Blair's co. 50th rgt.

Shaw, William C. Private in Capt. Moale's co. Columbian Artillery.

Shawan, James. Ensign in Capt. Turbett's co. 16th rgt. (Ap. 28, 1813).

Shea, Harvey. Private in Capt. Deems' co. 51st rgt.

Sheamer, James. Private in Capt. Kennedy's co. 27th rgt.

Shearman, I. Lewis. Private in Capt. Bunbury's co. Sea Fencibles.

Sheaves, Robert. Private in Capt. Miller's co. 39th rgt.

Shebboard, John. Private in Capt. Snowden's co. 36th rgt.

Sheckle, William. Captain in 42d rgt. (S. 21, 1813).

Sheebe, John. Private in Capt. Berry's Washington Artillery.

Sheffer, Jesse. Private in Capt. Horton's co. Maryland Chasseurs.

Shehey, Michael. Private in Capt. Addison's co. Sea Fencibles.

Sheldon, Curtis. Sergeant in Capt. McKane's co. 27th rgt.

Sheldon, James. Private in Capt. Chalmers' co. 51st rgt.

Sheldon, John. Private in Capt. Chalmers' co. 51st rgt.

Shelhouse, John. Private in Capt. Blair's co. 50th rgt.

Shellhorn, Henry. Private in Capt. McLaughlin's co. 50th rgt.

Shellman, Jacob. Private in Capt. Steiner's Frederick Artillery.

Shenton, Dennard. Private in Capt. Travers' co. 48th rgt.

Shenton, John. Private in Capt. Travers' co. 48th rgt.

Shenton, Richard. Private in Capt. Travers' co. 48th rgt.

Shenton, Thomas. Private in Capt. Travers' co. 48th rgt.

Shenton, William. Private in Capt. Travers' co. 48th rgt.

Shepard, Richard. Private in Capt. Hancock's co. 22d rgt.

Shepherd, John. Private in Capt. Blair's co. 50th rgt.

Shepherd, Samuel B. Private in Capt. Dyer's co. 17th rgt.

Sheppard, Basil. Private in Capt. Pinkney's Artillery co.; Sergeant in Capt. Wells' co. Ag., 1814.

Sheppard, David. Private in Capt. Rogers' co. 51st rgt.

Sheppard, James. Private in Capt. Chase's co. 22d rgt.

Sheppard, Thomas [1777-1848]. Captain in 6th rgt.

Sheppard, Yankey. Seaman of the privateer *Chasseur;* severely wounded in action with H. M. Schr. *Lawrence,* Feb. 27, 1815.

Sheridan, Thomas. Private in Capt. Brown's co. Eagle Artillerists.

Sherman, Nathan. Captain of the privateer *Torpedo,* Jan., 1815.

Shermentine, George. Private in Capt. Jarboe's co. 12th rgt.

Sherry, James. Private in Capt. McLaughlin's co. 50th rgt.

Sherwood, Philip. Private in Capt. Galt's co. 6th rgt.

Sherwood, Philip. Private in Capt. Dyer's co. Fells Point Riflemen.

Sherwood, William. Private in Capt. Massey's co. 38th rgt.

Shields, James. Private in Capt. Rogers' co. 51st rgt.

Shields, Leadman. 1st Lieutenant in Capt. Vinson's Artillery co. 12th Brigade (D. 10, 1813). Re-signed Ja., 1815.

Shields, William. Private in Capt. Pennington's Balto. Independent Artillerists.

Shields, William. Private in Capt. Stewart's co. 51st rgt.

Shinn, Joseph. Private in Capt. Getzendanner's co. 16th rgt.

Shinnick, J. Quarter-master Sergeant in Capt. Hanna's co. Fells Point Light Dragoons.

Shipley, Benjamin. Private in Capt. Hall's co. 3d Cavalry rgt.

Shipley, Brice. 1st Sergeant in Capt. Snowden's co. 36th rgt.

Shipley, Henry. Ensign in Capt. C. D. Warfield's co. 32d rgt. vice Welsh.

Shipley, John. Private in Capt. Quantrill's co. 24th rgt.

Shipley, Joshua. Sergeant in Capt. Smith's co. 51st rgt.

Shipley, Larkin. Quarter-master 3d Cavalry Dist. (O. 22, 1812).

Shipley, Lloyd. Cornet in Capt. Thomas' co. 3d Cavalry Dist. (My. 8, 1812); 2d Lieutenant (Jy. 6, 1814).

Shipley, Peter. Ensign in Capt. Bond's co. 7th rgt. (Je. 26, 1812).

Shipley, Samuel. Private in Capt. Stiles' co. Marine Artillery.

Shipley, Samuel. Corporal in Capt. Marker's co. 28th rgt.

Shipley, William. Private in Capt. Rogers' co. 51st rgt

Shipley, William. Private in Capt. Smith's co. 51st rgt.

Shipley, Zachariah. Private in Capt. Deems' co. 51st rgt.

Shircliff, Lewis. Private in Capt. Blair's co. 50th rgt.

Shirkey, James. Private in Capt. Oldham's co. 49th rgt.

Shirkliff, Leonard. Ensign in Capt. Beven's co. 50th rgt. (O. 16, 1810).

Shoat, Abraham. Private in Capt. Rogers' co. 51st rgt.

Shock, Henry. Private in Capt. Sterett's Independent co.

Shock, Peter. Captain in 41st rgt. (O. 30, 1794).

Shockey, John. Private in Capt. Blair's co. 50th rgt.

Shockney, John. Corporal in Capt. Blizzard's co. 15th rgt.

Shockney, Samuel. Corporal in Capt. Blizzard's co. 15th rgt.

Shoeff, Isaac. Private in Capt. Roney's co. 39th rgt.

Shoemaker, George. Ensign in Capt. Faster's co. 51st rgt.

Sholl, Christian. Private in Capt. Getzendanner's co. 16th rgt.

Shooke, George, Jr. Ensign in Capt. Blair's co. 50th rgt. (S. 22, 1811).

Short, John. Lieutenant in Capt. Williamson's co. 49th rgt. (Je. 26, 1810).

Short, John. Private in Capt. Waters' co. 22d rgt.

Short, P. Seaman of the privateer *Globe*, wounded in action, Nov. 1, 1813.

Shorter, Cain. Private in Capt. Mc-Namara's co. 48th rgt.

Shorter, William. Private in Capt. McNamara's co. 48th rgt.

Shortridge, John. Private in Capt. Levering's co. Independent Blues.

Shortt, John. Private in Capt. Nicholson's co. Balto. Fencibles.

Shoults, Abner. Private in Capt. Wells' Artillery co. 22d rgt.

Showers, Adam. Captain in 15th rgt. (D. 24, 1810).

Shreck, William. Private in Capt. Dyer's co. Fells Point Riflemen.

Shrim, John. Captain Balto. Light Infantry (Je. 26, 1795).

Shriver, Charles. Private in Capt. Pumphrey's co. 22d rgt.

Shriver, Isaac. Quarter-master in 2d rgt. 1st Cavalry Dist. (Ap. 23, 1813).

Shriver, Jacob. Captain in 2d rgt. 1st Cavalry Dist. (F. 13, 1812); Major (S. 18, 1812).

Shriver, Jacob. Private in Capt. Blair's co. 50th rgt.

Shrote, Mathias. Corporal in Capt. Smith's co. 51st rgt.

Shrote, Mathias, Jr. Private in Capt. Smith's co. 51st rgt.

Shroy, John. Private in Capt. John Miller's co. 2d D. I.; b. Germany; age 36; stone-mason.

Shryark, Samuel. Private in Capt. Addison's co. Sea Fencibles.

Shryock, George. Captain in 24th rgt. (Jy. 12, 1814) vice John Harry.

Shuck, George. Lieutenant in Capt. McLaughlin's co. 50th rgt.

Shuck, Jacob. Sergeant in Capt. Blair's co. 50th rgt.

Shuck, John. Private in Capt. Mc-Laughlin's co. 50th rgt.

Shuler, Frederick. Ensign in Capt. Galt's co. 47th rgt. (Je. 6, 1811).

Shull, John. Cornet in Capt. Zacharias' co. 2d rgt. 1st Cavalry Dist. (Je. 15, 1813).

Shultz, Jacob. Sergeant in Capt. Rogers' co. 51st rgt.

Shumack, Stephen. Private in Capt. Myers' co. Franklin Artillery.

Shutt, George. Private in Capt. Berry's co. Washington Artillery.

Shutt, John P. Private in Capt. Steuart's co. Washington Blues.

Shyrach, Charles. Private in Capt. Pinney's co. 27th rgt.

*Sibert, David. Private, command unknown. Widow pensioned by Legislature.

Sible, John H. Private in Capt. Sands' co. 22d rgt.

Sibley, James. Ensign in Capt. Jackson's co. 34th rgt. (Je. 27, 1812).

Siddler, Benjamin. Private in Capt. Haubert's co. 51st rgt.

Siford, David. Private in Capt. Blair's co. 50th rgt.

Sifton, John. Private in Capt. Hall's co. 34th rgt.

Sifton, William. Private in Capt. Howard's co. Mechanical Volunteers.

Sikes, John. Private in Capt. Blizzard's co. 15th rgt.

Silance, Richard. Private in Capt. Dobbin's co. 39th rgt.

Sillman, Thomas D. Private in Capt. Moale's co. Columbian Artillery.

Silver, David. Ensign in Capt. Stephenson's co. 42d rgt. (D. 10, 1807).

Silvers, William. Lieutenant in Capt. Jacob Albert's co. Extra Battalion Harford co. Transferred to cavalry, 1814.

Silverthorn, Henry. Private in Capt. Dobbin's co. 39th rgt.

Silvester, Thomas. Ensign in Capt. Chaffinch's co. 19th rgt. (Ag. 20, 1814).

Simes, John. Private in Capt. Pumphrey's co. 22d rgt.

Simes, Thomas. Private in Capt. Pumphrey's co. 22d rgt.

Simmering, Christian. Private in Capt. Miller's co. 39th rgt.

Simmering, John. Private in Capt. Miller's co. 39th rgt.

Simmonds, George G. Private in Capt. Griffith's co. 21st rgt.

Simmonds, John A. Private in Capt. Magruder's co. American Artillerists.

Simmonds, Samuel. Private in Capt. Magruder's co. American Artillerists.

Simmonds, Thomas T. Captain in 2d rgt.

Simmons, Edward. Private in Capt. Brohawn's co. 48th rgt.

Simmons, Elisha. Drummer in Capt. Sample's co. 49th rgt.

Simmons, Hezekiah. Private in Capt. Burgess' co. 43d rgt.

Simmons, James, Jr. Lieutenant in Capt. Easterday's co. 28th rgt. (Ap. 28, 1808).

Simmons, John. Sergeant in Capt. Porter's co. 30th rgt.

Simmons, John. Private in Capt. Brohawn's co. 48th rgt.

Simmons, John H. Captain in 13th rgt. (Je. 26, 1804).

Simmons, Moses. Fifer in Capt. Brohawn's co. 48th rgt.

Simmons, Richard. Corporal in Capt. Gray's co. 43d rgt.

Simmons, Samuel W. Ensign in Capt. Heater's co. 44th rgt. (D. 16, 1813) vice Geo. Heater.

Simmons, Simon. Seaman of the privateer *Surprise*, drowned, April 5, 1815.

Simmons, Thomas P. Captain in 2d rgt. (S. 23, 1807).

Simmons, William. Private in Capt. Page's co. 21st rgt.

Simmons, William. Private in Capt. Snowden's co. 36th rgt.

Simons, James. Private in Capt. Addison's co. Sea Fencibles.

Simons, John. Lieutenant in Capt. Faster's co. 51st rgt.

Simonson, John. Sergeant in Capt. Shrim's co. Balto. Light Infantry.

Simpers, Benjamin. Private in Capt. Miller's co. 39th rgt.

Simpers, Benjamin. Private in Capt. Howard's co. Mechanical Volunteers.

Simpers, Thomas. Private in Capt. Sample's co. 49th rgt.

Simpkins, Eli. Corporal in Capt. Sterett's co. 1st Balto. Hussars.

Simpson, Erasmus. Private in Capt. Berry's co. Washington Artillery.

Simpson, Henry. Cornet in Capt. Ford's co. 8th Cavalry Dist. (Je. 12, 1812); 2d Lieutenant (Jy. 7, 1814).

Simpson, John. Private in Capt. Horton's co. Maryland Chasseurs.

Simpson, John. Musician in Capt. Myers' co. Franklin Artillery.

Simpson, John D. Private in Capt. Watson's co. 39th rgt.

Simpson, Joseph S. Ensign in 14th U. S. Infantry (My. 11, 1814); 3d Lieutenant (My. 30, 1814).

Simpson, Richard. Major in 30th rgt. (N. 7, 1812).

Simpson, Samuel. Private in Capt. Stewart's co. 51st rgt.

Simpson, Thomas. Private in Capt. Maynard's co. 22d rgt.

Simpson, Walter. Quarter-master Sergeant in 6th rgt.

Simpson, William. Private in Capt. Burgess' co. 43d rgt.

Sinclair, —. Ensign in Capt. Galloway's co. 46th rgt. Resigned Jy. 14, 1814.

Sinclair, Alexander. Private in Capt. McDonald's co. 6th rgt.

Sinclair, James. Corporal in Capt. McDonald's co. 6th rgt.

Sinclair, James. Private in Capt. Howard's co. Mechanical Volunteers.

Sinclair, John. Ensign in Capt. Lawson's co. Balto. Patriots.

Sinclair, Matthew. Private in Capt. McConkey's co. 27th rgt.

Sinclair, Perry. Private in Capt. Lawrence's co. 6th rgt.

Sindal, Solomon. Private in Capt. Green's co. 46th rgt.

Sindall, John. Private in Capt. Howard's co. Mechanical Volunteers.

Sindell, John. Private in Capt. Peters' co. 51st rgt.

Sindell, Joshua. Private in Capt. Peters' co. 51st rgt.

Sindell, Thomas. Private in Capt. Peters' co. 51st rgt.

Sindle, Abraham. Lieutenant in Capt. Taylor's co. 46th rgt. (Jy. 8, 1814) vice Christopher.

Sindorff, Joseph. Corporal in Capt. Dobbin's co. 39th rgt.

Singer, George. Private in Capt. Sadtler's co. Balto. Yägers.

Singleton, Charles. Private in Capt. Moale's co. Columbian Artillery.

Singleton, Peter. Sergeant in Capt. Taylor's co. 46th rgt.

Sinley, Alexander. Corporal in Capt. Steever's co. 27th rgt.

Sinners, E. R. Private in Capt. Pennington's co. Balto. Independent Artillerists.

Sinton, Francis. Private in Capt. Addison's co. Sea Fencibles.

Sinton, Joseph. Private in Capt. Edes' co. 27th rgt.

Sinton, Joseph. Private in Capt. Peters' co. 51st rgt.

Sisser, Martin. Private in Capt. Haubert's co. 51st rgt.

Six, Leonard. Cornet in Capt. Thompson's co. 2d rgt. 1st Cavalry Dist. (Je. 26, 1812).

Skelton, John. Private in Capt. Mc-Conkey's co. 27th rgt.

Skiles, John. Sergeant in Capt. Myers' co. 39th rgt.

Skinner, Addington. Private in Capt. Beall's co. 34th rgt.

Skinner, Ewell. Private in Capt. Brown's co. 43d rgt.

Skinner, Fordyce. Private in Capt. Brown's co. 43d rgt.

Skinner, James. Ensign in Capt. Linthicum's co. 48th rgt. (S. 21, 1813).

Skinner, John. Private in Capt. Dent's co. 43d rgt.

Skinner, Oliver. Private in Capt. Brown's co. 43d rgt.

Skinner, Richard. Captain in 17th rgt. (S. 16, 1807).

Skinner, Richard. Private in Capt. Massey's co. 38th rgt.

Skinner, Richard. Private in Capt. Burgess's co. 43d rgt.

Skinner, Sylvester. Private in Capt. Brown's co. 43d rgt.

Skipper, David. Private in Capt. Addison's co. Sea Fencibles.

Skirven, William. Ensign in Capt. Chambers' co. 21st rgt.

Sky, Gattiel. Private in Capt. Lawrence's co. 6th rgt.

Slack, David. Corporal in Capt. Owings' co. 32d rgt.

Slack, James. Private in Capt. Stewart's co. 51st rgt.

Slade, William. Ensign in Capt. Almony's co. 41st rgt. (Je. 1, 1813).

Slater, Alexander. Private in Capt. Brown's co. 6th rgt.

Slater, Benjamin. Private in Capt. Ringgold's co. 6th rgt.

Slater, James. Corporal in Capt. Conway's co. 6th rgt.

Slater, John. Sergeant in Capt. Brown's co. 6th rgt.

Slater, John. Private in Capt. Green's co. 46th rgt.

Slater, William. Private in Capt. Green's co. 46th rgt.

Slaughter, Lee [-1842]. Private Corporal and Sergeant in 14th U. S. Infantry, 1813.

Slaughter, Samuel. 1st Lieutenant in Capt. Hughlett's co. 10th Cavalry Dist. (Je. 18, 1812); Captain (Ap. 23, 1813).

Slaughter, William. Private in Capt. Morgan's co. 49th rgt.

Slayton, David. Private in Capt. Myers' co. Franklin Artillery.

Sleekum, Peter. Private in Capt. Galt's co. 6th rgt.

Sleemaker, John P. Lieutenant in Capt. Taylor's co. 37th rgt. (Ja. 21, 1814).

Sleeper, Jonathan. Private in Capt. Sterett's co. 1st Balto. Hussars.

Slemaker, Jacob H. Lieutenant in Capt. Slicer's co. 22d. rgt. (Ap. 22, 1814).

Slemmer, Christian. Private in Capt. Peters' co. 51st rgt.

Slewman, William. Private in Capt. McDonald's co. 6th rgt.

Slicer, Andrew [1774-1865]. Lieutenant in Capt. Sand's co. 22d rgt. (Ag. 20, 1813); Captain (Ap. 22, 1814).

Slight, Thomas. Ensign in Capt. Hurley's co. 11th rgt. (Ja. 25, 1814).

Slingluff, Jesse. Private in Capt. Thompson's co. 1st Baltimore Horse Artillery.

Sliver, John. Private in Capt. Steever's co. 27th rgt.

Sloan, James, Jr. Private in Capt. McKane's co. 27th rgt.

Sloan, William. Surgeon's mate in 14th U. S. Infantry (Je. 28, 1814).

Sluk, John. Lieutenant in Capt. Knox's co. 47th rgt. (Ap. 18, 1809).

Slusman, Jacob. Private in Capt. John Miller's co. 2d D. I.; b. Chester Co., Pa.; age 32; wagoner; subs. for William Reynolds.

Sluss, Michael. Captain in 47th rgt. (Je. 12, 1812).

Sly, Richard of P. Private in Capt. Hance's co. 31st rgt.

Sly, Samuel. Sergeant in Capt. Hance's co. 31st rgt.

Slye, George. 3d Lieutenant in 36th U. S. Infantry (Ap. 30, 1813); 2d Lieutenant (F. 21, 1814).

Small, Jacob. Lieutenant-Colonel in 39th rgt.; Brigade Quarter-master 3d Brigade.

Small, John. Sergeant in Capt. Bader's co. Union Yägers.

Small, John. Private in Capt. Sterett's Independent co.

Smallwood, George. Private in Capt. Miller's co. 39th rgt.

Smallwood, John. Private in Capt. Burgess' co. 43d rgt.

Smallwood, Nicholas. Lieutenant in Capt. Van Horn's co. 14th rgt. (My. 23, 1799).

Smelser, Jacob. Captain in 28th rgt. (Je. 26, 1812).

Smewings, James. Private in Capt. Kennedy's co. 27th rgt.

Smith, Adam. Private in Capt. Galt's co. 6th rgt.

Smith, Adam. Private in Capt. Smith's co. 51st rgt.

Smith, Alexander. Quarter-master in 11th rgt. Resigned Ja. 25, 1814.

Smith, Alexander. Private in Capt. Bunbury's co. Sea Fencibles.

Smith, Andrew. Captain in 47th rgt. (N. 28, 1808).

Smith, Andrew. Captain in 51st rgt. (Jy. 28, 1813).

Smith, Andrew. Private in Capt. A. E. Warner's co. 39th rgt.

Smith, Andrew C. Captain in 49th rgt. (Mr. 25, 1811).

Smith, Anthony. Cornet in Capt. Hammond's co. 3d Cavalry Dist. (Jy. 6, 1814) vice Dorsey.

Smith, Arthur. Ensign in Capt. Chas. Jones' co. 7th rgt. (Ag. 30, 1808).

Smith, Augustin. Private in Capt. Blakistone's co. 45th rgt.

Smith, Basil. Private in Capt. Jarboe's co. 12th rgt.

Smith, Benjamin. Corporal in Capt. Quantrill's co. 24th rgt.

Smith, Benjamin. Private in Capt. Oldham's co. 49th rgt.

Smith, Benjamin B. [1786-1833]. Master's mate of the privateer *Joseph and Mary*, wounded in action, Oct., 1812; Private in Capt. Stiles' co. Marine Artillery.

Smith, Charles. Private in Capt. Burgess' co. 43d rgt.

Smith, Charles. Private in Capt. Piper's co. United Maryland Artillery.

Smith, Christian. Private in Capt. A. E. Warner's co. 39th rgt.

Smith, Clement. Lieutenant in Capt. Whann's co. 18th rgt. (Ag. 16, 1799).

Smith, Cyrus. Private in Capt. Mc-Kane's co. 27th rgt.

Smith, Daniel. Private in Capt. Quantrill's co. 24th rgt.

Smith, Daniel. Private in Capt. Shryock's co. 24th rgt.

Smith, David. Private in Capt. Mc-Kane's co. 27th rgt.

Smith, David D. Corporal in Capt. Smith's co. 51st rgt.

Smith, Dennis A. Private in Capt. Snowden's co. 36th rgt.

Smith, Edward. Private in Capt. Galt's co. 6th rgt.

Smith, Elie. Private in Capt. Smith's co. 51st rgt.

Smith, George. Private in Capt. Dillon's co. 27th rgt.

Smith, George. Private in Capt. Steever's co. 27th rgt.

Smith, George. Private in Capt. Levering's co. Independent Blues.

Smith, George. Private in Capt. Shryock's co. 24th rgt.

Smith, George A. Lieutenant in Capt. Styll's co. 19th rgt. (Ap. 12, 1814).

Smith, George W. Captain in 4th rgt. (N. 6, 1811).

Smith, Gerrard. Private in Capt. Shryock's co. 24th rgt.

Smith, Gilbert. Private in Capt. Moore's co. 49th rgt.

Smith, Henry. Lieutenant in Capt. Huston's co. 16th rgt. (Jy. 15, 1814).

Smith, Henry. Private in Capt. Blair's co. 50th rgt.

Smith, Henry. Prize-master of the privateer *Baltimore*.

Smith, Henry C. Private in Capt. Sands' co. 22d rgt.

Smith, Horatio. Private in Capt. Pumphrey's co. 22d rgt.

Smith, Hugh. Corporal in Capt. Patton's co. 30th rgt.

Smith, Hugh. Private in Capt. Stapleton's co. 39th rgt.

Smith, J. Job. Private in Capt. Sheppard's co. 6th rgt.

Smith, Jacob. Lieutenant in Capt. Snider's co. 8th rgt. (My. 20, 1809).

Smith, Jacob. Private in Capt. Stewart's co. 51st rgt.

Smith, James. 1st Lieutenant in 38th U. S. Infantry (My. 20, 1813); Captain (My. 20, 1814).

Smith, James. 2d Lieutenant in Capt. Wright's Artillery co. 6th Brigade (S. 10, 1814) vice Harrison.

Smith, James. Corporal in Capt. Galt's co. 6th rgt.

Smith, James. Sergeant in Capt. Dobbin's co. 39th rgt.

Smith, James. Private in Capt. Watson's co. 39th rgt.

Smith, James. Corporal in Capt. Stewart's co. 51st rgt.

Smith, James. Private in Capt. Wickes' co. 21st rgt.

Smith, James P. Private in Capt. Sheppard's co. 6th rgt.

Smith, James P. Private in Capt. Crawfurd's co. 17th rgt.

Smith, Job, Jr. Private in Capt. Warfield's co. Balto. United Volunteers.

Smith, John. Lieutenant in Capt. Flant's co. 47th rgt. (Mr. 15, 1809).

Smith, John. 2d Lieutenant of the privateer *Globe*, killed in action, Nov. 1, 1813.

Smith, John. Private in Capt. Sheppard's co. 6th rgt.

Smith, John. Private in Capt. Quantrill's co. 24th rgt.

Smith, John. Private in Capt. Snowden's co. 36th rgt.

Smith, John. Drummer in Capt. Smoot's co. 43d rgt.

Smith, John. Private in Capt. Peters' co. 51st rgt.

Smith, John. Private in Capt. Adreon's co. Union Volunteers.

Smith, John. Private in Capt. Posey's co. 1st rgt.

Smith, John E. Private in Capt. Lawrence's co. 6th rgt.

Smith, John S. Private in Capt. Stiles' co. Marine Artillery.

Smith, John S. Private in Capt. Levering's co. Independent Blues.

Smith, John Spear. Volunteer Aid to Genl. Smith in 3d Division M. M.

Smith, Josiah A. Paymaster 1st Rifle Battalion.

Smith, Levin. Lieutenant in Capt. Bowman's co. 18th rgt. (O. 10, 1799).

Smith, Major. Lieutenant in Capt. Graves' co. 21st rgt.

Smith, Mathias. Corporal in Capt. Barnes' co. 32d rgt.

Smith, Nathaniel. Corporal in Capt. Bouldin's co. Independent Light Dragoons.

Smith, Nathaniel L. Private in Capt. Berry's co. Washington Artillery.

Smith, Nehemiah. Fifer in Capt. Lake's co. 48th rgt.

Smith, Nicholas. Private in Capt. Sadtler's co. Balto. Yägers.

Smith, Paca. Captain in 7th Cavalry Dist. (Mr. 16, 1812).

Smith, Peter. Private in Capt. Quantrill's co. 24th rgt.

Smith, Philemon. Captain, 1813, command unknown.

Smith, Ralph. Corporal in Capt. Nicholson's co. Balto. Fencibles.

Smith, Richard. Private in Capt. Wickes' co. 21st rgt.

Smith, Richard, Jr. Lieutenant in Capt. McWilliams' co. 45th rgt. (D. 12, 1812).

Smith, Richard N. Ensign in Capt. Smoot's co. 43d rgt. (Ap. 27, 1813).

Smith, Robert. Private in Capt. McKane's co. 27th rgt.

Smith, Sabritt. Private in Capt. Linthicum's co. 22d rgt.

Smith, Samuel. Ensign in Capt. McConcking's co. 38th rgt. (Jy. 7, 1814) vice Blunt.

Smith, Samuel [1752-1839]. Major General in 3d Division M. M.

Smith, Samuel. Private in Capt. Snowden's co. 36th rgt.

Smith, Samuel. Private in Capt. Umsted's co. 25th rgt.

Smith, Samuel. Private in Capt. Pennington's co. Balto. Independent Artillerists.

Smith, Samuel D. Seaman of the privateer *Globe*, killed in action, Nov. 1, 1813.

Smith, Samuel L. 1st Lieutenant in Capt. Carcaud's co. 3d Cavalry District (Mr. 26, 1812).

Smith, Samuel W. Ensign in Capt. Graves' co. 21st rgt.

Smith, Solomon. Drummer in Capt. Lake's co. 48th rgt.

Smith, Stoughton. Private in Capt. Heath's co. 23d rgt.

Smith, Thomas. Quarter-master in 21st rgt. (S. 3, 1807).

Smith, Thomas. Corporal in Capt. Lawrence's co. 6th rgt.

Smith, Thomas. Private in Capt. Edes' co. 27th rgt.

Smith, Thomas. Private in Capt. McConkey's co. 27th rgt.

Smith, Thomas. Private in Capt. Adreon's co. Union Volunteers.

Smith, Thomas S. Private in Capt. Sands' co. 22d rgt.

Smith, Walter. Private in Capt. Gray's co. 31st rgt.

Smith, William. Lieutenant-Colonel in 42d rgt.

Smith, William. Captain in 4th rgt. (Je. 18, 1794).

Smith, William. Private in Capt. Addison's co. Sea Fencibles.

Smith, William. Private in Capt. Conway's co. 6th rgt.

Smith, William. Private in Capt. Kierstead's co. 6th rgt.

Smith, William. Corporal in Capt. Shryock's co. 24th rgt.

Smith, William. Private in Capt. McConkey's co. 27th rgt.

Smith, William. Private in Capt. Smith's co. 51st rgt.

Smithson, Archibald. Private in Capt. Stapleton's co. 39th rgt.

Smithson, Daniel. Private in Capt. Shrim's co. Balto. Light Infantry.

Smithson, Gabriel [-1862]. Private in Capt. John Smithson's co. 40th rgt.

Smithson, John. Captain in 40th rgt. Rifle co. (Ja. 2, 1808).

Smithson, Luther. Private in Capt. Addison's co. Sea Fencibles.

Smithson, Nathan. Private in Capt. Deems' co. 51st rgt.

Smithson, Thomas. Private in Capt. Roney's co. 39th rgt.

Smithson, William. Private in Capt. Haubert's co. 51st rgt.

Smoot, John. Paymaster in 11th rgt. (My. 31, 1808).

Smoot, John W. Ensign and 2d Lieutenant in 5th U. S. Infantry (Ja. 3, 1812); 1st Lieutenant (F. 21, 1814).

Smoot, Samuel. Lieutenant in Capt. Morton's co. 1st rgt. (My. 7, 1810).

Smoot, Walter. Private in Capt. Dunnington's co. 43d rgt.

Smoot, William H. Lieutenant in Capt. Edelin's co. 1st rgt. (Ja. 10, 1814).

Smoot, Wilson. Captain in 43d rgt. (Ap. 27, 1813).

Smuch, William. Private in Capt. Montgomery's co. Balto. Union Artillery.

Smull, Jacob. Surgeon of the privateer *Joseph and Mary*, Oct., 1812.

Smull, Jacob T. Private in Capt. Aisquith's co. Sharp Shooters.

Smyth, —. Colonel in 4th rgt. (My. 5, 1815).

Smyth, Ephraim. 2d Lieutenant in Capt. Dyer's co. Fells Point Riflemen (Ap. 4, 1812).

Smyth, Isaac. Private in Capt. Tilghman's co. 33d rgt.

Smyth, Lemuel. Sergeant in Capt. McConckin's co. 38th rgt.

Snecdor, John. Private in Capt. Quantrill's co. 24th rgt.

Sneed, Robert. Ensign in Capt. Ray's co. 26th rgt. (Jy. 8, 1813).

Snider, —. Ensign in Capt. Dedie's co. 10th rgt. Resigned S. 20, 1813.

Snider [Snyder], George. Captain in 8th rgt. (My. 20, 1809).

Snow, Freeman. 1st Lieutenant of the privateer *Perry*, Sept., 1814; Private in Capt. Stiles' co. Marine Artillery.

Snow, Isaiah. Captain of the privateer *Atlanta*, Dec., 1812; of the *Osprey*, March, 1814.

Snow, John. Lieutenant of the privateer *Rolla*, Oct., 1812.

Snow, Josiah. Lieutenant of the privateer *Orb*, Nov., 1814.

Snow, Robert. Corporal in Capt. Duvall's co. 34th rgt.

Snowden, Henry [-1868]. Cornet in Maryland Chasseurs (F. 28, 1812) ; Captain in 6th Cavalry District (Ja. 29, 1814).

Snowden, John B. Captain in 36th rgt. (D. 24, 1810).

Snowden, Joseph. Private in Capt. Warfield's co. Balto. United Volunteers.

Snyder, Andrew. Private in Capt. Nicholson's co. Balto. Fencibles.

Snyder, Frederick. Ensign in Capt. Murray's co. 15th rgt. (Ag. 22, 1812).

Snyder, George D. 2d Lieutenant in 5th U. S. Infantry (S. 1, 1812) ; 1st Lieutenant (Je. 25, 1814).

Snyder, Henry. Captain in 13th rgt. Resigned Aug., 1813.

Snyder, John. Paymaster in 6th rgt. (Mr. 16, 1812).

Snyder, John. Private in Capt. Piper's co. United Maryland Artillery.

Snyder, John. Sergeant in Capt. Schwarzauer's co. 27th rgt.

Snyder, John C. Corporal in Capt. Wilson's co. 39th rgt.

Snyder, Joseph. Private in Capt. Conway's co. 6th rgt.

Snyder, Richard. Corporal in Capt. Smith's co. 51st rgt.

Snyder, Valentine. Private in Capt. Shrim's co. Balto. Light Infantry.

Soaper, William. Private in Capt. Shryock's co. 24th rgt.

Sollers, Abraham. 2d Lieutenant in Capt. Sterett's co. 1st Balto. Hussars (Ap. 23, 1812).

Sollers, Bennett. 1st Lieutenant in Capt. Mackall's co. 3d Cavalry Dist. (Jy. 28, 1812).

Sollers, John. Private in Capt. Lawrence's co. 6th rgt.

Solley, John. Quarter-master in 42d rgt.

Solomon, Samuel. Private in Capt. Faster's co. 51st rgt.

Somers, John. Private in Capt. Deems' co. 51st rgt.

Somers, Philip. 3d mate of the privateer *Joseph and Mary*.

Somervell, Henry V. Private in Capt. Causin's troop, attached to 12th rgt.

Somerville, James. Private in Capt. Steiner's Frederick Artillery.

Somerville, Thomas T. Lieutenant in Capt. Naylor's co. 17th rgt. (Ap. 21, 1813).

Somerville, William C. Major in 12th rgt. (Ja. 27, 1811).

Sommers, Michael. Private in Capt. Piper's co. United Maryland Artillery.

Soper, Alexander. Private in Capt. Dyer's co. 17th rgt.

Soper, Nathaniel. Private in Capt. Dyer's co. 17th rgt.

Soper, James. Private in Capt. Hall's co. 34th rgt.

Soper, Jesse. Private in Capt. Brooke's co. 34th rgt.

Soper, Thomas. Private in Capt. Quantrill's co. 24th rgt.

Sotheran, James F. Captain in 45th rgt.

Sotheran, William. Surgeon's mate 45th rgt. (S. 21, 1813).

South, Thomas. Private in Capt. Wherrett's co. 24th rgt. ; court martialed for exciting mutiny.

444   APPENDIX

Southcomb, Carey. Private in Capt. Pennington's co. Balto. Independent Artillerists.

Southcomb, John. Captain of the privateer *Lottery*, killed in action, Feb. 8, 1813.

Southcomb, P. Private in Capt. Stiles' co. Marine Artillery.

Southcomb, Peter. Private in Capt. Conway's co. 6th rgt.

Southerland, William M. Private in Capt. Burgess' co. 43d rgt.

Southwait, William. Private in Capt. Stiles' co. Marine Artillery.

Sowers, Conrad. Private in Capt. Snowden's co. 36th rgt.

Sowers, John. Private in Capt. Shryock's co. 24th rgt.

Sowers, William. Private in Capt. Snowden's co. 36th rgt.

Sowerwein, Daniel. Private in Capt. Deems' co. 51st rgt.

Spalding, Clement. Private in Capt. Melton's co. 45th rgt.

Spalding, John. Private in Capt. Moale's co. Columbian Artillery.

Spalding, Reeves. Lieutenant of the privateer *Joseph and Mary*, Sept., 1812.

Spangler, Isaac. Private in Capt. Pike's co. Balto. Volunteer Artillery.

Sparkes, John B. [-1813]. 2d Lieutenant in 14th U. S. Infantry (Mr. 12, 1812).

Sparks, Bazilla. Private in Capt. Wickes' co. 21st rgt.

Sparks, John P. Captain in 35th rgt. (My. 6, 1807).

Sparks, Joseph B. Lieutenant in Capt. Hackett's co. 35th rgt. (My. 8, 1812).

Sparks, William. 2d Lieutenant in Capt. Godwin's co. 9th Cavalry Dist. (Je. 1, 1813) ; 1st Lieutenant (Jy. 8, 1813).

Sparks, William. Private in Capt. Bunbury's co. Sea Fencibles.

Sparks, William. Private in Capt. McConckin's co. 38th rgt.

Sparrow, John. Surgeon in 34th rgt. (Jy. 4, 1812).

Sparrow, Thomas. Private in Capt. Hall's co. 34th rgt.

Speak, Nicholas. Private in Capt. Burke's co. 6th rgt.

Speake, Edward. Sergeant in Capt. Faster's co. 51st rgt.

Speake, Francis R. 2d Lieutenant in Capt. Barnes' Artillery co. 5th Brigade (Ja. 21, 1814).

Speake, John B. 3d Sergeant in Capt. Brown's co. 43d rgt.

Spear, John. Private in Capt. Haubert's co. 51st rgt.

Spear, William. Captain of the privateer *Daedalus*, Sept., 1813; Sergeant in Capt. Stiles' co. Marine Artillery.

Spear, William. Private in Capt. Peters' co. 51st rgt.

Spears, James. Private in Capt. Stewart's co. 51st rgt.

Spears, John. Private in Capt. Snowden's co. 36th rgt.

Spears, William. Ensign in Capt. Decker's co. 7th rgt. (Jy. 24, 1813).

Specht, Cornelius. Private in Capt. Kennedy's co. 27th rgt.

Speck, Henry. Private in Capt. Dyer's co. Fells Point Riflemen.

Spedden, Edward. Surgeon's mate 26th rgt. (S. 13, 1814).

Spedden, Edward. Private in Capt. Watson's co. 39th rgt.

Spedden, John of John. Captain in Extra Battalion Dorchester Co. (Ag. 27, 1810).

Spedden, John of Robert. Lieutenant in Capt. Spedden's co. Extra Battalion Co. (Ag. 27, 1810).

Spedden, Levin T. Private in Capt. Hayward's co. 4th rgt.

Spedden, Robert. Armorer at Easton.

Spence, John. Surgeon in Extra Battalion Worcester co.

Spence, Thomas R. Surgeon's mate 9th rgt. (Mr. 9, 1808).

Spencer, Isaac. Paymaster in 8th Cavalry Dist. (Ag. 20, 1813).

Spencer, James. Private in Capt. Mackey's co. 49th rgt.

Spencer, Jarvis. Lieutenant-Colonel in 8th Cavalry Dist. (F. 28, 1812).

Spencer, John E. Ensign in Capt. Emory's co. 38th rgt. (Ag. 16, 1808).

Spencer, Jonathan. Captain in 26th rgt. (Je. 22, 1808).

Spencer, Moses. Private in Capt. McLaughlin's co. 50th rgt.

Spencer, Nicholas. Private in Capt. Wells' Artillery co. 22d rgt.

Spencer, Richard. Private in Capt. Wells' Artillery co. 22d rgt.

Spencer, Robert. Aid-de-camp to Genl. Benson, 12th Brigade.

Spencer, Robert. Private in Capt. Pinney's co. 27th rgt.

Spencer, Reuben. Private in Capt. McConkey's co. 27th rgt.

Spencer, Thomas. Private in Capt. Page's co. 21st rgt.

Spencer, Thomas. Private in Capt. Mackey's co. 49th rgt.

Spencer, William. Lieutenant-Colonel in 33d rgt.

Spencer, William. Private in Capt. Kennedy's co. 27th rgt.

Spicer, Jeremiah. Private in Capt. Brohawn's co. 48th rgt.

Spicer, Joseph. Private in Capt. Addison's co. Sea Fencibles.

Spicer, Thomas. Quarter-master in 5th Cavalry Dist. (Je. 26, 1812).

Spicer, Thomas. Private in Capt. Nicholson's co. Balto. Fencibles.

Spicer, Valentine. Sergeant in 38th U. S. Infantry (D. 5, 1813); Ensign (Jy. 14, 1814).

Spicknall, John. Ensign in 38th U. S. Infantry (My. 20, 1813); 2d Lieutenant (O. 1, 1814).

Spicknall, William. Private in Capt. Sadtler's co. Balto. Yägers.

Spiker, Adam. Private in Capt. Blair's co. 50th rgt.

Spillman, James. Private in Capt. Sterett's co. 1st Balto. Hussars.

Spillman, Peter. Private in Capt. McLaughlin's co. 50th rgt.

Sprague, Charles. Lieutenant in Capt. Coe's co. 17th rgt.

Sprague, Henry. Private in Capt. Burke's co. 6th rgt.

Sprigg, Daniel. 1st Lieutenant in Capt. Quantrill's co. 24th rgt.

Sprigg, Edward. Private in Capt. McConkey's co. 27th rgt.

Sprigg, Jenifer T. Captain in 10th rgt. (F. 1, 1814); Adjutant (Ag. 1, 1814).

Sprigg, Otho. 1st Lieutenant in Capt. Cook's co. 2d rgt. 1st Cavalry Dist. (N. 16, 1812).

Sprigg, Otho. Paymaster in 13th rgt. (Je. 26, 1812).

Sprigg, Samuel. Cornet in Capt. Herbert's co. 2d Cavalry Dist. (Ag. 20, 1814); App. 2d Lieutenant Jy. 7, but declined commission.

Sprigg, Thomas. Corporal in Capt. Hanna's co. Fells Point Light Dragoons.

Sprinkle, Daniel. Private in Capt. Chalmers' co. 51st rgt.

Sprole, William. Corporal in Capt. Pike's co. Balto. Volunteer Artillery.

Sprunig, George. Private in Capt. Magruder's co. American Artillerists.

Spry, George. Captain in 33d rgt.

Spurrier, Allen. Private in Capt. Pumphrey's co. 22d rgt.

Spurrier, Beale. Private in Capt. Stewart's co. Washington Blues.

Spurrier, Dennis. Private in Capt. Maynard's co. 22d rgt. 1813; Private in Ensign Brewer's detachment 36th rgt. at Bladensburg; Private in Capt. Slicer's co. 22d rgt., 1814.

Spurrier, Edward. Private in Capt. Sands' co. 22d rgt.

Spurrier, John. Private in Capt. McConkey's co. 27th rgt.

Spurrier, Rezin. Sergeant in Capt. Sands' co. 22d rgt.

Spurrier, William. Corporal in Capt. Steuart's co. Washington Blues.

Srimard, John. Private in Capt. Peters' co. 51st rgt.

Srit, John. Private in Capt. Quantrill's co. 24th rgt.

Stackers, Solomon. Private in Capt. Piper's co. United Maryland Artillery.

Stacks, John. Private in Capt. Snowden's co. 36th rgt.

Stacks, William. Private in Capt. Snowden's co. 36th rgt.

Stafford, Joseph S. Corporal in Capt. McLaughlin's co. 50th rgt.

Stafford, William S. Captain of the privateer *Dolphin*, which was captured in the Rappahannock River after a fierce engagement with boats of the British squadron.

Stahan, Robert. Corporal in Capt. Blair's co. 50th rgt.

Stake, Peter. Captain in 10th rgt. Resigned S. 20, 1813.

Stalker, John. Private in Capt. Maynard's co. 22d rgt.

Stall, Joseph. Private in Capt. Haubert's co. 51st rgt.

Stall, Samuel. Private in Capt. Myers' co. 39th rgt.

Stallings, Aquilla. Private in Capt. Ringgold's co. 6th rgt.

Stallion, John. Private in Ensign Brewer's detachment in 36th rgt.; in Capt. Wells' Artillery co. 22d rgt.

Staly, Moses. Private in Capt. Getzendanner's co. 16th rgt.

Standage, Thomas. Private in Capt. Brooke's co. 34th rgt.

Standfield, John. Private in Capt. Brohawn's co. 48th rgt.

Standley, George. Private in Capt. A. C. Smith's co. 49th rgt.

Stanford, Algernon S. Adjutant in 10th Cavalry Dist. (Jy. 8, 1813).

Stanford, Obadiah. Private in Capt. Heath's co. 23d rgt.

Stanley, Joseph. Private in Capt. Pennington's co. Balto. Independent Artillerists.

Stansbury, August M. Private in Capt. Steever's co. 27th rgt.

Stansbury, Benjamin. Private in Capt. Pumphrey's co. 22d rgt.

Stansbury, Caleb. Private in Capt. Blizzard's co. 15th rgt.

Stansbury, Charles. Captain Rifle co. 3d Brigade (Ap. 4, 1812); Captain in 38th U. S. Infantry (My. 20, 1813).

Stansbury, David. Private in Capt. Steever's co. 27th rgt.

Stansbury, Darius. Private in Capt. Howard's co. Mechanical Volunteers.

Stansbury, Dixon. 1st Lieutenant in 13th U. S. Infantry (Ja. 20, 1813); Captain (Je. 30, 1814).

Stansbury, Elijah [1791-   ]. Private in Capt. Montgomery's co. Balto. Union Artillery.

Stansbury, Hammond N. 3d officer of the privateer *Chasseur*.

Stansbury, James. Sergeant in Capt. Galloway's co. 46th rgt.

Stansbury, Joshua. Private in Capt. Fowler's co. 46th rgt.

Stansbury, Josias. Private in Capt. Hanna's co. Fells Point Light Dragoons.

Stansbury, Nicholas. Private in Capt. Lawrence's co. 6th rgt.

Stansbury, Richard. Private in Capt. Peters' co. 51st rgt.

Stansbury, Richardson. Ensign in Capt. Merryman's co. 41st rgt. (Je. 22, 1808).

Stansbury, Tobias E. [1756-1849]. Brigadier-General 11th Brigade (D. 6, 1809).

Stansbury, Tobias E., Jr. 1st Lieutenant in 6th Cavalry Dist. (Ap. 26, 1812) ; Captain (Jy. 8, 1814).

Stansbury, William. Private in Capt. Magruder's co. American Artillerists.

Stansbury, William. Sergeant in Capt. Myers' co. 39th rgt.

Stansbury, William. Sergeant in Capt. Horton's co. Maryland Chasseurs.

Stansbury, William. Private in Capt. Kennedy's co. 27th rgt.

Stansford, Aquila. Ensign in Capt. Howard's co. 46th rgt. (Je. 1, 1813).

Stansford, John. Lieutenant in Capt. Shock's co. 41st rgt. (Ap. 20, 1808).

Stanton, Joshua. Private in Capt. Blair's co. 50th rgt.

Stapleton, Joseph K. Captain in 39th rgt.

Stark, Sylvanus. Private in Capt. Massey's co. 38th rgt.

Starke, George. Private in Capt. Warfield's co. Balto. United Volunteers.

Starr, George. Private in Capt. Schwarzauer's co. 27th rgt.

Starr, Hezekiah. Private in Capt. Magruder's co. American Artillerists.

Starr, James. Private in Capt. Deems' co. 51st rgt.

Starr, William [1778-1819]. Private in Capt. Magruder's co. American Artillerists.

Statt, F. Seaman of the privateer *Globe,* wounded in action, Nov. 1, 1813.

Stavely, Isaac [-1814]. Ensign in Capt. Konkey's co. 33d rgt.

Stavely, John. Sergeant in Capt. Tilghman's co. 33d rgt.

Stavely, Wilson. Private in Capt. Hands' co. 21st rgt.

Staylor, Henry. Corporal in Capt. Piper's co. United Maryland Artillery.

Staylor, John. Private in Capt. Piper's co. United Maryland Artillery.

Staylor, Philip. Private in Capt. Piper's co. United Maryland Artillery.

Staylor, William. Private in Capt. Piper's co. United Maryland Artillery.

Steadham, Peter A. Private in Capt. Edes' co. 27th rgt.

Stebeck, John. Private in Capt. Lawrence's co. 6th rgt.

Steel, Joseph. Ensign in Capt. Garrett's co. 49th rgt. (Ap. 23, 1813).

Steel, Penson. Private in Capt. Ringgold's co. 6th rgt.

Steevens, Adam. Private in Capt. McConkey's co. 27th rgt.

Steever, Daniel. Private in Capt. Levering's co. Independent Blues.

Steever, George. Captain in 27th rgt. (My. 28, 1812).

Steffer, Frederick. Private in Capt. Wilson's co. 6th rgt.

Steidel, Gottlieb. Private in Capt. Bader's co. Union Yägers.

Steiger, Tobias. Private in Capt. Haubert's co. 51st rgt.

Steigers, George. Private in Capt. Smith's co. 51st rgt.

Steigers, Jacob. Major in 39th rgt.

Steigers, John. Private in Capt. Smith's co. 51st rgt.

Steinbeck, J. C. Private in Capt. Sadtler's co. Balto. Yägers.

Steine, George. Private in Capt. Hanna's Fells Point Light Dragoons.

Steiner, Henry [1775-1825]. Captain Artillery co. 9th Brigade Frederick Co. (Ap. 4, 1808).

Steiner, John Thomas. Private in Capt. Steiner's Frederick Artillery.

Steiner, Stephen. Captain in 16th rgt.; Major (Ag. 1, 1814).

Steiner, William. Corporal in Capt. Steiner's Frederick Artillery.

Steinforth, John. Private in Capt. Bader's co. Union Yägers.

Stemble, Frederick, Jr. Quartermaster in 28th rgt. (Je. 5, 1812) ; Transferred to U. S. Army.

Stembler, John. Private in Capt. Smith's co. 51st rgt.

Stemmin, Barnard. Private in Capt. Steever's co. 27th rgt.

Stephen, John. Private in Capt. Pinkney's Artillery co. 22d rgt.

Stephen, William. Private in Capt. Blair's co. 50th rgt.

Stephen, William. Private in Capt. Shryock's co. 24th rgt.

Stephens, Alexander [1794-1863]. Private in Capt. McConkey's co. 27th rgt.

Stephens, David. Captain in 8th rgt. (Ag. 9, 1808).

Stephens, George. Private in Capt. Blizzard's co. 15th rgt.

Stephens, John. Private in Capt. Galt's co. 6th rgt.

Stephens, John. Private in Capt. Hancock's co. 22d rgt.

Stephens, Timothy. Private in Capt. Bunbury's co. Sea Fencibles.

Stephenson, James. Captain in 42d rgt. (D. 10, 1807).

Sterett, Alexander. Private in Capt. Lawrence's 6th rgt.

Sterett, James. Captain 1st Balto. Hussars in 5th Cavalry Dist. (Ap. 23, 1812).

Sterett, James. Private in Capt. Quantrill's co. 24th rgt.

Sterett, Joseph [-1821]. Lieutenant-Colonel in 5th rgt.; Brigadier-General 3d Brigade (D. 20, 1814) vice Stricker.

Sterett, Robert. Private in Capt. Bunbury's co. Sea Fencibles.

Sterett, Samuel. Captain Independent co.; Major in 5th rgt. (D. 20, 1814) vice R. K. Heath.

Sterett, William. Private in Capt. Sterett's co. 1st Balto. Hussars.

Sterling, John. Lieutenant in Capt. Juett's co. 23d rgt. Resigned Jy. 14, 1814.

Sterling, John. Sergeant in Capt. Sterett's co. 1st Balto. Hussars.

Sterling, William. Private in Capt. Chalmers' co. 51st rgt.

Sterner, Jacob. Private in Capt. McLaughlin's co. 50th rgt.

Steuart, Ebenezer. Private in Capt. Linthicum's co. 22d rgt.

Steuart, George H [1790-1867]. Captain Washington Blues; wounded at North Point.

Steuart, Levin. Lieutenant in Capt. Linthicum's co. 48th rgt. (S. 21, 1813).

Steuart, Philip. Brigadier-General 5th Brigade (Mr. 23, 1814).

Steuart, Stephen. Private in Capt. Pumphrey's co. 22d rgt.

Steuart, William. Lieutenant-Colonel in 38th U. S. Infantry (My. 19, 1813).

Stevens, Darius. Private in Capt. Brown's co. 6th rgt.

Stevens, Jacob. Lieutenant in Capt. Page's co. 21st rgt.

Stevens, James. Lieutenant of the privateer *Rolla*, March, 1813.

Stevens, James H. Private in Capt. Stiles' co. Marine Artillery.

Stevens, James L. Gunner Capt. Addison's co. Sea Fencibles.

Stevens, John. Colonel in 37th rgt. (D. 7, 1813) vice Handy.

Stevens, John. 2d Lieutenant in Capt. Saulsbury's co. 10th Cavalry Dist. (Je. 15, 1813) vice Nicholls.

Stevens, John. Private in Capt. Edes' co. 27th rgt.

Stevens, John, Jr. Surgeon in 26th rgt. (S. 13, 1814).

Stevens, Mark. Private in Capt. Edes' co. 27th rgt.

Stevens, Peter. Private in Capt. Steuart's co. Washington Bues.

Stevens, Samuel, Jr. Captain in 4th rgt. (My. 27, 1811).

Stevenson, Alexander. Private in Capt. Chalmers' co. 51st rgt.

Stevenson, Basil. Lieutenant in Capt. Connaway's co. 15th rgt. (Je. 15, 1813).

Stevenson, George P. Cornet in 1st Balto. Hussars, 5th Cavalry Dist. (Ap. 23, 1812); Captain Fells Point Dragoons (Jy. 28, 1812); Adjutant (Je. 26, 1812); Aid-de-Camp to Genl. Stricker, 1814.

Stevenson, Isaiah. Private in Capt. Myer's co. Franklin Artillery.

Stevenson, John. Private in Capt. Deems' co. 51st rgt.

Stevenson, Joseph. Captain in 9th rgt. (Mr. 23, 1814).

Stevenson, Joshua. Private in Capt. Hanna's co. Fells Point Light Dragoons.

Stever, George. 1st Lieutenant in Capt. Bader's co. Union Yägers (Ap. 4, 1812).

Steward, James. Corporal in Capt. Foreman's co. 33d rgt.

Stewart, Alexander. Private in Capt. Sterett's co. 1st Balto. Hussars.

Stewart, Bennet. Captain in 42d rgt. (S. 21, 1810).

Stewart, Charles. Private in Capt. Haubert's co. 51st rgt.

Stewart, Dorsey. Private in Capt. Pumphrey's co. 22d rgt.

Stewart, Edward. Private in Capt. McConckin's co. 38th rgt.

Stewart, Ezekiel. Private in Capt. Pumphrey's co. 22d rgt.

Stewart, George L. Private in Capt. Pennington's Balto. Independent Artillerists.

Stewart, Henry. 3d Sergeant in Capt. Hall's co. 3d Cavalry rgt.

Stewart, Henry H. Private in Capt. Usselton's co. Artillery 6th Brigade.

Stewart, James. Sergeant in Capt. Howard's co. Mechanical Volunteers.

30

Stewart, James. Private in Capt. Sheppard's co. 6th rgt.

Stewart, James V. [-1812]. Surgeon Light Artillery U. S.

Stewart, John. Captain in 51st rgt. (Jy. 28, 1813).

Stewart, John. Paymaster in 10th Cavalry Dist. (My. 20, 1813).

Stewart, John. Private in Capt. Shrim's co. Balto. Light Infantry.

Stewart, John. Private in Capt. Hall's co. 3d Cavalry rgt.

Stewart, John. Private in Capt. Aisquith's co. Sharp Shooters.

Stewart, John I. [-1843]. Purser's steward under Capt. Huffington in Barney's flotilla.

Stewart, John N. Private in Capt. McKane's co. 27th rgt.

Stewart, Joseph. Private in Capt. Maynard's co. 22d rgt.; later, Capt. Sands'.

Stewart, Mordecai. Private in Capt. Hancock's co. 22d rgt.

Stewart, Nehemiah. Private in Capt. Dunnington's co. 43d rgt.

Stewart, Robert. Private in Capt. Maynard's co. 22d rgt.; in Ensign Brewer's detachment 36th rgt. at Bladensburg.

Stewart, Robert H. J. Lieutenant in Capt. Peters' co. 51st rgt.; Captain (D. 2, 1814) vice Peters.

Stewart, Thomas [1783-1830]. Private in Capt. Montgomery's co. Balto. Union Artillery.

Stewart, William. Hospital Surgeon's mate in 2d U. S. Artillery.

Stewart, William. Private in Capt. Smoot's co. 43d rgt.

Stewart, William P. Private in Capt. Steuart's co. Washington Blues.

Stewart, William S. Private in Capt. Moale's co. Columbian Artillery.

Stewart, Zachariah. Private in Capt. Boone's co. 22d rgt.

Sticher, John. 2d Lieutenant in 38th U. S. Infantry (My. 20, 1813); 1st Lieutenant (Jy. 9, 1814).

Sticher, Peter. Private in Capt. Getzendanner's co. 16th rgt.

Stickney, Henry. Private in Capt. Nicholson's co. Balto. Fencibles.

Stickney, John. Corporal in Capt. Galt's co. 6th rgt.

Stierley, Jacob. Cornet in Capt. Horton's co. Maryland Chasseurs (Mr. 27, 1813) vice Snowden.

Stiger, Peter. Private in Capt. McConkey's co. 27th rgt.

Stiles, George [1760-1819]. Captain Marine Artillery (S. 10, 1814).

Stiles, John S. 1st Lieutenant in Capt. Montgomery's co. Balto. Union Artillery (Mr. 25, 1814) vice Lewis.

Stilts, William. Private in Capt. Lawson's co. Balto. Patriots.

Stimple, Anthony. Private in Capt. Berry's co. Washington Artillery.

Stimpson, Stephen. Private in Capt. Addison's co. Sea Fencibles.

Stinchcomb, Aquila. Private in Capt. Dyer's co. Fells Point Riflemen.

Stinchcomb, Nathan. Private in Capt. Boone's co. 22d rgt.

Stinchcomb, Victor. Private in Capt. Smith's co. 51st rgt.

Stinson, Thomas N. Private in Capt. McConckin's co. 38th rgt.

Stites, William. Private in Capt. Conway's co. 6th rgt.

Stith, John. Cornet in U. S. Light Dragoons (Ag. 24, 1814).

Stocker, Charles. Private in Capt. Edes' co. 27th rgt.

Stocker, Elijah. Private in Capt. Stewart's co. 51st rgt.

Stocker, Zachias. Gunner in Capt. Addison's co. Sea Fencibles.

Stockett, John. Private in Capt. Hall's co. 3d Cavalry rgt.

Stockett, Dr. John S. Surgeon's mate in 2d rgt. (Ja. 11, 1815).

Stockett, Joseph N. Quarter-master in 2d rgt. (Ap. 17, 1813).

Stockett, Richard G. Surgeon in 32d rgt. (Jy. 24, 1807).

Stockman, Jacob. Private in Capt. McKane's co. 27th rgt.

Stocksdale, Elias. Captain in 15th rgt. (D. 4, 1810).

Stocksdale, Elisha. Private in Capt. Ducker's co. 7th rgt.

Stocksdale, Jesse. Private in Capt. Ducker's co. 7th rgt.

Stocksdale, Solomon. Private in Capt. Ducker's co. 7th rgt.

Stockdale, Thomas. Private in Capt. Ducker's co. 7th rgt.

Stockton, John. Private in Capt. Howard's co. Mechanical Volunteers.

Stockton, Richard C. Private in Capt. Thompson's co. 1st Baltimore Horse Artillery.

Stoddert, John T. Aid-de-camp to Genl. Steuart in 5th Brigade (Ag. 4, 1814).

Stokes, Horatio. Private in Capt. Wickes' co. 21st rgt.

Stokes, John. Private in Capt. Shryock's co. 24th rgt.

Stone, Francis. Corporal in Capt. Brown's co. 43d rgt.

Stone, George. Captain in 31st rgt. (Ag. 20, 1814) vice Wilson.

Stone, Harrison. Private in Capt. Brown's co. 43d rgt.

Stone, James, Jr. Private in Capt. Warfield's co. Balto. United Volunteers.

Stone, John. Captain in 45th rgt. Resigned Jan. 23, 1815.

Stone, John. Ensign in Capt. Mantz's co. 16th rgt. (Jy. 15, 1814).

Stone, John. Private in Capt. Green's co. 46th rgt.

Stone, John of Thomas. Private in Capt. Burgess' co. 43d rgt.

Stone, John of Wm. Private in Capt. Dunnington's co. 43d rgt.

Stone, Joseph. Major in 45th rgt. (1813).

Stone, Joseph. Private in Capt. Eversfield's co. 17th rgt.

Stone, Richard. Private in Capt. Montgomery's co. Balto. Union Artillery.

Stone, William. Private in Capt. Ducker's co. 7th rgt.

Stonebraker, Garrett. Captain in 24th rgt. (Mr. 9, 1808).

Stonesifer, Henry. Cornet Capt. Shriver's co. 2d rgt. 1st Cavalry Dist. (Je. 26, 1812); 2d Lieutenant (D. 22, 1812).

Stonestreet, Nicholas. Captain in 4th Cavalry Dist. (Mr. 25, 1812).

Stonestreet, William. Private in Capt. Causin's co. 4th Cavalry Dist.

Storey, Henry. Captain in 38th rgt. (My. 19, 1813).

Storey, John. Private in Capt. Berry's co. Washington Artillery.

Storey, John R. Lieutenant in Capt. Roe's co. 35th rgt. (N. 3, 1812).

Storey, Robert. Private in Capt. Horton's co. Maryland Chasseurs.

Storks, Levy. Private in Capt. Kennedy's co. 27th rgt.

Stoudt, George. Private in Capt. Myers' co. Franklin Artillery.

Stouffer, Jacob. Private in Capt. Thompson's co. 1st Baltimore Horse Artillery.

Stouffer, John. Musician in Capt. Steiner's Frederick Artillery.

Sturgis, Samuel. Captain in 35th rgt. (N. 3, 1812).

Sturr, Thomas. Corporal in Capt. Shryock's co. 24th rgt.

Styles, George. *See* **Stiles.**

Styll, Thomas. Captain in 19th rgt. (Ap. 22, 1814).

Suddon, John. Captain in 46th rgt. (Ja. 22, 1811).

Suddon, Zachariah. Ensign in Capt. Suddon's co. 46th rgt. (Ja. 22, 1811).

Sudler, William. Private in Capt. Miles' co. 23d rgt.

Suit, Oliver B. Private in Capt. Veitch's co. 34th rgt.

Suit, Philip C. Private in Capt. Brooke's co. 34th rgt.

Suite, John H. Ensign in Capt. Cawood's co. 45th rgt. (S. 21, 1813).

Sulivane, Joseph E. Cornet in Capt. Ennalls' co. 10th Cavalry Dist. (Jy. 29, 1812).

Sullivan, Clement [-1812]. Captain in 14th U. S. Infantry (Mr. 28, 1812).

Sullivan, Daniel. Ensign in Capt. Durbin's co. 20th rgt. (S. 12, 1814).

Sullivan, James. Private in Capt. Chase's co. 22d rgt.

Sullivan, James. Sergeant in Ensign Brewer's detachment, 36th rgt.; in Capt. Sands' co. 22d rgt.

Sullivan, James B. Surgeon in 48th rgt. (Jy. 8, 1813).

Sullivan, Jere. Private in Capt. Thompson's co. 1st Baltimore Horse Artillery.

Sullivan, Jeremiah. Division Quarter-master, 3d Division M. M.

Sullivan, John. Private in Capt. Edes' co. 27th rgt.

Sullivan, John. Private in Capt. Pinkney's Artillery co. 22d rgt.

Sullivan, John. Private in Capt. Miller's co. 39th rgt.

Sullivane, Daniel. Private in Capt. Jas. Massey's co. 38th rgt.

Sullyards, Jonathan. Lieutenant in Capt. Hunter's co. 8th rgt. (Ag. 14, 1810).

Sultzer, Sebastian. Private in Capt. Levering's co. Independent Blues.

Sumbleton, Palmer. Private in Capt. Snowden's co. 36th rgt.

Summers, Dawson. Private in Capt. Massey's co. 38th rgt.

Summers, George. Private in Capt. McConkey's co. 27th rgt.

Summers, Henry. Private in Capt. Travers' co. 48th rgt.

Summers, Judson. Private in Capt. Dyer's co. 17th rgt.

Summerville, John. Private in Capt. Peters' co. 51st rgt.

Summerwell, Richard. Private in Capt. Myers' co. Franklin Artillery.

Sumner, Henry Payson [1789-1839]. Sergeant in Capt. Sterett's Independent co.

Sumwalt, Daniel. Ensign in Capt. Gosnell's co. 7th rgt. (Jy. 24, 1813).

Sumwalt, George B. Ensign in Capt. Myers' co. 39th rgt. (Ja. 10, 1814).

Sumwalt, John. Private in Capt. A. E. Warner's co. 39th rgt.

Sumwalt, John Thornburg. Corporal in Capt. Berry's co. Washington Artillery; wounded at the six gun battery.

Sumwalt, John X. Private in Capt. Berry's co. Washington Artillery.

Sumwalt, Joseph. Sergeant in Capt. Levering's co. Independent Blues.

Sumwalt, Philip. Private in Capt. Magruder's co. American Artillery.

Sunderland, B. Private in Capt. Stapleton's co. 39th rgt.

Sunderland, Richard. Private in Capt. Stapleton's co. 39th rgt.

Sunderland, William. Private in Capt. Galt's co. 6th rgt.

Sunenshine, Michael. Private in Capt. Myers' co. Franklin Artillery.

Supper, John. Private in Capt. McConkey's co. 27th rgt.

Surratt, Nathaniel. Private in Capt. Dyer's co. 17th rgt.

Sute, John. Private in Capt. Kierstead's co. 6th rgt.

Suter, Henry. Private in Capt. Shrim's co. Balto. Light Infantry.

Suter, Jacob. Private in Capt. Myers' co. Franklin Artillery.

Sutherland, Daniel. Private in Capt. Stewart's co. 51st rgt.

Sutherland, George. Private in Capt. Ducker's co. 7th rgt.

Suthron, Thomas. Corporal in Capt. Cawood's co. 45th rgt.

Sutton, David. Private in Capt. Morgan's co. 49th rgt.

Sutton, James. Private in Capt. Mackey's co. 49th rgt.

Sutton, John. Private in Capt. Mackey's co. 49th rgt.

Sutton, Samuel. Ensign in Capt. Michael's co. 42d rgt. (Ap. 19, 1813).

Sutton, Solomon. Private in Capt. Thos. Warner's co. 39th rgt.

Suylavine, Dennis. Private in Capt. Massey's co. 38th rgt.

Swager, William. Private in Capt. Brown's co. 6th rgt.

Swagley, Michael. 2d Lieutenant in Capt. Cole's co. 10th rgt. Resigned Ag. 2, 1814.

Swain, Ebenezer. Ensign in Capt. McConkey's co. 27th rgt.

Swain, Henry. Lieutenant in Capt. Carter's co. 17th rgt. (My. 25, 1800).

Swain, John. Private in Capt. Faster's co. 51st rgt.

Swann, John. Private in Capt. Sterett's co. 1st Balto. Hussars.

Swann, John E. Private in Capt. Warfield's co. Balto. United Volunteers. Wounded at North Point.

Swann, Joshua. Private in Capt. Peters' co. 51st rgt.

Swann, Moses H. Lieutenant in Capt. Sprigg's co. 10th rgt. (F. 1, 1814).

Swann, Thomas M. Private in Capt. Cawood's co. 45th rgt.

Swann, William. Private in Capt. Warfield's co. Balto. United Volunteers.

Swartze, Henry. Private in Capt. Snowden's co. 36th rgt.

Swearingen, Henry Van [-1819]. 1st Lieutenant in U. S. Rifles (Jy. 6, 1812) ; Captain (My. 11, 1814).

Swearingen, John. 1st Lieutenant in Capt. Williams' co. 1st Cavalry Dist. (Mr. 16, 1812).

Swearingen, Joseph. Brigadier-General 9th Brigade (S. 25, 1810).

Sweeny, George W. Private in Capt. Brooke's co. 34th rgt.

Sweeny, Judson. Private in Capt. Brooke's co. 34th rgt.

Sweer, Peter. Private in Capt. Brown's co. 6th rgt.

Sweeting, Benjamin B. 2d Lieutenant in 38th U. S. Infantry (My. 20, 1813) ; 1st Lieutenant (Ap. 22, 1814).

Sweeting, Benjamin B. Private in Capt. Berry's co. Washington Artillery.

Sweeting, Joshua. Private in Capt. Dyer's co. Fells Point Riflemen.

Sweeting, Thomas. Adjutant in 51st rgt. (Je. 12, 1812).

Sweetman, Willis. Private in Capt. Faster's co. 51st rgt.

Sweetzer, John. Private in Capt. Stewart's co. 51st rgt.

Swern, William. Private in Capt. Deems' co. 51st rgt.

Swetzer, Samuel. Private in Capt. Levering's co. Independent Blues.

Swetzer, Seth. Private in Capt. Levering's co. Independent Blues.

Swift, Elisha. Private in Capt. Wickes' co. 21st rgt.

Swift, John. Quarter-Gunner in Capt. Addison's co. Sea Fencibles.

Swigert, Philip. Ensign in Capt. Brookbank's co. 10th rgt. (O. 1, 1799).

Swiggett, Robert T. Private in Capt. Thos. Warner's co. 39th rgt.

Switzer, Conrad. Sergeant in Capt. Kierstead's co. 6th rgt.

Swope, John. Private in Capt. A. E. Warner's co. 39th rgt.

Swoyer, Jacob. Ensign in 5th U. S. Infantry (My. 20, 1813) ; 2d Lieutenant (My. 1, 1814).

Syfert, Henry. Drum-Major in 15th rgt.

Sykes, James. Sergeant in Capt. Moale's co. Columbian Artillery.

Sylvester, Samuel. Private in Capt. Nicholson's co. Balto. Fencibles.

Symington, James F. Private in Capt. Steuart's co. Washington Blues.

T

Tabb, Moses. Captain in 1st rgt. 1st Cavalry Dist. (F. 28, 1812).

Talbert, Charles. Private in Capt. Dyer's co. 17th rgt.

Talbert, Peter. Private in Capt. Crawfurd's co. 17th rgt.

Talbot, Edward. Private in Capt. Levering's co. Independent Blues.

Talbot, Joseph. Captain in 19th rgt. (O. 3, 1807).

Talbott, Henry W. Private in Capt. John Wailer's co., Cramer's detachment.

Talbott, Richard [1785-c1840]. Ensign in Capt. John W. Dorsey's co. 32d rgt. (My. 13, 1813).

Tall, Anthony. Private in Capt. Brown's co. Eagle Artillerists.

Tally, Josiah. Private in Capt. Shryock's co. 24th rgt.

Tambo, David. Private in Capt. Deems' co. 51st rgt.

Taney, James. Corporal in Capt. Blair's co. 50th rgt.

Taney, Michael. Lieutenant-Colonel in 31st rgt.

Taneyhill, John of L. Private in Capt. Ireland's co. 31st rgt.

Taneyhill, Mordecai. Lieutenant in Capt. Leitch's co. 31st rgt.

Tanner, P. S. Private in Capt. Sterett's Independent co.

Tanner, Samuel. Private in Capt. McKane's co. 27th rgt.

Tarbutton, William. Private in Capt. McConckin's co. 38th rgt.

Tarlton, Elijah. Lieutenant in Capt. Young's co. 12th rgt. (O. 3, 1807).

Tarlton, George. Private in Capt. Walker's co. 45th rgt.

Tarlton, John. Surgeon in 45th rgt. (S. 21, 1813).

Tarlton, Robert. Private in Capt. Bean's co. 12th rgt.

Tarlton, Rudolph. Private in Capt. Shryock's co. 24th rgt.

Tarmer, James. Private in Capt. Magruder's co. American Artillerists.

Tasker, Elisha. Private in Capt. Blair's co. 50th rgt.

Tatcham, Daniel. Private in Capt. Schwarzauer's co. 27th rgt.

Taylor, Allen. Private in Capt. Dyer's co. 17th rgt.

Taylor, Aquila. Private in Capt. Stewart's co. 51st rgt.

Taylor, Archibald. Private in Capt. Steever's co. 27th rgt.

Taylor, Benjamin. Private in Capt. Brooke's co. 34th rgt.

Taylor, Benjamin. Private in Capt. Warfield's co. Balto. United Volunteers.

Taylor, Charles N. 1st Lieutenant in 38th U. S. Infantry (My. 20, 1813).

Taylor, Cromwell. Private in Capt. Berry's co. Washington Artillery.

Taylor, Elijah. Private in Capt. Magruder's co. American Artillerists.

Taylor, Elisha. Captain of the privateer *Active;* of the *Express,* June, 1814.

Taylor, Enoch. 1st Lieutenant in Capt. Gist's co. 2d rgt. 1st Cavalry Dist. (My. 31, 1813) ; Captain (Je. 15, 1813).

Taylor, Gamaliel. Private in Capt. Sands' co. 22d rgt.

Taylor, George. Private in Capt. McConkey's co. 27th rgt.

Taylor, Henry. Private in Capt. Edes' co. 27th rgt.

Taylor, Hezekiah. Private in Capt. Nailor's co. 17th rgt.

Taylor, Hugh. Captain in 19th rgt. (D. 10, 1807).

Taylor, Isaac. Corporal in Capt. Pennington's co. Balto. Independent Artillerists.

Taylor, James. Private in Ensign Brewer's detachment, 36th rgt. ;

originally of Capt. Slicer's co. 22d rgt.

Taylor, James. Private in Capt. Wilson's co. 6th rgt.

Taylor, James. Private in Capt. Berry's co. Washington Artillery.

Taylor, James. Prize-master of the privateer *Dolphin;* Captain of the *Wasp.*

Taylor, James W. Lieutenant in Capt. Tull's co. Extra Battalion Worcester Co. (Je. 18, 1812).

Taylor, Jenifer S. 2d Lieutenant in Capt. Hughlett's co. 10th Cavalry Dist. (Je. 18, 1812) ; 1st Lieutenant (Ap. 23, 1813).

Taylor, Jesse. Private in Capt. Moore's co. 49th rgt.

Taylor, John. Captain in 48th rgt. (S. 2, 1811).

Taylor, John. Private in Capt. Burke's co. 6th rgt.

Taylor, John. Private in Capt. Blizzard's co. 15th rgt.

Taylor, John. Private in Capt. Kennedy's co. 27th rgt.

Taylor, John. Private in Capt. Burgess' co. 43d rgt.

Taylor, John. Private in Capt. Taylor's co. 46th rgt.

Taylor, John. Private in Capt. Chalmers' co. 51st rgt.

Taylor, John B. Surgeon's mate in 5th rgt. (My. 13, 1813).

Taylor, John D. Captain in 38th rgt. (Ap. 23, 1812).

Taylor, John T. Captain in 37th rgt. (Ja. 21, 1814) vice Fleming.

Taylor, Joseph. Private in Capt. Sadtler's co. Balto. Yägers.

Taylor, Joshua. Captain in 46th rgt. (N. 8, 1811).

Taylor, Lemuel [1791-1859]. Captain in 5th Cavalry Dist. (Ap. 3, 1812) ; Adjutant (My. 3, 1813).

Taylor, Lemuel G. 2d Lieutenant Washington Artillery (Ag. 15, 1812) vice Berry.

Taylor, Lemuel G. Private in Capt. Sterett's co. 1st Balto. Hussars.

Taylor, Levi. Private in Capt. Mc-Conkey's co. 27th rgt.

Taylor, Levin. Private in Capt. Berry's co. Washington Artillery.

Taylor, Mal. Private in Capt. Blair's co. 50th rgt.

Taylor, Nathaniel. Private in Capt. Crawfurd's co. 17th rgt.

Taylor, Parran. Surgeon's mate in 9th Cavalry Dist. (D. 11, 1813).

Taylor, Philip. Private in Capt. Smith's co. 51st rgt.

Taylor, Robert [1781-1869]. Private in Capt. Pennington's co. Balto. Independent Artillerists.

Taylor, Robert A. Private in Capt. Moale's co. Columbian Artillery.

Taylor, Samuel. Private in Capt. Rogers' co. 51st rgt.

Taylor, Thomas. Lieutenant in Capt. Adreon's co. Union Volunteers (Ja. 10, 1814).

Taylor, Thomas. Private in Capt. Berry's co. Washington Artillery.

Taylor, Thomas. Private in Capt. Wilson's co. 6th rgt.

Taylor, Thomas. Private in Capt. Hands' co. 21st rgt.

Taylor, Thomas A. Private in Capt. Kennedy's co. 27th rgt.

Taylor, Thurston M. Prize-master of the privateer *High Flyer*.

Taylor, William. Private in Capt. McKane's co. 27th rgt.

Taylor, William. Private in Capt. Pinkney's Artillery co. 22d rgt.

Taylor, William. Private in Capt. Ringgold's co. 6th rgt.

Taylor, William. Private in Capt. Rogers' co. 51st rgt.

Taylor, William H. Captain in Extra Battalion Worcester Co. (F. 11, 1809).

Tayman, Levy. Sergeant in Capt. Eversfield's co. 17th rgt.

Teackle, Severn. Private in Capt. Pennington's co. Balto. Independent Artillerists.

Teal, Archibald. Private in Capt. McDonald's co. 6th rgt.

Teal, George. Musician in Capt. Pinney's co. 27th rgt.

Tebo, Peter. Private in Capt. Brown's co. Eagle Artillerists.

Tebo, Peter, Jr. Private in Capt. Brown's co. Eagle Artillerists.

Temple, Christopher. Private in Capt. Snowden's co. 36th rgt.

Temple, Samuel. Private in Capt. Snowden's co. 36th rgt.

Templeton, William. Private in Capt. Barnes' co. 32d rgt.

Tennant, Thomas [1767-1836]. 1st Major in 6th rgt.; Colonel (Mr. 3, 1815) vice McDonald.

Tennison, John. Private in Capt. Williams' co. 12th rgt.

Tennison, Samuel. Private in Capt. Burgess' co. 43d rgt.

Teplin, William. Private in Capt. Roney's co. 39th rgt.

Teppish, Caspar. Private in Capt. Dillon's co. 27th rgt.

Terry, Eli. Lieutenant in Capt. Thos. Jones' co. 30th rgt. (S. 5, 1812).

Terry, Hosea. Private in Capt. Mackey's co. 49th rgt.

Terry, John. Corporal in Capt. Roney's co. 39th rgt.

Terry, Jonah. Private in Capt. Sample's co. 49th rgt.

Terry, William. Private in Capt. Pinkney's Artillery co. 22d rgt.

Tevis, Benjamin. Lieutenant in Capt. Thos. Warner's co. 39th rgt.

Thaker, Walter. Sergeant in Capt. Edes' co. 27th rgt.

Tharp, James. Private in Capt. Wickes' co. 21st rgt.

Tharp, Joseph. Sergeant in Capt. Conway's co. 6th rgt.

Tharpe, George. Private in Capt. Steuart's co. Washington Blues.

Thelis, James. Seaman of the privateer *Globe,* killed in action, Nov. 1, 1813.

Thiel, Jeremiah. Private in Capt. Adreon's co. Union Volunteers.

Thistle, Archibald. Lieutenant in Capt. Tomlinson's co. 50th rgt. (F. 15, 1814).

Thomas, Abel. Private in Capt. Wilson's co. 6th rgt.

Thomas, Allen. Captain in 3d Cavalry Dist. (My. 8, 1812).

Thomas, Benjamin. Captain in 49th rgt.

Thomas, David. Private in Capt. John Miller's co. 2d D. I.; b. Washington Co., Md.; horse-farrier.

Thomas, David. Private in Capt. Shryock's co. 24th rgt.

Thomas, David T. Private in Capt. John Miller's co. 2d D. I.; b. Washington Co., Md.; age 25; joiner; subs. for Frederick Rohrer.

Thomas, Edward. Ensign in Capt. Gardiner's co. 1st rgt.

Thomas, Edward. Private in Capt. Bean's co. 12th rgt.

Thomas, Gabriel. Private in Capt. Dobbin's co. 39th rgt.

Thomas, George. 1st Lieutenant in Capt. Forrest's co. 4th Cavalry Dist. (Je. 5, 1812).

Thomas, George. Ensign in Capt. Woodburn's co. 45th rgt. (Je. 23, 1813).

Thomas, George. Private in Capt. Barr's Cavalry co. 1st Dist.

Thomas, George S. Private in Capt. Gray's co. 43d rgt.

Thomas, Isaac. Lieutenant in Capt. Decker's co. 7th rgt. (Ap. 27, 1813).

Thomas, Isaac. Private in Capt. Haubert's co. 51st rgt.

Thomas, Isaac. Sergeant in Capt. Miller's co. 39th rgt.

Thomas, James. Major in 4th Cavalry Dist. (F. 13, 1812).

Thomas, James. Sergeant in Capt. Dyer's co. 17th rgt.

Thomas, James H. Corporal in Capt. Galt's co. 6th rgt.

Thomas, John. Lieutenant and Quarter-master in 5th rgt.

Thomas, John. Quarter-master in 1st rgt. Artillery.

Thomas, John. Sergeant in Capt. A. E. Warner's co. 39th rgt.

Thomas, John. Sergeant in Capt. Ringgold's co. 6th rgt.

Thomas, John. Corporal in Capt. Haubert's co. 51st rgt.

Thomas, John. Private in Capt. Edes' co. 27th rgt.

Thomas, John. Private in Capt. McConckin's co. 38th rgt.

Thomas, John, Sr. Private in Capt. Linthicum's co. 22d rgt.

Thomas, John H. Surgeon's mate 33d rgt. (Jy. 18, 1812).

Thomas, John Hanson. Paymaster in 1st Cavalry Dist. (Jy. 14, 1814).

Thomas, John R. Private in Capt. Linthicum's co. 22d rgt.

Thomas, John W. Private in Capt. Magruder's co. American Artillerists.

Thomas, Joseph. Lieutenant in Capt. Biddle's co. 49th rgt. (Mr. 25, 1814).

Thomas, Joseph. Corporal in Capt. Howard's co. Mechanical Volunteers.

Thomas, Joseph. Private in Capt. Griffith's co. 21st rgt.

Thomas, Joseph. Private in Capt. Stiles' co. Marine Artillery.

Thomas, Joseph. Private in Capt. Sands' co. 22d rgt.; in Capt. Slicer's co.

Thomas, Lambert. Private in Capt. Shrim's co. Balto. Light Infantry.

Thomas, Lewis. 1st Lieutenant in Capt. Evans' co. 8th Cavalry Dist. (Ap. 23, 1812).

Thomas, Nathan. Private in Capt. Dunnington's co. 43d rgt.

Thomas, Oliver H. Private in Capt. Moale's co. Columbian Artillery.

Thomas, Otho. Lieutenant in Capt. Dawson's co. 28th rgt. (Jy. 8, 1814) vice Nicholls.

Thomas, Philip. Aid-de-camp to Genl. Foreman, 1st Brigade.

Thomas, Philip. Private in Capt. Barnes' co. 32d rgt.

Thomas, Philip. Private in Capt. Wells' Artillery co. 22d rgt.

Thomas, Richard S., Jr. Ensign in Capt. Hand's co. 21st rgt. (Jy. 12, 1812) vice Martin.

Thomas, Samuel. Captain Artillery co. 12th Brigade Talbot Co. (Ap. 20, 1808). Resigned July, 1814.

Thomas, Samuel. Lieutenant in Capt. Taylor's co. 38th rgt. (Jy. 28, 1812).

Thomas, Samuel W. Private in Capt. Massey's co. 38th rgt.

Thomas, Sterling. Corporal in Capt. Faster's co. 51st rgt.

Thomas, Thomas. Private in Capt. Lawrence's co. 6th rgt.

Thomas, William. Surgeon in 12th rgt. (D. 10, 1813).

Thomas, William. Corporal in Capt. Bouldin's co. Independent Light Dragoons.

Thomas, William. Private in Capt. Burke's co. 6th rgt.

Thomas, William. Private in Capt. Marker's co. 28th rgt.

Thomas, William. Private in Capt. Stiles' co. Marine Artillery.

Thomas, William P. Private in Capt. Dent's co. 43d rgt.

Thompson, Absalom. Private in Capt. Brohawn's co. 48th rgt.

Thompson, Alexander. Captain of the privateer Inca, Aug., 1812; Captain of the Midas.

Thompson, Alexander. Private in Capt. Haubert's co. 51st rgt.

Thompson, Alexander, Jr. Private Capt. Faster's co. 51st rgt.

Thompson, Andrew. Private in Capt. Taylor's co. 46th rgt.

Thompson, Aquila. Lieutenant in Capt. Ramply's co. 40th rgt. (Je. 16, 1812).

Thompson, Barzillai. Private in Capt. Causin's troop, attached to 12th rgt.

Thompson, Benedict. Private in Capt. Gray's co. 43d rgt.

Thompson, Bernard. Private in Capt. Watson's co. 39th rgt.

Thompson, Caleb. Private in Capt. Jos. Jones' co. 34th rgt.

Thompson, Charles. Lieutenant of the privateer Ultor, March, 1814.

Thompson, Clement. Private in Capt. Cawood's co. 45th rgt.

Thompson, David. Private in Capt. Dillon's co. 27th rgt.

Thompson, David. Corporal in Capt. Stewart's co. 51st rgt.

Thompson, David. Private in Capt. Pennington's co. Balto. Independent Artillerists.

Thompson, Edward. Musician in Capt. Myers' co. Franklin Artillery.

Thompson, Elias. Private in Capt. Haubert's co. 51st rgt.

Thompson, Francis. Captain in 43d rgt. (Ap. 20, 1813).

Thompson, George. Private in Capt. Massey's co. 38th rgt.

Thompson, George. Private in Capt. Blakistone's co. 45th rgt.

Thompson, Henry. Captain in 5th Cavalry Dist. (F. 13, 1813) ; Captain Ind. co. Horse Artillery, 3d Brigade, (D. 9, 1813).

Thompson, Henry. Sergeant in Capt. Maynard's co. 22d rgt.

Thompson, Hugh, Jr. Ensign in Capt. Knox's co. 47th rgt. (Ap. 18, 1809).

Thompson, James. Private in Capt. Lawrence's co. 6th rgt.

Thompson, James. Private in Capt. Steever's co. 27th rgt.

Thompson, James. Corporal in Capt. Patton's co. 30th rgt.

Thompson, James. Private in Capt. Levering's co. Independent Blues.

Thompson, James M. Private in Capt. Shryock's co. 24th rgt.

Thompson, John. Sergeant in Capt. Sands' co. 22d rgt.

Thompson, John. Sergeant in Capt. Owings' co. 32d rgt.

Thompson, John. Private in Capt. Pinkney's Artillery co. (Ag., 1813) ; Private in Capt. Slicer's co. 22d rgt. (N., 1814).

Thompson, John. Private in Capt. Pinney's co. 27th rgt.

Thompson, John. Private in Capt. Snowden's co. 36th rgt.

Thompson, John. Private in Capt. Dobbin's co. 39th rgt.

Thompson, John. Private in Capt. Stewart's co. 51st rgt.

Thompson, John. Private in Capt. Deems' co. 51st rgt.

Thompson, John. Private in Capt. Stiles' co. Marine Artillery.

Thompson, John F. Private in Capt. Stapleton's co. 39th rgt.

Thompson, John W. 2d Lieutenant in 14th U. S. Infantry (Mr. 12, 1812) ; 1st Lieutenant (Je. 26, 1813).

Thompson, Richard. Private in Capt. Bunbury's co. Sea Fencibles.

Thompson, Robert. Private in Capt. Fendall's co. 43d rgt.

Thompson, Samuel. Captain Artillery co. 1st Brigade Cecil Co. (S. 10, 1814).

Thompson, Samuel. Captain in 2d rgt. 1st Cavalry Dist. (Je. 26, 1812).

Thompson, Samuel. Private in Capt. Roney's co. 39th rgt.

Thompson, Stephen. Private in Capt. A. E. Warner's co. 39th rgt.

Thompson, Stephen Jay. 3d Lieutenant in Capt. Magruder's co. American Artillerists (Mr. 23, 1814).

Thompson, Thomas. Private in Capt. Levering's co. Independent Blues.

Thompson, Thomas. Private in Waters' co. 22d rgt.

Thompson, Thomas. Private in Capt. Dent's co. 43d rgt.

Thompson, Thomas. Private in Capt. Blakisone's co. 45th rgt.

Thompson, Walter. Private in Capt. Snowden's co. 36th rgt.

Thompson, William. Lieutenant in Capt. Matthews' co. 1st rgt. (D. 7, 1813); Captain (Jy. 11, 1814).

Thompson, William [-1844]. Ensign in 14th U. S. Infantry (Mr. 13, 1813); 2d Lieutenant (Ag. 5, 1814).

Thompson, William. Private in Capt. Levering's co. Independent Blues.

Thompson, William. Private in Capt. Lawrence's co. 6th rgt.

Thompson, William. Private in Capt. Sands' co. 22d rgt.; in Capt. Slicer's co. 22d rgt.

Thompson, William. Corporal in Capt. Hall's co. 30th rgt.

Thompson, William. Private in in Capt. Roney's co. 39th rgt.

Thompson, William. Private in in Capt. Stewart's co. 51st rgt.

Thompson, William. Private in in Capt. Myers' co. Franklin Artillery.

Thompson, William. Seaman of the privateer Surprise, drowned, April 5, 1815.

Thomson, Alexander. Private in Capt. Fowler's co. 46th rgt.

Thornburgh, James C. Private in Capt. Peters' co. 51st rgt.

Thornton, Aaron. Sergeant in Capt. Linthicum's co. 22d rgt.

Thornton, Edward. Private in Capt. Haubert's co. 51st rgt.

Thornton, Joseph. Private in Capt. Adreon's co. Union Volunteers.

Thornton, Sergood. Private in Capt. Brown's co. 6th rgt.

Thorp, William. Lieutenant in Capt. Griffin's co. 36th rgt. (O. 30, 1807).

Thraikill, George. Private in Capt. Chalmers' co. 51st rgt.

Thrasher, Peter. Private in Capt. Blair's co. 50th rgt.

Thrush, John. Private in Capt. Chalmers' co. 51st rgt.

Thrush, Nicholas. Private in Capt. Miller's co. 39th rgt.

Tice, Daniel. Private in Capt. John Miller's co., 2d D. I.; b. Washington Co., Md.; age 22; weaver.

Tice, John. Private in Capt. Shryock's co. 24th rgt.

Tidings, Rinaldo. Private in Capt. Chalmers' co. 51st rgt.

Tidings, Samuel. Private in Ensign Brewer's detachment, 36th rgt.

Tiernan, Michael. Private in Capt. Thompson's co. 1st Baltimore Horse Artillery.

Tilden, Charles. Surgeon in Extra Battalion Caroline Co. (My. 12, 1812); Surgeon in 8th Cavalry dist. (Ag. 20, 1813).

Tilden, Perry. Private in Capt. Stiles' co. Marine Artillery.

Tildon, William B. Surgeon in 33d rgt. (Ag. 20, 1813).

Tilghman, Frisby. Lieutenant-Colonel in 1st Cavalry Dist. (F. 13, 1812.)

Tilghman, Henry. Lieutenant in Capt. Hand's co. 21st rgt. (N. 7, 1812).

Tilghman, James. Lieutenant in 23d rgt.

Tilghman, John. Adjutant in 38th rgt. (Ap. 23, 1813).

Tilghman, Matthew. Captain in 33d rgt.; Adjutant in 3d Brigade.

Tilghman, Tench. Quarter-master in 9th Cavalry Dist. (Jy. 24, 1813).

Till, William. Private in Capt. Peters' co. 51st rgt.

Tillard, John. Ensign in Capt. Tillard's co. 2d rgt. (Je. 6, 1812).

Tillard, William S.. Captain in 2d rgt. (Ap. 5, 1808).

Tilly, Reuben. Private in Capt. Linthicum's co. 22d rgt.

Tilton, James. Surgeon in 4th rgt. (Jy. 4, 1812).

Tilyard, James. Private in Capt. Moale's co. Columbian Artillery.

Tilyard, John. Private in Capt. Stapleton's co. 39th rgt.

Tilyard, Philip. Sergeant in Capt. Berry's co. Washington Artillery.

Tilyard, William. Private in Capt. Levering's co. Independent Blues.

Timanus, Charles. Captain in 36th rgt. (N. 3, 1812).

Timanus, George. Major in 36th rgt. (D. 24, 1813).

Timanus, Henry. Ensign in Capt. Smith's co. 51st rgt.

Timanus, John. Private in Capt. Adreon's co. Union Volunteers.

Timbs, William. Private in Capt. Hayward's co. 4th rgt.

Tims, Benjamin. Private in Capt. Kierstead's co. 6th rgt.

Tincter, W. P. Private in Capt. Lawrence's co. 6th rgt.

Tingle, William. 2d Lieutenant in Capt. White's co. 11th Cavalry Dist. (My., 1812).

Tippett, Hezekiah. Private in Capt. Cawood's co. 45th rgt.

Tippett, John. Private in Capt. Dyer's co. 17th rgt.

Tippett, Robert. Private in Capt. Cawood's co. 45th rgt.

Tipton, Micajah. Lieutenant in Capt. Bond's co. 7th rgt. (Je. 26, 1812).

Tittle, Jeremiah. Private in Capt. Pinney's co. 27th rgt.

Tittle, Jeremiah. Private in Capt. Adreon's co. Union Volunteers.

Tittle, Samuel. Private in Capt. Adreon's co. Union Volunteers.

Todd, —. Surgeon in 36th rgt. Resigned July 13, 1814.

Todd, Bernard [-1816]. Private in Capt. Stansbury's co. 6th rgt. Cavalry.

Todd, Curtis. Private in Capt. Travers' co. 48th rgt.

Todd, James. Private in Capt. Roney's co. 39th rgt.

Todd, Lancelott. Private in Capt. Thos. Warner's co. 39th rgt.

Todd, Naboth. Private in Capt. McNamara's co. 48th rgt.

Todd, Nathan. Private in Capt. Fallin's co. 48th rgt.

Todd, Samuel. Private in Capt. Kierstead's co. 6th rgt.

Toelle, Frederick. Surgeon in 5th Cavalry Dist. (Je. 26, 1812).

Toelle, Garrard. Private in Capt. McKane's co. 27th rgt.

Tolley, Alexander. Private in Capt. Travers' co. 48th rgt.

Tolley, John. Quarter-master in 42d rgt. (Mr. 4, 1808).

Tolley, John. Private in Capt. Brohawn's co. 48th rgt.

Tolley, Travers. Private in Capt. Travers' co. 48th rgt.

Tolson, Francis, Jr. Captain in 14th rgt. (F. 4, 1808).

Tomlinson, Jesse. Private in Capt. Blair's co. 50th rgt.

Tomlinson, Joseph. Captain in 50th rgt. (F. 15, 1814).

Tongue, Thomas. Lieutenant in Capt. Tillard's co. 2d rgt. (Ap. 5, 1808).

Tonson, Nathaniel. Private in Capt. Hands' co. 21st rgt.

Tootle [Tootel], Richard. Captain in 10th Cavalry Dist. (S. 26,

1812); Major (Jy. 7, 1814) vice Enalls.

Torrance, Charles, Jr. Private in Capt. Thompson's co. 1st Baltimore Horse Artillery.

Torrence, George. Private in Capt. Warfield's co. Balto. United Volunteers.

Torrence, John. Private in Capt. Levering's co. Independent Blues.

Torrenson, John. Private in Capt. Schwarzauer's co. 27th rgt.

Totten, Edmond. Private in Capt. Barnes' co. 32d rgt.

Toulson, Andrew. Private in Capt. Chambers' co. 21st rgt.

Toulson, Thomas. Private in Capt. Pinney's co. 27th rgt.

Tower, James [-1813]. Captain of privateer *Comet*, 1812-13.

Town, John. Private in Capt. Magruder's co. American Artillerists.

Townsend, Dennis. Private in Capt. Galt's co. 6th rgt.

Townsend, James. Private in Capt. Stewart's co. 51st rgt.

Townsend, Jonathan. Sergeant in Capt. McDonald's co. 6th rgt.

Townsend, Nehemiah. Major in Extra Battalion Caroline Co. (Ap. 5, 1808). Resigned F. 19, 1814.

Townsend, Perry. Private in Capt. Stewart's co. 51st rgt.

Towsley, William. Private in Capt. Ringgold's co. 6th rgt.

Towson, Henry H. Private in Capt. Howard's co. Mechanical Volunteers.

Towson, John. Private in Capt. Rogers' co. 51st rgt.

Towson, Joseph. Ensign in Capt. Pinney's co. 27th rgt.

Towson, Joseph. Ensign in 27th rgt. (N. 8, 1814).

Towson, Joshua. Private in Capt. Montgomery's co. Balto. Union Artillery.

Towson, Nathan [1783-1854]. Captain in 2d U. S. Artillery (Mr. 12, 1812); Bvt. Major (O. 8, 1812) for capturing the enemy's brig *Caledonia* under the guns of Ft. Erie, U. C.; Lieutenant-Colonel (Jy. 5, 1814) for distinguished and gallant conduct in the conflict of Chippewa, U. C.

Towson, O. W. Private in Capt. Pennigton's co. Balto. Independent Artillerists.

Towson, Thomas. Lieutenant in Capt. Howard's co. Mechanical Volunteers.

Towson, Thomas. Private in Capt. Rogers' co. 51st rgt.

Towson, William. Private in Capt. Ducker's co. 7th rgt.

Toy, Isaac N. Sergeant in Capt. Dillon's co. 27th rgt.

Toy, John D. [1794-1875]. Private in Capt. Adreon's co. Union Volunteers.

Toy, Joseph. Private in Capt. Stewart's co. 51st rgt.

Travers, Benjamin. Private in Capt. Travers' co. 48th rgt.

Travers, Charles. Lieutenant in Capt. Travers' co. 48th rgt. (Jy. 8, 1813).

Travers, Henry K. Private in Capt. Brohawn's co. 48th rgt.

Travers, Hicks. Private in Capt. Travers' co. 48th rgt.

Travers, Jeremiah. Private in Capt. Brohawn's co. 48th rgt.

Travers, John. Captain in 48th rgt. (Jy. 8, 1813).

Travers, John. Private in Capt. Shryock's co. 24th rgt.

Travers, John of Matthew. Private in Capt. Travers' co. 48th rgt.; Lieutenant in Capt. Brohawn's co. 48th rgt. (S. 2, 1807).

Travers, John H. Private in Capt. Travers' co. 48th rgt.

Travers, Robert. Private in Capt. Travers' co. 48th rgt.

Travers, Samuel. Sergeant in Capt. Brohawn's co. 48th rgt.

Travers, Thomas. Private in Capt. Travers' co. 48th rgt.

Travers, William. Private in Capt. Brown's co. 6th rgt.

Travers, William B. Lieutenant of the privateer *Tyro*, Jan., 1813.

Travers, William H. Private in Capt. Travers' co. 48th rgt.

Traverse, Henry. Private in Capt. Lawrence's co. 6th rgt.

Travlot, John. Private in Capt. Bunbury's co. Sea Fencibles.

Treakle, James. Ensign in Capt. Burgess's co. 32d rgt. (O. 26, 1807).

Tregoe, John. Drummer in Capt. Brohawn's co. 48th rgt.

Tregoe, John, Jr. Private in Capt. Woolford's co. 48th rgt.

Tregoe, Levin. Private in Capt. Brohawn's co. 48th rgt.

Trehearn, James. Private in Capt. Heath's co. 23d rgt.

Trehearn, Teacle. Private in Capt. Heath's co. 23d rgt.

Trexlear, Ignatius. Private in Capt. Piper's co. United Maryland Artillery.

Trickett, John. Private in Capt. Pinney's co. 27th rgt.

Tridle, Jacob. Private in Capt. Sheppard's co. 6th rgt.

Trigger, Ezekiel. Fifer in Capt. Chase's co. 22d rgt.

Triggle, Dorsey. Private in Capt. Haubert's co. 51st rgt.

Trill, Samuel. Private in Capt. Faster's co. 51st rgt.

Trimble, John. Private in Capt. Addison's co. Sea Fencibles.

Trimble, Joshua. Private in Capt. Levering's co. Independent Blues.

Triplet, James. Private in Capt. Thompson's co. 1st rgt.

Trout, John. Private in Capt. Getzendanner's co. 16th rgt.

Trowbridge, Reuben. Private in Capt. Smith's co. 51st rgt.

Troxell, George. 2d Lieutenant in Capt. Thompson's co. 2d rgt. 1st Cavalry Dist. (D. 22, 1812).

Troxell, Jacob. Lieutenant in Capt. Cushwa's co. 8th rgt. (Jy. 4, 1812).

Troxell, John. Private in Capt. Shryock's co. 24th rgt.

Trucit, Robert. Private in Capt. Schwarzauer's co. 27th rgt.

Truit, John R. Lieutenant in Capt. Purnell's co. 9th rgt. (O. 31, 1812).

Truitt, Zediah. Private in Capt. A. C. Smith's co. 49th rgt.

Trull, Abner A. Private in Capt. Blair's co. 50th rgt.

Trull, John. Private in Capt. Sterett's Independent co.

Trundle, Daniel. Lieutenant in Capt. Trundle's co. 3d rgt. (Ag. 30, 1808).

Trundle, John L. Captain in 3d rgt. (Ag. 30, 1808).

Trundle, Otho. Ensign in Capt. Dawson's co. 28th rgt. (Jy. 8, 1814) vice Thomas.

Tschudy, David. Private in Capt. Shryock's co. 24th rgt.

Tschudy, Samuel. Private in Capt. Sterett's co. 1st Balto. Hussars.

Tschudy, Wimbert. Adjutant in 35th rgt. (S. 24, 1810).

Tubman, Charles. Private in Capt. Travers' co. 48th rgt.

Tubman, Richard. Private in Capt. Brohawn's co. 48th rgt.

Tuck, Washington G. Private in Capt. Hall's co. 3d Cavalry rgt.

Tucker, James. Private in Capt. Dillon's co. 27th rgt.

Tucker, Joseph. Private in Capt. Ringgold's co. 6th rgt.

Tucker, Joshua. Private in Capt. Lawson's co. Balto. Patriots.

Tucker, Samuel. Private in Capt. Sands' co. 22d rgt.

Tucker, Samuel. Private in Capt. Slicer's co. 22d rgt.

Tucker, Thomas. Private in Capt. Linthicum's co. 22d rgt.

Tucker, W. A. Private in Capt. Stiles' co. Marine Artillery.

Tucker, William. Private in Capt. Lawrence's co. 6th rgt.

Tucker, William. Private in Capt. Gantt's co. 31st rgt.

Tucker, Zach. Private in Capt. Pumphrey's co. 22d rgt.

Tuel, James. Private in Capt. Snowden's co. 36th rgt.

Tuel, Martin. Private in Capt. Brown's co. 6th rgt.

Tull, Elijah. Private in Capt. Travers' co. 48th rgt.

Tull, Elzey. Ensign in Capt. Harper's co. 11th rgt. (Ag. 20, 1814).

Tull, James. Ensign in Capt. Lambden's co. 9th rgt. (Mr. 23, 1814).

Tull, John. Captain in Extra Battalion Worcester Co. (Je. 18, 1812).

Tull, Samuel. Ensign in Capt. Thos. Handy's co. 23d rgt. (D. 10, 1813).

Tumbleson [Tumblinson], William [-1863]. Private in Capt. Brown's co. 6th rgt.

Tumbuster, Jacob. Private in Capt. McLaughlin's co. 50th rgt.

Tunis, Samuel. Private in Capt. Schwarzauer's co. 27th rgt.

Tunnell, Isaiah. Private in Capt. Brown's co. 6th rgt.

Tupper, Thomas [-1818]. Ensign in 11th U. S. Infantry (Ag. 23, 1813) ; 2d Lieutenant (My. 2, 1814).

Turbett, Nicholas. Captain in 16th rgt. (S. 18, 1812).

Turfield, Philip. Private in Capt. Burke's co. 6th rgt.

Turley, Enoch. Captain of the privateer *Water Witch*, Aug., 1814.

Turman, Patrick. Private in Capt. Nicholson's co. Balto. Fencibles.

Turnbull, Matthew. Sergeant in Capt. Taylor's co. 48th rgt.

Turner, Aquila. Private in Capt. Posey's co. 1st rgt.

Turner, Caleb. Corporal in Capt. Horton's co. Maryland. Chasseurs.

Turner, Caleb. Private in Capt. Brown's co. 6th rgt.

Turner, Charles. Private in Capt. Howard's co. Mechanical Volunteers.

Turner, David G. Private in Capt. Bader's co. Union Yägers.

Turner, Edward, Jr. Captain in 26th rgt.

Turner, Henry. Quarter-master in 45th rgt. (Je. 5, 1812).

Turner, Isaac. Private in Capt. Galt's co. 6th rgt.

Turner, Joseph A. Private in Capt. Thompson's co. 1st rgt.

Turner, Jesse. Sergeant-Major in 45th rgt. (1813).

Turner, John. Captain in 40th rgt. (Je. 16, 1812).

Turner, John. Private in Capt. Montgomery's co. Balto. Union Artillery.

Turner, Jonathan. Private in Capt. Robey's co. 43d rgt.

Turner, Joseph. Private in Capt. Myers' co. Franklin Artillery.

Turner, Joshua. Lieutenant in Capt. Brashear's co. 13th rgt. (Ag. 20, 1814). Cashiered Oct. 16, 1814.

Turner, Nathan. Private in Capt. Magruder's co. American Artillerists.

Turner, Philip. Lieutenant in Capt. Briscoe's co. 45th rgt. (My. 23, 1812).

Turner, Robert. 3d Lieutenant in 2d U. S. Infantry (Jy. 14, 1814).

Turner, Shadrach. Private in Capt. Beall's co. 34th rgt.

Turner, Stephen O. Lieutenant of the privateer *Wasp*, Feb., 1813.

Turner, Thomas. Ensign in Capt. Hatherly's co. 22d rgt. (Ap. 28, 1814).

Turner, Thomas. Private in Capt. Hall's co. 3d Cavalry rgt.

Turner, Thomas. Private in Capt. Hanna's co. Fells Point Light Dragoons.

Turner, William. Lieutenant in Capt. Talbot's co. 19th rgt. (My. 22, 1812).

Turner, William. Surgeon in 17th U. S. Infantry (Ap. 7, 1813).

Turpin, Francis. Captain in 11th rgt. (Je. 18, 1794).

Turpin, George. Private in Capt. Watson's co. 39th rgt.

Turpin, Sacka. Private in Capt. Dillon's co. 27th rgt.

Turpin, Thomas B. Lieutenant in Capt. McConckin's co. 38th rgt.

Turpine, Sewell. Quarter-master in 9th rgt. (N. 7, 1810).

Tustin, Samuel. Private in Capt. Levering's co. Independent Blues.

Tutts, George. Private in Capt. Peters' co. 51st rgt.

Tutwiler, David. Ensign in 14th U. S. Infantry (N. 22, 1814).

Tweeting, Thomas. Lieutenant and Adjutant in 51st rgt.

Twig, Robert. Private in Capt. John Miller's co., 2d D. I.; b. Balto. Co., Md.; age 23; shoemaker; subs. for Henry Keedy.

Tyar, Charles C. Private in Capt. Burgess' co. 43d rgt.

Tyar, John C. Corporal in Capt. Brown's co. 43d rgt.

Tydings, Edward. Private in Capt. Burgess' co. 43d rgt.

Tydings, Horatio. Corporal in Capt. Dent's co. 43d rgt.

Tydings, John. Private in Capt. Burgess' co. 43d rgt.

Tydings, Richard. Private in Capt. Dunnington's co. 43d rgt.

Tydings, Samuel. Private in Capt. Wells' Artillery co. 22d rgt.

Tyler, John. Bosu'n Capt. Addison's co. Sea Fencibles.

Tyler, John. Private in Capt. Brown's co. Eagle Artillerists.

Tyler, John C. Private in Capt. Howard's co. Mechanical Volunteers.

Tyler, Levin. Private in Capt. Thos. Warner's co. 39th rgt.

Tyler, Richard G. Sergeant in Capt. Chew's co. 31st rgt.

Tyler, William. Paymaster in 16th rgt. (Je. 22, 1808).

Tyson, William. Private in Capt. Sample's co. 49th rgt.

U

Uhler, Erasmus. Lieutenant in Capt. Miller's co. 39th rgt.

Uhler, Frederick. Private in Capt. Ringgold's co. 6th rgt.

Uhler, George. Private in Capt. Levering's co. Independent Blues.

Uhler, Henry. Private in Capt. Watson's co. 39th rgt.

Uhler, Philip. Private in Capt. Sterett's Independent co.

Umstead, —. Captain in 25th rgt. [1813].

Una, Joseph. Seaman of the privateer *Comet*.

Underwood, George. Private in Capt. Chase's co. 22d rgt.

Underwood, John, Jr. Private in Capt. McKane's co. 27th rgt.

Undrech, Henry. Private in Capt. Bader's co. Union Yägers.

Updicraft, David. Private in Capt. John Miller's co., 2d D. I.; b. Md.; age 35; wagon-maker; subs. for Jacob Baker.

Uppercoo, Frederick. Private in Capt. Ducker's co. 7th rgt.

Upperone, Jacob. Ensign in Capt. Stocksdale's co. 15th rgt. (O. 1, 1811).

Urie, Henry. Private in Capt. Wickes' co. 21st rgt.

Urie, Jeremiah. Private in Capt. Edes' co. 27th rgt.

Usher, James. Private in Capt. Stewart's co. Washington Blues.

Usher, John P. Adjutant in 46th rgt. (Ag. 1, 1814) vice Bowly.

Usselton, Aquila M. 1st Lieutenant in Capt. Morrison's Artillery co. 21st rgt. (Jy. 14, 1812); Captain (Ap. 21, 1814).

Usselton, James. Private in Capt. Usselton's co. 21st rgt.

Usselton, John. Private in Capt. Chambers' co. 21st rgt.

Usselton, William T. Private in Capt. Usselton's co. 21st rgt.

Utt, John F. Sergeant in Capt. Stewart's co. 51st rgt.

V

Valentine, Archibald K. Private in Capt. Ringgold's co. 6th rgt.

Valiant, John. Gunner in Capt. Bunbury's co. Sea Fencibles.

Valiant, Thomas P. Sergeant in Capt. Seth's co. 4th rgt.

Vallean, Henry. Private in Capt. Haubert's co. 51st rgt.

Valleau, Henry. Lieutenant in Capt. Courtney's co. 42d rgt. (Ap. 27, 1813).

Vallon, Peregrine. Private in Capt. Allen's co. 49th rgt.

Vanarsdale, James H. Ensign in Capt. Miller's co. 39th rgt.

Vanbaun, William. Private in Capt. Edes' co. 27th rgt.

Vanberger, John. Private in Capt. Steever's co. 27th rgt.

Van Bibber, James. Private in Capt. Ducker's co. 7th rgt.

Van Buren, Egbert. Sergeant in Capt. Stiles' co. Marine Artillery.

Van Buskirk, Daniel. Lieutenant in Stephen's co. 8th rgt. (Ag. 14, 1810).

Vance, James. Sergeant in Capt. Oldham's co. 49th rgt.

Vance, John. Private in Capt. Levering's co. Independent Blues.

Vance, Thomas. Sergeant in Capt. Pennington's co. Balto. Independent Artillerists.

Vance, William. Private in Capt. Nicholson's co. Balto. Fencibles.

Vanderford, John. Private in Capt. Massey's co. 38th rgt.

Van Harten, Gerrard. Private in Capt. Bader's co. Union Yägers.

Van Horn, Archibald. Adjutant in 14th rgt. (Ap. 18, 1798); Captain (My. 26, 1802).

Vanhorn, Fielding. Private in Capt. Ringgold's co. 6th rgt.

Vanhorn, James. Private in Capt. Burke's co. 6th rgt.

Vanlamp, Henry. Seaman of the privateer *Surprise,* drowned April 5, 1815.

Vanlear, John. Private in Capt. Steuart's co. Washington Blues.

Van Lear, Matthew. Private in Capt. Myers' co. 39th rgt.

Van Lear, Matthew Simms. Surgeon in 24th rgt. (Jy. 12, 1814) vice Downey.

Vanlill, Henry. Private in Capt. Snowden's co. 36th rgt.

Van Riswick, Thomas. Ensign in Capt. Geo. Morgan's co. 45th rgt.

Vansant, Benjamin. Ensign in Capt. Massey's co. 33d rgt. Resigned Aug. 4, 1814.

Vansant, Christopher. Private in Capt. Steever's co. 27th rgt.

Vansant, Ephraim. Captain in 33d rgt.

Vansant, John. Private in Capt. Miller's co. 39th rgt.

Vansant, Lemuel. Ensign in Capt. Massey's co. 33d rgt. (Ag. 4, 1814) vice Vansant.

Vansickle, Henry. Cornet in Capt. Smith's co. 7th Cavalry Dist. (Ap. 25, 1812).

Vansickle, Zachariah. Private in Capt. Blair's co. 50th rgt.

Vanwinkle, Samuel. Private in Capt. Dyer's co. Fells Point Riflemen.

Vanwinkle, William. Private in Capt. Dyer's co. Fells Point Riflemen.

Van Wyck, John C. Private in Capt. Sterett's co. 1st Balto. Hussars.

Van Wyck, Stedman R. Private in Capt. Warfield's co. Balto. United Volunteers; wounded at North Point.

Varden, Robert B. Corporal in Capt. Pinney's co. 27th rgt.

Varlinden, John. Private in Capt. King's co. 49th rgt.

Varnor, Robert. Private in Capt. Burke's co. 6th rgt.

Vashon, George [-1835]. 1st Lieutenant in 10th U. S. Infantry (Mr. 12, 1812); Captain (N. 29, 1813).

Veazey, Edward. Captain of the privateer *Baltimore,* Aug., 1812; of the *Lawrence,* 1814-15.

Veazey, John T. Private in Capt. Morgan's co. 49th rgt.

Veazey, Joseph. Corporal in Capt. Sample's co. 49th rgt.

Veazey, Peregrine. Adjutant in 49th rgt.

Veazey, Peregrine W. Private in Capt. Morgan's co. 49th rgt.

Veazey, Thomas B. Private in Capt. Morgan's co. 49th rgt.

Veazey, Thomas W. Lieutenant-Colonel in 49th rgt.

Veitch, James. Captain in 34th rgt. (Je. 27, 1812).

Veitch, John. Lieutenant in Capt. Veitch's co. 34th rgt. (Je. 27, 1812).

Vermillion, Joseph. Private in Capt. Smith's co. 51st rgt.

Vermillion, Thomas. Private in Capt. Crawfurd's co. 17th rgt.

Vial, Nicholas. Captain of the privateer *Fox,* Feb., 1813.

Vickers, Clement. 1st Lieutenant in Capt. Thomas' Artillery co. 21st rgt. (Ap. 20, 1808); Captain (Jy. 12, 1814) vice Thomas.

Vickers, James. Private in Capt.
Chambers' co. 21st rgt.

Vickers, James. Private in Capt.
Stiles' co. Marine Artillery.

Vickers, Jesse. Private in Capt.
Chambers' co. 21st rgt.

Vickers, Joel [1774-1860]. Corporal
in Capt. Stiles' co. Marine Artillery.

Vickers, John. Ensign in Capt. Hayward's co. 4th rgt. (Se. 10, 1814).

Vickers, Samuel. Private in Capt.
Hand's co. 21st rgt.

Vickers, Thomas. Private in Capt.
Hands' co. 21st rgt.

Vickers, William. Private in Capt.
Brohawn's co. 48th rgt.

Viers, Jesse. Ensign in Capt. Vincent's co. 3d rgt. (Je. 17, 1813).

Vincent, Jeremiah. Private in Capt.
Jas. Massey's co. 38th rgt.

Vincent, Thomas W. Captain in 3d
rgt. (Ja. 10, 1810).

Vinnemont, Hopkins. Private in
Capt. McConckin's co. 38th rgt.

Vinson, Benjamin. Ensign in Capt.
Milson's co. 37th rgt. (Jy. 8, 1813).

Vinson, Bruffit [-1814]. Captain in Artillery co. 12th Brigade
Talbot Co. (D. 10, 1813).

Vinson, John. Captain in 11th rgt.
(Ag. 20, 1814).

Vinson, Willis. Lieutenant in Capt.
Hodson's co. Extra Battalion Dorchester Co. (Ap. 21, 1814).

Vinton, Perry. Fifer in Capt. Colston's co. 48th rgt.

Vinyard, James. Private in Capt.
Addison's co. Sea Fencibles.

Voss, Ebenezer. Private in Capt.
Brohawn's co. 48th rgt.

Voyce, Thomas. Private in Capt.
Berry's co. Washington Artillery.

W

Waddam, George. Private in Capt.
Conway's co. 6th rgt.

Wade, George. Private in Capt. Dillon's co. 27th rgt.

Wade, James. Captain in 44th rgt.
(Ag. 22, 1812).

Wade, William. Captain of the privateer *Chasseur*, Dec., 1813; Private in Capt. Stiles' co. Marine Artillery.

Wadlow, John. Private in Capt.
Dillon's co. 27th rgt.

Wagers, Upton. Quarter-master in
13th rgt. (S. 10, 1814).

Waggaman, Henry. P. Surgeon's
mate Extra Battalion Dorchester
Co. (O. 12, 1807).

Waggoner, Jacob. Sergeant in Capt.
McLaughlin's co. 50th rgt.

Wagman, John. Private in Capt.
Quantrill's co. 24th rgt.

Wagner, J. C. Sergeant in Capt.
Sadtler's co. Balto Yägers.

Wagner, John. Private in Capt.
Snowden's co. 36th rgt.

Wagoner, George. Private in Capt.
Sheppard's co. 6th rgt.

Waile, George. Sergeant in Capt.
Stewart's co. 51st rgt.

Wailes, Benjamin. Private in Capt.
Naylor's co. 17th rgt.

Wailes, John. Lieutenant in Capt.
Dashiell's co. 25th rgt. (N. 15,
1809).

Wainwright, Joseph. Private in
Capt. Cawood's co. 45th rgt.

Waites, James D. Private in Capt.
Burke's co. 6th rgt.

Waites, Richard. Private in Capt.
Burke's co. 6th rgt.

Walgamot, John. Corporal in Capt.
Barr's Cavalry co. 1st Dist.

Walker, Benjamin. Private in Capt.
Schwarzauer's co. 27th rgt.

Walker, David. Private in Capt. Barnes' co. 32d rgt.

Walker, Francis. Private in Capt. Dyer's co. 17th rgt.

Walker, Frederick. Private in Capt. Oldham's co. 49th rgt.

Walker, Isaac. Private in Capt. Watson's co. 39th rgt.

Walker, Jacob. Private in Capt. Wilson's co. 6th rgt.

Walker, James. Captain in 45th rgt.; Bvt. Major.

Walker, John. Private in Capt. Ringgold's co. 6th rgt.

Walker, John. Private in Capt. Williams' co. 12th rgt.

Walker, John G. Adjutant in 7th rgt. (F. 1, 1814).

Walker, Jonathan. Private in Capt. Dyer's co. Fells Point Riflemen.

Walker, Peter. Private in Capt. Stewart's co. 51st rgt.

Walker, Samuel. Private in Capt. Piper's co. United Maryland Artillery.

Walker, Sater T. Private in Capt. Horton's co. Maryland Chasseurs.

Walker, Thomas. Private in Capt. Warfield's co. Balto. United Volunteers.

Walker, Thomas C. Hospital Surgeon's mate U. S. (Jy. 2, 1813).

Walker, Wesley. Forage master, 11th Brigade.

Walker, William. Private in Capt. Myers' co. Franklin Artillery.

Wall, John E. Private in Capt. Steuart's co. Washington Blues.

Wall, John T. Ensign in Capt. Skinner's co. 17th rgt. (S. 16, 1807).

Wall, William. Private in Capt. Sterett's Independent co.

Wall, William B. Private in Capt. Haden's co. 17th rgt.

Wallace, J. A. Sergeant in Capt. Nicholson's co. Balto. Fencibles.

Wallace, James. Captain in 18th rgt. (D. 4, 1810).

Wallace, James. Private in Capt. Brown's co. Eagle Artillerists.

Wallace, James. Private in Capt. Addison's co. Sea Fencibles.

Wallace, James. Private in Capt. Pinney's co. 27th rgt.

Wallace, James, Sr. 2d Lieutenant in Capt. Evans' Artillery co. 1st Brigade (O. 21, 1808).

Wallace, James B. Private in Capt. Moore's co. 49th rgt.

Wallace, John. Private in Capt. Travers' co. 48th rgt.

Wallace, John T. Lieutenant in Capt. Chalmers' co. 51st rgt.

Wallace, Joseph. Hospital surgeon's mate, U. S. (Jy. 15, 1813).

Wallace, Joseph. Private in Capt. Moore's co. 49th rgt.

Wallace, Joseph. Private in Capt. Pike's co. Balto. Volunteer Artillery.

Wallace, Matthew. Ensign in Capt. Taylor's co. 48th rgt. (S. 2, 1811).

Wallace, Robert. Quarter-master in 11th rgt. (Ja. 25, 1814) vice Smith.

Wallace, Solomon. Private in Capt. Magruder's co. American Artillerists.

Wallace, Thomas. Private in Capt. Edes' co. 27th rgt.

Wallace, Thomas. Sergeant in Capt. Mackey's co. 49th rgt.

Wallace, William M. Corporal in Capt. Pennington's co. Balto. Independent Artillerists.

Waller, Henry. Private in Capt. Barr's Cavalry co. 1st Dist.

Wallick, Mathias. Private in Capt. Shryock's co. 24th rgt.

Wallingsford, Joseph. Private in Capt. Veitch's co. 34th rgt.

Wallis, John, Jr. Private in Capt. Sterett's co. 1st Balto. Hussars.

Walls, Dawkins. Sergeant in Capt. Duvall's co. 34th rgt.

Walls, James. Corporal in Capt. Hook's co. 2d rgt.

Walmsley, Isaac T. Private in Capt. Mackey's co. 49th rgt.

Walmsley, Thomas. Private in Capt. Morgan's co. 49th rgt.

Walmsley, William, Jr. Private in Capt. Allen's co. 49th rgt.

Walpole, Gerard. Private in Capt. Dent's co. 43d rgt.

Walsh, Jacob, Jr. Captain in United Maryland Artillery (Ap. 30, 1813) ; 2d Lieutenant (Jy. 11, 1814).

Walsh, James. Private in Capt. Moale's co. Columbian Artillery.

Walsh, John. Private in Capt. Pennington's co. Balto. Independent Artillerists.

Walsh, John. Private in Capt. Warfield's co. Balto. United Volunteers.

Walsh, Moses. Private in Capt. Addison's co. Sea Fencibles.

Walstern, Samuel. Private in Capt. Conway's co. 6th rgt.

Walter, Benjamin. Private in Capt. Deems' co. 51st rgt.

Walter, Henry. Private in Capt. Bader's co. Union Yägers.

Walter, John. Private in Capt. Montgomery's co. Balto. Union Artillery.

Walter, John. Private in Capt. Adreon's co. Union Volunteers.

Walter, Joseph A. Private in Capt. Smith's co. 51st rgt.

Walter, Justus. Private in Capt. Sadtler's co. Balto. Yägers.

Walter, Philip. Private in Capt. Miller's co. 39th rgt.

Walter, William. Private in Capt. Faster's co. 51st rgt.

Walters, —. Captain in 23d rgt. [1813-14].

Walters, Alexander. Captain in 6th Cavalry Dist. (F. 13, 1812).

Walters, Alexander. Private in Capt. Cawood's co. 45th rgt.

Walters, Samuel. Cornet in Capt. Walters' co. 6th Cavalry Dist. (Ap. 26, 1812).

Waltham, William. Private in Capt. Galt's co. 6th rgt.

Walton, Charlton. Ensign in Capt. Galloway's co. 46th rgt.

Walton, Nathaniel. Private in Capt. Dillon's co. 27th rgt.

Walton, William. Lieutenant in Capt. Hatchison's co. 9th rgt. (Jy. 8, 1814).

Walts, John. Corporal in Capt. McLaughlin's co. 50th rgt.

Waltz, Otho. Captain in 16th rgt. (Jy. 15, 1814).

Wamaling, John. Private in Capt. Berry's co. Washington Artillery.

Wampler, Lewis J. Private in Capt. Pike's co. Balto. Volunteer Artillery.

Wampler, Nathaniel. Private in Capt. Galt's co. 6th rgt.

Wan, James. Private in Capt. Dillon's co. 27th rgt.

Wane, John. Corporal in Capt. Burke's co. 6th rgt.

Wane, Ralph. Drummer in Capt. Wilson's co. 6th rgt.

Waram, Abram. Private in Capt. Page's co. 21st rgt.

Waram, John. Private in Capt. Hynson's co. 21st rgt.

Ward, Edward. Private in Capt. Haubert's co. 51st rgt.

Ward, Hezekiah. Lieutenant in Capt. Phillip's co. 3d rgt. (O. 12, 1807).

Ward, James. 3d Lieutenant in 38th U. S. Infantry (My. 20, 1813); Captain Assistant Deputy Quarter-master General (Ag. 31, 1813).

Ward, James. Private in Capt. Faster's co. 51st rgt.

Ward, James. Private in Capt. Haubert's co. 51st rgt.

Ward, John. Lieutenant in Capt. Thos. Handy's co. 23d rgt. (D. 10, 1813).

Ward, John. Private in Capt. Dent's co. 43d rgt.

Ward, John. Private in Capt. A. C. Smith's co. 49th rgt.

Ward, John. Landsman of the privateer *Chasseur,* deserted Jan. 15, 1815 at St. Pierre.

Ward, John D. Private in Capt. Peters' co. 51st rgt.

Ward, John W. Private in Capt. Levering's co. Independent Blues.

Ward, Joshua. Private in Capt. A. C. Smith's co. 49th rgt.

Ward, Peregrine. Corporal in Capt. Kierstead's co. 6th rgt.

Ward, Samuel. Corporal in Capt. Thomas' co. 49th rgt.

Ward, Solomon. Private in Capt. Sterett's co. 1st Balto. Hussars.

Ward, William. Lieutenant in Capt. Wiggins' co. Extra Battalion Harford Co. (Jy. 8, 1814) vice Miller.

Ward, William. Private in Capt. Fendall's co. 43d rgt.

Ward, William. Sergeant in Capt. Thomas' co. 49th rgt.

Warder, John. Private in Capt. Brown's co. 43d rgt.

Warder, Walter. 1st Sergeant in Capt. Brown's co. 43d rgt.

Ware, John. Private in Capt. Faster's co. 51st rgt.

Ware, Nicholas. Sergeant-Major in 1st rgt.

Ware, Robert. Quarter-master in 36th rgt. (Je. 1, 1808).

Wareham, George. Private in Capt. Berry's co. Washington Artillery.

Wareham, Joseph. Private in Capt. Quantrill's co. 24th rgt.

Warfield, Alfred. Lieutenant in Capt. C. D. Warfield's co. 32d rgt. vice Welsh.

Warfield, Allen. Private in Capt. Hall's co. 3d Cavalry rgt.

Warfield, Basil H. Private in Capt. Smith's co. 51st rgt.

Warfield, Charles A. Lieutenant in Capt. Thomas' co. 3d Cavalry Dist. (My. 8, 1812); Captain (Jy. 6, 1814) vice Thomas.

Warfield, Charles D. Captain in 32d rgt. (Ap. 26, 1813).

Warfield, David [-1821]. Captain in Balto. United Volunteers. (Not at Bladensburg or North Point.)

Warfield, George. Private in Capt. Bunbury's co. Sea Fencibles.

Warfield, Gustavus. Surgeon in 3d Cavalry Dist. (O. 22, 1812).

Warfield, Philemon D. Lieutenant in Capt. Adam Barnes' co. 32d rgt. (N. 30, 1811).

Warfield, Surat. 1st Lieutenant in Capt. Clemson's Artillery co. 7th Brigade (Ap. 23, 1808).

Warfield, Surrat D. Captain in 29th rgt. (S. 20, 1813) vice Young.

Warfield, Thomas W. Private in Capt. Waters' co. 22d rgt.

Warfield, William. Private in Capt. Maynard's co. 22d rgt.

Warfield, Zadoc. Ensign in Capt. Austin's co. 44th rgt. (D. 16, 1813) vice Buxton.

Waring, Charles R. 2d Lieutenant United Maryland Artillery (My. 19, 1813) vice Butler.

Waring, Francis. Sergeant in Capt. Isaac's co. 34th rgt.

Waring, George W. Private in Capt. Sterett's co. 1st Balto. Hussars.

Waring, Henry. Major in 34th rgt.; Lieutenant-Colonel (O., 1814).

Waring, John. 2d Lieutenant in 14th U. S. Infantry (Mr. 12, 1812); Capt. (N. 14, 1814).

Waring, Max S. Private in Capt. Haden's co. 17th rgt.

Waring, Richard. Ensign in Capt. Lanham's co. 34th rgt. (S. 25, 1812); Lieutenant (Jy. 13, 1814) vice Lanham.

Waring, Thomas. Captain in 14th rgt. (Je. 18, 1794).

Warner, Alfred L. Private in Capt. Kennedy's co. 27th rgt.

Warner, Andrew E. Captain in 39th rgt. Mortally wounded at North Point.

Warner, George. Paymaster in 51st rgt. (Mr. 25, 1808).

Warner, Henry. Private in Capt. Roney's co. 39th rgt.

Warner, Henry. Private in Capt. Steever's co. 27th rgt.

Warner, John. Ensign in Capt. Jas. Massey's co. 38th rgt.

Warner, John. Private in Capt. Chalmers' co. 51st rgt.

Warner, John. Private in Capt. Aisquith's co. Sharp Shooters.

Warner, Michael [1774-1848]. Quarter-master in 51st rgt.

Warner, Overton C. Private in Capt. Brooke's co. 34th rgt.

Warner, Thomas. Captain in 39th rgt.

Warner, William. Private in Capt. Sterett's Independent co.

Warnkin, Henry. Private in Capt. Sheppard's co. 6th rgt.

Warren, Daniel. Private in Capt. Adreon's co. Union Vounteers.

Warren, John. Sergeant in Capt. McConkey's co. 27th rgt.

Warrick, John. Private in Capt. Addison's co. Sea Fencibles.

Warring, E. R. Private in Capt. Haubert's co. 51st rgt.

Warrington, John. Private in Capt. Deems' co. 51st rgt.

Warwick, S. Private in Capt. Heath's co. 23d rgt.

Washington, George. Private in Capt. Shryock's co. 24th rgt.

Washington, John. Private in Capt. Cawood's co. 45th rgt.

Washington, Lawrence. Private in Capt. Ringgold's co. 6th rgt.

Wason, Abraham. Private in Capt. Sands' co. 22d rgt.

Wason, Abraham. Private in Capt. Wells' Artillery co. 22d rgt.

Waterman, Warren. Private in Capt. McConkey's co. 27th rgt.

Waters, Allen. Assistant District Paymaster U. S. (Aug., 1814).

Waters, Asa. Private in Capt. Steuart's co. Washington Blues.

Waters, Henry G. 2d Lieutenant in Capt. Fulton's co. 2d rgt. 1st Cavalry Dist. (Mr. 23, 1814).

Waters, Jacob. Captain in 22d rgt. (My. 18, 1813) vice Weems.

Waters, John. Captain in 34th rgt. Died, 1814.

Waters, John. Private in Capt. Steever's co. 27th rgt.

Waters, John C. Captain in 42d rgt. Resigned S. 21, 1813.

Waters, John S. Private in Capt. Sterett's Independent co.

Waters, Joseph. Private in Capt. Magruder's co. American Artillerists.

Waters, Joseph. Private in Capt. Myers' co. Franklin Artillery.

Waters, Joseph G. Private in Capt. Magruder's co. American Artillerists.

Waters, Michael. Sergeant in Capt. Schwarzauer's co. 27th rgt.

Waters, Peter. Private in Capt. Steuart's co. Washington Blues.

Waters, Ramsey. Private in Ensign Brewer's detachment, 36th rgt.; Private in Capt. Maynard's co. 22d rgt.

Waters, Richard. Colonel in 10th Cavalry Dist. Brigade, Quartermaster at Baltimore, Jy., 1814.

Waters, Richard. Private in Capt. Sterett's co. 1st Balto. Hussars.

Waters, Stephen. Private in Capt. Myers' co. Franklin Artillery.

Waters, William. Private in Capt. Linthicum's co. 22d rgt.

Waters, William G. Paymaster in 23d rgt.

Waters, Zebulon. Private in Capt. Steuart's co. Washington Blues.

Wathen, Allen. Private in Capt. Edelin's co. 1st rgt.

Wathen, Charles. Private in Capt. Burgess' co. 43d rgt.

Wathen, Henry. Sergeant in Capt. Melton's co. 45th rgt.

Wathen, Sabine. Private in Capt. Sands' co. 22d rgt.; Private in Capt. Wells' Artillery co. 22d. rgt.

Wathen, Thomas. Sergeant in Capt. Posey's co. 1st rgt.

Wathen, Wilfred. Private in Capt. Edelin's co. 1st rgt.

Wathen, William. Seregant in Capt. Briscoe's co. 45th rgt.

Watkins, Archibald A. Sergeant in Capt. Schwarzauer's co. 27th rgt.

*****Watkins, Gassaway** [1752-1840]. Lieutenant-Colonel in 32d rgt. Resigned Jy. 7, 1814.

Watkins, Gassaway [-1814]. Ensign in 38th U. S. Infantry (My. 20, 1813); 2d Lieutenant (My. 20, 1814).

Watkins, Gassaway. Sergeant in Capt. Owings' co. 32d rgt.

Watkins, Gassaway. Private in Capt. Myers' co. Franklin Artillery.

Watkins, Henry. Sergeant in Capt. Cawood's co. 45th rgt.

Watkins, Horatio. Cornet in Capt. Williams' co. 1st Cavalry Dist. (Mr. 16, 1812); 2d Lieutenant (S. 12, 1814) vice Chaney.

Watkins, James. Private in Capt. Stiles' co. Marine Artillery.

Watkins, John Nelson [1790-]. Private in Capt. Maynard's co. 22d rgt.; Adjutant-General of Md. in 1835.

Watkins, Joseph. Captain in 2d rgt.

Watkins, La Fayette. Ensign in Capt. Dorsey's co. 32d rgt. (S. 20, 1808).

Watkins, Nicholas I. Sergeant-Acting Lieutenant in Capt. Sands' co. 22d rgt., April, 1813; Private in Capt. Magruder's co.; Sergeant in Capt. Chase's co.

Watkins, Samuel C. Lieutenant-Colonel in 2d rgt. (Jy. 23, 1807).

Watkins, Stephen. Corporal in Capt. Jackson's co. 34th rgt.

Watkins, Stephen. Private in Capt. Hall's co. 34th rgt.

Watkins, Stephen H. Private in Capt. Duvall's co. 34th rgt.

Watkins, Thomas. Private in Capt. Nicholson's co. Balto. Fencibles.

Watkins, Tobias [-1855]. Surgeon in 38th U. S. Infantry (My. 20, 1813); Hospital surgeon (Mr. 30, 1814).

Watkins, William P. Private in Capt. Barnes' co. 32d rgt.

Watson, Charles. 2d Lieutenant in Capt. Hall's co. 3d Cavalry Dist. (Jy. 28, 1812).

Watson, Daniel C. 1st Lieutenant in Capt. Bruff's Artillery co. 6th Brigade (My. 19, 1813).

Watson, George. Private in Capt. Blakistone's co. 45th rgt.

Watson, Hezekiah. Private in Capt. Nailor's co. 17th rgt.

Watson, John. Private in Capt. Schwarzauer's co. 27th rgt.

Watson, John. Private in Capt. Ireland's co. 31st rgt.; Sergeant in Capt. Freelands' co.

Watson, John. Private in Capt. Nailor's co. 17th rgt.

Watson, John T. Cornet in Capt. Ridgeway's co. 9th Cavalry Dist. (My. 25, 1812).

Watson, Joseph. Private in Capt. Dent's co. 43d rgt.

Watson, Robert. Private in Capt. McKane's co. 27th rgt.

Watson, Robert. Private in Capt. Sterett's Independent co.

Watson, Sylvester. Private in Capt. Aisquith's co. Sharp Shooters.

Watson, Thomas [-1864]. Captain in 39th rgt.

Watt, Joseph. Lieutenant in Capt. Little's co. 40th rgt. (Je. 16, 1812).

Watters, Benjamin. Captain in 38th rgt. (Ap. 18, 1808).

Watters, Isaac. Private in Capt. Faster's co. 51st rgt.

Watters, James. Captain in 25th rgt. (N. 26, 1807).

Watts, Andrew. Private in Capt. Tilghman's co. 33d rgt.

Watts, Dixon B. Private in Capt. Aisquith's co. Sharp Shooters.

Watts, Edward. Private in Capt. Dyer's co. Fells Point Riflemen.

Watts, Ezekiel. Private in Capt. Berry's co. Washington Artillery.

Watts, George. Private in Capt. Causin's troop, attached to 12th rgt.

Watts, George. Private in Capt. Chambers' co. 21st rgt.

Watts, Henry. Ensign in Capt. Williams' co. Extra Battalion Worcester Co. (S. 26, 1807).

Watts, John S. Private in Capt. Berry's co. Washington Artillery.

Watts, Joshua. Sergeant in Capt. Millard's co. 12th rgt.

Watts, Nathaniel. Private in Capt. Shower's co. 15th rgt.

Watts, Richard. Captain in 36th rgt. (O. 12, 1814).

Watts, Richard B. Quarter-master-Sergeant in Capt. Hall's co. 3d Cavalry rgt.

Watts, Richard K. 2d Lieutenant in 36th U. S. Infantry (Ap. 30, 1813); 1st Lieutenant (My. 1, 1814).

Watts, Samuel. Corporal in Capt. Brown's co. 6th rgt.

Watts, Thomas. Sergeant in Capt. Bean's co. 12th rgt.

Watts, Thomas B. Private in Capt. Aisquith's co. Sharp Shooters.

Waugh, John. Private in Capt. John Miller's co., 2d D. I.; b. Washington Co., Md.; age 23; distiller; subs. for Peter Shommon.

Wax, Henry. Private in Capt. Stewart's co. 51st rgt.

Way, Frederick. Private in Capt. Peters' co. 51st rgt.

Wayman, Perry. Private in Capt. Barr's Cavalry co. 1st Dist.

Wayman, Thomas. Captain in 26th rgt. (Jy. 8, 1813).

Wayman, Thomas. Private in Capt. Chase's co. 22d rgt.

Wayman, Thomas. Private in Capt. Waters' co. 22d rgt.

Waymann, Peregrine. 1st Lieutenant in Capt. Cost's co. 1st rgt. 1st Cavalry Dist. (Je. 16, 1812) vice Boteler.

Waypole, Avery D. Private in Capt. Dent's co. 43d rgt.

Waypole, Gerard. Private in Capt. Dent's co. 43d rgt.

Ways, William. Private in Capt. Thos. Warner's co. 39th rgt.

Wayson, Absalom. Private in Capt. Sands' co. 22d rgt.

Weakley, Otho. Ensign in Capt. Easterday's co. 28th rgt. (My. 22, 1811).

Weakley, Thomas. Private in Capt. Blizzard's co. 15th rgt.

Weaks, Edward. Private in Capt. Snowden's co. 36th rgt.

Weary, John. Private in Capt. Sheppard's co. 6th rgt.

Weary, William. Private in Capt. Brown's co. 6th rgt.

Weatherby, Elisha. Private in Capt. Galt's co. 6th rgt.

Weatherby, Thomas. Private in Capt. Galt's co. 6th rgt.

Weaver, Aquilla. Private in Capt. Miller's co. 39th rgt.

Weaver, Aquilla. Seaman of the privateer *Chasseur*, severely wounded in action with H. M. Schr. *Lawrence*, Feb. 27, 1815.

Weaver, Daniel. Private in Capt. Myers' co. Franklin Artillery.

Weaver, George. Private in Capt. Wilson's co. 6th rgt.

Weaver, Henry. Private in Capt. Faster's co. 51st rgt.

Weaver, James. Ensign in Capt. Brown's co. 6th rgt. (Jy. 12, 1814).

Weaver, John. Ensign in Capt. Shrim's co. Balto. Light Infantry.

Weaver, Joseph. Private in Capt. Smith's co. 51st rgt.

Weaver, William. Private in Capt. Usselton's Artillery co. 6th rgt.

Webb, Frederick. Private in Capt. Smith's co. 51st rgt.

Webb, James. Private in Capt. Steuart's co. Washington Blues.

Webb, John. Private in Capt. Brown's co. 6th rgt.

Webb, John. Private in Capt. Snowden's co. 36th rgt.

Webb, Lambert. Private in Capt. Galloway's co. 46th rgt.

Webb, Perry. Private in Capt. Schwarzauer's co. 27th rgt.

Webb, Richard. Private in Capt. Dent's co. 43d rgt.

Webb, William. Ensign in Capt. Ridenour's co. 24th rgt. (Ag. 1, 1814) vice Protman.

Webb, William. Corporal in Capt. Myers' co. Franklin Artillery.

Webster, John Adams [1789-1877]. 3d Lieutenant of the privateer *Rossie* under Capt. Barney; sailing-master of the flotilla. *See ante*, p. 177.

Webster, Richard, Jr. Ensign in Capt. Herbert's co. 42d rgt. (Ap. 4, 1808).

Webster, Thomas. Private in Capt. Dyer's co. 17th rgt.

Weddekin, John. Private in Capt. Bader's Union Yägers.

Wedding, Isaac. Private in Capt. Thompson's co. 43d rgt.

Wedding, Meshack. Private in Capt. Burgess' co. 43d rgt.

Wedge, Simon. Private in Capt. Pike's co. Balto. Volunteer Artillery.

Weed, Leven W. Private in Capt. Addison's co. Sea Fencibles.

Weedham, John. Corporal in Capt. Hanna's Fells Point Light Dragoons.

Weedon, Arthur. Private in Capt. Roger's co. 51st rgt.

Weedon, Ely. Private in Ensign Brewer's detachment 36th rgt. Private in Capt. Slicer's co. 22d rgt.

Weedon, Jonathan. Private in Capt. Maynard's co. 22d rgt.

Weeks, Benjamin. Sergeant in Capt. Stiles' co. Marine Artillery.

Weems, Charles. Captain of the privateer *Expedition,* Oct., 1812.

Weems, George. Captain of the privateer *Halcyon,* Jan., 1813; Private in Capt. Stiles' co. Marine Artillery.

Weems, Gustavus. Cornet in Capt. Mackall's co. 3d Cavalry Dist. (Ja. 31, 1814) vice Clare.

Weems, John B. Captain in 22d rgt.

Weems, William. Ensign in Capt. Franklin's co. 2d rgt. (Ag. 3, 1809).

Weems, William L. Major in 31st rgt.

Weir, John R. Private in Capt. Pennington's Balto. Independent Artillerists.

Weir, Lemuel. Private in Capt. Thos. Warner's co. 39th rgt.

Welch, Edward. Private in Capt. Dent's co. 43d rgt.

Welch, John G. Private in Capt. Kennedy's co. 27th rgt.

Welch, John of Samuel. Ensign in Capt. Hobbs' co. 32d rgt. (Ag. 20, 1814).

Welch, Mordecai. Private in Capt. Pumphrey's co. 22d rgt.

Welch, Richard. Private in Capt. McPherson's co. 43d rgt.

Welch, Robert of Ben. Private in Capt. Maynard's co. 22d rgt.

Welch, Robert of Robert. Private in Capt. Sands' co. 22d rgt.

Welch, Vachel. Sergeant in Capt. Blizzard's 15th rgt.

Welch, William. Sergeant in Capt. Sample's co. 49th rgt.

Welch, William. Private in Capt. McPherson's co. 43d rgt.

Weller, George. Private in Capt. Haubert's co. 51st rgt.

Weller, Martin. Private in Capt. Haubert's co. 51st rgt.

Wellford, R. T. Private in Capt. Warfield's co. Balto. United Volunteers.

Wellham, Wallace. Private in Capt. Linthicum's co. 22d rgt.

Welling, Henry. Captain in 32d rgt. (Je. 14, 1808); Major (Ag. 20, 1814).

Wells, Benjamin A. Sergeant in Capt. Hamilton's co. 17th rgt.

Wells, Cyprian F. Private in Capt. Warfield's co. Balto. United Volunteers.

Wells, Daniel. 1st Lieutenant in Capt. Pinkney's co. 8th Brigade (My. 9, 1812); Captain (Ap. 22, 1814).

Wells, Daniel. Private in Capt. Aisquith's co. Sharp Shooters; killed at North Point.

Wells, Elijah. Private in Capt. Pinkney's Artillery co. 22d rgt.

Wells, Frederick. Private in Capt. Slicer's co. 22d rgt.; in Capt. Sand's co.

Wells, George. Private in Capt. Sands' co. 22d rgt.

Wells, George W. Private in Capt. Hall's co. 34th rgt.

Wells, Harrison. Private in Capt. Howard's co. Mechanical Volunteers.

Wells, Isaac. Private in Capt. Burke's co. 6th rgt.

Wells, John. 4th Corporal in Capt. Chase's co. 22d rgt.; Lieutenant and Quarter-master of Col. Small's rgt., stationed at Annapolis, Dec., 1812.

Wells, John. Private in Capt. Travers' co. 48th rgt.

Wells, John. Private in Capt. Sample's co. 49th rgt.

Wells, John, Jr. Lieutenant and Quarter-master in 39th rgt.

Wells, John L. 2d Lieutenant in Capt. Shriver's co. 2d rgt. 1st Cavalry Dist. (Je. 26, 1812); 1st Lieutenant (D. 22, 1812).

Wells, Joshua. Private in Capt. Ireland's co. 31st rgt.

Wells, Richard. Surgeon's mate in 47th rgt. (Ja. 8, 1808).

Wells, Thomas W. Private in Capt. Berry's co. Washington Artillery.

Wells, W. T. Private in Capt. Pennington's co. Balto. Independent Artillerists.

Wells, William. Private in Capt. Snowden's co. 36th rgt.

Wells, William. Corporal in Capt. Piper's co. United Maryland Artillery.

Wells, William of George. Private in Capt. Hall's co. 34th rgt.

Wells, William of Richard. Private in Capt. Hall's co. 34th rgt.

Wellslager, George. Private in Capt. Chalmers' co. 51st rgt.

Wellslager, Jacob. Private in Capt. Wilson's co. 6th rgt.

Welsh, Benjamin. Private in Capt. Hall's co. 3d Cavalry rt.

Welsh, Daniel. Private in Capt. McConkey's co. 27th rgt.

Welsh, Francis. Private in Capt. Slicer's co. 22d rgt.

Welsh, George. Private in Capt. Myers' co. 39th rgt.

Welsh, John. Private in Capt. Bunbury's co. Sea Fencibles.

Welsh, John D. Lieutenant in Capt. C. D. Warfield's co. 32d rgt.

Welsh, Pierce. Private in Capt. Bunbury's co. Sea Fencibles.

Welsh, Singleton. Ensign in Capt. C. D. Warfield's co. 32d rgt.

Welsh, Thomas. Sergeant in Capt. Horton's co. Maryland Chasseurs.

Welsh, William [1800-   ]. Private in Capt. Levering's co. Independent Blues.

Welshoover, Henry. Private in Capt. Shrim's co. Balto. Light Infantry.

Welty, Henry. Lieutenant in Capt. Hauser's co. 10th rgt. (S. 20, 1813).

Werdebaugh, John. Private in Capt. Warfield's co. Balto. United Volunteers.

Werger, Michael. Private in Capt. Levering's co. Independent Blues.

Wertinberger, David. Lieutenant in Capt. Mills co. 10th rgt. (Jy. 13, 1812).

Wescott, William. Captain of privateer *Joseph and Mary*; captured by the frigate *Narcissus*, Nov. 25, 1812, and sent into Jamaca.

Wesley, John. Private in Capt. Barnes' co 32d rgt.

West, Amos. Private in Capt. Burke's co. 6th rgt.

West, Elijah. Private in Capt. Deems' co. 51st rgt.

West, Job. Captain of the privateer *Revenge*, March, 1813.

West, John. Private in Capt. Sadtler's co. Balto. Yägers.

West, John. Private in Capt. Montgomery's co. Balto. Union Artillery.

West, Levin. Private in Capt. Quantrill's co. 24th rgt.

West, Nicholas. Private in Capt. Berry's co. Washington Artillery.

West, Richard. Private in Capt. McConkey's co. 27th rgt.

West, Samuel H. Private in Capt. Shrim's co. Balto. Light Infantry.

West, Stephen. Brigadier-General 4th Brigade (F. 10, 1804).

West, William. Private in Capt. Montgomery's co. Balto. Union Artillery.

West, William. Private in Capt. Well's Artillery co. 22d rgt.; Private in Ensign Brewer's detachment 36th rgt. at Bladensburg.

West, William. Private in Capt. Dyer's co. Fells Point Riflemen.

Westby, Joseph. Private in Capt. Griffith's co. 21st rgt.; deserted Aug. 1, 1814.

Westby, William. Private in Capt. Griffith's co. 21st rgt.; deserted Aug. 1, 1814.

Westinberger, David. Lieutenant in Capt. Mills' co. 10th rgt. (Jy. 13, 1812).

Westwood, Thomas. Private in Capt. Addison's co. Sea Fencibles.

Wethered, Samuel. Paymaster in 33d rgt. (S. 12, 1808) ; Brigade paymaster, 6th Brigade.

Wetherstand, Jacob. Private in Capt. Shrim's co. Balto. Light Infantry.

Weve, James. Private in Capt. Stiles' co. Marine Artillery.

Whaland, Peregrine. Private in Capt. Hynson's co. 21st rgt.

Whaland, William. Private in Capt. Galloway's co. 46th rgt.

Whalley, Levi. Private in Capt. McLaughlin's co. 50th rgt.

Whann, Adam. Major in 8th Cavalry Dist. (F. 28, 1812).

Whann, William. Captain in 18th rgt. (Ag. 16, 1799).

Whealton, Elijah. Ensign in Capt. Low's co. 11th rgt. (Ag. 20, 1814).

Wheat, William. Private in Capt. Brooke's co. 34th rgt.

Wheatley, John. Private in Capt. McConckin's co. 38th rgt.

Wheatley, Joseph. Private in Capt. Jarboe's co. 12th rgt.

Wheatly, James. Private in Capt. Causin's co. 4th Cavalry Dist.

Wheatly, Joseph. Lieutenant in Capt. Harper's co. 11th rgt. (Je. 1, 1813).

Wheatly, William of Ed. Ensign in Capt. Turpin's co. 11th rgt. (O. 3, 1807).

Wheaton, Cloudsbury. Private in Capt. Rogers' co. 51st rgt.

Wheeden, H. Private in Capt. Sterett's Independent co.

Wheedon, Jonathan. Private in Capt. Sands' co. 22d rgt.

Wheeler, Austin. Private in Capt. Burke's co. 6th rgt.

Wheeler, Benjamin. Private in Capt. Deems' co. 51st rgt.

Wheeler, Bennett. Private in Capt. Briscoe's co. 45th rgt.

Wheeler, Charles. Private in Capt. Brohawn's co. 48th rgt.

Wheeler, Darius. Musician in Capt. Peters' co. 51st rgt.

Wheeler, Francis. Sergeant in Capt. Burgess's co. 43d rgt.

Wheeler, Hezekiah. Captain in 14th rgt. (F. 4, 1808).

Wheeler, Jacob. Private in Capt. Magruder's co. American Artillerists.

Wheeler, James. Private in Capt. Dent's co. 43d rgt.

Wheeler, James B. Private in Capt. Sterett's co. 1st Balto. Hussars.

Wheeler, Job E. Seaman of the privateer *Globe;* wounded in action, Nov. 1, 1813.

Wheeler, John. Captain in Extra Battalion Dorchester Co.

Wheeler, John F. Ensign in Capt. Bussey's co. 40th rgt. (Jy. 14, 1814).

Wheeler, Nehemiah. Private in Capt. Brohawn's co. 48th rgt.

Wheeler, Robert W. Private in Capt. Sadtler's co. Balto. Yägers.

Wheeler, Thomas. Private in Capt. Steever's co. 27th rgt.

Wheeler, Thomas T. Captain in Montgomery co. drafted infantry, 1813.

Wheeler, Walter R. Private in Capt. Hall's co. 34th rgt.

Wheeler, William. Lieutenant in Capt. Orrick's co. 41st rgt. Resigned Jy. 11, 1814.

Wheeler, William. Issuing Quartermaster, 6th Brigade.

Whelan, George. Private in Capt. Haubert's co. 51st rgt.

Whelan, James. Private in Capt. Haubert's co. 51st rgt.

Whelan, Thomas. Private in Capt. Levering's co. Independent Blues.

Wherrett, George. Captain in 24th rgt. Rifle co. (My. 9, 1808).

Whetcroft, William. Private in Capt. Chase's co. 22d rgt.

Whetson, David. Private in Capt. Berry's co. Washington Artillery.

Whistler, John [-1829]. Bvt. Major 1st U. S. Infantry (Jy. 10, 1812).

Whistler, John, Jr. [-1813]. Ensign in 19th U. S. Infantry (Mr. 12, 1812) ; 1st Lieutenant (N. 20, 1813).

Whistler, William [-1863]. Captain in 1st U. S. Infantry (D. 21, 1812).

Whirrett, Thomas. Private in Capt. Smith's co. 51st rgt.

Whitaker, George W. Private in Capt. Brooke's co. 34th rgt.

Whitby, Nathan. Quarter-master in Extra Battalion Caroline co. (My. 22, 1812).

White, Alexander. Landsman of the privateer *Baltimore.*

White, Allen. Private in Capt. Steever's co. 27th rgt.

White, Ambrose. Captain in 11th Cavalry Dist. (My., 1812) ; Colonel, 1813; Major (Ag. 5, 1814) vice Sturgis.

White, Benedict. 3d Lieutenant in 36th U. S. Infantry (Ap. 30, 1813).

White, Benjamin. Quarter-Gunner in Capt. Bunbury's co. Sea Fencibles.

White, Burgess B. 2d Lieutenant in 1st U. S. Artillery (Ap. 15, 1812) ; 1st Lieutenant (Jy. 29, 1814).

White, Caleb. Private in Capt. Hall's co. 3d Cavalry rgt.

White, Campbell P. Quarter-master in 5th Cavalry Dist. (S. 10, 1814) vice Spicer.

White, Charles. Private in Capt. Bunbury's co. Sea Fencibles.

White, Charles. Private in Capt. Snowden's co. 36th rgt.

White, Elisha. Private in Capt. Boone's co. 22d rgt.

White, Elisha. Private in Capt. Steever's co. 27th rgt.

White, Gavin. Lieutenant in Capt. Watters' co. 25th rgt. (Jy. 14, 1812).

White, George. Private in Capt. Pike's co. Balto. Volunteer Artillery.

White, Gideon. Private in Capt. Sterett's Independent co.

White, Henry. Private in Capt. Myers' co. Franklin Artillery.

White, James. Lieutenant in Capt. Gower's co. 50th rgt. (S. 10, 1814).

White, James. Private in Capt. Sheppard's co. 6th rgt.

White, James M. Sergeant in Capt. McLaughlin's co. 50th rgt.

White, James T. Private in Capt. Blair's co. 50th rgt.

White, Job. Ensign in Capt. Hudson's co. 32d rgt. (Jy. 7, 1808).

White, John. Lieutenant in Capt. Selby's co. 9th rgt. (N. 7, 1810).

White, John. Captain in 37th rgt. (S. 24, 1813).

White, John. Private in Capt. Levering's co. Independent Blues.

White, John. Surgeon in 32d U. S. Infantry (My. 17, 1813).

White, John M. Lieutenant of the privateer *Wasp*, July, 1812; Private in Capt. Stiles' co. Marine Artillery.

White, Joseph. Private in Capt. Sterett's co. 1st Balto. Hussars.

White, Joseph P. Gunner in Capt. Bunbury's co. Sea Fencibles.

White, Nicholas. Private in Capt. Shrim's co. Balto. Light Infantry.

White, Peter. Private in Capt. Adreon's co. Union Volunteers.

White, Peter L. Corporal in Capt. Pennington's co. Balto. Independent Artillerists.

White, Robert. Private in Capt. Snowden's co. 36h rgt.

White, Samuel. Private in Capt. McLaughlin's co. 50th rgt.

White, Stephen. Private in Capt. Chalmers' co. 51st rgt.

White, Thomas. Private in Capt. Pennington's co. Balto. Independent Artillerists.

White, Thomas. Private in Capt. A. E. Warner's co. 39th rgt.

White, Thomas. Private in Capt. Chalmers' co. 51st rgt.

White, William. Captain in 23d rgt. (Jy. 4, 1812).

White, William. Private in Capt. Brohawn's co. 48th rgt.

White, William W. Private in Capt. Addison's co. Sea Fencibles.

Whiteford, —. Captain in 42d rgt.

Whiteford, David. Private in Capt. Smith's co. 51st rgt.

Whiteford, Hugh. Surgeon in Extra Battalion Harford co. (D. 29, 1807).

Whiteford, Michael. Quarter-master in Extra Battalion Harford Co. (My. 8, 1812).

Whitelock, Charles. Private in Capt. Myers' co. 39th rgt.

Whitelock, John. Private in Capt. Stewart's co. 51st rgt.

Whiten [Whiting], William. Private in Capt. Gray's co. 43d rgt.

Whitlow, Thomas. Drummer in Capt. Moale's co. Columbian Artillery.

Whitmarsh, John. Private in Capt. Stapleton's co. 39th rgt.

Whitney, Simon. Private in Capt. Deems' co. 51st rgt.

Whittington, Benjamin. Private in Capt. Deems' co. 51st rgt.

Whittaker, George. Musician in Capt. Howard's co. Mechanical Volunteers.

Whittaker, Joseph. Musician in Capt. Howard's co. Mechanical Volunteers.

Whittington, Samuel. Private in Capt. Chase's co. 22d rgt.

Whittington, Thomas. Acting Surgeon in 33d rgt. [1814].

Whorley, Jonathan. Private in Capt. Dobbin's co. 39th rgt.

Whyte, Joseph. Private in Capt. Galt's co. 6th rgt.

Wichelhausen, H. D. Private in Capt. Thompson's co. 1st Horse Artillery.

Wickersham, William. Private in Capt. Piper's co. United Maryland Artillery.

Wickes, Joseph, 4th. Private in Capt. Chambers' co. 21st rgt.

Wickes, Matthew. Private in Capt. Usselton's Artillery co. 6th Brigade.

Wickes, Samuel. Lieutenant in Capt. Page's co. 21st rgt. vice Stevens.

Wickes, Samuel C. Private in Capt. Wickes' co. 21st rgt.

Wickes, Simon, Jr. Captain in 21st rgt. Rifle co. (Ja. 25, 1814).

Wickes, Thomas. Private in Capt. Chambers' co. 21st rgt.

Wickes, William, Jr. Private in Capt. Page's co. 21st rgt.

Widderfield, William. Private in Capt. Faster's co. 51st rgt.

Widrick, John. Private in Capt. Getzendanner's co. 16th rgt.

Wiegant, Daniel. Private in Capt. Bader's co. Union Yägers.

Wier, John. Lieutenant in Capt. Randall's co. 36th rgt. (N. 7, 1812).

Wiese, Frederick A. Private in Capt. Montgomery's co. Balto. Union Artillery.

Wiesenthal, Thomas V. Surgeon's mate in 6th U. S. Infantry (Jy. 16, 1813).

Wigart, Henry. Private in Capt. Berry's co. Washington Artillery.

Wiggins, John. Captain in Extra Battalion Harford Co. (Jy. 8, 1814) vice Quarles.

Wight, Jesse. Private in Capt. Berry's co. Washington Artillery.

Wigley, Edward. Private in Capt. Smith's co. 51st rgt.

Wigley, Henry. Private in Capt. Conway's co. 6th rgt.

Wigley, William. Private in Capt. Brown's co. 6th rgt.

Wilbee, Charles. Sergeant in Capt. Faster's co. 51st rgt.

Wilcox, Jacob. Private in Capt. Barnes' co. 32d rgt. Deserted.

Wilcox, James. Private in Capt. Hands' co. 21st rgt.

Wilcox, William. Private in Capt. Thomas's co. 49th rgt.

Wilcoxen, Jesse. Captain in 44th rgt. (S. 10, 1814).

Wilcoxon, William. Ensign in Capt. Dade's co. 3d rgt. (My. 17, 1811).

Wildman, Cornelius. Ensign in Capt. Floyd's co. 12th rgt. (S. 19, 1808).

Wiley, Alexander. Private in Capt. Magruder's co. American Artillerists.

Wiley, James. Private in Capt. Moore's co. 49th rgt.

Wiley, John. Private in Capt. Thomas's co. 49th rgt.

Wiley, Robert. Private in Capt. Myers' co. Franklin Artillery.

Wiley, William. Private in Capt. Brown's co. 6th rgt.

Wilhead, Conrad. Captain in 29th rgt.

Wilhelm, Adam. Bugler in Capt. Bader's co. Union Yägers.

Wilhelm, P. Private in Capt. Pennington's co. Balto. Independent Artillerists.

Wilkerson, Walter. Private in Capt. Robey's co. 43d rgt. Deserted.

Wilkins, Joseph. Private in Capt. Sterett's co. 1st Balto. Hussars.

Wilkins, John. Private in Capt. Sterett's co. 1st Balto. Hussars.

Wilkins, William. Private in Capt. Burke's co. 6th rgt.

*Wilkinson, James [1757-1825]. Major-General U. S. (Mr. 2, 1813).

Wilkinson, James. Private in Capt. Shryock's co. 24th rgt.

Wilkinson, S. Private in Capt. Stiles' co. Marine Artillery.

Wilkinson, Thomas H. Captain in 31st rgt.

Wilkinson, Thomas H.. Major in 3d Cavalry Dist. (F. 13, 1812).

Wilkinson, Walter. 1st Lieutenant in 2d U. S. Infantry (Jy. 2, 1812); Capt. (Ag. 15, 1813).

Wilkinson, William. Corporal in Capt. McDonald's co. 6th rgt.

Willard, Julius. 2d Lieutenant in Capt. Myers' co. Franklin Artillery (Ag. 11, 1813).

Willen, James. Private in Capt. Umsted's co. 25th rgt.

Willender, Thomas. Sergeant in Capt. Kierstead's co. 6th rgt.

Willett, Edward. Private in Capt. Brooke's co. 34th rgt.

Willett, George W. Sergeant in Capt. Brooke's co. 34th rgt.

Willey, Angelo. Private in Capt. Travers' co. 48th rgt.

Willey, Jacob. Fifer in Capt. Lake's co. 48th rgt.

Willey, John. Private in Capt. A. E. Warner's co. 39th rgt.

Willey, John. Private in Capt. Brohawn's co. 48th rgt.

Willey, Lemuel. Private in Capt. Travers' co. 48th rgt.

Willey, Patrick. Private in Capt. Travers' co. 48th rgt.

Willey, William. Private in Capt. Brohawn's co. 48th rgt.

Williams, A. A. Private in Capt. Sterett's Independent co.

Williams, Abell. Lieutenant in Capt. Stonebraker's co. 24th rgt. (Ag. 1, 1814) vice Wolfinger.

William, Abraham R. Private in Capt. Chalmers' co. 51st rgt.

Williams, Baruch. 2d Lieutenant in Columbian Artillery (My. 22, 1812); 1st Lieutenant (Je. 15, 1813) vice Heath.

Williams, Benjamin. Private in Capt. Ducker's co. 7th rgt.

Williams, Benjamin. Private in Capt. Peters' co. 51st rgt.

Williams, Benjamin, Jr. Lieutenant in Capt. Billingsly's co. 31st rgt. (Je. 12, 1812).

Williams, Charles. Private in Capt. Brohawn's co. 48th rgt.

Williams, Charles. Private in Capt. Haubert's co. 51st rgt.

Williams, Colmore. Quarter-master in 3d rgt. (Ja. 10, 1810).

Williams, Cumberland D. Private in Capt. Nicholson's co. Balto. Fencibles.

Williams, Edward Greene [1789-1829]. Captain in 1st Cavalry Dist. (F. 13, 1812).

Williams, George. Private in Capt. McDonald's co. 6th rgt.

Williams, George. Private in Capt. Nicholson's co. Balto. Fencibles.

Williams, Giles. Private in Capt. Lawrence's co. 6th rgt.

Williams Henry Lee. Private in Capt. Sterett's co. 1st Balto. Hussars; Captain Maryland Chasseurs (D. 2, 1814).

Williams, Horatio. Private in Capt. Myers' co. Franklin Artillery.

Williams, Isaac. Lieutenant in Capt. Walters' co. 23d rgt. Resigned D. 7, 1813.

Williams, Isaac. Private in Capt. Brown's co. 6th rgt.

Williams, Isaac. Private in Capt. Warfield's co. Balto. United Volunteers.

Williams, J. S. Private in Capt. Brown's co. Eagle Artillerists.

Williams, Jacob. Private in Capt. Hancock's co. 22d rgt.

Williams, James. Captain in 3d Cavalry Dist. (F. 13, 1812).

Williams, James. Private in Capt. Brown's co. 43d rgt.

Williams, James. Private in Capt. Edes' co. 27th rgt.

Williams, James. Private in Capt. Ringgold's co. 6th rgt.

Williams, James, 2d. Private in Capt. Bunbury's co. Sea Fencibles.

Williams, James. Private in Capt. Williams' co. 12th rgt.

Williams, John. Private in Capt. Blakistone's co. 45th rgt.

Williams, John. Private in Capt. Pennington's co. Balto. Independent Artillerists.

Williams, John. Private in Capt. Conway's co. 6th rgt.

Williams, John. Private in Capt. Kierstead's co. 6th rgt.

Williams, John. Private in Capt. Hancock's co. 22d rgt.

Williams, John. Sergeant in Capt. Dillon's co. 27th rgt.

Williams, John. Quarter-master in 37th rgt.

Williams, John. Private in Capt. Roney's co. 39th rgt.

Williams, John, Jr. Private in Capt. Roney's co. 39th rgt.

Williams, John J. Captain in Extra Battalion Worcester Co. (S. 26, 1807).

Williams, Jonathan. Private in Capt. Berry's co. Washington Artillery.

Williams, Joseph. Captain in 12th rgt.; in service, 1813.

Williams, Joseph. Corporal in Capt. Stapleton's co. 39th rgt.

Williams, Joseph. Private in Capt. Peters' co. 51st rgt.

Williams, Joseph, Sr. Private in Capt. Wells' Artillery co. 22d rgt.

Williams, Lewis. Quarter-master in 12th rgt. (Ap. 21, 1814).

Williams, Lewis. Private in Capt. Berry's co. Washington Artillery.

Williams, Nat. Private in Capt. Sterett's Independent co.

Williams, Nathaniel F. Private in Capt. Nicholson's co. Balto. Fencibles.

Williams, Osborn. Brigadier-General 8th Brigade (Je. 6, 1811).

Williams, Otho. Lieutenant in Capt. Magruder's co. 34th rgt. (S. 17, 1807).

Williams, Otho Holland [1784-1852]. Major in 1st Cavalry Dist. (F. 13, 1812).

Williams, Owen. Private in Capt. A. E. Warner's co. 39th rgt.

Williams, Richard. Private in Capt. Addison's co. Sea Fencibles.

Williams, Richard. Private in Capt. Deems' co. 51st rgt.

Williams, Richard. Private in Capt. Slicer's co. 22d rgt.; Private in Ensign Brewer's detachment 36th rgt.

Williams, Robert. Private in Capt. Snowden's co. 36th rgt.

Williams, Samuel. Lieutenant in Capt. Colston's co. 48th rgt. (Je. 26, 1812).

Williams, Samuel. Private in Capt. Snowden's co. 36th rgt.

Williams, Theodore M. Ensign in Capt. Bealmear's co. 2d rgt. (Jy. 6, 1814).

Williams, Thomas. Private in Capt. Montgomery's co. Balto. Union Artillery.

Williams, Thomas. Private in Capt. Levering's co. Independent Blues.

Williams, Thomas. Quarter-master pro tem. 30th rgt.

Williams, Thomas S. Ensign in Capt. Thomas Warner's co. 39th rgt.

Williams, William. Surgeon in 10th rgt. (Ag. 16, 1808).

Williams, William. Lieutenant in Capt. Hance's co. 31st rgt.

Williams, William. Ensign in Capt. Lee's co. 45th rgt.

Williams, William. Private in Capt. Ringgold's co. 6th rgt.

Williams, William. Private in Capt. Addison's co. Sea Fencibles.

Williams, William. Private in Capt. Warfield's co. Balto. United Volunteers; wounded at Bladensburg.

Williams, William. Private in Capt. Umsted's co. 25th rgt.

Williams, William D. Lieutenant of the privateer *Surprise*, March, 1814; Private in Capt. Stiles' co. Marine Artillery.

Williams, Woolman. Private in Capt. Massey's co. 38th rgt.

Williamson, David, Jr. 1st Lieutenant in Capt. Carnan's co. 6th Cavalry Dist. (Je. 26, 1812); Adjutant (Jy. 8, 1813).

Williamson, Henry. Private in Capt. Maynard's co. 22d rgt.

Williamson, James. Cornet in Capt. Hall's co. 3d Cavalry Dist. (Jy. 28, 1812).

Williamson, James. Private in Capt. Wilson's co. 6th rgt.

Williamson, Peregrine. Private in Capt. Smith's co. 51st rgt.

Williamson, Samuel. Captain in 49th rgt. (Je. 26, 1812).

Williamson, Thomas. Surgeon's mate 36th U. S. Infantry (Ap. 30, 1813).

Williamson, William. Sergeant in Capt. Galt's co. 6th rgt.

Willigman, C. H. Private in Capt. Pinkney's Artillery co. 22d rgt.

Willing, Alexander. Private in Capt. Umsted's co. 25th rgt.

Willing, Chaplin. Private in Capt. Umsted's co. 25th rgt.

Willing, Henry. Private in Capt. Kierstead's co. 6th rgt.

Willing, Josiah. Private in Capt. Howard's co. Mechanical Volunteers.

Willing, Louther. Private in Capt. Umsteds' co. 25th rgt.

Willing, William. Private in Capt. Crawfurd's co. 17th rgt.

Willingham, James. Private in Capt. Peters' co. 51st rgt.

Willis, Henry. Lieutenant in Capt. Willis' co. 19th rgt. (My. 10, 1808).

Willis, Henry. 2d Lieutenant in Capt. Hollingsworth's co. 2d rgt. 1st Cavalry Dist. (Je. 17, 1812); 1st Lieutenant (Ap. 27, 1814).

Willis, James. Ensign in Capt. Eccleston's co. 11th rgt. (Ag. 20, 1814).

Willis, John [1765-1839]. Private in Capt. Sprys co. 33d rgt.; Lieutenant in Capt. Eccleston's co. 11th rgt. (Je. 5, 1812).

Willis, John B. Ensign in Capt. Comegy's co. 21st rgt. (Ap. 22, 1813).

Willis, Joshua. Private in Capt. Sheppard's co. 6th rgt.

Willis, Justin. Private in Capt. Myers' co. Franklin Artillery.

Willis, Peter. Captain in 19th rgt. (Ag. 10, 1807).

Wills, Francis. Private in Capt. Levering's co. Independent Blues.

Wills, Richard. Private in Capt. McKane's co. 27th rgt.

Willson, Amos. Private in Capt. McLaughlin's co. 50th rgt.

Willson, Greenbury. Private in Capt. Horton's co. Maryland Chasseurs.

Willson, Isaac. Private in Capt. McLaughlins' co. 50th rgt.

Willson, Jonathan. Private in Capt. McLaughlin's co. 50th rgt.

Willson, Joshua. Private in Capt. McLaughlin's co. 50th rgt.

Willson, Richard. Private in Capt. Massey's co. 38th rgt.

Willson, Robert B. Ensign in Capt. Freeland's co. 31st rgt. (D. 23, 1813) vice Morsell.

Willz, F. M. Private in Capt. Sadtler's co. Balto. Yägers.

Wilmer, Henry. Private in Capt. W. H. Blake's co. 9th Cavalry Dist.

Wilmer, James J. [-1814]. Chaplain, U. S. A. (My. 20, 1813).

Wilmer, John R. Private in Capt. Hands' co. 21st rgt.

Wilmer, John W. Private in Capt. Sterett's co. 1st Balto. Hussars.

Wilmer, Lemuel. Private in Capt. Hands' co. 21st rgt.

Wilmore, William. Sergeant in Capt. Graves' co. 21st rgt.

Wilmot, John [1778-1858]. Ensign in Capt. David Warfield's co. Balto. United Volunteers (Jy. 29, 1811); received special mention for "conspicuous bravery" at battle of North Point; Lieutenant (N. 8, 1814).

Willmott, Thomas. Private in Capt. Fowlers' co. 46th rgt.

Wilson, Benjamin. Major in 6th Cavalry Dist. (F. 13, 1812).

Wilson, Benjamin, Jr. Captain in 6th Cavalry Dist. (F. 9, 1814).

Wilson, Charles. Private in Capt. Addison's co. Sea Fencibles.

Wilson, David. Private in Capt. Stiles' co. Marine Artillery.

Wilson, Dennis. Corporal in Capt. Travers' co. 48th rgt.

Wilson, Edward. 2d Lieutenant in 14th U. S. Infantry (Mr. 12, 1812); Lieutenant (My. 12, 1813).

Wilson, Edward H. Private in Capt. Barr's Cavalry co. 1st Dist.

Wilson, Edward J. 1st Lieutenant in Capt. Reid's co. 2d rgt. 1st Cavalry Dist. (S. 10, 1814) vice Hites.

Wilson, Edward M. Private in Capt. Levering's co. Independent Blues.

Wilson, Eli. Ensign in Capt. McElfish's co. 50th rgt. (F. 14, 1815).

Wilson, Fielder. Ensign in Capt. Welling's co. 32d rgt. (O. 31, 1809).

Wilson, Frederick. Captain in 8th Cavalry Dist. (My. 16, 1812).

Wilson, George. Private in Capt. McDonald's co. 6th rgt.

Wilson, George C. Quarter-Gunner in Capt. Bunbury's co. Sea Fencibles.

Wilson, Gerrard. Captain in 6th rgt. Mr. 14, 1810).

Wilson, Greenberry. Private in Capt. Linthicum's co. 22d rgt.

Wilson, Greenbury. Private in Capt. Chalmers' co. 51st rgt.

Wilson, Henry. Captain in 6th Cavalry Dist. (Ap. 4, 1812).

Wilson, Hillery. Captain in 31st rgt.

Wilson, Hosea. Private in Capt. Mc-Kane's co. 27th rgt.

Wilson, Isaac. Ensign in Capt. Timanus' co. 36th rgt. Resigned July 13, 1814.

Wilson, J. C. Private in Capt. Pennington's co. Balto. Independent Artillerists.

Wilson, James. Ensign in Capt. Hitchcock's co. 41st rgt. (Je. 26, 1812).

Wilson, James. Private in Capt. Mackeys' co. 49th rgt.

Wilson, James. Private in Capt. Chalmers' co. 51st rgt.

Wilson, James. Private in Capt. Kiersteads' co. 6th rgt.

Wilson, James [1792-1880]. Sergeant in Capt. Watson's co. 39th rgt.

Wilson, James. Private in Capt. Peters' co. 51st rgt.

Wilson, James C. Sergeant in Capt. Pennington's co. Balto. Independent Artillerists.

Wilson, John. Private in Capt. Sadtler's co. Balto. Yägers.

Wilson, John. Corporal in Capt. Watsons' co. 39th rgt.

Wilson, John. Private in Capt. Edes' co. 27th rgt.

Wilson, John. Private in Capt. Levering's co. Independent Blues.

Wilson, John. Private in Capt. Travers' co. 48th rgt.

Wilson, John. Private in Capt. Thompson's co. 1st Baltimore Horse Artillery.

Wilson, John. Seaman of the privateer *Globe;* wounded in action, Nov. 1, 1813.

Wilson, John C. Lieutenant-Colonel in 23d rgt. M. M. (in 1814).

Wilson, John C., Jr. Quarter-master in 23d rgt. (D. 24, 1810).

Wilson, John H. Sergeant in Capt. Dobbin's co. 39th rgt.

Wilson, John H. Lieutenant in Capt. Saunders' co. 1st Rifle Battalion (S. 20, 1813).

Wilson, John Sanford [1786-1881]. Private in Capt. Snowden's co. 36th rgt.

Wilson, Joseph. Private in Capt. Snowden's co. 36th rgt.

Wilson, Joseph. Private in Capt. Steever's co. 27th rgt.

Wilson, Joseph. Private in Capt. Dyer's co. Fells Point Riflemen.

Wilson, Lazarus. Private in Capt. Quantrill's co. 24th rgt.

Wilson, Nicholas. Private in Capt. Pumphrey's co. 22d rgt.

Wilson, Otho. Private in Capt. Smith's co. 51st rgt.

Wilson, Peter. Private in Capt. Dillon's co. 27th rgt.

Wilson, Richard G. Sergeant in Capt. Vansant's co. 33d rgt.

Wilson, Robert. 1st Lieutenant in Capt. Boyer's co. 8th Cavalry Dist. (My. 22, 1812).

Wilson, Robert. Private in Capt. Warfield's co. Balto. United Volunteers.

Wilson, Robert. Private in Capt. Adreon's co. Union Volunteers.

Wilson, Robert. Private in Capt. Mackey's co. 49th rgt.

Wilson, Robert. Private in Capt. Thompson's co. 1st. Baltimore Horse Artillery.

Wilson, Robert, Jr. Private in Capt. Wells' Artillery co. 22d rgt.

Wilson, Robert, Sr. Private in Capt. Pinkney's Artillery co. 22d rgt.

Wilson, Samuel. Cornet in Capt. Wilson's co. 6th Cavalry Dist. (Ap. 4, 1812).

Wilson, Samuel. Corporal in Capt. Sheppard's co. 6th rgt.

Wilson, Samuel. Private in Capt. Chalmers' co. 51st rgt.

Wilson, Samuel. Private in Capt. Quantrill's co. 24th rgt.

Wilson, Thomas. 2d Lieutenant in Capt. Wilson's co. 8th Cavalry Dist. (My. 16, 1812).

Wilson, Thomas. Private in Capt. Kennedy's co. 27th rgt.

Wilson, Thomas. Private in Capt. McConkey's co. 27th rgt.

Wilson, Thomas [1777-1845]. Private in Capt. Levering's co. Independent Blues.

Wilson, Thomas. Surgeon in 38th rgt. (Je. 1, 1813).

Wilson, Washington. Sergeant in Capt. Tilghman's co. 33d rgt.

Wilson, William [-1825]. Captain in U. S. Artillery (My. 12, 1814).

Wilson, William. 2d Lieutenant in Capt. Wilson's co. 6th Cavalry Dist. (Jy. 13, 1814) vice Fuller.

Wilson, William. Private in Capt. Bunbury's co. Sea Fencibles.

Wilson, William. Private in Capt. Steuart's co. Washington Blues.

Wilson, William. Private in Capt. Sterett's Independent co.

Wilson, William. Ensign in Capt. Juett's co. 23d rgt. Resigned July 14, 1814.

Wilson, William. Private in Capt. Watson's co. 39th rgt.

Wilson, William. Sergeant in Capt. Fowler's co. 46th rgt.

Wilson, William. Private in Capt. Blair's co. 50th rgt.

Wilson, William, Jr. Ensign in Capt. Levering's co. Independent Blues.

Wilson, William of Wm. Lieutenant in Capt. Jackson's co. 34th rgt. (Je. 27, 1812).

Wilson, William H. Lieutenant in Capt. Thos. Brookes' co. 34th rgt.

Wilson, Zachariah. Private in Capt. Travers' co. 48th rgt.

Wimmel, George S. Private in Capt. Montgomery's co. Balto. Union Artillery.

Wimms, Joseph. Private in Capt. Snowden's co. 36th rgt.

Wimsatt, Bernard. Private in Capt. Bean's co. 12th rgt.

Wimsatt, Samuel. Private in Capt. Posey's co. 1st rgt.

Wincett, Joseph. Private in Capt. Myers' co. 39th rgt.

Winchell, James F. Lieutenant in Capt. Dillon's co. 27th rgt.

Winchester, Jacob. Corporal in Capt. Ringgold's co. 6th rgt.

*Winchester, James [-1826]. Brigadier General, U. S. A. (Mr. 27, 1812).

Winchester, Richard. Corporal in Capt. Fowler's co. 33d rgt.

Winchester, Samuel. Private in Capt. Pike's co. Balto. Volunteer Artillery.

Winchester, Thomas C. Private in Capt. Berry's co. Washington Artillery.

*Winder, Levin [1756-1819]. Brigadier General Maryland Militia, 1812; Governor and Commander-in-Chief, 1812-15.

Winder, Rider Henry. Quartermaster in 1st rgt. Artillery (Ap. 23, 1813); Judge-Advocate U. S. (Jy. 9, 1814).

Winder, William Henry [1775-1824]. Lieutenant-Colonel U. S. Infantry (Mr. 16, 1812); Brigadier General (Mr. 12, 1813).

Winders, John. Private in Capt. Barr's Cavalry co. 1st Dist.

Windsor, John. Private in Capt. Posey's co. 1st rgt.

Winfield, Richard S. Private in Capt. Crawfurd's co. 17th rgt.

Wingate, Garrison. Private in Capt. McNamara's co. 48th rgt.

Wingate, James. Private in Capt. Morgan's co. 49th rgt.

Wingate, Lemuel. Private in Capt. McNamara's co. 48th rgt.

Wingate, Thomas. Private in Capt. McNamara's co. 48th rgt.

Wingate, Wallace. Private in Capt. Fallin's co. 48th rgt.

Wingert, Philip. Private in Capt. Shryock's co. 24th rgt.

Winkle, James I. Lieutenant in Capt. Woods' co. 27th rgt. (Ap. 21, 1814).

Winkler, John. Private in Capt. Horton's co. Maryland Chasseurs.

Winn, S. D. Private in Capt. Pennington's co. Balto. Independent Artillerists.

Winn, William. Private in Capt. Deems' co. 51st rgt.

Winnigden, Lewis. Private in Capt. Horton's co. Maryland Chasseurs.

Winsor, Arnold T. 1st Lieutenant in Capt. Linthicum's co. 2d Cavalry Dist. (My. 22, 1812); Captain (Jy. 4, 1814).

Winsor, Robert B. Ensign in Capt. Etichison's co. 3d rgt. (Je. 5, 1812).

Winstandley, William H. 3d Lieutenant in Capt. Magruder's co. American Artillerists (F. 14, 1815).

Winstanley, John. Sergeant in Capt. Haubert's co. 51st rgt.

Winstanley, John. Private in Capt. Galt's co. 6th rgt.

Winters, George. Private in Capt. Quantrill's co. 24th rgt.

Winters, Henry. Private in Capt. Deems' co. 51st rgt.

Winwright, John. Private in Capt. Brown's co. 6th rgt.

Winzett, William. Private in Capt. Blair's co. 50th rgt.

Wireman, William. Private in Capt. Sterett's co. 1st Balto. Hussars.

Wirt, Jacob. Private in Capt. Galt's co. 6th rgt.

Wisbaugh, Martin. Private in Capt. Steever's co. 27th rgt.

Wise, Augustus. Private in Capt. Edes' co. 27th rgt.

Wise, George. Private in Capt. Quantrill's co. 24th rgt.

Wise, John. Private in Capt. Rogers' co. 51st rgt.

Wise, John M. Private in Capt. Piper's co. United Maryland Artillery.

Wise, Samuel. Captain in 24th rgt. (Jy. 12, 1814) vice Shapleigh.

Wise, Samuel. Private in Capt. Williams' co. 12th rgt.

Wise, William. Sergeant in Capt. Vansant's co. 33d rgt.

Wisham, John. Corporal in Capt. Steever's co. 27th rgt.

Wissinger, George. Lieutenant in Capt. Getzendanner's co. 16th rgt. (Je. 26, 1812).

Witmore, John. Private in Capt. Barr's Cavalry co. 1st Dist.

Witterfield, James. Private in Capt. Steever's co. 27th rgt.

Woilds, David. Private in Capt. Steever's co. 27th rgt.

Wolf, Frederick. Private in Capt. Brown's co. 6th rgt.

Wolf, George. Private in Capt. Dobbin's co. 39th rgt.

Wolf, Henry. Private in Capt. Galt's co. 6th rgt.

Wolf, Isaac. Private in Capt. McConkey's co. 27th rgt.

Wolf, Jacob, Jr. Sergeant in Capt. Miller's co. 39th rgt.

Wolf, Michael. Private in Capt. Shrim's co. Balto. Light Infantry.

Wolf, Samuel. Lieutenant in Capt. Myers' co. 39th rgt. (Ja. 10, 1814).

Wolfe, Jacob. Private in Capt. Blair's co. 50th rgt.

Wolfe, Jacob. Captain in 10th rgt. (S. 20, 1813).

Wolfinger, John. Lieutenant in Capt. Stonebraker's co. 24th rgt. Resigned Aug. 1, 1814.

Wollaston, Joseph. Private in Capt. Garrett's co. 49th rgt.

Wollen, Zachariah. Private in Capt. Magruder's co. American Artillerists.

Wolleslager, Jonas. Private in Capt. Shryock's co. 24th rgt.

Wolverton, John. Private in Capt. Faster's co. 51st rgt.

Wood, Benjamin. Private in Capt. Thompson's co. 1st rgt.

Wood, Charles. Private in Capt. Cawood's co. 45th rgt.

Wood, George T. Private in Capt. Crawfurd's co. 17th rgt.

Wood, Henry H. Private in Capt. Horton's co. Maryland Chasseurs.

Wood, Henry S. Corporal in Capt. Burgess' co. 43d rgt.

Wood, Isaac. Private in Capt. Chalmers' co. 51st rgt.

Wood, Jesse. Private in Capt. Massey's co. 38th rgt.

Wood, John. Gunner in Capt. Bunbury's co. Sea Fencibles.

Wood, John. Private in Capt. Warfield's co. Balto. United Volunteers.

Wood, John [1785-1824]. Private in Capt. Berry's co. Washington Artillery.

Wood, John. Private in Capt. King's co. 49th rgt.

Wood, John G. Private in Capt. Myer's co. Franklin Artillery.

Wood, Joseph. Lieutenant, Harford co. drafted infantry, 1813.

Wood, Joshua. Major, Harford co., drafted infantry, 1813.

Wood, Leonard. Private in Capt. Ireland's co. 31st rgt.

Wood, Samuel. Sergeant in Ensign Brewer's detachment 36th rgt.; in Capt. Slicer's co. 22d rgt.; Private in Capt. Sands' co. 22d rgt.

Wood, Thomas G. Sergeant in Capt. Burgess' co. 43d rgt.

Woodall, Edward. Sergeant in Capt. Mann's co. 33d rgt.

Woodall, Isaac. Private in Capt. Mann's co. 33d rgt.

Woodall, James. Sergeant in Capt. Mann's co. 33d rgt.

Woodall, John A. Lieutenant in Capt. Boyer's co. 33d rgt. (Jy. 11, 1814) vice Boyer.

Woodall, John V. Lieutenant in Capt. Fowler's co. 33d rgt. (O. 13, 1814).

Woodall, Levin. Private in Capt. Sturgis's co. 35th rgt.

Woodall, Thomas. Private in Capt. Tilghman's co. 33d rgt.

Woodburn, William. Captain in 45th rgt. (Jy. 11, 1814).

Woodburn, William. Sergeant in Capt. Sotheran's co. 45th rgt.

Woodburne, Hezekiah. Private in Capt. Cawood's co. 45th rgt.

Woodfield, Thomas. Private in Capt. Wells' Artillery co. 22d rgt.

Woodland, Matthias. Private in Capt. Brohawn's co. 48th rgt.

Woodland, William. Major in 1st Rifle Battalion 3d Brigade (Ap. 4, 1812).

Woodrough, Samuel. Private in Capt. Blair's co. 50th rgt.

Woodruff, Ichabod. Private in Capt. Blizzard's co. 15th rgt.

Woods, Andrew H. Private in Capt. Levering's co. Independent Blues.

Woods, John. Private in Capt. Kierstead's co. 6th rgt.

Woods, Nicholas. Private in Capt. Stapleton's co. 39th rgt.

Woods, Samuel. Private in Capt. Berry's co. Washington Artillery.

Woods, Septha. Private in Capt. Piper's co. United Maryland Artillery.

Woods, Wesley. Captain in 27th rgt. (N. 8, 1814).

Woods, Wesley. Quarter-master Sergeant in Capt. Sterett's co. 1st Balto. Hussars.

Woods, William. Private in Capt. A. E. Warner's co. 39th rgt.

Woods, William H. Private in Capt. Levering's co. Independent Blues.

Woodward, Abraham. Private in Capt. Thos. Warner's co. 39th rgt.

Woodward, Amos. 2d Lieutenant in 14th U. S. Infantry (Je. 4, 1812); 1st Lieutenant (My. 13, 1813).

Woodward, Henry. Captain in 22d rgt.

Woodward, Nathaniel. Captain in Capt. Getzendanner's co. 16th rgt.

Woodward, William. Sergeant in Capt. Williams' co. 12th rgt.

Woody, William. Lieutenant in Capt. Watson's co. 39th rgt.

Woodyard, Joseph. Private in Capt. Brown's co. 43d rgt.

Woodyear, Edward G. Captain in American Artillery co. (Jy. 4, 1812); Aide to Genl. Stansbury (Jy. 8, 1814).

Woolen, William. Private in Capt. McConkey's co. 27th rgt.

Woolery, Jacob. Lieutenant in Capt. Blizzard's co. 15th rgt. (O. 22, 1807).

Wooles, Stephen. Private in Capt. Edes' co. 27th rgt.

Woolford, James. Cornet Capt. Woolford's co. 1toh Cavalry Dist. (S. 26, 1812).

Woolford, Roger. Captain in 10th Cavalry Dist. (S. 26, 1812).

Woolford, Thomas of Roger. Captain in 48th rgt. (My. 2, 1799).

Woolford, William. Sergeant in Capt. Woolford's co. 48th rgt.

Woolhouse, John. Private in Capt. Snowden's co. 36th rgt.

Woollen, Wesley. Private in Capt. Travers' co. 48th rgt.

Woollen, Wingert. Sergeant in Capt. Travers' co. 48th rgt.

Woollen, Zachariah. Private in Capt. Brohawn's co. 48th rgt.

Wooten, Richard. Private in Capt. Waters' co. 22d rgt.

Wootten, Bennet. Private in Capt. Williams' co. 12th rgt.

Woother, Thomas B. Private in Capt. Snowden's co. 36th rgt.

Wootton, Ignatius. Private in Capt. Bean's co. 12th rgt.

Wordle, Robert. Private in Capt. Ducker's co. 7th rgt.

Work, John. Private in Capt. Snowden's co. 36th rgt.

Working, Frederick. Private in Capt. Adreon's co. Union Volunteers.

Workinger, Jacob. Private in Capt. Shrim's co. Balto. Light Infantry.

Worl, Thomas. Private in Capt. Ducker's co. 7th rgt.

Worley, Joseph. Private in Capt. Thompson's co. 1st Baltimore Horse Artillery.

Worrell, Edward H. Surgeon's mate in 27th rgt.

Worrell, John. Private in Capt. Watson's co. 39th rgt.

Worthan, Damon. Private in Capt. Myers' co. Franklin Artillery.

Worthington, Beale M. Private in Capt. Waters' co. 22d rgt.

Worthington, Charles G. Surgeon's mate 32d rgt. (S. 20, 1808).

Worthington, Nicholas. Private in Capt. Dobbin's co. 39th rgt.

Worthington, Thomas C. Captain of Frederick Co. co., ordered to Annapolis in 1812.

Wren, James. Private in Capt. Wilson's co. 6th rgt.

Wright, Abraham. Private in Capt. Haubert's co. 51st rgt.

Wright, Clinton [-1818]. Cornet in U. S. Light Dragoons (Ja. 19, 1813); 2d Lieutenant (Ap. 19, 1814).

Wright, Daniel. Private in Capt. Oldham's co. 49th rgt.

Wright, Edward. Major in 33d rgt. Resigned May 4, 1815.

Wright, Edward. Ensign in Capt. Davis' co. 11th rgt. (Ja. 25, 1814); Lieutenant in Capt. Harper's co. 11th rgt. (Ja. 25, 1814); Lieutenant in Capt. Harper's co. (Ag. 20, 1814).

Wright, Edward. Private in Capt. Brown's co. 6th rgt.

Wright, Francis. Private in Capt. Oldham's co. 49th rgt.

Wright, George. Sergeant in Capt. Crawfurd's co. 17th rgt.

Wright, George. Sergeant in Capt. Fowler's co. 46th rgt.

Wright, Gustavus W. T. Captain Artillery co. in 38th rgt. 6th Brigade (Jy. 15, 1814) vice Larrimore.

Wright, James. Private in Capt. Naylor's co. 17th rgt.

Wright, James of John. Ensign in Capt. Blades' co. 19th rgt. (Ag. 20, 1814).

Wright, John [1789-1875]. Corporal in Capt. Myers' co. Franklin Artillery.

Wright, John. Private in Capt. Dyer's co. Fells Point Riflemen.

Wright, Joseph. Private in Capt. Eversfield's co. 17th rgt.

Wright, Joseph. Private in Capt. Dent's co. 43d rgt.

Wright, Malcolm. Private in Capt. Steuart's co. Washington Blues.

Wright, Nathan. Lieutenant in Capt. Davis' co. 11th rgt. (Ja. 25, 1814); Captain (Ag. 20, 1814).

Wright, Richard. Private in Capt. Wilson's co. 6th rgt.

Wright, Samuel. Lieutenant in Capt. Darby's co. 13th rgt. (D. 7, 1813).

Wright, Solomon E. Private in Capt. Jas. Massey's co. 38th rgt.

Wright, Stephen. Private in Capt. Fowler's co. 46th rgt.

Wright, Thomas. Lieutenant-Colonel in 38th rgt.

Wright, Thomas. Private in Capt. Chalmers' co. 51st rgt.

Wright, Walter. Private in Capt. Brown's co. 6th rgt.

Wright, William. Corporal in Capt. Deem's co. 51st rgt.

Wright, William [-1816]. Ensign in 12th U. S. Infantry (N. 13, 1813); 3d Lieutenant (Ap. 5, 1814).

Wright, William. Lieutenant in Capt. Betton's co. 38th rgt. (Jy. 28, 1812).

Wright, William. Private in Capt. Magruder's co. American Artillerists.

Wright, William E. Private in Capt. Rogers' co. 51st rgt.

Wroten, Gabriel. Private in Capt. Travers' co. 48th rgt.

Wroten, Philip. Private in Capt. Travers' co. 48th rgt.

Wroten, Thomas. Private in Capt. Travers' co. 48th rgt.

Wroten, Washington. Private in Capt. Travers' co. 48th rgt.

Wroth, James. Ensign in Capt. Buchanan's co. 21st rgt. (Je. 18, 1794).

Wroth, John. Private in Capt. A. C. Smith's co. 49th rgt.

Wroth, Peregrine. Surgeon's mate 8th Cavalry Dist. (Ja. 3, 1815) vice Scanlon.

Wroth, Samuel. Private in Capt. Morgan's co. 49th rgt.

Wry, John. Private in Capt. McConkey's co. 27th rgt.

Wulpy, William. Private in Capt. Bader's co. Union Yägers.

Wyant, George John. Private in Capt. Adreon's co. Union Volunteers.

Wyley, Joshua. 2d Lieutenant in Capt. Green's co. 6th Cavalry Dist. (Ap. 26, 1812); 1st Lieutenant.

Wyneman, John B. Private in Capt. Shrim's co. Balto. Light Infantry.

Wynn, Christopher. Corporal in Capt. McKane's co. 27th rgt.

Wynn, John. Private in Capt. Eversfield's co. 17th rgt.

Wynne, Edward. Sergeant in Capt. Stiles' co. Marine Artillery.

Wyse, John M. Private in Capt. Moale's co. Columbian Artillery.

Wysham, John. Corporal in Capt. Sands' co. 22d rgt.

Wysham, Thomas. Private in Capt. Adreon's co. Union Volunteers.

Wysham, William. Private in Capt. Sands' co. 22d rgt.; Corporal in Capt. Chase's co. 22d rgt.; Private in Ensign Brewer's detachment, 36th rgt.; captured at Bladensburg.

Wyvill, John R. Private in Capt. Travers' co. 48th rgt.

Wyvill, Robert. Private in Capt. Travers' co. 48th rgt.

Wyville, Marmaduke. Private in Capt. Pennington's co. Balto. Independent Artillerists. Wounded at Fort McHenry.

Y

Yäger, John. Private in Capt. Ringgold's co. 6th rgt.

Yäger, Joseph. Private in Capt. Pike's co. Balto. Volunteer Artillery.

Yam, Thomas. Private in Capt. Conway's co. 6th rgt.

Yanaway, Daniel. Private in Capt. Howard's co. Mechanical Volunteers.

Yates, Donaldson. Hospital Surgeon's mate (Ag. 16, 1814).

Yates, Henry S. Brigade Inspector 5th Brigade (N. 7, 1810).

Yates, John. Private in Capt. Nicholson's co. Balto. Fencibles.

Yates, William. Private in Capt. Millard's co. 12th rgt.

Yates, William of Edward. Private in Capt. Millard's co. 12th rgt.

Yeager, John. Private in Capt. Chalmers' co. 51st rgt.

Yealdhall, Aquila. Private in Capt. Linthicum's co. 22d rgt.

Yealdhall, Elijah. Ensign in Capt. Linthicum's co. 22d rgt. (S. 11, 1809).

Yealdhall, Robert. Private in Capt. Weems' co. 22d rgt.

Yeamon, Royal. Private in Capt. Smith's co. 51st rgt.

Yearley, John, Jr. Private in Capt. Page's co. 21st rgt.

Yeates, James. Private in Capt. Wickes' co. 21st rgt.

Yeider, John. Private in Capt. Shryock's co. 24th rgt.

Yeiser, Daniel. Private in Capt Reinhart's co. 20th rgt.

Yeiser, E. F. Private in Capt. Moale's co. Columbian Artillery.

Yeiser, John, Jr. Private in Capt. Thompson's co. 1st. Baltimore Horse Artillery.

Yerkess, Anthony. Private in Capt Edes' co. 27th rgt.

Yewell, John. Corporal in Capt. Howard's co. Mechanical Volunteers.

Yingling, Benjamin. Adjutant in 20th rgt. (Ag. 1, 1814) vice Matthias.

Yingling, Benjamin. Private in Capt. Blizzard's co. 15th rgt.

Yoe, Robert. Ensign in Capt. Broome's co. 31st rgt. (My. 20, 1814).

Yoe, Thomas. Private in Capt. McConckin's co. 38th rgt.

Yost, John. Private in Capt. Shryock's co. 24th rgt.

Yostler, William. Private in Capt. Shryock's co. 24th rgt.

Young, Adam. Captain in 29th rgt. Resigned Sep. 20, 1813.

Young, Edward. Private in Capt. Hance's co. 31st rgt.

Young, Henry. Ensign in Capt. Bowman's co. 18th rgt. (O. 10, 1799).

Young, Hugh. Sergeant in Stapleton's co. 39th rgt.

Young, Ignatius F. 1st Lieutenant in 36th U. S. Infantry (Ap. 30, 1813).

Young, Jacob. Private in Capt. Adreon's co. Union Volunteers.

Young, John. 1st Major in 51st rgt.

Young, John. Sergeant in Capt. Boone's co. 22d rgt.

Young, John. Private in Capt. Hance's co. 31st rgt.

Young, John. Private in Capt. A. E. Warner's co. 39th rgt.

Young, John. Private in Capt. Rogers' co. 51st rgt.

Young, John. Private in Capt. Stiles' co. Marine Artillery.

Young, John. Private in Capt. Berry's co. Washington Artillery.

Young, John. Surgeon in 14th U. S. Infantry (Je. 4, 1812).

Young, John A. Private in Capt. Ducker's co. 7th rgt.; Sergeant-Major in 15th rgt. (Ag. 20, 1814).

Young, John S. 1st Lieutenant in Schnebly's co. 8th rgt. (F. 9, 1814).

Young, John S. 1st Lieutenant in Capt. Aisquith's Sharp Shooters (Jy. 24, 1812).

Young, Jonas. Ensign in Capt. Hardy's co. 17th rgt. (Ag. 10, 1807).

Young, Joseph. Captain in 12th rgt. (O. 3, 1807).

Young, Peter. Quarter-Gunner in Capt. Bunbury's co. Sea Fencibles.

Young, Peter A. Private in Capt. Magruder's co. American Artillerists.

Young, Robert. Sergeant in Capt. Oldham's co. 30th rgt.

Young, Samuel. Quarter-master Sergeant in 39th rgt.

Young, Samuel. Private in Capt. A. E. Warner's co. 39th rgt.

Young, William. Private in Capt. Roney's co. 39th rgt.

Young, William. Private in Capt. Stiles' co. Marine Artillery.

Young, William L. Private in Capt. Warfield's co. Balto. United Volunteers.

Younker, Francis [-1849]. Private in Capt. Magruder's co. American Artillerists.

Yowler, Michael. Private in Capt. Getzendanner's co. 16th rgt.

Yuncet, Leonard. Private in Capt. Deems' co. 51st rgt.

Z

Zacharias, Daniel. 1st Lieutenant in Capt. Shriver's co. 2d rgt. 1st Cavalry Dist. (Je. 26, 1812) ; Captain (D. 22, 1812).

Zacharias, George. Private in Capt. Zacharias' co. 2d rgt. 1st Cavalry Dist.

Zane, Joseph. Private in Capt. Kierstead's co. 6th rgt.

Zane, Peter. Sergeant in Capt. Ringgold's co. 6th rgt.

Zeigler, Adam. Ensign in Capt. Huston's co. 16th rgt. (Jy. 20, 1812).

Zeiler, George. Ensign in Capt. Getzendanner's co. 16th rgt. (Je. 26, 1812).

Zellers, Daniel. Lieutenant in Capt. Schnebly's co. 8th rgt. (F. 9, 1814).

Zerne, Christian. Private in Capt. Peters' co. 51st rgt.

Ziegler, George. Private in Capt. Conway's co. 6th rgt.

Ziegler, Henry. Private in Capt. Pennington's Balto. Independent Artillerists.

Ziegler, Jacob. Private in Capt. Shrim's co. Balto. Light Infantry.

Zigler, John L. Private in Capt. Horton's co. Maryland Chasseurs.

Zigler, John W. Private in Capt. Horton's co. Maryland Chasseurs.

Zimmer, Peter. Private in Capt. Shryock's co. 24th rgt.

Zimmerman, Henry H. Private in Capt. Adreon's co. Union Volunteers.

Zimmerman, Jacob. Private in Capt. Deems' co. 51st rgt.

Zimmerman, John. Private in Capt. Myers' co. Franklin Artillery.

Zody, John. Private in Capt. Roney's co. 39th rgt.

Zorn, John. Private in Capt. Haubert's co. 51st rgt.

Zorne, Jabez. Musician in Capt. Sheppard's co. 6th rgt.

Zumbuly, Jacob. Private in Capt. McLaughlin's co. 50th rgt.

SOCIETY OF THE WAR OF 1812 IN MARYLAND

Addison, Taylor.
By right of descent from Peter Armstrong.

Alford, Albert Gallatin.
By right of descent from Ami Alford.

Armistead, George.
By right of descent from George Armistead.

Arthurs, Edward Ferguson.
By right of descent from William Ferguson, Private in Capt. John McNeal's co., Ohio Cavalry.

Bandel, Littleton Chandler.
By right of descent from William Bandel.

Baughman, Emilius Allen.
By right of descent from George Greer.

Beatty, John Edwin.
By right of descent from James Alexander Cole.

Bernard, Alfred Duncan.
By right of descent from George Gore.

Biays, Tolley Allender.
By right of descent from James Biays.

Boyce, Heyward E.
By right of descent from Dr. James Page.

Bradford, Samuel Webster.
By right of descent from Thomas Kell.

Branch, Henry, D. D.
By right of descent from Benjamin James Harris, Private in Capt. Wm. McCabe's co., 19th Va. rgt.

Brumfield, Jerome Edgar.
By right of descent from William Brumfield.

Bull, Robert Berry.
By right of descent from John Berry.

Carr, Alfred Jarrett.
By right of descent from John Wright.

Cathcart, Asbury Roszel.
By right of descent from Robert Cathcart.

Cherbonnier, Andrew Victor.
By right of descent from Pierre Cherbonnier.

Christhilf, Edward.
By right of descent from Henry Christhilf.

Colbert, Edwin Abbott.
By right of descent from Walter Cody Hayes.
Cole, John Carroll LeGrand.
By right of descent from Walter Cody Hayes.
Cole, Robert Clinton.
By right of descent from William Cole.
Collmus, Charles Carroll.
By right of descent from Levi Collmus.
Cooke, William Dewey.
By right of descent from Joseph Trout.
Dallam, Harry Gough.
By right of descent from Harry Dorsey Gough.
Dashiell, Nicholas Leeke, M. D.
By right of descent from Henry Dashiell.
Dell, Thomas Medairy.
By right of descent from Ezekiel Mills.
Dennis, James Teackle.
By right of descent from Thomas Wilson.
Dickey, Charles Herman.
By right of descent from Philip B. Sadtler.
Dickey, Philip Sadtler.
By right of descent from Philip B. Sadtler.
Downs, Samuel Addison.
By right of descent from Thomas Neven.
Dukes, Alexander Thompson.
By right of descent from Robert Neilson.
Dulany, John Mason.
By right of descent from Samuel Dulany.
Duvall, Richard Mareen.
By right of descent from Francis Waring.
Easter, Arthur Miller.
By right of descent from Lewis Klein, Private in Capt. G. W. Blincoe's co. Virginia Militia.
Easter, James Miller.
By right of descent from Lewis Klein, Private in Capt. G. W. Blincoe's co. Virginia militia.
Elliott, Thomas Ireland.
By right of descent from John Bunting.
England, Charles.
By right of descent from Richard Middleton.
Flower, John Sebastian.
By right of descent from Gustavus Flower.
Ford, Henry Jones.
By right of descent from Uriah Jones.
Foster, Clarence Dulany.
By right of descent from Samuel Dulany.

33

French, Chester Lee.
By right of descent from William French.
Gill, Robert Lee.
By right of descent from Stephen Gill.
Griffith, Louis Philip.
By right of descent from Howard Griffith, Jr.
Grindall, Charles Sylvester, D. D. S.
By right of descent from Thomas Armstrong.
Hall, Summerfield Davis.
By right of descent from John Perkins.
Hancock, James Etchberger.
By right of descent from John Despeaux.
Handy, John Custis.
By right of descent from William Matthews.
Harris, William Hall.
By right of descent from David Harris.
Henderson, Charles F.
By right of descent from Peter Henderson.
Hildt, John C.
By right of descent from John Hildt.
Hildt, Thomas.
By right of descent from John Hildt.
Hiskey, Thomas Foley.
By right of descent from William Shipley, Captain in 1st Delaware rgt.
Hite, Drayton Meade.
By right of descent from James Madison Hite.
Houghton, Ira Holden.
By right of descent from Samuel McMurray.
Huddleson, James Howard, Jr.
By right of descent from John Cox Stockton.
Hume, Edgar E., Jr.
By right of descent from Charles Hume, Lieutenant in Capt. Jos. Hume's co., 1st Virginia rgt.
Iglehart, James Davidson, M. D.
By right of descent from James Davidson.
Jenkins, Edward Austin.
By right of descent from Edward Jenkins.
Jenkins, Francis de Sales.
By right of descent from Edward Jenkins.
Jenkins, Michael.
By right of descent from Dr. William Jenkins.
Kaufman, John William.
By right of descent from Jonathan Kauffman.
Kenly, William Watkins.
By right of descent from Edward Kenly.

Keplinger, John Bernard.
By right of descent from Michael Keplinger.
Knott, Aloysius Leo.
By right of descent from Edward Knott.
Lake, Richard Pinkney.
By right of descent from George Lake.
Landstreet, John.
By right of descent from John Landstreet.
Langhorne, Charles McIndoe.
By right of descent from Maurice Langhorne.
Lee, Howard Hall Macy.
By right of descent from George W. Ford.
McComas, Henry Angle.
By right of descent from Zacheus O. McComas.
McDonald, William Bartholow.
By right of descent from John Perkins.
McDonnell, Austin McCarthy.
By right of descent from John Whitney Massie.
McGaw, George Keen.
By right of descent from John McGaw.
McNeal, Joshua Vansant.
By right of descent from James McNeal.
McDonald, John Stuart.
By right of descent from Francis Younker.
Mackenzie, George Norbury.
By right of descent from Thomas Mackenzie.
Mahool, John Barry.
By right of descent from James Biays.
Maltbie, William Henry.
By right of descent from Henry Van Deman.
Marine, Madison.
By right of descent from William Knowles, Private in Capt. Thos. Rider's co. 9th Delaware rgt.
Marine, Richard Elliott.
By right of descent from William Knowles, Private in Capt. Thos. Rider's co. 9th Delaware rgt.
Maynadier, Thomas Murray.
By right of descent from Dr. Thomas E. Bond.
Meigs, Henry Benjamin.
By right of descent from Luther Meigs.
Miller, John Henry.
By right of descent from Gabriel Smithson.
Mills, Ezekiel, Jr.
By right of descent from Ezekiel Mills.
Mills, George Albert.
By right of descent from Ezekiel Mills.

Morgan, John Hurst.
By right of descent from John Berry.
Nash, Charles Wesley.
By right of descent from Hugh Davey.
Neilson, George Peabody.
By right of descent from Robert Neilson.
Neilson, Robert Musgrave.
By right of descent from Robert Neilson.
Orem, John Henry, Jr.
By right of descent from John Henry Schuchts.
Owens, Edward Burnestone.
By right of descent from Joseph Owens.
Parrish, James Hagerty.
By right of descent from William Parrish.
Parrish, William Tippett.
By right of descent from William Parrish.
Pennington, Josias.
By right of descent from Josias Pennington.
Pentz, Franklin Eldridge.
By right of descent from Daniel Pentz.
Pentz, William Fletcher.
By right of descent from Daniel Pentz.
Perkins, William Henry, Jr.
By right of descent from John Perkins.
Phillips, George Thomas.
By right of descent from Benjamin Phillips.
Pritchard, Arthur John.
By right of descent from John I. Stewart.
Reese, Howard Hopkins.
By right of descent from Gilbert Cassard.
Reifsnider, John Milton.
By right of descent from Daniel Zacharias.
Riggs, Clinton Levering.
By right of descent from Elisha Riggs.
Rinehart, Evan Urner.
By right of descent from William Roney.
Rinehart, Thomas Warden.
By right of descent from William Roney.
Robertson, George Sadtler.
By right of descent from Philip B. Sadtler.
Rusk, Jacob Krebs.
By right of descent from George Rusk.
Sadtler, Charles Edward, M. D.
By right of descent from Philip B. Sadtler.
Sadtler, Howard Plitt.
By right of descent from Philip B. Sadtler.

Sheib, Samuel Henry.
  By right of descent from Samuel Elbert
Steuart, James Edmonson.
  By right of descent from George H. Steuart.
Stewart, Ambler Jones.
  By right of descent from Thomas Bay.
Strobel, Albert Perrigo.
  By right of descent from John Peter Strobel.
Strobel, James William.
  By right of descent from John Peter Strobel.
Summers, Walter Penrose.
  By right of descent from Charles Bosley Green.
Talbott, Hattersly Worthington, Jr.
  By right of descent from Otho Holland Williams.
Talbott, Otho Holland Williams.
  By right of descent from Richard Talbott.
Taylor, Benjamin Franklin.
  By right of descent from Robert Taylor.
Teale, Charles Edward.
  By right of descent from John Cranmer Teale, Private in Capt. John
    Martin's co. 9th New York Artillery.
Throckmorton, Charles Woodson.
  By right of descent from Josiah Throckmorton.
Tucker, James Armstrong Owings.
  By right of descent from Thomas Gardner Hill.
Wade, Samuel Henry.
  By right of descent from Thomas Samble (Sipley).
Warfield, Edwin.
  By right of descent from Gassaway Watkins.
Waring, Benjamin Harrison.
  By right of descent from John Beard.
Waring, William Emory, Jr.
  By right of descent from Peter Leary.
Warner Culbreth Hopewell.
  By right of descent from Michael Warner.
Williamson, Thomas Wilson.
  By right of descent from Charles Bosley Green.
Willis, William Nicholas.
  By right of descent from John Willis.
Wilson, John Appleton.
  By right of descent from Thomas Wilson.
Wright, George Mitchell.
  By right of descent from Alpha Wright, Sergeant in Capt. Rial Mc-
    Arthur's co. 4th Brigade Ohio Militia.

NATIONAL SOCIETY UNITED STATES DAUGHTERS OF WAR OF 1812, STATE OF MARYLAND

Agnus, Mrs. Felix (Annie E. Fulton).
By right of descent from Nathaniel Kimberly.

Baker, Mrs. Robert Quincy (Margaret Swindell).
By right of descent from Daniel Swift (Pa.), Private under Jackson at Battle of New Orleans.

Barry, Mrs. Robert C. (Johnanna McKean).
By right of descent from Nicholas Ruxton Moore.

Beall, Miss Susie C.
By right of descent from Col. William Williams, William Williams, Grafton Hall and John Perkins.

Bird, Mrs. William Sellman (Edith Bradford Wiles).
By right of descent from Major Isaac Winslow (Mass.).

Boone, Miss Elizabeth.
By right of descent from William Jenkins.

Boone, Miss Mary Kennedy.
By right of descent from William Jenkins.

Bosler, Mrs. Herman (Carolyne Dickey Dulany).
By right of descent from Samuel Dulany.

Bourne, Mrs. Thomas H. (Katherine Teackle Finney).
By right of descent from John Finney, Captain in 2d Virginia rgt., and Solomon Bunting, Private in Capt. Garrison's co. 2d Virginia rgt.

Bowie, Mrs. William D. (Marie Lee Bennett).
By right of descent from George Washington Jackson, Captain in 19th U. S. Infantry.

Brown, Miss Elizabeth Adele.
By right of descent from Abraham Simonton, Private in Capt. Elkanah Spear's co. 5th Mass. rgt.

Bullock, Mrs. Francis Simonton.
By right of descent from Samuel Alden Rich, Private in Capt. Gilbert's co. 5th Mass. rgt.

Butler, Mrs. John DeCamp (Louisa King).
By right of descent from Job Smith, Jr.

Byrd, Mrs. John Dozier (Clara Egerton Semmes).
By right of descent from Charles Calvert Egerton.

Callis, Mrs. Charles (Mary S. Codd).
By right of descent from James Hooper "Powder Monkey" on the privateer *Comet.*

Clark, Miss Anna E. B.
By right of descent from Dr. James Kendall Ball, Surgeon of 92d Virginia rgt.

Croxall, Mrs. Morris LeGrand (Agnes Browne).
By right of descent from John Browne, Private in Capt. Hearsey's co. 4th New Hampshire rgt.

Crozier, Miss Annie Lucile.
By right of descent from William Crozier.

Dade, Mrs. Joseph T. (Susan Ruth Dade).
By right of descent from Robert T. Dade.

Dashiell, Miss Mary Leeke.
By right of descent from Henry Dashiell and Benton Harris, Major on General Staff, Delaware Militia.

Dashiell, Mrs. Nicholas L. (Louisa Turpin Wright).
By right of descent from Benton Harris, Major on General Staff, Delaware Militia.

Dashiell, Mrs. Nicholas L., Jr. (Amelia Eleanor Marine).
By right of descent from William Knowles, Private in Capt. Thomas Rider's co. 9th Delaware rgt., John Perkins, Grafton Hall and William Williams.

Dickey, Miss Henrietta Sadtler.
By right of descent from Philip B. Sadtler.

Dove, Miss Beulah.
By right of descent from William Benson and Zachariah Dowden.

Dove, Miss Ida S.
By right of descent from William Benson and Zachariah Dowden.

Ehlen, Mrs. Frank (Florence Snowden).
By right of descent from John Thomas Richardson.

Emory, Mrs. John H. (Ella N. Applegarth).
By right of descent from Conrad Hook.

Fenwick, Miss Agnes Teresa.
By right of descent from Philip Fenwick, Private in Capt. Johns' D. C. Militia.

Fontaine, Mrs. John L. (Belle Harris).
By right of descent from Samuel Wilson.

Fulton, Miss Dollie Glorvina.
By right of descent from Nathaniel Kimberly.

Gaither, Mrs. Harry C. (Ida Blanche Wolfe).
By right of descent from Samuel Rust.

Green, Mrs. Charles F. (Mary Daugherty).
By right of descent from Daniel Daugherty, Private in Capt. Thomas Henry's co. 138th Pa. rgt.

Greenway, Miss Elizabeth Williams.
By right of descent from William W. Taylor and George Williams.

Greenway, Miss Mary Virginia.

By right of descent from George Williams and William W. Taylor.

Goodrich, Mrs. G. Clem (Ada Mercer Porter).

By right of descent from Conrad Hook.

Hadel, Miss Ada Amelia.

By right of descent from Nathaniel Kimberly and John Jory.

Hadel, Mrs. Albert K. (Florence M. Hough).

By right of descent from John Thornburg Sumwalt.

Hance, Mrs. Samuel B. (Tabitha M. Joynes).

By right of descent from Tully Snead, Private in Capt. Thomas Custis' co. 2d Virginia rgt.

Harris, Mrs. James Howell (Elizabeth A. Hardesty).

By right of descent from Isaac Hardesty, Drum Major in Capt. Morris' co. Virginia Militia.

Hatter, Mrs. Charles William (Mary Skipwith Coale).

By right of descent from Judge Samuel Chase.

Hogan, Mrs. Robert G. (Cornelia S. Heslep).

By right of descent from Col. Joel Lane of North Carolina.

Holloway, Mrs. Reuben Ross (Ella V. Houck).

By right of descent from Bernard Todd.

Homburg, Mrs. Albert H. (Gertrude Wight).

By right of descent from Andrew Slicer.

Houck, Mrs. George E. (Carolyne S. Porter).

By right of descent from Bernard Todd.

Hull, Mrs. William Skipwith (Caroline R. Sanks).

By right of descent from Alexander Boyd.

Iglehart, Mrs. James Davidson (Monterey Watson).

By right of descent from James Taylor, Lemuel Taylor and Thomas Watson.

Jefferies, Mrs. Ernest Smith (Virginia Leslie Holloway).

By right of descent from Bernard Todd and Reuben Ross.

Jenkins, Mrs. Spalding Lowe (Sarah K. Boone).

By right of descent from William Jenkins.

Johnson, Mrs. Andrew Green (Elizabeth P. Oakford).

By right of descent from Jacob Zollinger, Private in Capt. Thomas Walker's co. 1st Pennsylvania rgt.

Johnson, Mrs. Edward Thomas (Mary Avarilla Callis).

By right of descent from James Hooper, "Powder Monkey" on the privateer *Comet*.

Joynes, Miss Helen.

By right of descent from Tully Snead, Private in Capt. Thomas Custis' co. 2d Virginia rgt., and Smith Snead Private in 9th Virginia rgt.

Judik, Miss Florine J.

By right of descent from John Ordronaux, Captain of the privateer *Prince of Neufchatel*.

Judik, Mrs. Henry (Lillie A. Bringuls).
By right of descent from John Ordronaux, Captain of the privateer
Prince of Neufchatel.

Judik, Miss Lillie A.
By right of descent from John Ordronaux, Captain of the privateer
Prince of Neufchatel.

Kelly, Mrs. Andrew Jackson (Mary Park Redgrave).
By right of descent from Samuel Hance Redgrave.

Keys, Mrs. Charles M. (Martha Ray).
By right of descent from Enos Ray.

Lanahan, Mrs. Charles Miltenberger (Annie Snowden).
By right of descent from John Thomas Richardson.

Lee, Miss Elizabeth Collins.
By right of descent from John Wilson.

Lee, Mrs. James Williams (Emma Herbert Kronan).
By right of descent from Charles Herbert.

McClure, Mrs. James N. (Ida Louise Wight).
By right of descent from Andrew Slicer.

McGuire, Mrs. Robert Andrew (Mary Macon Hall).
By right of descent from Daniel Griffith Smaw, Private in Capt. Scarborough's co. Virginia Militia.

Marine, Miss Harriet Perkins.
By right of descent from William Knowles, Private in Capt. Thomas Rider's co. 9th Delaware rgt., John Perkins, William Williams and Grafton Hall.

Martin, Mrs. Guillumo Holte (Mary Eugenia Curlett).
By right of descent from George S. Eichelberger.

Maughlin, Mrs. James Boyd (Eleanor Ray).
By right of descent from Enos Ray.

Miller, Mrs. Alfred B. (Hannah Rebecca Sanders).
By right of descent from John Beard and Thomas Sanders.

Mohler, Mrs. Hugh P. (Alice Virdin Whiting).
By right of descent from John Kennedy, Private in Capt. Alex. Cummings, Pa. Light Dragoons.

Mohler, Mrs. I. Wimbert, Jr. (Ella Elzey).
By right of descent from Samuel Wilson.

Owens, Miss Katherine Cassard.
By right of descent from Joseph Owens, Benjamin Buck and Gilbert Cassard.

Owens, Miss Marie Purnell.
By right of descent from Joseph Owens, Benjamin Buck and Gilbert Cassard.

Perkins, Miss Laura Josephine.
By right of descent from John Perkins.

Rittenhouse, Mrs. John Edgar (Nina Roberts).
By right of descent from Joseph Blake.

Rous, Mrs. Charles (Frances Anderson Wood).
By right of descent from William Coleman Scott, Captain 28th Virginia rgt., James D. Wood and Thomas Scott (Va.).

Rowe, Mrs. Perry Belmont (Frances Elizabeth Marine).
By right of descent from William Knowles, Private in Capt. Rider's co. 9th Delaware rgt., John Perkins, William Williams and Grafton Hall.

Rowland, Mrs. Samuel Carson (Cornelia Talcott Ranson).
By right of descent from George Talcott, Lieutenant in 25th U. S. Infantry, 1814. *See* Heitman.

Sadtler, Mrs. Charles E. (Rosabella C. Slicer).
By right of descent from Andrew Slicer, Joseph Graham and Johnson Cooper.

Sadtler, Miss Florence Plitt.
By right of descent from Philip Benjamin Sadtler.

Sadtler, Mrs. George Washington (Delia Banks).
By right of descent from James Banks, Major-General 11th Division, Pennsylvania Volunteers.

Sadtler, Miss Sophia P. Banks.
By right of descent from James Banks, Major-General 11th Division, Pennsylvania Volunteers, Philip Benjamin Sadtler and John Reese.

Saul, Mrs. William Sawley (Mary Elma Ray).
By right of descent from Enos Ray.

Skinner, Mrs. Harry G. (Gertrude Thompson).
By right of descent from David Price, Private in Capt. McKnight's co., D. C. Militia.

Smith, Mrs. Charles E. Capito (Anna M. Eppley).
By right of descent from George J. Heisley, Private in Col. Kennedy's Harrisburgh, Pennsylvania rgt.

Smith, Mrs. Charles Howard (Jane Swindell).
By right of descent from Daniel Swift (Pa.) who served under Jackson at Battle of New Orleans.

Stansbury, Mrs. Harry (Jessie Benson Blake).
By right of descent from Joseph Blake.

Stone, Mrs. Frank Pellman (Lilly Catherine Moore).
By right of descent from John Moore, Lieutenant in Virginia Militia.

Streett, Mrs. John Rush (Katharine Busteed).
By right of descent from Samuel Vickers.

Swindell, Mrs. Walter B. (Margaret Ould).
By right of descent from Daniel Swift (Pa.) who served under Jackson at Battle of New Orleans.

Talbott, Miss Marie Hyde.
By right of descent from Henry W. Talbott.

Taylor, Miss Anna Stevenson.
By right of descent from Robert Taylor.

Taylor, Miss Virginia.
By right of descent from Robert Taylor.
Tormey, Mrs. Alfred J. (Florence Zollinger Oakford).
By right of descent from Jacob Zollinger, Private in Capt. Thomas
Walker's co. 1st rgt. Pennsylvania Militia.
Troupe, Mrs. Calvin Ferris (Hattie Ella Hull).
By right of descent from Joseph R. Foard and Alexander Boyd.
Trundle, Mrs. W. Burns (Anna Maria Dryden).
By right of descent from Joshua Dryden.
Tyler, Mrs. Erastus Barnard (Emilie Marcorelle).
By right of descent from Gilbert Cassard.
Wall, Mrs. William E. (Mary Catherine Dade).
By right of descent from Robert Townsend Dade.
Waring, Mrs. Robert K. (Kate Morten Sanders).
By right of descent from Thomas Sanders and John Beard.
Waring, Mrs. William Emory (Jane Leary).
By right of descent from Peter Leary.
Watts, Mrs. Philip Bartley (Helen Chase Cassard).
By right of descent from Gilbert Cassard.
Webb, Mrs. William Rollins (Cornelia Oakford).
By right of descent from Jacob Zollinger, Private in Capt. Thomas
Walker's co. 1st Pennsylvania rgt.
Willey, Mrs. Day Allen (Helen Muller).
By right of descent from Louis C. Muller.
Wilson, Mrs. J. Franklin (Clara Ray).
By right of descent from Enos Ray.
Wilson, Mrs. William L. (Sadie Waller).
By right of descent from Jonathan Waller, Captain of Delaware Militia,
and Thomas Waller.

INDEX

Gray, Henry W., 172.
Gray, Samuel, 173.
Green, Robert, 173.
Greer, George, 173.
Griffith, Capt. Samuel, 122, 123.
Grizel Joseph, 174.
Gross, John, 143.
Gruber, Rev. Jacob, 147.
Guerriere, 132.
Guns for defences, 145.
Gwinn, Edward, 9.

Hague, William, 123, 124.
Haley, James, 122.
Hall, John E., 9.
Hamilton, Lieut., 192.
Hamilton, Robert M., 174.
Hampton affair, 25-6.
Hands, Capt. Bedingfield, 119, 123.
Hanson, Alexander Contee, 7, 8, 9, 10.
Harbert, Zebedie, 122.
Hardy, Joseph, 173.
Harper, Robert Goodloe, 166.
Harris, Edward, 139, 143.
Harris, Jonathan, 123.
Harris, Samuel, 173.
Harrison, Capt. Jas. H., 73.
Harrison, Dr. Samuel A. (note), 56.
Hartley, Thomas, 123.
Harwood, Henry, 138, 142.
Hatcherson, James, 124.
Haubert, Jacob, 172.
Havre de Grace, attack on, 32.
Hawkins, James L., 173.
Hawkins, Jno. H. W., 191.
Hawkins, William, 139, 143.
Hawkins, Wm. Geo. 191.
Heard, Benedict I., 172.
Hearsey, George T., 172.
Heath, Major Richard K., 163, 165.
Hebrus, 73.
Henrix, Capt. Thomas, 55.
Herbert, Capt. J. C., 77.
Herring, Ludwick, 138, 143.

34

Hewitt. Eli, 138, 143.
Hickinbottom, James, 122.
Highflyer, 43, 45.
Hignet, John, 139, 143.
Hill, Dr. William, 190.
Hoffman, David, 9.
Hoffman, Henry, 174.
Holbrooks, Thomas, 174.
Holiday, Thomas, 174.
Hollingsworth, Edward, 113.
Hollingsworth, Horatio, 172.
Hollingsworth, Lieut. Jacob, 105.
Hollingsworth, Samuel, 133, 140, 143.
Hollins, John, 134.
Holtzman, George, 122.
Homespun Volunteer co. of Hagerstown, 21.
Hood, Col. Thomas, 77, 86.
Howard, Capt. Benj. C., 162.
Howard, Col. John E., 134, 136, 181.
Howland, Daniel, 138.
Howland, John M., 174.
Hubbard, Jacob, 171.
Hudson, James, 124.
Huffington, Jesse, 97, 174.
Hughes, Christopher, Jr., 176.
Hughes, Samuel, 40, 52.
Humphries, John, 124.
Hungerford, Capt. Jno. R., 53.
Hutton, James, 138, 143.
Hyland, John, 123.
Hyland, William, 123.
Hynson, Benjamin, 124.
Hynson, Capt. Thomas B., 119, 124.

Iler, Jacob, 174.
Inca, privateer, 17.
Independent Blues, 192.
Irvine, Alexander, 143.
Ivry, William, 124.

James, Thomas J., 123.
Jamison, Col., 53.
Jamison, Dr. Horatio, 145.
Jamison, Joseph, 134, 140.

CPSIA information can be obtained
at www.ICGtesting.com
Printed in the USA
FFHW012126230919
55162318-60889FF